Tony Benn has been the Member of Parliament for Chesterfield since 1984. He was elected to the National Executive Committee of the Labour Party in 1959, and was the Chairman of the Party in 1971–2. He has been a Cabinet Minister in every Labour Government since 1964, holding the positions of Postmaster General, Minister of Technology and Minister of Power. From 1974–9 he was Secretary of State for Industry, later Secretary of State for Energy and one-time President of the Council of Energy Ministers of the European Community.

He is the author of seven books including *Arguments for Socialism* and *Arguments for Democracy*, and holds four Honorary Doctorates from British and American Universities.

TONY BENN
Out of the Wilderness
DIARIES 1963–67

ARROW BOOKS

Arrow Books Limited
62–65 Chandos Place, London WC2N 4NW

An imprint of Century Hutchinson Limited

London Melbourne Sydney Auckland
Johannesburg and agencies throughout
the world

First published in Great Britain by Hutchinson 1987
Arrow edition 1988

© Tony Benn 1987

Made and printed in Great Britain by
The Guernsey Press Co. Ltd., Guernsey, Channel Islands.

ISBN 0 09 958670 3

Contents

List of Illustrations

Acknowledgments

My diary could never have been published without the help of many people over many years and to all these I am deeply grateful.

The decision to publish owes a great deal to Anne McDermid, who has always encouraged the idea, and particularly to Richard Cohen at Century Hutchinson, whose interest in the text and gentle but constant persuasion overcame my remaining hesitancy. I am also grateful to Century Hutchinson editors Kate Mosse and Stephanie Darnill, and to Heather Leithead, who all worked so hard and so enthusiastically against very tight deadlines.

I owe a great debt of gratitude to my sons, Dr Stephen Benn, who supervised the project from its inception, and Joshua Benn, who together devised the system for transcribing the diary on to word processors and advised on the many technical aspects involved.

Sheila Hubacher has tackled the huge job of transcribing hundreds of diary cassettes with equanimity and has worked perceptively on the edited text.

Most particularly I must place on record the central role played by Ruth Winstone who has managed the whole diary project herself, editing an original text of half a million words for this volume, undertaking a great deal of research and preparing the biographical and chapter notes.

Finally, I want to thank the Rowntree Trust for the funds which it generously provided to establish the diary office and start the typing, and for its confidence in the historical value of the archives; and Lord Chitnis for his personal encouragement throughout.

Illustration Acknowledgments

The publishers would like to thank the following for kindly supplying the line drawings and photographs used in this volume. Whilst every attempt has been made to trace copyright, in some cases this has not been possible. The publishers would like to apologise for any inconvenience this might cause.

Line drawings in text
Kingworth, © *Daily Mail*; Vicky, © *Evening Standard*; Trog, © *Observer*; Cummings, © *Sunday Express*; Papas, © *Guardian*; Newbury, © *Western Daily Press*; A. W. Lloyd, © *Punch*.

Photographs
Photo Source; Press Association; Popperfoto; Syndication International; Elliot-Automation; *Daily Herald*.

This volume is dedicated with love and affection to Caroline and all our family, and to those in the Labour Movement who gave us their friendship and taught us our socialism over the years.

Foreword

This first volume of my political diaries covers the period from January 1963 to December 1967, at the beginning of which the Labour Party was in its twelfth year of Opposition, after three consecutive General Election defeats; while I was still excluded from the Commons, having been disqualified, since 1960, from sitting as MP for Bristol South East by an old peerage law.

The diary opens with the death of Hugh Gaitskell* and the succession of Harold Wilson; my disclaimer of the peerage and re-election to the Commons; and Labour's narrow victory at the polls which took us into power and led to my appointment as Postmaster General. The volume goes on to record the Labour landslide of 1966, my entry in to the Cabinet as Minister of Technology and the abrupt end of Labour's honeymoon following the unpopular economic measures of July 1966. It finishes just after the 1967 devaluation, when Labour's high hopes had begun to evaporate.

I was initially optimistic about Labour's radical reforming possibilities, and fully supportive of the Government and the Prime Minister, but I began to form doubts during these events, in ways that will become clear.

I inherited strong radical instincts from my family, and by 1963 could claim more than ten years of Commons and constituency experience and great enthusiasm and energy. But I did not, at that time, have a real socialist understanding of the structure of our society. That came as a result of my experience over many years and in this sense the present volume and those that follow are the diaries of a socialist-in-the-making as well as the record of an active politician.

The main lessons I learned during the period dealt with in this volume may be summarised in four ways.

First, I learned how the permanent civil servants work to preserve

*See list of Principal Persons (I) for biographical details.

their policies against any Minister who wants to change them or challenge their power. This issue has become better aired recently, as a result of which more people understand how the Civil Service can frustrate the policies and decisions of popularly elected governments.

One of the Labour Party's failings is that it has never seriously concerned itself with State power and how it works, arguing that this is an academic matter of no direct concern to the people whom it represents, and hence almost a diversion from the real tasks facing Labour governments. In reality, it has been the existence of State power, entrenched in our constitution and reflected in the organisation of the civil, military and security services, which has prevented Labour Ministers carrying through any but minor changes in Britain's political and social system, a system which has retained many of its feudal features.

This feudal structure touched me in a directly personal way during my fight to get rid of the encumbrance of a peerage, inherited from my father, a former Labour MP. This battle, which began long before my father's death, lasted nearly ten years before victory was finally won in July 1963. During this campaign I learned more about the real nature of parliamentary democracy than most people could hope to discover in a lifetime at Westminster, and in particular the resolute way in which the Lords and the Commons, the Courts and the Palace defended the interests of privilege against the democratic rights of the electors.

Nobody had ever successfully challenged this particular aspect of our medieval law until then. Ironically the issue had far wider consequences for the Conservative Party than anyone could have known, by enabling two peers, Home and Hailsham, to renounce their titles and so be considered for the succession to Harold Macmillan.

The same lesson explains in part why there is a great deal in the present volume about the role of the Crown when I was Postmaster-General, for in those long drawn-out negotiations over stamp design, an issue which many might regard as peripheral, it was possible to see the same influences at work, and to study in microcosm how the Crown exerts its power, a subject rarely scrutinised or discussed in public.

The second lesson that I learned taught me a great deal about the way the Labour Party worked and how the Leader ran the Party almost as if it were his personal kingdom. Every Labour Prime Minister has available considerable powers of patronage and influence, many of them borrowed from the Crown, and can sustain himself by endless appeals for loyalty and unity, whatever may have been decided democratically by the Conference or the National

Executive Committee. This traditional centralisation of power within the Party was directly challenged by the campaign for democratic reforms years later, after the fall of the Callaghan government in 1979 – a campaign that will certainly come to be renewed.

Third, as a Minister, I experienced the power of industrialists and bankers to get their way by the use of the crudest form of economic pressure, even blackmail, against a Labour government. Compared to this, the pressure brought to bear in industrial disputes by the unions is minuscule. This power was revealed even more clearly in 1976 when the IMF secured cuts in our public expenditure, a process which will be described in a later volume of my diary.

The fourth lesson relates to the power of the media, in which I have had a continuing interest as a professional journalist, a former BBC producer and a Minister with responsibility for broadcasting policy. The power of the media, like the power of the medieval Church, ensures that events of the day are always presented from the point of view of those who enjoy economic privilege.

These lessons led me on to the conclusion that Britain is only superficially governed by MPs and the voters who elect them. Parliamentary democracy is, in truth, little more than a means for securing a periodical change in the management team, which is then allowed to preside over a system that remains in essence intact.

If the British people were ever to ask themselves what power they truly enjoyed under our present political system they would be amazed to discover how little it is, and some new Chartist agitation might be born and might quickly gather momentum.

My diaries will, I hope, give readers of different persuasions a new perspective on British politics. They should also allow readers to follow a wide range of issues and decisions as they were actually being discussed and made in the Cabinet, Parliament, the Civil Service, industry and the diplomatic world. The development of economic policies, industrial strategy, foreign affairs and nuclear power are some of the areas touched upon in this first volume, and expanded on more fully later as my own experience of Government grew.

To publish diaries while actively involved in politics may be unusual; most diaries, if they are published at all, appear after their author's retirement. My decision to publish now is a conscious political act, through which I hope that I may be able to contribute to the debate about the future of Britain. I hope that my diaries may be part of a movement that will eventually persuade people that democracy and socialism can and must be a major influence in British politics.

In recording events, I have tried to make my diary as full and accurate as possible, though considerable cutting and editing has been required to prepare it for publication. Here I have followed the 'Hansard rules' which permit an MP to improve the grammar or to clarify, but not to change in any way the sense of what was said.

Over the years the form of my diaries has changed, starting with fragmentary records going back to my youth, and forty manuscript volumes of intermittent diaries and letters written during the war and immediate post-war years. Since 1948 I have kept a brief manuscript diary meticulously every night, and from 1950, when I was first elected to Parliament, until 1963 there were bursts of full manuscript or typescript diary, though not continuous. From 1963 until the present, with one exception, I have dictated a day-to-day diary.

The one exception will be apparent in the last section of this volume, since from September 1966 I discontinued my dictated diary for fifteen months, partly because of the immense pressure of the Ministry of Technology and the demands on a new member of the Cabinet, partly because, at that time, it seemed wrong to dictate Cabinet proceedings to someone not covered by the Official Secrets Act. However, from brief manuscript notes made each day during that period I have reconstructed the most memorable events during those fifteen months, with some reflections on them.

On 1 January 1968, when the next volume begins, I started to dictate my diary on to tape every night but did not have the recording transcribed until very recently.

Diarists do not enjoy the advantages of the writers of memoirs, who have the benefit of hindsight, and who must inevitably be tempted into self-justification. However, if diarists set out accurately their account of the day and do not tamper with the text, they leave behind a valuable contemporary record from which, later, they may feel – as I do about this book – almost as detached as would any other reader.

Of course, no two diarists will interpret and describe experiences in the same way, and to illustrate one amusing example of this I have printed alongside my entry for the evening of 22 February 1965, when we went to dinner with Dick Crossman, Dick's own diary and Tam Dalyell's (as yet unpublished) account, each of which reflects the distinctive approach of its author.*

The diaries are primarily about day-to-day events and do not include the texts of contemporary speeches and articles in which my political opinions were expressed. These, together with other archival material, have been collected and filed alongside the diary over many

* See pages 310–11.

years and may assist those who wish to study the period in greater detail. Included in these archives are many examples of national and international political ephemera – posters, handbills, banners, placards and journals – collected by Caroline Benn. This whole collection, including the full and uncut diary, will ultimately be deposited in a national library in Britain.

The record of these years will be of most value seen in the context of the general development of British politics in the years following 1945 when Labour enjoyed its landslide victory. That Labour Government, coming out of the war-time coalition headed by Churchill, laid the foundation for a consensus which lasted until the IMF cuts in 1976 and can be seen as having ushered in, and later seen out, a new era in which there was a general agreement that full employment and the welfare state were to be permanent features of British society. The central tenets of this consensus were accepted almost uncritically by each of the major party leaders, and for a while it appeared that all that was at issue was which party could best demonstrate its competence in administering that system.

The consensus itself rested upon the wealth created by the post-war boom which had given British capitalism an unexpected Indian summer. It could not last. As other industrial countries developed or reconstructed, the pressure on the British economy increased, and the political consensus began to break up.

The resulting crisis revealed starkly the failure of those post-war consensus governments to tackle the underlying problems of a slowly declining British capitalism, so that when the crisis sharpened – after the OPEC oil price increase in 1973 – it was resolved by governments becoming progressively more authoritarian and seeking a remedy at the expense of working people and their living standards.

Some of those developments were emerging as early as the years covered by the present volume – with the abandonment of the National Plan and the imposition of a statutory pay policy in 1966 and the devaluation of 1967; but the full significance of what was happening was not then apparent to me, and the early volumes of my diaries record a certain optimism that if we did the right things our mixed economy could be made to work effectively. For what we were attempting to do during those years was to shore up the existing consensus by direct action.

Our policies were not adequate then, and I have no reason to believe they would work any better now, when the decline of our economy has gone so much further.

For an apprenticeship in the keeping of political files I owe a deep debt of gratitude to my father, whose filing system – on which I worked under his supervision from my earliest childhood – was a model and whose papers are now in the Record Office of the Houses of Parliament.

My diaries, like his, are political and not personal, so that family news and activities are not dealt with except in the occasional references to holidays with the children or, perhaps, birthday parties at home. However, in separating the public and the private in the diaries there is one point that needs to be made about my own family, which has had a major role in shaping my own understanding of politics.

First from my own parents, and later even more, and consistently, from the advice of Caroline and our children Stephen, Hilary, Melissa and Joshua,* I have been able to draw upon a fund of wisdom and understanding that was all the stronger because it was slightly detached from the daily argument. Had I listened more carefully to them, I would have avoided many mistakes, and for their advice as well as for the unceasing love and care with which they have always surrounded me I am profoundly grateful.

* See list of Principal Persons (II) for family details.

1
Back to the Commons
January–August 1963

Friday 18 January
Hugh Gaitskell died today after a terrific fight for his life over the last week or so. Nobody had realised how serious it was and it has dominated the press and television in an astonishing way. It is a terrible personal tragedy for him as he was closer to Downing Street than at any time in his life.

The odious thing about the obituaries is the way the Tories are building his death up with half an eye to suggesting that there is no possible successor. Macmillan's tribute was the most revolting since he and Gaitskell hated each other. Indeed one of the curious factors operating to check bi-partisanship in politics has been this personal hatred.

For me, Hugh's death produced mixed reactions. I have worked closely with him for twelve years and when he was at his nicest he could be very kind indeed. After the 1959 Election he put me on the Front Bench as Shadow Minister of Transport which was an extraordinary promotion.

On the other hand he was a divisive leader of the Party. He had a real civil servant's mind, very little imagination and hardly any understanding of how people worked. His pernickety mind always managed to engineer a confrontation of principles which he would then seek to resolve by brute force. I fell out with him on Clause 4 and later still on the defence issue[1] at the Scarborough Conference of 1960. From then on I was in outer darkness as far as he was concerned. If you didn't agree with him 100 per cent then he wasn't interested in you at all.

He never could understand the force or logic of views with which he disagreed. He projected the unilateralists as Communists and fellow-travellers and those who supported the Common Market as traitors to the Commonwealth and extremists. He thus isolated himself from an increasing number of colleagues as time went on.

But his death seems a disaster because it looks as if George Brown will succeed him and for a number of reasons he is totally unsuited to be Leader of the Party.

During the first seven months of 1963, I was preoccupied personally with the progress of my campaign to renounce the Stansgate peerage.

My father, William Wedgwood Benn, was elected to Parliament as a Liberal in 1906, and served as a whip in the Liberal Government but joined the Labour Party in 1926. He resigned his seat and was re-elected for North Aberdeen in a by-election in 1927 as a Labour MP, becoming Secretary of State for India in the 1929–31 Labour Government. At the end of 1941, he was created Viscount Stansgate. From 1945–6 he was Secretary of State for Air.

At that time, all peerages were hereditary and the title would have devolved upon my elder brother Michael on my father's death. But, in 1944, Michael was killed while serving in the Royal Air Force and I became the heir to the peerage. In 1955, I introduced a Personal Bill to allow me to renounce, which was rejected by the Personal Bills Committee of the House of Lords, and in April of that same year my father moved the same Bill as a Public Bill, which was voted down by the House of Lords as a whole.

After my father's death in 1960, I returned my 'Letters Patent' to the Lord Great Chamberlain, claiming that I had renounced them, but this had no legal validity and I was therefore summoned to the Committee of Privileges of the House of Commons which reported, in the spring of 1961, that I had inherited a title and that I was therefore not eligible to be a Member of Parliament. My seat was consequently declared vacant and a writ was issued for a by-election. However, I was readopted as the Labour candidate and the by-election took place in May. My Conservative opponent, Malcolm St Clair, issued a warning to the electors of Bristol that any votes for me would be thrown away: my majority more than doubled and I turned up at the House of Commons to take up my seat as the newly-elected member for Bristol South East. But the doorkeeper had received instructions from the Speaker that force was to be used, if necessary, to keep me out. The House then voted to refuse to seat me and St Clair took me to the Election Court where I was disqualified and my seat awarded to him, the losing candidate. Subsequently, owing to the public outcry on the matter, the Government agreed to set up a Joint Select Committee of Members of both Houses to consider possible changes in peerage law. In January 1963, as this volume begins, the Joint Select Committee had just reported in favour of renunciation but everything depended on the readiness of the Government to accept and implement the report.

Sunday 20 January

Rang Edward Boyle[2] today and he told me that the Cabinet would soon be deciding what line to take on the Joint Select Committee report. He was extremely friendly, as always, and promised that he

Daily Herald

No. 14047   Friday, May 5, 1961   Price 3d.

BENN WINS—NOW FOR COMMONS CHALLENGE

Gaitskell triumphs— now unity

By GEOFFREY GOODMAN and TREVOR WILLIAMS

THE growing demand in the Labour Party for unity now overshadows the bitter two-year

BUMPER MAJORITY FOR THE RELUCTANT PEER

By HAROLD HUTCHINSON and HUGH PILCHER

ANTHONY WEDGWOOD BENN, the Reluctant Peer, has won a sensational victory in the South-East Bristol by-election. The result, declared early today, gave him a crushing majority of 13,044—an increase of 7,217 on the General Election.

And now begins the **REAL** fight to take his seat as an M.P. For Mr. Benn, who inherited the title of Lord Stansgate from his father, has been barred from the House because he is a peer.

THE CENSOR AND THE SPY CASE

By the Editor

A FREE newspaper has to reconcile its re-

Why can a man lay down a crown—but not a peerage?

May 1961: the peerage battle as reflected in the press. The Cummings cartoon appeared in the *Express* before the by-election, above a sympathetic article by A. J. P. Taylor.

would ring me when the Cabinet had reached its decision. I therefore decided that this was the moment to put on some pressure.

This evening I rang four Cabinet ministers. I rang Enoch Powell who listened very correctly and said that he presumed it would be in order for him to transmit what I had told him to the appropriate quarters. I rang John Hare[3] who was friendly and said that he would do what he could. And I rang Bill Deedes[4] who was more than friendly and said that the arguments I had given him would be very useful in shifting some of his colleagues. I rang Hailsham but he was in America. To each of these people I made the same four points, which I advanced as arguments that they might find useful if they were hoping to influence their colleagues.

Firstly, the Labour Party would accept the Committee's report and would facilitate the passage of a Bill to implement it.

Secondly, there was considerable pressure on me from Bristol to fight again whether the law was changed or not and in a sense I had nothing to lose by agreeing to this since I was out. I added that it was particularly gruesome to be out just when the Party was electing its new Leader.

Thirdly, a Labour Government would go a great deal further in dealing with the Lords if they won the Election, and it would be a priority if nothing had been done by then.

Finally, this was a popular issue that cost no money and should recommend itself to the Government for that reason.

This was all rather difficult to say because it implied threats of one kind or another. But since these threats are much easier to make than to carry out I thought my points worth getting over to them before they decided. It's all very well being polite and modest and holding back and trusting them but it has never paid off, and my case has shown that it is only by being unpleasant and pushing that anything gets done at all.

Friday 25 January
In Poland for a week at an Anglo-Polish conference held in the Palace of Jablonna to discuss European security. There were a number of MPs on the trip and Peter Kirk[5] told me that he had seen Macleod about my case and that it will be okay before the Election. He also told me that it was generally thought that Hailsham would not renounce and that this would simplify the issue. I am not sure whether he is right about that. If Hailsham is likely to renounce it stirs Conservative interest in reform among the Hailsham fans but naturally it worries Hailsham's rivals in the Cabinet.

One other interesting conversation about this in Poland was with Oscar Langer, who is the Polish economic expert and is on their

Central Committee. He was most cordial at dinner when we sat next to each other and he told me about Molotov describing the House of Lords as 'the British Outer Mongolia'. This was the story that I had started and was quoted in the *Observer* from a speech I made in San Francisco a year before, and had got back to Poland by a roundabout route.

Langer also said that he could see a strong case for having a sort of House of Lords (non-hereditary, of course) in Poland. The problem of what to do with older politicians is a serious one in Poland and an appointed second chamber where they would have status and influence without power offered many advantages. Undoubtedly if you don't shoot them or send them to Siberia there is a lot to be said for some Marxist way of kicking them upstairs. Langer, like all the other Poles I met, had followed the peerage case with interest.

Thursday 7 February
Harold came out well ahead on the first ballot. This news was wonderful and incredible to me, knowing the PLP [Parliamentary Labour Party]. George Brown's arm-twisting produced a strong reaction and helped to contribute to Harold's success.

Thursday 14 February
Tonight Harold was elected Leader of the Labour Party. It is a great shot in the arm and opens up all sorts of possibilities for the Party. I have known him well personally, have always agreed with his general line and voted for him against Gaitskell in November 1960. He is an excellent chairman, gets on well with people and has some radical instincts where Hugh had none.

Wednesday 20 February
Went to see Rab this morning in his office, the very office Father had used when Secretary of State for Air in 1945. Rab had 'flu and looked rather baleful.

I thanked him for agreeing to see me and said I had come to ask what the prospects were and to put one or two points to him. The conversation progressed along these lines:

Butler: We have a general disposition to implement the report and do it soon. Of course the Committee only agreed by a majority of one but I think we shall accept it. The Leaders of the Lords and Commons [Hailsham and Macleod] agree on this.
Benn: In fact my position was covered unanimously and it was on the right of sitting peers to renounce that the Committee divided.
Butler: Well, we shall have a debate in both Houses and see what it's like. We shall put our toe in and feel the temperature of the bath water.

Benn: I just hope the debate reflects the real view of the two Houses. Compromises – like this one – usually attract vociferous criticism but rarely attract enthusiastic support.

Butler: Our chaps are generally in favour of this with a few exceptions. But you do understand I can't give you a pledge now on behalf of the Cabinet.

Benn: I understand that. Well, then, there's nothing much more for me to say.

Butler: Well, make your points anyway.

Benn: First, I gather that our chaps (Butler always talks about our chaps versus your chaps, and so whenever I see him I do the same) will accept the report as a package deal, though many of them don't like it, and will facilitate passage. There may be one or two amendments moved; for example, Lord Pakenham feels he is a special case.[6]

Butler: We shan't accept any amendments. We will take the report as a whole.

Benn: I realise that and it is agreeable to us as well. It won't take much time. Of course, if it isn't done, a Labour Government is pledged to help me and if we win the Election our solution will be more radical.

Butler: How do you mean?

Benn: Well, there has been a subtle change of view inside the Party and we will probably end all hereditary sitting. Also Bristol wants to put me up again, whether the law is changed or not. I feel I must accept since I have nothing to lose.

Butler: Surely the best thing would be for you to be qualified in time to stand at the next Election.

Benn: Of course – if you act in time.

Butler: What about St Clair? He can't be very happy?

Benn: He's not standing again and in any case if the report goes through he will be allowed to renounce the Scottish peerage to which he is heir, so I've done him a good turn. He's pledged to resign from Bristol when the law is changed anyway . . . I am glad Hailsham can renounce, for I think Attlee treated him shabbily.[7]

Butler: He won't renounce now. Of course he'd like to be Prime Minister but he feels that his job in the Lords is just as important. Alec Home won't because his is a very old title.

Benn: I'm not surprised. In fact I am glad because all the press comments have suggested that the only reason anyone wants to be in the House of Commons is because he wants to be Prime Minister.

Butler: I know. Everybody always writes about me as a possible successor to Macmillan. When the Prime Minister's popularity slumps, which it often does, my name always pops up. Nobody ever writes about what I do. It's getting me down. And we're told that because of Wilson we need a younger man too. But the PM will carry on. He's in good shape. And we may win the Election.

Benn: I know. It must be very difficult for you having been the heir apparent for so long.

Butler: Yes, and you know the Common Market breakdown was a much bigger shock for us than your chaps realised. I am very doubtful about it and I only supported it because of our exports.[8] If we had gone through with it we might have faced a real farmers' revolt.

Benn: I was against it but I never thought we would get in anyway. Was it really the defence issue with de Gaulle?[9]

Butler: Macmillan and de Gaulle had been going different ways for some time, especially with regard to the Americans in Europe. I always thought those shooting parties at Château Rambouillet were a mistake, especially getting Lady Dorothy out of mothballs for the trip. No truths were ever exchanged.

Rab looked exceptionally gloomy and picked his nose with his little finger which is what he always does when you go to talk to him, and which he sometimes does on the Front Bench in the Commons as well.

Benn: In a way, de Gaulle was right. Britain was not ready for the Common Market. You said you only supported it for our exports and they knew that was the motive.

Butler: Yes, but it may make it easier for us to win the Election. What do you think about Wilson?

Benn: He's a very formidable political leader.

Butler: Yes, I agree. Of course, Brown is very able too, but they tell me he drinks too much.

Benn: That has never been held to be a bar to high office but I think that had he been Leader of the Labour Party the nation would have been consolidated too much on class lines.

This brought the interview to an end and I thanked him and left. As I was going out of the door he particularly asked to be remembered to Caroline, although I don't think he knows her. But he always refers to her as 'your charming wife'. This was a useful interview. It told me all I wanted to know. I always enjoy my talks to Butler as he is easy to get on with, wildly indiscreet and of course utterly unreliable. I felt rather sorry for him this time as he obviously sees the premiership slipping away for ever. I'm sure he's right. That sort of chance never comes twice.

Went to Bristol this evening for a meeting of Brislington Ward. This is the ward that moved a resolution while I was in America last September, asking the Party to start selecting a new candidate. I gave a report on the general political situation and told them as much as I could about the prospects of early legislation on the peerage issue. Ted Bishop* then moved a resolution welcoming the Committee report, pledging continuing support and urging a campaign to bring about a change in the law. Tom Martin refused

* Bristol councillor, MP for Newark, 1964–79.

to accept it, as chairman, and the resolution was referred to the local Executive Committee. It was a typical Martin manoeuvre and I would have been a lot more depressed if it hadn't been so unimportant in view of the moves to put it right which Butler had told me about.

Sunday 24 February
Harold Wilson phoned me today and said that he would like to talk to me about broadcasting and to hear my views on the forthcoming debate on Lords' Reform. It was encouraging that he should have taken the trouble to do this and I noticed immediately the change in my prospects of re-entering the Commons if a Labour Government is returned.

Wednesday 27 February
Today we had the National Executive Committee and I went from there to the BBC studios at Lime Grove with John Harris and Harold Wilson for his television programme. It was the first that Harold had done straight to camera and he insisted on using a teleprompter. However it was a competent performance and I had a good opportunity to talk to him at the BBC. He gave me a firm pledge of action on peerages by a Labour Government and repeated his suggestion that I come along and have a talk with him. I also put to him the idea that we should have a Cabinet minister at the UN and he seemed very much taken by it.

I am going to work out a plan for this and submit it to him. I wrote to Phil Noel-Baker[10] to congratulate him on his appointment as Shadow Minister of Disarmament and mentioned this as well. I can think of nothing that would make more immediate difference to Britain's standing at the UN than such an appointment.

Tuesday 5 March
I came down from Cheshire on the sleeper last night especially to attend a meeting of the Joint NEC/Shadow Cabinet Broadcasting Committee – the first for six months. This was called at our request to consider Election planning. Hugh Gaitskell had been trying to kill our Broadcasting Advisory Committee, of which I was chairman, and this was our great chance to re-establish its authority under Wilson.

We brought forward our plans for Election broadcasts – in outline – and then Alice Bacon simply proposed that our Advisory Committee should be wound up. I looked surprised and Harold Wilson said rather coldly to me, 'Would you like your committee to finish or should it go on?' I thought this was a hostile question, so I just explained what the committee did and how essential it was if our broadcasts were to be serious and good in the next Election. He quietly said, 'Very well then, continue as before.'

I went away feeling this was a narrow escape and it wasn't until I heard from Peter Shore and Dick Crossman, and later still from Harold Wilson himself, that this was a great triumph. Apparently it means that Wilson wants me to run the Election campaign for the Party not just in television but spreading out into other fields as well. When I saw Harold later he was rubbing his hands and saying, 'I thought that went rather well, didn't you?'

Sunday 10 March
The *Sunday Express* – 'Crossbencher' – says that the Prime Minister himself has intervened to prevent Lords' Reform going through. This is attributed to his dislike of Hailsham, which is well known. I rang Douglas Clark ['Crossbencher'] at home and he said that he had heard it from one of the Prime Minister's closest aides. Somehow when he explained this it sounded pretty improbable but it did raise doubts in my mind about the certainty that this would go through with his approval. Macmillan has been hostile to the idea from the beginning and I remember Butler telling me that he was originally much opposed to the life peerages idea.

Sunday 24 March
The *Sunday Times* this morning said that a Labour Government would go much further than the Tories if they came to power and found the peerage business unsettled. I was delighted at this since it had exactly the effect that my article in the *Guardian* in January was intended to have but came with much greater authority from the political correspondent, James Margach.

I wondered who had put it in and it was only later that I discovered that Macleod had. Harold Wilson told me that Margach had come to see him with this story that a Labour Government would go further and had asked Harold to confirm it. Harold, who is no fool, said of course it was true and then enquired where the story had originated. Margach said it had been put out by Macleod. Macleod is obviously using it to railroad his colleagues into passing the law before the Election. This is because he is a bright tactician and realises that it could be damaging to the Tory Party if it were to crop up again during the next General Election campaign.

Monday 25 March
This evening I had fifty minutes with Harold in his room. It was a delight to find him so relaxed and easy. Gaitskell used to be so tense and tired and often signed his letters while I presented my points to

him. I gave Harold all the stuff I had prepared for the debate next Thursday and he seemed pleased with it.

Then he walked up and down beside the long table and talked in an expansive way about how he was going to run the Election. He plans to have a mobile headquarters of personal staff and writers moving from city to city with him and do a daily press conference and one or two major evening appearances. He's not going to hundreds of village courts and market squares.

He said, 'I'm not going to sit in my hotel room putting shillings in the gas and writing an article for the *Sunday Times* in my pyjamas as Hugh used to. If I have to do articles I'll have J. B. Priestley* travelling with me writing them for me.'

This is a most imaginative idea and we must gear our TV and radio to it. He seemed to want me to be with him all the time during the Election, which would mean even less time in Bristol than I had in 1959. He obviously expects me to do most of the working out of this.

Thursday 28 March

Both Houses debated the Joint Select Committee report. Mother was in the Commons most of the day. Stephen came with me and sat in the Commons gallery all day too. I sat under the gallery, separated by only a two-foot partition from the House. It was a weird feeling and everybody came up and said hello, including Harold and George and a number of Tories as well as loads of Labour MPs.

The debate was as dead as could be. At first it was depressing but then I suppose the fact was explained by the collapse of the other side. Like all issues that have been won, you can't find anyone who ever took the losing side. One or two good speeches were made and I feel now that I am really on my way back.

Thursday 4 – Monday 8 April

Went to Germany today for the annual Anglo-German Königswinter Conference until Monday. It was very depressing in a way because the Germans are so rigid in their Cold War approach and the German Social Democratic Party just wants to join the Adenauer coalition. They have no guts or sense of purpose and are licked before they start. Dick Crossman, Barbara Castle and I made speeches at the plenary session on the Sunday and tried to reflect something of the new energy of Wilsonism. The rest of the Labour delegation were pretty fair deadbeats.

Had a long talk to Dick about the Profumo-Keeler scandal.[11] He

* Socialist author and broadcaster.

said that Dr Stephen Ward, the Harley Street osteopath procurer, ran a sort of brothel on the Astor estate at Cliveden. Profumo lied in his statement in the Commons and Wilson is putting in a note of what happened to Macmillan with a warning that it will be raised if something isn't done about Profumo. I'm not in favour of private life scandals being used politically but it certainly makes the Government look pretty hypocritical.

The GMC [General Management Committee] met in Bristol tonight. I had sent them a full report on my year's activities which was read out and evidently approved. A resolution of support was passed and all seems to be going well.

Tuesday 16 April

To see Dick Crossman this afternoon to discuss Election strategy. Peter Shore was there and we had a couple of hours on it. Dick was in a defeatist mood, particularly in respect of getting our distinctive international policy over to the electorate. Peter and I both felt that he was a bit of an old man and he didn't understand what the younger generation wanted a Labour Government to do.

Peter and I had a talk afterwards and he is going through a very interesting stage. Since Cuba he has moved away from CND towards a sort of British Gaullism. His idea is that British influence should be used independently to try to bring the major powers together and I am inclined to agree with him.

We agreed to invite Harold Wilson to spend an evening with the three of us to discuss Election strategy in the near future. I rang Harold later and he has agreed.

Thursday 18 April

Went with Caroline to the *New Statesman* jubilee party. There were about 700 people, including all the well-known figures of the Left. Vicky was there and so was Norman Mackenzie and his wife, K. S. Carol, Jim Cameron, Mrs Ronald Searle, and the Townsends. The main guests were Jean-Jacques Servan-Schreiber and his wife, Sabine, from *L'Express* in Paris.

We have heard so much of him that it was like meeting an old friend. He invited Caroline and me to go to Paris to visit him any time we liked. I was a little disappointed to find him so smooth and well dressed, but he is a remarkable man and I would like to have the chance of a proper talk sometime. Afterwards a group of us went to dinner together in Soho.

Saturday 20 April
To Bristol by car today for the new Bristol Group which was as usual at John Ollis's house.[12] We had a final run through on the educational broadsheet which is an attack upon the present set-up in Bristol and an appeal for more comprehensive schools. The Group has been much smaller than we originally hoped for when it was set up, but it has produced eight or nine broadsheets and they will be published together in June, which is the anniversary of our foundation.

Tuesday 23 April
Went to Lime Grove this morning to help George Brown practise a TV broadcast. He was very relaxed but his content was absolutely meaningless – full of phrases like 'priorities', 'planning' and 'fair-shares' and 'get Britain moving', which without examples are completely colourless. But he was very friendly and he is a human man – both his strength and weakness being essentially human.

Friday 26 April
Peter Shore rang to say Harold Wilson wanted to have my notes on Macmillan's period as a director of the Great Western Railway which I had used in a transport debate in April 1960. I typed them out and sent them off so that he could get them over the weekend. It is sickening being out of Parliament at this particular moment.

Tonight we had a dinner party for Lucy and Norman Morris, Liz and Kenneth Robinson and the Townsends.[13] We had an interesting evening talking about the Health Service and agreeing that a Labour Government must be very radical as it probably only has five years in power and may as well do as much as it can to reconstruct Britain during that period.

Saturday 27 April
Valerie worked like a beaver all day on the major document on Election Broadcasting for the Advisory Committee next Monday. If it is agreed there it will go up to the senior Joint Broadcasting Committee and then it will be a firm programme on which we can work.

It'll be interesting to see if there are any objections from Alice Bacon and others to our work on Election strategy. I'm sure she will feel that we are overstepping the limits of the Advisory Committee. But nothing whatsoever has reached us from the Campaign Committee, and if we do not get guidance we must do the work ourselves as in 1959.

Monday 29 April

The papers this morning are full of the Tory weekend conference at Chequers. Apparently they are planning a campaign under the title 'Britain in the Seventies' – which is designed to make Britain in the sixties look old hat. This is all part of Macmillan's 'modernisation not nationalisation' theme which is obviously going to be one of the main planks in their Election programme. It makes the task of our strategic propaganda high-command much more urgent.

Worked in the office and then to the Broadcasting Advisory Committee to present the document which is to go up to the senior committee. Tom Driberg and Chris Mayhew were the only political people there and we made a few amendments. Tom Driberg was insistent that a specific reference should be made to public ownership – although it had been implicit. I'm sure he's right that we must be offensive about this and not defensive.

Harold sent a draft of his TV broadcast to me and others for us to scribble our comments on. What a change from Hugh! That man knows how to get the best out of people.

In Bristol in early 1963 a public row had developed because the bus company, owned by Transport Holding Company, had imposed an unofficial colour bar on employment on the buses, supported by some trade unionists. Paul Stephenson, a young black in the city, had brought this into the open and then demanded a boycott by passengers of the buses to get it reversed.

Thursday 2 May

The colour bar employment policy on Bristol buses is headline news and I spent a lot of the day writing round to Oliver Tomkins, Bishop of Bristol, Frank Cousins, Marples[14] and Bristol people about it. It really is monstrous that this should go on and I am sure we shall soon have it licked. I also rang Harold Wilson, who is including a couple of sentences about it in his speech at the African Freedom Meeting tonight.

To the Fabian International Bureau where I took the chair. Afterwards had tea with Tommy Balogh and we talked about building up the necessary brains trusts to take over each department after the Election. There is all the excitement of a revolutionary movement, with plans for this and that already afoot – just as if we were partisans poised for a victorious assault upon the capital.

Friday 3 May

Harold's speech last night referring to the colour bar in Bristol got good publicity in the local papers. He has a very sure touch.

Wrote an article for the *Sunday Citizen* as part of the revived 'You

Are The Judge' series which I do. With Caroline's help I tried to open up the whole question of the monarchy.

Desmond Brown of the TGWU in Bristol rang me today to say that I had been severely criticised at the regional committee for having jumped in on the colour bar dispute. He gave me all the familiar stuff – Stephenson is a Communist, the trade union has been working for years behind the scenes to get this put right, this would set it all back, Stephenson was unrepresentative of the West Indian community, I should have consulted the union, etc, etc. I didn't consult the union because they had issued a statement saying it was nothing to do with them. Anyway, Caroline wisely advised me not to get my colleagues agitated.

To Oxford this evening, in place of Tony Crosland who was sick, to talk to the Labour Club on 'Approach to Power'. It was based on my paper for Harold on Election strategy and I added a section on the first things a new Labour Government should do. Among these were some 'mood changing measures' – like no dinner jackets for Labour Ministers at Buckingham Palace, mini-cars for official business and postage stamps without the Queen's head on them. This last suggestion was the most popular thing in the speech. Republicanism is on the increase.

This afternoon I went to see Auntie Rene* with a tape recorder to take down some of her recollections of Father and the early days before 1914. She had prepared some handwritten notes and I also got an hour on tape.

Sunday 5 May
Joined the Bristol May Day march and had a long talk to Ron Nethercott, the local TGWU organiser for the region. He was very angry with me on the colour bar issue but I can't stand the equivocation and hypocrisy of pretending that this is caused by troublemakers. Wilson's intervention (about which they were also very angry) saw to it that this was not Communist led.

The Bishop of Bristol issued a statement today with the Church Council. It blamed the trouble on 'an unrepresentative' group of West Indians, then deplored the attitude of the busmen and called for a Christian approach. But nowhere did it say explicitly that the bus colour bar was wrong and should go. Just short of what was required and anxious to keep impartial by smacking out at everyone else.

---

* Irene Benn, sister of my father, William Wedgwood Benn.

Tuesday 7 May

To the Fabian Executive this afternoon and afterwards a long talk to Tommy Balogh. He is delighted with Wilson and regards himself as one of the principal advisers on economic affairs. After seven years 'out', he now feels he is 'in'. We discussed the United Nations and Civil Service reform and he promised to send me some papers.

This evening the Bishop of Bristol rang and we had a talk about the colour bar issue. He said he knows Paul Stephenson, thinks he is not a Communist, but said that he is one of those enthusiastic idealists who could easily become a tool of the Communists. What a typical Church attitude to a basic principle! I was as tough as I could be.

Wednesday 8 May

The Bristol colour bar is over. The papers announced that Transport Holding Company have issued a directive to the General Manager of the bus company ordering him to abandon it. I was so glad, I rang Sir Reginald Wilson, the Managing Director of THC.

To Lime Grove studios all day, helping Harold Wilson. The trouble is there are too many advisers – John Harris, Clive Bradley, the Party's Broadcasting Officer, Harold's secretary, Marcia, and of course John Grist, the TV Producer. He stuck to the teleprompter but did a competent job. His script had been in draft for well over a week and many people had done comments on copies of it. He takes trouble.

He said to me that I must get re-adopted by Bristol at once and suggested that I should get Herbert Rogers to write to the Organisation Sub-Committee before next Wednesday's meeting. His interest has made a sensational difference.

Thursday 9 May

This afternoon Harold asked another peerage reform question of Macleod, who re-affirmed in the most solemn terms his pledge that the law will be changed before the Election. He confirmed that peers could now get nominated and said the Bill would be published in a few weeks. If I have to record any one day as the day of total victory it would be today.

Caroline went to dinner with the Tunisian Ambassador and met a young Tory peer called Viscount Colville of Culross. He made a patronising remark – 'we decided to let your husband off' – and she just turned her flamethrower on him and told him exactly what she thought of him and the House of Lords. I met him briefly when I got there after the dinner and I found him badly mauled.

Friday 10 May
The *Daily Telegraph* confirms yesterday's statement by Macleod and its significance. Today is Father's birthday and he would be so pleased.

Lunch with the chairman of Anglia TV – Aubrey Buxton – and scared the pants off him about what a Labour Government would do to commercial television. They are worried I think.

To the BBC this evening for a forty-five minute talk on the trans-Atlantic telephone with Alger Hiss, whom I am interviewing for the Third Programme in a couple of weeks. He had a nice voice and his arguments were impressive. I desperately hope that one day he can prove his innocence.[15]

On to Bryan Magee's* party and then to Tony Crosland's for a couple of hours. I had a long talk to Tony about his attitude to Wilson, who he still thinks is a shit, but who he also thinks has done very well and would like to help in any way he could. I must try to pass this on to Harold since Tony is too good to waste. But the simple fact is that with Hugh's death his old courtiers feel out in the cold – exactly as I felt with Hugh. Roy Jenkins is bitter about it and jealous of what he conceives to be my relationship with Harold, which frankly is similar to his relationship with Hugh. Tony is getting nicer and nicer as the years go by and, as he is a very old friend, that is rather pleasant.

Sunday 12 May
At 10.30 Andy Roth† came for a couple of hours' discussion on a book on the honours system in Britain which he is writing. I gave him as much as I could about the Labour attitude to honours and some inside stuff on the Party machine's attitude to my case. It's easier if he says it than if I do.

My mind is working now on a logical Labour alternative to the honours list. I think it is very important that we should do something about it along the following lines.

1. A humble address passed by the Commons praying that Her Majesty discontinue the granting of all hereditary titles (peerages and baronetcies) and possibly all other awards except those for gallantry.

2. A firm decision by a Labour Prime Minister that he will not forward to the Crown any lists whatsoever of people to be honoured in the Birthday and New Year Honours Lists.

---

* Labour MP until joining the SDP in 1981. Lost his seat to Labour in 1983.
† Author and publisher of reference books listing MPs political and business affiliations.

3. The establishment of a small permanent select committee of very senior Members of the House to replace the Political Honours Scrutiny Committee which would consider names referred to them for honours by the Prime Minister.

4. The incorporation of these names in an annual Resolution of Thanks tabled by the committees and passed by the House. Within this Resolution of Thanks there might be certain grades of gratitude: 'high commendation', 'special thanks', and so on down to 'general thanks'. Those who were mentioned could then be invited to a reception as guests of the Speaker which would be held in the Palace of Westminster that afternoon.

5. Each person honoured in this way might be entitled to bear the initials PC – for Parliamentary Citation – and to wear a plain green ribbon after decorations for gallantry but before all other orders.

The great advantage of this scheme would be that Parliament would be the fount of honour instead of the Crown, scrutiny of purely political honours would be tighter, and it would just keep the Palace in its place. Happily none of it would require legislation.

This afternoon to speak to the Marylebone Youth CND group about South Africa. They were a nice, keen crowd, though mainly middle class – one of CND's greatest weaknesses.

Monday 13 May
This evening went to St Mary-le-Bow, Cheapside, for a meeting of the Christian Agnostics to hear the Bishop of Woolwich, John Robinson, talking about his book *Honest to God*, which we had gathered to discuss. The Reverend Joseph McCulloch has organised this group, justifying its name by reference to the line (from Oranges and Lemons) which runs: 'I do not know – says the great bell of Bow'.

At this gathering were Canon John Collins of St Paul's Cathedral, Father Corbishley (a Jesuit writer), George Dickson (an industrialist), Duncan Fairn (who took the chair), Gerald Gardiner, Dr Graham Howe (the humanist psychiatrist), the Earl of Longford, Canon and Mrs Milford, Mrs J. B. Priestley and a number of others.

The Bishop opened by saying that secularism was not basically anti-Christian and that Christians must understand and even welcome the revolt against dualistic supernaturalism, the mythological view of the world and the religiosity of the Church. He said his book was designed to help those who were in revolt to see the basic validity of the Christian message.

Mrs Priestley asked him if he was right to leave the mythological

Christians to go on in the old way. Woolwich said he thought if they wanted to believe this sort of thing he saw no objection to it.

Canon Collins asked about Christ's resurrection and the empty tomb. Woolwich replied that he really was an agnostic on this. He did not know.

Father Corbishley pointed out that the witnesses to the resurrection believed in physical resurrection. Woolwich said that of course they also believed in the physical ascension and no one now accepted that. Corbishley replied that Jesus had to leave the world somehow and he could see no difficulty in his ascending into a cloud (a splendid Jesuit view). Woolwich said that he thought the concept of Christ beginning a space journey was not very helpful.

Graham Howe asked if Woolwich was concerned with communicating Christ or communicating reality. He thought we must communicate in terms of experience. Resurrection is not within the experience of a congregation but the idea of death and the idea of fatherhood are within human experience. The trouble with the Church is that it's all mother and no father.

Duncan Fairn asked whether God was Love, or Love was God. Woolwich replied that for him personal relationships were everything and he deified them and believed that Christians should say that they are the most important things.

Corbishley said that you must have some sort of mythology because you were trying to unscrute the inscrutable.

I said that I found the book a flood of light because having visited Jerusalem and having seen the Church of the Holy Sepulchre and Christ's last footprint in the Chapel of the Ascension, it had added nothing for me. Similarly, having spent three hours in the anti-religious museum in Leningrad which had mocked Christian mythology and riddled the record of the Church, I found it had detracted nothing.

I welcomed the idea that we had the right to think for ourselves about Christ and were not bound to take it or leave it. The idea of depth instead of height reconciled Christianity with the scientific method and substituted understanding for magic. But since it would lead to a new conception of Christian political commitment, it would challenge the supernaturalists in the Church and divide the Church, and Woolwich must be ready for a battle. As he had said in his foreword he suspected that he should have gone much further.

Canon Collins asked whether Christ was perfect, for if he was he was then God. Woolwich replied that he wanted to write a book about Christ and that the Virgin birth made Christ seem unreal. Woolwich's interest in Christ lay in his normality, not his abnormality. He felt he could not make sweeping statements about Christ's moral life, for what was significant was his obedience. Collins replied that if you simply say Christ was 'the best man I know', Christianity could never get started.

We broke up for supper and resumed for another hour and a half. Later we had a much deeper discussion about the supernatural in which I had a long confrontation with Corbishley about whether the evidence for the supernatural came really from external manifestations or the discovery of hidden depths. Corbishley was splendidly Jesuitical in saying that you had to have mythology 'to get people to pray'. Here is the real nub of the question. Is prayer a duty or a need?

I attacked the double standard by which the in-group of Christians know that the mythology is bunk but they don't discuss it publicly for fear of offending the faithful. Moreover, if the maintenance of the idea of the supernatural is justified on the grounds of practical necessity, it must be judged by results. And by results it has failed to stem the rising tide of secularism.

Woolwich summed up briefly. He is really an academic with guts but he is coming under such heavy fire now that I wonder if he can stand up to the pressure. The Anglican hierarchy is beginning to sense that his vibrations may start an avalanche and ruin its plans for Christian unity. But then unity on those terms is death. I hope he has the courage to go on and see it through. *Honest to God* is certainly the most helpful Christian theology that I've ever come across and I'm sure millions of others feel the same.

Tuesday 14 May
This evening to dinner with the Zanders. Also there was Eliahu Elath* who is such an old friend. He was excited by the Bishop of Woolwich, full of news of what was happening in Washington, where Kennedy relies solely on the advice of his brother Robert, Ted Sorenson, McNamara and George Bundy. He also described tea with Macmillan at Admiralty House and said that the PM had taken him to see a bust of Disraeli (a great Jew and a great Prime Minister). Elath always makes me feel that he believes in the potential of the Labour Party and of its power to do good in the world if it can get a little bit outside its welfare objectives and visualise a role that will help to bring East and West together. I find him most inspiring and greatly value his friendship and the occasional opportunities for a talk.

* Israeli Ambassador to London, 1952–9, later President of the Hebrew University, Jerusalem.

Wednesday 15 May

A letter from Harold Wilson this morning, saying that he had seen Ray Gunter and Len Williams about the problem of readopting me and they share his view that it should be done as soon as possible. The Organisation Sub-Committee is meeting this very morning. It is impossible to describe the difference it makes to have a man at the top who is keen to get this settled.

At lunchtime I rang Sara Barker to find out what had happened at the Organisation Sub-Committee. She told me that they had decided that Bristol should proceed with a selection conference in the normal way, as if a vacancy had occurred. Nominations are to be invited, a shortlist drawn up and a selection conference held.

This is the most ridiculous nonsense I have ever heard. It is the final answer of the bureaucratic mind. It entirely disregards the victory we have just won and suggests that this is just an ordinary event instead of the culmination of ten years' work. It puts the NEC into conflict with the PLP who voted to seat me though disqualified. It doesn't even follow the precedent set by the adoption procedure in April 1961 when I was picked for the by-election without formal nominations.

I shall oppose this at the National Executive next Wednesday and will try to arrange an emergency meeting of the GMC this Sunday at which the Bristol Party can pass a resolution adopting me and call on the National Executive to endorse it. There will be a hell of a row about it, of course, but unless you make a fight nothing ever happens. My God, the Labour Party makes you sick.

To the Commons this afternoon and heard Macleod make his statement. The Peerage Bill will be published shortly and will undoubtedly go through by the end of July. It was interesting to hear Macleod speak as if this had long been Conservative policy instead of being an admission of defeat.

On to Bristol to do the 'Arena' programme on television and I telephoned Ted Bishop to tell him what had happened. He went to see Bert Peglar [chairman of Bristol South East Labour Party] who has always been very unenthusiastic. Bert's comment was to ask whether I was on the panel of approved parliamentary candidates, as if I somehow might not even be eligible to be considered for a constituency. It makes you laugh.

It's interesting that the press haven't tumbled to it. It would make such a wonderful story. But then the press aren't like that. They're much more interested in finding out how a viscountess will feel at losing her title than in unearthing the real tensions that exist inside this business. They have almost all missed the biggest news angle they could have had – the failure of the Party to support this. And the lobby tradition of good will and gossip, under the umbrella of which confidences are exchanged and never broken, is an excuse for doing no nosing around.

Friday 17 May
Had to catch the night sleeper back from Teignmouth to London and got to Exeter station at 10.30 with three and a quarter hours to wait. The refreshment bar was closed of course. The waiting room was bare with a few hard-backed chairs, so I blew up a beach mattress, had a cup of tea from my thermos, set my alarm, stuffed the earpiece of my transistor under my pillow and went to sleep.

The alarm went off at 1.30 and I found the room full of football fans who had been eyeing me as if I was a drunk, or a crank, or both. The train was on time and I got to sleep quickly.

Saturday 18 May
Home at 8 am and off at 9.30 to Yarmouth for a Festival of Labour Rally. It was so cold on the pier that the band was playing with literally nobody in sight. However, about a thousand people turned up for the meeting inside. I travelled back with Harold Campbell, the new Secretary of the Co-operative Party, and he explained to me the inside story of the London Co-op row in which John Stonehouse, a former director of the Co-op, has become involved. It is a complicated story but John doesn't come out of it very well. Also heard from him what a difference it had made to Labour – Co-op relations to have Harold Wilson in the job. Wherever you look his touch is evident.

Monday 20 May
Ted Castle* rang to say that the *Herald* was thinking of doing a major article against the monarchy and wondered if I would write it. I'm tempted to do this but decided not to, because I want to write a serious piece in my own way in the planned peerage book, summing up the role of the Crown and why it is bad. I don't want to commit myself in advocating a definite republican constitution which will get bogged down with the question of who would elect the President and when. Also, until the law is actually changed I don't want to run the risk of queering my pitch. Maybe over-cautious, but I am vulnerable at the moment and I don't want to be impatient and take on more of the battle than I can manage.

Wednesday's Executive is going to be tricky. There are three points on the Organisation Sub-Committee report.

* Husband of Barbara Castle. Journalist on the *Daily Herald* at the time. Created Baron Castle in 1974.

1. My readoption in Bristol, which it will be hard for me to raise since it concerns me but where the Executive is behaving very foolishly.

2. The refusal to allow Frank Beswick[16] to be a sponsored Co-op candidate at Deptford. He ought to get back in the House, was accepted as a sponsored candidate for Bromwich (which fell through owing to a muddle) and Deptford is an old Co-op seat anyway.

3. The row over Putney Labour Party who took their Party banner on the CND march to Aldermaston.[17] This could develop into an absurd dispute.

To a meal with Michael Flanders, which was great fun. Also there were Joe Horowitz, the conductor, and one or two others.

Tuesday 21 May
Jeffrey Boss, a doctor from Bristol, wrote today to say he was thinking of resigning from the Party and from Bristol Council because of the threatened action against Putney. I wrote a long letter back trying to dissuade him. What folly it all is!

Talked to Dick Crossman and wrote to George Wigg about the report that appeared in *Newsweek* suggesting that British Polaris submarines could only receive radio signals via the US Communications Centre in Maine. If this is true, it means that there will be a US veto on their independent use. It absolutely torpedoes the idea of an independent British deterrent.

This evening to the Commons to have a meal with Dick Crossman and Peter Shore and later to talk to Harold Wilson about campaign planning. We hope to get a regular group set up which will act as a strategic and tactical high command to work through to the Election and also to think about drawing up the 'War Book' and sketching out the tasks of the first one hundred days. Dick was very critical of Mary Wilson, who didn't want Harold to be Prime Minister and hated politics and didn't realise that Harold had to be cosseted now that this colossal burden had fallen upon him.

We went in to see Harold at 7.30 and he looked terribly tired. His left eye was swollen with a sty and although he was as alert as ever it confirmed Dick's anxieties as to whether he could stand the pace. We discussed what was needed and he agreed that there should be a committee once a week with general terms of reference and that George and Herbert Bowden, the Chief Whip, should be on it, that Gerry Reynolds should be put on it to please George and that Alice Bacon should be kept off it if possible. Officially it is to review the text of our advertising copy and look at Party political broadcasts.

Wednesday 22 May
The National Executive this morning and the main item of interest was the Organisation Sub-Committee report. It had recommended an inquiry into the Putney Party because they took their banner to Aldermaston and it also wanted to defer Hugh Jenkins's endorsement as candidate until after the enquiry. Mikardo raised this question and I cross-examined Sara Barker on her one-sided account of the position there. It emerged that those Members who were protesting about the banner had no complaint against Jenkins or his selection. I therefore moved that Jenkins be endorsed and this was carried by ten votes to seven. It was rather a pleasant victory. However, Dick Crossman's attempt to substitute a talk with Putney officers for a formal enquiry was defeated so that part of the folly must now be played out.

I did not raise the minute on my readoption for Bristol South East, though Sara Barker suggested that the Party had got what it wanted.

Lunch in Hampstead with Miroslav Jirasky, the Czech counsellor. He was a fat, slightly unattractive man who was mainly concerned to impress on me the desirability of trade. However he did not want cultural agreements, which fitted in with one's impressions of the Czechs as the most Stalinist of the Eastern Europeans. I raised with him the question of rehabilitating Mordecai Oren, who was arrested and imprisoned while on a visit to a peace congress in Czechoslovakia in 1951 during the Slansky trial.[18] I met Oren when he was released, and again in Israel this January. Jirasky replied that I should write to the Ambassador. He then invited me to go and give a lecture in Prague at their Institute of International Affairs. The snag is I have to pay the air fare.

Thursday 23 May
To the BBC this afternoon to do my interview with Alger Hiss. He was much tenser than when we had our informal talk but he brought out all his points and I underlined their significance. There is to be a playback for American correspondents in London before transmission and I think the programme will cause quite a stir there.

Friday 24 May
To a film studio this morning to see six films which I have collected over the years. Mother, Dave and June and Caroline came too. It was an hour of real enjoyment. Father's television programme, 'Speaking Personally', done in 1957 was superb and I am so glad that his grandchildren will be able to see their grandfather and hear fifteen minutes of spoken autobiography. There was also another

charming little short interview of his recollections from the First World War and the RAF.

This evening Caroline and I went to Mervyn Stockwood's[19] fiftieth birthday party at Bishop's House in Tooting Bec. His chaplain, Mr Mayne, had organised it and it was a very amusing do. He called Mervyn 'My Lord', which was slightly overdone. Mervyn was wearing a huge purple cassock with a clanking pectoral cross.

The first people we met were the Attlees. Clem was sitting in the garden in an overcoat, looking terribly frail. I had a talk with him about the 1945 Election and how he came into Transport House blinking from the sunshine and someone shouted, 'Here's the next Prime Minister'. He chuckled as he remembered Churchill's discomfiture at his defeat in 1945 – an echo of old political fighting now forgotten with Churchill's canonisation. We also talked about the Party and Harold Wilson. And Macmillan who he said was terribly insincere. 'It shows every time you see him on television.' He said my battle was a historic achievement and I thanked him for his support from the beginning.

Vi Attlee said what a great failure Herbert Morrison had been as Foreign Secretary – 'he just didn't understand it'.

Next Caroline and I had a delightful talk with the Bishop of Woolwich and later with his wife. He is under fire and I think he's glad of friends. Kingsley Martin[20] said that just as T. H. Huxley had debunked the Old Testament, so Woolwich later debunked the New Testament. Woolwich looked a little bleak. Later Caroline heard the Archbishop of Canterbury asking him 'What naughty things have you done now', and Woolwich blushed.

Mervyn introduced the Archbishop to us at the end – the first time I have met him. He is a mountain of a man and so plump and smooth that he looks like some medieval prince of the Church. I thanked him for his kindly reference to my case and said I had never had any sort of Archiepiscopal blessing for anything else I had ever done. Ramsey gave a watery smile and indeed looked at Mervyn most of the time he was talking to me. He said that he had made five speeches in the House of Lords this year, two of them Right, and three of them Left. A very silly comment. Alas he is only fifty-seven though he looks seventy – so we shall probably have him for the next twenty-five years.*

I also met a man called Oliver Cutts, the son of a costermonger who bought a lorry in 1946 and I imagine is now a millionaire who owns a chain of filling stations, a road haulage fleet and a great deal of land. He retained all his Cockney charm and obviously was a man

* Michael Ramsey was Archbishop of Canterbury, 1961–74.

of great drive. He's a friend of Bob Mellish's and shocked me by saying he hoped Bob would one day be Sir Robert Mellish, Bart, in view of his services to the Queen and Empire.

I said I very much hoped no such thing would happen and that Bob had been serving the people of Bermondsey and not the Queen and Empire at all. Here was a guy who left school at nine, licked the Establishment, and got to the top, and was now yearning to be a part of that Establishment. If politics is only about who is to get peerages and honours – our chaps or their chaps – then I'm not very interested in it. But I liked him all the same.

We went from there to Elwyn Jones's flat in Gray's Inn Square where he and Polly Binder live. He is a dear man and she is a tough and delightful woman. They had some Chinese author there and a few others. Elwyn is working with Gerald Gardiner on a book on law reform to be published soon. Apparently they have a scheme for appointing a vice-chancellor who would sit in the Commons as Minister of Justice responsible for legal reform. I hope they are getting this all through to Harold Wilson. If we are going to do the job that has to be done quickly, everybody must be ready to carry through some pretty fundamental changes as soon as we get into office.

Geoffrey Bing would like to leave Ghana now and would also like the Woolsack. But I hope that goes to Lynn Ungoed-Thomas who was really forced out of politics by Gaitskell but being a judge could come back that way. Lynn has a fire in his belly, like Elwyn – but unlike most lawyers.

Saturday 25 May

Tommy Balogh rang this afternoon and I went up to see him in his house in Hampstead. At Harold's request he has prepared a major document on Civil Service reform which he claims could be started within two weeks by dividing the Treasury into two halves and giving half of it over to a Ministry of Expansion or Production. The rump of the Treasury would handle financial matters and would act as a Bureau of the Budget. The Prime Minister's office would then be expanded to absorb the National Economic Development Committee and all disputes between the Treasury and the Ministry of Production would automatically be settled by the Economic Committee of the Cabinet, under the chairmanship of the Prime Minister.

One other implication of the paper is the need to set up regional planning boards – which in turn means the reform of local government. Tommy gave me this document to take away and read and I am delighted to think that Harold is working on such radical plans. If we get fundamental parliamentary, Civil Service, local government, legal and educational reorganisation we shall have gone a long way to reshape Britain.

Sunday 26 May
Stayed in bed till 11.30 – for the first time for five years at least, and then in the garden sitting in the sunshine while the kids screamed their heads off and splashed each other with the hose.

Monday 27 May
Paul Carmody, the deputy regional organiser in Bristol, rang today about the procedure to be adopted in Bristol South East for the selection of a new candidate. He told me that all the NEC is insisting on is that each ward and affiliated organisation should have the right to nominate a candidate and that the period for nominations should be four weeks. If only one nomination came in – mine (as he thought likely) – it would be open to the GMC to adopt me immediately. Endorsement would be automatic.

This is much more reasonable and, as Paul pointed out, if the constituency made a row about the recommended procedure it would only delay things. I said I was inclined to agree with this view and he asked me if it was my intention to come to tonight's local Executive. I said I couldn't and anyway was planning to keep out of it all. On the assumption that there are no other nominations, I should be able to be adopted on 4 July and could then go to the conference as the prospective parliamentary candidate and would be eligible for the NEC in that capacity.

This evening to speak on Parliament in the Stern Hall for the Friends of the Hebrew University. Dr Walter Zander was in the chair and he and Norman Bentwich[21] spoke. It was a delightful evening and audience – as all Jewish audiences are.

Wednesday 29 May
Clem Attlee wrote this morning in answer to my query about why he had dropped Father from the Cabinet in 1946. It was, as I thought, to bring on younger men.

To Harold Wilson's office this afternoon for the first meeting of the committee which we persuaded him to set up when we met him last week. When I got there I found Dick Crossman, John Harris, Gerry Reynolds, Peter Shore, John Scholefield Allen, and the Chief Whip just going into the office. Harold came through us and was the first to enter his own room where Len Williams was already sitting. Len Williams said gruffly, 'What is this meeting, who called it and what is it to do?' Harold said, 'I am Leader of the Party and I can call a meeting in my room whenever I like, to discuss what I like.

This is primarily to discuss the text of the very expensive advertising which we are putting in the papers. If Transport House can't do the job properly, we must do it.'

Seeing a row brewing up, everybody quietly picked up their papers and left. We waited in the corridor talking disjointedly when George Brown arrived and went straight in. At about 2.50 we were called in again and Harold began speaking. He said that this was a liaison committee to consider the text of advertising material and day-to-day tactical matters concerning the Party and the PLP. It was not an Executive committee and would not deal with Executive matters. The only full members of the committee were himself and George, myself, the General Secretary and the Chief Whip. Others attending in an advisory capacity would come from the publicity, research and broadcasting branches and Gerry Reynolds and Dick Crossman were there as advisers. 'Is that all right, Len?' said Harold. Len grunted. I have never seen Harold being tough before and it was impressive.

The committee then discussed the text of the latest ad, the publicity the Tories had got for their new housing plan, the coverage for George Brown's visit to America, the fact that the USA could jam British messages to our new Polaris submarines, and the ITA's and Serjeant-at-Arms' refusal to let a Granada defence programme be shown in the Palace of Westminster. We also discussed the desirability of Harold and George appearing in the defence and foreign policy Party political broadcast.

I then raised my idea that the Party should buy one share in each of the five hundred largest companies and send someone along to the shareholders' meetings to ask whether they were contributing to Tory Party funds, the Aims of Industry or the Economic League. If we got the facts, we could publish them, if we didn't we could then take legal action to force them to publish and use the whole campaign to build up the issue of business contributions to the Tories. I was told that this was not the appropriate committee in which to raise this matter but the seed had been planted and Harold said that discussions were going on about legislation to compel companies to publish this information.

The meeting ended just after 3.30, having achieved an astonishing amount. It was agreed that it should meet every Wednesday at about 2.30 and George Brown insisted that we should continue during the recess. I must say that George was not only very able in his contributions but a tower of strength to Harold in beating off Len Williams.

Tea with Dick Crossman, and we discussed the need for institutional reconstruction by the Labour Government. The five major institutions requiring reconstruction are: Parliament, the Legal System, the Civil Service, Local Government and Education. Work on some of these has already begun but if we are to get the benefit of any changes they must all be started in the first year.

We also talked about the idea of instituting 'national service' for a year for all university graduates to meet the critical shortage of teachers. If we are to abolish university fees it would not be unreasonable to ask all graduates to teach for twelve months. This is a most exciting idea that arose out of Dick's talk with Nigel Calder, the editor of *New Scientist*. We also discussed an idea of mine that at some stage an appeal should be made by Dick or someone to all academics abroad to come home and help Britain get on its feet again. Many would and this is our answer to the drift into exile under the present Government.

To Bristol and met the Councillor Vyvyan-Jones on the train. He is the chairman of the Bristol Education Committee and was sitting there with a Penguin book on comprehensive schools and a notebook, trying to think of what to say at tomorrow's first meeting of the Education Committee since Labour won the council in Bristol. He really didn't know what to say or do. It was a most vivid example of the acutest problem of all in modern politics, especially for us – what to do with power when you've won it. Happily I was able to tell him about the New Bristol Group broadsheet and he decided to drive straight from the station to collect a copy of it and read it before tomorrow's meeting. That is exactly the job the Group was set up to do.

Thursday 30 May

To the Commons this afternoon and sat under the gallery to see the Government present the Peerage Bill. There was no statement but the Bill was nodded in by Macleod and was available in the Vote Office immediately afterwards. There are no surprises in the text except that the Bill does not come into force until the dissolution of the present Parliament. Maybe an amendment can be moved on this during the debate. To the Strangers' Cafeteria with the Bill to talk to my lobby friends, and made the following comment.

'The Bill published today is the product of over ten years' campaigning. Without the unfaltering support of my constituency in Bristol South East throughout the whole of this period, this Bill would never have been produced. It throws an interesting light on the Conservative attitude to modernising Britain.'

I saw Charlie Pannell and we agreed to start planning the victory party which will involve about five hundred people and will be held in the Members' Dining Room at the House of Commons at the end of July. Each day brings the victory nearer. But today is particularly satisfying – to hold a printed Bill presented by Macmillan, who so resolutely stood out against the change and who has been forced to bow to public opinion.

Tuesday 4 June
Caroline and I went to a Tunisian Embassy party tonight and met Fenner Brockway who gave Caroline a big kiss and me a warm hug to celebrate the victory. He does so remind me of Dad and is a great man.

Wednesday 5 June
This afternoon Profumo wrote to the PM, admitted that he lied in his personal statement to the House of Commons, and resigned. The BBC asked me to do a discussion about the political implications of this in their ten o'clock programme but I refused. I can't think that the Opposition rubbing its hands in glee can do anything but political harm. It's a bit like wrestling with a chimney sweep.

This evening Caroline went to dinner with Lois and Edward Sieff[22] and there she met a man called David Pelham who is making a film of Christine Keeler's life. She had a long talk with him and he said that Christine Keeler was absolutely determined to bring the Government down. She was 'a woman scorned' and felt bitter about being dropped by the top people. It is all a very murky world.

Friday 7 June
Lunch with Duhacek, the Yugoslav Minister. He is very interested in the stimulation of European trade following the breakdown of Britain's entry into the Common Market – but can make no progress with the present Government who still live in hopes of getting into Europe.

He also thought that the Sino–Soviet split would get worse after the July meetings in Moscow with Wilson and that Khrushchev would be rigid until they were over. However, he thought then things would ease up and that the Russians were interested in the potentialities of a Wilson Government, which he also thought would break the impasse in European politics generally.

Mother came home for a birthday tea party here. We are renting her a TV set for twelve months as a birthday present – on the excuse that she must be able to watch the Election on TV.

Tuesday 11 June
Caroline and I set off for Heidelberg. We drove to London Airport, boarded a BOAC Boeing 707 and were in Frankfurt after just over an hour's flying. An hour along the autobahn and we were in Heidelberg, the most beautiful city on the River Neckar nestling between

the wooded slopes of the mountains. There Dr Heinz Walz was waiting and after lunch in the Schloss Hotel he took us back to his house to meet his wife Rosemary, who is English.

Walz was at Heidelberg before the war when it was a great centre of Nazi propaganda. He himself was arrested by the Gestapo and escaped to England where he naturalised. He is now back again and says that some of the old Nazi professors are also back. One of them worked with Eichmann on the background documents which led to the preparation of the final solution to the Jewish problem but since it cannot be proved that he killed a single Jew he is allowed to go on unhindered.

I gave my lecture, 'Beyond the Cold War', in the old Aula of the university with perhaps 700 people there – mainly students but with representatives of the city university, American officers from the huge HQ and citizens associated with the Atlantic Association and the German-British Association. I was very tough on the Oder-Neisse[23] issue but they took it all without criticism because the Germans are so disciplined that almost anything said from the rostrum is accepted.

Thursday 13 June

I had to go to Leeds to speak for Merlyn Rees[24] who is fighting Hugh Gaitskell's old seat. The political situation is fantastic at the moment with the Cabinet deadlock and rumours rife that there are more scandals to come, and that Enoch Powell will resign. *The Times* is now leading a campaign to get rid of Macmillan and there is a real possibility of so many abstentions on Monday that the Government might fall.

The PM himself is almost bound to have to go. If I were a Tory I should insist on this just out of an instinct for survival. But they are such sheep that I do not expect a revolt and if Mac can go on I think he will be massacred in the Election. This cannot be buried, as Dr Stephen Ward will be on trial in October and there is bound to be a tribunal or enquiry. It is all terribly bad for politics and Parliament and is an indication of the decay of the old British Establishment. But in the long run it may do good by forcing us to re-examine some things we have ignored and creating the sort of crisis atmosphere which will make it easier for the Labour Party to reform.

Friday 14 June

We had a party this evening. Among those who came were Robin Day, Val and Mark Arnold-Forster, Liz and Peter Shore, Michael and Claudia Flanders, Simon Watson-Taylor with Carmen Manley and another girl, David Hockney, Shirley Fisher and a host of others. Obviously the main topic of conversation was the Profumo business which produces new sensations every few hours. Mark assured me that the Tories had decided that Macmillan must go but he would be given his majority on Monday on the understanding that he would resign in August. Apparently the two main contenders now for the succession are Butler and Hailsham – with Hailsham edging ahead since his television broadcast last night when he slashed out at the decline in public morals and attacked *The Times*, the Bishop of Woolwich, the Labour Party and the Welfare State which encouraged people to believe they could get something for nothing. This sort of maniacal outburst is exactly what the Tory rank-and-file want and no one can give it to them better than Hailsham.

By an extraordinary coincidence Hailsham is able to be considered for the premiership only because of my campaign which has led to the Peerage Bill at exactly the critical moment for him. All the Government have to do is to amend it so that it comes into operation immediately and Hailsham can then renounce next month. Mark Arnold-Forster has suggested to the Tories that Hailsham should then stand as Quintin Hogg for Profumo's old seat at Stratford-on-Avon. This is a master stroke that will provide exactly the sort of opportunity the Tories are looking for to obliterate the traces of the scandal. Quintin is then elected an MP during August and immediately succeeds Macmillan so that when the House meets in October, Mr Hogg is the Prime Minister of a new administration with twelve months to try to persuade the country that this is a new, forward-looking, vigorous, proud administration that will make Britain great again. Hogg is to be our de Gaulle. Of course, it may not happen but it is true that the only circumstances under which Quintin has any chance of success are exactly these.[25]

Saturday 15 – Sunday 16 June
The Profumo business is still headlines morning and evening in all the papers. The weekend press seems to think that Macmillan will have to go and the Tories are now just looking round for an opportunity to do it decently. There's no reason why the Labour Party should help them to regroup under a new leader in this way.

Monday 17 June
Joe Cort[26] looked in. He is hoping that with the return of a Labour Government he and Ruth can live in Britain and he can get an academic job here. If he goes back to the US he might well be grilled by the Un-American Activities Committee and his career would be ruined. I discussed with him the case of Mordecai Oren. He has been in touch with me to see if I can get him rehabilitated. What an

extraordinary story of two cases of injustice from opposite sides of the Iron Curtain – both men ironically Jews.

The Commons all day debated the Profumo case. The place was besieged by people hoping for tickets and the House of Commons' telephone line was actually engaged when I tried to ring them. I carried a transistor all day to hear the bulletins and also watched TV when I could. Here was the Commons doing its job – making and unmaking Ministries – and acting as the Grand Inquest of the nation, the great forum of debate. Macmillan acquitted himself of any charge of conspiracy but, by all accounts, his competence was brought into question and the security services seemed to be operating both inefficiently and without proper political control. Macmillan will have to go and the fight for the succession will be on. Interestingly, Hailsham was near destroyed by George Wigg who described him as a 'lying humbug' for saying on television that a three-line whip was only an order to attend and not to vote. Nigel Birch[27] made the deadly quotation from Browning's 'The Lost Leader':

> . . . Let him never come back to us!
> There would be doubt, hesitation and pain,
> Forced praise on our part – the glimmer of twilight,
> Never glad confident morning again!

It is now only a matter of time.

Tuesday 18 June

Rang Dick Crossman and we agreed that we should try to plan a terrific thrust now to get rid of the Government. The important thing is to prevent them from having time to regroup under a new leader and present themselves as being 'under new management – no connection with the old firm'. All the papers this morning said that Macmillan was on the way out and so I wrote a paper for Harold, intended to suggest ways in which we could keep the pressure up and thus retain Macmillan or bring down the whole Government. Dick Crossman independently wrote a paper saying the same thing and we exchanged them.

This evening Messaoud Kellou came to see us. We hung out our old Algerian flag to welcome the new Ambassador. He greeted me with a kiss on both cheeks and we sat and talked for an hour about his struggles here from 1957 to 1961, during the bitter dark days of the war. I asked about all my old friends and no fewer than five of them who were here at one time or another as representatives of the Algerian National Liberation Front are now Ambassadors. Djoudi is in Tanganyika, Sherif Gelal is in Washington, Ben Yahia is in

Moscow, Hedi Ghany is in Stockholm. What a fantastic story of French obstinacy and British stupidity!

Wednesday 19 June

Dick rang this morning to say he thought we should press for an amendment to the Peerage Bill to keep Hailsham's candidacy alive[28] and thus to give Macmillan an excuse for staying on – which is what we want. The second reading is this afternoon and this point can be made from the Front Bench in anticipation of an amendment to the Bill in committee.

Mordecai Oren came and asked me to go to Prague at once to plead for his rehabilitation. I said I couldn't and didn't think it would help but I will try to keep the pressure up by correspondence.

After lunch to a meeting of the Vetting Committee in Harold Wilson's office. We discussed the situation in the light of the Profumo debate and agreed to reconsider next Wednesday's broadcast after the weekend. If the row does not subside we may move over to an offensive with a call for an immediate Election.

Caroline and I went to Bristol and I spoke at a meeting in Brislington for the Reverend Peter Allen, who is the candidate in the council by-election tomorrow. The Tories were there in force and it was a stormy meeting.

Saturday 22 June

This afternoon Tommy Balogh came for two and a half hours to discuss the 'War Book' idea, a book of immediate action to be undertaken as soon as Labour comes to power. He feels we should start work on this and let Harold see it when it is finished. I rang Peter Shore, who agreed, and we decided to bring in Dick Crossman of course. The idea is that each of the four of us should write a brief outline and we should then set aside an evening, after which the paper would be written and Harold would get it via Peter Shore, on an informal basis.

Balogh is very keen on the idea of building up a Prime Minister's Office at Number 10 with Ministers of State, one for the home front and one abroad. I suggested that the Cabinet Minister responsible for information policy should also move in there to co-ordinate things under the PM.

To Donald Swann's party this evening. He and Michael Flanders sang some of the numbers they have written for their new show.

Sunday 23 June

Nineteen years ago today Mike was killed* and Melissa and I went over to see Mother.

Monday 24 June

Drafted a short memo on the 'War Book'. Caroline and I had lunch with Joe Murumbi and Tom Mboya from Kenya.[29] It was nice of them to ask us and they are so happy to have won independence.

To Harold's office to discuss his broadcast on Wednesday. We agreed to do an interview with him, opening and closing straight to camera.

Had a brief talk to Dick Crossman about the 'War Book' idea which interested him and he agreed that we should tackle this.

Tuesday 25 June

Charlie Pannell has seen the Serjeant-at-Arms, who had told him that he had seen a mention of my party to celebrate the victory and had given special orders that I couldn't hold it in the House. Charlie replied, 'Mr Wedgwood Benn knows the rules of this place a great deal better than you do, and would never dream of trying to hold a party here without the sponsorship of a Member.† You will never be any good at this job,' he added, 'until you get as much feeling for it as you had for the Navy.'

Wednesday 26 June

The National Executive this morning was interesting. Three slightly disturbing decisions were reached.

1. It was decided not to set up an Appeals Tribunal, as had been requested, to deal with expulsions. Dick and I and Harold had spoken in favour of an appeals procedure.[30]

2. It was decided not to issue a new policy statement on agriculture and cotton‡ but to launch the policy by means of speeches, depriving the Conference of its policy-making function.

3. It was decided not to issue a speaker's handbook to candidates as such, complete with a summary of Labour proposals on different aspects of policy, but to cut out the policy and make it a factual

---

* Michael Wedgwood Benn, fighter pilot in the RAF, born 5 September, 1921, died 23 June, 1944.
† Charles Pannell himself sponsored the victory party.
‡ The British cotton industry was being severely affected by cheap imports from Third World countries.

encyclopaedia of twelve Tory years. This means that it will not be possible to find our views drawn together anywhere. Again this was for fear of counter-attack.

We did, however, succeed in getting a decision in favour of sending free to every constituency copies of our *Talking Points* and *This Week* which had been deleted from the budget to save £900. This is fantastic when we are spending £170,000 on the pre-Election campaign. Dick and I, talking as we came out, agreed that it was sinister to see the role of the Party and its membership being demoted and everything being subordinated to the desire to win the next Election.

This evening to Lime Grove for Harold's Party political broadcast, in which he was questioned first about international problems. He was extremely good and is better when questioned than he is straight to camera. Today Profumo left the Privy Council. He only has his OBE to go now.

Thursday 27 June
To dinner this evening with Lynn and Dorothy Ungoed-Thomas. We hadn't seen him since he was made a judge last year and it was a delightful evening with just the four of us. He is such a fiery Welsh radical with all the right instincts and he only left Parliament because he could see no future under Gaitskell's leadership. Before he went he saw Hugh and was told that his only hope was to be Attorney-General with no prospect of Cabinet appointment. He thus joined Robens, de Freitas, Younger, Marquand, Chetwynd and others who pulled out from disappointment.

His only way back would be to appoint him as Lord Chancellor. But on legal reform I'm not sure that he really is so go-ahead. He was rather critical of Denning who is certainly the most progressive judge on the Bench and I think maybe he would have to be promoted upwards to the Court of Appeal. Gerald Gardiner is the obvious man to be our Lord Chancellor. He is well respected by the Bar.

Friday 28 June
Twenty nomination papers arrived from Bristol this morning. It clearly will be a unanimous selection by the constituency Party.

To the BBC to record my talk on the Hiss case, and dashed from there to catch the train for Lincoln where I spoke at the Annual Women's Dinner – more than 200 of them. Done to repay Dick Taverne for his support during the peerage case.

Monday 1 July

Caroline and I looked in briefly at the Ghanaian party and then on to the annual dinner of the Society of Labour Lawyers. More than twice as many people were there as last year and the old hands were cynically saying that this was the bandwagon pure and simple, with hopes of getting promoted to the Bench under the new regime. Father used to say that he knew the Labour Party would win the 1929 Election when he saw so many lawyers joining the Party. There was even a rumour that Shawcross[31] had rejoined and expected the Woolsack.

Gerald Gardiner was the first speaker – tall, austere and incredibly frank. He praised the Labour Government of 1945 to 1950, but said that then the Party had gone to the Right to win the floating voters and the floating voters knew it. What mattered was sincerity, and in our new Leader we had a man who stood up for things because they were right and not because they were popular – citing Harold's speech on arms to South Africa.

Harold himself spoke next. He said he had read the new book, *Law Reform Now*, and was deeply impressed by it. He was sure that permanent machinery for law reform was necessary and said that structural reorganisation was an essential part of the new Government's talks, though this was not a thing to talk about publicly at this stage. He also said that he was sure that the first Private Member's Bill to abolish capital punishment would get through the House and be made law. This is very close to Gerald Gardiner's heart and was almost an invitation for him to join the Government. Finally, he said that he thought future historians judge a period of government far more by the structural changes that it makes than by changes of policy. This was exactly the point I was going to make.

I was the next speaker, proposing the health of the Society. I began with a few peerage jokes, including the difference between a life peer and a life commoner: that whereas a life peer was noble to his fingertips but was sterilised from transmitting his nobility to his children, I, who was now prevented by statute from ever holding a hereditary peerage myself, contained within me a capacity to fertilise endless generations of future peers.

Then I tried to draw the two lessons of my years of exile – the need to correct institutional obsolescence and the need to change the public mood. Measures for the latter included no evening dress at Government functions, new postage stamps and a general playing up of dynamism and playing down of pomp. Five institutions needed reform – Parliament, the Civil Service, the Law, Education and the United Nations. In fact, it was my 'War Book' paper and I was glad to get a chance to put it to Harold in this unusual way.

Dingle Foot replied for the Society and then called Clem. The old man looked so fragile and spoke so modestly and was given such a wonderful cheer. He made some very friendly references to my battle and welcomed Harold Wilson as the next Prime Minister.

Wednesday 3 July

Dick Crossman phoned this morning and we had a talk about security. The Party is making a great fuss about this over the Vassall, Profumo and Philby cases. It is obviously better than taking up the personal scandals but I am afraid that it's giving the impression that we want to institute a police state. Dick, who worked for Intelligence during the war, is a fierce security man and said that, as a Minister, he would think it right that his phones should be tapped and all his letters opened. This is quite mad. I am terrified that George Wigg may be made Minister for Security and given power over all our lives.

Thursday 4 July

This afternoon I went by train to Bristol where Caroline met me at the station. We had a meal in our usual place – the refreshment room at Temple Meads station – and then drove up to the Walter Baker Hall. There members of the General Committee were assembled and the formal business began. Paul Carmody, from the Regional Office, was there to see the formalities were correctly observed.

Bert Peglar was in the chair and he explained that it was necessary for me to speak briefly before the resolution of adoption was put to the meeting.

I said that it was a very moving occasion for us and wished Father could have seen it. We had a long association with the constituency and today was a day of victory. The Lords had passed the Peerage Bill on second reading and we had made history together. The real lesson was that when people discovered their power and used it there was nothing that could not be done. I read the opening and closing words from my selection conference speech in 1950 and said that if they chose me, I would do my best to work for the constituency.

Bert Peglar (who had read out the list of twenty nominating organisations, which included every ward except Brislington) then reviewed the story of the battle and moved that I be selected as prospective parliamentary candidate. Tom Martin tried to second it but was pushed aside as it had been arranged that Ted Bishop should do it. After that Gus Trathen spoke for Kingswood and Tom Martin for Brislington, (hard not to remember his hostile line throughout the Peerage campaign). Then Frank Jones from Hanham and Helen Bloom, who made a characteristic speech stressing how hard she had worked and how busy she was, etc, etc. Finally Harold Warfield and Reg Gregory spoke from Stockwood and St George West wards.

I was then unanimously selected and had to say one or two words more. I told them that invitations for the party in the House of Commons were available and a great number of people came up and took tickets and they are thinking of booking a coach.

The next business was the resolution nominating me for the National Executive. I can now go to Conference as the prospective candidate and as a delegate from the constituency. The meeting then adjourned while the press and television cameras were brought in from the BBC and TWW [Welsh Television]. They took a number of pictures showing Caroline and me coming in and being cheered by the meeting and I made a half-hour political speech, setting out the tasks which the Party had to undertake up to and after the next Election. Finally at 10.15 Caroline and I left for London.

Friday 5 July
Letter from Arthur Schlesinger, Kennedy's special assistant at the White House arrived this morning. I had written at the end of last month: 'No doubt you are following the political situation here. The Tory Party are working hard to find a new Leader under whom they can regroup for a year's build-up before the Election. Macmillan has threatened that if they force him out he will precipitate an immediate Election . . . Macmillan is hoping to use [Kennedy's] visit to buttress his own position just as he was able to use Eisenhower's visit before the 1959 Election to help in that campaign.' In fact Kennedy had been extremely brusque with the PM and his departure on television showed him to be most perfunctory in his farewells. Schlesinger, writing in reply said that 'the considerations you mention have been much in our minds . . . I do think though that this will not turn out too badly.' I am awfully glad I wrote and it is nice to have a private 'hot line' to the White House.

Caroline and I went to the party at the Soviet Embassy tonight for Madame Furtseva. As we were talking we saw Macmillan about four feet away, looking his odious self, surrounded by all the Bolshoi Ballet people.

On the way out I said to Romanov, the Russian Minister-Counsellor, 'Why do you invite these has-been politicians instead of Wilson?' He became very animated and said he hadn't seen Wilson since his return from Moscow and had asked him and Gordon Walker and Healey and me and only I had come. I explained that the invitation came late and that they were desperately busy, but he seemed hurt by their absence. So I later rang Marcia Williams and suggested that Harold might devise some system for sending people to represent him on these occasions. He must not get over-worked and kill himself but, as Romanov said, 'Good relations do depend upon good personal relations'.

Saturday 6 July
This afternoon to Transport House for the National Committee of the Young Socialists of which I am an NEC member. Bessie Braddock was in the chair and was brutal and tactless and as out of touch as anyone could be. It's so silly to bully these young people and does no good. Bessie spent a lot of time telling me about the secret anti-Communist intelligence digest to which she subscribes. It's like meeting a Protestant who is full of Papist plots.

Monday 8 July
Heard from Mrs Karmi from Israel that her brother, Jacob Frankel, had had his death sentence commuted to life imprisonment. He was sentenced for economic offences and I had cabled Khrushchev from Jerusalem appealing for mercy in January. A subsequent letter to the Ambassador had led to rather a brush-off. It shows it is worth trying.

Thursday 11 July
Bill Epstein,* his wife and son, came for an hour this morning on his way from the Geneva disarmament talks and was full of ideas on how Britain should behave at the UN. 'Your special relationship with America is dead and a new one is growing up between Washington and Bonn,' he said. 'De Gaulle has kept you out of Europe and the economics of nuclear policy are forcing you to go non-nuclear. Britain should become the leader of the "Scandi-Canadian Club" at the UN, working to make the UN effective and being one of the natural leaders of the small nations through the Commonwealth group.' It all makes sense to me.

Drove to Dover with David Ennals tonight to do two meetings for him, one at Sandwich and one at Deal. We had six hours of talk which gave me a chance to catch up with all his news and hear in depth about his visit to Russia with Harold and Patrick Gordon Walker.

He thinks very little of Gordon Walker and we both prayed that he wouldn't be Foreign Secretary. David has now met Khrushchev four times, twice on this trip and twice in 1959 with Hugh and Nye. He said Khrushchev didn't take Hugh seriously at all but that Harold had been brilliant. However, Khrushchev had exploded with wrath at various stages in their first interview saying, 'I would much rather

* Liberal Canadian official at the UN, whom I had met on a visit to the US.

deal with the Conservatives. I always could get on very well with
Selwyn Lloyd.'[32] This of course was what Khrushchev said after his
visit to Britain in 1956, that he preferred to deal with the
Conservatives.

When he was tough on Berlin, Harold said, 'That would create a
very dangerous situation.' Khrushchev shouted, 'Don't threaten me
with war or I will destroy London.' Harold said that he wasn't
threatening but that a dangerous situation would develop, and Khrushchev shouted again, 'There you are, threatening me with war.'
David didn't know whether this was done to test Harold's mettle or
to try to provoke him or what, but at the second interview Khrushchev was all sweetness and light and said he looked forward to seeing
him again as Prime Minister. Of course the great thing about their
visit was that they actually negotiated at the technical level with the
Soviet Foreign Office officials. Unfortunately, Patrick had not done
his homework and was full of guff.

David and I spent a lot of our time reflecting on the great change
that had come about with Harold's leadership and how awful Hugh
had been.

Bed at 1.

Friday 12 July
Had a long and interesting talk at lunch with George Ivan Smith of
the UN. He is an Australian who took over the UN operation in the
Congo, where he was nearly killed in 1961. He still limps badly. He
is now head of the eight-strong UN mission in East and Central
Africa. He gave the most fascinating account of the Addis Ababa[33]
Conference and of his talks with Kenyatta, Mboya, Kaunda, Nyerere,
Banda and Winston Field.[34]

Not only is he doing a first-rate job on the technical side, providing
advisers and help for these countries as they seek to federate, but he
is also about the one trusted channel of communication between the
whites and the blacks. He showed me a number of his confidential
reports to the Secretary-General of the UN, U. Thant, about the
situation and told me how he saw the South African crisis developing.
America and Britain must support UN intervention in South Africa
(by way of South West Africa). He told Field that it was only the
moderate Africans outside Rhodesia who were keeping law and order
for him by holding off the bomb throwers from starting work.

He saw the role of the UN as a natural meeting ground for the
super-powers, providing proper auspices for East/West agreements.
The Secretary-General acted as the Prime Minister of the developing
countries, representing their interests and working to bring about big
power agreement. The staff of the UN should provide technical aid

without neo-colonialist overtones and try to exercise political skill to resolve differences. He said the UN must intervene positively during and before major crises like Suez, the Congo and South Africa with an effective police force for this task. Here was a mission in which one really could believe. It was international and peaceful and constructive and entirely free from the taint of national aggrandisement. This man – he's probably around sixty – roams like an Ambassador at large all over East and Central Africa with his Land Rover and a dictaphone, with access to anyone, trusted by everyone and representing the might and authority of the UN.

His priorities were for Britain to give Kenneth Kaunda a new constitution and independence as soon as possible so that he can rid himself of the artificial necessity for an alliance with Harry Nkumbula.[35] Coupled with this must be a constitution based on parity for the Africans in Southern Rhodesia and a tough line on South Africa.

He also agreed with Bill Epstein that when Britain could clear up its Central African colonial encumbrances and deal with one or two other areas such as Aden and Oman, we would be free to lead the Commonwealth group at the UN in support of the developing countries and in line with the Scandinavian approach. All this is becoming much clearer in my own mind now.

If I dare confide an ambition to paper, the job I desperately want in the Labour Government is to be a member of the Cabinet as our permanent representative in New York at the UN to get this policy started there and fly the Atlantic every week for Cabinet meetings. I believe it is the single most important job there is to do.

Monday 15 July
Wrote to the American Ambassador about the refusal of the American Government to grant a visa to Willie Gallacher* on the grounds that he is a Communist. The old man is eighty-one and his sister is sick in Chicago. It really is heartless.

Lunch with Tommy Balogh at St Stephen's Restaurant to discuss his various projects. He is rather a nuisance in that he is always wanting to see me and it does take up such a hell of a lot of time. However, I am interested in what he is working on. He is jealous of the others who advise Harold and I think regards me as a useful link. He feels that his economic advice is negatived by the right-wing economists who advise Jim Callaghan. I can't help with that and I suspect that Harold deliberately keeps all his advisers, including me and Dick and Peter, at arm's length so that he is always in complete

---

* Communist Party MP for West Fife, 1935–1950.

command. If I were him I should probably do the same, not wishing to be 'taken over' by anyone.

Tuesday 16 July
Drove to Northampton with Reggie Paget to speak at his Labour Women's Supper Club. As I entered the Mayor's Parlour, the Mayor handed me a card on which was written: 'House of Lords defeated Government by 125 to 25 in favour of amendment that the Peerage Bill should come into force as soon as Royal Assent is received.'

What a message to get from the Mayor of Northampton in Bradlaugh's[36] own constituency! It represents a total breakthrough. The Government cannot resist this and their retreat has turned into a rout. I shall be back in the Commons before Christmas and maybe even sooner.

Wednesday 17 July
The press this morning is full of yesterday's news and it is accepted that the Government will acquiesce. I wrote to the Clerk of the Crown to set in motion the renunciation procedure and to Sara Barker and Herbert Rogers to alert them to the organisational problems.

On the way out of the Fabian Executive, I met Will Wilkins, MP for Bristol South, who had just come back from a Buckingham Palace garden party where he and his wife had been introduced to the Queen Mother. She had said, 'I hear you are from Bristol.' 'Yes,' said Mrs Wilkins, 'we are, and we still regard Mr Wedgwood Benn as our MP.' The Queen Mother gave a watery smile and said that she had been following the case with interest.

Went to bed about 8.30 and almost slept the clock round which is what I needed.

Thursday 18 July
The Peerage Bill had its report stage in the Lords today and some consequential amendments were made – the main one being to give sitting peers twelve months in which to renounce.

To Bristol for a public meeting which was crowded. I had issued a press release saying that we were near the end of the battle and we must now work for the return of a Labour Government.

Felt rather funny during my speech but finished it and answered a couple of questions. Then decided to withdraw while they looked for a doctor. None was available so Herbert Rogers drove me to Cossham Hospital, where I was admitted to casualty ward. Various doctors examined me and decided to keep me in for a series of tests. I felt lousy and was very glad when they put me to bed and knocked me out. Decided to tell Caroline in case she heard from other sources.

It must have scared her to get a phone call from the night sister and a Ghanaian doctor to say that I was in hospital.

Saturday 20 July

Caroline had cancelled most of my engagements for the next couple of weeks. It's so nice to have an excuse like this. She came down to Bristol yesterday and today stayed all day at the hospital and there were masses more visitors.

Dr Poku, at my request, took a hypodermic full of blood and put it in a test tube for me, as a reminder of the 'noble blood' which I shall lose in a few days. He mixed it up with some anti-coagulant so that it wouldn't clot and it turned blue most appropriately. He said he quite understood as his father was an Ashanti chief who had given it all up.

Sunday 21 July

It was a lovely, sunny day and Caroline and I walked in the garden and sat on the grass and I felt we had stolen a little time from the hurly-burly of daily life. It somehow reminded me of a military hospital during the war where everything was different because it was so peaceful.

Afterwards Caroline went back to London.

Monday 22 July

More tests today. The Consultant, Dr Page, said he was sure that this had not been a heart attack and that physically I was OK. So after an inspection of the hospital with the matron I came back to London and Caroline met me at the station.

Among the pile of letters was one from Sir George Coldstream, the Clerk of the Crown, who answered all my questions about the Instrument of Renunciation. It is very simple and I don't think I can go wrong.

Monday 29 July

I had Roger Baldwin of the International League for the Rights of Man in for a talk about Labour and the UN. The phone rang incessantly and we had to take it off the hook.

Buddy[37] was with us, cleaning up the children.

At 2.45 Mr Yavar Abbas of BBC Television News arrived to film us leaving for the Commons, and he then drove us to the Commons and filmed us greeting the coach party from Bristol (seventy strong) as it got to St Stephen's entrance.

It was a perfectly glorious, cloudless day and we stood and chatted outside St Stephen's and then poured in in a solid phalanx, led by

Charlie Pannell, up through the central lobby to the Members' Dining Room. The Bristolians settled themselves down in the chairs all round the room and watched the other guests arrive.

Caroline and I stood at the door and greeted them all as they came in. We don't know exactly how many came but it was well over 300. Among those who were there were Clem Attlee, (who had a talk to Stephen), Dora Gaitskell, Harold and Mary Wilson, Gerald Nabarro, Lady Violet Bonham Carter, Lynn and Dorothy Ungoed-Thomas, the Bishop of Woolwich, Arthur Lourie (the Israeli Ambassador), Messaoud Kellou, the Algerian Ambassador and two members of the Soviet embassy staff who had come to represent Mr Romanov. Also there were Canon Collins, Lady Jowitt, Cassandra, John and Patsy Altrincham, A. V. Alexander and a host of Labour MPs.

At 4.50, Charlie banged on the table and I jumped on a chair and made a speech that lasted about ten minutes. I summarised the history of the case and how long it had taken, and thanked the Party and especially Charlie Pannell. Also the Young Liberals like Lady Violet and Young Tories like Churchill. I also thanked the lobby and the lawyers, especially Michael Zander, and those who had given to the Bristol Fund, especially Lynn [Ungoed-Thomas]. I reserved the main bouquets for Bristol and for Herbert Rogers.

Finally, I thanked the family and said I wished Father had been there. Then I made a few jokes about the Peerage Bill and produced the test tube of blood taken in the hospital. I finished by saying that the time had come to put pomp and pageantry back in the museum and that this fight was the beginning of a much bigger fight which I was sure we would win too.

I walked back to the North Court Restaurant with the Bristol party where Mother had arranged a sit-down high tea for them all before they drove back to Bristol in their coach. At the restaurant there was another round of speeches and bouquets were presented to Mother and Caroline. Those people radiated warmth and affection and it was quite an experience for us all.

While getting us some tea, the phone rang. It was Herbert Bowden. He told me that he had seen Martin Redmayne, the Tory Chief Whip, and had been told the following: 'The Government will accept the Lords' amendments tomorrow and St Clair will announce, during the course of the debate, that he intends to resign immediately. He will be given the Chiltern Hundreds (or the Manor of Northstead)[38] on Wednesday, and the Royal Assent is likely that day as well. The Tories will not put up a candidate in Bristol South East if the Liberals do not put one up either and when an assurance from the Liberals is given, the Government will move the writ for Bristol this week, so that the election, if one is necessary, will come in August.' Bowden swore me to secrecy and said he would ring back when he had heard further news.

This was almost too good to be true for it was the final end of the whole of the story that I was hearing unfolded and I could hardly believe it.

I at once rang Lady Violet Bonham Carter and without telling her the source of my information said I understood that it depended on the Liberals not putting up a candidate. She said of course they wouldn't and would check it with Jo Grimond when he returned from the Stratford-on-Avon by-election. I know she is right and it was very nice to be able to set the Liberal machine in motion.

Later, Michael Zander phoned to say that he had seen Macleod at 5.30 and he had been very cagey about Government intentions but had said that in his opinion I had greatly damaged my cause by standing in the by-election in 1961 and this had annoyed a lot of Tories. Macleod is not a stupid man and if you exclude that explanation of that comment he is just a liar. But of course had I not stood, nothing whatsoever would have happened.

To bed a very happy man.

Tuesday 30 July
The Crown Office rang to tell me that the Royal Assent will definitely be tomorrow at 6 pm.

Caroline and I took the boys to dinner with her folks and we went to see *Oh What a Lovely War*. Afterwards I turned on my transistor radio and heard the news bulletin. St Clair spoke when the Lords' amendments came up, announced his resignation and said that he hoped I would not be opposed. The Government accepted the Lords' amendments.

And so to bed, my last night as a peer.

Wednesday 31 July
The phone rang so incessantly that I couldn't even shave so we took it off the hook. CBS Television sent a unit to film the family and Hilary [aged nine] gave a sensational interview in which he said, 'The hereditary system is ridiculous and Britain ought to have a President who was elected instead of a Queen who was not.' The interviewer asked him if he had studied the American system of government and Hilary replied, 'Not in any detail, but I know what it adds up to.' We had no idea what he was going to say, but after they told him they were going to ask him some questions, Caroline found him in the bathroom washing his face, and saying, 'I am really nervous.'

The reporters were coming to the door every few minutes and

Caroline and I had a job finding time to sign the Instrument of Renunciation. We did three copies, one on cardboard as a show one, one to keep and one to use. Stephen was watching cricket at the Oval all day. Caroline took Melissa and Joshua out to lunch and Hilary handled the telephone.

I went to the Commons for the weekly meeting in Harold Wilson's office and then to Transport House for a broadcasting meeting. From there I picked up Mother and we met Caroline at 4.45 pm outside St Stephen's entrance. There were two film cameramen and about thirty photographers. It was another lovely day and I took off my coat while we were photographed with the Instrument. The three of us went to have tea in the Strangers' Cafeteria, and then at about 5.50 we took our seat in the second row of the Lower West Gallery of the House of Lords. It annoyed me very much that the attendant kept calling me 'My Lord'.

The defence debate was in progress and just before 6 the House suspended itself, while the Commissioners came to sit on the Woolsack. They were the Lord Chancellor, the Archbishop of Canterbury and Lord Morris. Black Rod was sent to get the Commons and they arrived with the Speaker, though we could not see them below the gallery.

There were fifty-seven Acts requiring the Royal Assent and the Peerage Act was somewhere in the middle. The ceremonial seemed awfully silly especially when the Clerk read out the names of some Bills like the 'Public Lavatories (Turnstiles)' Bill and the other Clerk said '*La Reyne la veult*'. As soon as the words of assent were given to the Peerage Act, we got up and walked out and Caroline accidentally banged the door of the gallery which rang like a shot through the chamber. *The Times* said we left 'as if a starting pistol had been fired'.

Downstairs a Badge messenger* escorted us straight to the Clerk of the Crown's office, where one of his officials was waiting for us. Two *Daily Express* men were standing outside and asked if they could be with us. We said firmly 'No', and closed the door. By then it was 6.12 pm and just after 6.15 we were ushered into the office of the Clerk of the Crown, Sir George Coldstream. Sir George himself came in in his full-bottomed wig, took it off and put it on the table. I had a bag full of documents in case any of them were needed but none was asked for.

Sir George glanced at the Instrument and went through it quickly and said it was in order. At 6.22 pm exactly, with Caroline and Mother beside me, I put my right thumb on the green seal and as I handed the Instrument to Sir George Coldstream, I said, 'This is my

---

* 'Badge messengers' have custodial duties within the Houses of Parliament.

deed and my act.' As the paper passed into his fingers, the peerage disappeared from me and became dormant, in which state it will remain until my death, when it will be wholly and fully revived in the person who is my heir at that time.

Sir George was absolutely charming and his face was wreathed in smiles. He said that he was glad I was the first to renounce and he showed me the Register of Renunciation which had been specially prepared pursuant to the Act, in which the names of those who had renounced would be written. My name will go as No 1. Sir George then said to Mother how much everyone missed Father and what a popular Member of the House he had been.

At our request he let us out of the side door and we slipped down the stairs into the Chancellor's Courtyard and through the arches in the open towards the Strangers' Cafeteria, where the lobby were waiting. As we passed one of the Badge messengers of the House of Lords he said, 'Goodnight, Sir!' It was all over.

The press lobby were their usual selves and we talked to them for some while. They really are a lot of deadbeats with no enthusiasm for anything – not even for digging out the story behind the story. They have always missed the really interesting angle of my battle – how the Labour Party machine tried to obstruct – and they're just sponges that mop up the official story with a special personality angle and miss the main political importance of things. I simply couldn't get them to see the significance of the Act if any conflict developed in the future between the two Houses. For then, the 800 hereditary peers, who might have renounced under the Act but did not, would be represented as having opted for privilege and discounted accordingly.

Caroline and I went over to Kenneth Rose's* flat. Among his other guests were John and Patsy Grigg. John had renounced eight minutes after me and the Clerk of the Crown had said, 'I hope you don't regret it!' As he left, one of the secretaries in the office said, 'We have been dreading this day, but it hasn't been too bad.' I suppose this was a reference to my appearance. I must seem an ogre and monster to that department. Also there at dinner were Lord and Lady Freyberg. He is a major in the Guards, with special responsibility for ceremonial. We felt so 'one up' on him. If status symbols mean anything, far and away the best is to have had it and given it up.

---

* An historian, and 'Albany' of the *Sunday Telegraph*, who was a contemporary of mine at college.

Thursday 1 August
There were some lovely press photos this morning and we had
German TV to do an interview. Stephen went to the Oval to watch
the West Indians and I sent my passport to the passport office by
Post Office messenger to have the words 'Viscount Stansgate' deleted.
They did this without any trouble.

The Executive met in Bristol this evening to consider what sort of
campaign to fight if it became necessary to have one. They agreed
to limit themselves to an Election address to be distributed by hand,
and a simple window bill and to campaign for only a few days at the
end.

Friday 2 August
The Certificate arrived from the Lord Chancellor's office this morning
resplendent with blue ribbon and a red wafer seal, certifying that my
Instrument (of which a photostatic copy was attached) had been
received.

At 11.20 am I went to Harold's office for a meeting on
broadcasting.

At 1.15 pm I went to the BBC to do an interview for the North
American service. How elaborate and clumsy their preparations are!
There was a programme engineer, a producer, an interviewer and a
big studio – all for four and a half minutes. Compare this with the
number of overseas radio correspondents who come with their midget
recorders and do it in ten minutes. Also they were very cross when
I made some points about the political and social consequences of
the hereditary system. What they wanted was a lot of gooey 'women's
column' stuff about how it felt to have 'dropped my nobleman's
coronet'. Ugh! I'm sure they will cut out the useful bits.

Sunday 4 August
Mother came to lunch and said that she had seen Mr Justice Gorman
at church this morning. He came over and shook her warmly by the
hand and said how delighted he was by the news. 'Now I can be
impartial about it, at last,' he added. A curious choice of phrase for
a judge but what he meant was that he felt no longer bound by his
own judgement[39] and need to uphold the law. I have an affection for
that old man, despite his ghastly judgement.

*On 8 August the family went on holiday to France, long arranged and much
needed, but coming at an awkward moment as the writ for the by-election for
20 August had been moved and the campaign was about to begin. Edward
Martell had been nominated as an Independent right-wing candidate, with Mrs
Dorothy Lloyd, a London caretaker, also Independent, and a Mr Geoffrey Pearl,*

*who described himself as an anti-socialist, which meant that my absence would
attract unfavourable comment. I therefore decided to go with the family for three
days to get them settled into the flat we had rented and then fly back to London
for the election. The next few days' diary were contained in a letter sent to
Caroline from Bristol.*

Tuesday 13–Thursday 15 August

'It's three days since I left you all and this is really the first moment
that I've had to write. Valerie is typing it so that I can get through
more news quickly.

'It was an awful wrench leaving you at St Raphael but as soon as
the bus disappeared round the corner I turned my mind to Bristol
and being busy is making the time fly by.

'The drive along the motorway to Nice was very beautiful and we
can come back that way to Cannes next week. The flight home was
uneventful and I got a taxi back home from the airport to leave me
time to make some 'phone calls to Bristol and plough through the
mountains of mail.

'The press had just begun to hint at my absence and Martell was
mocking it. So this was obviously the right day to return – late
enough to make a triumphal entry but not too late. I rang Herbert
to catch up with the news and the Election addresses were going out
as planned by door-to-door distribution. It has saved hours of work
addressing envelopes and is far more efficient.

'Up early on Wednesday and had to push the car to get it started
as the battery was dead – a real sign of Election time. Valerie arrived
and we loaded the car up with tons of junk because there was too
little time to sort it out. Bought a roof rack to hold my posters and
we set off for Bristol, arriving just in time for the press conference
we had fixed. Unity House was purring with the usual sorts of
activities and Ted Rees* and his staff had moved in and were boiling
tea on a new primus stove.

'The press were there in force, just as the Stratford by-election† is
closing – and there were some old faces like Paddy Travers from the
Telegraph. Martell is a brilliant publicist and has been filling the
papers with bets that he won't lose his deposit, reports that he has
been threatened over the telephone, challenges to the Bristol Tory
machine to support him and all the rest. He uses his printing press
to produce thousands of an 'Election Special' and I have a job
knowing how to deal with him. If I launch in as I could it would

---

* Full-time South West Regional Organiser of the Labour Party.

† John Profumo's seat was contested and won by Angus Maude. The Labour candidate was Andrew Faulds.

only make him seem more important – but if I don't my stuff is a bit pedestrian. Anyway it doesn't much matter.

'Jennie Lee came down and we had three wonderful adoption meetings with over eighty at each and although they were mainly supporters it was an indication of interest and enthusiasm which will reflect itself in our week's campaign.

'On Thursday I was up at 6 doing the bus queues and then we had the press conference at which I released the text of a telegram to Hailsham, asking him when he was going to renounce. The *Telegraph* was right to call it a gimmick but there you are.

'Harold Wilson sent a very friendly message from the Scilly Isles. By the way, the press is full of pictures of him on holiday. How Mary Wilson must be cursing the press!

'This afternoon we planned to launch a committee to be called Citizens for Labour. This is the scheme I have had in mind for a very long time. It has the personal blessing of Herbert Rogers (strengthened by the possibility that Transport House may be against it), Ted Rees and Leslie Bridges.* John Harris is also very keen, as he has been trying to get the idea approved by the Organisation Department under Sara Barker.

I tried a new sort of bus canvassing – getting on a bus and meeting everyone on the top and bottom decks and getting off again at the next stop. People are delighted as they have nothing to do or read on a bus and are anyway quite captured. Many conductors won't take any fare money. It has suddenly hit me like a shaft of light that there are such public meetings criss-crossing my constituency all day just waiting to be addressed. It is a splendid way of getting round.

Did a factory lunchtime meeting at Britton's, the shoe people in Kingswood. Of course we are all very bucked by the result at Stratford-on-Avon where Angus Maude's majority dropped from 14,000 to 3,000 and the Labour vote increased absolutely and, taken with the Liberals, means the Tories are in on a minority vote.

It's awfully hard to know what will happen here. Quite frankly there has been absolutely no canvassing whatsoever and the ward organisation is virtually non-existent. This by-election is a publicity exercise, pure and simple, and if we do well it will suggest that the traditional methods are just out of date as I have long suspected. If I have to guess, I would give us 18,000 votes and Martell 5,000, which would mean about the same absolute majority as last time. I shall certainly be very disappointed if our vote drops below 15,000 or the majority below 10,000.

* Secretary of Bristol Borough Labour Party.

'The time is flying and I can't tell you what it means to be able to look forward to coming back again on Wednesday – even for so few hours. I think such a lot of you all on the beach in the sunshine and hope it isn't complete hell coping by yourself.

With love to all those children, collectively and individually, and a special hug for you.'

Friday 16 August
Martell's press campaign is extremely effective. He manages to catch the headlines every day with something – threatening telephone calls, a bet with the local editor, help for a woman who is looking for a house, etc. Also he has a very good theme to play on – he is against the big battalions representing the right of ordinary people to stand for Parliament and opposed to the caucus decision that led to my being returned unopposed.

He has also hit upon the secret of good political organisation – building up a card index of people who will do something. This is far more important than canvassing or our traditional methods of trying to build a mass membership. He keeps a careful list of his supporters all over the country and can call on them for money and support when and as he needs it.

This evening I went to an Amalgamated Engineering Union meeting in the Crispin Rooms and found that because of Martell's anti-union activities they were going all out to help. In a way it is a good thing to have a serious crank who stirs genuine opposition. Our constituency organisation is in its usual state of chaos and in some areas is virtually non-existent.

Sunday 18 August
Valerie worked up at the headquarters all day today helping Joyce Perham and preparing two more issues of 'The Campaigner', dealing with Martell's 'Election Special', which was a real smear sheet. It reproduced my *Who's Who* entry, suggesting I had two houses, falsified the Election results over the last few years to show a steadily declining majority (the first figures he gave were for Cripps[40] in 1950, and not me, and he left out the redistribution boundaries, and the by-election of 1961). He also said I had done nothing for the constituency but was hawking my peerage around.

Monday 19 August
Eve of poll and the last press conference at Unity House. Factory gate meeting at Strachan and Henshaw. Mother arrived after lunch and we went round the Co-op Clothing Factory.

Jim Griffiths[41] came down to the meetings and we had three of them, ending up in St George's Park, again by the headlights of the cars, in a semi-circle around the wagon. I should think there were 200 or more there and it was a traditional Bristol occasion.

Tuesday 20 August
Polling Day and Mother came round with me to thirty-four polling stations – a journey we didn't finish till 6. Very few committee rooms were in operation and the turn-out was so low as to be absolutely frightening. In some areas it was only 8 per cent by 6 o'clock and I thought that the majority would be slashed to about 5,000 in a 25 per cent poll. After a meal I did some last-minute loud-speaker work and the rain was coming down, with the street lights reflecting in pools of water in the empty streets. But the voting was a little brisker near the end.

At about 10 o'clock Mother and I collected Valerie and we went to St George's Grammar School for the count. The television units were setting up their lights and cameras outside and there were quite a few people gathering idly.

Inside was the familiar scene as the boxes were emptied out into a huge wooden tray and distributed to the tables to the counters. At first peek it looked as if Martell might lose his deposit – all the more so when it was clear that nearly 25,000 people had actually voted. He looked very gloomy and was surrounded by a hard-faced group of men and women each wearing a white carnation.

Mrs Lloyd was absolutely alone – not even her husband had come. Pearl had withdrawn from the contest the day before and had asked his supporters to vote for Martell.

Soon after midnight the Sheriff began consulting with the agents and then declared the result as follows:

Benn	20,313
Martell	4,834
Lloyd	287

Majority 15,479 representing 79.7 per cent of the votes cast. Lloyd and Pearl lost their deposits.

Wednesday 21 August
After the result we went out on to the stone parapet illuminated by the television lights and down in the road was an enormous crowd entirely blocking the highway. It's hard to say how many people were there but I shouldn't be surprised to find there were nearly 2,000. I made my speech and then Martell was called. There was such a lot of shouting that I had twice to ask the crowd to be quiet so that he could complete what he had to say. He was so angry that

August 1963, after the renunciation: Lord Hailsham in fact needed little
encouragement to cast his votes aside.

he made the great mistake of turning on them and saying that I was
better than they were. Mrs Lloyd made a short speech thanking them
for 'tolerating' her.

From the parapet we went down into the street and I was hoisted
on the shoulders of two strong supporters and then put on top of the
car which was pulled (with the help of the car engine) up to the
Walter Baker Hall which was crowded with people. There I made
another speech of thanks and after a couple of radio and TV interviews went back to bed about 3.

Up at 6 and set off from Bristol. We had a puncture on the way
which delayed us a bit. Went to London Airport to catch the plane
for Nice. The TV newsreels covered my departure – the first time I
have ever been filmed doing that platitudinous walk up the steps into
a jet complete with a wave at the end.

Arrived in Nice and caught the airport bus to St Raphael, where
Caroline and the children met me and we drove back to Pampelonne
and dropped exhaustedly into bed.

Thursday 22 August
To St Tropez to celebrate the end of our holiday. It was awful for them being left alone there but I'm glad they stayed and didn't cancel out.

Sunday 25 August
How lovely to be home. Unpacking and household jobs, and beginning to sort out the office which has been knee-deep in miscellaneous papers, letters, Election addresses, notes, telegrams and muddled files.

Monday 26 August
Rang the House of Commons about taking my seat on 24 October – the day Parliament resumes for prorogation. The clerk said it might mean that Black Rod was kept waiting. They still don't understand what it's all about. The very fact that he would be was enough to confirm my determination that that should be the day. Charlie Pannell, to whom I told this story, agreed strongly. The other reason I want to do it this way is that it means I am in on the 1962–3 session and will only have missed one complete session as a result of my disqualification.

I also ordered some House of Commons notepaper so as to start work properly.

Thursday 29 August
We watched the march on Washington on TV last night – a historic day in the Negro struggle for equal rights.

Office work again all day and I lunched at St Stephen's with the journalist John Guinery whom I like very much but who has absolutely no zip and no enthusiasm and the fact that he says he's going to vote Labour excites me as much as if a millstone declared its intention of coming swimming with me. I discovered that he's an ex-Communist and this I think explains it all. Before that he was a keen Christian and the disillusioned, licked ex-leftist is the worst of all, for he dare not be enthusiastic, recollecting his errors of judgement in the past.

After lunch I went to the Commons – the first time for nearly three years as an MP. I wandered into the Chamber which was absolutely deserted – no crowds, no messengers, no police, nobody. I just sat in my old seat on the Back Benches and looked around and thought. It was an extraordinary experience, incredible and exciting and vaguely unreal, like a man coming back from the dead. I stayed for about ten minutes there, then wandered around for a while and came home.

NOTES
Chapter One

1. After the defeat of the Labour Party in the 1959 General Election, Hugh Gaitskell recommended to the National Executive that Clause 4, which contains the basic socialist principles of the Labour Party, be amended, an attempt which failed. At the Scarborough Conference of October 1960 a motion was carried in favour of unilateral nuclear disarmament and it was then that Hugh Gaitskell said, 'We shall fight and fight and fight again to save the Party we love.' Just before the 1960 Conference met, I had tried and failed to persuade the National Executive and the TWGU (the main force behind the unilateralist motion) to seek a compromise on the nuclear arms question, and I resigned from the Executive. At the Conference in 1961 Gaitskell succeeded in reversing the Party's commitment to unilateralism.

2. Sir Edward Boyle, then Minister of Education, and Conservative MP for Handsworth, 1950–70, was a contemporary of mine at university and we went together to the USA in 1947 on a debating tour. He was created Baron Boyle of Handsworth and became Vice-Chancellor of Leeds University in 1970.

3. John Hare was Minister of Agriculture in 1963 and Conservative MP for Sudbury and Woodbridge from 1950 until 1963 when he was created Viscount Blakenham. He was always personally very friendly.

4. William Deedes, Conservative MP for Ashford, Kent, 1950–74, was then a Cabinet Minister without Portfolio. In 1974 he became editor of the *Daily Telegraph*.

5. Peter Kirk won Gravesend from Labour in 1955, after the resignation of Sir Richard Acland on the nuclear bomb question. In 1963 he was Under-Secretary in the War Office. He became very active in the European Movement.

6. Frank Pakenham was heir to the Earl of Longford, an Irish title, but as he was not a Member of Parliament and Attlee wanted to put him in the Government, he created Pakenham a lord with a UK peerage. Lord Pakenham then wanted to be free to renounce that title when renunciation came into force in 1963, but this was not agreed.

7. When Lord Hailsham died in 1950, his heir, Quintin Hogg, MP for Oxford City, wrote to Attlee seeking legislation to allow him to stay in the House of Commons, while remaining a peer. Attlee refused and Hailsham went to the Lords. In October 1963, after the Peerage Act was passed, Hailsham, with the premiership in mind, announced his decision to renounce his title under that Act so that he could stand for the Commons again.

8. It was argued that we should be a part of the EEC because if we were not, our exports would be excluded by Common Market tariff barriers.

9. De Gaulle was very angry with the British Government for agreeing to buy the Polaris submarine, thus retaining a nuclear partnership with the US at the time that Britain was seeking membership of the Common Market. It is widely thought that this was one of the major factors leading to de Gaulle's veto of Britain's first application.

10. Philip Noel-Baker was a lifelong campaigner for disarmament and held

office in the 1946–51 Labour Government. He was MP for Coventry, 1929–31, Derby and Derby South, 1936–70 and in 1977 he was created Lord Noel-Baker.

11. John Profumo was forced to resign as Secretary of State for War and as MP for Stratford in June 1963 after denying an association with Christine Keeler, whose relationship with the then Russian naval attaché in London presented a supposed 'security risk'. Macmillan's reputation as Prime Minister was damaged by the fact that he said publicly that he had not been told about this affair. The scandal led to prison sentences for Christine Keeler and others. On 3 July, Stephen Ward was found guilty under the Sexual Offences Act, 1956, but on 3 August, before the sentence was announced, he died after a barbiturates overdose.

12. The 1961 by-election campaign had attracted a whole new group of people into the Bristol Party. The New Bristol Group was set up in order to keep in touch with these people and to use their expertise to advance policy-thinking in the city. The Group met regularly from 1961–5 and published policy broadsheets which were reported and discussed in the local papers and sometimes adopted by the Party locally. But this aroused resentment among the old guard of the Labour Council. The City Librarian actually refused to stock the broadsheets because one of them had criticised the Library service. Active members were John Ollis, Roger Gill and Frank George.

13. Professor Norman Morris was then gynaecologist at Hammersmith Hospital, and delivered our two youngest children, Melissa and Joshua. Peter Townsend was Professor in Social Administration at the London School of Economics. He was chairman of the Fabian Society, 1965–6.

14. Ernest Marples was Minister of Transport, 1959–64, and a former Postmaster General, 1957–9. He was MP for Wallasey, from 1945 until 1974 when he was created Baron Marples.

15. Alger Hiss, an official in the US State Department in the 1930s, was named as a Soviet agent in evidence to the US Un-American Activities Committee during the McCarthy period. In the subsequent trial of 1949 the jury failed to reach a verdict and after a retrial, Hiss was found guilty of perjury and jailed for five years in disgrace. The case became a *cause célèbre* in the US and in Britain, Hiss continuously protesting his innocence declaring that typewritten documents used in evidence against him were forged.

16. Frank Beswick, former Labour and Co-operative MP for Uxbridge, was defeated in 1959. In 1964 he was made a peer and served subsequently as my Minister of State in the Department of Industry, 1974–5.

17. The right wing of the National Executive was bringing heavy pressure to bear upon unilateralists within the Party and their initial refusal to endorse Hugh Jenkins as the Labour candidate for Putney (although he had been properly selected) was one aspect of this.

18. This was a notorious show trial in Czechoslovakia in 1951 in which Rudolf Slansky, former Secretary General of the Communist Party, was accused of being an American agent. During the course of his trial a number of people were named CIA agents, including Israeli socialist Mordecai Oren,

who was sentenced to fifteen years imprisonment. The inclusion of a famous British socialist MP, Konni Zilliacus threw extra doubt on the legitimacy of the trial.

19. Mervyn Stockwood was Curate and Vicar of St Matthew Moorfields in Bristol between 1936 and 1955, a Labour Councillor and a member of the General Management Committee of the Bristol South East Party which selected me as its candidate to replace Stafford Cripps in November 1950. Became Bishop of Southwark in 1959 and retired in 1980.

20. Kingsley Martin, a well-known socialist journalist, had formidable influence throughout the 1930s, 40s and 50s when he was editor of the *New Statesman*. His partner was Dorothy Woodman and they lived in a flat at the Adelphi which became a centre of a great deal of socialist discussion.

21. Dr Walter Zander was the father of Michael Zander. Professor Norman Bentwich, a distinguished Jewish lawyer and philosopher, was associated with the movement for reconciliation between Jews and Arabs.

22. Joseph Edward Sieff was then Vice-Chairman of Marks and Spencer, later President. He was vice-president of the Zionist Federation, during which period (1973) he was shot and severely injured at his home, apparently by a Palestinian assailant.

23. The Oder-Neisse line was the line drawn by agreement between the Allies at the end of the war delineating the Eastern boundary of East Germany in such a way that territory which had belonged to pre-war Germany was incorporated in the new Poland, to compensate for the loss of Polish territory taken over by the Russians in 1945. The validity of the Oder-Neisse line as an international frontier became a dominant issue and many West Germans, including Adenauer, refused to accept the frontier. An agreement confirming Oder-Neisse was signed by Poland and East Germany in 1950.

24. Merlyn Rees won Gaitskell's old seat of South Leeds in June 1963. He was Under-Secretary of State at the Ministry of Defence 1965–8, Northern Ireland Secretary 1974–6 and Home Secretary 1976–9.

25. In the event, of course, Home was Macmillan's immediate successor not Hailsham. In November 1963 Hailsham renounced his peerage and Sir Wavell Wakefield, MP for St Marylebone, resigned his seat, so that Hailsham could be elected as Quintin Hogg, MP, at the December by-election. He returned to the Lords in 1970, having been given a peerage in his own right as Lord Hailsham of St Marylebone, subsequently becoming Lord Chancellor. He and Lord Home were thus the only men in history to sit in the Commons and the Lords and then the Commons and the Lords consecutively. (See Principal Persons.)

26. Joseph Cort was an American physicist working at Birmingham University, who appealed for my help in 1954 after coming to Britain when his US passport had been withdrawn due to McCarthyite pressures. He was exceptionally short-sighted and manifestly unfit for military service but the American Government demanded his deportation by the British authorities. His wife Ruth was a doctor and I did my best in the House of Commons to protect them from deportation. Ultimately, he was accepted by the Czechs as a political refugee. By an extraordinary chance, the Polish boat in which

he and Ruth left was the same boat from which a Polish sailor escaped and sought political asylum in Britain. Joe Cort later came back to Britain, won his case in the Supreme Court in the United States for the return of his passport and now lives in the US.

27. Nigel Birch, MP for West Flint and Economic Secretary to the Treasury, 1957–8, had resigned along with Chancellor Peter Thorneycroft and Financial Secretary Enoch Powell in January 1958, when Macmillan insisted upon a higher public expenditure than Thorneycroft, as a right-wing Chancellor, was prepared to accept.

28. Crossman's point was that if we could amend the Peerage Act to come into force as soon as the Bill received the Royal Assent, Hailsham would be able to renounce his peerage and provide a credible alternative candidacy to Macmillan.

29. Joseph Murumbi from Kenya was Secretary of the Movement for Colonial Freedom and became Minister of State for African Affairs in the Kenyan Government after independence in 1963. He later withdrew from politics and became an industrialist. Tom Mboya was the young General Secretary of the Kenya African National Union, who rose to become Minister of Economic Planning in the Kenyan Government. He had links with the American Committee for Africa. He was assassinated in 1969.

30. It had been argued in the NEC that appeals against expulsion should be in the hands of an independent appeals tribunal. However, the decision was taken not to do this, in part because Wilson's election led to a much greater atmosphere of tolerance.

31. Hartley Shawcross was Labour MP for St Helens, 1945–58 and Attorney-General in the post-war Government, becoming President of the Board of Trade when Harold Wilson resigned in the spring of 1951. After leaving Parliament, he was created a life peer and held many business and City appointments.

32. Rt Hon Selwyn Lloyd, Conservative MP for Wirral from 1945–76, was a former Chancellor of the Exchequer and Foreign Secretary 1955–60 in which capacity he was very much involved in the Suez War. He was sacked by Macmillan in the Night of the Long Knives in the summer of 1963 but came back to be Leader of the House of Commons and later Speaker, 1971–6.

33. The Addis Ababa Conference was a gathering of heads of African states and governments, and African nationalist organisations, which met from 22–6 May, 1963. It was the first of its kind since 1958 and established the charter of the Organisation of African Unity.

34. Jomo Kenyatta, President of the Kenya African National Union, and first President of Kenya 1964–78; Julius Nyerere, President of Tanganyika, later Tanzania, 1961–85; Hastings Banda, Prime Minister, then President of Malawi (Nyasaland) since 1963; Winston Field, Rhodesian Front Party Prime Minister in 1962, replaced by Ian Smith in 1964.

35. Kenneth Kaunda and Harry Nkumbula formed a Coalition Government in December 1962 in what was Northern Rhodesia. Kaunda, a son of the manse and leader of the United National Independence Party, became President of Zambia. Harry Nkumbula, leader of the African National

Congress, was a much less reliable man and by the date of the Presidential Elections in August 1964 had fallen out with Kaunda.

36. Charles Bradlaugh was MP for Northampton between 1880–91. He was the first atheist to be elected to Parliament who, on principle, refused to swear an oath of allegiance to the Crown. Because of his refusal his seat was vacated but he was re-elected and was again refused permission to take his seat without the oath. The third time he was re-elected, he agreed to take the oath, but was then told he couldn't take it and he was evicted once more. It was as a result of this famous Victorian radical's stand that the law was changed to allow MPs to affirm rather than to swear an oath of allegiance. Out of respect for Charles Bradlaugh, I have from 1963 always affirmed rather than sworn an oath of allegiance as an MP and a Privy Councillor.

37. Buddy (Olive Winch) came as a children's nurse to look after my brothers and me in November 1928 and left in 1940, remaining a very close and intimate friend of the family. She is always present at my own family's celebrations.

38. Steward or Bailiff of the Chiltern Hundreds, or the Manor of Northstead, are 'offices of profit under the Crown' and are devices to allow an MP to vacate a Parliamentary seat. Malcolm St Clair had pledged to resign his seat at once to allow a by-election to be held.

39. Mr Justice Gorman and Mr Justice McNair were the two judges presiding at the Election Court which had unseated me in 1961. Both of them were always friendly and this particular slip of the tongue threw some light on the way in which the judges regarded their function.

40. Sir Stafford Cripps was my Labour predecessor in Bristol who retired in October 1950 aged sixty-one. He was knighted in 1930 and served in governments before and during the war, which included a spell as Ambassador to Moscow in 1940. In the 1945 Labour Government he was Minister for Economic Affairs and then Chancellor of the Exchequer until his resignation. He died in 1952.

41. The Rt Hon Jim Griffiths, former President of the South Wales Miners' Federation and MP for Llanelli, 1936–70. He replaced Herbert Morrison as Deputy-Leader of the Labour Party in 1955, and was succeeded by Nye Bevan in 1959. He was Minister of National Insurance in the 1945 Labour Government and first Secretary of State for Wales in the 1964 Labour Government with a seat in the Cabinet.

2
Campaigning for Victory
September 1963–October 1964

Sunday 1 September
Geoffrey Bing rang up. He has just come in from New York where he has been laying on the arrangements for a debate in the Security Council on the situation in Southern Rhodesia. Since the Addis Ababa Conference the African states have been working more closely together and on this issue every single one of them is united in their determination to force a UN role into the situation. Geoffrey told me that when the Algerian Prime Minister Ben Bella was visiting Nkrumah in Ghana to discuss this and other things, he had said that the Africans should not ignore British public opinion and had mentioned the work I had done for the Algerian cause, during their long war against the French. I am lunching with him tomorrow.

We have just got a copy of the new record 'Fool Britannia' which Peter Sellers, Antony Newley and Joan Collins recorded a few weeks ago in New York. It is all about the Profumo-Keeler-Ward case and is the most biting satirical comment on the state of Britain under the Tories.

Monday 2 September
Lunch with Geoffrey Bing and three Ghanaians, a lawyer Dr Ekow Daniels, Mr Harry Amanoo, Deputy-Secretary to the Ghanaian Foreign Office, and Mr J. A. Afari, Ghanaian High Commissioner in London, to discuss Southern Rhodesia. I promised I would try to get the issue raised at the Labour Conference and would submit a resolution to the Overseas Committee of the Executive when it meets soon. It will also make an excellent subject for my maiden speech in the foreign affairs debate on the Address on the Queen's Speech.

Thursday 5 September
Journalist Larry Thaw came to see Caroline for his interview for the *Woman's Mirror*. He hasn't the slightest idea of what the peerage battle

has been about or why and is only interested in the ludicrous status aspects and what it means not to be a peeress and all that crap.

To a party at Sir Andrew and Lady Cohen's house. Cohen was the Governor of Uganda when the Kabaka [King 'Freddie' Mutesa II] was deposed in 1954. He is one of those Colonial Office officials who maintains his membership of the Fabian Society as a sort of insurance policy to keep him in good odour with the Labour Party in case they ever win an election. He became head of the Department of Technical Co-operation.

Friday 6 September
Messaoud Kellou came along this morning, bringing with him A. M. Khourredine who is a member of the Algerian National Liberation Front Politbureau. We had a long talk about the world situation. He confirmed that there was a strong racial element in the Chinese propaganda against the Russians and in the Chinese attacks on the European socialists.

Had a chat with Robin Day.[1] He recently saw Hartley Shawcross and thought that Shawcross was beginning to consider the possibility of an appointment under Wilson. Day said, thought he would be an excellent man to send to the UN. God forbid! Shawcross is a complete careerist who wouldn't even help us indirectly in the last General Election when I asked him to do a quote on film for our TV programmes.

Monday 9 September
The Post Office telephone engineer came to the house this morning to discuss our new telephone system and I think there is one which will exactly meet our needs. Just after that, a man came and demonstrated the Ansafone. This is a tape recorder that answers the phone, repeats a recorded message, records an answer and signs off. Not only would it mean that the house was manned telephonically while I was out or away, but would also mean that I can monitor incoming calls to decide whether it's necessary to phone them back.

Wednesday 11 September
Worked today further on the political expenditure issue and I gather that I have to answer for the Executive on this at Conference, which will be my first speech from the platform. I am writing to a number of Bristol firms to ask them if they contribute to the Tory Party and am also writing to the Tory front organisations to ask them if they publish their accounts. I think if every candidate did that it would put the business contributors to the Tory Party on the spot.

Friday 13 September

Today the whole family drove to Bristol for the local victory party after our ten and a half year campaign to renounce the viscountcy.

First we called on Mrs Kiff who is an old-age pensioner living in a housing estate in Hengrove. Two years ago she started to send ten shillings a fortnight for the fund and has written the most wonderful letters. She is seventy-six, lives alone, and the warmth of her welcome was touching.

Then we went to Fairfax House where the party was being held. There were nearly 600 people crowded into the restaurant and it was a superb evening. The children enjoyed it enormously and Melissa danced the twist till 11 o'clock when it ended. I made a short speech of thanks and they presented me with a photograph taken after the declaration of the result on 21 August. There were so many friends from all over Bristol and it does show you need a little bit of social activity in addition to stern politics to keep the Party together.

Saturday 14 September

In the afternoon I worked on my speech for the Wilson meeting in the Bristol Central Hall. There were about 1,500 people there from Bristol and the nearby areas. Harold spoke for an hour and was very good. I had to raise the collection and we got £177. The first woman who gave a £5 note got a handkerchief autographed by Harold.

I drove John Harris back to London and we had a long talk on the way. He told me some hair-raising stories about George Brown which confirmed my clear view that he was quite unfitted to be Leader of the Labour Party. Apparently he caused Hugh Gaitskell a great deal of anxiety the year before he died. However, it seems generally agreed that George should not be opposed for the Deputy-Leadership this coming session.

Ten years earlier, in 1953, the Central African Federation, comprising Southern Rhodesia, Northern Rhodesia and Nyasaland, had been set up by the British Government to entrench white power in Central Africa. Now, towards the end of 1963, the Federation was to be officially dissolved. It was one of the anxieties of the African states that the Southern Rhodesian Government should not be left in eventual charge of the Federation Air Force, because that would give them considerable strike power in that part of the world, whereas the other states, Nyasaland (now Malawi) and Northern Rhodesia (now Zambia) would be bereft of the necessary air force for self-protection. In the event, the Southern Rhodesian Government did retain the air force and it became a factor leading a later British Government to decide not to use force against Rhodesia at the time of the Unilateral Declaration of Independence in November 1965.

Tuesday 17 September

At the Overseas Committee of the NEC today my draft resolution on Southern Rhodesia came up for discussion. This was based on my talk with Geoffrey Bing and he thinks (quite rightly) that it is important that the Labour Party's view should be made clear. There are two points of substance.

One is that we should pledge ourselves to consult with the United Nations, and the other is that the powerful air force of the Central African Federation should not be transferred to the control of the Southern Rhodesian Government. Harold was sympathetic but thought the air force question required further study. A special paper will be produced for the National Executive when it meets at Scarborough next week.

Harold was anxious that the Party should not be identified with the conference in November called by the Movement for Colonial Freedom to discuss a total trade embargo on South Africa. I am a sponsor of this conference and feel strongly that the matter should be studied. On the other hand, I don't want to do anything this coming year which might look like rocking the boat or embarrassing the Party.

Dinner with Peter and Liz Shore. Also there were Dick Crossman and Richard Titmuss.* There was a most interesting discussion, of which I was only a spectator, about Labour's educational policy. Should universities be under the Minister of Education? What are we going to do about integrating the public schools? I wondered whether there has been as much preparatory work on these questions as should have been.

Dick was very friendly about Citizens for Labour and I think I can count on his support.

Wednesday 18 September

Citizens for Labour was discussed at the Organisation Sub-Committee today and the minute which later reached me included a recommendation more or less condemning it as being 'neither desirable nor necessary'. So I decided to send the memorandum to half a dozen other members of the National Executive in order to lobby them before the meeting in Scarborough.

Saturday 21 September

This evening Caroline and I went to the Ghanaian party to celebrate President Nkrumah's birthday. The High Commissioner, Kwesi Armah, has a most comfortable house and it was an enjoyable evening.

* Professor of Social Administration at the LSE, 1950–73.

When we got home there was a phone call from New York from Geoffrey Bing. The poor man had cerebral malaria and was unconscious for two days and was thought to be dying. But he recovered and was full of bounce. He gave me some more useful information on the Southern Rhodesian issue which I can utilise to convince the National Executive next week.

Then Tony Crosland came in for a drink – self-invited. Susan is in Baltimore and we had a talk about George Brown and the state of the Party and our prospects – personal prospects – of office. He is busy preparing himself and I think would make an excellent Minister. We are very old friends now and although we don't agree about certain fundamental things I greatly enjoy talking to him, and after all these years it would be hard to have a serious cleavage.

Tuesday 24 September
To Bristol this evening for a meeting of the New Bristol Group. There were about eighteen people and they discussed my latest paper on race relations. Their reaction was rather typically liberal middle class, feeling that to stress race as an issue was to accentuate differences which morally ought not to exist. But race is an explosive issue and cannot be pushed under the carpet. Anyway the Group is going fine.

Thursday 26 September
The Denning Report on the security aspects of the Profumo case was published this morning and is creating a storm. The confusion at the top is very evident. Denning skates over the other scurrilous scandals that have been circulating.

Caught the 1 o'clock train to Scarborough [for the Labour Party Annual Conference] with Peter Shore, Barbara Castle and Tom Driberg. We stayed at the Royal Hotel and a whole flood of hideous memories of 1960 – when we had the nuclear disarmament clash – came back. What a ghastly conference that was and how different this one is going to be!

Friday 27 September
To the National Executive this morning. The atmosphere was very cordial and only two points that affected me came up. I strongly urged that we issue a statement announcing our opposition to the transfer of the Rhodesian air force to Southern Rhodesia and supported David Ennals's paper which hinted at UN conciliation. However, Sam Watson[2] killed my suggestion, despite Harold Wilson's readiness to go half way to meet my points. I can see in the Labour Party all the elements that led the French socialists astray on Algeria and it is rather frightening.

After lunch Ray Gunter delivered the report of the Organisation Sub-Committee on Citizens for Labour and he warned about its subversive potentialities and all that rubbish. Quite a number of other people chipped in and I delivered a long speech, accepting the need for its integration with the Party but asking for the right to experiment. As there was no vote on the recommendation it skidded through safely and it is now a question of getting it set up on the right basis in Bristol South East.

Saturday 28 September
Walked to Scarborough Castle with Barbara Castle and Merlyn Rees, talking about the African situation. I think the younger ones see the danger that Central Africa involves us in.

Composite sessions this afternoon, and this evening to Bridlington Labour Party by car for their annual dinner. I dashed back in time to watch 'That Was The Week That Was', which returned to TV tonight. It was savage and brilliant in parts, and the room was packed with Labour leaders and journalists. Not a single anti-Labour joke was made and even I wondered if it had gone too far.

Sunday 29 September
Worked in my room all morning on an idea for the National Executive this afternoon that we should have another look at our Annual Conference to see how it might be improved. It came up under 'any other business' but was quite sympathetically received and I have promised to submit a paper.

This evening to the Party demonstration where Willy Brandt made a very tactful speech and Clem Attlee was given a pair of pipes in a case. He made a short and moving speech and got a rapturous reception. He is a dear old boy and the affection for him is completely genuine.

Monday 30 September
The Conference opened this morning but it was not a very exciting day. As it happened, the big news came at the Fabian tea, when Harold announced his support for the idea of a Ministry of Planning or Production and thus publicly settled the dispute that has gone on under the surface between him and George Brown and Jim Callaghan.[3] George is anxious to muscle in as overlord on the home front and Jim, who is a lightweight, is very resentful about his projected demotion.

Harold also announced his idea for a UN Minister, a Minister of Overseas Development, and a Disarmament Minister. But he rather rejected the idea of a Prime Minister's Office or major importations into the upper Civil Service appointments. These latter points threw Tom Balogh into utter gloom and he saw Dick Crossman who fell into a similar state of depression and quite upset poor Pat Blackett, who had come up to have dinner with them and found long faces and moans. They were very silly but I suppose they are nervous of losing their role as Harold's private advisers.

Caroline arrived – O joy! – and we went to the agents' ball. There we met Barbara Castle who was almost in tears because Alice Bacon had been given a major speech and she had not. She said Harold was good on the machinery but always sold the Left down the river and she would quit politics if she did not get a major Shadow Cabinet appointment. She was outraged that Shirley Williams should have been put on the TV presentation team. It was almost hysterical and reflected the great uncertainty of the Left at Harold's success and the unaccustomed unity of Conference. I tried to calm her down and no doubt she will soon forget it.

Tuesday 1 October
In the National Executive elections this morning I moved up a place to No 3 and my vote went up from 612,000 to 715,000. All being well, I should be on the Executive for life.

At this morning's session we had the great science debate which Wilson opened brilliantly. It was Peter Shore's day too, for he is the one who thought of the idea of making public enterprise the agency for bringing growth to our lagging economy, instead of just nationalising dying industries.

This afternoon Caroline and I went to hear Malcolm Muggeridge* 'Looking at the Labour Party' at the Labour Parliamentary Association tea party. He was hilarious and reminded us that the Labour Party had never liked its leaders and had never been a happy band of brothers and he thought it would be very unhealthy if they ever liked authority. His personal reminiscences had us in fits.

Wednesday 2 October
Jim Callaghan made an indifferent speech in the incomes policy debate this morning and Harold is thought to be angry with him for having continued the argument against a planning ministry. George Brown made his speech and pledged his support for Harold, which led to a huge ovation.

At the new National Executive meeting Harold told me what I could say tomorrow about a Labour Government's attitude to Tory political funds. Tony Greenwood was elected chairman. Caroline

* Journalist and critic, editor of *Punch*, 1953–7.

went and had a drink and dinner with Roy Jenkins and the Right. Most of them have conceded Harold's successes but are uneasy about their personal positions. Caroline also heard that George Strauss* is worried that I will be made Shadow Minister of Transport instead of him. I don't really want the job back and I hope I don't get it.

Meanwhile I went to Whitby with Bessie Braddock, where an absolutely packed meeting of 450 people were crowded into a school room. It is hard not to sniff the scent of electoral victory in the air.

Worked until 4.30 am on my speech for tomorrow's debate.

Thursday 3 October
Only had about twelve minutes for my speech on Tory Party political funds but it went down all right. Caroline went home this afternoon and I went to the Mayor's reception, to the *Daily Mirror* party – where I had a talk to Frank Cousins – and then had dinner with the Crossmans, Lena Jeger and Alastair Hetherington.[4]

Friday 4 October
Last sessions at the Conference and Harold Wilson got in with a short speech at the end which was most sensible as it gave the newspapers some hard news and helped to offset the damage which the Conference Arrangements Committee annually tries to do to the Party by guaranteeing that we end on a massive and carefully contrived anti-climax.

I came home in the train with Peter Shore. It has really been his Conference and the chairman, Dai Davies, mentioned him by name when giving thanks just at the end. The next thing is to get Peter into the House, where he desperately wants to be. We talked about a number of things, including the tremendous challenge that the Post Office would offer a Labour Minister.

Home to find the family well and Stephen, who is quite a mathematician, still working on the graph and calculations for fixing the optimum speed of vehicles on roads.

Sunday 6 October
The boys are frantically tunnelling in the garden, following a film they saw about POWs escaping during the war. They are way under the concrete path and will be in the next garden unless stopped. It is a beautifully concealed tunnel with a wooden top covered with mud and can already hold two full-sized people. Joshua gives it away by removing the lid and disappearing himself when the other boys aren't there.

* MP for North Lambeth and Lambeth Vauxhall, 1929–79, except between 1931–4. Father of the House in 1979.

Wednesday 9 October
Caroline's article on 'The New Britain' for *Look* magazine is brilliant.

Macmillan's prostate operation has suddenly changed the whole political scene and, coming on the eve of the Blackpool Conference, has led to wild speculation. Few papers now think he can carry on. This new element could affect Labour's chances.

I went to the Battersea College of Technology to talk on Parliament at a lunchtime meeting. I think Wilson's scientific speech has made some impact on these sort of people – though the staff are very Conservative with a real grammar school outlook that is harder to stomach than almost anything else.

On TV, the Tory Conference showed Hailsham trying to control himself and looking like a man in the grip of suppressed hysteria, smirking and protesting loyalty to Macmillan. It was odious.

Thursday 10 October
To the House of Commons for a meeting under the chairmanship of Arthur Bottomley[5] to consider Labour's attitude to the Rhodesian question and especially the transfer of the air force to the settlers. David Ennals was good and with the help of Dingle Foot and Maurice Foley[6] we were able to stiffen Arthur up a bit. His attitude was that the prospect of our gaining power meant virtually abandoning our line. I fear that he will capitulate to Civil Service and settler pressure.

This afternoon to the Annual Rally of Kent Women with Shirley Summerskill[7] who is a fanatical feminist like her mother, and just as tough.

Home to hear the news of Macmillan's decision to resign. At 9.30 Robin Day phoned from the Tory Conference in Blackpool to tell me that Hailsham had just announced his intention to renounce his peerage and could I let him have a quote that he could throw at Hailsham in a TV interview later that evening. I gave him one: 'It is a sad comment on Lord Hailsham's respect for the House of Commons that he is only prepared to give up his hereditary privileges when he stands to gain something from it personally.' Robin put this to Hailsham and I'd hoped he would explode but he is so determined to keep a grip on himself that he gave a pompous reply about 'my great sacrifice'. David Butler phoned to tell me that the Tories were so busy committing themselves to one or other candidate that when the choice was made it would tear them apart. Macmillan could hardly have done them a worse turn and there simply is no machinery for settling the leadership.

Today's *Telegraph* promises a Gallup poll tomorrow.

Friday 11 October
Up before 7 and to the paper shop in my pyjamas to buy the *Telegraph* to read the Gallup poll. They had not published it. I rang Dr Durant of the Gallup poll and he refused to give me the figures but said he would ring the editor. I tried the *Telegraph* several times but they wouldn't give the figures. Later Durant rang back to say the editor had authorised him to release them and they show a Labour lead up to 12.5 per cent, a 1.5 per cent increase. It also showed Wilson's popularity is up and that the Labour Conference has made a favourable impression on all issues except on nationalisation and our decision not to abolish private education.

Wrote a letter to *The Times* attacking the idea of a Royal Choice when a new Prime Minister is selected,[8] and sent it by special messenger.

Dr Leo Szilard came in for an hour's talk about nuclear policy. He is a University of Chicago professor, a nuclear strategist advising President Kennedy. The Cuban crisis had convinced him war was possible and he really wanted Britain to become semi-neutral, keep a small nuclear deterrent 'the sting of a bee', and try to see that Europe survived even if America and Russia wiped themselves out. It was curiously naïve and pessimistic but if I worked in the atmosphere of American public opinion, I might take the same view.

Bed early, feeling lousy.

Saturday 12 October
The Times gave pride of place to my letter and obviously want to start a controversy on this subject. The main thing is to show how the Tories use the Crown for their own purposes and to go on pushing them to say whose decision will be behind the new Leader. If they say it is the Queen then we can charge them correctly with using her, and in the process can frighten her back into a rubber stamp position. The whole feudal façade is cracking fast.

To Transport House for the Young Socialists' National Committee. It was a long and weary tussle between Bessie Braddock and Reg Underhill against these active Young Socialists. The Labour bureaucratic mind is quite impervious to enthusiasm and new ideas.

I left at 5 and went back to bed with a temperature of 103.

Sunday 13 October
Caroline felt lousy today and was in bed all morning although it was her birthday. The children got their own breakfasts and went out to the Wimpy Bar for lunch by themselves. We had some birthday celebrations this afternoon.

Monday 14 October
The correspondence in *The Times* is now well under way and it looks as if Lord Home may be the acceptable third choice, able to unite the Butlerites and the Hailshamites. He will, however, be a dud when it comes to exciting the electorate and Wilson will make rings round him. The only men I fear – Macleod and Maudling – are both out of the race.

Friday 18 October
Macmillan resigned this morning and Home was asked to form a Government. It is incredible that such a thing should have happened. From the Labour Party's point of view he is much less dangerous than Maudling but I am disturbed that my battle should have paved the way for a Conservative peer to come back to the Commons as PM.

Saturday 19 October
To Bristol for a day school on disarmament, organised by the United Nations Association. Wayland Young came down from London and he spoke on the political developments in the first session. After tea, with Professor Dickinson in the chair, I spoke on the economic consequences of disarmament. It was quite a good crowd of over 100 but there is something flabby about the UNA.

Long talk to Wayland on the train back to London. He would be a great Minister for Disarmament in a Labour Government. I gather he is working on some aspects of this for Harold Wilson.

Wednesday 23 October
National Executive this morning. Harold and George were away. It was agreed that my paper on reorganising the Annual Conference should go forward for discussion with an office paper on the same subject. Also we agreed a good tough statement on Southern Rhodesia which goes 90 per cent of the way towards meeting Geoffrey Bing's pressure.

With Dick to see Harold to discuss last night's TV. Harold was bullied mercilessly by McKenzie* and Day on TV. We are shaky on the deterrent issue. Harold was furious with the way the BBC had treated him – especially having refused to do it in his room in the Commons and even to discuss the studio set they had prepared. It was all most undignified.

The Chief Whip told me that as the new parliamentary session is

---

* Robert McKenzie, political broadcaster and Professor of Sociology at London School of Economics, 1964–87.

not to be opened on Tuesday, I could take my seat tomorrow.[9] I decided to make my 'maiden' speech on the implications of Lord Home's appointment as Prime Minister and stayed up all night preparing it. It is a bit forward, jumping in straight away, but this issue is ready-made for me and there's something to be said for getting back to normal as quickly as possible. Charlie agreed I should. A bit nervous but then I always am.

Thursday 24 October
Today was the day I have been dreaming about for many a year. Although the peerage battle has been a long one and at times the exile has seemed interminable and the outlook hopeless, in fact I have only missed one complete session of Parliament. I sat in the first week or so of the 1960–1 session and am taking my seat at the very end of the 1962–3 session. Father would have been amazed and delighted to see it end so quickly. It certainly is something to be the first man who has come back from a peerage into the House of Commons, though Lord Home will be the first man to have come back from the House of Lords to the House of Commons, since I did not take my seat there and he did.

Caroline and I went in by car just after 10 am and there was the usual battery of press photographers at St Stephen's entrance.

At 10.45 I went to the Chief Whip's office where Charlie Pannell and Will Wilkins, MP for Bristol South, were waiting. We stood in the Members' Lobby during Prayers and as the doors opened afterwards moved through the Churchill Arch where – two and a half years ago – the chief doorkeeper had stopped me on the Speaker's instructions.

The first business was the announcement of the death of two Members and then Selwyn Lloyd – the new Leader of the House – made a short business statement. Then came the introduction of the new Members.

First Angus Maude, who got some ironical cheering from our side. Then me and it was with very mixed feelings that I walked up to the table and affirmed. The Labour Members cheered of course but what was so annoying was the ironical cheering of the Tories and the waving of their order papers to celebrate Lord Home's appointment as Prime Minister, which my Act has made possible. This discomfited the Labour Members and confused the nature of the victory. What should have been the celebration of the clear defeat of the Lords by the Commons looked like a victory by a hereditary peer over the dignity and privileges of the Commons.

The Speaker was very embarrassed as he shook me by the hand and I thanked him and said I hoped to catch his eye during the course of the debate. Harold was waiting at the back of the Speaker's chair to shake me by the hand which was decent of him. I slipped through the Division Lobby and back to my old place on the Back Benches. There was no pleasure in it and none of the excitement of being back in the Commons that I had expected was there. I felt very uneasy.

Harold made a good speech, Selwyn Lloyd an appalling one and Jo Grimond an inconsequential one. Manny Shinwell was all knockabout and no substance and the House was pretty empty when I was called, having been encouraged by Charlie to plunge in. I was afraid of mocking laughter from the other side but this was the one opportunity to set the record straight and show the relevance of my campaign and contrast it with Home's return.

Friday 25 October
To Bristol to speak to the University Labour Club on 'The Regeneration of Britain'. It was a packed meeting with every seat taken and three rows of standing students surrounding the whole room. University interest in the Labour Party is very high at the moment.

Sunday 27 October
Spent the whole day in the garden, mowing and clearing. Worked in the office till 1.30 in the morning, clearing up and preparing for the indefatigable Valerie.

Wednesday 30 October
Dictated the first draft of an outline for a Post Office development programme to send to Harold Wilson, stimulated by the science debate and incorporating a lot of ideas which have been buzzing round in my mind for many years. Here is a science-based industry, already in public ownership, which could be made to serve the more sophisticated needs of a modern community and make a profit.

To the Algerian party this evening where the Ambassador, Messaoud, presided with his newly acquired diplomatic charm. He is an old and dear friend and his country is going through great difficulties. Talked to David Ennals, who is utterly disheartened and demoralised by Home's selection and, like many Labour people, more than half-seriously angry that I should have made it possible. Of course the Election is not a foregone conclusion for us, but most of the Labour anxiety is because Tory demoralisation has been halted by Macmillan's departure and the feeling that there is a new man around whom the Tories can rally. Any Leader would have given them the same sense of relief.

Thursday 31 October
Tam Dalyell came to see me this afternoon to plan the proposed
Bristol science conference. He is a decent, serious person and one of
a number of new Labour MPs whom I must get to know in the new
session.

Friday 1 November
Peter Carter* came for lunch. He is here to be interviewed as a
possible architect for the new National Theatre and his proposed
layout is most imaginative and is based on a three-year study project
which he has done while in Mies Van der Rohe's Chicago office. He
is one of those I hope will come back if Labour wins.

Sir Wavell Wakefield has been made a hereditary peer today so
that Hailsham can have his constituency of St Marylebone. It is the
grossest abuse of the honours system I can recall.

To Luton to speak at a by-election meeting. It was a blue collar
audience in a post-war school and they are optimistic about the
outcome. What a pity that Party HQs aren't better decorated and
more efficiently run so that they would be less repulsive to those who
want to help.

Saturday 2 November
To a party for Fenner's seventy-fifth birthday. All the Movement
for Colonial Freedom crowd were there. The Maoist wing of the
Communist Party has captured the MCF now and it reflects Peking
rather than Moscow in its outlook. I am sure it still does a good job
but it really would be too much of a sweat to fight that battle when
there is so much more to be done working inside the Party.

On to dinner with friends, and also invited were the actress
Vanessa Redgrave, who is both charming and intelligent, and the
writer Alan Sillitoe, who looks quiet but is seething with passion and
has a sharp American wife.

Monday 4 November
This evening Wayland Young rang and asked us to go round and
advise him as to whether he should renounce his peerage. Ideally I
would like all Labour peers to renounce and those who don't will
have lost something in effectiveness. Wayland senses this too but
Harold Wilson advised him not to. I greatly hope he will be made a
Minister for Disarmament in the new Government. However this
may not be possible if he renounces and doesn't find a constituency
so that he is cut off from both Houses of Parliament. He would, I
think, be wiser not to renounce.

* Family friend who subsequently returned from the US and practices in Swindon.

Also there was Peter Scott, the naturalist, who is his half-brother, a nice gentle fifty-year-old and friend of the Duke of Edinburgh, with whom he shares all the innocuous interests of yachting, boys' clubs and nature conservancy. He has a real Gordonstoun outlook – all brawn and lusty amateurism, but so nice you couldn't help liking him.

Tuesday 5 November
Over the weekend I had a letter from Alastair Hetherington, offering me Dick Crossman's weekly column on the *Guardian*. I rang Dick to tell him this and he was delighted as apparently Harold Wilson suggested to Hetherington that I should do it. I don't write well, dread deadlines and expose myself enormously by the necessity to say something every week. But it will finance the inflated office expenses to which I am now committed and does give me an outlet for saying something useful to an influential audience. So I agreed.

Working in the office all day and fireworks in the garden this evening. The rain had only just stopped and the fireworks take an interminable time to go off and are also quite dangerous and should really be banned. But the squeals of joy from the children make it an inevitable annual event.

Friday 8 November
To Bristol, where I looked in on a reception for three Argentinian trade unionists and then to speak to the Movement for Colonial Freedom on Southern Africa. There were seventeen people there. Sean McConville, the secretary, was a Communist but is having a row with them. This is partly, I suspect, because he is selling Chinese literature from his bookshop in Bath. The Moscow–Peking row is undoubtedly splitting the world Communist movement and its implications and ramifications are endless.

Sunday 10 November
Mother came to lunch and we put a poppy in for Mike at the Field of Remembrance. Then, with all the children, Caroline and I went on to Blackheath to see Dave's new house.

Tuesday 12 November
To the Commons this morning where Parliament was opened for the new session. As the Queen is pregnant it was done by a commission – the Lord Chancellor read the Queen's Speech from the Throne – and I didn't bother to go along and hear it. In fact it is an Election manifesto and very thin in substance.

I went to the PLP meeting at 12 and was a little nervous, like a schoolboy at the beginning of a new term, especially as Home's arrival has blurred the nature of my victory.

Harold was in the chair – the first time I have seen him there as a Leader. He welcomed the members of the NEC and the Party after the recess and then came to new Members. He referred to me first and mentioned the great constitutional battle especially. I had to stand awkwardly for a moment and there was a general grunt of approval. Then Will Howie was welcomed as the victor of Luton.* After reference had been made to the death of two Members, we stood for a moment as always.

Harold went on to deal with the Queen's Speech briefly and there was a general but straggly series of speeches in which Jim Callaghan got attacked for his weekend speech suggesting that a Labour Government couldn't pay for the Tory Election promises.

Lunch with Barbara and Tony Greenwood and back to see Home introduced and to hear Harold's speech. I had to go out before Home spoke as the Overseas Committee of the NEC was meeting. Tom Driberg was defeated as chairman by Walter Padley (in absentia) by twelve votes to four. But will be an improvement on Sam Watson.

Then to the Fabians for a discussion on the situation in British Guiana. Sandys' constitutional proposals for proportional representation will force Cheddi Jagan[10] out under American pressure and there will be serious trouble in the colony as independence has been refused. We agreed an article which was highly critical of Sandys and I managed to get included a phrase that 'a Labour Government would fix a date for independence'.

Back to the Commons to go to a dinner at which about sixteen Labour MPs under forty were entertaining Sidney Bernstein,† including Tam Dalyell and Jeremy Bray, as well as others I knew already. We had an interesting discussion about television, including the televising of Parliament and Sidney Bernstein said that he would finance a mock up of some kind if I could get together a little committee including members of all parties to urge it. I think I'll get in touch with Jeremy Thorpe and Humphrey Berkeley and see what we could agree.

Home at 10.30 and beginning to feel the yoke of long days and late nights pressing on my shoulders again.

---

* Will Howie won the seat from the Conservatives at the by-election caused by the bestowal of a life peerage on Dr Charles Hill, who became chairman of ITA.

† Founder and chairman of Granada, a strong Labour Party supporter. Created Baron Bernstein in 1969.

Tuesday 19 November

Lunch with the Polish Ambassador to meet the Deputy-Minister of Foreign Affairs on his way back from the UN to Warsaw. He said that the smaller nations were beginning to show some signs of resentment that the big powers are getting on so well together and are negotiating directly rather than through the UN. This is a reversion to 1945 and confirms me in my view that a Labour Government which threw in its lot with the General Assembly of the UN would have far more influence than one that hung about in the lobbies hoping for a special relationship with the USA.

Wednesday 20 November

PLP meeting this morning on the Immigration Bill. It was a highly successful meeting and justified all the work that Peter Shore had done on the prepared statement.

Harold said that Commonwealth Immigration was a difficult problem and give-and-take would be necessary, and he recommended that a statement by the Party be made. He said that when the Bill was introduced we should say that firstly, it was based on race discrimination, secondly, it discriminated between the Commonwealth and Europe and thirdly, it was not based on an agreement with Commonwealth countries but was unilateral in character. We would make clear that we supported, and do support, a health check for immigrants which should be made more effective and that there should be the right to deport illegal immigrants, and these powers should be strengthened and should extend up to five years.

He said that the Labour Party does not contest the need for control but we have to be positive and that it was important that there be Commonwealth consultation and implementation of the controls at the point of exit. Until this was agreed he recognised that the hiatus would stimulate immigration – ie people would try to rush in before the new rules came into effect. If the Government would open negotiations, Labour should accept the Act to give time to complete the negotiations. He said this was the only condition we would insist on and we can't amend the Act. If the Government won't negotiate we have no choice but to oppose it.

There was also the problem of immigrants living in Britain. To deal with that, it was necessary to insist on the following points. First, that racial discrimination be made illegal. Second, that greater help be given in housing and education and there should be proper rent control and control of the law. Third, that we should help local authorities with their efforts, particularly in respect of the establishment of working parties. Fourth, he believed there should be maximum facilities for Commonwealth students, including the inter-change of visits.

He said this problem could not be solved by controls alone and it was an index of poverty in the Commonwealth and we must therefore increase aid through the Commonwealth, the United Nations and trade.

Frank McLeavy [MP for Bradford East] said, 'I will not vote against the Act. The main issue is controlled immigration and there is no question of compromise.' He said Bradford has 661 unemployed coloured people and the case for immigration control was strong. Howell said we should deal with the Irish problem by making people living in Ulster show their passports. Christopher Mayhew said that if we voted against the Bill it would be comparable to Labour's votes against the defence estimates in the 1930s. John Silkin* and Maurice Foley were against it. Dick Marsh was for it.

George Brown, winding up, said that he resented the charge that he was in favour of no control. He said, 'Deep down there is the question of prejudice, and the Jews and the Irish know it, and I know it because I am Irish.' He said without immigrant doctors we couldn't run the Health Service. He said he couldn't accept the idea that we only represent our constituents. Labour will tackle the social problems and this is not a compromise.

The vote in favour of Harold's statement was 85 for and 8 against and there was a two-line whip announced. We were told we could pair if we didn't agree with the decision, but we couldn't vote against.

To Oxford this afternoon to give a lecture at the Nuffield political seminar on the reform of British political institutions. Warden Chester was intolerably dull in opening the discussion and most of the arguments centred around the desirability of specialist committees.

Thursday 21 November
The usual agony over the *Guardian* article – this time on race relations – and then to the Commons. As I was walking along the corridor behind the Speaker's chair, I saw the Prime Minister, Home, coming from the other end with someone else and so I looked down very firmly at my papers to walk by. I have never spoken to him in my life and I had a sort of idea that he would want to speak to me. This was the last thing I wanted. But sure enough, after I had passed him he caught me by the arm and when I turned round there he was with his vacuous expression and he said, 'I see you short-headed me to it.' There was a pause for me to answer and as I said nothing at

---

* MP for Lewisham, Deptford, 1963–87. Government Whip and Chief Whip, 1964–9.

all he went on, 'What a strange experience.' I could think of nothing to say that wasn't rude so I just said with a wry smile, 'I see we have another recruit', and walked away. The truth is Home wants to be friendly and popular and this was his way of showing it. But the last thing I wanted was to discuss renunciation as if it was a sort of game that he and I had engaged in and that gave us a special bond against everyone else.

Tea with John Guinery and to the Party meeting to hear the result of the Shadow Cabinet election. I got 82 votes which was far more than I had expected and only missed election by three places. How scandalous that Dick Crossman wasn't elected and that the same old crew got back.

Friday 22 November

Just as I was leaving home to speak in Acton the phone rang and Hilary answered it and it was one of his friends. When he rang off he said that Kennedy had been shot and I didn't believe it. But we switched on the television and there was a flash saying that he was critically ill in Dallas. I drove to Acton and heard the 7.30 bulletin, just before going in to the meeting, which announced that Kennedy had died. It was the most stunning blow and at the beginning of the meeting we all stood in silence for a moment in tribute.

I dashed home to watch TV and hear the details. George Brown was drunk when he was interviewed but everyone else who spoke was sensitive and touched and it was a most moving evening.

Saturday 23 November

Kennedy's death blotted out all other news and we watched a film transmitted via Telstar during the night. Melissa and Joshua drew the most wonderful pictures of what they had seen and it helped to get it out of their system.

This afternoon I took Hilary and his friends to a birthday treat to see Fifty-five Days in Peking. Caroline and I went to the Shores this evening. I heard from TV producer Jeremy Isaacs what happened when George Brown was on TV last night. He was so tight that he nearly got in a fight with someone else who had also come to pay tribute to Kennedy and they almost had to be separated. He is a complete disgrace and one day it will all blow up. One almost wishes it was more obvious so that Harold would have Party backing for removing him.

Sunday 24 November

Worked all afternoon and most of the evening. The papers are still full of Kennedy and today Lee Harvey Oswald, his alleged assassin, was shot while in police custody. The whole thing is so fishy and the shame of the Dallas police is complete.

Wednesday 27 November
To the National Executive. The only points of interest were firstly, that broadcasting will be on the agenda of the Campaign Committee in future; secondly, the Party is urgently discussing the idea of an Ombudsman; thirdly, it was agreed that I should submit a paper on the honours list to the Home Policy Sub-Committee.

Back to the House and worked on a speech on the Commonwealth Immigration Act. The debate lasted for just over three hours and although the whips passed round a note asking us not to speak I was so provoked by Cyril Osborne and his racial venom that I launched into him. In fact, we were only defeated by fifty votes which was very good.

Thursday 28 November
Looked in at the Party meeting where George Brown made a brief statement apologising for his tribute to Kennedy last week. It was acutely embarrassing and there was no comment, nor even grunts of sympathy from MPs there.

Friday 29 November
Up at 6.30 and left home after 7 to drive to Bristol. Met the governors of Kingswood Grammar School to discuss their building programme for the provision of a new science block.

Then to lunch at the New Senate House with Tam Dalyell to meet about ten University, College of Advanced Technology and other people to discuss the science conference which we are holding next year. It was a most successful lunch and the interest and enthusiasm is high. Moreover we are building on the solid foundations of the New Bristol Group.

Drove to Cirencester to do 'Any Questions'. The panel included Bronowski, who is a very bright scientist but rather a poseur, Sir Stephen McAdden, MP for Southend East, and William Hardcastle, former editor of the *Mail*. Afterwards drove home and got in at 1 am.

Saturday 30 November
Home preparing for a party. About thirty-five people came, including the Ungoed-Thomases, the Youngers, Anthony Sampson and Ivan Yates, Dave and June, Crosland and Susan Catling, Bryan Magee, Freddie Ayer and Dee Wells, Jan Le Witt, Michael Flanders, Donald

and Janet Swann, John Gross, Robin Day and Katherine Ainsley, and the Labovitches.

It went well though there was a tremendous row before the party broke up at 3 am about George Brown. Tony Crosland thought this was a left-wing plot to ditch George and it was all malicious and unnecessary. Unfortunately it is not as simple as that.

Monday 2 December

A letter has come in from Rear-Admiral Bonham Carter, treasurer of the Duke of Edinburgh's Household. It was in response to a letter I had forwarded him from a madwoman, saying he was dead. His letter described me as the Rt Hon Anthony Wedgwood Benn DSO, DFC, MP, which gave me a wonderful chance to point out to the Palace that decorations are not hereditary titles!

To the Commons for lunch in honour of Creech-Jones, who is retiring after twenty-three years as chairman of the Fabian Colonial Bureau.[11] I was put next to Harold and much to my embarrassment he raised the subject of George Brown's behaviour. I warned him that there was the danger that if this was badly handled, it might look as if he, Harold, was trying to knife George. He was aware of this and said that that was why he had not accepted George's offer to resign. The idea of making an apology at the Party meeting had been George's and he thought it was a good thing – especially after the Profumo business – that it had been made clear to the public that the Party took this very seriously. A hundred MPs had protested and something had to be done.

He then raised the question of the Shadow Cabinet reshuffle and said it was difficult to do this in case people thought that the new names he might bring forward involved a commitment for future use. I was embarrassed since it might look as if I was hoping to be one of the new names, but I did say that I thought Tony Greenwood and Barbara Castle should be brought in. He said it would be much easier to make his own appointments in the Government than in the Shadow Cabinet. He said he wanted to see me this week.

Tuesday 3 December

To see Harold Wilson at 6 o'clock at his request. Caroline had said some time ago that she thought Harold was anxious for people to advise him on what he should do and that I should think some things out in case I was summoned. In fact this was exactly what he wanted and I had some points ready. The Labour campaign has lost its impetus and must be begun again in the New Year, with a series of meetings that Harold is to address. I suggested that he anticipate our Election manifesto with one major keynote speech in which he outlines the programme of a Labour Government. This programme must have a specific name like the 'New Britain' programme – an idea Caroline had suggested – comparable to Kennedy's 'New Frontier'. It would be printed as a leaflet and in other major speeches he would take up the points from it and elaborate them at greater length. On the basis of this a number of our supporters and backroom brains trusters would come out and announce their support for the 'New Britain' programme – as distinct from coming out as members of the Labour Party.

Thus Citizens for Labour would become a reality without having any organisational existence whatsoever. People who support and work with Wilson would become New Britons. I also put it to Harold that the answer to modernisation as a theme was regeneration, since this suggested that Labour would permit Britain to do things to itself rather than have things done to it by a benevolent Government. Moreover regeneration has a spiritual flavour and a suggestion of youth (new generation) about it which differentiates it more forcibly from Tory philosophy.

Harold more or less asked me to become his principal speech writer and personal adviser. He said we should meet regularly to talk and I could consult with others like Peter Shore and Ted Willis[12] in order to prepare and polish phrases for this great speech and others. I asked about using Dick Crossman but he said that Dick was 'going through one of his moods', which suggests there might be a slight estrangement there.

He then raised the question of his difficulty in reshuffling the Shadow Cabinet, especially at the moment with the George Brown episode so freshly in the minds of the press. He is already being accused of having knifed George and said quite frankly that if he appointed Tony Greenwood and Barbara Castle to high Shadow offices it would look as if he was taking advantage of the difficulties created by George Brown to impose people unacceptable to other members of the Shadow Cabinet. He was therefore going to postpone everything until the New Year and was half apologising to me for not giving me a Shadow ministry. I said, which was true, that I didn't mind a bit, but that I did think that he should now demonstrate his new-found authority in the Party by picking a much younger and stronger team for the Front Bench as the present crowd were not very exciting and rather old. He said he couldn't sack any member of the Shadow Cabinet since they were elected but he might consider bringing in more people from the Back Benches to speak from the Front Bench. His Government would be of his own making and would include some surprising and exciting choices. And he added,

'You'll be in it.' This is the first time he has ever made any such suggestion.

We then got on to the Speakership and I said I thought we ought to have a Labour Speaker but he disagreed and said this would cause the maximum of provocation with the minimum of return. I said I had thought Frank Soskice would be a good choice and anyway it would keep him off the Woolsack. Harold then said, 'My Lord Chancellor will surprise and delight everybody and it certainly won't be Frank Soskice. I'll probably make him a peer and leader of the House of Lords.' He must of course mean that Gerald Gardiner is going to get it and that would be a brilliant choice.

Anyway it looks as if I am going to stand in relation to Harold as Tony Crosland did in relation to Hugh – rather more a backroom adviser than a Front Bench figure. It is obviously more influential but means hitching my wagon to his star, at any rate until the Election. As I left he told me to keep up on transport which suggests that I am going to have that, which is a most difficult job, posing problems that no Labour Government can actually solve within five years. I would much rather be out of the Cabinet and in New York doing the UN job.

Thursday 5 December

At home this morning working on my *Guardian* article. Marcia rang to say that Harold wanted a speech for tomorrow when he was addressing 6,000 graduates from Pitman's College. I promised to think about it and ring him back. I must brace myself for writing drafts of all his speeches over the next few months. It will drain me of ideas and I don't know how I'm going to have enough to spare for my *Guardian* column and my own speeches, and whether I have got to keep off points I put to him.

To Bristol for the GMC – a crowded meeting which, with one dissentient, approved the idea of setting up a Citizens for Labour Committee. I put it to them that once again they were pioneering a new technique, and this appeals to them.

Monday 9 December

To the Campaign Committee this morning to present the recommendations for future broadcasts. Harold arrived late and I was afraid we might be torpedoed but in fact it went through without a murmur.

This evening Caroline and I went to the French Embassy for a party. We had no idea why we had been asked and judging from the blank look on the Ambassador's face he had no idea why he'd asked us. We saw hardly anybody we knew and the few people who were introduced to us were a duchess, several French countesses and all that. It was pretty grim. We were glad to get on to Shirley and Bernard Williams' for dinner.

At 10.45 we left there and went to the Foreign Office for a party given by Ronald Higgins who is the duty officer and has a flat there. That was a much more interesting crowd and I greatly enjoyed a long talk to the cartoonist Abu Abraham and his beautiful Indian wife.

Saturday 14–Sunday 15 December

Up at 6 to Bristol for a surgery. About eighteen people turned up with a variety of problems, from redundancy in a commercial vehicle factory to widows' pensions and the inevitable housing. Home this afternoon and lazed about with 'TW3' on Saturday night telly.

Rang Harold Wilson and he was pleased about the 'New Britain' idea.

Chris and Cicely Mayhew and eight children to Sunday lunch and they went off with Caroline and the three elder children to a Christmas concert. It took me two hours to wash it all up.

Monday 16 December

To Bristol and I was interviewed for the New Bristol Group broadsheet on race relations. Just had time to drive up to Horfield Prison where the vigil organised by the Campaign for the Abolition of Capital Punishment was in progress. Russell Pascoe is to be executed tomorrow morning and the whole thing is very gruesome. I was so steamed up about it that I wrote my *Guardian* column all about it on the way back in the train.

Caroline met me and we went on to a buffet supper at the Tanganyikan High Commissioner's, Sam Ntiro, and his wife Sarah, who is a charming woman. Also there was the new Kenyan High Commissioner and Messaoud Kellou, the Algerian Ambassador. I had a long talk with Messaoud about Israel.

Tuesday 17 December

They hanged Russell Pascoe in Horfield Prison this morning at 8 am. The protests in Bristol reached an enormous volume and I think it'll probably be the last hanging there, for capital punishment is on the way out and in the new Parliament it will certainly be abolished.

Had an hour with Harold Wilson discussing the 'New Britain' campaign. He is delighted with it and I can see that I am firmly entrenched as his speech writer. The speeches will be made in the New Year and the first one will be published as a pamphlet. The organisation is very simple. Dick, Peter, Tommy and I are the inner circle and round us will be the phrase-makers, like Ted Willis, Jim Cameron[13] and Hugh Cudlipp.

From there to a teachers' reception and home. Caroline has a bug of some kind and I put her to bed early and worked late.

Wednesday 18 December

To the National Executive this morning. My proposals for a working party to discuss Conference arrangements had produced a completely negative paper by Len Williams and after a discussion all but three of the Executives voted to defer action until after the General Election. Like 'Citizens for Labour', it was another idea turned down. The report of the Putney Labour Party enquiry came up and the recommendation that it be censured was passed. The Party finances were discussed at length as we will have a deficit of £11,000 next year. I proposed that we launch a general appeal but after a lot of discussion nothing was done. Frankly the NEC is such a conservative body that one despairs of getting it to do anything to bring the Party up to date. If we lose the Election I shall write a pamphlet to start a real campaign to modernise the Party.

Claudio and Paula Veliz came to lunch at the Commons.* They said they could easily arrange for an invitation for me to visit Cuba, which I would very much like to do. Claudio also had some useful ideas on the sort of economic aid that a Labour Government could give. He said that it would be a great mistake to try to diffuse our efforts over a wide field and that we ought to concentrate on things we could do well.

The first was educational assistance, especially by the teaching of English, by universities here adopting new universities abroad, by bringing more foreign students here and by providing technical training.

In addition, we should develop a new approach to investment abroad. The old division between industrial nations and primary producers is out; the old ideas of foreign businesses exploiting raw materials in poor countries is out and the old idea of trying to shape their economic development for them and limiting it to simple industrial processes is out.

What is required is long-term credits at a low rate of interest to buy advanced plant and equipment from Britain and to provide all the educational and technical training package for their technicians that goes with it.

He thought that English language, culture and equipment could

---

* Claudio Veliz was a Chilean professor of history and a Latin American correspondent.

be spread very effectively over the whole world in a way that would leave the decision-making entirely in the hands of under-developed countries and would bring prosperity to our home industries. It all made very good sense to me.

To South Dorset with Guy Barnett[14] to speak at his annual Christmas dance. It was a pleasant evening, though I had ten minutes of speaking to a huge ballroom where even 500 people look miles away round the fringe of a blank dance floor.

Thursday 19 December
Early train back to London. To Transport House with Caroline this evening for their Christmas party. The new bright young guys there put on a satirical show which effectively mocked the old Labour Party and did not go down very well with the old boys. But it was the first sign of life in the machine for years.

Saturday 21 December
This evening we went to Wayland Young's party and met Mikhail Lyubimov and his wife from the Soviet Embassy. In looks and behaviour they were indistinguishable from some sleek diplomats from the French or Italian embassies and the smoothness of his conversation gave the discussion a character quite different from any other I have had with a Soviet diplomat. He was criticising the Labour Party for being so unspecific in its foreign policy and unforthcoming in its attitude to further initiative to improve Anglo–Soviet relations and settle the German question.[15]

Sunday 22–Thursday 26 December
Christmas. Very little contact with anyone politically. Six Labour peers were announced and I thanked God I was not stuck in the Lords and welcoming new recruits, as I would be if I were there.

Friday 27 December
To Bristol to do a TWW programme where I spoke for five minutes and answered questions for twenty-five minutes from a handpicked, bitterly hostile Tory and Liberal audience. These sort of things do no good to politics, for they seek to make entertainment out of it all.

Herbert Rogers rang to tell me that I have been reported to the Executive of the Borough Labour Party for writing to the Lord Mayor about the New Bristol Group's proposal for a Citizenship Council to improve race relations. This is taken as an indication that the New Bristol Group has entered politics. Of course it is no such thing, for I wrote as an individual and the New Bristol Group has done nothing about it. But what a fantastic situation. The Party machine in Bristol has done no new thinking for years and is trying to commit suicide with the help of its own rule book. Moreover the NBG broadsheet is just anticipating the lines on which a Labour Government will be tackling this very problem.

Finished the evening at a party in Clifton where the artists and architects and designers had all gathered. I had a long talk with them.

Tuesday 31 December
Lunch with Peter Shore to discuss Election arrangements. Harold's idea that everything is to be run from a 'caravan' is basically all right but you can't shut Transport House down and you must have all the key people in the caravan. Neither of these conditions are met.

Wrote a memo on the honours list for the Home Policy Committee and to New Year's Eve party at Michael Flanders' flat. Home just before midnight where the boys and Melissa were welcoming in the New Year, twisting and shouting.

The end of 1963 and what a year politically and personally! First the dead – Pope John XXIII, Kennedy and Gaitskell. The collapse of the Common Market application. The Profumo affair, and Macmillan's resignation. Now, Home versus Wilson and the fortunes of the Party are reversed. The year of the test-ban treaty and the end of Adenauer and the beginning of a new era.

Personally it has been just as sensational – beginning with me still in exile and only the faintest glimmering of hope that the law might be changed. Then the sudden rush of legislation, renunciation and re-election. I feel now as if I had never been out of the Commons at all.

On to 1964 which will be the busiest and most important politically and personally. At the moment a Labour victory seems virtually certain and with it a complete change in our lives seems certain too, though in what capacity I shall have to work I just don't know.

Thursday 2 January 1964
To Bristol for a New Bristol Group meeting with the usual fifteen very keen and intelligent people. We discussed a broadsheet on voluntary services. That venture really is a success.

Back to stay with the Bishops at 11 pm and had an hour with Mike Cocks [Labour candidate in Bristol West] about the TSR2,[16] where the Tories are warning of unemployment if Labour is returned. The political risks of disarmament are considerable.

Monday 6 January
Flew to Glasgow to do a Scottish TV interview called 'They Made News' with three journalists. The other half of the programme was the Duke of Argyll, whose recent divorce case was so sensational.[17] He looked like Maurice Chevalier and his bored affirmation of the value of the hereditary system was belied by his own mediocrity.

Back on the sleeper which was the first of a new service called the Night Limited and had a bar on it. The station master in his top hat was greeting important travellers including the chairman of the Scottish region of the railways, McSomething of McSomething. He was another of these aristocratic executives with no imagination and very patronising.

Wednesday 8 January
Spent half the day on the phone, trying to sort out the latest muddle over Party political TV. The divided control between the Leader, the Chief Whip and the General Secretary has reached a point of chaos.

To see the chairman of the Tilling Group, Mr Holmes, this afternoon. Bristol Commercial Vehicles, which is part of his group, and whose shares are wholly owned by the Transport Holding Company, is prohibited by law from selling its vehicles in the open market because it is wholly nationalised. I suggested the workers should buy one share from THC and thus free the firm from this unnatural proscription. This seems to be a workable scheme and we are going to try it.

Thursday 9 January
To see Peter Shore for a talk about Election arrangements before a joint interview with Harold, who was almost deliberately vague and slightly testy. He quite wrongly thinks that he can shut Transport House down and imagines that his caravan can consist purely of himself, Ted Willis and John Harris as the top-level brains trust. Clive Bradley and Percy Clark came in later and we are gradually getting the 'New Britain' theme incorporated in other propaganda, but the co-ordination is very poor.

Saturday 11 January
Worked at home this morning and to Transport House this afternoon for the Young Socialists' National Committee. One of the things that came up was their attitude to the United Nations. Up to now by a majority they have opposed support for the UN, which confirms my suspicions of Trotskyist influence on the committee. Normally I don't

vote as a member of the Executive but this time I did and we got through, by a majority, a resolution supporting the UN.

Monday 13 January
To the Campaign Committee this morning in Harold Wilson's office. He was a bit late and was not there when broadcasting came on to the agenda. Len Williams launched a great attack on the handling of the last Party political broadcast. He complained that he had been told nothing and especially nothing about the decision to use Granada. Of course I had notified Harold Wilson about this in November, and, at his suggestion, had not told the Campaign Committee about it. I think Harold is rather devious and I must be careful to keep myself covered when this sort of thing happens again.

This evening the family and Mother came with us to the theatre to see Michael Flanders and Donald Swann.

Tuesday 14 January
Lunch at the House of Commons with Mr Kostarkis of the Polish embassy. He is an agreeable man and we had a long and interesting talk about his reasons for joining the Communist Party during the war. We both felt that the Cold War was completely over and what was needed was a new approach to European politics. I would like to see a pan-European conference with Russians and Americans attending only as observers, in which East and West Europe could try to plan a new approach to its own problems.

Then to *The Times* building for a party of some visiting American senators and congressmen.

Thursday 16 January
Early train back to London and to see Harold Wilson with Peter Shore for the script conference about next Sunday's 'New Britain' keynote speech. It looked a mess but we managed to clean it up quite a bit and he was very easy to work with. He was very relaxed and wandered about talking expansively about how he saw the campaign developing.

This afternoon the *Spectator* came out with Ian Macleod's review of Randolph Churchill's* new book *The Fight for the Tory Leadership*. This article has created a major political sensation, since it gives Macleod's own account of what happened. He says quite plainly that the processes of consultation were unsatisfactory and he more or less accuses Lord Dilhorne [the Lord Chancellor] of having misled

---

* Randolph Churchill, Conservative MP for Preston, 1940–5, son of Sir Winston Churchill.

Macmillan as to the views of the Cabinet. It couldn't come at a better moment from the point of view of Wilson's weekend speech, for one of the major themes he is taking up is the rotten aristocratic element in our society which is at the moment holding Britain back.

After the division at 10 pm I had a talk to Dick Crossman and explained the current difficulties with Harold Wilson. He knew what I meant and feels a bit left out of things now.

Friday 17 January
Macleod's article is still major political news in all the papers and the Gallup poll in the *Telegraph* continues to give us a lead of 10.5 per cent. I decided to send a letter to Herbert Rogers, saying we must be ready for an Election at any time.

To Bristol this afternoon and went to the College of Commerce to talk about world affairs. The audience included a lot of Tories. One girl of twenty wanted us to issue an ultimatum to Russia to get out of East Berlin. Another was absolutely opposed to economic aid. I think they must be grammar school Tories who have come to the college. I find them unattractive.

From there to Kingswood Youth Club at St Stephen's Church, Soundwell. About sixty youngsters were there and I don't think most of them wanted to listen to me at all, but the vicar had invited me and they sat there while I talked. As soon as I had finished and the questions had stopped, they leapt up and got on with their dancing and I was sorry I had accepted. I sometimes wonder whether it is true that young people are supporting us. They were so defeatist about Britain and thought that nothing could be done to improve things.

Tuesday 21 January
Two issues have arisen in Bristol that exactly demonstrate what is wrong with the Labour Party as it is now organised for municipal work.

The first is that Bristol Education Committee has decided on a very rigid scheme of educational reorganisation which involves reducing the role of the ancient grammar schools to becoming the upper half of a two-tier comprehensive system for a narrow geographical area. This has produced an outcry in Bristol and will stir up tremendous resistance from the public. If the Labour Group had kept in touch with current thinking on this they would have suggested an alternative scheme under which the ancient grammar schools become sixth form colleges, maintaining a high academic record and being open to people from all over the city. I wrote to

Vyvyan-Jones, chairman of the Education Committee, in the hope that it was not too late for the position to be reconsidered.

The second row is because the Kingswood Labour Council – 100 per cent control – have negotiated in secret with a property company to develop the centre of Kingswood. They signed the contract with the company before making it public. The layout of the scheme is quite imaginative but it is the denial of a fundamental right of public discussion that has caused the trouble. Moreover, the scheme of bringing in private property companies is contrary to the latest Labour thinking and will probably not be approved by a Labour Minister. Kingswood people are up in arms about it and it could have serious consequences in municipal elections.

If either Bristol or Kingswood had kept in touch with the Labour Party and its experts in these two fields they would never have fallen into these errors. If ever there was a case for the New Bristol Group, this is it.

Thursday 23 January
Into the Commons at 10.30 this morning for an hour's session with Harold Wilson about the speech he is delivering in Swansea on Saturday. Tommy Balogh and Peter Shore were there too and we went through it quite successfully. It was full of turgid economic policy but Harold is amenable to suggestions and has none of Hugh Gaitskell's rigidity in sticking to dull economic phrases that could and should be simplified. Back to the office and wrote my *Guardian* piece. Spent the rest of the day clearing up mail.

When I was in Wilson's room today, Marcia came in to say that Robert Carvel of the *Evening Standard* was on the telephone to enquire whether Harold had any speech writers. Harold said, 'No. I am working on a speech now, every word of which I have dictated.' Marcia looked at me and asked if I minded. I said, 'Of course not.' The last thing I want is to be known as Harold's speech writer and I think it is the last thing he wants too.

Friday 24 January
Worked in the office this morning and had lunch with Vassev of the Soviet Embassy at the Coq d'Or. We had a general talk about foreign affairs and he expressed considerable disappointment with the caution that Harold Wilson has shown in his statements. Apparently the Russians feel there will be no real difference when there is a change of Government. I pointed out that Harold would need a year to work himself into the leadership and win over the Shadow Cabinet and the Executive to his point of view. I rebuked him for his naïveté in not distinguishing between a lieutenant of Aneurin Bevan and

Lord Home, a man of Munich. I pointed out the areas in which Labour policy would be quite different. The Russians' great interest now is in carrying the test-ban treaty a stage further. When Harold makes his foreign affairs speech in Leeds on 8 February, the distinctive nature of Labour's policy must be spelled out more fully.

Saturday 25 January
This evening Harold made his second speech in the 'New Britain' series, at Swansea, on economic policy. I came across a cutting from yesterday's *Evening Standard* in which it was made clear that he has no speech writers.

Monday 27 January
To the Campaign Committee where I reported on the work of our informal group preparing for the Election. The trickiest point was getting them to accept the arrangement under which we would meet every morning at Transport House to discuss broadcasting. The plan is that I should take the chair, Peter Shore will be there with Chris Mayhew and Shirley Williams and it will in practice be the London end of the campaign organisation, in regular telephone contact with Harold. Ray Gunter smelt a rat and I had to fight off resistance to the idea. So I played it all down as a purely technical discussion and it was more or less accepted.

This evening Caroline and I went to the reception at India House to celebrate Republic Day. The new High Commissioner is Mr Mehta. He is a very old man and it rather suggests that the Indian Government does not think that the London post matters very much.

Afterwards we had a quick meal at the Commons and Caroline went into the gallery for the last half hour of the debate. Meanwhile, I had two Southern Africans come to see me, Mr Mutasa, who is the London representative of the Zimbabwe African National Union, and Simpson M'tambanengwe, a Southern Rhodesian lawyer and also a member of ZANU. This is the breakaway movement from Joshua Nkomo's organisation, Zimbabwe African People's Union.

They were a little hesitant and embarrassed but I gather that their real anxiety was to maintain some contact with the Labour Party. My sympathies are largely with Joshua but one has to keep in touch with everybody. They are afraid that Winston Field will make some progress in his appeal for independence for Southern Rhodesia, or that he will do a 'Boston Tea Party'. I told them the way I believed Labour thinking was going and then went to vote in the division at 10.

Tuesday 28 January
David Ennals and Peter Shore came here at 9.30 this morning to discuss Harold Wilson's next speech on foreign affairs. I had done a draft for them and we were in almost complete agreement about the general line he should take. Peter and David certainly are the two ablest people in the Party.

Wednesday 29 January
Went to have my polio shot this afternoon with Melissa.

Harold phoned this afternoon to say that he had decided to postpone his foreign affairs speech and to do homes, education and land instead. He feels that the Cyprus crisis will help the Tory Government and therefore wants to bring the campaign back to domestic issues. His instinct is probably right. I also raised with him the question of Election arrangements and the hideous new Labour newspaper advertising campaign which speaks of 'Labour's New Britain'. It is so exclusive and narrow and contains the phrase that under a Labour Government 'everybody will have it good'. Harold agreed to get these deleted.

This evening Caroline and I went to the Columbia Theatre to see the première of *Dr Strangelove*, in which Peter Sellers plays three parts. It is a superb film about a mad American general who sends atom bombs to Russia because he thinks that fluoridation of water is a Communist plot to sap the energies of the West. The film hovers between gravity and farce but always keeps its balance and reminds us how near we are to obliteration and how little we should repose our confidence in computers and security arrangements and a strict chain of command. We thoroughly enjoyed it.

Sunday 2 February
Drove to Bristol University for the science conference. Thirty were invited and 120 people turned up, including five professors. Dick Crossman was absolutely brilliant and we had some excellent discussions on the Robbins Report[18] and the application of science to industry.

Then to Mr Adams's house, where Labour candidates and leading Party workers met Dick Crossman. Vyvyan-Jones was there and we had a short discussion about education.

Thursday 6 February
To the Commons this morning for an hour or more with Harold Wilson to discuss the weekend speech. He has decided not to do foreign affairs because he feels that it is home issues that really pull

in the support and so he concentrated primarily on housing and town planning.

I am afraid we are getting away a little bit from the 'New Britain' theme but you can't be too rigid. After the others had left, Dick Crossman, Harold and I had half an hour on the problems of dealing with direct grant grammar schools. Harold is a bit worried about the way things are going generally.

This evening Caroline and I went to the Soviet party to meet Valentina Tereshkova, the first woman cosmonaut. Afterwards Peter and Liz Shore came and had a meal with us.

Tuesday 11 February
Lunch with Sergio Romano of the Italian embassy and Joe Fromm of US News and World Report, and a man called Barnes from the Foreign Office. Fromm came out with the argument that a Labour Government would be neutralist and we had a fierce discussion that went right through lunch. The Italians were really on my side and I felt a European against what was of course a very right-wing American view. The Foreign Office man was full of smiles and ineffective comment. They are awful.

The Young Socialists Youth Unemployment Rally took place today and there was a lobby at the Commons. I spoke at the Central Hall to a meeting to which only a smattering of the young people had come.

Saturday 15 February
Janet Stewart, a sociologist, came to see me this morning as she is writing a piece on race relations in Bristol. I hope it helps to get things moving there again. In the evening, went to Abingdon School to give a Foyle's lecture. This is a direct grant school with a history going back 500 years or more. The headmaster was a retired Lieutenant Colonel and the discipline was rigid to a degree. There was an audience of boys from eleven to eighteen who listened to me in silence for an hour talking about Parliament. The questions were not bad but I got the feeling of a completely repressed school in which all the natural irreverence and genius of the children had been stamped out. The headmaster was full of criticism of American education, a firm believer in the elite, very doubtful about the Robbins Report and the general plans for the expansion of education. I went away quite depressed if these are the sort of people who have got to be won over to the new policy.

Sunday 16 February
A day at home and Mother came over for lunch and tea. This evening
Tommy Balogh called. He stayed for half an hour and said how
anxious he was about Jim Callaghan and would I talk to Harold
about it, and so on, and so on. Of course, I have no influence in
these fields and the trouble with Tommy is that he hasn't got enough
to do. I believe he just pursues people who are in his immediate
circle and makes life hell for them by 'phoning and insisting they
have lunch and calling round at weekends. I like him and he is a
very able person but he just gets in my hair.

Monday 17 February
To Bristol this morning to speak at the Bristol Rotary Club. About
150 people were there, representing middle range leaders of city life
with whom I get very little contact. I talked about the way in which
technical change made the machinery of Government obsolete. It
was highly political but by not mentioning the Labour Party or the
Conservative Party once they all congratulated me afterwards on
having stayed off politics. This is the curious thing about speaking
to Tories, they never can see anything political unless it is spelled
out by mentioning a political leader or party. If I had made a
most innocuous speech about road safety and had mentioned Harold
Wilson and Marples all the time, they would have gone away feeling
somehow I had brought politics into it.

From there to Colston Girls' School where I was speaking to the
Political Club. I talked for half an hour on the Labour Party and
in the questions that followed, lasting an hour and a quarter, the
overwhelming majority were about educational policy. I simply made
the case for comprehensive education as formidably as I could. In
the end the teachers got so angry they kept chipping in and it
developed into quite a battle.

Back to London to vote at 10 o'clock.

Tuesday 18 February
Working at home this morning and tea in the House of Lords' Dining
Room with Wayland Young this afternoon. It was the first time I
had been in the Lords' Dining Room since Father died and it felt
very strange. How glad I was just to be there as a visitor. Wayland
is worried that the Party is going to commit itself finally and firmly,
and irrevocably, against the Polaris submarine deal before the Election. He feels that the decision should be kept open until after the
Election, and if there is no disarmament in the next five years it
would be impossible for Britain to be able to slip back to being a
non-nuclear power at a period of history when perhaps eight other

countries have become nuclear powers. He had written to Harold Wilson about this. Later I saw Dick Crossman and he too thought we should keep everything open, partly because we shan't know the truth about the exact military position until we come to power.

Wednesday 19 February

Lunch at the House of Commons with Eric Wright of the *Sunday Citizen* for whom I am writing articles on the next three Sundays.

At 4 o'clock Colonel Kenneth Post of the Arndale Property Company came to see me to discuss the Kingswood development plan. He had been with the Civic Trust and had moved to one of the property companies. He didn't really know much about the scheme and appeared to be a real creature of public relations.

To the Foreign Press Association reception at the House of Commons, and then on to a party with Caroline at the Argentinian embassy. All the Latin American diplomats were there and it was the usual cocktail party small talk – so different from the Soviet and African parties. These people looked as if they were bored stiff with each other's company and hardly any politics was talked.

Thursday 20 February

Began the move to my basement office today. At last there will be room for all my papers and the arrangement is going to work out very well indeed. It was quite a wrench leaving that upstairs room where I have been for twelve years. Melissa's seventh birthday party this afternoon, and then I had to hurry off to Transport House to discuss George Brown's TV broadcast next Wednesday.

This evening Sir Alec Douglas-Home was on television and it was clear that he simply didn't understand most of the questions. He is a real asset to us.

Saturday 22 February

To Newark to speak for Ted Bishop. He has become very popular there by his hard work and imaginative approach to the electorate. I was collected from my hotel at 8.30 am for a motorcade through the constituency. It was icy cold and we went through ten villages and I had to make six open-air speeches. At 12 we ended up in a wooden hut where the women's section had got a cup of tea and from there I was dropped at a roundabout on the main road to Leicester where I was collected and taken to the Party's policy briefing conference. That lasted for two hours, with a lot of questions and discussion and then on to two evening meetings.

The first was at Calverton which was pretty empty. They took me to the Miners' Welfare Club where I was allowed on to the platform for a moment though there was a strict rule about no politics. From there I was driven to Alveston for a crowded meeting and a social and finally got back to Nottingham after midnight, having made about ten speeches and holding two press conferences and feeling pretty tired.

Tuesday 25 February
Worked at home this morning. This afternoon to the first meeting of the working group on immigrants which Tony Greenwood is chairing for the National Executive. It was a very good group and the people who came had a lot of experience. But it's a massive undertaking and it will take six months or longer to complete the report.

Caroline came to the House to collect me and we went to Transport House for a party for Rose Davy, who had been in the office for forty years. Then we went on to a party at Grosvenor House, given by the Kuwaiti Ambassador and we slipped out of the fire exit as soon as we had shaken hands.

Then to the Soviet Embassy for a farewell party for Romanov, the Minister-Counsellor. Romanov has been in London on three separate occasions from 1947–52, 1955–8 and 1960 till now. He is going on to Lagos as Ambassador. He is a most kindly man and it was a very nostalgic party for he was sad to be leaving. We had a talk to Ted Hill[19] and his wife, Anna – mainly about whether he should accept a peerage. He would quite like to go to the Lords when he retires from his union next year but his wife is dead against it.

We chatted to Mr Ossipov who is the *Izvestia* correspondent. He was very critical of Wilson and I described Wilson's background and achievements as Leader of the Party. We ended with Trofimenko who is the Radio Moscow correspondent in London. Harold Wilson had turned up at the party which was decent of him as he is just leaving for America. He and Romanov have known each other for a long time. The Russians all think there will be no change when a Labour Government is elected and indeed some of them are quite naïvely sympathetic to Home. This is partly because their philosophy doesn't allow them to admit that there is much difference between parties in a bourgeois state and partly because they would like the Labour Party to be much more specific about Anglo–Soviet relations and can't understand why we are not.

Wednesday 26 February
To the National Executive this morning for an hour and then to the BBC Television Centre with Dick Crossman and George Brown to record the Party political broadcast on 'Labour and the Scientific Revolution'. I did have a chance for a short talk with George about

difficulties with Clive Bradley, the broadcasting officer. Clive has sent George up the wall with his continual choppings and changings and I think this will make it easier for me to get full authority during the Election to reach final technical decisions. The broadcast went moderately well, although it was not a complete success. Originally Dick Crossman was to have done it but Harold Wilson imposed George Brown on the programme for personal and political reasons.

Saturday 29 February

Surgery in Bristol this morning and eleven people came with a host of problems. I have never known my constituency work heavier. About a hundred letters a week coming in and about two hundred a week having to be written. Home this afternoon.

Wednesday 4 March

To the Commons this afternoon and saw Harold Wilson with Peter Shore about Harold's speech in Liverpool this Saturday. He has just come back from America where he had got on excellently with President Johnson. I think they are both highly political animals and understood each other well. He was very worried about the report that had appeared concerning his alleged proposals to hand the Navy over to the United Nations.[20] For my part I found it a very exciting idea and was rather sorry to see him back-tracking so fast.

Monday 9 March

After lunch Caroline and I drove to Oxford where I spoke at Ruskin College about the second chamber. They followed me on the necessity for cutting the powers of the Lords and ending hereditary membership but were sceptical of any plan for appointing people to an advisory second chamber. Caroline thought they were suspicious of the creation of a new privileged class based on merit. Maybe nothing can ever be done but it is a job that needs clearing up.

We went and sat on our bench (or the one that replaced it)* and then to the Union where there was a dinner organised by the City Labour Party and University Labour Club. This was followed by a public meeting in the Union and we drove home late.

Tuesday 10 March

Lunch with Kostarkis of the Polish embassy. We discussed increased cultural contacts. He is an Anglophile Communist, but even so it is difficult to make much progress as they are all suspicious of ideo-

---

* I proposed to Caroline on a park bench on 11 August 1948 when she was on a summer course at Oxford. I later bought the bench which rests in the garden at home.

logical coexistence. But he did say that he thought it was remarkable that Britain had been able to take the loss of her empire and he thought that Wilson's programme for restoring self-confidence to Britain was very necessary.

At Messaoud Kellou's farewell party later we had a long and delightful talk with Mr Shen Ping, the Chinese chargé d'affaires. This is the first time a Chinese diplomat in London has been friendly for years and I hope to follow it up.

Wednesday 11 March

Figuerido, the London representative of General Delgado, leader of the Portuguese opposition in exile, came to see me. He has just come back from a conference in the Netherlands and thinks the Common Market countries might be a force for liberalising the regime in Portugal and opening up the possibility of Delgado's succession.

Tea with Ted Willis who is very embarrassed still by being a peer and told me what a cold reception he had had from the Labour peers.

Friday 13 March

To Bristol this evening for a meeting organised by the Medical Practitioners' Union, attended by about twenty GPs to discuss the future of the Health Service. I gave a speech for twenty minutes and then we had a most informative exchange of ideas. It was useful to me and also I think indicates that it is much better to try to talk to people gathered in groups according to their work rather than according to where they live.

Saturday 14 March

Home to London and to the Young Socialists' National Committee this afternoon. There was the usual bitter row with the five alleged Trotskyists on one side against the rest of us. They defeated a resolution endorsing 'Signposts for the Sixties' and I then moved that the committee adjourn. This precipitated a great row and it was reversed. Obviously youngsters will be critical of the Labour line but their hatred for the UN carries it beyond this point. I really don't know what the conference will be like but I'm fearful.

Monday 16 March

To the Youth Sub-Committee where we had the row all over again. I defended the right of one of the Young Socialists, Barrie Evans, to write a vitriolic article against the role of conscription. The trouble is the official Party attitude is entirely negative.

Tuesday 17 March
To the Commons this morning to take a party of schoolchildren round. There were about twenty girls between fourteen and sixteen and not one of them had ever heard of Attlee or Eden. Only two had ever heard of Churchill.

This evening to Caxton Hall for a debate organised by Mary Adams and the Television Viewers' Council about the televising of Parliament. Marcus Worsley [Conservative MP for Louth] and I were for it and Cyril Osborne [Conservative MP for Keighley] and Dr Eric Taylor [one of the Clerks of the House] were against it. The case against televising Parliament reveals a prehistoric attitude to Parliament and Taylor was worse than Osborne. He said that debates had deteriorated since the press was allowed into the House. This was fantastic. He also argued Parliament was 'the High Court of Parliament' and therefore TV could not be present. A Labour Government will have to televise the House of Commons as it will be the only way of getting our case across to a country which will be receiving most of its news from a Tory press.

Wednesday 18 March
Up at 5.30 and fixed my New Year Planner on the ceiling. With the help of little self-adhesive stickers one can see a year's engagements at a glance. It is a brilliant step forward in organisation! Working at home today and to the House of Commons to see Peter Shore to discuss Harold's next speech. We both agreed that he should deal with foreign affairs, the United Nations, and help to under-developed areas. But when we went to see Harold at 6.30 pm he said that he was going to 'beat the big drum for Britain' at Edinburgh this weekend, showing how Britain had fallen behind under the Tories. I put it to him that a foreign affairs speech was necessary even if only to influence opinion formers. But he would not have it. I'm afraid he is disappointing at the moment on these issues. He is almost more closely tied to the Gallup polls than Hugh Gaitskell was.

Thursday 19 March
Bought a second-hand photocopier this morning. It is the most fabulous machine and when I have got over using it as a toy I think it will be very handy. Caroline and I went shopping this afternoon and went out for a meal.

Saturday 21 March
Caught the early train to Bristol for a liaison committee meeting between the Labour parliamentary candidates* and the leaders of the Labour Group. We discussed race relations, education and the future of the College of Advanced Technology. On race relations, Wally Jenkins and Bert Peglar are absolutely dead against a Citizenship Council, an idea I had been urging for some time and which was more important in the light of the bus boycott. They think they know how to handle it. I didn't press the point beyond saying that Labour policy was to encourage these councils. Next time there is a big row about it the move to get the Citizenship Council established will probably succeed. On education they have decided to withdraw the free places they take at the direct grant grammar schools progressively over the next eight years. This will cause a storm of protest and of course will run counter to the official Labour Government policy of integrating the public schools. I pointed this out but said no more.

This seemed an opportunity for conciliation and I think relations are improved.

Back to London this afternoon.

Monday 23 March
Campaign committee this morning and Len Williams explained the set-up for the Election period. This suits us in broadcasting though no decision has been taken about the executive command structure, which will have to be clarified.

Harold rejected my proposal for a programme on world poverty on TV on the eve of the municipal elections.

Tuesday 24 March
This afternoon to India House to see Mehta, the High Commissioner, about the Rivonia trials[21] in South Africa. I was leading a deputation including Dr Yusuf Dadoo (ex-president of the Indian National Congress) and Tom Kellock, on behalf of Anti-Apartheid World Campaign for the release of these prisoners. Mehta was very pleased and agreed to try to put pressure on the British and American Governments to implement the resolution.

To the Commons and saw Harold Wilson, to tell him I was going to meet the Chinese chargé d'affaires, Shen Ping, and could I transmit his greetings. He said, yes in general but that we could do nothing publicly now without disturbing the American impartiality towards Labour in the forthcoming Election.

* Bristol comprised six constituencies in March 1964; three were Labour, three were Conservative.

I also told him that George had asked me to set up a working party on urban congestion and did he mind. He looked at me as if I was asking him whether I was to be Minister of Transport (which I wasn't), and said it would be all right if it was entirely informal.

Friday 27 March

Reorganised my books this morning.

This afternoon to see Shen Ping at the Chinese embassy in Portland Place. Mr Ping received me in the embassy and we had an exchange of pleasantries in which we asked about each other's children. He had arranged for some wine, tea and pastries, and was accompanied by a younger man who occasionally acted as interpreter, though he did not speak English much better. I told him that Mr Wilson knew of my visit and conveyed his greetings formally.

I asked first how Britain could improve relations with China and why they had exchanged Ambassadors with France but not with us. Mr Ping said that France had wholeheartedly supported China, did not recognise Chiang in Taiwan, had refused his Ambassador at the Common Market and had voted for Peking at UN technical organisations. Britain, by contrast, was only half-hearted in supporting Peking. China rejected the 'two Chinas' policy. If American forces were withdrawn from Taiwan and the Straits, the Taiwan problem could be settled by China internally.

I asked him whether China would take her seat in the UN if she was admitted – before the Taiwan question was settled. Mr Ping replied that China was a founder member of the UN and would take her seat, provided that Chiang did not continue to represent Taiwan in the General Assembly.

Mr Ping then asked whether the Labour view would be different. I replied that it would. A Labour Government had recognised Peking in 1949 and did not recognise Chiang's regime in Taiwan. We always regarded the Taiwan question as being one that would have to be settled after China had been restored to her rightful place.

I asked him what attitude China took towards the disarmament conference in Geneva. Mr Ping replied that China was not a member of it. China wished comprehensive disarmament that went far beyond the partial test ban. This conference was set up by the UN from which China was excluded.

I asked if China would feel herself bound by UN resolutions if she were a member of it. Mr Ping said, 'Yes.' I then questioned him on why China thought that the partial test-ban treaty was unsatisfactory. Mr Ping said it was because the monopoly of nuclear weapons by the US and USSR was not acceptable to China. 'If you have three people,' he said, 'and only two of them have sharp knives, they can blackmail the third unless he has a sharp knife too.' I said, 'Would it not be better if everybody's sharp knives were taken away and we all paid for a policeman.' He said, again, that China would not accept a monopoly held by others.

I asked whether a total test-ban treaty would be better, in China's eyes, than a partial treaty. Mr Ping said that personally he thought it would be better but that the real answer was to end the monopoly. I asked if he did not think there was a danger in the spread of nuclear weapons. Mr Ping said that China recognised nuclear weapons were very destructive but ('you will not agree with this', he added) socialist countries would always be peace-loving and would never use nuclear weapons to make war. I said I thought this was too optimistic. For example, would he be happy if Yugoslavia had nuclear weapons? He replied that Yugoslavia was an agent of US imperialism. I said this confirmed my view that socialist countries might later develop in different directions and it would still be dangerous, for this reason, for nuclear weapons to spread.

I asked if China accepted the Colombo powers'[22] attitude to the Sino-Indian border dispute and stressed the strong Labour links with India. Mr Ping said that China accepted their view in principle but there could be no preconditions to the negotiations, which must be based on the present line of control and could allow either side to raise points of concern to them.

We talked about Hong Kong and I handed him an extract from ex-President Truman's book which quotes from a State Department paper on US policy to China in 1945, calling for Kuomintang-Communist reconciliation, the strengthening of China and the restoration of Hong Kong to the mainland. Mr Ping was very interested in this but said that China's policy towards Hong Kong was realistic. China recognised the present position and was even making arrangements for the water supply to be trebled to meet the needs of the colony. But China did want proper consular representation which now did not exist.

Mr Ping then asked me about the Labour Party's attitude towards trade. I explained the two strategic embargo lists limiting trade with Communist countries, one for the Soviet bloc and one for China, and that this was not altogether a matter for Britain alone. I pointed out that the Government had taken an independent line on trade with Cuba and that the Labour Party, I thought, was in favour of expanded trade with China.

I sounded him out on how China would react to the establishment of a Sino-British parliamentary group to improve contacts and Mr Ping said that such a group would be welcome and he would like to discuss it further. He asked about the unity of the Labour Party and

I described the set-up of the Party embracing Christians, Fabians, trade unionists, co-operators and Marxists and described the effect of Mr Wilson's election as Leader on the unity of the Party.

Mr Ping asked what effect a Labour Government would have on British foreign policy. I replied that I could only answer personally but I hoped there would be a big change especially in relation to the United Nations, through which I thought a Labour Government would conduct its foreign policy more fully. I said that when a ship changed course, only fractionally, its position sometime later was far further from where it would have been had it not changed course than might appear from the small change of course it had made.

He said he hoped the Labour Party would win the Election and that it would pursue an independent foreign policy. De Gaulle had done this and had made France great as a result. Britain should do the same. I said I didn't agree with de Gaulle's policy but I saw what he meant. Mr Ping asked why de Gaulle had objected to Britain's entry into the Common Market. I explained the economic and military motives and de Gaulle's concept of a world dominated by Europe, dominated by the Common Market, dominated by a Franco-German alliance, dominated by France, dominated by de Gaulle.

The conversation lasted for over an hour and a half and Mr Ping was most civil and friendly. It was a great deal easier than talking to Soviet diplomats during the Stalin period. I invited him to tea at the House of Commons, when I shall have a chance of continuing the discussion.

Later Peter Blaker[23] told me that he was resigning from the Foreign Office, had joined the Tory Party and hoped to get a constituency next month. Well, well.

Monday 30 March–Easter Monday
Up at 5 and to Brighton for the Young Socialists' Conference. This has been a shambles with a strong Trotskyite element which has defeated resolutions supporting 'Signposts for the Sixties' and the UN. Today there was a flaming row over foreign policy and I was down to speak on incomes policy. This came at the very end of the conference after a short and indifferent debate. I was not interrupted but my plea for a withdrawal of the resolution against the UN was rejected on a show of hands.

Sunday 5 April
To the Albert Hall for the Greater London Labour Party rally. It was a tremendous gathering which reminded me of 1945. Clem Attlee was there and Tony Greenwood took the chair. George Brown and

Harold Wilson both spoke. With the first Greater London elections coming up this week it had a double significance. It was also the first time I had heard Harold make one of his 'New Britain' speeches.

Tuesday 7 April
Back home from Bristol and hurried to Lime Grove to record the Party political broadcast. It consisted of questions filmed up and down the country and put to our leaders. It went over very well.

To the Commons this afternoon and saw William Collier just before he renounced the barony of Monkswell. He is a country doctor and a good socialist and is doing it for reasons of principle.

This evening to dinner in honour of James Chuter Ede* who is retiring at the end of this Parliament. Bob Mellish took the chair and Harold Wilson and Clem Attlee made the main speeches, while Manny Shinwell made an appallingly egocentric one.

Thursday 9 Saturday 11 April
Up early to vote in the Greater London Election and the children all went off to Stansgate for the weekend. I went into the Commons for the publicity committee and then Caroline and I went out to dinner. We are trying to have a few days' holiday.

A late start on Friday. Valerie came as usual and Caroline and I had lunch at the Wimpy Bar. Labour has won the Greater London Elections by a majority of 64 to 36. It is wonderful. Caroline and I went to Bristol and I spoke at two eve-of-poll county council election meetings in Hanham.

Up early on Saturday and to Unity House and then to do some loudspeaker work in Kingswood. We came back on the midday train and had a delightfully lazy afternoon. Then went to the movies.

Tuesday 14 April
To the Tunisian embassy for a party to meet Mongi Slim, the Tunisian Foreign Minister, and delegates to the international conference on sanctions against South Africa which opened in London today. The organisers had done a brilliant job in getting Slim and Mboya and Swai, the Minister of Development in Tanganyika, to come and take part personally in an unofficial conference. Harold Wilson's message was equivocal and said that 'Britain cannot act alone', but there is no suggestion she should. I hope Harold is better in office on this sort of issue than he is in Opposition.

Barbara Castle confided in me last night that she had grave reservations about Harold, and I have myself. He just doesn't like a

* Labour MP for South Shields, 1935–64, Home Secretary, 1945–51.

showdown and yet until a political leader is prepared to fight a stand-up battle with his colleagues for the things in which he believes he can't be tempered by the fires of controversy and win the dominance and respect he must have to lead.

Wednesday 15 April
Vassev from the Soviet Embassy came to have drinks here and then I took him out to lunch. He is very worried about the Chinese and says they cannot afford nuclear weapons. 'They have copied all that is bad from our own experience and nothing that is good.' Stalinism certainly bit very deeply into the soul of that generation of Communists and it has even opened up the possibility of re-examining the Cold War in a detached spirit. I tried out a reassessment of the Korean War and he said that he thought that the photo of Dulles looking northward through binoculars might have triggered off a North Korean attack – a perfectly rational explanation.

He found it difficult to believe that we could ever have expected a Soviet attack in Europe in the 1940s. I told him that I had never been sure whether it was likely or not but that I had never believed the stories that circulated about Stalin at that time in America, though it appeared now that these were not exaggerations. The truth is the Communist–anti-Communist gulf in the world socialist movement has shrunk to practically nothing and we discussed the way in which it could be bridged. The economic case for socialist planning in the West, together with the slow development of inner Party democracy in Russia are paving the way for socialist co-operation.

To the Commons for the Fabian autumn lectures sub–committee where we agreed to run a series on institutional reform covering Government, Civil Service, Parliament, Regional and Local Government and the Law.

Saturday 18 April
Addressed the Annual Conference of the Pioneer Women – the Mapai* affiliate in the UK. I was asked to speak on Israel and the Middle East and concentrated almost entirely on Israeli attitudes to the Arabs and the urgent need for a fresh approach. It went down all right with the audience, but there were a few Jewish men who were passionate Ben-Gurion fans and they were frighteningly rigid.

Thursday 23 April
Bristol this afternoon for a meeting in the Bristol Commercial Vehicles canteen about their future. The Transport Act prohibits

* Moderate Israeli social-democratic party affiliated to the Socialist International.

normal trading to nationalised industries, and the company cannot sell the workers the shares they wanted to get round the restrictions. I was able to give them the Wilson pledge that all restrictions would be lifted.

Saturday 25 April
Edith Sorel, who is the Paris correspondent of the Cuban paper *Revolution*, came and spent two hours at home. We have many mutual friends. She has a great contempt for Servan Schreiber who, she says, is just engaged in a long-term attempt on the presidency of France. She interviewed me for her paper. Her views on Cuba were extremely interesting and she knows Castro well.

Monday 27 April
After a Sunday spent in the sun in the garden pottering – the first really warm day this year – back to work.

Tommy Balogh rang to say that he had just come back from Peru and the US, where he visited the White House. He says the White House is passionately committed to a Labour victory in Britain – more so than when 'that Eastern aristocrat, Kennedy, was in charge'. Johnson is an old-style, folksy, warm-hearted New Dealer with much more in common with Wilson than Kennedy had or than he (Johnson) has with Home. All that is very encouraging. The only trouble is that Johnson, being a Texan, is very poor on Latin America, where things are going to get a lot worse before they get better.

This evening to speak in Kensington Town Hall. I told the Chairman to skip the peerage business in introducing me, so he confined himself to saying that I was the man who had made Douglas-Home Prime Minister and then said that despite a 'dubious upbringing' I had joined the Party and 'mixed well'. It made me hopping mad as I made rather clear. But I think many people must have got the idea from the peerage battle that I came from a long line of Tory aristocrats.

Tuesday 28 April
Lunch with Ian Waller of the *Sunday Telegraph* at the Reform Club. We discussed the general prospect and especially the flare-up of the class issue in British politics which is affecting both the Tory Party and the Labour Party.

To the Commons and then to a party given by Kenneth Rose, where we met Gulbenkian, the oil multi-millionaire, who was very amusing.

Thursday 30 April
The usual nightmare with the *Guardian* article. Caroline and I to lunch at the Café Royale where Signor Moro, the Italian Prime Minister, was the guest of the Foreign Press Association. I met him briefly and we listened to his long and boring speech in which he gave a view of world affairs comparable with that given by Churchill in May 1953 after the death of Stalin. It was really the worst type of European Christian Democratic stuff and made one wonder how the socialists could have agreed to an 'opening to the Left'.

This evening to supper with Dick Clements and his wife. The Shores were also there and we had a great political evening.

David Butler phoned to tell me Peter Blaker has been adopted as Tory candidate for Blackpool.

Friday 1 May
Lunch with Tommy Balogh and Peter Shore today. Tommy is over-joyed at Labour's 13 per cent lead in the polls but Peter is very depressed that Harold has done nothing to get him a constituency. We discussed the line that should be taken in the next few months.

This evening 'Any Questions?' in Aldershot with Lord Mancroft, Bob Boothby[24] (who came out strongly against the independent deterrent and for the nationalisation of the arms industry) and Lady Violet Bonham Carter, with whom I travelled home. Lady Vi goes to visit Churchill every week and says the old man's mind has almost completely gone. He cannot even remember the early days and is like a child.

Sunday 3 May
To Bristol this afternoon for May Day and back in the train with Jim Callaghan. Jim commented on Harold's technique of leading the Party by means of a succession of bilateral interviews – resisting committee discussions and not keeping people informed about where they stand. Jim thought this might make for admiration while it succeeded but would fail to build personal loyalty on which to rely in bad days. He thinks he himself will last about two years as Chancellor and is worried about the enormous bill he will have to meet. He told me he thought Frank Cousins would come in as Minister of Transport and asked me what office I would like. I said, 'The UN or the Post Office.'

Monday 4 May
To Lime Grove to record the Party political TV broadcast on waste with Denis Healey, William Ross and Jim Callaghan. There was some panic because of a rumour that two British soldiers had been

beheaded and their heads displayed in Taiz in the Yemeni-Aden fighting. Denis was saying we ought to stay in Aden but it seems to me the sooner we extricate ourselves from colonial commitments the better.

Tuesday 5 May
David Butler called this morning. I have never known him surer of a Labour victory. He says that Home really did believe that he would win the Election for the Tories until Tory Central Office told him defeat was certain in a June Election and he would have to go on. The thought of defeat has completely unnerved him.

To the Commons this afternoon and a meeting of the Council for Freedom in Portugal and her Colonies. We agreed to set up two sub-committees, one to deal with Angola and the other to deal with the Portuguese Democrats in exile. I think this will be a much more informal arrangement and will leave the Council as a shadow organisation doing what is necessary.

Harold Wilson and I were invited to dinner tonight with the staff of the *Guardian*. They sent a car for us and we drove to the Connaught Hotel where we met Alastair Hetherington, John Cole, Mark Arnold-Forster, Peter Jenkins, Harford Thomas, Brian Redhead, Geoffrey Taylor and Francis Boyd.

After dinner Harold answered questions on a whole host of subjects and it gave me a unique opportunity to catch up with his thinking on various points.

1. He is worried that the Home Government may be trying to make the Yemen crisis into a little Suez to win public support.

2. He believes that a Labour Government would be able to establish a much more informal relationship with the American President than Home has been able to do and imagines that he can telephone and fly over as and when necessary, without the usual fuss of top level meetings. He also hopes to have an Ambassador there who is in and out of the Administration's meetings all the time. He thinks a Labour Government will get on better with Washington than the German Government, and the French are out of it anyway.

3. As soon as the Election is over, he and his top colleagues will fly to Washington to renegotiate the whole basis of Anglo-American relations in the field of defence and foreign affairs. They will be pleased that we are giving up Polaris and will probably approve the idea Harold has that British naval power and command structure should be available for UN and Commonwealth purposes and for

'brush fires'. We must therefore keep our bases in Singapore and Aden for these purposes. Otherwise we may have to find or develop some islands for bases. Meanwhile the Germans can provide the main strength of the land forces in Central Europe. He doubted whether the French would ever really develop their own independent nuclear deterrent.

4. On domestic affairs a Labour Government would have a dramatic programme for the first 100 days and this would include a number of changes in the machinery of Government. These certainly would be a great extension of Number 10 Downing Street and there would also be a division between the Treasury and the new Ministry of Production. Regional centres would be established for the traditional twelve regions and all this can be done quite quickly.

5. Incomes policy involves close negotiation with the trade union leaders in the first instance, and the hammering out of the programme which they will accept in the new atmosphere of a new Government. Public support for this wages policy can be expected to last for at least eighteen months. After that, all that will be required will be a 'floating light' which the Government will insist on. People will have to get used to the fact that they may be taking their rise in living standards in the form of social dividends rather than in the form of personal income.

6. On the public schools Harold said he had no guilt complex like his predecessor.* The educational trust would be set up to examine this and he agreed that there were no votes from a Labour point of view in being very tough with the public schools. What interested me was that the *Guardian* staff were all passionately keen on getting the public schools dealt with drastically and at once. Harold said that the supply of money by family business and tax subsidies could and would be cut off and that the special advantage the public schools have in getting their boys university places would also be stopped. In this way they would become irrelevant to the general state structure. This did not satisfy the questioners but it was clear that Harold had other things to do and to think about in the first five years. He made great play of the fact that he had not yet read the Fabian report on this subject which has been submitted to him.

I said practically nothing in the course of the evening, since I didn't think that either the *Guardian* staff or Harold wanted to hear my

* Wilson went to Wirral Grammar School, Gaitskell to Winchester Public School.

views. But I did get this opportunity of hearing his thinking on all these and many other subjects and seeing something of the mood in which he approached his job. He was weakest was on the future of Parliament itself. He simply had no ideas as to how Parliament could be usefully modernised or developed when we were in Government.

We left the hotel well after midnight and drove back to the House of Commons.

Wednesday 6 May
Worked at home today and this evening to the House of Commons for an adjournment debate on Bristol Commercial Vehicles. This debate ended about six months' hard work on this case and it is clear that one of the first things a Labour Minister of Transport will do is to lift the restrictions now operating on this and other firms.

Friday 8 May
Lunch with Demajo of the Yugoslav Embassy at the Savoy Hotel. We went round a series of problems from British Guiana to Malta and Aden, Southern Rhodesia, South Africa and the future of the United Nations. There really is no barrier at all between a Yugoslav Communist and a British socialist nowadays.

This evening to Stroud in Gloucestershire to speak for the candidate, Dennis Hunt. It is a primitive and feudal part of Britain and I always find it depressing.

Saturday 9 May
Surgery in Bristol this morning and among those who came were a group of schoolmasters to discuss teacher supply problems. One of them was the secretary of the Teachers' Consultative Committee who has been intimately involved in the new educational development plan which is being worked out. He told me that he had been converted from opposition to comprehensive schools and that he knew of no teachers in comprehensive schools who were not enthusiastic for them.

Home for Joshua's birthday party.

Sunday 10 May
Worked in the office part of the day and this evening to dinner with Shirley and Bernard Williams. Among those there were Richard and Caroline Miles. He and I had a long and interesting talk about Britain's role at the United Nations, where he was seconded for a time. He said that Britain was thought of as being entirely negative in its approach to practical UN problems and also that the quality of our people on the expert committees was not as high as those for

other countries. He agreed that what was wanted was a really tough political directive and then things might work out better. We also discussed the desirability of having a small ministerial cabinet available to ministers in their departments. He was very much against it but I didn't think his case was all that strong.

Monday 11 May
To lunch today with Denis Healey in Highgate. It was for Mr Walter Lippman, the distinguished American commentator, and his wife, and George Thomson,[25] Chris Mayhew and Roy Jenkins were also there. We had a long discussion which ranged round the situation in Vietnam. Afterwards I went up to see Karl Marx's grave in Highgate cemetery with the Lippmans and Roy Jenkins.

Tuesday 12 May
To the Commons, where Tony Howard of the *New Statesman* interviewed me for the 'Profile' series, which they are doing on Labour leaders. Tony is the only lobby journalist who does his homework thoroughly and retains a duty to his profession that overrides political loyalty to the Labour Party or the requirements of friendship with the MPs. He put a dozen very difficult points based on a real research job on my political past. He's frightening because he is so good at his job.

This evening Caroline and I went to dinner with Mr Shen Ping, the Chinese chargé d'affaires, and Mrs Shen Ping. They had with them an interpreter and the five of us sat down to a long meal of course after course of rather unattractive food.

They were extremely friendly and we asked all about their family and background and children and where they met. They were both guerrilla fighters in the Communist army and he went to university to study agricultural problems. They have three children, two girls and a boy, who are in China. My guess is that they never get out and see anybody in London and probably few people ever visit them. Caroline found her interested in everything about Britain. They talked in French.

Mr Shen wanted to know what the Labour attitude was towards Taiwan. Did the Labour Party believe in the 'two Chinas' policy? I said we did not. We wanted China to occupy her rightful place in the UN, Chiang Kai Shek to be removed from the UN and American forces to be withdrawn from Taiwan.

I asked Mr Shen what he thought about the future of Kashmir and he said there should be a plebiscite which would decide whether Kashmir should join India or Pakistan, or be divided, or become independent. I said that there were people who thought that the future of Taiwan should also be decided by a plebiscite. He replied that it was an internal affair of China's. I said that India thought Kashmir was an internal Indian affair and I had only drawn the parallel in order to show that those who rejected the 'two Chinas' policy might still feel that the future of Taiwan permitted alternative solutions.

I reminded Mr Shen that when we last talked he had described Yugoslavia as an agent of imperialism. He corrected me and said that Yugoslavia was now a capitalist country again and it would require another revolution to bring socialism. I asked him whether revisionism in the Soviet Union was comparable to Yugoslav revisionism, and he said that it was of the same order but not as far advanced. I asked if it was going to be necessary for a violent revolution in Russia to liquidate the Khrushchev group. He said that this was for the Soviet Communist Party to decide. It was a great Party and they would best know how to deal with Khrushchev's clique. I asked what was the theoretical explanation of how revisionism and the road to capitalism could open up again in a country where there was no property-owning class interest to restore it. He said this would take a long time to explain but it was due to the combination of bourgeois influences at home and capitulationism abroad. Khrushchev was in contemporary terms a Menshevik. In Yugoslavia capitalism had returned and the workers' councils were a cover for private ownership but Russia had not travelled as far along this road. I asked whether private ownership necessarily involved a betrayal of the revolution, since Lenin's new economic policy had permitted some capitalism to remain. He said that was necessary at the time.

I asked whether Khrushchev was right in his description of the breaches of socialist legality committed by Stalin during the 1930s. He said that Stalin was a great socialist leader and that Khrushchev had presented a very negative picture of what Stalin had done. Stalin had made certain mistakes but the overall achievement of his administration had been to build the great Soviet Communist Party. In any case, Khrushchev had been deeply implicated in the whole Stalin policy and was trying to off-load the blame that he properly should share. I asked if it was true that Stalin had ordered the murder of Trotsky. He said he did not know.

I wondered if he thought it possible that socialism could come to Britain without a violent revolution. He said he did not think the British Labour Party was socialist but merely reformist and that in any case Britain was not yet ripe for a revolution. I asked him whether the Labour or Conservative Parties were more likely to make Britain ripe for revolution. He laughed and said that he did not know. But a revolution would be necessary. So I then said that if countries that had had a revolution, like Yugoslavia and Russia, could return to capitalism via revisionism, was it not possible that a longer slower progress might prove better in the end. I compared it to the race between the tortoise and the hare, where the revolutionary hare leapt ahead and then fell into a deep revisionist sleep while the reformist tortoise won the race. He laughed and said it would take too long to explain and Britain's internal affairs were for the Government. He wanted us to pursue an independent foreign policy free from American influence. I said I thought that British capitalism was a paper tiger that would not be so difficult to defeat.

We discussed further the possibility of establishing a Sino-British group. We agreed that the next stage would be to arrange a dinner at the House of Commons where he could meet some interested MPs to discuss it. We parted on cordial terms and I hope to arrange such a meeting after Whitsun.

Wednesday 13 May
Just after 8 o'clock this morning Professor Samuel Becker came to see me to discuss educational radio and television and the use of the mass media for political purposes. He is an American, over here on a Fulbright Scholarship and his ideas on the integration of educational TV with education, rather than with broadcasting, seemed to me to make very good sense.

This afternoon I went to Devizes to speak at the by-election eve-of-poll there.* There were two meetings, both pretty well attended. Beforehand I had been sent round to canvass some doubtfuls and I must say the reception I got was very favourable. We had a first-rate meeting. George Brown made a moving speech in which he said that politics was not about power but about people and their relationship one with another and with the community. It was George on an ethical level, which I must say I prefer.

Thursday 14 May
Back to London this morning and the newspapers are full of a statement made by Harold Wilson to the press lobby in which he repudiated the plan for part-time schooling as one way of meeting the current teacher shortage. The plan was one of ten points included in a report on teacher supply, which had been approved by the Home Policy Committee and by the Executive. Dick Crossman had been asked to make these points at a Party press conference in the presence of George Brown and under the chairmanship of Tony Greenwood.

* Irving Rogers, my agent Herbert Rogers' son, was the Labour candidate in the Devizes by-election caused by the death of the Conservative MP, Percival Potts.

Thus the whole Party leadership was deeply committed to it as Harold Wilson was a member of both the Home Policy Committee and the Executive.

I rang Dick Crossman to find out what had happened. It seems that some teachers in the PLP had objected and protested to the Shadow Cabinet and that was how the repudiation came about. Dick felt badly let down by Harold and said he had spent about an hour with him to discuss it. Harold blamed George Brown and the Chief Whip. He said he was very tired and the trouble would soon blow over and he asked Dick to forgive him. But Dick said, 'You can't run a Government like this, you know.' Harold said it would be different then. But Dick didn't quite believe him and neither do I. Dick evidently went on to say that he was happy with his farm, and politics was only worthwhile if you could rely on loyalty from your superiors and colleagues. Then he told Harold that he had been asked to go on 'Gallery' on TV tonight and this evidently worried him a great deal, but he did appear and did extremely well.

David Butler and Marilyn came to lunch today and he said he thinks we shall win Devizes quite comfortably.

Friday 15 May
We have lost Devizes by over 1,000 votes, which is a real set-back for our hopes. On the other hand, the Gallup poll this morning showed us still to be seventeen points in the lead. It does make you wonder how reliable the polls are. One amusing sideline on it which also throws doubt on their reliability was a suggestion that 2 per cent of those questioned wanted me as Prime Minister!

Wrote my *Sunday Citizen* article and then away with the family to Stansgate for the weekend. It was the first time that we had spent a night there for nearly four years.

Saturday and Sunday, 16–17 May
We spent three days at Stansgate. The sun was hot and bright all the time. I didn't do a hand's turn of work, just sat on the grass or on the beach, with the children playing about. They love the place.

Friday 22 May
This evening to Faversham to speak at the by-election for the candidate, Terry Boston. This constituency has a gross income of £25,000 a year and has about 5,000 members. There are eight Labour halls. It is the best organised constituency in Britain, but with a majority of only 253 it needs to be.

Monday 25 May
This evening Caroline and I went to Holland Park School to talk to the headmaster. For a long time we have been very discontented with the prospect of Westminster for educational, social and political reasons. Holland Park is new and vigorous and active and we were much impressed by it when we went round.

Tuesday 26 May
Caroline went to a party to launch *Antiphon* which the editor, Melville Hardiment, has organised, to link together various school magazines. I went to a debate with the Bow Group at the Royal Commonwealth Society to discuss foreign policy and defence. The Tories were mainly concentrating on the details of defence and we, David Marquand[26] and myself, were dealing more with the change in the international situation in recent years. There was very little meeting ground between us.

Wednesday 27 May
National Executive this morning. There was a long discussion about whether or not we should hold the Annual Conference and later a short and potentially acrimonious discussion about Harold Wilson's repudiation of Dick Crossman over the plan for part-time education up to the age of six to help meet the teacher shortage. Harold handled it very tactfully but I didn't feel that he had done very well. Dick was glad that it had been limited to this and had not developed into a major row.

Lunch at Dick and Anne Crossman's house with Peter Shore. We discussed the University of the Air. There is a lot more thinking to be done about this.

Pandit Nehru died today. It is a terrible loss.

Wednesday 3 June
Lunch with Miroslav Jiraska, the Czechoslovak diplomat, at Scott's restaurant. Now that Czechoslovakia is de-Stalinised, relations are much easier. The fact is the Eastern Europeans are pathetically anxious to improve relations with Britain and fear that we are not interested in them. There should be a good-will delegation to Eastern Europe.

This evening I went to Eton to speak for Fenner Brockway in a hall just opposite the college. He made a long speech about Labour's educational policy, including its plans for the public schools. Only four or five Eton boys were there and I think they were all Labour.

Saturday 6 June
Peter Jones from Washington came for a talk this morning. He is
Deputy Secretary of Commerce in Johnson's administration – aged
thirty-two and a very bright guy indeed. He described how much
more popular President Johnson was than Kennedy and how you
had to be a real politicker to get things done. He thought Goldwater
had no chance of election but was nervous lest the campaign was
fought out too far to the Right and in case the civil rights issue
produced a white reaction.[27] We also talked about Cuba and he
defended the American line of weakening Castro by the blockade. 'It
would be different if Castro were like Nasser,' he said. But of course
he really is, and this is what the Americans don't understand.

This afternoon to the first meeting of the Young Socialists' new
National Committee. Outside was a lobby of young members who
had come to protest about the suspension of the Streatham Young
Socialists by their local Party for issuing a leaflet which said, 'Up
the mods, up the rockers, against police violence. Join the Labour
Party'. The leaflet was probably ill-advised but the Streatham Party
had issued press statements savaging the YS and I suggested an
enquiry.

But the new National Committee is heavily weighted with the
'Keep Left' brigade and they passed a resolution condemning the
Streatham Party and then moved that this resolution should be
reported immediately to the press lobby. To go out of a confidential
committee with a news item to a group of indeterminate status was
clearly impossible. Mikardo pointed this out and was accused of
blackmailing the committee. He asked the chairman to insist on a
withdrawal of this word and when he wouldn't Mik walked out.

The resolution to report to the lobby outside was carried by the
chairman's casting vote and Reg Underhill suspended the meeting.
The 'Keep Left' people are obviously hoping that the NEC will shut
down the YS so that they can take it over. We would be foolish to
fall for this one.

Monday 8 June
To the Home Policy Committee to present my paper on honours and
awards. I introduced it and Jim Callaghan said he was against
tinkering with the House of Lords, thus proving that he had not read
the paper. Peggy Herbison said she thought titles were quite irrelevant and Jennie Lee preferred hereditary titles and was dead against
a nominated second chamber. This is the policy of total conservatism,
doing nothing until you can do everything and never being able to
do anything. Dick said it was important to eliminate political honours
and we should make this clear. Jim said it was not a case for the first

100 days. I pointed out that since Harold would have to make a dozen life peers at once, any benefit from ending political honours would disappear. Also, were we to make the law officers knights? Were we to make the Lord Mayor of London a baronet annually? George Brown said that we had spent too long on an unimportant subject and brought the discussion to a close. My paper was noted and effectively killed. The only hope is whether I can interest Harold in some of its proposals but he is so terribly conservative that I am not optimistic.

Afterwards to the Fabian International Bureau meeting and then on to do a recorded question and answer discussion with Enoch Powell at London House for the BBC Overseas Service programme 'People and Politics'.

Tuesday 9 June
To the Overseas Sub-Committee where we heard a report on Harold Wilson's trip to Moscow. He had to leave but David Ennals answered some questions. Khrushchev is evidently in favour of arms control in the Middle East imposed by the great powers and a 'rational solution' of the Palestine question without force. This is very encouraging. Khrushchev also said that the MLF would wreck any progress in signing an anti-proliferation agreement on nuclear weapons.* But he made no mention of the Polaris agreement.

From there to the Commonwealth and Colonies Group to hear Abdullah Alasnag, the Secretary General of the Aden TUC, talking about Aden. He opposed the present constitutional conference on the grounds that the delegation was not representative. The traditional rulers had been forced on the tribes by the British and the Federal Council was only nominated. He pointed to the support for his cause from the UN and said, 'We are agents of nobody – just Arab nationalists wanting fully constitutional progressive rule – but if Nasser and Sallal support us we will accept their support. We believe we have a majority. The People's Socialist Party policy towards the elections has not yet been decided. We want independence first for the entire territory and then will negotiate about any possible arrangements about the naval base.'

He said the British could and should democratise the protectorates to break the grip of the tribal rulers and that international supervision of the elections would be necessary to secure public liberties and democratic rights. Britain should recognise the new regime which depended on Egyptian support. I found Alasnag an extremely

* The Multi-Lateral Force was a project for a NATO mixed-manned nuclear submarine force.

impressive and able man and considering that he is on the eve of taking power at the age of twenty-nine, would rate him with the best of the nationalist leaders.

From there to the Transport Committee joint meeting with the Science Group to hear Mr Duckworth, the managing director of NRDC, Mr Hennessy, his deputy, and Mr Kennington, the chief engineer of Hovercraft Development Ltd, describing their plan for the tracked Hovercraft as a means of three-hundred-mile-per-hour inter-city transport, which offers higher speed, lower passenger costs, lower track costs, and lower fares than any other form of transport. It was an impressive presentation. It may be that this is the right way of tackling the London Airport link instead of monorail.

Wednesday 10 June
To the House of Commons this afternoon and took part in the debate on the Finance Bill on the fuel tax for public service vehicles. It gave me an opportunity to make quite a serious speech about the need for developing public transport and the way in which we had to achieve a steady shift from private to rented vehicles.

Thursday 11 June
This afternoon Caroline went to the Conway Hall, Red Lion Square, to hear the American lawyer Mark Lane deliver his lecture on Kennedy's assassination. I heard the last hour of it and thought that Lane spoiled a very interesting case that could have been built with ice-cold judicial skill on half a dozen major inconsistencies in the evidence, by making it a political knockabout turn in which he made the usual leftist comments about the FBI and the John Birch Society and so on. That is not to say that he hasn't got a case, but he certainly puts it over badly and I think is beginning to suffer the consequences of the persecution complex which he is acquiring.

Afterwards Caroline and I went to the House of Commons for the vote and then we marched to South Africa House with about fifty MPs to present a petition on the Rivonia trial, in which Nelson Mandela has been sentenced to life imprisonment with others. After that we went on to St Paul's Cathedral to join in for a while in the vigil which was being held there. It was all very moving.

Friday 12 June
This evening I went to the Young Fabian School at Guildford to talk about 'The Government and the Individual'. It was quite an interesting group of people, aged below thirty, of different occupations but I found them fairly conservative, or else I am out on a limb as a radical. But the Young Fabians have done well and do reflect the

increased interest in the Labour Party of the new professional and executive classes. A storm and my windscreen wipers didn't work so I limped home, getting back at 3.30 am.

Sunday 14 June
This afternoon Caroline and I went to Hyde Park Corner to join the head of the procession to march to Trafalgar Square about the Rivonia trial. Most of the banners there seemed to be for the Committee of 100 and the London Anarchists and the Trots and others. That's the trouble about these demonstrations; they are always taken over by those who are keenest. Anyway we marched to Trafalgar Square and I took the chair. Among those who spoke were Bertrand Russell, the Bishop of Woolwich, Elwyn Jones, Fenner Brockway, David Ennals, Angus Wilson the author, Andrew Faulds,* and someone called First, who had been the editor of a magazine in South Africa. There were two or three thousand people there and we collected £300 from them. Afterwards a few of us marched to Number 10 and handed in a letter to the Prime Minister.

Monday 15 June
I went to the House of Commons and then Caroline and I met at the Mahatma Gandhi Hall where I was asked to pay a tribute to Jawaharlal Nehru. Also invited to speak were the Duke of Devonshire, a tall, elegant, weak-kneed aristocratic member of the Government, Jennie Lee, who was firm and vigorous, and one or two others. We came home after a meal and Caroline worked late on her article on Mark Lane which is appearing in *Tribune*.

Tuesday 16 June
Up at 6 and working in the basement till breakfast. Then to the House of Commons, where the foreign affairs debate began with an extremely wet speech by Rab Butler. His theme was that the Russians had de-Stalinised and that the West had decolonised and if we remained tough and flexible and kept the bomb everything would be all right. I had to go out for part of the time to attend the study group on Commonwealth immigration, set up by the National Executive.

There was an interminably long discussion here about the draft Bill, which had been presented by the League of Labour Lawyers, incorporating a proposal that would make it illegal to issue a statement that would induce hatred or contempt for a racial or religious group. The Bill was far too wide and would have involved an intolerable infringement of liberties. Frank Soskice in reply was most ineffec-

* The actor and Labour MP for Smethwick, 1966–74, and Warley East since 1974.

tive and muddled and in fact his draft Bill widened it still further. We more or less agreed to let it drop and concentrate on ending discrimination in public places, which is what Fenner Brockway always wanted.

Wednesday 17 June
Up at 5.15 this morning. It was our fifteenth wedding anniversary. I drove to Covent Garden and got fifty carnations to give Caroline with her breakfast in bed.

At 8 o'clock Douglas Verney, the Head of the Department of Political Sciences at York University, Toronto, came to see me to discuss a book he is writing on the British constitution. He emigrated to Canada three years ago and finds the freedom of academic endeavour there exciting after the limitations of a British provincial university. I found him an agreeable man and had an idea he might be interested in coming back to Britain one day.

To the House of Commons and had lunch with Dick Crossman and Charles White, from Reading. He is the European Manager of General Electric and wrote to me, following a *Guardian* article I had written, saying he was prepared to give up his job at £4,000 a year if he could perform some useful political service. I introduced him to Dick Crossman and they had a very productive lunch. I think there is no doubt that he has a place either in Parliament or working as one of our temporary civil servants in the new Ministry of Technology that will be set up after the Election. This sort of man is worth a hundred votes and indicates that there is a shift at the top among seriously minded people.

I went into the foreign affairs debate to hear the Prime Minister open the second day. To my astonishment I was called immediately after him – the prime time of the debate – which really caught me quite unprepared. I spoke for about half an hour and it pleased our people. But I wish I had prepared it more carefully!

Thursday 18 June
At 8 o'clock Professor Stanley Donner came to see me about the 'University of the Air'. He is from Stanford University and he is one of the five Fulbright Professors who are spending a year over here studying educational television. He is keen on us launching straight out on a scheme for appointing a vice-chancellor and a technical director and starting broadcasting in spare time not wanted by the BBC and ITA. I found him very interesting and there is a certain simplicity about his scheme for a general degree in higher education which has great merits about it.

The Broadcasting Advisory Committee this afternoon. We

discussed the technique for running the Party political broadcasts yet
again but some useful ideas came out of it. We have drawn in Ted
Willis and our old faithfuls.

In the House of Commons this afternoon there was a Private
Member's motion put down by the Tories against nationalisation.
Dick Marsh, speaking from our side, demolished the enemy and it
was a notable parliamentary triumph.

Friday 19 June

Lunch with Dick Crossman again, this time at his house, with
Tommy Balogh and Peter Shore. It is the first of a regular series of
weekly lunches the four of us are going to have together to discuss
Election tactics. We discussed the general conduct of the Tory
campaign and the urgent necessity for Harold not to muck in with
personal abuse against Home. We talked about what Labour should
be trying to get the BBC to do by way of coverage, and the economic
crisis which will develop by the autumn and how we should handle
it. Peter suggested that Harold should write to the Prime Minister
now about this. I followed up by suggesting that Harold should ask
for private talks to concert our activities and to prevent the Election
from having any adverse effect on the pound. We are meeting again
on Monday to discuss it further.

Saturday 20 June

George Harris* turned up. He has been in Dallas a great deal,
covering the story of President Kennedy's assassination and is absolutely certain that it is a straightforward case involving Lee Harvey
Oswald. As Caroline has agreed to serve on the committee set up by
Bertrand Russell[28] and has taken an interest in Mark Lane, there
was an interesting discussion. The one question to which I think
there may well be some substance is whether Oswald was actually
taken on by the FBI as a potential double agent and received money
from them. If this could be proved it would be dynamite politically.
Maybe this is what the Warren Commission are anxious to keep
under. I never believed the conspiracy theory of Kennedy's death
but there are some unanswered questions. George hadn't been in
England for sixteen years and we tried to put him in the picture on
the new Britain which is emerging and what a Labour Government
will mean. I think even he felt excited by it.

Monday 22 June

To the Campaign Committee this morning, where we settled the
question of broadcasts between now and the beginning of the Election

* Editor of various American journals, he introduced Caroline to me in 1948.

campaign. We [Wilson's informal committee] got another £2,500 out of them. I asked whether we could be included in the master plan for the Election campaign and got a lot of blank looks. Of course they're doing no planning at all.

Lunch with Dick Crossman and Peter Shore and Tommy Balogh today. We discussed three papers which I had prepared, one on Tory funds and how to carry the campaign a stage further forward, another on the possible use of the American election campaign to help us with our own fight here, and a third on the things we would like to see the BBC do that would help us.

We also discussed the draft letter that Peter Shore had written from Harold Wilson to the Prime Minister, asking for secret talks on the state of the economy as a way of forestalling the danger that they might blame a crisis in the autumn on the possibility of a Labour Government. This is a brilliant strategic stroke.

Tuesday 23 June
Lunch today with Mr Kostarkis from the Polish embassy. I took him to the local Lyons Corner House as part of my campaign to break away from the formality of diplomatic entertaining. He's a very agreeable man.

Caroline went out this morning to record a CBS interview on the Kennedy assassination. Then she went to have lunch with Ralph Shoenman[29] and Mark Lane. They are very discouraged because they are finding it hard getting the committee established and they wanted Caroline to take it on. She simply hasn't got the time and told them so but she would like to prevent it getting into the hands of those who want to use the committee to discredit the United States. There is much official and unofficial disapproval of the committee and this makes it especially difficult and also important to keep it at the strict judicial level.

She regards Mark Lane as being a good American liberal. He was a friend of Eleanor Roosevelt and served in the New York State legislature. Shoenman is more of a puzzle and she suspects that he is really just running a shell known as Bertrand Russell. The important thing is that she should not get mixed up in something which is really engaged in quite a different sort of operation. But she is right to keep at it because there must have been many people who stood back when Zola was doing the same over the Dreyfus case.

This evening at the House of Commons the younger Labour MPs met and Clem Attlee was our guest of honour. I realised that I was the only one there who had sat in the House of Commons when he was Leader of the Party. Dick Mabon[30] introduced all of us to him and it was necessary to say in each case who the newcomer had replaced. Clem was in fine form despite the death of Lady Attlee last week and he gave good answers to the questions. He was at his best on the need for some sort of world government but on some other questions was very old-fashioned. For example, he wanted the public schools established as great Commonwealth and international schools to which people would come from all over the world.

He also was anti-American in a superior way and suggested that they needed our advice as they were so inexperienced. Also when questioned he couldn't think of any mistake that his Government had made. But he was excellent value and very charming and kind and he has got a most formidable character which stands out.

Wednesday 24 June
Up at 5 and worked until breakfast. Arriving at Transport House this morning for the National Executive meeting, I heard a lot of chanting and shouting and saw a number of people with placards outside the building. It was a demonstration laid on because of the suspension of the Streatham Young Socialists. I don't know how many of them there actually were Young Socialists and how many of them had been whipped up by the Socialist Labour League and its leader Gerry Healy. The place was crawling with police and while we were sitting at the meeting we could hear people running round the roof just above us. Alice Bacon was nearly knocked over and Bessie Braddock was manhandled. The demonstration had clearly been laid on by those who wanted us to disband the Young Socialists but there really is no inclination to do this and I think what will happen is that a counter-attack against the SLL will be mounted from inside the movement. But we did expel two Young Socialists and there was no discussion of this at all. I would certainly have raised it but for the demonstration.

The only other thing of interest this morning was that we approved the Ombudsman[31] proposal which I think is very important indeed.

Saturday 27 June
A lovely hot day and the family was in the garden most of the time. I spent the afternoon working to get the basement kitchen organised. Caroline went to the hospital to see June and baby Frances. Every few minutes the phone seems to ring with another American who's in town and hopes to see us. We have almost got to the point of taking the telephone off the hook.

Sunday 28 June

Full of energy and spent the whole day from 9 am to 5 pm spring cleaning the kitchen and all the cupboards and scrubbing and repairing the drawers.

Caroline wrote a long letter to Shoenman about Mark Lane and the future work of the committee. It represents a clear statement of her attitude to the committee. It would be a great pity if it could be represented that she had joined in an organisation designed primarily to discredit the United States, rather than to find out the truth about Kennedy's assassination. The difficulty is that she will be working with people whose motives may not be exactly the same as her own. But I am sure it's worth doing.

Monday 29 June

I went to the New Bristol Group which about twenty-five people attended. We reviewed the work of the last year and planned our programme for the coming year. There is no shortage of projects and no shortage of enthusiasm to carry them through. It is well and truly launched.

Today Mark Lane gave a press conference and reported that the Warren Commission had asked him to return to America. Afterwards Shoenman told the press that as a result of pressure from the American embassy, Caroline had given up her job as secretary of the 'Who Killed Kennedy?' Committee. The press rang and she pointed out that she had never accepted the secretaryship of the committee and that the American embassy had never communicated with her on the subject at all. It is a warning of the difficulties of relying on people not altogether reliable.

Tuesday 30 June

Back to London by train and took a party of schoolgirls round the House of Commons.

On to lunch with Dick Crossman, Tommy Balogh and Peter Shore. We discussed fully Harold Wilson's complete failure to consult with us collectively and felt that he had much more time to see journalists than he had to discuss future strategy with colleagues. The disillusionment with Harold has set in quite firmly now. He is doing a great job but doing it alone and this is not calculated to stimulate loyalty. We agreed that we must make some arrangements to see him together – even if only on the pretext of discussing speeches. I reported on the state of play with Tory funds and we discussed the proposed private letter to the Prime Minister asking for confidential talks on the state of the economy.

To the House of Commons and the first meeting of the Urban

Study Group of which I am chairman. This was set up at George Brown's request and with Harold Wilson's knowledge, to consider the problem of urban commuters and work out some action points for a future Minister of Transport.

Ian Grimble came to the House and we had a couple of hours together. He has now made great progress with his campaign to revitalise the Highlands. His book on the evictions gave the background to the present situation and means that he has a deep knowledge of the origins of the problem. He is now studying Scandinavian laws to prevent absentee landlordism and excited me with the possibilities in Scotland along the same lines. The feudal system exists there and the landlords own huge tracts – the largest holding being half a million acres – and control the lives of those who live there. Apparently this is a very live issue now, partly because of his work. He is now going to study in greater detail how the landlord system could be altered.

This evening Tam Dalyell and I wandered round the House of Lords' end of the building to find out just what accommodation was available there if the Commons were to take it over. We walked along deserted corridors, looking in offices and making a note of the accommodation. We stumbled on the Civil Defence Room and found on the wall huge charts showing the rooms on each floor and roughly specifying their purpose. We were going to copy them all down but it would have been too big a job. What is needed is a photograph of them or to go along with a tape recorder and read off all the names on to a machine. At one stage we were stopped by a policeman who sent us away. Then we met a custodian – Mr Wilkinson, who used to be a dustman at Grosvenor Road when I was a child – and he took us and showed us many other rooms. I have arranged to go and see the whole palace one night with him. What is required is a blazing attack on the whole system.

Wednesday 1 July

To the House of Commons where I attended the Transport Group, which was addressed by Sir Philip Warter and Sir Reginald Wilson of the Transport Holding Company. I was not impressed with Warter at all. Wilson was a much more active and energetic looking person. But when the Tory Establishment gets its hands on nationalisation it certainly does make it look pretty unattractive.

Then to the Immigration Group to hear Michael Duane, the chairman of the Anglo-Cypriot committee, discussing his problems with immigrant children. He is the headmaster of the Risinghill Comprehensive School and was accompanied by one Greek and one Turkish Cypriot.

This evening it was very warm and I turned on the floodlight in the back garden and sat out till about 11 o'clock at night, reading my papers and delighting in the new office suite.

Thursday 2 July
Simha Flapan* came to lunch today and we ate in the garden – the first time the basement kitchen had been used for a business meal. Simha brought me up to date with news from Israel. He said there was a new tension in Egypt between the capitalist-military-expansionist bloc and the left-wing civilian group, who are anxious to democratise and develop and carry the internal revolution a stage further. Nasser supports the latter.

Eshkol [the Israeli Prime Minister] visited America and was a great success. Simha stressed the reduction in tension and the hopes for better relations with the Arabs and the need for a US–USSR detente. Eshkol is conservative domestically but progressive externally and Ben-Gurion, Dayan and Peres are trying to topple him.

Simha saw Bertrand Russell in Wales to talk about a plan Russell was sponsoring, under which the West Bank of the Jordan and the Gaza Strip would become a Palestinian state with a corridor access across the Negev. Flapan suggested as an alternative that Nasser should give Gaza to Jordan to make a bigger Jordan, which would be viable.

The colloquium organised by the Mayor of Florence failed because of the irresponsible publicity announcing that the Arabs were sending a delegation to meet Goldman† and the Jews. So Arab-Israeli relations had to be taken off the agenda. Flapan did have talks with some Arabs informally and found the atmosphere changing. Apparently if Eshkol could make some offer on refugees and stress that the water pipe for irrigating the Negev would also make possible their resettlement, this would be a very useful gesture.

The Givat Habiba centre is going well but it is mainly useful for training welfare people to work among the Israeli Arabs. The younger Arabs tend to be a rootless nomadic urban proletariat in revolt against the feudal paternalism of the Arab village and humiliated by the Jews. Simha thought that the position was comparable to the alienation of the American Negro or the persecuted Jews in the diaspora and could lead to a movement akin to the Black Muslim.

Harold's office for a briefing on the line I am to take tonight in the radio debate with Sir John Eden [Conservative MP for Bournemouth

---

* Editor of the Jewish socialist journal *New Outlook*.
† Nahum Goldman of the World Jewish Congress.

West] on arms for Spain where I argued for an embargo on supplies to Franco.

A huge row has developed about my nocturnal prowlings with Tam Dalyell around the Lords. The Lord Great Chamberlain wrote to the Serjeant-at-Arms and it was reported to Bowden who went to see Harold. Harold said that we should apologise to the Lord Great Chamberlain. Bowden asked us to do so. Tam and I refused. But I did write a letter to Bowden admitting that it was I who had wandered round with Tam (the LGC thought that it was John Mackie).

> Dear Mr Bowden,
> I understand that some question has been raised about my visit round the Palace of Westminster on the evening of June 30. I have frequently walked through the corridors of both Houses, sometimes with visitors, and sometimes late at night. I might add that I entered no rooms that were occupied.

Meanwhile, Tam and I are circulating a motion as follows:

> *Control of the Palace of Westminster*
> That an humble address be presented to Her Majesty praying that the control of the Royal Palace of Westminster be transferred to a House of Commons Commission under the chairmanship of Mr Speaker; and to amend the powers of the Lord Great Chamberlain accordingly.

We plan to make this into a Back Bench revolt on 13 July, when accommodation is discussed. Harold takes no interest in this point and has got to be forced to realise that it is a live issue.

To the BBC this evening to do the debate with Eden. It was the usual predigested spot-timed cockfight.

Friday 3 July

To lunch today with Paul Hasluck at Australia House. He is the Minister for External Affairs and invited about eight younger MPs, as he wanted to meet those who were likely to be in politics in ten years' time. Hasluck was a pretty quiet and unexciting person and when pressed admitted that the Commonwealth was, for him, primarily sentimental. He had few suggestions to make about how it might be developed. He was contemptuous of the Australian Labour Party and expressed curiosity about our policy. Dick Marsh pointed out that Menzies was the one Commonwealth PM who had not asked to see Wilson. Hasluck seemed surprised.

We also asked how long the white Australia policy could last with the pressure of a rising Chinese population. He agreed it was difficult but felt that the pressure from China would make it easier for Australia to get on with her neighbours who were also afraid of China.

The only reason Australia does not recognise Peking is because of American disapproval.

We tried to persuade him that Australia had a role in helping to ease the Rhodesian crisis and influence the settlers there. He did not sound keen about this.

Saturday 4 July
Breakfast in the garden and a lovely morning. To Bristol for a Co-op international day which was held in Fairfax House. Back this evening. A great row is developing in Bristol about the plan to withdraw the free places from the direct grant grammar schools and there is a silly argument about a compulsory purchase order which has led to some abuse between leading members of the Labour group.

Monday 6 July
Lunch with Dick Crossman. Peter Shore was there but not Balogh. We are all extremely anxious now about the way the political situation is developing. Harold is principally concerned with his own position and we have lost the initiative. We are increasingly on the defensive on nationalisation and the exchange of abuse between the two political leaders is leading to a rising irritation among the public. Somehow we have got to break this vicious circle.

At home this afternoon and into the House to vote this evening at 10. This was my third visit to the Commons today, involving six journeys – all because there are no proper office facilities there. Though quite frankly I much prefer my office at home.

Tuesday 7 July
To the Commons for the Overseas Committee of the Executive. We had a long discussion about Southern Rhodesia. I urged that it would be better for us if Rhodesia did declare its independence before we came to power. Others thought this might be right but couldn't see how we could achieve it or whether it was wise even to think about it. But I am sure it is right.

Caroline went to tea with all the wives of Labour MPs, entertained by Mrs Wilson, Mrs Brown and Mrs Bowden. Then we met and went to have dinner with David and Marilyn Butler at the United University Club.

Thursday 9 July
Tommy Balogh rang – almost in hysteria – to complain about the defensive attitude the Party is taking towards nationalisation and urging me to see Harold about it at once. He really is the most flappable politician I know.

I wrote a *Guardian* article on the Crown which I have been longing to do.

Lunch at the House of Commons with Mother and about twelve others who had come for the annual meeting of the Society for the Ministry of Women. The Bishop of Woolwich was also there. They are rather an ageing crowd and contain a feminist element from the past. What they need is some fight if they are ever going to win.

After lunch to the Immigration Committee to consider a further draft of a Bill to outlaw discrimination and incitement.

Then to see Harold Wilson briefly about his TV broadcast next Wednesday. He wants me to do a three-minute introduction, saying that the Labour Party has explained its policy and attacking the Tories for attacking us for not explaining it, etc. I said I wouldn't do it and that he shouldn't be so defensive. He really has been worried too much by Tory attacks and is very defensive. He had a terrible cold and I felt sorry for him.

Mohammed Khider came to see me this evening. He is one of the original leaders of the Algerian Nationalist Movement and has spent twelve years in prison in the course of his life. He was for six years in the French Assembly and was one of the founders of the FLN and was later with Ben Bella in prison after the French arrested them.

When Algeria became independent he became Secretary-General of the FLN but disagreed with Ben Bella when Bella became President and he left on 8 June 1964, under a cloud and fearing arrest. He is now set on starting a new civil war to free Algeria from Ben Bella. I pressed him continuously on the real source of the disagreement: was it ideological, was it anything to do with Arab nationalism, had it to do with the Muslim religion? But there were no satisfactory answers. I came to the conclusion that this was a personal difference with Ben Bella. It then turned out that he had got control of sixty million new francs which he had deposited in the Swiss banks during the revolution and which was available on his personal signature. With this money he intended to finance the revolution and he was cocky and confident of success. Considering all the suffering Algeria has had to undergo in the last ten years I could find no sympathy for him.

Sunday 12 July

This morning to the weekend conference on regional planning, organised by the Party at the Bonnington Hotel. George Brown was in the chair and there were various Front Bench and Executive spokesmen, academics and local authority people and industrialists.

This morning we dealt with physical planning, including land use and after lunch there was a session on transport. Although George

Strauss was there, George Brown asked me to wind up and I spoke
for about a quarter of an hour. It did rather indicate which way the
wind was blowing. Then George Brown wound up the conference
with a speech on the way he sees the Ministry of Planning developing
and the regional centres which will be set up in every region.

Monday 13 July
The postal strike means that no letters are coming in which is a great
relief.

To see Harold Wilson with Clive Bradley and John Harris to
discuss his TV broadcast on Wednesday. Harold wanted to use it
for fighting a rearguard action but I persuaded him to forget the
Spanish frigates and talk about the first 100 days of a Labour Government and let the issues of the Election emerge out of his discussion.

This afternoon Dick Crossman went to see him and he told Dick
that he had decided to do the 100 Days idea. He also told Dick (who
passed it on to me) that he was going to make me Postmaster General,
give me a chance there for eighteen months and then to the Ministry
of Transport. I have no idea whether this is true or not (not Dick's
story, of course, but Harold's intention). If it is, I don't think there's
much point in sweating my guts out on transport policy between now
and the Election. I'll borrow a book on the Post Office and take it
on holiday instead. It would be a most interesting job to have and
if I got it it would be attributable entirely to the memorandum I
wrote to Harold last October. Such are the uncertainties of politics.
But it is the first time that it has even been indicated officially that
I am going to get anything.

We had the debate on office accommodation in the House this
afternoon and I spoke. There was a near unanimity of view that a
vast extension was necessary.

Tuesday 14 July
At Transport House for a run-through of the TV broadcast tomorrow.
Harold and I tried out a discussion on something else, so as not to
get stale. With the risk of being phoney, he wants me to appear with
him discussing the priorities, the problems, the economic inheritance,
the machinery and the mood of his new Government. 'I want some
of your youth to rub off on me,' he said. 'As I am at least seven years
younger than you,' I replied, 'that should be relatively easy.'

Wednesday 15 July
George Wigg rang to ask for details of Mohammed Khider's interview
with me last Thursday. I had mentioned it casually and George took
all the details down in his usual conspiratorial way to report to the

Algerian Ambassador. He is, I think, a complete madman, and if, as Dick Crossman thinks, he will be the Minister of State at 10 Downing Street, we shall soon have a police state run by Colonel Wigg on the security side.

With Harold Wilson by car to Lime Grove to record the television interview – discussion with him. He adopted the 100 Days idea and it went off quite well on the first take – underrunning by three minutes. Rather than do it again and get stale, we accepted it. Harold was friendly and the whole atmosphere was very cordial.

Thursday 16 July
To the Commons and started looking through all the books on the Post Office. Most of the histories were written in the last century or the 1920s. It confirms my impression that the GPO has not (except possibly when Marples was PMG) been an up-to-date, go-ahead organisation.

Friday 17 July
Caroline and I went to Durham and attended the pre-Gala dinner. Also there were Harold Wilson, Frank Cousins, Will Paynter, Sam Watson and others.[32]

At dinner I could hear Sam asking Harold who would be doing what in the Labour Government and I could just hear Harold giving some names. Afterwards when I was alone Harold came up to me and said, 'Tony, I thought it would be helpful if you knew that I want you to be Postmaster General in the Government.'

I wasn't, of course, at all surprised since Dick had told me this on Monday. It is a job I would very much like to have, but seemingly Harold thought I would be very disappointed at not being Minister of Transport to which I could reasonably lay some claim and which had confidently been expected by all the papers predicting the Government he would set up. He also knew that it was not a Cabinet job and therefore went out of his way to repeat what he had said before to me, that this was only for eighteen months. 'My real Cabinet will be made in 1966 – just as Clem's was made in 1947,' he said.

He told me that Frank Cousins would be Minister of Transport and he also told me the names of a number of other appointments. Frank Soskice for the Home Office (if he lives), Tony Greenwood for the Colonies, Sir Hugh Foot (with a peerage) to the UN, Gerald Gardiner on the Woolsack, Peggy Herbison at Pensions, Barbara Castle (in the Cabinet) at Overseas Aid.

I asked about the Assistant Postmaster General and he said that it would be Joe Slater, his PPS, who is very nice. Roy Mason is to go as Minister of State shared between Dick Crossman at Education and Science and the Minister of Labour to deal with re-training. Dick's other Ministers are to be Reg Prentice[33] for schools and Lord Bowden for universities.

Harold stressed that I would be the only one of the newcomers to be Head of a Department, ie a Departmental Minister of Cabinet rank, outside the Cabinet, and that he thought that would be extremely important with University of the Air to launch and the Giro system to introduce. I reminded him that I had sent him a memo on the Post Office last November and he said he remembered it but had intended this earlier. 'I had thought of you doing a Bill Deedes – PRO for the Government – but decided against it.' I told him I was very glad he had as it is a job I would hate.

This does now give me a few weeks to do some preliminary work on the Post Office and I decided to get down to it at once so that if we win I shall have some clear idea as to what to do. Caroline and I talked about it as we walked round Durham Cathedral close and castle which were both floodlit.

Saturday 18 July

Breakfast in bed and on the balcony at 8.30 for the arrival of the miners with their banners. There was a cloudburst and thunder and it rained solidly till 11.30. Caroline and I stood on the open balcony throughout it all and waved. Then it cleared and we marched to the platform. We were sopping wet. But just as I got up to speak it began to pelt again and we walked back to the hotel, dripping and sodden. We decided to go straight to the station and travelled back with the Yugoslav Ambassador, Prica.

Monday 20 July

To the Campaign Committee to discuss broadcasts and then to Dick Crossman's for lunch with Peter and Tommy. Our big anxiety is whether Goldwater is likely to become a big issue and whether our defence policy will come in for attack. I am really a Gaullist and in favour of positive neutralism. Harold and Patrick are committed special-relationship men, who prefer the Washington link to the Common Market. We are seeing Harold tomorrow.

After lunch I told Peter about the Post Office job and he told me that at last Harold is working to get him a safe seat which has excited him greatly.

The Urban Traffic Congestion Study Group met again and I must begin to withdraw from it. We plan to have one more meeting next week and submit our report to George and Harold, for the consideration of the incoming minister.

Spent most of the day frantically photostating pages of articles and memoranda on Post Office matters, together with the *Who's Who* entries on all key GPO officials so as to know a bit about the people with whom I would be working. It is all very exciting and I feel like a revolutionary who has been told by the insurgent general that when we capture London I am to take over the Post Office. My reading of the personal information is that the top GPO brass are rather limited, ageing and unimaginative.

Tuesday 21 July

The postal strike still means that the flow of letters is much reduced and my workload correspondingly easier.

To the Commons for the first collective talk that Harold and Dick, Thomas and Peter and I have had for many months. We discussed the September period and considered the possibility that with an impending economic crisis the Election date might be advanced. When the trade returns are published, Harold will probably write a confidential exchange to Home that can be revealed if necessary, should the Tories blame a worsening crisis on the prospect of a Labour victory. The fact is they are now racing against time, with a distinct possibility that a run on the pound will begin in August.

On the Goldwater question, Harold agreed that we should de-emphasise the Anglo-American link, stress the need for Britain to speak up for peace, and possibly say at the end that a Labour Government will 'do whatever is necessary to defend itself'. We don't want to raise Goldwater but it is likely to be raised. We cannot shift from our existing defence commitment without appearing to retreat and endangering the unity of the Party.

Harold said that the *Daily Mirror* will campaign for the Party 'as no newspaper has ever campaigned before' – these being the words of Cecil King and Hugh Cudlipp.

Wednesday 22 July

Missed the National Executive today because I had such a lot of work to do in the office. In fact nothing much happened, I believe, except that Barbara Castle raised the Southern Rhodesia issue and pressed her view to a vote against Harold.

There was also a discussion afterwards informally about Malta. The British Government have rushed through the independence provisions and are pushing a Bill through in one day. This Bill entrenches the rights of the Catholic Church at the expense of the civil rights of others and is really a monstrous proposal. But apparently the Shadow Cabinet bullied Harold Wilson into accepting this, more or less uncritically, because they didn't want a Labour Government to be landed with the problem of Malta. Harold was actually outvoted on the Shadow Cabinet – an extraordinary procedure.

Lunch today at the House of Commons for Shen Ping, the Counsellor from the Chinese embassy. He came with Mr Hsieh. The interested MPs we had got together included Julian Snow, William Warbey, Judith Hart and Sir Cyril Osborne. However, Sir Cyril got into a huff in the middle of dinner and walked out – which was very stupid. The Chinese talked continuously about Taiwan. After lunch Harold Davies joined us and we discussed the possibility of setting up a Sino-British parliamentary group. The Chinese were doubtful about this but in the new Parliament we can look at it again.

Caroline, Melissa and Joshua came to the House of Commons for tea on the terrace today. Afterwards they all went into the House of Commons just as Churchill was leaving the debate. It will be quite a thing for them to be able to say that they actually saw Churchill. If they live to be ninety – his age – they will be saying in 2040 that they remember seeing a man who was elected to Parliament 150 years before.

This evening to Broadcasting House to help Denis Healey do a Party political broadcast on Labour defence policy.

Tuesday 28 July
Worked at home this morning and completed the paper on the machinery of government for the Urban Traffic Congestion Study Group, which had its last meeting at the Commons this afternoon. We have only met four or five times but are able to put in quite a reasonable report which, though not definite in all its policy recommendations, does provide an extended agenda for an incoming Minister of Transport. I am glad to be clear of it now as I shall not have the responsibility for it.

Peter Shore and I had a long talk afterwards. Apparently Dick Mitchison [MP for Kettering] is being forced to resign because he is seventy-four and Harold has hinted that Peter might get the seat. However, Harold has not spoken to Frank Cousins about it, which will be necessary as Peter is a Transport Workers' candidate. We were planning how to carry this project forward.

Wednesday 29 July
This evening to dinner with Peter Shore. He is hoping that Harold will urge Frank Cousins to get him nominated by a local Transport Workers' branch and I promised to watch over things while he went on holiday to France. Also there was Roland Brown and his wife. Roland is Attorney-General of Tanganyika and gave an interesting insight into the Commonwealth Conference and the prospects in

Rhodesia and elsewhere. He thought that Labour's reluctance to terminate the Simonstown[34] agreement was causing a lot of ill will among African states.

Friday 31 July–Saturday 1 August
To celebrate the beginning of the holiday I slept in the garden with Stephen and Hilary and we ate sausages and had a hurricane lamp. Tommy Balogh phoned. Ian Grimble came for lunch. The trouble is you can't cut the phone off. Started work on sticking in the family snapshots since 1959. All day in the office on Saturday on the photographs and went out with the children to a Chinese restaurant.

Thursday 6 August
Stephen went with Benjy Zander and George Malcolm to Westminster Cathedral to a summer school for choirboys. Stephen did extremely well and was invited to attend a day's rehearsal and sing on Sunday. Ruth Khama telephoned to say that she and Seretse were in London for the day, so we went and had a drink with them. They had some of their Bechuana friends with them. We had a brief discussion about politics. Seretse is very worried that he is going to be pushed into a direct confrontation with South Africa which he is simply not equipped to tackle effectively. He is, I am afraid, a real aristocratic African nationalist leader, a bit like the Sultan of Morocco, made secure by the fact that the British persecuted him. But he is also a dear friend.

Monday 10 August
To Transport House this afternoon to see the set which has been prepared for the Election broadcasts. Then to the House of Commons to see Harold Wilson who had flown back from the Scilly Isles today in view of the serious crises in Vietnam and Cyprus.[35] He looked fit and well. We are saying nothing about Cyprus because there is nothing to be said, and on Vietnam we are terrified of saying anything that might upset the Americans. The British Government needs American support against Sukarno, who is attacking Malaysia and Wilson is particularly anxious not to upset Johnson at this stage. That is the way politics go.

Wednesday 12–Thursday 27 August
This was our first holiday ever with the children and away from either Caroline's family in America or mine here. The Hotel Kursall, Rimini, was right on the beach and we were able to lie in the sun every morning and some of the afternoon. The children thoroughly enjoyed it and made friends with lots of other children. We had two

trips, one to Venice, which was quite a success, and the other to San Marino which is just as romantic as the tourist posters suggest. Except for two telephone calls from Peter Shore about the prospects of his candidature, there was no link with home at all and I became so lazy that I couldn't even read detective stories. The journey home was long, taking about thirty-six hours, and we arrived back pretty tired on the evening of 27 August.

Friday 28 August
Valerie came in this morning and we began clearing off the backlog of work, though most of it had been done in my absence. To Bristol this evening and looked in at the Hanham Labour Party meeting and then to the presentation to Helen Bloom* in the Walter Baker Memorial Hall. Seeing about sixty people there in that grim building, all of them over sixty, and with the rain leaking through the ceiling on to the floor, was a reminder of how unrepresentative the local Labour Party has become in that constituency. It is absolutely essential to make fresh contact with the people there and organise a more or less new Party which can somehow be latched on to the old one.

Monday 31 August
Felt lousy today with a very heavy cold. This evening I went to see Harold Wilson to discuss the TV broadcast which is going to launch the manifesto on 11 September. He seemed very cheerful and I think that we are not taking too seriously the slight Tory recovery evident in the polls.

Afterwards Peter Shore gave me a copy of the manifesto he has written and which will come before the NEC next week.

Tuesday 1 September
In the office all day and Valerie began preparing a mailing list of people to whom I intend to write in Bristol South East in anticipation of the campaign. These fall into three groups. First, members of the GMC, to whom I shall write two or three letters during the campaign, keeping them up to date and helping to mask my absence in London. Secondly, a trial mailing to all the doctors in the constituency, to a selected group of those people whose cases I have taken up over the past eighteen months, and to some shopkeepers who wrote to me about re-sale price maintenance. To these people I am sending the Citizens for Labour letter with a reply postcard. It will be interesting to see what sort of response one gets with a controlled list of this kind. The third group I am going to write to as soon as the date of

---

* Labour councillor and sometime Lady Mayor of Bristol.

the Election is announced is all those people I have in my card index who are Party members in the constituency. This is a very obsolete list and one advantage of writing now is that it will give me a chance of bringing the list up to date and checking how much support there really is in it.

Thursday 3 September
Tommy Balogh called this morning and we sat in the garden and worked out notes for Harold Wilson's speech at the TUC on Monday. In the evening I went to Bristol for a meeting of the General Management Committee. The main item on the agenda was Election plans but there was a terrific volume of trivia first and we came to it very late. There was some criticism of me for having to cancel a meeting in Kingswood next week because the National Executive had been called to discuss the manifesto. The only troublemaker is Tom Martin. Otherwise relations are very good.

Sunday 6 September
Worked on my fact sheet based on a study of White Papers, blue books and letters from local government departments bearing on housing, education and other conditions in the city. Also transferring the principal fighting points from all our literature on to cards which I am going to use in a mobile research library, carrying it round with me. It is based on the report I read of Kennedy's mobile reference library and I think will be very useful for speeches. The office is now almost fully devoted to the Election job.

Monday 7 September
Went to the Farmers' Club today to lunch with Dick Crossman, George Wigg and Tommy Balogh. It is the first time I have worked closely with George Wigg. Up to now he has always been rather unpleasant, but he has a certain tough capacity and I think is a useful person to have on this sort of operation. We all agreed that the arrangements made for the running of the campaign were totally inadequate and it surpasses our understanding why Harold Wilson should have been so much weaker than Hugh Gaitskell was in imposing his own framework on to the Election campaign. There is no real provision for morning brains trusts meetings. Dick Crossman has a much reduced role and I have no real authority to deal with the broadcasting side. We worked on some papers to present to Harold. This is our only hope of being influential. This evening Harold made his speech at the TUC and it was very effective.

Tuesday 8 September

I had lunch with Ned Sherrin from 'That Was the Week That Was' at Lime Grove. Also there were Norman St John Stevas[36] and others. The idea was to discuss the new programme that is to come on for three nights each weekend to replace 'TW3'. Ned Sherrin's idea was that in addition to satire there should be serious political discussion and comment. I told him I thought these were quite incompatible and that an MP really could not appear in an entertainment programme. I felt like a wet blanket and I sensed an enormously powerful anti-political feeling. It wasn't anti-political in the way that CND or the real Left is anti-political. It was anti-political in a scornful and contemptuous way, and I thought the whole lunch was a waste of time from my point of view.

This evening I went to the National Executive meeting at Transport House for the joint meeting with the Shadow Cabinet to agree the Election manifesto. One thing that we had agreed at lunch yesterday was that the immigration issue ought to be taken by the horns. In the draft manifesto it was not mentioned at all and so when we came to that section tonight, I put in a draft, having given notice earlier in the meeting that I intended to do this.

The draft drew attention to our determination to outlaw racial discrimination and our intention of helping local authorities in areas where immigrants had settled. The draft also made clear that the Labour Party accepted the necessity for some form of control and said that, until this was agreed with the Commonwealth, we should have to maintain existing immigration controls. There was some discussion about this and Harold Wilson had an open mind. But my draft was ultimately accepted and put into the manifesto, and I think has succeeded in killing immigration as an issue during the campaign.

The meeting was made somewhat difficult by the fact that George Brown was drunk and at one stage, just couldn't answer some perfectly straightforward questions that were being put to him about the report of the Home Policy Committee. It was an incredible meeting that went on until midnight. Tony Greenwood was a poor chairman and when we finally left the Drafting Committee was still finalising one or two details.

Peter Shore looked very ill and I was worried to think of him doing this manifesto job. Liz collected him about 2 am and took him home to bed where he should have been. But it is a good manifesto. Later I heard that Jim Callaghan woke up in the middle of the night and realised there was nothing about Scotland or Wales in it. We also forgot to mention the agricultural policy. This was only discovered just before the manifesto was launched. It is an impossible committee to do any serious work.

Wednesday 9 September
This afternoon to see Harold Wilson to discuss the Election programmes. With him were George Brown, John Harris and Clive Bradley. The position quite simply is this. Harold wants to do the first and fifth broadcasts and realises that this makes it difficult with regard to George and some of the other leading figures. So he has more or less agreed to hand over programmes two, three and four to them. This has the effect of making the programme rigid and incapable of last-minute adjustment. This is what Clive Bradley has worked at for about a year, although officially our policy has been to retain complete flexibility. Harold has given me no authority whatsoever to act and since I am not in the office at Transport House all the time, Clive Bradley simply carries on with his own line. It does pose serious problems.

Thursday 10 September
Valerie worked all day on Election preparations. She is checking through the list of Party members that I had, to see if they are still on the register and to put in Christian names and correct addresses. Meanwhile I have prepared a pile of material to go to them. The first is a letter telling them how important the campaign is and this is accompanied by the fact sheet on conditions in Bristol, and a summary of the Election manifesto. Also going in is a Help card addressed to me for return and an excellent card on my advice service.

David Butler came to tea. The National Opinion Poll has come out with a slight Tory lead, although Gallup still shows us leading by 5.5 per cent – a drastic cut from what we had earlier. The polls must be worried to be so far apart and straddling the point of victory. David still thinks it more likely that we will win but the Conservatives have had a tremendous boost.

Friday 11 September
Dick Crossman, George Wigg, Tommy Balogh and John Allen came to lunch today to have another discussion. It went well and we agreed that material must be prepared on the question of how to pay for our programme and on defence. But we are all a lot of prima donnas and spend a great deal of time arguing about the structure of the campaign about which we can do nothing. The plain fact is that we have to try to make the present system work as best we can. Harold's great weakness is his reluctance to confront anybody with an unpopular decision and thus things drift on with no one knowing quite where they are. This is a grave weakness and one wonders whether it will carry on when he is Prime Minister. The difficulty is

also that if he succeeds people admire him, but if he fails nobody will feel responsibility for it.

Afterwards to Lime Grove for the TV programme to launch the manifesto. Harold opened and closed it and others taking part were Dick Crossman, Michael Stewart, Jim Callaghan and Gerald Gardiner. It was dull and earnest and good – and in marked contrast to the Tory commercial technique which is being used. I had to leave afterwards to take Peter Shore and Liz to Stepney where he had an important meeting with the Transport and General Workers' Union delegates. It was a real shock to see him. His mind was working slowly and he was slurring his words, and his left arm and leg were partially paralysed. I wondered if he had had a heart attack or a stroke but Liz says it is a virus that has attacked his central nervous system. I had actually offered to speak in case he was too unfit for it but I was not allowed into the meeting and I sat outside in the car.

Saturday 12 September
Dutch television came this morning to do an interview with me and then this afternoon Caroline and I went to Wembley for the great Labour Rally. The manifesto was launched yesterday and this was a crowded gathering of about 10,000 who had come by bus and coach and train from all over Britain. It began with an American convention-style entertainment with actors and actresses and a pageant. It was good but much too long. We stayed to hear Harold Wilson and then left.

Sunday 13 September
To the candidates' conference at the TUC this morning and afternoon. It was a briefing conference and the questions were good, and although I had no part whatsoever to play I think it was a good thing to turn up.

This afternoon Caroline went to do a television programme on childbirth with Professor Norman Morris and Dr Tizard, who had both been involved in delivering some of ours.[37]

In the evening I went to Tommy Balogh's house for a general talk. This had been arranged at Harold Wilson's request and also there were Dick Crossman, George Wigg, John Harris, John Allen, and Marcia Williams. We discussed the poll published this morning which showed that we had fallen to 5.5 per cent lead – which really means 2.2 per cent if you average it out. We discussed the tactics of the campaign and I said that I thought that the natural Tory come-back would be: 'They want to build a New Britain but they're not prepared to defend it.' Obviously the nuclear deterrent is going to be used at some stage in the campaign and we have to be ready for it. Harold commissioned a special paper to be written on this subject.

I made the suggestion that when the Tory manifesto was published we should challenge Home to a confrontation. This had been hoped for earlier but had never come off and it seemed that it would be a good time to do it so as to steal the headlines the following day. There was a terrible idea that the Duke of Bedford should be brought in and a debate should be done at Woburn Abbey. Happily I was able to kill that. It was a useful evening and if only such a group had met regularly over the last six months I think we would have done better. We're meeting again next week.

Monday 14 September

To the last meeting of the Campaign Committee today. They simply rubber stamped the general outline of the Election programmes and we were able to get away quickly.

This afternoon to Broadcasting House for a long meeting of the Broadcasting Group. This led to an awful row with Clive Bradley. He has simply gone ahead with his own idea for the programmes, which bears little relation to what we had originally planned. Clive got into a terrible temper and said that he was not prepared to take instructions from anyone else. He is a difficult customer and I can anticipate growing problems with him throughout the campaign.

After that very prolonged meeting I went to Billericay to speak at Eric Moonman's adoption meeting. He tells me that he is hopeful that Peter will get Stepney on Wednesday night.

Tuesday 15 September

Worked in the office this morning. The first edition of the new *Sun*[38] newspaper was published today – after a huge press and advertising bally-hoo build-up. It is appalling. It is slightly bigger than the *Herald* but basically the same – minus the limited *Herald* political content. It is a pale wishy-washy imitation of the *Daily Mail* and I don't honestly see how it can survive as a daily. It is the product of market research, without any inner strength and message. There is little hard news – pages of fluffy features and nothing hard to bite on. I am afraid that it may not be as much of a help to us between now and polling day as we had hoped.

To Bristol this afternoon and had a surgery and then went back to Unity House to discuss the Election plans with Herbert Rogers. The fact is that he has been able to do practically nothing and all the work on the Election which is being done in London by Valerie is going to be essential.

This afternoon the Prime Minister announced the date of the

Election: which is to be Thursday 15 October, as we had all anticipated for so long.

To Holland Park School to talk to the Senior Society on the Election. It was a good meeting and I enjoyd it.

This evening Peter Shore limped to Stepney again and was adopted as the candidate. I am delighted. Even though he is clearly a sick man and will need at least a month's complete rest he will be an MP at the end of it, whatever he does.

Thursday 17 September
To Transport House this morning for another broadcasting discussion with Chris Mayhew and Shirley Williams. Chris is profoundly unhappy at what is happening and feels that control of the programmes has passed out of our hands and that it is being dealt with by Harold on the old, old basis of using the men who must be got in without regard to presentation, life and content. Shirley is worried too because she is being brought up and down from a marginal constituency but feels that there is no real part for her. I just feel I have to bumble along and not make trouble. But at this stage I don't think the programmes are going to be any good and I ought to go to Harold and be perfectly frank with him about it.

Meanwhile Valerie is mailing off the first letters to the Citizens for Labour mailing group. These are all the doctors in the constituency, plus a number of businessmen who wrote and complained about resale price maintenance, plus a number of personal cases for whom I have tried to do something over the last year. It is an experiment but I feel the 'Citizens for Labour' idea must be developed if we are ever to break out of the tight character of our local Party. Bristol South East Labour Party is made up of ageing manual workers and has got no contact with new people.

I drove to Bristol this evening for the annual general meeting of the New Bristol Group, when our new edition of *Output*, covering the last year, was published. Brian Abel-Smith[39] had kindly agreed to come and speak and he gave a brilliant talk on poverty. About forty people turned up and we distributed copies of the booklet which has been published at £83 for 1000. It is full of really good material – but unfortunately the announcement of the date of the Election has overshadowed publicity for our booklet. At any rate the New Bristol Group was a product of the 1961 by-election and has certainly justified itself.

Friday 18 September
To Unity House and then to the printer, followed by an intensive midday period writing and designing the new Election address. It is

going to be a terrible rush to get everything out. We agreed that in the Election address would go my message, a special folder dealing with my advice service, a leaflet with the main points of Labour's manifesto and also a yellow reply card inviting people to say whether they would like to help, whether they needed or would lend a car on polling day. On the back is space for questions and comments and I am hoping in this way to get in some material which will be useful at my meetings.

This afternoon I went to a tea meeting organised by Mrs Kenwood in Kingswood and from there to Temple Meads to meet Caroline, who had come down from London for my adoption meeting. The formal business was conducted upstairs and then we went downstairs to the public meeting in the Walter Baker Hall. It wasn't very well attended but there was a great deal of enthusiasm and we didn't finally get away until late.

Saturday 19 September
This morning Caroline and I went to Monks Park Comprehensive School with all the other Labour candidates in the city. Mr Waley, the headmaster, talked about the comprehensive school and what notable successes he had achieved there with university entrance, A-level and O-level passes. Then Vyvyan-Jones came along with Bob Glendinning and Claud Draper from the Education Committee of the Council to explain the plans for the city. These are now finalised and involve converting the municipal grammar and old secondary modern schools in East and Central Bristol into a sort of modified Leicestershire form. In addition they are quite firm in deciding not to take free places at the direct grant schools. This is causing a terrific storm in Bristol.

I said quite frankly that I had not been consulted at any stage. I told Vyvyan-Jones that I had had to deal with the mail that Harold Wilson had received on this subject without being fully informed. He had got the idea that I was hostile to the scheme and had no idea that our boys were at a comprehensive school. When I told him I think he was a bit surprised as he had regarded me as being unfriendly. But I also told him that the Labour Party was committed to having talks with the direct grant schools to fit them into the state educational pattern. I asked him what, if he had complete power, he would do with Bristol's direct grant schools. He said that he really could think of no way of fitting them in. While I am absolutely opposed to selection at eleven or the maintenance of an examination to feed the direct grant schools, I think it is pretty foolish to say that there is no place at all for them in the Bristol system.

Also, I doubt whether Dick Crossman, as Minister of Education, would be prepared to let the city go on with its plans. Frankly, Dick is thinking of making the public schools into direct grant schools and then either integrating them entirely, or cutting them off and leaving them quite on their own to fend for themselves as best they can. In these circumstances, I think that with stricter rules for family allowances and the tax structure and the attack upon the exclusive entry that the public and direct grant schools have into our universities, it would be possible to have a state system that was so good that only a few would want to go outside it.

Sunday 20 September
The Gallup polls this morning show our lead at 2.5 per cent, which means that there has been no change for a week. This is the first evidence that the Tory revival has been halted and I am hoping that from now on we shall be able to lift our lead a little bit.

I worked in the office all morning on Election preparations and this afternoon John Allen looked in. We agreed that there must be a major shift of emphasis from talking about our policy and how to pay for it, to attacking the Tories on the points at which they are susceptible. Caroline put me up to this and Peter Shore agreed on the telephone. He is now in hospital with this virus. But he is able to talk on the telephone from his hospital bed and wants to be kept in touch. He agreed we must go over to the attack and he fed me with some useful ideas.

At 7 this evening I went back to Tommy Balogh's for another evening meeting with Harold Wilson and the same crowd. I made the point about going over to the attack. This was generally agreed. Specifically, we agreed that on Tuesday Harold should invite Clem to visit him in his house. The Prime Minister has his last Cabinet meeting on Tuesday and it is important that we should be in the news too.

After a study of the Conservative manifesto it seemed that the most curious and sinister part of it was the reference to recasting social security. It was agreed that Dick Crossman should make a serious warning speech on Thursday about this and that it should be given the full build-up. We also discussed the *Sun* and what a disaster it was for us as well as for Cecil King. It can't survive if it goes on like this. Harold agreed to see King or Cudlipp and urge them to come out strongly for us now – even if only to hold their old *Herald* readers, who are now clearly discouraged. We then went on to various strategic plans and anticipated that defence would be thrown against us. Various papers had been prepared and circulated and this seemed all right.

Monday 21 September
I went to Transport House at 11.15 to discuss the TV programme in which Patrick Gordon Walker, Denis Healey and Jim Callaghan are to take part. Clive Bradley has a rigid format to which he wishes to adhere and I explained that it might well be that we should have to change the subject and either we would not want them or we would want others to appear. Jim was absolutely furious with Clive Bradley because he had been asked by 'Panorama' to appear in a programme and then Clive Bradley had notified 'Panorama' that he was not doing it.

Back to Transport House this afternoon for another meeting of the Broadcasting Group. I explained that I thought these programmes had to be flexible, that we should not think in terms of programmes but items, and that each item should be an attacking question on 'why the Conservatives had failed to do this or that'. We could then develop this and show that things were getting worse, that the Tories were incapable of solving these problems and finally come to our Party spokesman who would show in brief what we would do.

In the evening Ken Peay* telephoned me and said he was very worried and that I should go and speak to Harold to say I must have authority and that these progammes were going to be disastrous unless he gave me that authority. Ken thought that I really might have to contemplate resigning from the operation and I feel the same. When I talked to Peter Shore he thought I should raise it directly with Harold and so I think I shall have to face him frankly. I am extremely unhappy about the way it is going.

Tuesday 22 September
To see Harold Wilson. I put it to him plainly that I really had to be given the authority if I was to do the job required of me. I didn't threaten in any way but made it very clear that this was necessary. He agreed to dictate a minute to this effect. We also discussed the press release that I put out for my Young Fabian meeting, taking the confrontation theme a stage further. In this I said that confrontation was desirable, that debate was essentially a British rather than an American practice and that it was time the Tories modernised their campaign techniques.

Wednesday 23 September
Harold Wilson phoned at 10.30 pm last night – and I was in bed – to say that my press release had been on the news and how effective

* Former Labour Party agent and Party official, who maintained connections with Transport House.

it had been. He has never rung me at home and I have no doubt that he did it because I had been to complain yesterday about the broadcasting position, and he wanted to keep me sweet.

Ivan Yates called this morning to interview me for an *Observer* article on Transport House and how the campaign was working. I played down my role so that it didn't appear in the article. The fact is that Harold doesn't want any people to know that anyone helps him at all. He wants it all to be his show and Dick and Tommy and I have to pretend we don't exist. Kennedy never minded it being known that he had speech writers and advisers, but Harold does. It's very silly but I know that my capacity to influence him depends upon total self-erasure. Dick finds this unbearable and is always leaking how central he is.

To see Harold at 11 and went over his future speeches. He couldn't have been more friendly.

To Bristol for the debate, with Stephen O'Brien, my Tory opponent, in St Matthews parish hall. O'Brien is one of these rather wet do-gooder stockbroker Christian Tories. But very nice. Afterwards watched Harold on 'Election Forum'.

Thursday 24 September

At the printers this morning checking the Election material, on to a coffee meeting of women and then to Queen's Square, where I spoke for an hour and a quarter without a loudspeaker. About a hundred people were there and there were some excellent questions.

Back to London. David Butler came to dinner. He still thinks that Labour is most likely to win. But the polls are now meaningless. I just wish they were meaningless in our favour. Home was on 'Election Forum' and really was pathetic.

Saturday 26 September

This afternoon to Bristol with Caroline and Hilary, and to the Central Hall meeting where Harold spoke to about 2,500 people. I spoke after him and then we went back to the Grand Hotel and Caroline and Hilary and I watched the Tory Party political in his room with his huge staff. Afterwards the three of us had dinner with him. It was a successful start to the campaign.

Sunday 27 September

We came back to London. In the afternoon I went and had a long talk to Peter Shore. As Harold has opened up on the trade gap in speeches in Cardiff and Bristol, Peter thinks we must shatter Tory complacency and really go for them on the whole front. Peter was in good form, though still in bed and very tired.

Tuesday 29 September
Another early start at Transport House and to Len Williams's meeting. The economic crisis is now major news and the Tories are on the defensive. But there is a certain flatness about the campaign and I am profoundly doubtful as to whether we can win.

There is a great row raging now between me and the *Western Daily Press* on the way they reported Harold Wilson's 'Election Forum' last Wednesday. They ran a headline saying, 'Wilson snubs Bristol's schools plan'. I rang to complain last Thursday, having consulted Harold, and I have written to the Press Council. The Bristol papers are furious.

Wednesday 30 September
To the office this morning to see Herbert Rogers. All the Election printing is finished and so are the envelopes. Otherwise there are no signs of activity and he sits there with a part-time secretary, running an imaginary army and sending them duplicated instructions. We are worried about apathy and the women's vote.

After lunch John Guinery came for a talk. Then he took me to meet Mr Cooper, the new editor of the *Evening Post*, and into the *Western Daily Press* reporters' room. I thought it would show there was nothing personal and I think it was a good move.

This evening to a meeting for Ray Dobson, the Labour candidate in Bristol North East, and back to the hotel at 10. I watched the Election reports on TV and was profoundly distressed. Home is out stomping the country and dealing with hecklers. Harold is always at a press conference and never with people. There is a real danger, Caroline thinks, that he is great for the in-people but is not getting over to ordinary people. Today's *Mail* poll puts the Tories 2.9 per cent ahead, which would be a repeat of 1959 – and a disaster for the Labour Party.

I spent the day thinking about what to do if 1959 is repeated. It will be necessary, I think, to launch a national programme of action, no individual membership, but the support of radical Liberals and de-Stalinised Communists who will bind themselves together for one Election. It would destroy the terrible handicap of trade-union leadership and the generally illiberal reputation of the Labour Party and provide something new and dynamic. Even to think such thoughts is treason but we cannot go on as we are.

Thursday 1 October
Up at 6 and to London and straight to Len Williams's meeting. Harold's pledge yesterday about enquiries into election strikes provoked deliberately by employers to damage Labour's chances was

discussed over the radio telephone with George Brown. I gather the trade union people are furious but I am sure that Harold was right.

Harold arrived from Norwich and I talked to him and Dick, Tommy and Peter by phone link. The trade crisis has given us our opening and a chance to alert a partly apathetic public to the consequences of Tory rule if they are returned. I also raised with Harold the effect that is created by his daily press conferences. It looks as if he is always commenting on the campaign, whereas Home is out in the streets plugging the two themes of prosperity and the need for the Polaris submarine. Harold was a bit touchy about this and said that if he had not been in London the whole campaign would have floundered. I'm not sure that he's right but that certainly is what he thinks. He is also on the defensive about his pledge to enquire into strikes that have taken place during the campaign.

Friday 2 October

Woke early and to Transport House at 9 o'clock where we had a long and rather bitter discussion about this evening's broadcast on television. Against my wishes I was told I had to introduce it myself and so I cancelled 'Any Questions', which Christopher Mayhew did instead.

Went on to Lime Grove, where Peter Parker and Wilfred Brown were talking about the industrialists' attitude to planning.[40] George Brown arrived at 3.30 tired, having done fifty meetings. He was simply furious that he was not to be allowed to do the whole thing straight to camera and Tom Driberg took the brunt of his rage. In the event, he recorded two pieces, one of two minutes and one of four minutes, which had considerable force. We added film of Willie Ross from Scotland and Lady Megan Lloyd George from Wales. I introduced the programme, did the commentary on the film and also briefly interviewed the two industrialists. All in all it was quite a successful programme. George had a few drinks and headed off for Fulham. Had it been necessary to do the programme live I don't think he would have been in a fit state. I am still profoundly depressed by the way the campaign is going and there is just something wrong about it. Harold insists on making a different speech every day – 'He thinks he's writing the chapters of a book,' said Tommy Balogh on the phone. But Tommy was delighted with the TV and we felt we had shattered the mirror of complacency with it.

Saturday 3 October

Went on the 7.45 am train to Bristol, was formally nominated as candidate at the Council House at 10.30 and then to Transport House, Bristol, where there was a meeting of about sixty or seventy trade union officials and shop stewards. Will Wilkins was in the chair and after I had spoken Victor Feather of the TUC spoke. He made an excellent speech about strikes and it was a good conference.

I had lunch with Desmond Brown of the TGWU and this afternoon went out in the car, visiting a number of Party stalwarts. All the printing is done and the people were busy in the committee rooms putting material into the envelopes. I think I probably am criticised for being so little in Bristol, but the job in London, though depressing, is important.

This evening I went by train to Swindon and spoke for Irving Rogers and then caught the last train home.

Sunday 4 October

This morning the news that the Gallup poll had swung from 1.5 per cent in favour of the Tories last week to 4.5 per cent in favour of us this week was a wonderful tonic. We must really carry it a stage further now and Peter Shore, Dick Crossman, Tommy Balogh and I all agree that Harold must really play down his press conferences and concentrate on repeating the same points again and again. Harold is too much absorbed with the press lobby and the in-group and much too little concerned with the electorate as a whole. He ought to throw away his notes and just make these speeches in general terms to alert people to what is happening.

I'm afraid he won't like it when we tell him this but it is the right advice. Unfortunately the papers were full of Dick and Tommy this morning. Dick undoubtedly leaks everything to the press and it makes Harold very angry and will probably diminish Dick's influence as a result. It is a curious thing that Harold doesn't like it to be known he has any advisers. Partly this is because he doesn't want to upset the Party machine and partly because he likes everyone to think that all his successes are his alone. It is a part of his character which makes him difficult to work with but there it is.

John Allen telephoned when he got back to London with Harold Wilson's caravan. He is working for Harold during the campaign. He said Harold had been furious at all the news reports of Dick Crossman's role in the campaign and especially at the photograph of Dick and Tommy Balogh which had appeared in one of the papers. I suppose Dick desperately wanted to be Leader of the Party and, not being able to achieve that, this is the way he compensates. But it makes things impossible for Tommy Balogh and also could make them impossible for me. I have no doubt that the mention of me last Sunday as one of Harold Wilson's 'telephone set' came from Dick too.

John Allen also told me that Dick had told Harold that I had supported Jim Callaghan for the leadership eighteen months ago. This is totally untrue as I was campaigning hard for Wilson. John had told Harold several times in the course of the week that he thought it unlikely to be true, but I shall have to deal with it myself and intend to do so by talking to Marcia direct. It's a small point but it does indicate that Dick can't altogether be trusted.

Monday 5 October
To Len Williams's meeting. Harold was there. We discussed the progress of the campaign and we tried to get across that there should be much less diversification of energy and much more concentration on the economic front where we really have the Tories on the defensive. I think Harold is coming round to see this. But he is certain that he is the one that is winning the campaign for us single-handed and I don't think he quite believes that he can be doing anything wrong.

On to Lime Grove for the preparation of the broadcast. It was an incredible afternoon. Dick Crossman, Michael Stewart and Kenneth Robinson were the principal participants. Shirley Williams was to link it. Everything went wrong and we had to re-shoot many of the bits twice and even three times. Michael and Kenneth were delightful but Dick Crossman got into a tremendous temper and stamped up and down, shouting and swearing at everybody for having been kept waiting. He really is the most appalling prima donna. After he had recorded his piece he apologised, and then stayed for a drink and by the time he finally left, at 7.45, he had resumed his aggressive posture.

I went to Television Centre to be there while the editing took place and was then told that they had not had time to make the cuts and joins required and that it was quite possible that the film would break down. At 9.15 I returned to Lime Grove, was put in the set which was lighted and the whole crew was standing by. I had to watch the programme on a monitor and if at any point it broke, the camera was to come to me and I had to carry on as best I could until they could find a part of the tape which was good, in which case I was to hand back to it. It was the most appalling sweat and strain sitting there watching, expecting a break at any moment. In the event, one didn't happen and I got back home at about 10 o'clock, really washed out.

Tuesday 6 October
All the reports suggest the campaign is now going very well and I am longing to get back to Bristol to see if there is any reflection of it there.

At the meeting this morning we planned the sound broadcast

tomorrow at which we are bringing in a number of distinguished people like Bishop Ambrose Reeves [Assistant Bishop of London] and the scientist, Lord Bowden.* I am to link it. Thursday's TV is a great gamble with a household full of people to be gathered together to put questions to Jim Callaghan, Gordon Walker, Healey and Ray Gunter.

This morning's meeting with Len Williams was very funny. John Harris was describing the market surveys on reactions to our TV broadcast last Friday with George Brown. Len Williams exploded with contempt and said he thought it was a 'bloody waste of money interviewing ten people', as he put it. John said it had been agreed that this should be done and Len got very red and repeated his statement. This made John very pompous, and Len shouted at him, 'Don't you dare speak to me like that!' Len was red and John white and the rest of us examined our pencils and found papers we had to look at until it was over. At this moment, George Brown came through on the telephone to ask advice but the conference telephone link machine had not been set up. There was another explosion and we were all slightly punch-drunk by the time Harold arrived to recount his latest successes to us.

I said I thought the campaign was getting too diversified, that the press didn't matter much now and we should stick to certain simple things and hammer at them. I don't think Harold liked it very much but this is the advice he is getting from most of his friends. The campaign is getting us all down. Harold looks tired, and I am beginning to feel a bit exhausted myself.

Peter rang at lunchtime and we discussed the campaign. We then got on to Dick's story to Harold that Caroline and I had been Callaghan supporters. Peter was shocked. He too thought I should raise it and could not find words to explain why Dick should have done it. I can't say it has altered my view of Dick but it has reminded me of what he is like.

Wednesday 7 October

The *Western Daily Press* had a banner headline, 'Wilson's Snub. He Ignores Schools Protest Telegram', based on the fact that he was supposed not to have replied to a telegram sent to him on behalf of 28,000 parents protesting about the educational plans for the city. In fact he had not replied but at the same time I discovered that the woman who had sent it had not checked to see whether it had been received by Harold before she gave her statement to the press. Paul

* Lord Bowden became Minister of State at the Department of Education and Science, 1964–5.

Fluck, the *Western Daily Press* reporter, had telephoned Transport House but had not asked to speak to Harold Wilson's secretary. I therefore rang Fluck, and tape recorded the conversation, and issued a statement to the evening papers. I later discovered on Harold's return from Birmingham that the telegram had been handed to him but that it had no name or return address on it and that this alone was sufficient explanation for his failure to reply. I dictated a reply for him to send and sent the text of it to the Bristol papers. So the story was killed and I am going to take it to the Press Council again. The *Western Daily Press* really is a scandalous newspaper and this battle is well worth having – on principle alone.

This afternoon I went to Broadcasting House and cut and edited and linked a number of voices on tape for our 10 o'clock programme. They included Lord Bowden, Vanessa Redgrave, Bishop Ambrose Reeves, and others. It was good.

Back home David Butler and Tony King* called. They told me that the Tory Party was in a state of great disarray and that the NOP on the marginal constituencies is showing a terrific Labour swing. They said that Sir Keith Joseph, amongst others, was completely dejected by the way the Tory campaign was going and thought it might be a Labour landslide. Tony King said he could not understand why the Labour Party had not made a big issue of recalling the record of the Tories over the last two or three years. What we should be doing is reminding people of the circumstances in which the great swing to Labour took place. I agree absolutely about this and shall put it to Harold tomorrow.

At 11 o'clock this evening I telephoned Marcia at home to kill the story that I had supported Callaghan at the time of the leadership contest.

Thursday 8 October
The *Western Daily Press* this morning ran a huge headline, 'Benn's Blunder'. This attacked me for saying that the *Western Daily Press* had distorted the report of the Wilson telegram.

Travelled to Bristol this afternoon and Bert Peglar and Les Bridges met me at the station. I pointed out that I was entirely right in the charges that I had made. They were satisfied with this but felt that I should not have used the tape recorder with Fluck.

I went to the BBC Bristol studios to do 'Question Time' with Mark Bonham Carter and Edward du Cann. One of the panel of

* Anthony King. Joint author with David Butler, of a series of political handbooks, and Professor of Government at Essex since 1969.

journalists was Eric Price, the editor of the *Western Daily Press*, and I had a clash with him both on education and the role of the press.

Afterwards I went to the meeting of the NUJ chapel in Bristol and Paul Fluck came and raised a complaint against my behaviour. It was decided that this had to go in writing and that two weeks must elapse, so in fact nothing happened. Back to the hotel, where Stewart Steven of the *Western Daily Press* came on a peace mission. I met him with Herbert Rogers and we had a long talk. It was most unsatisfactory and I didn't budge.

Friday 9 October

To London this morning and straight to Transport House and back home by 11.30. The *Western Daily Press* telephoned to suggest that they might make a statement and that I might apologise. I said this was quite unacceptable and typed out a form of their apology which I thought *they* might consider.

This afternoon I went to film Clem Attlee at his new flat in the Temple. He was in fine form, telling lots of stories about the past. He has a great contempt for Home whom he described as 'the Tory disc-jockey'.

I came home after this and we had a family evening.

Sunday 11 October

To the last meeting at Transport House this morning and then collected Mother from the flat and took her home for lunch.

Afterwards Caroline and I loaded the car with all our equipment and drove to Bristol – staying at the Grand Hotel.

This evening I spoke at two meetings, one at the Ruskin Hall and one at the Walter Baker Hall. There was some heckling but that helps to keep the atmosphere exciting. The Gallup poll today showed a 6 per cent Labour lead which is very encouraging. But it's still not quite enough.

Tuesday 13 October

Caroline's thirty-eighth birthday and I went out to the market and bought her some flowers before breakfast. The *Western Daily Press* published a very churlish apology and I issued a statement about it (which they did not publish the next day). Valerie hard at work in the office and more and more yellow cards coming in from our publicity drive.

Caroline and I visited the new Health Centre in Bristol and then went to a short factory gate meeting at the Douglas Works in Kingswood. This afternoon we went to the Women's Co-op Guild and did loudspeaker work and had a number of evening meetings. Thank goodness there are only two more days to go.

Wednesday 14 October
A number of Indian journalists came to interview me this morning and Caroline and I had lunch at the Co-op and then to a factory gate meeting and went round the Co-op tailoring factory. This afternoon we did loudspeaker work and finally there were four eve-of-poll meetings and the usual rally in St George's Park.

Thursday 15 October
Caroline and I followed Bert Peglar to all the thirty-six polling stations and committee rooms – it lasted till 5 o'clock. We had lunch at the Co-op with Herbert Rogers who was extremely gloomy and predicted a majority of about 4,000. We did some last-minute loudspeaker work and at 9.30 were back in our hotel, having a snack and watching the beginning of the results programme. David Butler, Richard Dimbleby,* Robert Mackenzie and others were on it. By the time we left for the count at about 11 o'clock, it was pretty obvious that Labour was winning the Election. St George's Grammar School was crowded with people and we stood in the side room as usual with the transistor radio, and notified all those in there of what was happening.

Friday 16 October
The result was declared about 1.15 and I had a majority of 9,800 – 4,000 better than last time. There were quite a few people in the street for the declaration and then we were towed in the traditional way, sitting on top of our car up to the Walter Baker Hall. After that we went to BBC Bristol for a television insert into the results programme. Then on to the TWW interview, followed by a radio interview and finally got to bed about 4.30. It is clear that Labour is winning.

Up at 8 and drove home listening to the results programme on the radio all the way. Lunch at London Airport and home by 2.30. There is an overall Labour majority of four only. Home has resigned the premiership and Harold Wilson has formed a Government. We've waited thirteen years for this.

* BBC broadcaster who became most well known for his 'Panorama' presentation on Radio 4.

Giles in the *Express* reflecting the attack on Wilson and comprehensive education just before the 1964 Election.

NOTES
Chapter Two

1. Robin Day, a contemporary of mine at university, was a barrister before becoming a radio and television journalist. He was knighted in 1984.
2. Sam Watson was General Secretary of the Durham Miners Association, 1936–63, and a member of the National Executive Committee, 1950–62.
3. There has been traditional tension in the concept of the Treasury running our economic, and effectively industrial, policies as opposed to a strong Ministry of Production, able to challenge the Treasury and its basic financial assumptions. Historically, Labour Governments have been defeated by City pressure brought to bear on the Cabinet through the influence of the Treasury and it has been a policy of the Left, when in Opposition, to press for a powerful counterbalancing Department of Production, or Economic Affairs. In this particular case, the conflict lay between Jim Callaghan, Shadow Chancellor, and George Brown, who had aspirations to introduce the National Plan when Labour came to power. Harold Wilson resolved to support the idea of a division in the Treasury, and it was as a result of his decision that the Department of Economic Affairs was set up in 1964 with George Brown as its first Secretary of State. It was wound up in 1969.
4. Alastair Hetherington was editor of the *Guardian*, 1956–75, becoming Controller of BBC Scotland, 1975–80. This was followed by a short spell as Manager, BBC Highland Radio.
5. Rt Hon Arthur Bottomley, Labour MP for Middlesborough East, 1962–74, and previously for Rochester and Chatham, was Secretary for Overseas

Trade in the Attlee Government. In his role as Secretary of State for Commonwealth Affairs, 1964–6, he became involved in the negotiations with Ian Smith about the future of Rhodesia.

6. Maurice Foley was Labour MP for West Bromwich, 1963–73. He held junior ministerial posts, 1964–70, and then became active in Common Market institutions.

7. Shirley Summerskill, daughter of Baroness Edith Summerskill, who was Chairman of the Labour Party, and Minister of National Insurance in the 1945–51 Government. Mother and daughter were both doctors and Labour MPs, Shirley for Halifax, 1964–83, and Edith for West Fulham, 1938–55, and Warrington, 1955–61. Dr Shirley Summerskill later became Under-Secretary of State at the Home Office in the 1974–9 Government.

8. In my letter to *The Times* I wrote: 'In the case of the Labour Party it is well established that no one would accept a commission to form a government until he had been elected Leader by his colleagues in the House of Commons. Even Labour peers do not vote in such an election. If the Crown consults ministers about the choice of a successor to Mr Macmillan, it is their plain duty to tender exactly the same advice. . . Why is this advice not tendered? The answer is simple. If Conservative MPs were permitted a secret ballot the result might not please those powers within the Party, Lord Home, Lord Poole and others, who, though not themselves elected to Parliament, nor accountable for what they do, still wish a controlling voice in the choice of a Leader. For these people, it is much more convenient to conceal their influence discreetly behind the myth of a continuing Royal Prerogative. . . In this way the Conservative hierarchy, under the guise of defending obsolete royal privileges, is in effect trying to link the monarchy with its own political purposes.'

Subsequently in 1980 when the PLP was discussing the electoral college, one leading Labour ex-Minister said that the electoral college would not be acceptable to the sovereign because it would impair the Crown's absolute prerogative in choosing a Leader. This interested me because it indicated that the last resort of the Right has always been to fall back on the feudal nature of our constitution.

9. The opening of Parliament had been postponed until 12 November 1963 to allow the new Prime Minister, Lord Home, to renounce and contest Kinross and West Perthshire and thus enter the Commons. Home was (at any rate notionally) a peer and Prime Minister from the moment he was asked to form an administration to the moment when he renounced.

10. Cheddi Jagan was leader of British Guiana's Progressive People's Party, which in 1953 formed the first Government to be elected under universal suffrage. Jagan became premier in 1961. The influence of the socialist PPP and Jagan was undermined by proportional representation introduced by the British Government in 1964.

11. Rt Hon Arthur Creech-Jones, former Colonial Secretary, 1946–50, was defeated in the 1950 election and was one of the candidates short-listed alongside myself after the resignation of Sir Stafford Cripps in 1950. He subsequently returned as Labour MP for the Wakefield constituency vacated on the death of Arthur Greenwood in 1954.

12. Ted Willis, playwright and TV producer, best known for his 'Blue Lamp' series on TV, subsequently made many films and programmes. He was created a peer in 1963.

13. James Cameron was a distinguished and internationally regarded foreign correspondent renowned for his liberal views. A founder member of CND, he marched to Aldermaston with Michael Foot.

14. Guy Barnett won Dorset South for Labour unexpectedly in a by-election in 1962 caused when the Conservative MP Viscount Hinchingbrooke succeeded his father as the Earl of Sandwich. Barnett lost the seat in 1964 but was subsequently Labour MP for Greenwich 1971–1987.

15. In 1964 the Cold War was waning and it was possible to speak candidly with the Russian and Eastern European diplomats about peace and detente in Europe. The Russians were always very disappointed with the line taken by the Labour Party and, being realists, they knew they had to maintain their contacts with the Tory Government, with whom they felt they knew where they were.

16. The TSR2 was a British designed and developed swing-wing fighter bomber which was subsequently cancelled by the Labour Government when it came to power in 1964 and was replaced by an order for the American F1–11. This caused great anger in the industry and particularly in Bristol, where the TSR2 was being built. Subsequently, after devaluation, the F1–11 was cancelled as well.

17. The 11th Duke of Argyll was married four times. His third marriage was dissolved in 1963 on grounds of his wife's misconduct, in a court case which captured the public's attention. The Duchess of Argyll claimed condonation of her affairs.

18. The Robbins Committee on Higher Education was established in 1960 and the recommendations in its Report resulted in the vast expansion of higher education by creating new universities, and upgrading other higher education institutions.

19. Ted Hill was General Secretary, then President, of the Boilermakers (since the Amalgamated Society of Boilermakers, Shipwrights, Blacksmiths and Construction Workers) 1948–65 and long-standing member of the TUC General Council. He was created Lord Hill of Wivenhoe in 1967.

20. Harold Wilson's plan was to earmark a powerful conventional naval force under British command to be made available for specific international peace-keeping duties.

21. The Rivonia trials began in October 1963 against a number of anti-apartheid activists in South Africa and resulted in life sentences for eight men – six Africans, one Indian and one European. Seven men remain in prison, of whom Nelson Mandela is the most celebrated.

22. At the Colombo Conference of December 1962 representatives of Ceylon, Burma, Ghana, Indonesia, the UAR (Egypt and Syria) and Cambodia met in Sri Lanka (Ceylon) and put forward proposals for ending the border dispute between India and China.

23. Peter Blaker, a contemporary of mine at university after the War, trained as a lawyer, then joined the Foreign Office and in 1964 was elected MP for

Blackpool South and subsequently became a junior Minister in successive Conservative Governments.

24. Lord Mancroft was a junior minister in the Conservative Governments of the 1950s, and a contributor to *Punch*. Lord Boothby was the Conservative MP for Aberdeen and PPS to Churchill in the 1920s. Created a life peer in 1958.

25. George Thomson was Labour MP for Dundee East from 1952 and until 1972, when he resigned to become a Commissioner to the EEC and later chairman of IBA. He was Secretary of State at the Commonwealth Office, 1967–8.

26. David Marquand, the son of Hilary Marquand, a post-war Labour Minister, was himself elected for Sutton-in-Ashfield in 1966. He resigned in 1976 to go to the EEC. In 1981, he was one of the former Labour MPs who resigned from the Labour Party and joined the SDP.

27. Senator Barry Goldwater was a Republican who stood as a right-wing candidate against Lyndon Johnson in the 1964 Presidential Election and whose views were treated with great anxiety by the liberal Establishment in the United States. He took an aggressive Cold War stance and was rigid in the traditional views he held on economic policy. He was heavily defeated.

28. Bertrand Russell and others established the 'Who Killed Kennedy?' committee, to investigate the circumstances of Kennedy's and Lee Harvey Oswald's murders.

29. Ralph Shoenman was an American student living in London in the early 1960s, who became Bertrand Russell's 'amanuensis' through their mutual activity in CND. He subsequently became Secretary General of the Vietnam War Crimes Tribunal. Towards the end of his life, Russell repudiated Shoenman.

30. Dr Dickson (Dick) Mabon was MP for Greenock, 1955–83. He joined the SDP in 1981 and unsuccessfully fought Renfrew West for the SDP/Alliance in 1983. He held ministerial posts in the Scottish Office, 1964–70 and was my Minister of State at the Department of Energy, 1976–9.

31. The Ombudsman idea was discussed and agreed by the National Executive before the 1964 Election and subsequently came to be established by the Labour Government as the Parliamentary Commissioner for Administration.

32. Will Paynter was President of the South Wales Miners and General Secretary of the NUM 1959–68. He was a very highly trusted figure in the Labour movement and a life-long Communist.

33. Reg Prentice was a Minister in Education and Science, Public Building and Works and Overseas Development in the 1964–70 Labour Governments. He was a Labour MP from 1959–79 but in fact resigned from the Labour Government in 1976 as Minister of Overseas Development and crossed the floor to join the Conservative Party. In 1979 he was elected Conservative MP for Daventry.

34. Simonstown, in the Republic of South Africa, had been used as a base by the Royal Navy for many years and remained a British naval base right into the 1970s, even though South Africa had been expelled from the Commonwealth. This issue of joint South African-British naval manoeuvres

continued to be controversial right up until the Labour Government of 1974 was formed.

35. In early August 1964 President Johnson alleged that a US destroyer had been the subject of two unprovoked torpedo attacks by North Vietnamese patrol boats and he used this as an excuse to begin the bombing of North Vietnam. It later emerged that the attacks as described did not take place. The affair became known as the Gulf of Tonkin incident.

The Turkish Air Force attacked Greek Cypriot targets in Northern Cyprus in August 1964 after fighting had broken out between Greek and Turkish Cypriot communities.

36. Norman St John Stevas, a barrister and writer, became Conservative MP for Chelmsford in 1964. He was Minister of State for the Arts 1973–4, and Leader of the House and Minister for the Arts, 1979, from which posts he was dismissed by Margaret Thatcher in 1981.

37. This programme was an early contribution to the changing concept of childbirth, directed towards mother and child and away from medical procedure. Dr Tizard was a professor of paediatrics and Professor Morris was also a pioneer of these new ideas.

38. The *Sun* was, in fact, a re-naming of the old *Daily Herald* after Odhams press took responsibility from the trust that had previously run it. It was considered important that the first issue of the *Sun* should come out just before the 1964 Election because it was avowedly pro-Labour but later it was bought by Rupert Murdoch, turned into a tabloid and became a viciously anti-Labour newspaper. However, to this day, there are still people who believe that the *Sun* is a Labour paper because of its original links with the *Daily Herald*.

39. Brian Abel-Smith was a consultant to the UN and the World Health Organisation in the late 1950s and early 1960s, and became Professor of Social Administration at the London School of Economics in 1965. He was very active in hospital administration and was adviser to the Department of Health and Social Security in 1964 and 1974 Labour Governments.

40. Peter Parker had been a Labour candidate in 1951 for Bedford and was one of a group of industrialists and businessmen in 1964 sympathetic to a Labour Government. Among many posts held, he was chairman of British Railways Board 1976–83. Wilfrid Brown was a Labour industrialist, managing director and chairman of Glacier Metal Co. Ltd, who was created a life peer in 1964 and was Minister of State at the Board of Trade 1966–70.

3
Postmaster General
October 1964–August 1965

Sunday 18 October
One of the oldest jokes in politics is about hopeful candidates for office who stay by their telephones when a new Government is formed, just like husbands waiting for their wives to have their first babies. For both it's awful.

The TV and news bulletins kept describing people who were turning up at Number 10 and I was getting gloomier and gloomier and planning a completely new life. Then at 4.45 Number 10 phoned. Would I stand by for tonight or tomorrow morning. It was a great relief. I worked till about 2 am, reading all the Post Office stuff that I had collected and just couldn't go to sleep.

Monday 19 October
Up early and still waiting for the phone and still hearing of other people going down to Downing Street. I had completely given up hope again. Then at 10.55 am the phone rang and I was summoned.

There was a huge crowd of photographers outside and inside Bob Mellish and Lord Bowden were waiting. Finally I went in and there was Harold looking extremely relaxed. I shook him by the hand and we had a chat about the general situation and then he said, 'By the way, I want you to take the Post Office. I am giving you Joe Slater as Assistant PMG. Then in about eighteen months time I shall be reshuffling the Government and you will be in the Cabinet.'

Then he beckoned me over to the window, and pointed into the garden. 'Look at that. It's the last of Reggie Maudling's* luggage going,' he said with schoolboy enthusiasm. He told me he didn't know yet whether PMGs were Privy Councillors but that I would be one if it was customary.

I asked his Private Secretary to ring the Post Office and tell them I was coming. I told the press that all I could say was that I *hadn't* been made a peer. I then went to a call box and phoned Mother, came home and after lunch telephoned the Post Office and asked for the PMG's office. 'What's your name?' asked a gruff voice. I gave it

* Chancellor of the Exchequer, 1962–4 and Conservative MP for Barnet and Chipping Barnet, 1950–79.

and a few minutes later came a different and oily voice:' Good afternoon, PMG. I think the DG wants to speak to you.' A minute later the Director General came on the phone, said he had a lunch appointment and would come to see me at 3 o'clock. I said I would like a car to take me there immediately.

At 1.30 an enormous limousine arrived with a uniformed chauffeur and Mr Henry Tilling, my principal Private Secretary, pale and tense and drawn. In the car he told me that his great interest was heraldry and orders and decorations – not the best start. He said there were no decisions waiting to be taken and that the Post Office ticked over quietly. Apparently Bevins* made a practice of being in his office from 10 am to 2 pm on Tuesdays, Wednesdays and Thursdays only and had not been there for a month or more.†

At the GPO headquarters at St Martins-le-Grand a man in a full-length red frock coat and top hat opened the door and a messenger opened my car door and I went into a high-ceilinged office containing a desk, a conference table and a television set. I sat down and Mr Tilling said, 'How do you want to play it?' as if it were a game of cards. 'I want the names of all the people in my private office, doorkeepers, messengers, typists and clerks,' I said. He gave me the names and I wrote them down. I told him I also wanted a memorandum on the powers of the Postmaster General. Then we talked until the Director General arrived.

The DG, Sir Ronald German, came in. I had wished him a happy birthday on the telephone earlier, based on the preparatory work I had done on the Post Office last July when I photostated the principal officials from *Whitaker's Almanac* and *Who's Who*. I said I would like to see all the directors at ten-minute intervals throughout the afternoon.

The Director General described the Post Office as a business comparable to a nationalised industry. He said that the finances were on a sound basis but that there was a case for increased charges which had been delayed by the outgoing Government and that he was in favour of making these soon. The principal financial problem was to get the Treasury to agree to a bigger capital programme.

He suggested reconstituting the Post Office Board on a smaller

---

* J. R. [Reginald] Bevins, my Conservative predecessor as Postmaster General, 1959–64, and MP for Liverpool, Toxteth, 1950–64.

†This and later references to Reginald Bevins' working pattern are as reported to me and noted down in my diary at that time, but I now accept Mr Bevins' assurance that he spent the rest of his working day at the House of Commons and that he also went to the Post Office on Mondays on returning from his Liverpool constituency: he had not been at the Post Office for the previous month because he was defending his Liverpool–Toxteth constituency in the General Election. It was and is not my intention to throw doubt on his record as a conscientious Conservative Postmaster General.

scale and abandoning the larger Board which had not met and was really a formality. He also thought that the Assistant Postmaster General should be given specific responsibilities and ultimate disciplinary power.

The directors of Post Office departments came in and the DG stayed with each of them. He had expressed this desire and I couldn't very well say no. But in fact he simply talked about each of them in their presence and it was hard to get anything out of them at all. I thought they all looked slightly pale and anxious. I don't think they expected me to work any harder than Bevins and were surprised to find that I wanted to know what was going on and that I had done so much preparation.

They had all read my *Guardian* article on the Post Office* and were bracing themselves for the first changes which they imagined I would make. I touched on one or two of these things but had not the slightest intention of showing my hand at this stage. This, I think, made the suspense worse for them.

I discovered I have a gigantic industry to control, employing about 390,000 people. Among the departments are the Post Office Savings Bank, which is the biggest bank in the world by far, having deposits totalling £6,200 million. As PMG I also have a private railway line in London and am in Space through the International Satellite Progamme. In American terms I am PMG, chairman of the Federal Communications Commission, president of the largest bank and president of the Bell Telephone Company all rolled into one. It is quite a job, and except for buildings, wage levels and the capital investment programme, it is entirely free from Treasury control.

Toby O'Brien, Public Relations Officer, came with a list of questions the press were likely to ask. I told him that I was not prepared to make a statement at the moment as I first had to work myself into the job but would meet the press later. He thought that I should meet the industrial correspondents soon. I said I would also like to meet the scientific correspondents and the women's correspondents, since any attempt to stimulate the use of the telephone would depend to a great extent on women feeling that a telephone was as useful and desirable as a washing machine or an electric mixer.

Mr Peter Lillicrap, director of Radio Services, described his responsibilities, namely broadcasting, independent television, frequency allocations and ship-to-shore broadcasting. He said that legislation was at an advanced stage of development on the radio pirate ships. A Convention is to be signed soon and when this is through, our

* 'The Future of the Post Office', *Guardian*, 19 July 1964, reproduced in *The Regeneration of Britain*, 1965.

legislation could be put forward for implementing it. It is based on the idea of making it illegal to advertise or to supply pirates with certain services.

He raised the question of the BBC licence fee, which he thought the BBC would want to increase to £6. He also said the question of pay-television and local broadcasting would be sure to come up soon.

Colonel Donald McMillan, Director of External Telecommunications Executive, is a member of the International Satellite Committee in Washington which he or his deputy attends every month. Britain's contribution is £8 million a year: still only a quarter of what the Americans are paying in.

With regard to satellite tracking stations, our Gonhilly station was very successful, being more accurate than the American station and costing only a quarter as much. He said that Britain had scope here for selling complete tracking stations abroad but that industry was slow in getting on with the job. I raised with him the possibility that the Post Office might go into this as part of a consortium including some big contractors – a mixed enterprise. He seemed interested and this is something to watch.

After the directors had gone I called in my typist, Mrs Funnell, a nice Irish woman. It was only with her that I was able to unbend at all and say how strange it was, and how I should rely on her to help.

I left at 7.15, having told Mr Atkins, my principal messenger, that I should be bringing a pint mug, a packet of teabags, a big spoon and a box of saccharin to save him the absurdity of making me trays of tea.

I then went to Transport House where Caroline was waiting for the celebration party. Harold was there and we had a pleasant talk in which he reiterated that Ministers were to be seen but not heard at the moment. He didn't want a whole host of press conferences. He also told me about the legislation that used to force a PM to have a high proportion of his Ministers in the Lords. He said the press had noticed that all his early appointments had been in the Commons and had said, 'We presume, Prime Minister, that your PMG will be a peer.' Harold said he had replied, 'You don't know how funny that is.' Later at the party, he told this story amid general laughter.

I told them about my final word to Sir Ronald German after we had had about three hours together at the Post Office. 'Sir Ronald, you have been telling me about your job, and I want now to tell you about mine. Would you read this?' I said, and I handed him a copy of our manifesto. He picked it up with a look of infinite disgust and carried it out of the office with two fingers. Later I shall examine him on it to see if he noticed the many points in it that relate to the work of the GPO. I also intend to send copies to all the other directors, drawing their attention to certain passages and asking them to consider how the points can be implemented.

Afterwards, I came home with Peter Shore who is Harold's PPS at Number 10 – a key job which will be a great help to me.

Still couldn't sleep tonight with excitement.

The General Post Office, as it was then called, was one of the oldest and biggest public enterprises in Britain and, with responsibilities ranging from posts and telephones to broadcasting and satellites, was effectively a ministry of communications. But the restraints imposed on the GPO and the apathy into which it had fallen, mainly as a result of its anomalous position as a Civil Service department instead of an independent public corporation, were immediately apparent. My overall objective therefore was to restructure internal management and establish a new public status for the Post Office, working from the outset in the closest relations with the Post Office unions.

On appointment as Postmaster General, one major consideration – which reflected the economic crisis inherited by Labour generally – was the reduction of the Post Office deficit which had been concealed by the outgoing Government, through raising postal charges (tariffs), through mechanisation and in departmental economies. At the same time, demand for telephones was explosive and a capital investment programme was required to meet this and to exploit the growth area of computers and data processing – the beginnings of 'information technology'.

Beside the dominating financial deficit, there were certain compelling problems confronting the Post Office in October 1964.

In the first place was the persistent illegal activity of pirate radios. In the early sixties, radio stations such as Radio Caroline and Radio London began to appear around the shores of Britain. These were run by fly-by-night companies which employed a crew to man either a moored ship or some offshore structure from which was broadcast continuous pop music, interspersed with advertisements, and introduced by disc-jockeys who became household names amongst their mainly young audience in Britain. The outgoing Conservative Government, realising that pirate radio was popular and having some sympathy with piratical entrepreneurs of that kind, decided to do nothing about it and the problem landed on my plate when Labour came to power. A narrow majority and the likelihood of another Election made it a sensitive and difficult subject.

The main argument used by the Post Office against pirate radio stations was that they were breaching the international allocation of wavelengths, thereby causing interference on the Continent, and Continental countries were threatening to take over some of the wavelengths allocated to us. This would interfere with our domestic transmissions if we did not take action. It was also argued that essential police, fire and hospital services were being interfered with by pirate radio broadcasts. In addition, the Musicians' Union and some of the record companies naturally objected to loss of royalties. The Ministry of Defence were the owners of some of the offshore structures built during the war that were now being used for the pirate radio stations but expressed no interest in taking action; the Board of Trade said that although they had responsibilities for shipping, they had no disciplinary powers outside the three-mile territorial limit.

In dealing with the pirates one line of attack was to use the popularity of the pirate stations to persuade the BBC to reschedule its own programmes so as to provide a channel of continuous popular music comparable to the pirates. BBC radio was at this time divided into three channels – the Home Service, the Light Programme and the Third Programme – and, with its paternalistic attitude, declined to do that and said it was not there to pander to popular taste. Ultimately, the pirate radio stations had the effect of altering the pattern of broadcasting at home, not only in the BBC but, of course, in forming a beach-head for the development of commercially-owned radio, to which I was opposed.

In addition to sound broadcasting problems, I was confronted with important decisions over television broadcasting. In October 1964 there were three television channels in existence – BBC1, BBC2 (opened in April 1964 on a very small scale) and independent television, comprising commercial companies such as ATV. A fourth television channel was being considered. There was the problem of raising the BBC licence fee from £4. A decision as to which channel should be allocated, in part, to the new University of the Air had to be made by the Post Office and the Ministry of Education, within which Jennie Lee became the Minister responsible. In addition, licences had been granted by my predecessor to five groups for experiments in pay-television. Under this system viewers would be charged for watching programmes transmitted through a particular cable network and, of course, the BBC and ITV were doubtful about this potential threat. There was also a decision to be made on which colour television system Britain should adopt.

The Post Office Giro Bank was a major innovation of the Post Office during the 1964–70 Labour Government. Giro banks had been instituted in many Continental countries as early as the nineteenth century. These Giro banks, which were popular banks operating through Post Office counters, provided working people who did not have commercial bank accounts with a convenient way of transmitting and accounting their money. However, the British banks had always resented the idea of a Giro bank in Britain because they saw it as a threat to their own appeal to working class customers and since the Treasury represents banking interests inside Government, the Treasury had killed off earlier attempts to bring it about.

One of the other preoccupations of my first months as Postmaster General was stamp policy. The GPO had a narrow and limited view about commemorative stamp issues which were primarily connected with State or Commonwealth occasions and one or two other international events. Above all, they were determined that British stamps should not become 'cheap and flashy' which was the way they interpreted the mass of modern design that was emerging all over the world. Indeed it was impossible to do a good design when about a third of all commemorative stamps were occupied by a large portrait of the Queen which, in effect, involved attaching a regular stamp to the side of every commemorative stamp, thus destroying any integration of design or free-flowing picture across the whole. I therefore urged a more imaginative policy, which was greatly resented, and invited designers to put in their own designs for public display. The Stamp Advisory Committee under Sir Kenneth Clark argued that the Queen herself did not wish to appear with faces of other people, however famous, who were dead. The ordinary, or definitive, postage stamp had always carried the monarch's portrait and because Britain was the originator of postage stamps, it was and is the only country whose stamps do not bear the country's name.

Historically, sovereigns in this country have been intensely interested in the design of coinage, stamps and all medals issued. It is reported that after the Victory service that took place in St Paul's Cathedral in 1945, King George VI, on leaving the Cathedral, noticed a retired Admiral wearing on his uniform decorations that had been given to him by the Emperor of Japan after the First World War and stopped and rebuked him for this. The poor old Admiral had retired long before the war against our former ally, Japan, broke out in 1941 and had never thought to have his Japanese medals removed.

Tuesday 20 October

My car arrived at 8.15 am and I was at the Office by 8.40, hours before anyone else. Appointments had been made with several more directors.

Mr George Downes, Director, London Postal Region, has 52,000 postmen under him and of course has felt the main impact of the recent pay dispute. We discussed the need for improved working conditions for London postmen, which he said were very bad in parts. He also said it was the custom to ask the Lord Mayor of London and the Sheriffs to Mount Pleasant just before Christmas. I said I was in favour of also inviting the Chairman of the LCC [London County Council] and would like to do this. The Director General, who was sitting in, said this might not be popular with the Lord Mayor.

Mr Henry Smart, Director of Savings, came in and told me he was the biggest banker in the world, holding more than £6,200 million in deposits. I asked about establishing Giro and got the impression that he personally was in favour of this but that the real opposition came from two sources: firstly from the postal order and inland money order departments of the Post Office which would lose business; secondly, from the Joint Stock Banks who would feel the hot breath of Giro competition. This is, I presume, why Bevins did not do it. Mr Smart promised to put a paper in on this and I got the feeling he would like the chance to establish Giro – provided the system could be computerised from the outset.

The DG and Tilling raised with me the question of my PPS – as I had told them that I intended to invite Charles Morris, MP for

Openshaw, who is young and competent, and from the Union of Post Office Workers. The DG has no business whatsoever to comment on this, but he said he thought it would be undesirable as it would lead to a conflict of loyalties for Morris and would make the other unions jealous. I pointed out that Marples, when Minister of Transport, had awarded large contracts to his own company in which his wife retained shareholdings even if he did not. I said conflict of interest was a matter that could never be resolved except on the basis of a man's integrity.

The next point was the suggestion that I should follow the usual practice and have a sherry party for the thirty-six unions that deal with the Post Office. I said I would not do this but would, instead, invite them to an all-morning working conference and we would have tea and biscuits at 11. With obsequious frowns, this was set in motion.

Just before lunchtime fifty press and TV photographers came and took pictures of me at my desk in my shirtsleeves. The room is very warm and I had taken off my coat as I always do. Indeed, last night I met all the directors in braces, with my tie loose at the neck. This is to be a workshop not a front parlour.

I lunched in the staff canteen and was told that this was the first time a PMG had ever done so. Naturally nobody recognised me. Tilling warned me that someone might come up to him and ask, 'Tell us, what's he like?' In fact no one did.

Wednesday 21 October

At the office at 9 and phoned Charles Morris to ask him to be my PPS, which he willingly accepted.

The DG came in and I told him that I had considered his points but could not accept them. He was somewhat shaken. He then advised me not to hobnob with the unions and I pointed out that personal friendship would not interfere with the exercise of my responsibilities and I could not believe that Mr Bevins had been asked not to get too friendly with the chairman of a large electronics firm which might be doing business with the Post Office.

The fact is that my private office is utterly decayed and does practically nothing. I put a point to Mr Hesketh, the Parliamentary clerk, yesterday about expanding the explanatory memoranda on Bills and possibly furnishing MPs with duplicated notes on committee points to help them, and to shorten debates. Hesketh, who was sitting doing nothing in his office when I asked him about this, returned a memorandum late last night saying it couldn't be done. I called him in this morning, thanked him for his note, told him it could be done, and asked him to prepare a memorandum showing how. He had been chattering in the outer office where the private staff and even the DG are huddled together like a lot of cattle in the Chicago stockyards.

The only real welcome I had was from two old London postmen who recognised me as I was stuck in a traffic jam this morning, and when I wound down the window put in their hands and shook mine warmly, wished me luck and said how delighted they were. These are the guys who matter.

Joe Slater turned up yesterday morning and I gave him a chance to sit in with all the people I met. In the afternoon he came in again for an hour of pure tea-room gossip. He's a miner and a lay preacher. He's thrilled to have been appointed and touchingly glad that it's me.

At 11.30 I had to go to the Privy Council Office for a rehearsal of the ceremony of admission into the Privy Council. We were greeted by the most awful stoogey-looking people, real Crown Office–House of Lords types. Among those there were Peggy Herbison, Kenneth Robinson, Roy Jenkins, Charlie Pannell and Elwyn Jones. I asked Elwyn if he was going to be knighted. He said yes, and I said, 'I'm sorry to hear it.'

The rehearsal was terribly degrading as we were told that we had to kneel on a footstool before the Queen and assent to the Privy Council oath which had a real Mau-Mau quality. Charlie and I chattered during the rehearsal and tried to look as if we were not taking it too seriously. I'm afraid the officials were profoundly shocked. I made no attempt to conceal my feelings.

Then, each in our own limousines, we were driven to Buckingham Palace where we had to be by 12.30. There an officer in breeches, spurs, a sword and full Court dress greeted us and we went into a drawing room. Herbert Bowden, the new Lord President of the Council, was there, and I asked him whether I had to go through with it, as I did find the terms of the oath so degrading and distasteful. He said that he knew I would but that I had to do it because if I didn't I couldn't get Cabinet papers. Many of the others with me felt the same but I suppose it was particularly unpleasant for me. Charlie said I ought to do it for the sake of the Party and it was really for that reason that I did. I have always wanted to be a Privy Councillor because it is the greatest honour in the parliamentary field but when it came to it, it was terrible.

We were summoned in one by one to the Queen's drawing room and she shook us by the hand. Then we stood in a row and the oath was administered to those who were swearing, whereas Kenneth Robinson, Charlie Pannell and I affirmed. I think they are atheists. I did it because I disapprove of a religious oath for any but religious purposes and because I wanted to pay a tribute to Charles Bradlaugh who had fought four elections to establish this right.

We then went up to the Queen one after another, kneeling and picking up her hand and kissing it, and then bowing. I did the most miniature bow ever seen and returned to my line. When it was over she made a couple of remarks and we all walked by and shook hands. After that I had the oath of the Postmaster General administered to me. I left the Palace boiling with indignation and feeling that this was an attempt to impose tribal magic and personal loyalty on people whose real duty was only to their electors.

Lunch at home. I didn't go back to the Post Office early because Bevins was going to say goodbye. I thought he would prefer not to have me there. I went in at about 5pm and they told me Bevins was broken up at having lost his position and his job as MP in one fell swoop. I decided to write him a little personal note.

Thursday 22 October
At 8.30 this morning, I saw Mr Eric Shepherd, Director of Finance and Accounts, and Mr Bill Ryland, Director of Inland Telecommunications. Ryland is a very bright man. He told me that the big problem was to overcome the arrears due to the restriction of years gone by; that there was a buoyant demand for telecommunications and that telephones were becoming progressively cheaper as prices were rising less than for other services.

We discussed computers which are already being used for technical billing purposes but there is no dynamic operational planning in existence, covering the service as a whole. This might be associated with a forward planning unit of the Post Office entirely divorced from any departmental responsibilities and free to range over the whole field; especially studying technical developments, making statistical calculations and reporting from time to time on what is likely to happen.

Ryland also talked about the role of the telecommunications network in meeting the requirements of industry for the transmission of data. In this connection I suggested that we might consider developing within the Post Office a computer service which small firms could use to do their calculations on a rental basis. Altogether a most stimulating discussion.

Eric Shepherd is responsible for the accounts, which includes postal orders and money orders, and is a general financial adviser under Sir Kenneth Anderson. I asked him to prepare a paper on increased postal charges, arguing that if charges were to be increased, they should be done soon.

Ron Smith, General Secretary of the Union of Post Office Workers, came to lunch. I told him how rarely Bevins visited the Office and he said that explained a great deal. We talked for nearly three hours, having lunched together in the staff cafeteria. I have met him once or twice but this was the first proper chance for talk. He is a powerful man physically and temperamentally and one felt one was rubbing against granite. He wants me to meet the UPW Executive soon – with my wife – for lunch and an informal chat.

We had a completely informal discussion about pay and conditions. He said that the work conditions of postmen were very poor, especially in the older offices such as Mount Pleasant. All the capital investment had gone into telecommunications and the postal services were the Cinderella left to rot.

On pay we discussed the difficulty of establishing comparability since the postman does four jobs – all of them responsible. He is a sorter of letters, involving a high degree of attention and care. He is a driver of vehicles. He is a deliverer of letters – and in the last capacity almost a social service worker, in country areas at least. Because the postman does not adopt restrictive practices and does them all must not lead to his being judged simply as a manual worker to be compared with any other lower paid worker.

Smith raised the question of establishing an informal committee, to be known as 'The Postmaster General's Informal Committee', bringing in the principal union figures with the PMG to discuss forward policy. He said that Ness Edwards* had planned this years ago and that it tied in well with the Guild Socialist ideas with which the UPW was historically associated. It tied up in my own mind with the future of the Post Office Advisory Council, which is moribund if not actually defunct and which it had been suggested should be reconstituted on an entirely new basis. Ron Smith said he thought this might be the right way of bringing the union leaders in.

I asked him what his attitude would be to a slight formalisation of the role of postman as social service worker – perhaps by equipping him with a guide to local social services which he would be able to use if asked for advice by the people whose homes he served and who might need help. Smith thought this had merit, provided we did it slowly and did not create the idea of a snooping service always nosing around to see if Mrs Buggins was having a row with her husband and needed the services of the Marriage Guidance Bureau!

This afternoon Toby O'Brien came in and we had a talk about public relations. I'm arranging that the acknowledgement of all letters addressed to the Postmaster General is in a facsimile of my hand-writing and also that the clerks-in-waiting have a telephone answering

* Former Labour Postmaster General, 1950–1, MP for Caerphilly, 1939–68.

machine with a short message from me, asking callers if they would be so kind as to leave a note of their complaint so that it can be dealt with.

Home a little bit earlier as it was Prize Day at Holland Park School. It was a wonderful evening.

Friday 23 October
I took a taxi to the Post Office this morning as I discovered that Mr Wilson, my driver, has to leave home at 6.45 in order to be here at 8.30.

I am anxious to make some economies in the huge personal staff to offset the expenditure that the Office is going to incur in providing me with a dictating machine and modern office equipment. I had a talk to Mr Tilling about this today and he told me that as we were in effect treated as a nationalised industry we were free from Treasury control and he was rather in favour of us organising ourselves along modern lines. There is no reason why the Post Office should be lumbering on using the techniques and filing systems of the twenties. It is a modern communication industry and should reflect this in its practice.

I drafted a message to all Post Office staff which is to be circulated to them. This is really in the nature of an 'Order of the Day'. Tilling suggested toning it down slightly as he thought it too heady a draught of wine. I agreed. After three or four days I am getting to like Tilling. He comes from a Post Office family – like so many people who work here – is free from the usual Civil Service rubbish and has a very dry sense of humour. His caution is also a good thing in damping down my over-enthusiasm.

I had Charles Smith of the Post Office Engineering Union to lunch and we had two hours' talk. He was an MP for Colchester from 1945–50 and I was much struck by his imagination and energy. Among the points he raised were these: the quality of the telephone service is falling partly because of shortage of equipment, partly because of shortage of staff especially in London, and partly because maintenance quality has been cut by economy measures. This is destructive of staff morale. Sales aggressiveness is required and the market research work should be extended and developed.

He said that the GPO is a family business with many hereditary postal workers but it is too inbred and would benefit by borrowing good people – perhaps even exchanges with universities. More GPO people should have a chance of going abroad. The Swedish telephone service is excellent, so is the Swiss, and no doubt the Bell Telephone Company would be interested in having some visitors from Britain.

Post Office factories have been allowed to degenerate into repair

depots since 1951, because of the pressure of private business interests. Post Office technical maintenance has recently been sub-
contracted out, which is reasonable if Post Office staff are being
overstretched, but in general is not desirable.

On monopolies and price rings in the supply of Post Office equipment, Smith hopes I will ask for a report and he said that the
Pye Company (excluded from these agreements) had prepared an
interesting report attacking them.

The POEU, and Smith, pride themselves on speaking out frankly
on Post Office matters. I said I understood and appreciated it. Smith
added that the POEU affiliation to the Labour Party was still only
a year old and it was especially important that he should be able to
maintain an independent attitude.

This afternoon Mrs Indira Gandhi and the Indian High
Commissioner, Dr Mehta, came to see me for about twenty minutes.
She is the Minister of Communications and Information and we had
some talk about educational TV but she took little interest in the
conversation and seemed so anxious to go that I didn't seek to detain
her.

Saturday 24 October
Began sorting out all the papers in my office. I intend to bombard
each department with a barrage of minutes and requests and questions and see how things work. I must also begin to do some serious
basic thinking about major fields of policy – like broadcasting – for
which I am responsible. Meanwhile I must somehow try to clear the
tons of mail which are waiting for me to handle.

Sunday 25 October
John Allen came to see me. He is now a civil servant at Number 10.
He, George Wigg and Marcia have lunch with Harold Wilson every
day so he does provide an excellent channel of communication to the
PM. We agreed that it would be a good thing to try to restart the
lunches with Peter Shore, Dick Crossman, Tommy Balogh, John
Allen and myself. We are aiming to have the first one this Wednesday.
I feel terribly isolated at the Post Office and don't know what's going
on elsewhere.

John and I agreed that we both feel weighted down by the security
side. We all had the feeling our letters were being opened and our
telephones bugged – though we suspected the security people were
as inefficient as the government departments over which we had some
control.

Then there was the secondary problem as to whether the Civil
Service staff were politically reliable. Obviously one can safely send

a Cabinet paper through the secret channels and know it won't reach the press, but are we so sure that some political intelligence isn't being leaked through to the Tories? John said that the secretaries working at Number 10 were deb types and he wouldn't trust any of them. It's all highly complicated and we shall just have to see how it works. I am going to get a scrambler put on my telephone at home so that I can have a discussion with people without feeling that it's an open line.

Monday 26 October
Up at 6.30 and dictated a lot of letters before breakfast. Left for the Office at 8.30. At 10.30 the radio announced the economic measures being taken by the Government and soon afterwards I went to the Director General's meeting. Present were the top directorate and they explained what they did at these meetings. It is perfectly obvious that Bevins has done nothing since he was PMG – not having met the directorate for years and having allowed both the Post Office and the Post Office policy committees to fall into disuse. I listened to all this and then gave them eight points of Post Office policy which I wished to be reviewed.

1. Broadcasting policy, covering the BBC licence fee, local broadcasting, the future of colour television and the provision of facilities for the possible introduction of the University of the Air.

2. Telecommunications generally, to include a review of the investment programme and charges. Under this heading I have included the possibility of establishing a data network serving industry.

3. Postal services: the most urgent problem here is charges. I should also like to have a further look to see if we could give greater impetus to mechanisation and review the services offered.

4. The Prime Minister and other Ministers have expressed an interest in the Giro and we shall have to look at this in detail.

5. Post Office administration: the proper constitution of the Post Office Board, the role and membership of the Advisory Council, the possible establishment of a directorate of forward planning and the relationship between the Post Office and the House of Commons.

6. In view of the unhappy experience of the postal strike last year, I think staff relations merit special consideration.

7. The work of the Post Office in relationship to the work of the new Government generally. I am sending round a copy of the Election manifesto with passages marked that have some bearing on our work. I have included the possibility of diversifying our activities to be sure that we are always in at points of growth.

8. Finally the new economic measures announced by the Government will affect us and we shall have to study their implications carefully.

At 12 o'clock my new PPS, Charles Morris, came to see me, a very keen guy who began as a telegraph boy and has built himself up into a person of great authority and integrity and intelligence. We had lunch together in the staff cafeteria.

At 2.30 Sir Kenneth Anderson came to see me about Giro. He told me the background to the story. Immediately after the Radcliffe Committee had reported[1], a major study was undertaken on the basis that the Post Office might start a Giro service computerised from the beginning. By 1960 a report had been prepared and the Post Office and Bevins wanted it to go to Cabinet, and a modified version of it published. However the Cabinet delayed it and would not allow anything to be published. This was because of the opposition of the Joint Stock Banks and not because of any opposition among the Post Office staff. Finally on 4 March 1963, Ray Mawby, the then Assistant Postmaster General, was put up to kill the idea, which he did.

Anderson raised a number of points in connection with our decision to review it again. It would take four to five years to carry through. The planning would involve 500-man years. The capital would be £4–5 million and a staff of between 3,000 and 5,000 would be necessary. The big problem is whether we could get the big money through our Giro. It is unlikely that a Giro would produce much new business but it might succeed in getting business from the banks and replacing GPO and other Government remittances. Sir Kenneth thought that the banks would fight it bitterly and that if the Giro were to succeed it would have to be competitive in price and service. It would require the goodwill of the banks and it would be ludicrous if it were separated from the Joint Stock Bank clearing houses. We certainly could not afford to fight the banks. I formed the impression that he was open-minded on it but not all that enthusiastic.

After signing letters I went to the PLP meeting at Church House. Ted Short was in the chair and Clem and Harold were warmly cheered as they entered. Manny Shinwell and Jim Griffiths moved and seconded Harold's formal election as Leader of the Party and this was carried unanimously. So was George Brown's election as Deputy Leader, moved by Herbert Bowden.

Then Harold made a short speech in which he said we had a very tough job. He said he realised it was a difficult job to form an administration. He was sorry about people who had been left out – but we were all on trial. Herbert Bowden then dealt with Party organisation, including the establishment of a liaison committee. Ted Short talked about Party discipline and the need to maintain rigid control to be sure we held our tiny majority.

Home about 8 o'clock, listened to Harold on TV and then worked till 11.30.

Tuesday 27 October
My first job this morning was the security briefing given by Mr Thistlethwaite from the security services. With him was the Director General, Tilling and Joe Slater. We had about an hour and a half and he went through all the material that is in the security services' book, *Their Trade is Treason*. It was a most unattractive hour and a half. This man, though very intelligent, was deep in the heart of the James Bond world and whatever else one may think about espionage and counter-espionage there is no morality in it either way.

After he'd gone I went on working at minutes, and turned up for the first meeting of the new Parliament. It was funny to be on the Government side of the House again after thirteen years and there were many new faces on both sides that I didn't recognise. We elected the Speaker after the usual hypocritical speeches about his defence of the rights of individual members against the power of the Government. He was the man who had ordered me to be kept out by force and I found it hard to stomach.

Wednesday 28 October
To the National Executive this morning and as my car went past Buckingham Palace we overtook Quintin Hogg in a bowler hat on one of those Moulton bikes. He looked ridiculous.

I had a word with Peter Shore afterwards and told him about the Post Office. Not only had Bevins turned up for only three days a week and the postal services allowed to go into decay, but he removed from the annual report in July the page prepared by the director of Finance and Accounts which had forecast a deficit of £100 million over the next few years in the postal services. This is the GPO equivalent of the balance of trade crisis which the Tories concealed before the Election.

The Fabian Society phoned to say that as Tommy Balogh had got a Government job he would have to resign the vice-chairmanship of the Society and so I shall now be vice-chairman and shall be elected chairman in December. This will be an additional chore, but it is an important year to have the job.

Frank Longford wrote and said he wanted Charles Hobson* to be my spokesman in the Lords. I rang him and persuaded him to agree to allocate C. P. Snow as well. A £6,000 mailbag has been lost and so I called in Mr Osmond, the head of the Investigation Department.

Thursday 29 October
This morning I invited eighteen of the clerks-in-waiting to come to see me with the press officers. I did this because they bear the brunt of public criticism of the Post Office, have wide experience of the sort of telephone complaints and queries that come in and do a job which is a real chore.

I was told that about one-third of telephone queries were from the press and one of the difficulties was that Fleet Street was at its most active between 6 o'clock and midnight, when the clerk-in-waiting is responsible, the press officer having gone off duty.

They made some helpful suggestions and what is necessary is this. The job should be changed from being clerk-in-waiting, which is entirely Dickensian and inappropriate, to senior duty officer. A telephone answering machine should be installed for an experimental period on to which I shall record a short message and the senior duty officer will then invite people to record their complaints on to the machine, to be dealt with as part of the PMG's correspondence next morning. I was told that this was the first time that the clerks-in-waiting had met the PMG in person or had been in his office.

Friday 30 October
I began drafting minutes which I am going to send out to get my ideas launched in the Office.

This afternoon I had a series of people to see me, including Mr T. H. Southerton, Controller of Factories and Dr Long, the Chief Medical Adviser. Mr Southerton is an engineer and he is in charge of the eight Post Office factories which employ 2,500 people. 85 per cent of the work of these factories is the repair and overhaul of telephone equipment. At the turn of the century the Post Office factories were major manufacturing establishments. By about 1910 the manufacturing had begun to ease off and though the factories did some manufacturing during the last war – because of the need for national self-sufficiency – in 1951 manufacturing more or less stopped, partly as a result I am told of a select committee report. In 1947 and 1948 Nye Bevan as Minister of Health got his new Health

* Former Labour MP for Wembley North, 1945–50 and Keighley, 1950–9. Created life peer in 1963 (died in 1966).

Mervyn Stockwood, the flamboyant Bishop of Southwark, who was a vicar in Bristol and member of the General Management Committee of the Bristol South-East Labour Party which first selected me as its candidate in 1950

Gaitskell speaking at a rally in Glasgow faces angry heckling from CND demonstrators

With five other Labour MPs advertising a rally in 1954 for the H-Bomb National Committee, forerunner of CND. *Left to right:* George Craddock, Fenner Brockway, Sir Richard Acland, Tony Greenwood and George Thomas

With Jo Grimond during my 1961 by-election campaign in Bristol. Grimond, the son-in-law of Violet Bonham Carter, was replaced as Leader of the Liberals in 1967

On the buses: canvassing a captive audience on a Bristol Corporation Bus during the 1963 by-election

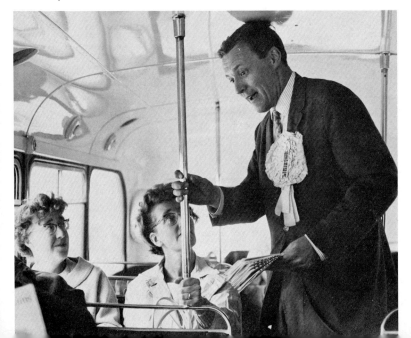

John Profumo, Secretary of State for War 1960-3, receiving a supporting hand from his wife, actress Valerie Hobson

With Caroline outside the Commons with the Instrument of Disclaimer — signed on 31 July, 1963 after over ten years of campaigning

Left: Back to the Commons: in August 1963, following the renunciation, I was re-elected as MP for Bristol South-East and carried from the count to the Labour Party headquarters, opening the way for Home and Hailsham

A triumphant Lord Home outside Number 10 on his appointment as Prime Minister in October 1963. Within five days he had disclaimed his six peerages to become Sir Alec Douglas-Home, and the following month fought and won a by-election taking him back to the House of Commons

Left: Planning the Campaign with Wilson in 1964

Gerald Gardiner, Labour's Lord Chancellor, whose attempt to see his own MI5 file was thwarted by the security services

Tony Crosland, who was Minister of State for Economic Affairs 1964-5 before moving to Education as Secretary of State

August 1964: on holiday in Rimini just before the onset of Labour's electoral campaign

Service deaf-aid designed by the GPO, though the PO factories did not actually produce them.

A number of questions arose from this discussion. Would it be possible for Post Office factories to build and manufacture some equipment now bought from outside contractors? Should the factories be allowed to go in for normal trade – selling the goods that it now manufactures, burglar alarms for example. It certainly will be the policy of the new Government to see how our nationalised industries can be stimulated.

Where bulk supply agreements have been entered into by the Post Office there is a case for setting up a joint company in which the Post Office and the manufacturer would be represented and which would be an independent subsidiary manufacturing for us, and we would share in the profits. This is a part of present Government policy and we ought to consider carefully its application to the Post Office.

Dr Long, the Chief Medical Adviser, has been in the Post Office service since 1938. He gave me a copy of his annual report which shows that the problem of absence through sickness is a very serious one. It may be due to the fact that poor wages in the Post Office have led to a higher age-range of men being recruited, with a proportionately higher sickness absence. I was much struck by Dr Long and enjoyed my talk with him.

Saturday 31 October
Caroline and I went to Bristol this morning and Mr Tilling came with us on the train. In Bristol we were met by the Regional Director, Mr Scott and spent the morning with him and his staff. At the end of this talk, after hearing all his problems, I asked Mr Scott, 'What would you like me, as Postmaster General, to do?' 'Frankly, Minister, sit quiet,' he said. For about two weeks this has been hinted at broadly to me by all the people with whom I've come in contact and now at least someone has had the guts to say it out loud. It·was a significant comment.

Monday 2 November
I went to see Tommy Balogh in his new room in the Cabinet offices. I told him what I had discovered at the Post Office – particularly the £100 million deficit which had been intended for publication in the annual report but had been deleted by order of Mr Bevins. This is as near to cooking the books as you could find and may lead to a big row.* I don't know whether the civil servants ought to have told me this but they have done, and it is in my hands now and must be

*This was my contemporaneous judgement: by 2 February 1965 (see pages 214 to 215) I had concluded that there had been no falsification of accounts.

dealt with. I also showed him the list of the five principal committees and how rarely they had met over the last five years.

Tuesday 3 November
Into the Post Office and at 12.45 met the directorate – the head-quarters directors and the regional directors – who had come in for a meeting. I gave them a tough quarter of an hour talk, explaining the main problems that seemed to be waiting for me and also describing to them the policy of the Government as I understood it. Afterwards I went over to the Commons, had a quick lunch, and heard the opening of the debate on the Queen's speech in which Harold Wilson got himself involved in the tremendous controversy over the 'parliamentary leper', Peter Griffiths, the man who beat Patrick Gordon Walker in Smethwick after having fought a racialist campaign.[2]

Today is polling day in the United States and all the evidence suggests that it will be a Johnson landslide over Goldwater. This should exorcise the ghost of extreme right-wing Republicanism created by the Cold War and Senator McCarthy. It could release some progressive forces in the United States at long last.

Wednesday 4 November
We all got up very early this morning to watch television at 6.30 for the result of the American elections. It is a gigantic Johnson landslide. Goldwater has been destroyed as a serious political force and the effect of this on American politics cannot be calculated yet, but it looks as if it could liberate them for a shift to the left inside both the major parties.

At noon there was a service in the Crypt for members of the Government, held at Harold Wilson's suggestion. Mervyn Stockwood and Donald Soper* took it and it was well attended. It was an imaginative idea and except for Mervyn's egocentric sermon, every-thing went well.

After a quick lunch I went to the Post Office for a meeting with the staff associations. This was instead of the sherry party which is traditionally held by an incoming Postmaster General. I had written them all a letter explaining that I preferred to have a working meeting over a cup of tea. I gave them all a copy of our manifesto, 'The New Britain'. I told them I have presented each director in the Post Office with it as well and the meeting almost broke up with astonishment and suppressed laughter. But the reason for it is obvious and it was right to have done it.

* Socialist Methodist minister, created a Labour peer in 1965.

Thursday 5 November

I spent a great deal of the morning talking to Mr Tilling about the idea I have for establishing a directorate of forward planning, especially in the field of computers. This is the field that needs developing. I have now agreed to re-establish a smaller Post Office Board, which is really the general directorate plus myself.

I also raised with Tilling my desire to get the stamps altered so that commemorative issues did not have to have the Queen's head on them. Joe Slater came in at this stage and was absolutely shocked by the idea. He said it was dynamite and that it would cause a major storm and the women in Britain would hate it and the Cabinet would not agree to it and that people on our side of the House would be opposed to it. It was a frightening experience to hear him talk. Obviously it is going to be necessary at some stage to declare myself openly as a republican and see what happens. It's no good pretending one is a monarchist and then have difficulties with ideas of this kind. I shall have to leave the stamp question for a bit but I intend to come back to it and won't funk it unless Harold Wilson tells me that I must just drop it.

This evening I went to see Michael Stewart. I am delighted he is the Minister of Education rather than Dick Crossman. He is a passionate believer in comprehensive education and sees the danger of allowing the direct grant schools to obstruct the development of fully comprehensive education.

Friday 6 November

This evening Caroline and I went to the Soviet Embassy for the celebrations of the Revolution. We saw all our old friends – Chizov, Vassev and his wife, Voronin and Rogov. Rogov has been away for two years and has now come back to the Embassy. He let slip one remark to Caroline which, on analysis, surprised us both. He said that he knew she came from Cincinnati and that we knew Mr X, who supplied such wonderful laundry equipment to the Soviet Union. How he knew this I don't know. It showed that he had been giving a great deal of attention to us and had linked Caroline up with Cincinnati and with Mr X.

Mr X had told me some years ago that when he went to Russia to do a business deal, the Central Intelligence Agency had asked him for information about any potential military targets that he saw. One in particular was a ball bearing plant in Odessa which he had to visit. I had mentioned the incident – changing the name and the place and all relevant details – on a broadcast I once did about espionage following the Profumo, or it may have been the Vassall, case. It just occurred to me that the Soviet Intelligence might have put two and two together and come to the conclusion that Mr X was spying for the Americans and thought that we might be involved. Coming so soon after MI5 had warned me about the number of Soviet Intelligence agents operating in the Soviet Embassy in London, it certainly made us both much more cautious about Rogov.

This evening Tilling phoned to say that there had been a post office raid in Remnant Street and that a man had shot the branch supervisor, Mr Frederick Long. I telephoned the police and asked them for details and when we discovered he was in the Middlesex Hospital Caroline and I went along there. We talked to the doctor and the staff, and saw the bullet that had been removed from his back. Mrs Long came in so we were able to speak to her briefly. Happily he is likely to recover.

Monday 9 November
To the Post Office where a number of pressing problems were waiting. Tomorrow is my day for Parliamentary questions and I had to check through the drafts that were put in. I found that the answers and notes given to me were based on the assumption that there had been no changes of policy whatsoever as a result of the General Election. I sent several questions back for redraft and also crossed out many of the notes put down to help me deal with supplementaries.

The two most pressing questions that had to be answered were about the last Government's decision to move the Post Office Savings Bank to Glasgow and about the state of Post Office finances. The Glasgow business was the most complicated. The staff all wanted to go to the North East of England and the Tory Cabinet had overruled them and decided to send them to Glasgow. The staff were absolutely wild with rage and the whole of the voluntary basis of our dispersal policy was threatened. Sir Kenneth Anderson and the Director General put in a minute asking me to get the matter reviewed and Sir Kenneth said he could not guarantee that it would be possible to move the staff to Glasgow in the face of their bitter opposition.

Caroline and I went to the *New Statesman* party at the Stationers' Hall. We saw the Bishop of Woolwich and his wife. When I told her about my system of carrying cards around in case ideas struck me in the middle of the night, she said, 'You must be very difficult to sleep with.' I replied, 'You'll never know', and the Bishop roared with laughter. Afterwards we came back to the House of Commons with the Castles and Ted Castle had a meal with us in the Dining Room. He feels terribly shut out as Barbara tells him nothing. It must be hell to be a Cabinet Minister's husband.

Tuesday 10 November

Waiting on my desk this morning was a parliamentary question about the Post Office finances put down by Robert Cooke.* He obviously hoped to embarrass me for this afternoon. But in fact it gave me a supreme opportunity of revealing the state of finances left by Bevins. I had been shown a copy of the deleted paragraphs from the Post Office accounts, stating that the accumulated deficit over five years amounted to something like 100 million pounds. The question was, should I bring these facts out in answer to this particular question? Tilling thought I should not do this without letting my Cabinet colleagues know in advance. So did Jack Diamond whom I phoned. However, when an appointment was made for me to go to Number 10 to discuss the Post Office Savings Bank-Glasgow move I decided to put the question about the deficit before the Prime Minister myself. Tilling said I should write the PM a minute – which would have meant that Tilling would have kept a copy of it. I said that I would write a letter which would be entirely personal.

At 12.30 I arrived at Number 10 and was taken into the Cabinet room where the Prime Minister was sitting with the Chief Whip and the Lord President. George Brown and Willie Ross were there and also Woodfield, the Prime Minister's Private Secretary. I opened and made the case for a review of this decision. From the point of view of the staff, the Giro, and the impact of computerisation, it seemed to me that there was a strong case for a rapid review. Willie Ross gave the Scottish view and George Brown backed him up. I said that, as a politician, I accepted their arguments but that I thought they should give us time to consider the implications of the new factors.

However, it was eventually agreed that I should confirm the decision to move the POSB to Glasgow. I then handed Harold the letter setting out the basic position on Post Office finances and asked him if I could bring this out in answer to the question this afternoon from Cooke. He said yes indeed, and he thought it might even merit an enquiry and I was to make the statement at the end of questions and possibly see the lobby afterwards.

I then went back to the Commons but by the time I got there and began drafting my answer, Woodfield had phoned Tilling to tell him that under no circumstances should it be revealed that a paper shown to the previous Government had been shown to me. This was the inner Civil Service network in action. So I drafted the statement in such a way as to leave open the question of fact – as to whether

* MP for Bristol East and chairman of the Conservative Parliamentary Broadcasting Communications Committee.

Bevins knew about the deficit. Even so, Woodfield had said the Prime Minister wished to see my statement. So at 2.40 pm I went to see Wilson and handed him the statement which he approved. Then I went on to the Front Bench.

This was my first day of questions and I had a rough passage. At 3.30 I rose to make my statement and it did shock the House – as it was expected to do. But all the Tories did was to complain that I had answered it in this way without giving Cooke notice. Afterwards I went to a lobby meeting and explained the background to it.

That was not the end of the story. During the afternoon, Edward Heath notified Bowden that he intended to raise the matter and this he did. He said that my statement had been 'disreputable' and that it was 'designed to mislead the House'. I intervened and said that my statement had been made in response to a Conservative question, that it contained facts known to the previous Government, and that it had deliberately suppressed them for political reasons. The House was by now in uproar. When Bowden got up to speak, he said to Heath that he would be well advised to study the six deleted paragraphs of the report before making such a statement. This added to the air of mystery.

I have learned some interesting lessons today. First, if you want to get a decision the thing to do is to create a situation in which the decision has to be reached.

Second, there is an inner Civil Service network protecting itself and this is quite distinct from the political network which we desperately need to keep the Government going effectively. I discussed this with Marcia and with Peter Shore and George Wigg. Unless there is some way that we can exchange political information rapidly without the Civil Service knowing what is going on, it will be impossible for us to govern. Peter Shore is in fact hoping that he will be responsible for this at Number 10. He told me incidentally that the PM wanted him to be positively vetted before he became his Private Secretary. George Wigg wanted Ministers to be positively vetted too – but Harold Wilson had refused.

Wednesday 11 November
The press this morning was absolutely full of the Post Office story, including the background briefing that I had given the lobby. I went to the Office and Tilling told me that as a result of the disclosures the previous night about the six deleted paragraphs, he would get into appalling trouble with the Secretary of the Cabinet. I told him that if such a thing happened he must inform me and I would raise it personally with the Prime Minister. If Heath had not said that my

statement was 'disreputable' the further facts would not have come out. The DG came in and didn't seem a bit worried about this.

I also discussed with Tilling the business of 'the network'. He said it would be disastrous if I kept papers that he couldn't see. I pointed out that he had all the papers of the previous administration that I couldn't see and that we should have to respect each other's need for privacy in certain matters. I think he understood.

This morning Lord Normanbrook and Sir Hugh Greene came to discuss the future of the BBC. We discussed the proposed £6 licence, colour television, pirate broadcasting, local broadcasting, and the need for educational television. Normanbrook is a real old Establishment figure and not at all knowledgeable on broadcasting. Hugh Greene is much brighter but I think he was shaken when I shamed him with some of my thinking on local broadcasting and my desire to ease the BBC monopoly. I feel no sense of loyalty to him since the BBC is wildly right wing. I feel it only to public service broadcasting.

Caroline came in this morning and we went to lunch with the Union of Post Office Workers at Crescent House in Clapham with Joe Slater and Charles Morris. I spoke to the full Executive for about five minutes and answered questions and then we had the most delightful lunch in the UPW staff canteen. Ron Smith made a most affectionate speech and I replied for a few minutes. Then we went into the kitchen to meet all the staff and came back to the House of Commons.

This evening I went to a dinner laid on by the Society of Industrial Artists in the House of Lords. The guest of honour was Dr Beeching*. Also speaking was Stuart Rose, the Postmaster General's adviser on layout and design. Everyone was in evening dress except me; I was wearing a red tie and a rather dishevelled shirt and was late. All these designers are an informal crowd but they feel they must join the Establishment. Here were guys of real ability but they had been sucked into a hierarchy of alleged merit which completely took the spirit out of them. Talking to them afterwards, I found that I was surrounded by four members of my Stamp Advisory Committee whom I had not met. Some of them were saying how vital it was to keep the Queen's head on the stamps. I shall make some changes there.

Coming back to the Commons I discovered that I had made one minor and inconsequential slip in answering Cooke's question yesterday and the Tories had banged down a motion of censure against me. As far as I am concerned, this is worthwhile and I hope

* Dr Richard Beeching was chairman of British Railways Board 1963–5. He became associated with the closure of many branch lines.

time is given to debate it. I accidentally transposed two quotations and that is easy to deal with. The important thing is that Bevins now admits that he did cut some passages out from the Post Office accounts on the grounds that they were 'too verbose'. It is these passages which reveal the true state of the Post Office finances. We are heading for a big parliamentary row on this.

At 11.30 pm the *Daily Telegraph* rang up to ask if it was true – as reported in the first edition of the *Daily Express* – that I had sent my sons to Holland Park School, a question Caroline had answered when the *Express* had asked earlier. I hope it does something to get comprehensives moving.

Thursday 12 November
This morning I had another interview with Tilling. He asked me if I had told the Prime Minister that the last Cabinet had ruled the Giro out. Evidently the Post Office is under heavy attack from Helsby, the Secretary of the Cabinet, for having given me the deleted paragraphs from the Post Office accounts, and now this second charge has been made. Tilling said that he has committed a Civil Service offence by allowing these documents to come from Sir Kenneth Anderson to me, and his question was really impertinent, enquiring about my statements to the Prime Minister.

This led to a tough conversation with Tilling. I told him that I respected the fact that he had to maintain the standards of the Civil Service and that there were many things that he could not show me. But, at the same time, I pointed out that I had to have my own private security system and that in future he was not to look in my steel filing cabinet. He told me that he opened every letter that entered my office, whether it was marked Secret, Personal, Private or anything. It is clear that a political Intelligence system of our own has got to be established and I shall dictate some letters for the Prime Minister or other Ministers to Valerie and send them by Post Office messenger to Marcia Williams or to Members by hand. I told Tilling this frankly.

Moreover, in order to rub it in, I told him that I would have to see a number of people without him being present. I also told him that if there was any trouble about what had happened, I would see the Prime Minister personally. This is a most interesting controversy but it is clear that I shall have to establish my own gradings of secrecy and maintain them rigidly.

At 12.15 John Ollis, Frank George and Roger Gill of the New Bristol Group came to lunch. I had just fifteen minutes to talk to them before Mr Cadbury, the head of mechanisation, came in to join us. I told them of the uses that might be made of computers as I understood them in the Post Office, including the use of computers for dynamic operational planning, and the establishment of a data processing network using computers that we own or spare capacity that we can link up with potential customers. They were very excited by all this.

Cadbury is an extremely able man although he has no expert computer knowledge. But he told us what was already being done in the field of clerical mechanisation and said that Sir Albert Mumford, on the engineering side, used computers for certain design problems. We had about two hours' talk and at the end Cadbury said that he would prepare a short paper on the use of computers in the department, and Frank George and Roger Gill and John agreed to do a note on their potential use. I shall set up a technical group of some kind and if it is necessary for these people to do work for us it will be on a consultancy basis. I am sure this is the right way of tackling it and I am also sure that Cadbury is the only man in the department who could become the Director of Forward Planning. We also discussed the possibility of exporting computer time by means of a telecommunications link under the Channel, which would also permit us to import foreign computer time.

After that I went to the House of Commons and was there when the Leader of the House, Herbert Bowden, had to deal with the motion of censure on me put down by some Tory Members, claiming that I misled the House about Bevins' statement on postal charges. In fact I had wrongly quoted Bevins' statement in July 1963 as having been made in July 1964. But he had made the identical statement in July 1964 and I had simply picked up the wrong quotation from Hansard. So there is no substance in the motion of censure and I think that one is finished.

Friday 13 November

To the Office today and Lord Hill came along to talk for an hour. He discussed the possibility of the Independent Television Authority playing a part in educational television and we talked about the banning of smoking advertisements on TV and a number of other things. He is a jolly and agreeable man but the role of the chairman of ITA is merely to be a glorified public relations officer for the commercial companies, and I don't think he uses his powers to the full.

At 11 o'clock we had the first meeting of the new Post Office Board which I had set up. Present were the Director General, Mr Wolverson, Mr Wolstencroft, Sir Albert Mumford, Joe Slater and myself. The Secretary is Mr Smith, the DG's Private Secretary. Later we were joined by Mr Ryland, Brigadier Holmes and Mr O'Brien.

Our first job was to establish terms of reference for the Board and I modified these slightly to safeguard my right to act in between meetings. We then moved on to the financial report presented by Sir Kenneth Anderson. It was a long document which I was not well qualified to judge but the key to it came in the last page where the estimates of future profitability, productivity, telephone and postal demand, and financial out-turn was shown. It was clear that the figures were largely guesswork. They were based on Sir Kenneth's desire to show the necessity for immediate tariff increases, based no doubt on his fear that I might not agree. In fact I did agree that we needed to raise between £40 and £45 million a year and this satisfied him. At the same time one cannot run a major business on long-term predictions based on hunches. It is obvious that there must be some proper estimating done and a computer team working flat out could probably produce far more accurate figures.

I also made out a strong case for second class or unsealed mail which would go more slowly but which could contain written as well as printed material. There was a long discussion about this throughout which they all seemed to react rather negatively. After that we went through the tariffs one by one and agreed the increases we would recommend. I kept them there till 3.30 pm and they had no lunch. I can't have been popular.

Then the DG came to see me urgently. He said that Helsby had summoned him to find out if I had told Harold Wilson that the Giro had been stopped by the previous Government. Also he was doubtful about the release of the fact that there had been suppressed paragraphs in the Post Office accounts published in the summer. The DG had said that his department had done nothing wrong but that when you had an 'alert Minister' it was impossible for him not to discover what had gone on before he took over. I told the DG that I well understood that civil servants had to preserve the security of the papers of the previous Government but that I had to have a security network of my own for political links with my colleagues. He said that he hoped I would trust him implicitly, and I do. But I must be free to establish my own lines of communication.

Saturday 14 November

Tommy Balogh came to see me this morning and we had a discussion about the urgent necessity of establishing direct links with each other. He told me that his own secretary actually telephoned Helsby with the text of a letter he was writing to Wilson privately. The way we are to communicate with each other is by letters marked 'Personal and Private' sent to Marcia Williams at Number 10. She keeps a black box for Harold which nobody else sees. This is the only method of doing it. Tommy said that he was appalled by the lack of expertise in the Treasury and the failure of other departments to have skilled people operating round the Minister. He thought that I would have no difficulty in appointing advisers to the Post Office and this I intend to do.

Monday 16 November
To the Office where I found an invitation waiting for me to a sherry party at Buckingham Palace. This is what I have been dreading and I have now got to find some way of establishing from the outset that I don't have to go. There was the usual stream of parliamentary questions to be approved and at 12 I had a press conference for radio and TV correspondents. Beforehand there had been anxious consultations. I decided simply to share my thinking with them and to concentrate on five questions I was asking myself. Such a thing had never been done before and there were grave doubts as to whether it would work. We also decided that it had to be non-attributable.

The five questions I discussed with them were:

1. Are we making the most of radio and television in Britain?

2. Have we thought through the impact of technical change on the structure of broadcasting?

3. Does broadcasting offer an adequate publishing outlet or is it for ever to be left to the editors?

4. Do future financing arrangements have to follow the same division between all-licence and all-advertising, as has been followed in the past? Or are there other means of financing, or a mixture of the two?

5. Is public service synonymous with monopoly? Is advertising synonymous with commercial broadcasting?

It was a good conference. I confided these questions to the correspondents and then had a host of questions back. I think the correspondents enjoyed the opportunity of thinking about the future in this way. The only risk is what they make of it. I told them that if this was abused it would simply be the last press conference of this kind.

Harold Wilson had asked me to lunch with him at the Commons. I think he had heard from Marcia, George Wigg and Tommy Balogh that I was feeling a bit lonely and we had an hour together which allowed me to talk to him about what I was doing. His Private Secretary had queried the reports that I had decided to ban cigarette advertising and I told Harold this was pure speculation. He is not against it and was only keen that I should follow normal procedures.

I mentioned that the DG had been summoned by Helsby about the revelations of the last Government's attitude to Giro. He was extremely angry and said he would take this up with Helsby.

We also discussed the future of the postal service and he was a little nervous of an increase in the postal charges. But I told him that we did need capital to modernise the postal services and that we ought to make some contribution towards this from our own resources. I think he sees political dangers in raising charges.

I described my plan for the Post Office to own a bank of computers and make them available along our Datel[3] network. I said we could become brokers in computer time and might even export computer time by cable to other countries. He seemed very keen on this and told me to discuss it with Frank Cousins whose Ministry is to be the new sponsoring Ministry for computers. We also discussed the BBC licence fee and he was anxious to avoid an increase to £6 as this is such a regressive form of raising money. He understands everything so quickly and one doesn't have to explain anything at all. He turns his mind to any problem, picks its essentials up, conducts a searching cross-examination and leaves you refreshed, if slightly breathless. He said to me at the end, 'You're working hard – does it mean long hours?' I said it did but that I was greatly enjoying it.

I went to the Youth Sub-Committee of the Executive which was entirely taken up with a discussion as to what we should do with the Trotskyites. All but two members of the National Committee of the Young Socialists have been expelled and Ian Mikardo made the point that we should not take drastic action. If local Labour Parties have exercised disciplinary powers of their own and if there are now appeals against expulsion from the people concerned (which there have not been) it's better for us to keep out of it.

I came home to change and Caroline and I went to the Lord Mayor's banquet. It was a scene of splendid pageantry. Everyone is expected to wear a white tie but I went in a black one. The only other person in a black tie was George Brown and it established a warm bond of sympathy between us.

Before dinner Mountbatten came up and I had a long talk to him. It was the first time I had ever spoken to him and he spent the whole time name-dropping. His conversation consisted of a long list of well-known people whom he described by their nicknames and claimed to know very well. For the uncle of the Queen and an earl and Admiral of the Fleet, it was astonishing that he wanted to impress.

After that we went in to dinner and sat between Lord Chief Justice Parker and the President of the Admiralty, Probate and Divorce

Division, and opposite a former Lord Mayor and Cecil King. Lady Parker who was on my left is an American woman from Kentucky. During the Archbishop of Canterbury's speech she wrote me a note on the back of her menu, 'When you are Prime Minister will you decree that there shall only be two speeches? I cannot bear another Archbishop.' I wrote back underneath, 'By that time, you will need every Archbishop you can lay your hands on.' She laughed – and handed it to the Lord Chief Justice.

Cecil King was completely lumpen and defeatist about the *Sun* and when we both tried to persuade him that its role was to criticise the Labour Government from the Left, I don't think he understood what we meant.

As we left dinner, some City bigwig shouted, 'Why aren't you properly dressed?' I didn't hear him but he caught Caroline by the arm and repeated it to her. She was extremely angry. I had the opportunity for a word with the Lord Provost of Glasgow about the Post Office Savings Bank move.

Tuesday 17 November
Today is the fourth anniversary of Father's death – and of my expulsion from the Commons.

I went to the Post Office and tried to cope with parliamentary questions all morning. In order to understand the financial ones, I brought Sir Kenneth Anderson in and cross-questioned him closely. He is in fact neither an accountant nor an economist and I am beginning to have the gravest doubts about his figures. He is just an ordinary administrator responsible for the accounts of this enormous department. We must have an economic adviser.

To the House of Commons for our big day with questions. Caroline and Mother were in the Gallery. The Tories were gunning for me and anything I said might have caused a riot. I did make a couple of minor slips which gave them their opportunity. It was a tough day but I stayed firm and found it quite bracing, though extremely exhausting.

Afterwards I had to go to the Legislation Committee of the Cabinet to urge the case for passing our pirate radio Bill this session. It was referred to the Home Affairs Committee for consideration.

Wednesday 18 November
We had a meeting of the Post Office Board to consider the amended proposals for the increase in postal tariffs. We shall have a fight on our hands and there is no harm in asking for a little bit more than we are likely to get.

At the Commons Charles Morris told me that this morning Peggy

Herbison had had a rough time at the Party meeting from Members who felt that it was only the bureaucratic obstruction of the Civil Service that was preventing the payment of the recently agreed increase in old-age pensions before March. Some sharp things had been said and it had been hinted that the Post Office staff were one of the barriers to a quick payment of the increase. I rang Brigadier Holmes, the Director of Postal Services, and told him that I wanted to be kept fully informed and avert an apparent crisis between pensioners and the UPW. This is important and I shall take responsibility for it myself.

I went to Television House to do an eight-minute interview for 'This Week', which is being shown tomorrow night. It was my first official appearance as PMG. The amusing thing was to find that the bigwigs had come out to meet me. I still feel the whole PMG red-carpet treatment is weird and am much more at home with the producers.

Thursday 19 November
Today I went to Reading to open a new trunk switching centre. O'Brien and Tilling came with me and we were greeted at the station by the station master and all the top brass. I met the senior officials and then had ten minutes with the telephone staff representatives without any of the management present and picked up a number of useful points. From there I went to the Head Postmaster's office and then saw the postal staff representatives. After that I went to the Mayor's parlour, then had lunch in the cafeteria at the new switching exchange. After lunch I was shown round the equipment which looked pretty old-fashioned to me in that it was still electro-magnetic rather than electronic. At 3 o'clock we had the opening ceremony and I made my first speech as PMG.

This evening Caroline and I went to a party given by Lord Mountbatten at his house in Wilton Crescent. He introduced me to his son-in-law Lord Brabourne, who is a film producer. I had heard of this man and thought I would not like him but in fact he was intelligent and had some ideas on pay-TV which may be worth considering. After that we went on to a party at Kenneth Rose's. I had a brief word with Nubar Gulbenkian and raised the possibility of getting a grant for the establishment of a fellowship in minuscule design.

Friday 20 November
Today I replied to the invitation to the sherry party at Buckingham Palace next Wednesday. I simply said, 'Mr and Mrs Wedgwood Benn thank the Master of the Household for conveying Her Majesty's

kind invitation for November 25 but beg leave to be excused from attending.' I wrote it in my own hand and sent it over to Buckingham Palace. It is now up to them to query it. All I have done is to ask leave to be excused and if they say that I can't be, I shall ask them to put it in writing. I haven't said I won't go or given any reason which might be taken to be insulting. I am sure this is the right thing to do and once I have established my right to refuse an invitation the position will be much easier. My colleagues who have been assured by their civil servants that these invitations are commands have, I think, been taken in by the official network. The actual words of the invitation are that the Queen has commanded the Master of the Household to invite. The command is to him, not to us. This is exactly where the civil servants exercise their most pernicious influence – perpetuating a concept of society which is out-of-date.

This morning the Irish Postmaster General, Michael Hilliard, came for an informal visit. I told him that Father had been a passionate supporter of the Irish cause and he said that he remembered it and that was why he had wanted to come.

At 3 o'clock I had to make bravery awards to two men who had been attacked with iron bars and an axe in a raid on a post office in Shepherd's Bush in September. They both looked shaky.

One issue on which I am now working is the BBC licence fee application. Lillicrap is the man in charge and I sent him a minute today asking him to think of alternative ways in which the money could be raised. These would include applying the TV levy to the BBC as a grant-in-aid,[4] taking over the Light Programme and financing it by advertising, running a big Post Office commercial light music programme, or taking away BBC2 and using the channel for educational television with advertising. I hope Lillicrap is discreet and that these ideas do not get conveyed at this stage to the BBC.

A rumour that Lord Normanbrook is threatening to resign reached my desk today and I decided to disregard it. I am sure that the BBC must be worried. I daresay the network conveys information to them in the same way that it does to other departments. But Harold has no particular love for the BBC and I don't think I should get into difficulties on this score.

Monday 23 November
To the House of Commons for a vote at 10 o'clock. After that I went to join Caroline at dinner with the American author Dee Wells who said that she thought that Britain was such a defeated and conservative country that she couldn't see it pulling itself up by its own bootstraps. This made me angry but she may be right. It is most depressing to have been born in a country at a time when things are

going downhill so fast. One just wonders how far individuals can change this by their efforts, or whether one just has to accept the inevitable and sit back and administer a ruin.

Tuesday 24 November
Early to the Post Office this morning and at 10.15 Monsieur Jacques Marette, the French Postmaster General, made the first dialled call from Paris to our office. I had prepared an elaborate reply in French and we exchanged courtesies. In fact I was nearly unable to do it as I was summoned to the Cabinet at twenty minutes' notice. It would have been fatal to have had him call and find the Postmaster General of Britain had disappeared.

To the Cabinet at 10.30. It was the first time I had ever attended it and it was an interesting experience. The emergency payment of pensions was decided against on economic grounds.

In the afternoon I went to the Party meeting where Douglas Houghton explained the position about payment of old-age pensions. Nobody suggested that this was due to practical difficulties and the Post Office came out of it well.

Wednesday 25 November
Another meeting of the Post Office Board this morning. We met from 10.30 till 2.45 with sandwiches and tea brought in at 1 o'clock but no break from our discussions.

The agenda was a long one. First we considered the tariff increases again. George Brown wants us to have a more thorough survey of the position to satisfy himself and the Cabinet that we could not absorb the higher costs by greater efficiency without increasing charges.

On the question of stamp design, I rejected the old criteria applied by the Post Office and said that our new objectives of policy would be to celebrate events of national or international importance, to commemorate appropriate anniversaries and occasions, to reflect Britain's unique contribution to the arts and world affairs, to extend public patronage of the arts by promoting philately and to raise revenue. I announced that I intended to appoint a new advisory committee with complete freedom to recommend any type of design they thought appropriate. Thus the question of the monarch's head will be subject to review. The Sovereign had already indicated that she did not wish ever to appear on a stamp with another person. This was after appearing jointly with Shakespeare. Since we decided to introduce a Burns stamp, this makes the issue a live one and at the Queen's request.

For the 1965 programme the Board agreed to do stamps on the

Battle of Britain, the twentieth anniversary of the United Nations, the 700th anniversary of Parliament, the Salvation Army centenary, Robert Burns, the Post Office Tower, the Commonwealth Arts Festival, and the International Telecommunications centenary. This means eight stamps, which is twice the number done hitherto and each will be in two denominations.

Next we considered BBC financing and I said that the BBC were to be asked to conduct a private review similar to our own, showing what economies would be possible and what they would produce, and we would then have to examine ways of meeting the cost.

We had a discussion about the new data transmission services. We shall also have to look at the possibility of the Post Office using banks of computers to service industry which will require authorisation for capital investment.

Then we went on to my numbered minutes and I got a survey of the work going on. The one that interested me most was the possibility of appointing a Director of Forward Planning and I told the Board what I had in mind.

Under any other business we discussed my decision to continue with the Santa Claus scheme, under which children writing to Santa Claus receive letters from the Post Office. It is to be coupled with an appeal for money for UNICEF.

Finally I discussed with them my desire to get operational research considered much more seriously and also to appoint a consultant designer to review the whole of Post Office design.

It was quite a meeting.

Afterwards I went to Sir Albert Mumford's office to listen to the demonstration of the two-speed tape recorder for use by the telephone and telex service. The loss of quality even at twice the normal speed was great and intelligibility was low. But it did alert me to the possibility of building telephone answering machines in conjunction with automatic dialling so that in fact you could get messages transmitted at night between business houses when the trunk lines were not used. I like the engineering people and they are the most adventurous of the lot.

To the House of Commons, discovered that I could pair, and was home by 6 o'clock.

Friday 27 November
Attended the Home Affairs Committee of the Cabinet at 9.45 am to discuss pirate radio. We shall get our convention but the legislative pressure may keep the Bill back. I was urged to prepare a plan for local sound broadcasting at the same time, which suits my book perfectly.

To the Office by 10.30. I summoned Mr Lillicrap, the director of Radio Services, and told him to get cracking on a number of alternative schemes for providing a nationwide pop music service financed by advertising which would be a revenue raiser for the Post Office and help to meet the BBC deficit. This could be achieved by splitting the BBC Light Programme VHF transmitters off. There would be a terrible squeal from some people but since pop music and advertisers both seek mass audiences there would be no conflict of interest and the Post Office would pocket the cash.

On educational broadcasting I asked him to prepare a plan under which a vice-chancellor of the Air would be given a grant-in-aid to enable him to buy programmes from the BBC or ITA or anywhere and pre-empt time on BBC2 to show them. To begin with this would come in the daytime and as it began to spill into the evening peak it would be transferred bodily to the fourth channel. The vital thing is to stop the BBC running the University of the Air which would be disastrous.

After lunch I got out my camp bed and went soundly asleep for forty minutes behind my desk, having arranged to be woken with a cup of tea. It was the first time I had tried it and it worked like a dream. I suspect that Tilling and Co think I am completely nuts. One of the delights of getting older is that you can do what you like and not care what other people think.

Saturday 5 December
Surgery in Bristol this morning and home by late lunch. The telephone answering machine is an absolute Godsend. I sit in the office and hear the thing ringing and ringing and then the machine answers and the telephone stops. Without changing my number it gives me exactly the privacy that I need. I suppose one could just not answer the phone and it would have the same effect.

Monday 7 December
At the Post Office this morning an MI5 man came along to interview me about a political adviser who has given me as a reference for the positive vetting procedure in order to work at Number 10. The chap was a real pudgy flatfoot police type, and very friendly. But it is an odious business being asked to answer personal questions such as drinking habits, sexual deviations and private life.

I had the first of my informal lunch meetings with thirteen people from the Building, Welfare and Transport departments. They sat round my table drinking beer and eating sandwiches and apples like a lot of middle-aged bankers on a church outing. There was not a spark of enthusiasm, imagination or excitement of any kind to be seen. I am really talent-spotting and even a person of average intelligence would shine out of that sort of group.

To the Commons and Sir John Macpherson, the chairman of Cable & Wireless, came to see me. He is a retired colonial official and his company is progressively being squeezed out all over the world. He brightened visibly when I said that I thought perhaps he might be the instrument by which Britain sold satellite tracking stations round the world. But the DG was there with a million reasons why it couldn't be done. I have been PMG for seven weeks now and not a single bright idea has come up from below. It's like trying to resuscitate a dying elephant – tiring and almost hopeless.

Stayed at the Commons till 1 am working, voting and talking to the Serjeant-at-Arms about Commons postal, messenger and telephone services.

Friday 11 December
This morning I had a delegation from the Radio and Electrical Manufacturers Association, consisting of Mr Stanley of Pye, Sir Jules Thorn, and Mr Allchurch. They represent the radio and TV manufacturers and are extremely disappointed that the arrival of BBC2 has not stimulated sales of TV sets on the scale they need to bring the industry up to full capacity. In fact they are operating at about 50 per cent of the peak they reached some years ago when TV sales were approaching saturation point. What they want is a second entertainment channel to create a mass demand for them. I found them an extremely unimaginative lot. Frankly we cannot reach a decision of the kind they want just to give them work. What is required is an assessment of the unused capacity and then a decision as to how best it can be used in the national interest for exports or essential production. If these were the leaders of British industry in this field, they were a poor lot.

The timing of the General Election had led to the cancellation of the annual Labour Party Conference, so on 13–14 December we had a two-day conference in Brighton which was little more than a victory celebration for the Party after thirteen years in Opposition. However, National Executive Committee elections were held as usual in which Anthony Greenwood came top of the constituency section, I came second, and Barbara Castle third.

Monday 14 December
To the Economic Development Committee in the Cabinet Office this morning to discuss the new prices and incomes policy. I was only there as an observer.

At lunch today I had representatives from the Central Organisation and Methods Branch. They were a bright crowd and we had an interesting talk about their computerisation programme which involves the purchase of two and a half million pounds worth of computers immediately and more computers at the rate of about a million pounds a year, which I am to announce later this week. Again I looked round to find the bright young guy with drive and energy and didn't quite see him. This time it was like meeting a lot of intelligent signals officers in the services, basically conservative but engaged in a field that called for some degree of flexibility.

Tuesday 15 December
Mount Pleasant for the traditional Postmaster General's Christmas press conference. There were a mass of press and television people and I was photographed holding up the turkey whose wrapping had come unstuck in the post and spent a lot of time in 'heartbreak corner', with other parcels which had come undone.

In a written answer today I announced the new criteria for stamp design and invited MPs and the public to make suggestions as decisions have to be reached rapidly. I think this will have the effect of stimulating ideas on design policy generally and I'm looking forward to it.

Wednesday 16 December
At 3.15 the Lord Mayor of London and the two Sheriffs came to the East Central Office and we took them round. This visit was switched from Mount Pleasant and I wondered if there would be any comment. No doubt the Lord Mayor's flunkey, Brigadier Clapham, complete with tail coat and monocle, had noticed it. But frankly, none of the party did. I was very jovial, but what a lot of deadbeats they are.

Thursday 17 December
This morning Bessie Braddock brought some pools promoters from Liverpool to see me about postal tariffs. They were the hardest, seediest crew I have seen for a long time, and we had some tough bargaining. I had to refuse to pay them £40,000 compensation for losses during the postal strike and fight off their appeal not to raise charges.

With Caroline to Mount Pleasant where the Chairman of the LCC, Arthur Wicks, and his wife paid a visit. They had never been there and knew the significance of my invitation. What was interesting was the subtly different tone of the Post Office welcome as compared to the obsequiousness shown to the Lord Mayor.

Rushed to the Commons for the first meeting under the chairmanship of Kenneth Robinson to discuss the question of banning cigarette advertising on television.

Then to the Fabian Executive where, on the principle of Buggins' turn next, I was elected chairman. I put up an idea for a committee to study the first reaction of Ministers to the problems of their new departments and it was welcomed. When I put in my first 100 days' report to Harold I shall be able to summarise my impressions and this will be relevant to such a study.

Back to hear Stephen and Hilary in the Holland Park School concert at St Mary Abbots and returned for the end of the defence debate, where Harold Wilson finally destroyed the pretence that we have an independent nuclear deterrent.

Friday 18 December
My next big job in the Post Office is to get in consultants on a host of subjects, especially in the field of management. I am not at all satisfied with the quality of the very top chaps and it is becoming increasingly clear to me that a Civil Service department cannot generate the impetus to make a growth industry grow and expand at the necessary rate. The attitudes are too rigid, the wage structure is too tightly under Treasury control and the political supervision of prices and practices makes the job impossible.

I must therefore charge my consultants with the job of reviewing the whole structure and give them freedom to recommend a separation of the Post Office from the Government. Quite where this would leave the PMG I'm not sure. I have an idea that he would be a Minister of Communications responsible for the overall direction and development of a number of different enterprises, each under its own management but answerable to him on questions of high policy. The organisation of each section – broadcasting, posts and telegraphs, savings bank and Giro, national computer service, and so on – would depend upon its own needs and would blend off into mixed enterprises that would emerge from total government ownership at one end to government shareholding in major private enterprise undertakings with which we had dealings at the other. Unless we break up the monolithic structure that now exists and encourage some younger leadership there will never be the great leap forward that is required.

Sunday 20 December
The Mayhews to lunch and to the carol concert at the Albert Hall. Chris is so enthusiastic about the Admiralty, thinks its civil servants are wonderful and efficient and that the admirals are so go ahead. It tells you a lot more about Chris than it does about his department.

This evening to the BBC recording of the GPO Show with Spike Milligan and Harry Secombe which was most enjoyable.

Monday 21 December

Negotiations began with the Post Office Engineering Union over their wage claim. Now that the National Union of Railwaymen have accepted the arbitration award there was no reason why we should not go ahead and agreement was reached within a few hours. It is a massive increase based on pay research findings.

This afternoon we had the private office party with colour TV laid on by the BBC and it went well.*

This evening to the Commons to vote for the abolition of capital punishment – which was carried overwhelmingly. At last the gallows have gone.

Thursday 24 – Monday 28 December

Did no Post Office work of any kind for five days and felt much better for it. A real family Christmas.

Tuesday 29 December

John Allen came to lunch and to have a talk. It took some time to get out the real object of his visit. But in fact Harold had asked him to look at the increase in postal tariffs both from an economic and a political point of view. With an Election likely this spring, the political impact could be difficult. This is a new point, additional to George Brown's special economic difficulties arising from his wages and prices agreement so recently signed. I hope it doesn't scupper us at a critical juncture.

Wednesday 30 December

I received a royal warrant giving me a quarter of a doe, shot in Windsor Great Park – one of the perks of Ministers. The only question is, what to do with it?

John Allen came to see me over lunch to follow up his enquiries on Harold Wilson's behalf about postal charges. Harold hadn't realised it had gone as far as it has done. John agreed that on the merits, my proposals were right but pointed out that they would be politically unattractive with the possibility of an Election. Of course, that is so. The trouble is that the decision, when it is taken, will not be related to the merits but to the extraneous factors which bedevil the Post Office.

* This was a purely experimental demonstration. Colour television was introduced commercially in 1967.

I did score one success today which gives me great pleasure. My scheme for using every post office as a mini art gallery has not presented the insuperable difficulties I expected and we are going ahead. It means that possibly 2,000 post offices will have pictures on display as a result of cooperation between curators of local museums and Head Postmasters. This is Arnold Wesker's dream – or part of it – coming about.[5]

Thursday 31 December
To the Office at 8.30 am and mulled through some papers. There is nobody here at the moment. I can get more work done in that way.

At 10.30 I left for Leicester Square and queued up on my shooting stick for an hour for tickets to see the latest Disney film. There were eleven of us – the Gibsons and ourselves. Afterwards we had a meal at a Chinese restaurant.

I had a scandalised telephone call from Tilling who told me that tomorrow's New Year Honours will not include Mr Wolverson's name. Number 10 told the Post Office that this was because I had deleted Wolverson's name from the list. In fact, when asked to comment on Bevins' honours list (a day or two after taking office) I had made Tilling write to Number 10 stating my views on the honours system but saying that, if the system remained unchanged, I would not think it right to vary the recommendations made by my predecessor in respect of Post Office staff. In my whole time in the Post Office I have never known Mr Tilling so galvanised by anything as he was by this – and the disposal of the venison from Windsor Great Park.

This evening Mother came over to spend the night and Caroline and I went to a party at Lord Snow's. There was a mixed bag of people, including Bernard Braden and Barbara Kelly, Kenneth Rose, Alan Sillitoe and his bright wife Ruth, who is a poet. As we left Snow leaned over to me and said, 'I really should have gone to the Commons and Frank [Cousins] should have gone to the Lords. My experience of speaking would have been such a help. I'm not sure he'll do very well. It's a pity I didn't speak to Harold about it.' It all rather reinforced my feelings about Snow's inadequacy. But he was friendly and said that he heard that I was doing well at the Post Office. Such a remark, however meaningless, raises morale.

Thus ended an eventful year for us, and ushered in another that is likely to be busier than any we have ever had.

Friday 1 January 1965
After lunch James Margach of the *Sunday Times* came to see me. The press this morning carried a story that there was a clash between

Brown and me over the postal tariff increases. I don't know where this came from but certainly not from the Post Office. Margach was keen to draw me on this but I diverted him on to broadcasting policy which is much more interesting. I kept Tilling with me all the time which I think upset Margach but was some sort of guarantee that I had not said anything I should not have said. These are hot issues and I have to be careful.

Bed, extremely tired.

Saturday 2 January
The Times this morning carried a centre-page story developing the alleged argument between George Brown and me over whether postal charges should go up. They reminded readers of the charge I had made against Bevins and hinted that George Brown had proved me to have been exaggerating. This puts me in an acute political difficulty. I am still wondering where the story came from.

Monday 4 January
Dictated minutes on the reorganisation of the Post Office into a Ministry of Communications and another one on the use of cybernetics as a management aid. These are fundamental issues but as I am alone with nobody who is remotely sympathetic politically, I wonder how much progress can be made. The Establishments Branch came to lunch – twelve more bank managers glaring unenthusiastically. I'm beginning to wonder if these lunches are a waste of time.

This evening to see *Pickwick* as guests of Harry Secombe. He was delightful with the children afterwards, and gave them his old Pickwick hats and the LP of the show. He radiates kindness.

Tuesday 5 January
To Dollis Hill* all day with the Engineering Department. We discussed the work of the station and its future. Particularly worthy of consideration are:

1. The need to prune the non-qualified tail and build up the scientific and engineering staff;

2. The need for a better balance between pure research and development;

3. The expansion of the research budget subject to improved recruitment of qualified engineers;

---

* Headquarters of the Post Office research laboratories.

4. The possibility of graduate work by staff; and

5. Closer links with the universities.

Afterwards I went round the various departments and was subjected to a battery of demonstrations covering a host of different technical problems. It tested my mind to the full but was stimulating and maybe encouraged the staff too.

During the course of the day I heard that the Prime Minister wanted to see me on Friday and it was made to sound as if he was angry at the press reports of my broadcasting ideas and that he intended to intervene to stop the tariff exercise.

Thursday 7 January
I spent the whole day in the Office on tariffs and broadcasting problems, preparing for my meeting with Harold tomorrow. I wrote to him to say that the speculation in the press was without basis and this will relieve his doubts. I also heard from Derek Mitchell, his PS, that the Honours List is to go unchanged and I must therefore submit names. I hate doing it but you can't reform everything at once.

On broadcasting I wrote a paper and discussed it with the DG and Lillicrap. They were skeptical and negative and I didn't feel that I had established any sort of understanding of what I was seeking to achieve. But it is obvious that the BBC licence fee has got to be seen in the context of broadcasting policy generally and there will have to be many changes.

Friday 8 January
My scheme for turning post offices into mini art galleries is coming along nicely. Though small, this achievement and the new stamp policy represent a real stimulation of the arts. But I got a knock on another issue. The PM has intervened to prevent the taking of a photograph of the Commons at the 700th anniversary meeting on 20 January, which I wanted for the stamp.

I went to Number 10 in fear and trembling, expecting a rocket. In fact, it was a delightful hour and a quarter. 'I hope you don't have to rush away,' said Harold as if I was the busy one. That is his charm and his ability to remain calm at the centre of a storm.

We talked about his Christmas in the Scilly Isles, the acute difficulties facing the Tories and Election prospects. On that he doesn't need advice from anyone. He thanked me for the idea of an export award* which I had transmitted from Bristol. There was no

* An idea which became known as the Queen's Awards for Industry and Exports.

trouble on tariffs and he is keen to play up the modernisation. On broadcasting our minds were working closely together and it restored my confidence in my own sanity. We shall have to have a ministerial committee. I discussed briefly my ideas for a Ministry of Communications which appealed to him and I can see the pattern clearly, with a Minister working with five boards – posts, telephones, bank, broadcasting and data processing. I came out feeling as if I had had a month's holiday.

I saw the DG and the ADG and conveyed the news to them while eating a sandwich lunch, slept for twenty minutes, was woken with tea, amended the White Paper for the printers, gave a bravery award, had two hours of tough niggling negotiations with the Society of Civil Servants about the POSB move to Glasgow and came home exhausted but very happy at about half past seven. I am inching my way forward.

Tuesday 12 January

A letter from the PM today, asking for details of some of the plans I have to submit for his major statement on exports next week. These include the export of earth satellite tracking stations, postal mechanisation equipment, the national data processing service and electronics.

Most of the morning was taken up with the first meeting of the 'informal' committee. Ron and Charles Smith are the leading members. I floated my idea of a Ministry of Communications with five boards. Charles Smith passionately wants a separate telecommunications board, but Ron Smith fears that if posts are separated they will shrivel away. The important thing is to fight the battle to get the Post Office out of the Civil Service and established as a nationalised industry. This is big enough without raising difficulties between the UPW and the POEU.

I wrote a six-page 'Hundred Day Report' for Harold and sent it over to Marcia Williams at Number 10 marked 'Reserved'.

This evening the DG and I went to have dinner with the top brass of GEC. Our hosts were Lord Aldington (Toby Low), the chairman, Oliver Humphreys, the vice-chairman and Arnold Weinstock, the managing director. Aldington is a real Tory amateur and knew practically nothing. Humphreys is an engineer, and bright. Weinstock is brilliant and delightful, about my age, and obviously one of the top tycoons in British industry. He told me about his efforts to get into Mexico, the effect of the Arab boycott of firms with Israeli connections and the way his competitors used it, and his belief that a vast increase of trade with China was necessary and required Government action. We discussed politics and he was very impressed with Frank Cousins.

On the issue of bulk supply agreements covering telephone apparatus, I said these must end altogether, and on electronic exchanges they must be revised to a new formula within six months with a profit-sharing element for the Post Office. If I can win on this it will be a notable move towards mixed enterprise. Hitherto, we have not realised our power as the main customer.

On earth satellite tracking stations, I told them that British industry had been slow and that the Post Office intended to give a lead by proposing a consortium in which we would play a part. They were dead against being forced to link with their competitors but in the tough international market I see little alternative.

Wednesday 13 January

I was asked to approve two new appointments for regional directors, so I called in the DG and asked the names of alternative people who had been considered. He was rather shaken. But if I am to be responsible for appointments, I wanted him to know that I intend to take a real interest.

This afternoon Sir Kenneth Clark and Paul Reilly of the Council of Industrial Design came at my request to discuss stamp design. I read out the list of issues to be made which is far and away the most exciting ever attempted. I then outlined my plan for a treble-size stamp which would give the designer a panel he could use absolutely freely, on the right of which the definitive stamp would be printed in one piece. Thus on the envelope it would look as if a stamp without the Queen's head had been stuck next to the definitive. This is as far as I can go at the moment without precipitating a row in which I might not even carry Harold's support. Of course I sold it to them on design grounds – that it would widen the designer's freedom of action. They pressed me as to whether there would be a perforation between the panel and the Queen's head. I said, no. But of course it does pave the way for a second stage which I would dearly like to carry through.

There was one sharp clash when Sir Kenneth Clark said that stamps were 'basically heraldic devices'. I challenged this and he hastily withdrew and said he meant they were 'symbolic art'. Sir Kenneth wants a new portrait of the Queen on definitive stamps and offered to draft a letter to the Palace for me to send on this point. He thinks that one of Lord Snowdon's photographs would be best and proudly said that he thought he had the Duke of Edinburgh's support. I agreed to try this out and experiment with them alongside the new commemorative.

I mentioned that the Post Office is establishing a Fellowship of Minuscule Design to encourage this neglected art. They said it had to be at the Royal College of Art but I intend to send it elsewhere if I can. It was a depressing but amusing interview.

Thursday 14 January

To the Cabinet this morning with my major document on postal tariff increases. It was a tough occasion. Gerald Gardiner said it was a 'capitalist document'. Frank Cousins said the Post Office should seek to absorb the whole increase in productivity. George and Jim were absent. Harold supported the principle, but left the timing for further discussion with him. I was asked to review the parcels rate again. It convinced me that the GPO as a Government department, politically accountable in every detail, could never make progress. I shall have to press on with my major scheme for making it a nationalised industry. The public sector cannot survive if it is always underpriced.

Then Sir Willis Jackson, the chairman of the Television Advisory Committee, came to see me and we discussed the colour system to be adopted in Europe at the March conference. Whereas the French are pulling out all the stops and have sent a ministerial delegation to Moscow to win support for the French system, we have, characteristically, sent a couple of engineers to demonstrate ours. I was so concerned with this that I decided to write to the Board of Trade at once. I discussed with the DG the question of Britain's participation in the European Launcher Development Organisation, ELDO,[6] on which a five-hundred-page brief had been prepared for a meeting tomorrow which I cannot attend. He is going in my place. We agreed that the GPO interest was limited to satellite communications through the international committee.

Defence, colour television, Concorde, rocket development – these are all issues raising economic considerations that reveal this country's basic inability to stay in the big league. We just can't afford it. The real choice is, do we go in with Europe or do we become an American satellite? Without a conscious decision being taken the latter course is being followed everywhere. For personal reasons, I would see much attraction in an English-speaking federation, bringing in Canada, Australia, New Zealand and Britain to a greater United States. But this is a pipe dream and in reality the choice lies between Britain as an island and a US protectorate, or Britain as a full member of the Six, followed by a wider European federation. I was always against the Common Market but the reality of our isolation is being borne in on me all the time. This country is so decrepit and hidebound that only activities in a wider sphere can help us to escape from the myths that surround our politics. I do not know yet what the answer is but I do know that the questions cannot be dodged.

To see Reg Prentice at the Ministry of Education about educational TV. Until the University of the Air can be launched later, his only short-term plan is for four extra hours of education on BBC2. I am passionately keen that the BBC should not gain control of the University of the Air and proposed an alternative idea, that we would withold some of the increase from the higher BBC licence and pay it direct to an educational TV commission set up by the Ministry of Education, which would then buy programmes and rent transmitters from the BBC to put them on. Prentice is only anxious to get on with the job and didn't care how I organised it. I see it as a move towards publishing and towards a proliferation of programme planning functions.

Friday 15 January
To the Home Affairs Committee of the Cabinet this morning. We agreed to ban cigarette advertising on television and I will make a parallel statement when Kenneth Robinson announces it. There may well be repercussions from Bristol.*

At 11.15 am Dr Beeching came to sign the long-term parcels agreement under which he gets our parcel trade for ten years and we save about £4 million a year. We gave a joint press conference, signed the agreement like a treaty and then I took him to see the Post Office railway. At lunch he launched into an attack on what he called 'overblown democracy', said Britain was heading for catastrophe and politicians would not speak the truth. Government could not do what it claimed it could and even full employment was a myth. He hinted at the desirability of a limited vote based on educational qualifications and said that Parliament should pass a law to provide that Trade Union leaders should be fined if they did not compel their members to fulfil agreements. This was neo-fascist talk and I think Beeching imagined himself as a new de Gaulle, emerging from industry to save the nation. He was heated and arrogant, and I gave as good as I got. After this clash, I had a pleasant talk to him. He told me that he was going back to ICI, not into politics as I thought he might. Here is a man with a scientific training, a brilliant analytical mind, but no understanding of politics and scarred by the experience of trying to work under a political directive that was itself woolly and lacking in analytical content. But he probably thinks that politics would be easy for him to run, just as many misguided people think that the railways are easy to run.

* Bristol was a centre of cigarette manufacture, home of Imperial Tobacco.

To Bristol for an executive. There was a storm of criticism, both personal and political. On the personal level they complained that I had neglected the constituency since the Election, had sent the thank-you letters out late, had not sent them Christmas cards, and even that I didn't write to everyone who was married or promoted in the way that some Tory MPs do using the local press to keep them informed.

This was followed by an outcry of political protest. I could understand their terrific anxieties about the aircraft industry, which could acutely affect Bristol. But it was broadened out into a general attack on the bank rate, rising income tax, foreign policy and the lot. They are unaware of the critical economic situation, or of the achievements of the 100 days and emerged as a most short-sighted group. There must be much more political education and active campaigning. All in all, a discouraging meeting. Coming after Beeching, my faith in democracy was a bit shattered from both ends.

Churchill is gravely ill and it looks like the end.

Saturday 16 January
Spent this morning drafting a letter to Buckingham Palace about the new stamps issue. I was also preparing my scheme for co-operation with the Citizens Advice Bureau to try to give the Post Office some role in improving communications between the social services and the public.

To the House of Commons this afternoon where everybody was waiting to hear news of Churchill's illness. All major Government policy statements have been postponed, the Prime Minister having cancelled his visit to Bonn. The crude fact is that everybody is waiting for the old man to die. Parliament will probably have to adjourn for five days when he does, since we can hardly meet while his body is lying in state in Westminster Hall. Yet he may well drag on for days, weeks or months. It is macabre and grisly.

Home this evening fairly early. Peter Shore came along from 10.15 to 12.45. I confided in him my pessimism at the prospect of getting Britain moving again in the absence of any evident public desire. I told him that I thought decisions about Britain's future – as an independent island, as an American satellite, or as a member of a wider Europe – were being taken by default without any real consideration of what was involved. I also told him that I had become profoundly convinced that although the Civil Service was a good administering body, it did not have within itself the necessary impetus to stimulate economic growth. We went on to discuss reorganising the Post Office as a nationalised industry and ideas for broadcasting development. It was just good to hear his views. He's a most wise and intelligent person and I greatly regret not having him at the Post Office.

Wednesday 20 January

I went to the Commons and had a talk with Charlie Pannell who is upset by the delay in implementing his scheme to take over the Palace of Westminster from the Lord Great Chamberlain and put it in the hands of a committee. He says the Queen is agreeable and the opposition is coming from the Labour peers led by Longford and Gardiner who have mobilised Tory support against him. He is hopping mad and thinks that Harold is being a bit weak about it.

At 6.15 pm I went to the Department of Economic Affairs for a talk with George Brown, Jim Callaghan and Tony Crosland about the timing of our statement on tariff increases. I knew George was inclined to a later date but managed to win him round on the grounds that we had it before his machinery had been set up and could say – as I intend to – that we had been through the most rigorous price review machinery. He finally agreed. He was very tired, had flu, and had to go to Patrick Gordon Walker's election meeting in Leyton. But I find him extremely agreeable and we talked about a number of other problems.

Thursday 21 January

To the Commons this afternoon where Sir Harold Banwell chairman of the National Citizens Advice Bureau came to discuss the ways in which the Post Office might help the social services. I am keen that postmen should carry a reply postcard containing the names of local social services. Linked to this, telephone operators would take down details from those who called to enquire and forward these names to the Citizen's Advice Bureau.

At midnight, after we were both asleep, Peter Shore rang up to tell us the appalling news that Patrick Gordon Walker had been defeated in the Leyton by-election by 200 votes. This is a terrible shock to the Government and reduces our majority to three. It poses immediate problems for Harold. What is to be done with Patrick? He cannot be made a peer as Foreign Secretary, he can hardly be exposed to another by-election, and he cannot be left any longer as Foreign Secretary without being in Parliament.

Our first reaction was to gather together the same group that met throughout the summer – Dick Crossman, Peter Shore, myself, John Allen, George Wigg, and Tommy Balogh – to try to restore some central direction to our campaign. We have neglected the public since we came to power and undoubtedly are paying the price for this now. This will just confirm the prejudices that each of us have about what is wrong.

My own feeling is that Gordon Walker's defeat is partly attributable to the crude manipulation of the Honours List in order to make room for him. Quintin Hogg had a similarly humiliating result in his 1963 by-election. People who have elected a Member of Parliament whom they know and trust cannot like it much if he is bought off with a peerage so that the Prime Minister can impose upon the constituency someone else of his choice for reasons of his own. I put this to Peter Shore and it had never occurred to him that this might be the case.

Friday 22 January
The press this morning blew up the Leyton defeat – inevitably – as the Waterloo of the 100 days. There were urgent talks at Number 10 all day as a result of which Michael Stewart was moved to the Foreign Office and Tony Crosland to the Ministry of Education. I'm sorry that Michael has moved from a more important to a less important job and particularly that he has given up education where he was an anchor man who knew what he wanted. Also I have some doubts about Tony who has a middle-class obsession with the public schools issue and may be weak on the comprehensives, behind-hand on the real issue of streaming versus non-streaming and too keen on extending the direct grant idea.

To the Europa Hotel to speak at a huge lunch organised by the Institute of Public Relations, attended by about 400 people. Toby O'Brien, our PRO, is president this year and I talked about GPO public relations and my understanding of the Post Office as the Ministry of Communications responsible for developing them in every conceivable way. Caroline talked to O'Brien at lunch and discovered that he thought Bevins had been a disaster.

Back to the Office to make a bravery award and then a discussion with the Post Office solicitor Sir John Ricks about the pirate radio Bill. The title 'Marine Etc Suppression' Bill is impossible and the Bill itself is clumsy and unattractive. I shall have to see the Attorney-General about this.

Home this evening, working through my papers until late. The new Government announcements were made. Peter rang to say that he is being taken on as strategic political thinker with special links between Harold and Transport House.

Sunday 24 January
Winston Churchill died this morning. I heard it on the news at 8.45. Thus ends the life of one of the greatest Englishmen of our time. Our family have much cause to be grateful to him. He it was who gave Father his extra twenty years of active life in the House of Lords. Also he was one of those who supported me so much during my long constitutional struggle and that support was of great practical value.

In 1940 he noticed my brother David's letter in the *Times* and sent him his book and a covering note to Father which is now an historic document.[7] He has had such a long retirement that his death means more to middle-aged people than it does to those under thirty-five. But even with the many years of waiting for this moment it is nonetheless a shock.

The effect of all this is to put politics into cold storage for a week.

Monday 25 January

I called Brigadier Holmes into the Office this morning. He had produced an incredible report examining the proposal I had made that we should introduce Post Office Christmas cards experimentally this year. By fiddling with the figures – the only way of describing it – the report suggested that we would have to sell 15 million cards before we could even expect to break even. There can hardly be a simpler task than printing Christmas cards and of course few of the manufacturers – many of whom make enormous profits out of it – ever approach a turnover of one million, let alone 15 million. This is the way the Civil Service undermines you if it doesn't want to do something. It simply produces a paper to say that a thing cannot be done. It is all so discouraging.

I had the internal telecommunications people to lunch today. I'm not sure these lunches are turning out to be much of a success. Occasionally one meets a bright chap and Mr Jones, who is the head of the particular branch that I met, was undoubtedly one of the brighter characters but the rest seemed to me a bit scornful. The trouble with the Civil Service is that it wants a quiet life. The civil servants want to move slowly along the escalator towards their knighthood and retirement and they have no interest whatsoever in trying to develop new lines of activity. For this reason, the Civil Service is totally unfitted for the main functions the Post Office performs. But if you did make it into a nationalised industry, would you get any greater incentive for action?

To the House of Commons this afternoon to hear the statement on Churchill's death. It was very moving but the tributes have been in the press for so long that there was nothing new to be said. Lady Asquith made far and away the best speech in the House of Lords.

Tuesday 26 January

O'Brien came and we had a talk about the public relations policy of the Post Office. I asked him to prepare a complete paper on this so that we could consider it at a Board meeting. O'Brien is a man of some imagination and it seemed sensible to bring him on the Board and try to raise the status of public relations in the Office. There will be some resistance to this but I intend to go ahead with it.

To the House of Commons at lunchtime and right up to the last minute we didn't know whether we were going to get questions or not. In the end there were no questions asked. I now go to the bottom of the queue and will not come up again until 11 March. This will prevent me from making a number of important announcements which I would like to make. I had decided to write to Harold to get his general consent about a Churchill stamp and was told that his main anxiety was whether the Queen would agree to share a stamp with the face of Sir Winston. It's perfectly obvious that far from being able to get the Queen off the stamps, I'm going to fight like a tiger in order to get the right to put some other faces on. However, I happened to see him later in the evening and I told him that the design would have to be approved by the Palace in any case and then he gave me the go-ahead. I suspect that the network has been feeding information in to him to suggest that I want to get the Queen off the stamps and this has been reported tactfully to him.

This evening Caroline and I went to a party at St Stephen's Restaurant attended by all those who had helped in the '64 General Election on the publicity side. They are working to furnish a publicity programme for Labour for the next Election and my neglect over the last three months has resulted in my being forced out of the broadcasting work. I think it is essential to get back into this and I propose to devote a great deal more time to Party politics from now on. This means partly working with people on publicity, partly working in the constituency and partly making more public speeches. The trouble with us now is that we are a Government but we are not a Party and the physical isolation is producing disintegration of the common mind on political things. I believe this happened in 1945 but we don't have a big enough majority to be able to afford to let it happen again.

Afterwards Caroline and I had dinner at St Stephen's and as we looked out of the window we saw the coffin of Sir Winston being brought in and carried on the shoulders of the pallbearers to the catafalque in Westminster Hall where it is to lie in state tomorrow, Thursday and Friday.

Wednesday 27 January
Went to Westminster Hall to see the lying-in-state.

At 10 o'clock we had the National Executive. There was a short discussion about the political situation and by general agreement the Executive decided that the publicity effort would have to be stepped up. Part of the difficulty here is that Harold continues to believe that his relations with the lobby are the key to the whole business. This was the mistake he made during the General Election when he concentrated on press conferences in London rather than getting out to the people as a whole. In fact, the lobby is coming under heavy attack now as being a little in-group of bought journalists who are not only contemptuous of those who concentrate solely upon them but are incapable of exercising the major influence on public opinion which is attributed to them.

Just as during the Election George Brown's vigorous public campaign did us more good than Harold's TV press conferences, so now the public image of George in his war against higher prices is doing us more good than the weekly briefing which the PM gives to the lobby. It is undoubtedly a grave weakness but there is no point in trying to persuade him that he is wrong as he is not receptive to that idea.

Another point highlighted this morning was the need to increase the salary scale at Transport House. The Head of the Research Department is expected to start at £1,200 which for a man with those responsibilities is a laughable salary. The reason it is not increased is that the trade unions provide most of the money and their own salary scales are deliberately kept low by their members. They are therefore not willing to contemplate higher salaries in Labour Party headquarters. They are, however, ready to provide hundreds of thousands of pounds so long as it is spent on publicity and not upon higher administrative remuneration. The control of the National Executive of the Labour Party by the trade union leaders with their built-in resistance to modern methods and financing is undoubtedly one of the sources of Conservative strength in Britain today. The others are the Palace which is very influential, the Civil Service and the Conservative Party itself. One day I shall write a serious book on Britain's conservative bias and analyse it in full.

During the Executive I had a short talk to Jennie Lee about her White Paper on the arts. She is very keen that the art in Crown Offices should be the work of living artists and not pictures from museums on loan.

Jim Callaghan came up to warn me of the effect of the Leyton by-election on the thinking of the Cabinet on my own departmental problems. He was extremely anxious about this and so am I.

Back to the Office where I heard that Number 10 had approved my announcement about the Churchill stamp but that, in order not to upset the Queen, the Prime Minister intended to raise with her in his audience tomorrow the question of whether Churchill's face should be allowed to appear beside her own.

Last night I read the long document submitted by Brigadier

Holmes about my GPO Christmas card idea. It was ten pages of entirely negative comment. It consisted simply of a list of every conceivable – and some inconceivable – difficulties that could be dredged up. The financial calculations, that the sale of 15 million Christmas cards would be necessary to break even, could only be interpreted as a final attempt to kill the idea off. I therefore wrote a minute saying that I had decided to drop the idea entirely not because I was convinced by the arguments but because it was obvious that the department did not wish to do it and that were I to insist the prospects of success would be non-existent if it were launched in the negative spirit evidenced in the document.

I handed this to Tilling and told him to circulate it as a numbered minute. He came back into my room looking very white and said that he could not circulate it and I would have to tell Brigadier Holmes personally what I thought. I'm sure it wasn't Brigadier Holmes's fault but I sent for him, told him what I had written and said that would be all. He was very shaky when he left. It is just not worth pursuing a minor thing like this. But the department had better realise that on major things there's got to be co-operation.

This afternoon I went to see the Attorney-General about the pirate broadcasting Bill. Most of the discussion was about the title of the Bill which is currently called the 'Suppression of Marine etc. Broadcasting Bill'. It is a massive document creating dozens of new offences, all designed to strangle the pirates. I have the greatest doubt as to whether it will be effective and the Government have no time to introduce it in this session. It is obvious that before this is done, an alternative of our own will have to be put forward. The pirates are establishing themselves firmly in public favour and if we killed them it would be extremely unpopular. I can see ourselves moving steadily towards the starvation of the BBC through a failure to raise the licence fee and ultimately capitulation in favour of commercial sound broadcasting. That is unless we permit the expansion of broadcasting on the basis of public service with advertising revenue to finance it.

Afterwards, I took all the children to see the lying-in-state. They were much impressed except for Joshua, aged seven, who thought we were going to 'Lyons Steak' which he believed to be a restaurant. He declared that he was delighted as he was very fond of steaks. When he saw Westminster Hall he couldn't understand and said he knew there was a coffin under the flag, but he clearly didn't know what a coffin was or what it contained. The thing that made the biggest impression on him was the sight of the television cameras.

Friday 29 January

I am coming to see things more clearly on the constituency side. The Bristol South East Labour Party is, effectively, dead. Some wards are active but the Party does not reflect the new broad base of our support and cannot, in my view, be re-formed to serve this purpose on its present basis. Two years ago I tried to launch Citizens for Labour to fill in this gap. However, it ran into bitter opposition from the National Executive and was as hard to establish locally as the Party itself. It was also open to the objection that it was a parallel organisation and not a very clear one at that. People don't like being lined up in organisations.

The two most neglected fields at the moment are the Party machine – especially the staff at Transport House – and Back Bench Labour MPs. Both are suffering from an acute feeling of neglect and both are essential for the long-term development of the Party. With Terry Pitt, Percy Clark and Gwyn Morgan [International Secretary] just appointed, I must try to establish a working relationship with them.

I have been pretty gloomy myself over the last few days and I think I keep going only on the bicycle theory – if you stop you fall off.

Saturday 30 January

This morning Caroline and I went to Sir Winston Churchill's funeral service at St Paul's Cathedral. We left at 8.45 and joined the huge crowd of cars queuing up in the Mall to enter the funeral route. There were thousands of troops standing there and the crowds on each side were extremely heavy. We got to St Paul's at 9.50, and found ourselves sitting in the dome about five rows from the front. The cathedral had television sets put all around it so that we could see the BBC programme, and it was crowded with TV cameramen and photographers. The most interesting part of the day was to see the world leaders who had attended. General de Gaulle, taller in real life than in cartoons; Ben Gurion, short and vigorous; Chancellor Erhardt of Germany, looking prosperous and German; and Earl Warren from the United States. We didn't see Eisenhower but he was there. Also President Tshombe, Habib Bourguiba Jr, and Kenneth Kaunda from Zambia. The book of ceremonial was far longer than the book containing the funeral service itself. The sight of the Establishment coming out with all its pagan clothes was slightly jarring. It was the last great Victorian festival and I suppose one had to accept it as that. Afterwards, we stood on the steps while the cars came and drove the various leaders away and then slipped up to the Post Office where our car was waiting.

Sunday 31 January

This morning Percy Clark, the new Director of Publicity at Transport House, came for a couple of hours' talk. The danger is that the advertising groups have gathered round the Party machine and they have little political sense and pursue the market research approach to politics much too crudely.

Today, there was a sensational article by Bevins about his period at the Post Office,* describing in detail the clash between him and the Cabinet on the subject of postal pay. It contains such a detailed account of what happened that I should think it possibly constitutes a breach of the Official Secrets Act. It is a complete abandonment of collective responsibility and will furnish me with useful material in fighting the defensive battle that lies ahead. I have some sympathy with Bevins and it just confirms my general view about a greater degree of separation of the Post Office from the Government machine.

Tuesday 2 February

Frank Cousins and Jim Boyden, MP for Bishop Auckland, came to my room to discuss the development of educational broadcasting, all part of the major decision making about broadcasting.

I wandered round the Commons and talked to a few people. The trouble about being PMG is that every other Member stops you with some local query about a telephone kiosk or a sub-post office and it's just impossible to keep abreast of all their complaints.

I saw Herbert Bowden and the Chief Whip, Ted Short, about the Broadcasting Committee. Harold was approached by Herbert Bowden and has agreed that I am to serve on it in a personal capacity. Harold is very much against Party political broadcasts at the moment, feeling that his appearances on 'Panorama' are enough. He doesn't seem to see that we are failing to get our case over to the public, partly because we are not using Party politicals.

I also had a short talk to Tony Crosland and Austen Albu about my plans for taking the Post Office out of the Civil Service and making it a nationalised industry. They are interested and I think I might be able to build up some support.

Wednesday 3 February

This morning began with an explosion from Sir Kenneth Anderson about a clash in the House of Commons last night. George Brown had intervened during Maudling's speech to say that the Tory Government had cooked the Post Office books and falsified the

---

* An extract from his autobiographical book *The Greasy Pole*, 1965.

accounts. In fact, of course, Bevins had not falsified the accounts but had eliminated the forecasts of future losses. Sir Kenneth was talking about the possibility of a libel action against George Brown. It was all very embarrassing as I knew George was wrong but was not prepared to listen to my civil servants criticising a political colleague. So I simply ignored it. But I do think this business has gone far enough. Bevins should have raised the postal charges earlier but did not do so for electoral reasons.

This evening with Charles Morris for a tour of the BBC Television Centre and dinner with Lord Normanbrook and Sir Hugh Greene. It was an interesting evening though it began with a great deal of small talk by Normanbrook who is at the very centre of the Establishment. I think he's a stupid man and highly suspicious of me. After dinner had progressed on this basis, I raised some problems to discuss. The first was whether the BBC could meet the need for light music that has been demonstrated to exist by the audiences which the pirate radios are getting. They said that if you had continuous light music, it would be like keeping the pubs open all day – a real BBC view that it is bad to give people what they want.

The next issue I raised with them was the way in which we might impose a Pilkington solution[8] on the ITA by gathering advertising centrally and gradually diminishing the commercial role of the programme companies. They were frankly not interested in this, being keen to keep the BBC going and to keep their hands clean.

I had a long and rather fierce discussion with them about the desirability of having some broadcasting council, comparable to the Press Council, to which people could take complaints. I cited the case of the savage attack on Henry Brooke, the former Conservative Home Secretary in 'TW3'. Since I hate Brooke this took them a little bit by surprise. They really couldn't answer but said that it was up to the Board of Governors to take the necessary action. But it's no good going to the Governors as they are the people who run the organisation that is doing the damage.

At the end of the dinner I said to Greene and Normanbrook, 'I hear from everybody that you are very worried about my appointment.' They both looked rather sheepish. Indeed, I said that not long ago a note was put in my in-tray to say that Lord Normanbrook intended to resign, but that when I questioned my office about it they could not say any more. Greene was not surprised but Normanbrook did not deny it and it is clear that he had wanted it conveyed to me. I'm glad I said it.

Thursday 4 February

To the Post Office this morning and told Lord Hill about the proposed ban on cigarette advertising. I then went on to a number of other discussions with him including the need for some sort of broadcasting council. He said the Independent Television Authority was much more of a censor for this purpose than the BBC Board of Governors since it did not produce any of the programmes itself.

After Hill had gone, two of the staff from McKinsey, the management consultants, came to see me. I told Tilling that I was not prepared to have the DG with me while we talked. It was necessary to do this because I wanted to tell them quite frankly and in confidence my impressions of the Post Office. They made a keen note of it all.

This evening I went to Bristol for a meeting at Hanham and then to the GMC. There was a very great deal of personal and political criticism from the GMC. They said I had neglected the constituency and that the Labour Government had greatly disappointed them. It was all very discouraging.

Saturday 6 February

Spent the whole day preparing for our party. About seventy-five people came from 9 pm till 2.30 in the morning, among them Tony Crosland, the Mulleys, the Robinsons, the Shores, the Townsends, Lady Asquith, Harry Secombe and his wife, Ghislane and Stefan Leven, the Ungoed-Thomases, the Bishop of Woolwich, and so on. Everybody seemed to get on well. Bed very late and very tired.

Monday 8 February

I went to the Post Office Savings Bank headquarters at Blythe Road this morning to see the Glasgow Exhibition. Mr Smart received me, I met the senior officials and walked round. In one room there were 500 girls doing nothing but sorting out withdrawal forms that had poured in from every Post Office in the country. It was a fantastic sight. A complete computerisation programme had been set in hand. I also saw the staff side representatives very briefly to discuss the meeting in the Albert Hall.

This evening to dinner at the White Tower with Percy Clark and advertising people he had got together. We had a discussion about advertising and PR and the state of the Party. The trouble is of course that they see things a bit too much from the technical point of view and one suggestion that we should have some debs to the Labour Women's Conference with a fashion show seemed to me to be very shallow. No doubt they regarded me as a terrible old stick-in-the-mud.

Tuesday 9 February

To A. V. Alexander's memorial service at St Martin's-in-the-Field.[9] It had all been arranged by the Navy and the address was given by the Chaplain of the Fleet who had hardly known A. V. He described him as 'this great Christian gentleman' and made no reference at all to the fact that he had been active in the Labour and Co-operative movements all his life. It was like a farewell oration to some retired admiral. After the address we had a message from the Grand Preceptor of the Water Rats who described what a keen friend A.V. had been of the organisation. I walked back to Westminster with Charlie Pannell and Jennie Lee and we agreed that it had been an appallingly inappropriate service.

This evening I spoke at the Telecommunications Equipment Manufacturers' Association [TEMA] dinner which represents all the main manufacturers of equipment with whom we have bulk supply agreements. They ask about fifty or sixty Post Office people to their annual dinner and in this way keep us sweet. It is normal to make a completely anodyne speech about telephone progress. But I decided that I would use the occasion to explain what the Government was trying to do: firstly, how the planning machinery would work, secondly to talk about the Post Office as a Ministry of Communications, and thirdly to speak as the biggest customer of the industry. In the last section, I had decided to refer to the bulk supply agreements. The DG was extremely worried about this and when I did finally write out my speech and sent it in, the press office at the Post Office said that it was political and could not be put out as a release. So I simply had to put my foot down and say it was to go out. It did go out in the end.

The dinner itself was all horribly ritualistic. There was a band playing, and everyone slow handclapped as the guests came to the top table. I sat next to a tough guy called John Clark of Plessey who was wildly right wing and greatly resented having to meet me. I made my speech in a friendly way and on the whole I think it went down reasonably well.

Wednesday 10 February

An extraordinary storm in a teacup today. A new MP, Ted Leadbitter from West Hartlepool, has written to complain about a telegraph pole being put up in front of one of his constituents' houses. Joe Slater replied in a very nice letter, saying that they had consulted the local authority and there was in fact nothing that they could really do to help. So Leadbitter put down a question to me and I replied very briefly saying that the Post Office did always consult local authorities. He then rang up my office and left a message to say, 'Mr Leadbitter regards the Postmaster General's reply as so rude and evasive that he does not propose to come to the House or to accept the Labour whip until the answer is withdrawn and the pole is removed.' I rang up the whip to tell him what had happened and left a message for Leadbitter to come to see me. Leadbitter received the message, rang up my office again and said under no circumstances would he see me and rang off in a temper. The Chief Whip had to summon him and he refused to attend. He was finally pushed in and told that it was a very serious offence to resign from the Labour Party and that if he resigned from it on the grounds of a telegraph pole he would be a laughing stock. Apparently he's now prepared to see me.

Thursday 11 February
Working away at accumulated papers. Among the most interesting letters that came in was one from David Gentleman, the famous stamp designer, who complained bitterly about having the Queen's head on the stamps. My office had handed me a letter to reply to him, saying that under no circumstances was there the slightest prospect of varying this. I of course refused to sign the letter and now see a way forward. I rang him up and asked him if he'd come to see me and whether he'd give permission for his letter to me to be published in the *Philatelic Bulletin*. If I can get this done, it will open up a controversy about the Queen's head at exactly the right level – design-wise rather than politically. I can see some trouble but it is an opening which has come to me quite unexpectedly.

Friday 12 February
To the Office where I found a letter waiting for me from Ray Mawby, former Tory Assistant PMG, asking me to provide the evidence on which George Brown had charged the last Government with falsifying the Post Office accounts. This is a very finicky one, as George clearly went wrong and should never had said what he did say. It is all very embarrassing.

To lunch with Roy Thomson* and a distinguished crowd of guests. Thomson is a self-made Canadian tycoon. He had a photographer photographing us having drinks beforehand and at lunch, and presented each of us with the *Sunday Times* colour supplement and at the end with the most expensive cookery book. He told me with great pride that his grandson would inherit the title and how many houses he had in England, Scotland and Canada. He is a simple-minded

---

* Lord Thomson, chairman of the Thomson Organisation Ltd, then publishers of *The Times* and the *Sunday Times*.

soul who must have some great skill as a businessman or he would never have got as far as he has done. After lunch he banged the table and some of those present asked me questions. I enjoyed it. This was the top Establishment meeting and I suppose now I must expect to find myself amongst its members.

Monday 15 February
David Gentleman, came to see me for breakfast this morning. He's about my age and is undoubtedly one of the best – if not the best – stamp designers in this country. The visit was a follow-up of his letter and he wanted to stress that it was impossible to get a decent quality of stamps in this country until the Queen's head was removed. We discussed it at great length and he had brought along an album of foreign stamps showing what was possible if the designer had a completely free hand.

We discussed how this issue could be most respectably brought to the fore and I promised that I'd consider publishing an article from him in the *Philatelic Bulletin*. He said he had a Churchill stamp ready with a tiny Queen's head on Churchill's massive shoulder and asked whether he could have the stamp reprinted without the Queen's head to see what it looked like. I said I could see no objection to this and that it would go before the Stamp Advisory Committee.

Then I went to the Office and had a long talk to Brigadier Holmes. I told him that I wanted the *Philatelic Bulletin* zipped up, that I wanted rejected designs published in it so people could judge for themselves, and that I'd like Gentleman's letter published as an article. I asked if there would be any objection to Gentleman's own Churchill without the Queen's head being essayed, and he said he didn't see why there should be.

This afternoon Mrs Gentleman came by with the artwork for the simplified Churchill and it was beautiful.

Tuesday 16 February
Arnold Wesker came to see me for breakfast this morning at 7.30, to persuade me to put out a stamp in support of the arts and sports which would sell for 3d plus 1d and the extra money would go to this cause. However, we calculated that the amount this would yield in a year for the arts would be very, very small and it may well not be worth trying. We went on to discuss the question of the royal head and I told him that I thought a discussion of this issue would not be a bad thing at all. But it is important that it should be kept entirely divorced from me. The real risk is that this will leak and I shall be hauled over the coals by Harold Wilson who I cannot think would be at all sympathetic, even on artistic grounds.

Afterwards to the House of Commons for a while and then with a huge crowd of people to the Albert Hall for the meeting with the Savings Bank staff who don't want to go to Glasgow. There were about a couple of thousand there and I was pretty nervous. I walked on to the platform with Mr Smart who introduced me briefly and then it was my turn to speak. I had a throat microphone and I sat on the front of the table and talked for about twenty-five minutes. Afterwards, there was an hour of questions, most of them very tough. One man said that 'it was like Hitler's Germany' and to prove this point he said he had a stopwatch and would time everyone while they clapped for a whole minute to show they agreed with him. I sat for a minute of clapping and then at the end I said that I had never heard anything so like Hitler's Germany as that.

The only thing I could really do was to stress that the decision was firm and that it was in their interests as much as ours that they should fill in the questionnaire on their personal situation. At the end we saw a film about Glasgow to promote the city. It was not a successful nor an unsuccessful meeting but I think it may have helped to clear the air a little and perhaps they will have appreciated the fact that I had come to talk to them about it. It had never happened before and the word will spread around the Savings Bank that I am genuinely taking a personal interest.

Wednesday 17 February
To the Cabinet Office for a committee meeting and then back to the Office where I heard that Gentleman's Churchill stamp without the Queen's head had not been submitted to the Stamp Advisory Committee yesterday afternoon. In fact I found a total paralysis in the Office on this subject. They were just not prepared to do what I told them to do. I've no doubt that the Post Office network has already got to work on Number 10 about this and that they have been notified by the PS at Number 10 that I am not to do anything else, while no doubt at the same time the PS at Number 10 is telling the Prime Minister that the Post Office is extremely worried by what I'm doing, and in this way effectively blocking all action. I shall either go to see Harold or write to him and see what happens – but not through my office. The only way to defeat the Civil Service network is to establish personal contact.

At noon I went to open the Stanley Gibbons Centenary Catalogue Exhibition and found a whole host of bigwigs there in the Festival Hall. I made a speech in which I tried to explain our new stamp policy and afterwards went round the exhibition and was presented with a gold reproduction of a penny black.

At 3 o'clock I went to see Herbert Bowden at the House of

Commons and was told that the Prime Minister was worried at rumours about what was going to happen to the BBC and felt sure that this must be due to leaks from me. This is the BBC pressure group operating again and I am absolutely fed up with it. I have given no interviews whatsoever to anybody on broadcasting. There is a delay because politically we can't afford to raise the licence fee to £6. As a result, people are thinking of all sorts of other ideas for raising finance, and Lord Normanbrook is just busy working away to undermine my position with the Prime Minister, using Sir Burke Trend or Sir Laurence Helsby for the purpose. Whether Harold is genuinely worried or whether it's just his Private Secretary who is putting it about, I don't know.

At 4 o'clock Ted Leadbitter came to see me about the telegraph pole in West Hartlepool. He was a bit shamefaced and apologised for having spoken to my secretary in the way he did. I promised to write to the man.

Then to the Central Hall for a fabulous illuminated and illustrated lecture on how colour television works.

Afterwards Caroline and I went to the Institution of Electrical Engineers for an informal dinner with Hugh Greene and all the top Post Office people. I was expected to make a speech but this was indicated to me about five minutes before I got to my feet so I just had time to scribble down a few jokes and one or two serious points. Caroline sat next to Hugh Greene and told him how delighted I was that he was at the BBC and what a great respect I had for him, and so on. This is necessary in view of the massive campaign the BBC are waging against me at the moment. She also told him what difficulties there were at the Post Office and how the Post Office people were just all Tories. Greene replied by saying how pleased he was that there was somebody in the Post Office who was capable of thinking about broadcasting problems.

Thursday 18 February
Alf Robens* came to see me at the House of Commons and we had an hour and a quarter discussing the Coal Board and the Post Office and how one runs a big industry. He was strongly in favour of us moving to a nationalised status and also said that he made a particular point of seeing that in his private office all the guys were socialists so that their loyalty was to him and not to the department. He told me the most hair-raising stories about the last Government where the network would report Ministers they didn't like to the

* Lord Robens, chairman of the National Coal Board 1961–71, Labour MP for Wansbeck, 1945–50 and Blyth, 1950–60.

Prime Minister and he would get rid of them. Obviously this is what is happening with the BBC. Lord Normanbrook has lunch with Derek Mitchell and triggers this controversy off. I found Alf stimulating and it was good of him to have spared the time to see me.

While we were there Jennie Lee came in to say that she'd had lunch with Lord Snowdon and Princess Margaret yesterday and had mentioned to them that the best designers thought that you'd never get decent stamps unless some of them were free to submit designs that didn't include the Queen's head. Apparently, so Jennie said, they didn't mind a bit about it and thought it must be some officials lower down who were causing the trouble.

Enoch Powell came to see me at 7 o'clock to say that a Post Office official in Wolverhampton was an alcoholic and would I deal with it. Afterwards he stayed and we chatted for a while.

Just as I was going home I looked in at George Wigg's room and found Peter Shore there. He was shortly joined by Tommy Balogh, John Allen and Marcia Williams and we had the most hilarious hour discussing the Civil Service and how we could beat them. It was lovely to have the chance of discussing things in this friendly atmosphere. Our main concern was to try to turn the network on itself. For example, why don't we spread the word among the civil servants that the others are gossiping about them so that there is a complete breakdown of confidence?

Friday 19 February
To the Treasury this morning for a meeting on educational broadcasting, with Reg Prentice presenting his plan that the BBC would be given money to carry a few hours of genuine educational broadcasting on BBC2 at night, starting in September. Judith Hart was representing the Scottish Office and Jack Diamond was in the chair. There was a bevy of officials.

When I was asked for my comments I said I thought it would be much better to give the money to an educational committee and let them spend it, commissioning programmes from the BBC or ITA to get them on the air. If all programmes were repeated on the ITA during the daytime they would get a far bigger audience than on BBC2 at night. The intervention more or less killed the existing proposal stone dead, as it clearly showed the way to a larger audience at a lower cost and introduced the possibility of something that was quite different from just an extension of the BBC empire. The whole matter was referred back for further consideration.

I went to Number 10 with the car to bring Harold's personal secretaries Marcia Williams and Brenda Dew over to the Post Office for lunch. Joe Slater and I took them to the canteen and when he left for his train north they stayed for an hour's talk with me in my room. We discussed the network at great length. They hate Derek Mitchell who is Harold's principal Civil Service secretary. We discussed in detail how these men operate, why their loyalty is to each other rather than to the Government, the techniques they use for evaluating the standing of Ministers and their power to undermine them and influence events. I mentioned the stamp business and the BBC lobby as examples. Marcia and Brenda are very nice and Harold leans heavily on them. No doubt there was a buzz of conversation in the Office to find out exactly why I had had the Prime Minister's personal secretaries to lunch and what we were talking about.

We discussed the honours list and I said what I thought about it. They told me what a fantastic struggle Harold had had to get the footballer Stanley Matthews his knighthood. He is obviously in just as great difficulty as I am.

Monday 22 February
The DG was very friendly and I think had been a bit uneasy over the last few days. He did not know that I had made a private arrangement to see the Prime Minister this evening. This is the only way in which I can get anything done.

I went to lunch with Sir Leon Bagrit, Chairman of Elliot-Automation, to whom I had written some time ago after having read his Reith lectures. I had also met him at Lord Thomson's lunch and he was evidently impressed by what I said there. He greeted me in his fancy London headquarters. We discussed the best way in which we could release the energies of the Post Office with the possibility of future development. He thought that it was no good setting up a separate Directorate of Forward Planning and that the best thing to do would be to try to get a general feeling abroad that new ideas were welcome, which is what I have done. We also discussed the possibility of a weekend conference to consider the application of cybernetic techniques. He went on to say that he thought it would be a good idea if we asked all our major suppliers if they would think ahead and prepare plans for the development of apparatus that we might be able to use ten or fifteen years hence. This is rather comparable to what the American Post Office did under Kennedy. I think I shall prepare material for this and perhaps send a personal letter to all the heads of the great undertakings that work for us.

I got a message that Harold would see me this evening so I went over to Number 10 at 6.30. Marcia was sitting in her little waiting room and I had about ten minutes' talk to her before Harold appeared. She had to draw the curtain before he came into the room in case somebody should take a pot shot at him from the park. This is evidently one of the security precautions. We had an hour and a half talking about various things.

First of all I raised the issue of the BBC licence fee and said that I presumed that he was not in any great hurry to get this one settled. I told him that I had been subjected to a vigorous BBC lobby and he assured me that he had not indicated to anybody any dissatisfaction with the way I was doing my job and that if he had any complaints he'd tell me so to my face. I said I didn't believe in the conspiracy theory of politics but that of course the pressure was considerable and the longer the delay the more anxious the BBC became.

Secondly we discussed the politics of the tariff increases. I told him that the situation had become much more serious and that it would be impossible for me to publish a White Paper next month revealing starkly the extent of the deficit without having something that I could say about it. He inclined to the view that we ought to increase charges earlier rather than later, in view of the impending decision on an Election date. In this connection I asked him whether Tommy Balogh could be spared to come and have a look at some of my figures and also to look at my Giro paper when it arrives. Whether or not I shall get an economic adviser out of this I'm not sure. In many ways it's better to have Thomas coming in and doing the work himself if he can spare the time.

Next we came to the question of stamps. I told him that the 'release of energy was beginning to get out of hand'. The designers were pressing for the right to do commemorative and pictorial stamps without the Queen's head and I asked whether I could have an audience with the Queen to ask her permission to submit some non-traditional as well as traditional designs. Harold said that he had an audience with the Queen tomorrow and would ask her whether she would agree to receive non-traditional designs and consider them. This gets me off the hook completely and it'll be interesting indeed to hear what the result of the audience is. I'm determined to hear it from Harold personally and not through Mitchell.

Mitchell sneaked in and out once or twice to see who was in with Harold. Marcia hates him.

We went to the Crossmans for dinner.[10] Tam Dalyell was there too. We had a general talk about politics and then after dinner I began raising some questions about the BBC. Dick Crossman is on the ministerial committee and I thought it would be interesting to test out what he thought. I put to him the problem of the £6 licence fee and he was in favour of granting it – though not at once for political reasons. He said that he was an old-fashioned Reith man who thought the BBC ought to be a public service without making concessions to the desires of the viewers. However, for reasons of economy, he would scrap BBC2 and just limit TV to the existing BBC and ITA channels. His main desire seemed to be to get rid of Hugh Greene. It was the old prickly Dick but Caroline always reminds me that he's just a teacher and not a politician and I shouldn't take any notice of what he says. He certainly is a stimulating person to talk to.

Home at 12.30.

Tuesday 23 Feburary

I had lunch today with Sheikh Ahmad Zardan, the Deputy Minister of Communications from Saudi Arabia, who has come to London on a junket and is interested in getting some postal advisers to help him. He was an engineer of about fifty and non-political. I had to take him to lunch at the Royal Festival Hall and it was rather sticky finding things to talk about. The only time he warmed up was when we told him about the great mail robbery and he said that in Saudi Arabia they cut off the hands of robbers and this was a very good idea that we ought to consider.

Wednesday 24 February

To the Executive this morning at Transport House. Two or three items of interest came up. The first was the announcement that the Labour Party staff had turned down the 10 per cent pay offer made by the staff board and wanted an independent enquiry into comparability. Dai Davies, Party Treasurer, was angry about this but I supported it on the grounds that the Labour movement did underprice its services and that we might be much better advised to spend our existing money on better staff salaries than on some of the publicity items that are presented to us. This caused something of a storm but Dick Crossman supported me.

Thursday 25 February

To the Office this morning and saw Mr Lillicrap about the possibility of getting a greater degree of accountability of BBC and ITA broadcasts. This is a difficult issue as there is such a strong tradition of no political interference, which I share. But we could make a move by insisting on the availability of scripts to MPs and perhaps by aggrieved individuals and organisations appealing to the General Advisory Councils of the two bodies.

I rang Marcia Williams at Number 10 and she told me that the Queen had readily agreed to give me an audience to discuss stamps, which is most encouraging.

To the Commons this afternoon and there was a deputation from the Phonographic Society and the Musicians' Union brought by Brian O'Malley [MP for Rotherham]. They wanted to know how quickly I could kill pirates. Both are deeply affected. I told them that the legislative programme was congested and that there were political difficulties. We must have an alternative to propose.

I asked them to think hard about the problem of an alternative which would perhaps mean a national programme of light music made up of records and live orchestras, interspersed. This might be run by the BBC or possibly by a Post Office network called POP. It might be linked to local stations which could opt in and out of the network if their local resources were unable to fill the full day. The Phonographic interest is to plug new records sufficiently to sell them but not sufficiently to make people feel they needn't buy them. The Musicians' Union is afraid for the employment of its members and frankly doesn't like records at all. This leads both sides to be restrictive about needle time. I suggested that they might like to get together on an informal basis with Frank Gillard* to see if the Light Programme could be revamped to meet this need. I kept quiet on the topic of financing it, since this raises other issues which will have to be looked at by the Government. It was an exercise in diplomacy to try to get them to see how popular demand could be met without damaging their own legitimate interests.

Afterwards Tommy Balogh came to see me and we had an hour together. He has agreed to act as my economic adviser. He was full of gloom about the sabotage of the Civil Service and we compared notes on this.

Lunch with Paul Stephenson. Paul is back from six months in America and the West Indies and full of plans for stepping up the civil rights campaign in Britain. He and I think alike – integration is not enough and the idea of tolerated acceptance has got to be replaced by the idea of unselfconscious equality while maintaining fruitful cultural distinction.

To the Office for the afternoon, clearing papers. I sent off some documents to Tommy Balogh. Tilling was furious as he said that the suggestion that I needed an economic adviser was a vote of no confidence in the department. I was too kind to say how right he was. The Civil Service is a nightmare, God knows how you can instill real excitement into it. I think I may hold another Albert Hall meeting in a few months to report on the progress made and try to stimulate some of the lower echelons with what is happening.

* Former BBC war correspondent and director of Sound Broadcasting, BBC, 1963–8. Later Managing Director, BBC Radio.

Working through the top brass restricts the flow of ideas both upwards and downwards.

Liz Shore looked in this evening to collect Mimi from the Youth Club while Caroline was out at the first meeting of the Comprehensive Schools Committee. She said the middle ranks of the Civil Service retain some initiative but Ministers never meet them.

Tuesday 2 March
My first meeting was with F. H. K. Henrion from 11 until about 12.15. He brought along Alan Parkin from his office and they explained the work they had been doing on Post Office design co-ordination. Three immediate issues are coming up that they would like held for the moment. One is the design of kiosks, the second is the design of postmen's uniforms, and the third is the house style which Stuart Rose proposed. Rose is our typographical adviser. They suggest that a design co-ordinator be appointed from within the Office to work with the consultant designer. Then individual designers would be briefed on design policy generally and asked to get on with the job. It was an exciting plan and I intend to back them to the hilt.

Mr Wolverson looked in and I discussed art in Crown Offices with him. The department is paralysed with fear at the thought that Head Postmasters would have to select the paintings to be hung. I will have to take this up with Jennie Lee.

Then Cadbury came and I discussed with him the national data processing service plan. He says that he and Jeremy Bray do not altogether agree but that nothing should now hold up consultations with the Ministry of Technology at official level with a view to presenting a paper to the Cabinet. I think there will be some difference as to whether this is just to be a small-scale co-operative computer service comparable to that offered by computer firms or whether it is to move into the higher range of management.

At 4.45 Judith Hart joined me to receive a delegation from the University of Strathclyde who have developed a simple TV studio and want a licence to broadcast a one kilowatt signal covering the inner Glasgow conurbation. They were tremendous enthusiasts, led by a tough physicist and it was like being transplanted suddenly to America or Israel. We may need to use them for rather different purposes in the short run but my heart warmed to them. I would like to give them what they want.

This evening Tony Smith [BBC producer] called and told me the inside story of Baverstock's fall from power.* Baverstock is a hopeless administrator and has made many enemies. It is clear that the whole

* Donald Baverstock, Chief of Programmes BBC TV, 1963–5.

pattern of broadcasting needs looking at again and there may be a case for taking BBC2 away from the BBC and setting it up under a separate corporation. I doubt if I can get my colleagues to agree but it's certainly worthwhile knowing what one wants.

Wednesday 3 March
Went to the BBC to watch a demonstration of the rival colour TV systems, NTSC and SECAM. The Soviet Ambassador had also been invited and had come along with a number of his counsellors and attachés. The whole BBC top brass were there together with senior Post Office people. Afterwards we lunched together. It is very difficult because the BBC want us to give a firm date for the introduction of colour and frankly I am not optimistic about this, since the cost of colour would be astronomical in terms of public expenditure on sets and I don't think it's justified in the present circumstances.

Afterwards to the Commons and then at 4.15 to see George Brown about tariffs. We had a stand-up row about it. He is absolutely opposed to any increase and thinks we ought to survive a year on borrowing in order to save his prices policy. I told him I thought this showed lack of nerve and even a certain lack of integrity. It's only by standing up to George Brown that you can ever make any progress and I don't think I've done any good by sitting back and letting him make the running. He is an appalling bully and I'm afraid he may succeed in bullying Harold Wilson on this. Jim Callaghan at the Treasury is of course on my side. But I'm not sure whether I shall carry the day.

I felt tired and came home to lie down for a couple of hours, going back to the House from 10 till 11.30 for a couple of votes.

Thursday 4 March
After Cabinet I went to Riverside Studios to record an interview on the telephone service with Derek Hart for 'Choice', the TV consumers' programme. I read the script and saw the film they'd collected and it was obviously a *News of the World* type exposé of the telephone service, making no attempt to set it at all in perspective.

I went to listen to the end of the defence debate. Quintin Hogg made a rip-roaring knock-about speech and Denis Healey wound up. He attacked Reggie Paget and Konni Zilliacus[11] and said they were the most curious partnership since 1939 – a reference to the Hitler-Stalin pact. It was a cruel personal attack and Denis's speech was typical of him – full of unhappy phrases.

Afterwards I stayed working until 11.20 but there was no division. The queue for taxis was so long that I came home on the underground.

Monday 8 March

To Norwich this morning to see the sorting machines in action. I travelled with Brigadier Holmes and had an interesting talk with him there and back in the train. He is strongly in favour of taking the Post Office out of Government and making it a nationalised industry. He also strongly supports separating Posts from Telecommunications in order to restore their morale and give them a chance. He agreed that there was a great need for strengthening the first line supervisors and the middle and upper management in the postal services. He was in favour of a deeper analysis of costing to try to make some sense of the pattern of charges and the pattern of services. I think Holmes is a good chap, though he is a bit too anxious to please and may not be tough enough when he doesn't agree.

Norwich was interesting but not sensational. I met the staff and found them unenthusiastic about mechanisation. They said it destroyed their skill and craft as manual sorters.

Tuesday 9 March

David Butler came to see me. He is anxious about the way the Boundary Commission is going about its work and also thinks the Speaker's Conference[12] is rather a disaster. David said that if we had not accepted the postal vote in 1948, we would have won the 1951 Election and would have had a majority of twenty-six now. So it does pay to think about these things.

Then Jennie Lee came in and I had an hour with her. She has been put in charge of the University of the Air and has all sorts of ideas for taking BBC2 and running it as an educational channel. She is in contact with Sidney Bernstein and Arnold Goodman and I think the plan would be to take over the network, put educational programmes on that would be repeated on ITA in the daytime and then advertise in order to get revenue to finance it. It would be an exciting project, although it'll undoubtedly precipitate the threatened resignations of Normanbrook and perhaps Greene as well. Who cares!

Wednesday 10 March

David Gentleman came to breakfast this morning at my request as today is the day that I am seeing the Queen. He brought along the most beautiful designs for Battle of Britain stamps made up of silhouettes of RAF and Luftwaffe planes in combat, which could be sold in blocks of twelve. I didn't tell him I was going to see the Queen but I think he must have guessed it. He also brought along some models for Christmas cards and I shall take these into the Office and get them done.

Then to the House of Commons for an hour and at 12.20 to

Buckingham Palace for my audience with the Queen. Yesterday I received a notification that the court was in mourning so I had to wear a black tie.

As my car arrived I was greeted by Sir Michael Adeane, the Queen's private secretary, and taken up in the lift to the private apartments. Adeane went out of his way to be friendly and was somewhat nervous of my arrival. He said, 'Don't you think our stamps need some new ideas?' and, 'There's a real danger we will get out of date, don't you think?' This was obviously designed to draw me out about the subject of my audience and also to suggest that the Palace was a great modernising influence. I nodded gravely, and agreed with him, and admired the view and looked at the paintings and then, at 12.40, one of the big flunkeys called out my name and I went in to the state apartment grasping a huge black official box, bowed, shook hands, the Queen beckoned me to sit down and I started on a carefully prepared speech.

I said that I was very grateful to her for seeing me as I knew the keen interest that she took in postage stamps. I said that I had some stamps for her approval but didn't want to worry her to approve them there and then. What I wanted to do was to talk about stamp design policy generally. I said that the new Government saw stamps in an entirely new context as part of the arts and not just as adhesive money labels for postage purposes. That was why we had set up a Fellowship in Minuscule Design and wanted to improve design generally. Miss Jennie Lee was greatly concerned, and the Prime Minister had kindly arranged this audience so that I could discuss it with the Queen. There were many things about Britain that we ought to project abroad, perhaps through postage stamps.

Specifically we would like to have new definitives which would have a more beautiful picture of the Queen on them. She smiled graciously. On commemoratives, I said that we had broadened the criteria to many subjects that had previously been excluded and I thought this was the right technique. Also I said the designers were keen to produce pictorial stamps depicting perhaps our composers, our landscapes, our architecture, our painters, our kings and queens and this was a most exciting field that had never been explored.

'However,' I said, 'this raised the whole question of the use of the head on the stamps.' The Queen frowned and smiled. I said that there was a view held by many designers that the necessity of depicting the head on the stamp was restrictive and embarrassing. For example, the Burns stamp would be difficult to put out as a two-head stamp. Similarly, the United Nations stamp which the UN was trying to get issued all over the world in identical design would be excluded under our present rules. And even the Battle of Britain stamp might not be appropriate for a head. On the other hand, I added hastily, the Parliament stamp was absolutely right for the royal head and so of course was the Commonwealth Arts Festival and the 900th anniversary of the Abbey.

I said that the real difficulty was that, up to now, it had been understood in the Office that by the Queen's personal command stamps that did not embody the head could not even be submitted for consideration. I said this had led to a most unfortunate situation in which designers were full of new ideas but these were not allowed to be transmitted because it was generally thought that the Queen herself had refused to consider them. I said I didn't know whether this was true or not but it seemed to me the straightforward thing to do was to come along and ask whether this was as a result of a personal command of this kind. The Queen was clearly embarrassed and indicated that she had no personal feeling about it at all. I said I knew she wouldn't and that I knew this was all a misunderstanding but that it was rather ridiculous that there should be these lovely stamps available which she wasn't even allowed to see.

She of course was extremely anxious not to give the impression that she was the obstacle to new design. I said that I foresaw a controversy developing about the heads on stamps which I thought would be most undesirable. I said the pressure to review this particular aspect of our stamp design policy was growing and at the same time there would be great opposition to taking the head off the stamps unless it were done with royal consent and approval. In these circumstances it seemed to me that the right thing to do was for us to establish that designers could put in any designs they liked, that they could all be submitted to the Queen for approval, and that I should be able to say in answer to a question in the House of Commons that the Queen had approved a procedure under which all stamps of all kinds were submitted to her for consideration. This seemed to me to be the best way of tackling it and I hoped she agreed.

This speech must have lasted for about ten minutes and she listened and then indicated that she knew that in some Commonwealth countries the head had been removed but in others a crown had been substituted. I said a crown was an interesting idea and I thought in many cases the head would be right, but there were all sorts of other ways of doing it, such as embossing the head in white or having a silhouette, or a definitive stamp affixed to a commemorative or pictorial stamp, and that all I wanted – as I was not a designer or a philatelist – was the right to submit stamps of all kinds to her. She indicated that she had never seen any of these stamps and would be interested to see them. I said, 'Well, I've got some in my bag' (having brought David Gentleman's collection as provided this morning). The Queen wanted me to leave the new designs with her but I explained the difficulties and she agreed to see them on the spot.

This was exactly what I had hoped would happen so I unlocked my bag and spread out on the floor twelve huge design models of the stamps provided by Gentleman and also brought out his album of foreign stamps. I then knelt on the floor and one after the other passed up to the Queen the Battle of Britain stamps bearing the words 'Great Britain' and no royal head on them. It was a most hilarious scene because I had my papers all over the place and she was peering at something that had obviously never been shown to her or even thought about at the Palace before.

At the end I packed up and said I would take them away but that I was delighted to hear that she approved of a scheme under which we could submit things to her for her consideration. I said I hoped I might come back in a few weeks and that was the end of the audience. It had lasted about forty minutes instead of the expected fifteen.

As I was going out, Sir Michael Adeane – who I suppose might have been listening via a microphone during the audience – assured me that there had never been any indication whatsoever from the Palace that non-traditional stamps would not be acceptable. It was most amusing because of course it was quite untrue. But I said I was delighted to hear this and that now we could submit all sorts of designs. 'But I think the monarch's head has to be on the stamps, doesn't it?' he said. I replied that there was no rule about it but that it had always been done; but now that we could send in the new designs we could see where and when it was appropriate. He looked extremely uncomfortable.

So I went back to the House of Commons feeling absolutely on top of the world. The fact is the Palace is determined not to get into any controversy in which they might be seen to be responsible for holding back popular clamour for change. The real enemies of course are those forces of reaction – the Tory Party, the Civil Service, the Palace flunkies and courtiers – who use the Queen as a way of freezing out new ideas. No doubt she herself shares the views of the flunkies but the Crown has to be extremely careful. I had always suspected this was true but am now convinced that if you went to the Queen to get her consent to abolish the honours list altogether she would nod and say she'd never been keen on it herself and felt sure the time had come to put an end to it. Of course when you do that you have to be terribly charming and nice and I tried as hard as I could to do a little Disraeli on her with all the charm I could muster.

I went back to the Office and called the Director General and Mr Wolverson in and told them about my visit to Number 10 and the Palace. They were a bit astonished I think that I had gone straight to the Queen and raised the question of the head with her. I then dictated a letter in order to consolidate my victory and will send it off tomorrow.

To dinner with the Yugoslav Ambassador, Mr Prica, and his wife. Also there were Denis Healey, who told blue jokes throughout the whole of dinner, and George Thomson and one or two others.

Bed very late. It had been the best day since I took office with almost complete victory on the whole front. Now I must be sure to follow it up.

Thursday 11 March
I dictated a letter to the Queen following my audience and it is all ready to go off except that I must clear it with Harold Wilson.

Caroline and I went to dinner at the Dorchester. It was the annual dinner of the Screenwriters' Guild and a real showbiz occasion. We met Huw Weldon, Lew Grade, Michael Peacock, Charles Hill, and a host of others. Ted Willis was in the chair. The only speeches were his and mine. Then Caroline gave the awards and there was dancing and a film in place of a cabaret which we couldn't hear.

I had arranged to have a telephone call from Harold at home at 11 o'clock but as I was still at the hotel I rang him from the porter's lodge. I told him about my audience with the Queen yesterday and he listened with great interest. All he said was, 'Did she get down on the floor with you?' Obviously he was surprised and relieved that it had gone well and saw no objection to my writing to her. He also told me that the postal tariffs ought to be all right. I gather that George Brown has been making further trouble but it looks as if we are home and dry now.

Friday 12 March
Up early and to Bristol with the usual hoo-ha. The station master at Paddington saw us off personally and the train was brought in to a different platform in Bristol where the station master there greeted me. Everywhere I went there were policemen saluting and standing to attention. I began in the telephone exchange and tried my hand at the switchboard, then I had lunch with the regional board and discovered one or two interesting things.

Firstly, there is pressure from the staff controller to break with the Civil Service altogether. Secondly, a simple and unpublicised cancellation of a 9 am collection in one part of Bristol saved £5000 – the only consequence being that fifty letters a week for Dublin were not delivered until about twelve hours later than they otherwise would have been. Thirdly, the cost of some rural deliveries is as much as two shillings per letter. These are all things worth chasing up.

At 4.45 to the BBC for a short television interview and then to the sorting office near Temple Meads. I met the staff representatives and then went to see the highly-mechanised office.

At 7 o'clock I spoke at the Bristol College of Commerce on 'Parliament from the Front Benches', a speech I had written on cards at various free moments during the day. Then at 8.45 to a meeting organised by the AEU to allow us to hear the views of their district committee on the possible consequences of cuts in the TSR2 programme.

Saturday 13 March
Home by train and David Gentleman and his wife, Rosalind Dease, came to tea. I told them about my audience with the Queen and he is ready to prepare a sample album of stamps, showing what could be done with different treatments of the head, royal ciphers, crowns, etc. He was delighted with the way things had gone and I just hope to God he is discreet. He also told me that Stanley Gibbons, the stamp dealers, were producing a sample series of pictorial stamps next week.

Sunday 14 March
This evening Caroline and I went to dinner with Patrick Gordon Walker and his wife. It was the first time they had ever invited us to anything and we accepted because of our sympathy with them in their plight. Also there were the Greenwoods, Roy Jenkins, Marjorie Durbin, Shirley and Bernard Williams, and some children. Poor Patrick is very down. His wife showed me a copy of the filthy Nazi propaganda cards that had been distributed at Leyton.

Monday 15 March
Lord Normanbrook came to see me to discuss the new appointments to the BBC Governors. He is anxious that I should reappoint one woman, a friend of Henry Brooke's, about whose original appointment there was an appalling row five years ago. Also he was keen that I should appoint Lord James, the former headmaster of Manchester Grammar School. I listened most intently and flattered him and the main thing I learned from the interview was that he knew what he wanted and was coming round to it by degrees. I also caught him exchanging glances with Sir Ronald German. I am quite clear now about what I am going to do.

I asked him what would happen if the BBC did not get the £6

licence. German had put in a memorandum to me warning that any radical attitude towards BBC2 would probably lead to resignations from the BBC Board of Governors. The Establishment hangs together and what a battle it is to get anything changed.

There was a letter from the Palace today – from Sir Michael Adeane – confirming that the letter I had written to the Queen was acceptable. I can now arrange for the parliamentary question and answer, and wrote in my own hand to Harold Wilson to tell him so. The way is completely clear now and the next thing is to get some beautiful stamps prepared to show what can be done. I shall commission Gentleman for this purpose. I have to see the Stamp Advisory Committee to tell them what happened. There will no doubt be some trouble from them but it is not a discussable issue any more since it has already been settled with the monarch.

To the Commons for the Youth Committee of the Executive. The Trotskyite Young Socialists have broken away and the whole thing has become farcical. One just couldn't help laughing hilariously. But Sara Barker sat there with her lips drawn tight with disapproval.

Tuesday 16 March
Up late last night preparing for questions today and spent most of the morning going over them and checking them and thinking of supplementaries. Then to the House after lunch. It went well. I tried to be a great deal nicer than I was last time and Caroline – my sternest critic – who was in the Gallery seemed pleased with it.

Wednesday 17 March
At 8 o'clock this morning Kenneth Harris came with two BBC people to record a tribute from me to Harold Wilson. They are doing obituary tributes for a number of people and I prepared a few notes and talked on tape.

To the Office where I received a deputation of greeting card manufacturers who are protesting about the possibility of standardisation of envelopes.

Most of the morning occupied with the Post Office Rifles. I inspected 114 veterans of the First World War, attended the service at which the memorial was being unveiled and then took the march-past the Lord Mayor and finally spoke at the lunch. It was all rather moving.

Worked again in the Office and had a message from Number 10 to say that it was all right to go ahead with the parliamentary question on stamps. That is the end of this phase of the battle.

Thursday 18 March

Today we had the first Post Office Board lunch, bringing members of the Board and distinguished visitors together – Sir Alec Valentine, chairman of London Transport; Sir John Macpherson, chairman of Cable & Wireless; Sir Willis Jackson of Imperial College and Ron Smith were our guests. After lunch I banged the table and asked their view as to whether we ought to become a nationalised industry in place of a Government department. The response was interesting. Valentine said how useful the Transport Tribunal was in fixing fares and that we might gain by being able to appeal to a similar tribunal. Ron Smith was doubtful from a union point of view. We also discussed the possibility of mixed enterprise and whether there was a case for the Cable & Wireless solution[13] – a limited liability company with Government control of shares. Altogether a successful start and the first occasion that the Postmaster General's dining room had been in use since before the war.

Then a Fabian Society meeting and stayed at the House till 10 o'clock for the vote. Afterwards Jennie Lee told me she had a new plan for educational broadcasting under which the ITA would be given the fourth channel and with the money they make they would finance University of the Air until 8 every night. This is an appalling solution – just as bad as Reg Prentice's scheme for handing it over to the BBC. I shall have a fight on my hands. The trouble is that neither she nor Reg know anything about the broadcasting problem as a whole.

Friday 19 March

Today Mr Wolverson had come to see me in a state of great anxiety about the parliamentary question which is to be tabled next week about stamp design. He said that he had read Sir Michael Adeane's letter most carefully and from it it was clear that the Queen did want her head to appear on every stamp. He had therefore – on his own authority – tried to modify the parliamentary answer that I had agreed with the Palace. It shows how terribly carefully you have to watch these civil servants. Of course Adeane's letter was an attempt to retrieve the situation but he had consented – on behalf of the Queen – to the words of my parliamentary answer and I intended to consolidate the gains that I had made. Wolverson was anxious about it but I just insisted on restoring the original answer. There may be a public row but I am on absolutely sure ground. Now we must commission Gentleman's album and things will be almost settled.

Monday 22 March

This morning Mr Wolverson and Brigadier Holmes came to see me to finalise the question and answer on Wednesday in which I am going to reveal the Queen's consent to the new policy for stamp design. Wolverson was again very agitated and I discovered that he *had* actually modified the draft answer in order to exclude the phrase, 'In future designers may submit any designs that they wish'. He read me Adeane's letter and said didn't I think that it showed that they still wanted the head on the stamps. I said then, of course Adeane wanted the head on the stamps but I had got an agreement and intended to stick by it. Wolverson is terrified of controversy and I just had to rewrite the draft question and answer as I wanted. Thank heavens I did it, otherwise I could have lost out at the last moment.

Home early this evening feeling tired and then summoned to the House of Commons by the whips for a vote at 10. When I got there, I discovered there wasn't a vote so I got a pair and came home again. Just after 11 Caroline and I went off to the midnight show put on in aid of anti-apartheid at the Prince of Wales Theatre. The only other Minister there was Barbara Castle. The Bishop of Woolwich and a number of MPs were present. It was a very good show with Eartha Kitt, Frankie Vaughan and Vanessa Redgrave singing one of her own songs. We left after the first half and were in bed by 2.

Tuesday 23 March

Went to see Fred Lee, Minister of Power, about the use of coal in heating Post Office buildings and on to lunch with Sydney Jacobson at Kettners. Also there was the editor of the *Sun*, Dinsdale, and the political correspondent, Joe Haines. It was rather a dull meal. I talked a bit about the stamp policy and they said they thought there would be public support for a new and more venturesome series. They also asked me directly about postal charges and I simply couldn't answer.

Back to the Commons and had a talk to Jennie Lee about the scheme for displaying art in crown Post Offices. I told her that the Head Postmasters were nervous at having to make the choice themselves, being subject to public criticism. We decided to press ahead with a pilot scheme in the North East in co-operation with the North East Arts Association which receives a grant from the Arts Council.

This evening Judith Hart and Jennie and I had a meal together to discuss the University of the Air. Harold is keen to get this going as he is being mocked for having proposed a scheme that was ill thought out and impracticable. Jennie wants the fourth channel. Meanwhile I suggested that she took all the free time on BBC1,

BBC2 and ITA and that the Post Office would provide her with the technical facilities for doing this if she would set up a vice-chancellor of the Air to provide the programmes. Home with bad sinus and indigestion and feeling lousy.

Wednesday 24 March
With Caroline to the last meeting of the Stepney Borough Council where I had been asked to speak because of Father's connection with the constituency.[14] It was an interminably long meeting mixing up a little bit of political business with the granting of the Freedom of the Borough to three people including the Town Clerk. I was called about 9.30 and spoke about Grandpa Julius, Grandpa and Father and their links with St George's that now go back 115 years. Afterwards we stayed for a short reception and then home.

Thursday 25 March
At 10.30 this morning, Sir Kenneth Clark, Paul Reilly and James Fitton came to see me about stamp policy. I told them about my interview with the Queen and the new free policy for designers. They seemed excited by it and were not as critical as I had feared, but Sir Kenneth Clark said that George V had told him when he was a young man and first appointed to the Stamp Advisory Committee, 'Never let the sovereign's head come off the stamps.' Sir Kenneth had promised that he would not. At this stage I expected that he would announce his resignation. But he said that he felt that this pledge would be honoured provided they remained on the definitive stamps which is perfectly agreeable to me. All in all it was a much more successful morning than I had expected.

Afterwards I worked hard in the Office preparing the statement on postal tariff increases in the afternoon.

I went into the House and made the statement at 3.40. The Tories jeered throughout the statement but for everybody else it was old hat. They had known about it for months. Afterwards, I dashed back to the Post Office for a poorly attended press conference and then did a couple of TV interviews.

At 7 o'clock Susan Crosland came to see me to do an interview for the *Sun*. She stayed for just over an hour and asked a hundred trivial questions. Why do you keep your hair short? What do you think the *Evening Standard* meant by saying that you were a Scoutmaster? . . . and so on. It was entirely inconsequential and I cannot think that anything helpful will come out of it.

The whips said I could come home provided I was on half-hour call. They had arranged an all-night filibuster to prevent Airey Neave's Bill to extend the pension scheme to those who have not paid contributions from coming up for debate. Rather a shabby business.

Monday 29 March
Up at 5.45 this morning and Lew Grade, chairman of ATV, and Ted Willis came to breakfast. Lew is a dramatic, vigorous and attractive Jewish businessman. He wanted to try to sell me the idea that the fourth channel should be given to commercial companies. He was almost naive about it, having prepared a memorandum showing me how much money ATV could make out of the deal. I listened intently and then discussed the project with him. I said, 'The fourth channel is a valuable piece of property. The public owns it and you want it. Suppose that we went in on a 40–60 basis, so that 40 per cent of the profits accrued straight to the Post Office and could be used to finance broadcasting development.' He brightened immediately I had mentioned a figure and we began bargaining as if this really was going to happen.

I don't know whether it's a practicable proposition or not but the idea of mixed enterprise still has to be fully explored and I wouldn't be sorry at all to see us becoming shareholders in a big commercial company. It would be better than giving it to the BBC, though not as good as setting up another public corporation which would be a public service and inspiration, but would be allowed to take advertising. Somehow one has got to combine profitability for the public sector with the sort of drive and business sense which someone like Lew Grade has got.

Back to the Office where I did some more work on my speech for tomorrow's motion of censure put down by the Tories.

Tuesday 30 March
Up early this morning and working at home and the Post Office on my speech for today's motion of censure against me. I looked in to see Harold just before the debate began and he was encouraging. In fact, the debate was a quiet one. Sir Peter Rawlinson, the Conservative spokesman on Law, opened poorly from a lawyer's point of view. He obviously knew nothing about the Post Office and was even less interested. I spoke for about fifty minutes and although there was a good attendance of our members, there were only thirty or forty Tories. Caroline and Mother were in the Gallery. Macleod wound up and was offensive but Jack Diamond finished him off. Afterwards I took the DG, Sir Kenneth Anderson, Tilling and Miss Goose for a cup of coffee and Harold joined us. I think they were glad to meet him. He said again, 'Why don't you solve the BBC's problem by

allowing them to advertise on BBC2?' This certainly is one of the lines we shall have to consider.

Thursday 1 April
This afternoon we had the first ministerial committee on broadcasting and to my surprise and delight I found that most of the members agreed that we should not simply hand the BBC the £6 fee and let them get on with it. There is to be a full review and I have been asked to put in a paper. Meanwhile we shall have to find some money to tide the BBC over its immediate problems.

Friday 2 April
To Brighton this morning to receive the Reginald M. Philips collection of early Victorian stamps worth £250,000. The old boy was a property developer aged seventy-seven who had retired thirty or forty years ago. Since then he had concentrated on collecting these stamps and was determined that in giving them to the Post Office he should force us to set up a national postal museum. I enjoyed meeting him. There was big television and radio coverage and we had lunch afterwards.

Back to London to do an ABC television programme on the House of Lords. It was the usual Establishment crap. They had Professor Bromhead of Bristol University to say that old controversies were sterile and Lord Mancroft to say how wonderful the Lords was. I lashed into them and said that I thought it was a complete anachronism and all hereditary peers should be driven out, and that you should be able to devise some way of having an advisory second chamber without hereditary or even non-hereditary titles at all. They all gazed in horror that I should have been so extreme. But I am sick of this non-partisan approach to an entirely Tory chamber.

Saturday 3 April
My fortieth birthday. The family came in early with gifts. Then we had tea this afternoon with Mother. It was a lovely day and we sat in the garden for a bit.

This evening Susan Crosland brought her unspeakable article for me to vet. It was the bitchiest, most horrible thing I've ever read and I decided to be bold and rang her up and asked her not to publish it. She was much taken aback, no doubt hurt, but she assented immediately. I should never have accepted in the first place.

Sunday 4 April
Melissa was ill in bed today. I played around with the family, romped and played rugger and chess with Hilary in the evening. Then I

settled down and dictated letters. We go to America at the end of next week and it hardly seems possible.

Monday 5 April

Had Mr Grady in to the Office to discuss the Giro. I told him that there was a strong case for us using the Giro to pay the social wage – state benefits and so on. He had some doubts on this, based I think on what Sir Kenneth Anderson thought ought to be done. But I decided to write to Peggy Herbison and get that idea across.[15]

At lunch I entertained Mr Geneen, the president and chairman of International Telephones and Telegraphs, a giant American enterprise with manufacturing firms all over the world including Standard Telephones & Cables in this country. Also there were Mr Dunleavy, the president of ITT in Europe, and the two managing directors of ST&C here.

Geneen is a compulsive talker and a big tycoon in the best style. What impressed me about him was his passion for efficiency and self-improvement all the time, the degree of devolution which he gave to his subsidiaries and the establishment of a central staff responsible to him for reviewing the work of others. He declared his great belief in free enterprise and I said that I thought that he was efficient but that he was not efficient for the reason he thought he was.

I said I thought that free enterprise was part of the American mythology and it was rather charming to meet a man who actually believed it. The Office people looked awfully stick-in-the-mud as compared with him. The fact is you've got to have some mythology and believe in it and what these men ought to believe in is the mythology of vigorous public enterprise. But I'm not sure they do.

Tuesday 6 April

This morning I had a deputation from the National Union of Printers about a row between them and six women who work at the Post Office Savings Bank printing branch. These women failed to turn up at a branch meeting and were fined £5 each which they refused to pay. Since then they have fallen out of membership of the union which likes to maintain a closed shop. It was a scandalous fine to impose, representing something like two and a half years' contributions. The women refused to use the machinery of appeal and now the union want me to put pressure on them. There is nothing that we can do so I suggested that we simply took the pressure off the women for six months to see if they could be persuaded to rejoin next January. Unions can be pretty intolerable in their behaviour.

Afterwards we had a board meeting to consider the most elaborate investment plans for the next five years. There was a thick wad of

documents full of figures which had been given to me thirty-six hours
before the meeting. It was a perfect example of the way in which
the Post Office treats its Ministers, leaving them to rubber-stamp
documents, having meanwhile sent them off to other departments as
if they had been approved. I simply said I would not accept the
document which allows for a waiting list of telephone subscribers
rising from 50,000 to a quarter of a million or more during this
period. They were a bit taken aback. But it exactly illustrates the
need for proper machinery at headquarters which can review plans
submitted by subordinate bodies.

Afterwards to the Commons to hear the Budget. Jim's speech was
long and detailed but I think it's good. We made a ghastly error in
including the TSR2 cancellation in it and then leaving it to Denis
Healey to fill in the details. He had foolishly released the text of his
speech to the press, and owing to hundreds of points of order the
speech appeared publicly before he was able to complete it in the
House. It was a perfect example of the bad management of the House
of Commons.

Wednesday 7 April
To the Commons this morning. Peter Shore came to discuss the Giro.
His point was a simple one – that you start with 7 million people
receiving the social wage in one form and another and if each of them
has a Giro account this sets up the Giro instantly, makes the payment
of this money straightforward and makes the case for the Giro on
economic efficiency grounds as well as on grounds of economic return.

Ron Smith came to see me most urgently about postmen's pay.
Also there were the DG, Wolverson, Joe Slater and Charles Morris.
Ron is under very heavy pressure from a highly dissatisfied member-
ship and talked in terms of a 13 per cent increase as the absolute
minimum. This would mean almost 20 per cent last year plus 3.5
per cent this year plus 5 per cent equivalent for reduction in hours.
It is a very difficult situation indeed. This is likely to blow up when
I'm in America and will probably wreck my whole American tour.

Then Jennie Lee came to tell me again about the University of the
Air. She is working hand in glove with the commercial companies
and they are hoping to get the fourth channel from eight to midnight.
Though she has fine ideas I think her plans are impracticable. The
trouble is that neither she nor I can rely on our civil servants for
schemes of this kind. We are really on our own.

Thursday 8 April
To the Office this morning where a deputation came to see me
from the National Guild of Telephonists. This is a breakaway union

founded in 1929 or 1930 from the UPW representing male telephonists. The Tories recognised them in 1932 and since then there has been a state of uneasy truce between them, the UPW and management. They're not on the departmental Whitley committee but they are officially recognised. They came to see me to ask if they could be given permission to represent women telephonists. I had no intention at all of agreeing and I turned it on them by suggesting the time was ripe when they might open negotiations with the UPW to see if they could be reunited. This had been attempted before without success but I felt that now was the time for a second start. They were not altogether hostile to the idea and favoured the suggestion that a mediator should be appointed to discover ground common to both sides.

At 2.30 the DG came to see me and I unfolded to him the problem of upper management structure. He agreed that McKinsey should be invited to look at this. This is all I wanted. But in saying this the DG said he recognised that I was unhappy and felt that the Civil Service was obstructive. I said that this was nothing personal but that there was a creative tension between myself and the department which probably had its merits. Later I asked Miss Goose what she thought about it. She said that I was good for the department but that the department did feel that I ought to be more appreciative of the good points and not appear to be so critical. There may be strength in this argument and I had better make a fresh try at being friendly. The fact is I do feel isolated here and this drives me into a slightly defensive position.

At 4 o'clock Charles Smith and the POEU delegation arrived to discuss outstanding points in wage negotiations and particularly the question of hours. They were upset that the shorter hours had been delayed till the last possible date and felt it was sharp practice. On other points they thought we were being pernickety over trifling sums of money. I said this was all the product of pay research which took such an interminable time to process and settle. They said that it was a product of our being a part of the Civil Service which deprived me of any authority at all in reaching agreements on individual wage claims. They are right and it strengthens my view that a separation from the Civil Service is essential. We ended on a jovial note.

A taxi arrived today for me to examine as an alternative form of transport. It is big and rather uncomfortable and a hundred pounds more expensive than a Humber Hawk. But of course it holds far more people and is extremely agile in traffic. I think I shall go ahead with it and the Austin Princess can go into the pool and be available as and when required. This is part of the image changing of the Post Office. Other measures of this kind are the decision to use 'Mr' instead of 'Esquire' in all my correspondence, the new personal note-paper that I am having designed, the new stamp policy, and my decision to take the men in red coats and top hats and put them in the new grey Post Office uniform. These are all very important though minor changes.

On the telephone to Ron Smith tonight I said that I was extremely concerned about the way that the postmen's pay claim might develop and was terribly keen to avert what happened last year. I suggested to him that he might informally write to Ray Gunter, Jim Callaghan and George Brown to say how worried he was by the way pressure was building up. This will strengthen my hand on Tuesday and I intend to do the same thing. I think he was grateful for this sugges-tion. Meanwhile, I must get in touch with Harold early and alert him to the danger in the situation.

This evening Shirley Williams rang me up to say that the editorial in *Venture* which attacked Labour policy on Vietnam had greatly upset Harold Wilson and that he was considering resigning from the Fabian Society. She is of course the chairman of the editorial committee but had not had a chance of seeing the article before it was published. She said she was going to issue a repudiation. I read the article and agreed almost entirely with it. I urged her strongly not to issue a repudiation since it would force everybody else to take up a position and was unlikely to avert Harold's resignation from the Society. Anyway the Fabians have a tradition of freedom of expression and if there was a great row, it is certain that it would lead to my forced resignation from the chairmanship which would have a most undesirable effect. In the end she did agree just to write a letter to the *Sun* to say that the editorial did not represent her view.

Saturday 10 April

This evening Caroline and I went and had dinner with Peter and Liz Shore. Also there were Richard Titmuss, Arnold Rogow and his wife Pat. Arnold is a professor of political science at Stanford Univer-sity and is an old friend and associate of Peter. Also Dick and Bridget Clements. It was an enjoyable evening and Titmuss was extremely interested in the idea of elevating postmen to become social service workers. I think I need a social service adviser in the Post Office to see how far these projects can be stimulated.

Sunday 11 April

At home all day and did a little work. Hilary is now sick and we are wondering whether we shall ever get off to America.

Monday 12 April

The DG, Joe Slater, Miss Goose and I sat round and talked about the postmen's pay issue. Harold has assented to the personal letter that I wrote him on the subject and it looks as if things may be clear for tomorrow's prices and incomes meeting. The question then will be how we put it across to Ron Smith. The DG has been in the habit of telling Ron Smith confidentially what it is that he can have and allowing him to play it his own way. That is to say Ron would be told that the maximum would be X per cent and we would then by agreement start at about half that figure and he would press and we would yield, and he would press and we would yield, and finally it would be settled at X per cent which he had known about all along.

Joe Slater was appalled to hear that negotiations took this form. In the mining industry it is very different. He also said – quite truthfully – that if Ron Smith's executive knew what was happening, they'd murder him. But this is in fact what does happen and it has for some time. Indeed the DG was afraid that if we didn't tell Ron Smith the full extent of the authorised increase at the beginning and he discovered it later, he would feel that he had been tricked and would then lead his men out and demand a far bigger percentage than we could offer. You cannot evidently run the wage negotiations with the union on any other basis. The DG and Ron Smith are very close and a degree of confidentiality exists between them that doesn't exist between the DG and the Cabinet or Ron Smith and his more militant executive members.

Home after this and telephoned America. Now that Hilary has got a confirmed case of scarlet fever, we are in a real difficulty. We just don't know whether I shall be able to go on my official US trip, or whether the family will go and I will postpone my official trip.

Tuesday 13 April

To the Office this morning and I called Lillicrap in to go over the BBC licence issue. He explained it all and I think I got it straight.

Then to the Cabinet, which agreed to the BBC licence fee increase and discussed the UPW pay claim. Coming out of the Cabinet I had a short talk with Jim Callaghan, who suggested a way of solving the postmen's pay dispute involving a phasing operation. I told him I doubted whether it would work.

I went into the Commons and Sir James Duff, the vice-chairman of the BBC, came to see me and I conveyed to him in advance the Cabinet decision. He was grateful for small mercies.

My case about postmen's pay came up at the Prices and Incomes Committee at 6, and I went in and did the best I could but I got a rough passage. George was extremely aggressive and Jim was against me and was instead proposing his alternative scheme. Ray Gunter said nothing at all. I pointed out the risks of a strike and George spoke as if he would be prepared to run them. Also I got a flea in my ear for having written to Harold on the subject and was told that this was settled not by him but by this committee. All in all it was a most unpleasant experience. I returned to the DG, Wolverson, Daniels, Charles Morris, Jean Goose and Joe Slater who were waiting. I told them the news and they were all pretty pessimistic about it. We discussed endlessly the tactics and how we should present them. Finally we agreed that Ron Smith should be told part of the offer we were going to make in advance confidentially, but that something would have to be held in reserve for me. Throughout these talks Charles Morris was a tremendous help because he could see it from the union point of view.

We talked about it right through till 8.45 over a meal, and agreed that since this was the best we could get and as going back to the Prices and Incomes Committee would not necessarily meet our further claim, the best thing to do was to put a brave face on it and sell it as a tremendous victory for the union and for us and a new deal for postmen. As part of the goodwill on both sides, we could throw in the idea of a three-year settlement, part-timers and women as a concession by the union, and suspend the household delivery of commercial literature as a concession by us. Put that way, I think there is a reasonable chance of getting it accepted.

Today I had to reach a firm decision about our plans for America. Hilary is much better but will not be fit to travel on Thursday. So it was agreed that Caroline should go on Thursday with Stephen, Melissa and Joshua, Hilary will stay with me and I will cancel my official visit to the US. Then as soon as Hilary is fit and the postmen's pay issue is settled, I will take him over for about a week which will be entirely in Cincinnati. This could go wrong for a number of reaons. He could have complications, the postmen's crisis could blow up into an explosion, and a number of others things could happen. But it is the best we can manage. Meanwhile, I will postpone my official visit until the Whitsun week.

Back home about 10.45 and Caroline and Stephen came back from the *Messiah* at the school which Hilary had had to miss. Liz Shore came with them and she said there was no reason why Hilary shouldn't go to America on Friday if the swab revealed that the throat infection had cleared.

At 11.30 we had another phone call to Cincinnati and we told them the decision had been reached.

Altogether a confused and exhausting day. But it is nothing to what tomorrow will be.

Wednesday 14 April

Left for the Office at 8.30 and dictated a long memorandum on the postmen's pay negotiations for the DG, Mr Wolverson and Mr Daniels. This was designed to put a bit of stuffing into them as they were much too pessimistic and their capacity to convince the union that this is a reasonable offer will much depend on their believing themselves that it is a reasonable offer. This was typed out first thing when I got to the Office.

The Board met at 10 o'clock and we had a discussion about the handling of the negotiations. Ron Smith was meeting the DG this morning and the DG was to tell him *privately* that we would go up to 5 per cent, having started at 3.5 per cent. They have left me half a crown or 1.5 per cent that I can add tomorrow when I meet the union executive. It's not much but it may help.

Meanwhile I began thinking hard about the problem of presenting this both to the union negotiating team and to the press and television if it is going to be necessary tomorrow. I decided to call the plan a Fair Deal plan for postmen and to itemise it under ten points. I called in someone from the Public Relations Department – an artist who can present it graphically. I am having these duplicated for each member of the union executive. I shall also make it available to the press and I shall illustrate it on television if need be with a big placard and a ruler, pointing out exactly what has been offered. Last year Ron Smith had it all his own way with the press and Bevins was poor at presenting his case. This time I intend to be just as good as Ron Smith if it does have to come to a public discussion about our offer and his rejection of it.

The Board meeting this morning was very quick. We accepted a vastly increased investment programme which will bring the telephone waiting list down to nothing within four years. Whether it is practicable to do it is another question.

I also got what I wanted – namely the extension of McKinsey's brief to do a study of the top management of the Post Office. This will not be publicised. I got it agreed that three firms of operational research experts and consultants shall study our system of forecasting telephone demand and put in feasibility studies for improving it.

Then further talks on the postmen's claim. The Chancellor's office had rung up to say that there had been a misunderstanding and he had not agreed to 3.5 per cent for 1966. I was sure he was wrong about this and it certainly made things difficult. Ron Smith has said informally this morning that the offer was not satisfactory and we are not hopeful about this afternoon's negotiations.

After lunch I went to the House of Commons and announced the increase in the television/sound licence fee from £4 to £5 and an extra

5s for sound only. The Tories were in a difficult position. But a number of questions came, including one about pensioners from our own people. I did as well as I could.

Then to our room at the Commons, waiting to hear news of the negotiations. We decided in the end to go back to the Post Office for further consultations. There the DG and Mr Wolverson and Mr Daniels came in and reported what had happened. They had gone up to their limit and the unions are not satisfied. They are meeting tonight to consider their attitude and have asked for an interview with me tomorrow. I rang the Chancellor and told him that I *must* be able to go up to 3.5 per cent for next January. He agreed to this provided it was a final offer. He is going to be in London tomorrow until 3 o'clock so that I can consult him if necessary. But it is perfectly clear that neither he nor the First Secretary of State are prepared to go beyond what I've said and so there's no point in my even promising the union that I will look at it again. It may well be that there will be unofficial action and even a strike. I have written to warn the Prime Minister of the position. But George Brown simply will not allow us to move and is ready for a fight with the postmen. It's too late to cry over that, I've just got to make the best of it. Jim was very nice on the phone and I think he realised that I was under heavy pressure.

I completed the Fair Deal plan tonight and it's all going to be ready for me in the morning. Then I came home. The DG rang to tell me that he had heard the UPW had rejected the offer and had sent out a branch circular advising members not to do anything unofficially until I had a chance of considering further representations.

I also had a message to ring Ron Smith who said that he had one of the roughest meetings of his executive ever and that it was going to be a tough job stopping unofficial action. The full executive is coming to meet me tomorrow morning. He wished it could only be the negotiating team but could not resist his executive's request.

Caroline, Stephen, Melissa and Joshua are all packing and are very excited about their trip tomorrow. I'm still hopeful of getting to America with Hilary early next week.

One amusing thing today. I read the Lords Hansard for yesterday when they were criticising the appointment of McKinsey's. Lord Erroll said I had had an expensive business lunch with McKinsey's and had been won over by their salesmanship. He also said that I had done it without the advice of my officials. In fact George Brown suggested McKinsey's. My officials examined alternatives and agreed that McKinsey was best and I didn't see them until the decision to engage them had been made. After I had seen them, I took them to the Post Office canteen and gave them a 3s lunch each for which I paid personally. I never went to lunch with them at all. I'm rather tempted to write to Erroll and say this to him.

Thursday 15 April
Up early and kissed goodbye to Caroline, Stephen, Melissa and Joshua who went off to America. I arrived at the Office just after 9. I dictated the notes for my first speech at the negotiations with the UPW. I also cleared the text of the ten-point Fair Deal plan for postmen and the graphic representation of it.

At 10.30 I went up to Room 401 where the whole executive of the UPW was waiting for me. Joe Slater, the DG, Mr Wolverson, Mr Daniels, Mr Lawrence and Mr Tilling came with me. . . .

The notes made during the day-long negotiations with the UPW are too long for inclusion in the diary but the occasion was memorable for me for a number of reasons. The first was that it was the first time I had negotiated with a union as a Labour Government Minister and I found the harshness of the argument used by the other side difficult to contend with. I was also under the tightest possible control from the Treasury and had little room for manoeuvre. The proposals and counter-proposals were made in a slightly ritualised form because, of course, the whole negotiation had been conducted unofficially in advance between the Director General and Ron Smith. But at the time, it was extremely tense and I did succeed in getting a concession over the telephone from the Chancellor, allowing me to go further than had originally been authorised, I was subsequently blamed by some sections of the press and indeed by certain members of the Cabinet for having given way on a critical part of the pay policy front, at a time the wages control policy was becoming increasingly dominant in the thinking of the Cabinet.

. . . At 8.20 pm I came downstairs fully expecting the whole thing to break down and I was preparing a statement. We were all desperately tired. Joe Slater had been at the House of Commons till 3 o'clock this morning and I was physically exhausted by the six rounds of negotiations we had had with no proper food. Then, at 8.50, Ron Smith and his negotiating committee came out and said they had decided to accept. I could hardly believe my ears. I said how delighted I was, not only that we had reached an agreement but that all the other things we had hoped to do would now be possible. Ron and I went and gave a joint press conference. Then I thanked everybody and went to do a joint TV programme with him. He evidently said to Joe Slater that I had been tougher to deal with than Bevins, which I took to be a compliment.

I got home absolutely exhausted at about 11 o'clock. Hilary was still awake and we sat and watched the TV discussion and at midnight

I rang Caroline who by that time had arrived in Cincinnati, 4,000 miles away, only fourteen hours after I had said goodbye in London.

That was the end of one of the toughest days I've ever had and my first wage negotiation. Obviously one requires to do a great deal more thinking about these negotiations and the tactics of them. One thing is certain, one should never get excited – as I did today – and one should always fight a rather subtler campaign.

Good Friday 16 April
There were no newspapers today and Hilary and I had breakfast downstairs in the office kitchen. Hilary was much better and bounced about. This afternoon we played in the garden a bit and I tidied and threw out tons of junk from all over the house. It was just what I needed to forget the Post Office for a while.

Saturday 17 April
The Times and the *Telegraph* ran leading articles attacking the postmen's settlement and Ian Coulter of the *Sunday Times* rang up in preparation for tomorrow's piece.

The doctor came and said that he thought Hilary ought not to go to America. I don't know what to do. This evening I went down to the office and started throwing out papers. It requires a certain attitude of mind to throw out old papers and I was in a particularly ruthless mood.

Easter Sunday 18 April
Hilary and I had our breakfast and ate our Easter eggs and then came down to the office and Hilary painted all morning while I threw out more rubbish.

In the *Sunday Times* Ian Coulter said that the settlement had 'disturbed my senior Cabinet colleagues' – this was very damaging.

This afternoon I decided to ring Caroline to tell her what the doctor had said and she said she had spoken to the City Health Commissioner in Cincinnati, whom she knew, who had told her that scarlet fever was no longer taken at all seriously and that children go back to school after a week but are watched for a while for complications. I therefore decided to go to America tomorrow, rang Pan Am and changed the reservations and began dictating spools and tidying up my Post Office papers.

Hilary is very excited and I'm sure is perfectly able to travel.

Monday 19 April
Everything is set and Hilary and I went to London Airport and caught a Pan American Boeing 707 jet. The plane left at 12 and we

arrived in Cincinnati 6 pm local time. We were actually home by 6.30. I hadn't told Caroline we were coming and she was walking down the stairs as she spotted us coming up the drive with our baggage. It was a tiring flight but an enjoyable one.

Tuesday 20 April

Phoned London this morning and discovered that there was not much news from the Office. However, there has been some criticism of the Post Office wages settlement and the press have suggested that my colleagues are furious with me for having settled for such a high figure.

I had lunch with Sharon Schmidt, a journalist working for the *Post Times Star*. She interviewed me and it was a job to remember that I was not a lecturer free to comment on everything but a member of the Government who had to weigh every word. I refused to comment on Vietnam. Sharon is an ardent Goldwater supporter and of course the gap between that view and the central British view is so wide as to be completely unbridgeable.

Wednesday 28 April

Arrived in London at 6.40, the end of a lovely holiday. Stephen and I didn't sleep at all on the plane but the others dozed off.

I went straight off to the National Executive at the House of Commons and then to the Post Office. I discovered that in my absence a tremendous row had blown up over postmen's pay and the *Economist* had published a savage article calling for my dismissal by Harold. Evidently this had been raging all the time that I was away but Tilling didn't tell me. I felt very uneasy about it. The fact is the department had said that they didn't think we could get a settlement for under 8 per cent and in fact we had got one for under 6 per cent. It is obvious that they are not reliable advisers on matters of this kind.

I presume that George Brown must have been responsible for some of the leaks, but Tilling told me that Jim Callaghan had telephoned to say that I was not to be worried by the hostile press, which was decent of him.

Thursday 29 April

To the Post Office this morning for the Post Office Board. We spent most of the time discussing the press reaction to the Post Office settlement. The officials were embarrassed, I think, by what had happened and stuck to the fact that they could have justified an 8 per cent increase. It also appears that a final vote on the UPW executive was only narrowly in favour of accepting the settlement.

Apparently it was only 12 to 10. But there was a competitively militant element, due to the fact that the elections for the UPW executive are coming up soon.

We discussed what must now be done to prevent us from getting into a position where we shall need higher charges next March. I insisted that there must be economies and proposals were made for providing these economies by cutting out the second deliveries in certain rural areas, spreading the night mail deliveries and making some of the collections a little earlier. We also agreed that certain other productivity changes must be insisted upon and I intend to make my speech at the UPW conference an appeal to them to co-operate in productivity measures, including the recruitment of women and part-timers to which I know they are hostile. This speech is going to be a crucial one since I want to consolidate the good atmosphere created by the settlement but at the same time point out the necessity for big changes in the service to meet the needs of the future.

There is another strike brewing on the Post Office Engineering Union side. Members of the POEU in the Supplies Department, who are responsible for stamps, are going slow and the DG said he intended to authorise an interim pay award of 3 per cent, whatever the Treasury said. I had to stop him quite firmly and make it clear that this could not be done without my authority.

Saturday 1 May

In Bristol for May Day. Up early and collected a Hertz rent-a-car and then to a surgery at Unity House from 9 till 11.

I had lunch with Paul Stephenson who has just been acquitted on a charge of disorderly conduct which was really due to a landlord refusing to serve him on grounds of race. Paul is an able man and I hope he stays in Bristol and gives leadership to the coloured community.

Monday 3 May

To the Commons to meet the Bristol Siddeley deputation who have come about the cancellation of the TSR2.

Back to an informal lunch with the postal services department who made some useful suggestions. I was not much impressed by them. Their top management are mainly ex-army people without much imagination and they said that what was required to make the postal services pay was 'an honest day's work for an honest day's pay'. I'm sure there's more wrong than that!

During the course of today I had rather a row with Tilling, who is being promoted, about his successor. He told me that I was more or less bound to accept the DG's suggestion and I said that an appointment of this kind was so personal that I had the right to reach my own decision. It is monstrous to regard the Minister as being such a temporary visitor in the department that he can have anybody pushed upon him whether he likes them or not. I have in mind another man – Wratten – who was with Unilever for a year and I shall certainly see him as well as Morris, the DG's man.

Tuesday 4 May
O'Brien came with a huge press advertisement explaining the new postal charges. Instinctively I am in favour of this but I wonder whether it is open to criticism that a Minister uses a press advertisement to justify his policy. Trevor Lloyd Hughes* at Number 10 is going to check this with Harold. Meanwhile I went over the text very carefully.

Today I had a lunch for a number of stamp designers. We agreed that unsuccessful designs should be released to the press; that designers should have a chance of meeting the Stamp Advisory Committee to discuss their stamp design; and that designers should be given the opportunity to do the stamps they would like to tackle. Some useful comments came out of this meeting though inevitably the designers didn't agree much themselves. But now I have the right to release to the press rejected designs, I am halfway to a solution of my problem of dealing with the Queen's head.

Then to the Commons where Ysrael Barzilay, the Deputy Speaker of the Knesset, came to see me. He is an old friend who was Minister of Health for many years and is a member of Mapam. I met him last in Israel two and a half years ago. His main concern was to see whether the British Government could play any part in exploiting the new situation created by President Bourguiba's statement that there should be direct talks between Israel and the Arab states. I said I would make enquiries through Michael Stewart but am not optimistic.

First of all the Israeli Government do not attach much importance to this statement since it helps to destroy their own militancy. Secondly Mapam are suspect because they are not affiliated to the Socialist International. And thirdly, the Foreign Office do not want to do anything which will interfere with their impartiality towards the Arabs.

Fenner Brockway may be able to do more and of course if I were a Back Bench Opposition member, I would certainly make indirect contact with the Tunisians to find out what possible progress might

* Press Secretary to the Prime Minister 1964–9, knighted 1970.

be made. Bourguiba has since qualified his statement and the Israelis are settling down to their usual reaction of hostility. There is a real danger of armed action by the Arabs to divert the water north of Israel and the situation remains extremely tense.

Tilling went over some papers with me this afternoon and one of the things he gave me was an invitation from the German Minister of Posts and Telegraphs, inviting Caroline and me to go to Germany in June for a big international telecommunications conference. This letter was dated 23 February and appealed for a reply by 31 March. It had not been handed to me until today. In addition to the discourtesy of not replying before now, I find that we have lost the chance for the Post Office to exhibit, and it is a scandalous piece of inefficiency.

I talked to Peter Shore and David Ennals who are thinking of forming a new group to counter those who are working for Britain to join the Common Market. Their group would be an *all*-European group which I wholly support and have done for many years. I suggested that their first objective should be to cultivate an atmosphere favourable to a successful European security conference which Michael Stewart has been working for and mentioned during his visit to Czechoslovakia. It was just like the old times and I suppose there's no reason why a Minister shouldn't encourage his colleagues to take up issues even though I'm tied hand and foot and confined to Post Office matters. Peter Shore and I are both really Gaullists nowadays.

Wednesday 5 May
To the Cabinet at 10.40, then to the Commons for the big debate on steel. Everyone wondered how it would go in view of Woodrow Wyatt and Desmond Donnelly's revolt.[16] But George Brown promised he would 'listen' to new proposals involving less than 100 per cent ownership. This brought Wyatt and Donnelly into the lobby but caused something of an uproar among the left of the Party who felt they were being let down.

Friday 7 May
Tilling has been promoted to head of Organisation and Methods Branch and he wrote me this assessment of my period as PMG to mark the occasion.

A new era was opened when Mr Anthony Wedgwood Benn became Postmaster General in October 1964. Mr Benn, young and forward-looking, was determined that the Post Office should become a science-based industry. He applied this principle not only to his Department's services but also to his own post, and at the General Election in April 1969, the ancient office of Postmaster General was abolished and a

'Rapidec' Mark 999 computer was installed in Room G1 at Post Office Headquarters in St Martin's-le-Grand.

Meanwhile, the Post Office had undergone rapid expansion and change. Its capital investment rose to £ quinillions annually as its Headquarters, Regional Headquarters and local Telephone Area and Head Offices were all replaced by computers of increasing size and complexity. All the staff of these offices were retained as programmers, translating their previous work into binary code for the computers. Indeed, so great was the programming programme that the staff of the GPO had increased to over a million by 1 January 1984: 500,000 programmers and 500,000 engineers to tend the computers. All the staff had been transferred to the Central Organisation and Methods Branch on temporary promotion.

At their head was Sir Henry Tilling, GCB, who had been appointed head of the Central Organisation and Methods Branch soon after Mr Wedgwood Benn became Postmaster General, and these revolutionary changes had been made under his baleful supervision. In an age dominated by machines, Sir Henry maintained the antiquated principle that machines existed to serve mankind, and, while he remained in office, the Post Office continued to serve the public's needs – unlike the rest of the public services which were run entirely for and by computers. Sir Henry, in his fortress in Stepney, retained not only these out-of-date principles but also old fashioned habits which marked him as one of an earlier generation of administrators. He had his room heated by a coal fire and his tea served every afternoon from a silver teapot made 200 years before his birth. Needless to say, these unhygienic habits and his backward-looking, humanist-based policies caused resentment and discontent among his staff and the computers, and, when he eventually retired on 24 January, 1984, he was replaced by an Omniscient Mark 5 Computer.

By 1 February, 1985, there was a marked deterioration in the quality of the Post Office services, and with the collapse of the communications network in 1999, the world entered a new dark age, in which the darkness was more profound and prolonged than that which succeeded the fall of the Roman Empire.

Saturday 8 May
I wrote this verse today to celebrate Tilling's departure and promotion.

A PMG's PS named Tilling
To contemplate change was unwilling
He'd detected decay
Since Sir Brian Tuke's day
And the future appeared to him chilling.

The Department admiring this trait
Picked him out for promotion one day
Each new project he'd stop

Brought him nearer the top
Till as DG he had his own way.

The savings in manpower he made
Were a hundred per cent a decade
He brought back the horse
And the whole postal force
Were retired with their full pensions paid.

The most famous speech that he spoke
Was dismissed by the press as a joke
But ignoring their moans
He ripped out all the phones
And reverted to signals by smoke.

His achievements were legion I'm told
And historians now make so bold
As to claim he undid
Just to save a few quid
Innovations five hundred years old.

His Knighthood he felt that he'd earned
By the millions of letters he'd burned
And he always did boast
That they played the 'Last Post'
On the day the PO Board adjourned.

His retirement to live in his den
Was marred by a fellow named Benn
For – still PMG –
He chuckled with glee
And built up the service again.

Messaoud Kellou telephoned to say he had just come in from New York where he'd been attending the UN debates on Rhodesia and the Dominican Republic. He was on his way to Prague where he is Ambassador. We had a couple of hours' talk. He said the non-aligned world is very disappointed with the Labour Government, which it believes is entirely subservient to the United States. In marked contrast to this, de Gaulle is following a logical policy of national independence which is much appreciated by the non-aligned countries.

The Labour Government is weak on Rhodesia and could at least be as tough with the white Rhodesians as de Gaulle was with the colonialists in Algeria. Sir Hugh Foot, our representative at the UN, had been much attacked in New York on this. Africans did not want to get involved in the Peking-Moscow row any more than in the Cold

War, but of course the Chinese view was prevailing because of the behaviour of the Americans in Vietnam and the Dominican Republic.

It was nice to see Messaoud again and I hope we can keep in contact even though he is discouraged by the policy the Government is pursuing.

Monday 10 May
In the morning Caroline and I went to Hampstead to present the ten millionth telephone to an engaged couple. It was really a GPO stunt to publicise the new Trimphone.

To the House at 3.30 where Brian O'Malley [Labour MP for Rotherham] brought a deputation from the Musicians' Union and the record industry to protest about the rumours that we might ask the BBC Light Programme to provide a pirate radio substitute. I could not say much but will certainly take their interests into account. But they are very restrictive.

The Home Policy Committee of the NEC met today and Dai Davies raised George Brown's gaff on steel. Johnnie Boyd attacked vigorously and George exploded and had to leave the chair while a most violent argument developed which got us nowhere. It was reminiscent of the Clause IV argument and George hinted darkly that if pressed he would reveal the names of Ministers who pretended to be in favour of steel nationalisation but really were not. Fears were expressed about leaks and the following day the *Guardian* contained a very accurate account.

Then to the Youth Committee which agreed constitutional changes in the Young Socialists, designed to keep the Trots out.

Tuesday 11 May
Made a short film on the Churchill stamp for Commonwealth use.

Then on to the House of Commons for the Ministerial Committee on Broadcasting to discuss next Thursday's broadcasting debate. My memorandum went through with only one amendment, to exclude the mention of financing the BBC out of taxation. Otherwise it was accepted and marks the first stage towards fundamental changes in broadcasting policy which will include the ending of the BBC sound monopoly, the introduction of mixed revenue into the BBC, and the development of genuinely local and regional radio and TV. I was delighted.

Vote at 10.

Wednesday 12 May
I saw John Morris and Wratten this morning. They are both able people and it is hard to choose who should succeed Tilling. But

Wratten is younger, was at LSE and had a year with Unilever. Morris is steadier but a more typical Post Office product and less imaginative. I hope Wratten is the right decision.

First STD call to the Lord Mayor of Plymouth and then an urgent meeting which led to a decision to postpone the Churchill stamp issue because of the ban on overtime in supplies. The expected public outcry did not materialise. I think the public are getting a little bored with the Churchill story.

First for questions today. It is a tremendous strain doing nearly an hour without a break. But nothing went wrong.

This evening Caroline and I went to a party at the American Embassy for the cast of James Baldwin's play, *Blues for Mr Charlie*. The Embassy obviously thought it was a good occasion to invite the Left and many members of the Government were there.

I met Groucho Marx who said, 'I like England and its people but this quaintness has gone too far and has got to be stopped. I ordered a suit and it was four weeks before the first fitting. I asked about another firm of tailors who had made me a suit years ago and they said, "It's still going but the head of the firm is dead at present".' This is how the world looks at us, but we are still resolutely blind to it.

Bed 2 am.

Thursday 13 May
Worked all morning on my broadcasting speech and to the House after lunch.

The debate was quiet and dull, as there were no announcements I could make. The BBC – through the grapevine – had got to know what was in the air and had sent a memorandum to many Members denouncing the idea of any advertising on the BBC. I found it difficult to speak from a text but had to get the words right and put it all on the record. I feel sure that opinion is moving this way and we must now get on and reach our agreement, including the creation of real local stations.

Friday 14 May
With Tilling, Brigadier Holmes and Mr Mead to visit Harrison's, the printers, at High Wycombe. I spent the day going through the factory and seeing the stamp process from beginning to end. The most interesting thing was to see the whole sheets of mistakes worth hundreds to thousands of pounds that are all destroyed under security conditions.

In discussion with the firm we considered how we could help them with their exports and the possibility of putting their imprint on each stamp together with the name of the designer. They are not satisfied with the present Stamp Advisory Committee and we considered the possibility of working with project teams instead.

We are definitely going to publish rejected essays which will help to focus public attention on the design of stamps.

Monday 17 May

Up early this morning and with Tilling to Manchester by train.

We had lunch with the Lord Mayor at the City Hall to discuss the proposal that Manchester might have a local sound radio station. Among those there were representatives from the city, the university, and the college of science and technology. They pressed for a broadcasting corporation which they would run, to be licensed by us and they didn't want it to be under the BBC. It was an interesting proposal and I told them that if they formulated it more carefully, I should be glad to consider it. If such a thing were done it would obviously have to be organised in such a way that there was no more local government interference than there is Government interference with the BBC. It would also require a mixed revenue, including some advertising.

Wednesday 19 May

There was a private notice question today about a shortage of stamps.

This has been caused by an unofficial ban on overtime at the Supplies Department depot at Hemel Hempstead. But the Tories tried to make out that it was incompetence and Heath put in a vicious supplementary question. In fact I think some Head Postmasters may have slightly underrated the demand for 1d and ½d stamps but the problem arises from a much more fundamental difficulty caused by the strike which was made official yesterday by the union.

Friday 21 May

Home at 5.15 am after an all-night sitting by which time the sun had almost risen. I worked till 7.30 when Henrion came to breakfast. He has completed his survey of Post Office design and the scheme that he puts forward is, I think, a good one under which we would have a design administrator and a consultant designer working together.

In to the Office feeling extremely tired and spent almost the whole day discussing the strike at the stamp depot. I decided to take emergency action, including issuing a message to Head Postmasters that packets could be handed in with cash if someone is unable to buy stamps.

Saturday 22 May
Up early to do a surgery this morning in Bristol which raised a number of personal problems. Then home and worked a bit this afternoon. This has been an appalling week and I feel pretty tired.

Monday 24 May
To the office this morning and John Beavan of the *Daily Mirror* came for an hour to discuss the stamp shortage. I invited him to come because of the unpleasant leading article in the *Daily Mirror* last Friday. I tried to put him in the picture as best I could and we went on to have a general talk about the role of the Post Office. I'm not getting a good press at the moment.

My chauffeur, Mr Wilson, asked me this morning if I had considered the possibility that the shortage of stamps was a piece of deliberate sabotage to help to bring the Government into disrepute, organised by top officials of the Post Office, who had no particular love for me or the Government. I said I hadn't but he was so serious that it rather affected me. Frankly if there is sabotage – instead of sheer inefficiency which I suspect is responsible – there's nothing whatsoever that I can do about it. But I have noticed a certain woodenness in my officials in the last month verging almost on non-co-operation. I think the reason for this is that having achieved the tariff increase which they desperately wanted for the sake of the department, and having got the highly generous UPW wages settlement which they wanted just in order to get peace and quiet, they have more or less lost interest in me and are just deliberately slowing down all the things that I wanted to get moving.

I don't know what one can do in these circumstances but I despair of making real progress. Of course they hear the local election results and think to themselves, this Government and this man won't last much longer so all we've got to do is play for time and we can minimise the damage. If only we had a bigger majority and a real prospect of a long run. It just makes you think that Castro was right and that you can't organise change on the basis of the old centres of power.

I spent the rest of the day talking to people. Charles Morris is a great comfort and he said that the time had come now to press ahead with recruiting part-timers and women and one or two other changes. I saw the DG who has been away for a couple of weeks touring round the country and I told him that this must be done at once. But everything is so interminably slow.

I had a meal with Joe Slater and afterwards a long talk to Ernest Marples who's absolutely full of computers. He thinks that because he is learning about them nobody else understands them. He says he's writing a great book on how the British Constitution can be reorganised. He was full of scorn for us. I pointed out to him that more had been done about computers in the last six months than in the previous thirteen years. Frankly we didn't get far because the only thing that might have interested me related to the machinery of Government and he didn't want to be specific about this. He just kept assuring me that everything he had done had been brilliant, that nobody worked harder than he did and that he could earn three times as much as he earned in Parliament in petty cash if only he got an outside job. I both like and dislike him very much.

Afterwards I moved to the corner of the smoking room to talk to Shirley Williams. Shirley thinks that race is going to be the dominant issue at the next Election and is rather pessimistic. Indeed my colleagues generally are pretty pessimistic about our prospects of survival.

Home about 12.30 and worked down in the office until just after 1.

Tuesday 25 May
This morning I gave some BEM medals to four Post Office people who had been mentioned in the New Year's Honours. It was revolting to hand these medals which said on them 'For God and Empire' but of course nobody notices these things any more.

This afternoon Roger Morrison and Alan Stewart of McKinsey's, came to see me and I kept them for nearly two hours and let my hair down. I told them of the organisational difficulties in the Post Office structure and they went over the areas where they felt they might produce results. I told them a little bit of the inside story of the recent wage negotiations and of the difficulty I had in getting the department to accept changes in the status quo.

This evening we went to the Africa Day party organised by the heads of the African missions. I was one of the few members of the Government invited and there were very few white people at all. They don't need us any more. Those who did speak to us were highly critical of the policy of the Government towards Indonesia and I found it difficult to say anything. My heart is rather heavy.

Afterwards Caroline and I went to Holland Park School for a meeting of the boys' house to which parents had been invited. It was delightful.

Wednesday 26 May
To the National Executive this morning which was held at the House of Commons. Only two things of interest came up. One was the statement on Vietnam which did nothing more than to explain the

Government's policy, including the reasons why we have supported the bombing of North Vietnam by the Americans, which I found and find hard to take. Harold explained the position and his general argument is of course that public declarations are less effective than private pressure. I didn't feel it was the time to say anything but I'm sure that a lot of people there, like myself, are extremely unhappy about the way in which things are going.

The other issue was the decision by the Organisation Sub-Committee not to approve Illtyd Harrington's inclusion in List 'B' of parliamentary candidates.* Apparently it had been said that he had written articles in the *Daily Worker* attacking the Government and this was one of the main reasons why the interviewing committee of three had felt unable to recommend his inclusion. Ian Mikardo raised this and he said he'd been through the whole file of the *Daily Worker* since last October and there had been no article whatsoever written by Harrington. I knew Illtyd from two years ago when we did a programme called 'Arena' in Bristol. He is a fiery and rather irresponsible but attractive bearded Welsh schoolteacher and if the Party won't have *him*, I just don't know where we'll be.

I spoke up for him and so did Dick Crossman and Tom Driberg and by a majority of one we agreed to get the decision postponed till next month. The GLC Labour Group will then write a letter to the Party and we can consider it in the light of what they say. The illiberal instinct of the Executive was revealed again.

The rest of the afternoon was spent working on my papers and this evening to the Guild of TV Directors' dinner at St Stephen's Restaurant. There were about twenty people there, most of whom I know. We had a discussion interrupted by about seven divisions, each of which necessitated my walking back to the House and voting. They were keen to get on with colour television – that emerged clearly – and were interested in pay-television. They were also interested in the idea of community television which would involve licensing regional stations and allowing them to be networked together for educational and community purposes. It was a pleasant evening.

Thursday 27 May
Arrived at the Post Office late this morning and worked through my papers and signed letters. I must sign 150 letters of apology for service failures a week and it is rather a burden.

---

* Harrington was a member of the GLC and Chairman of the GLC, 1984–5. List 'B' is the Labour Party's list of members recommended for consideration by local constituency parties as parliamentary candidates.

This afternoon to the Commons and talked to Frank Barlow, the Secretary of the PLP, who told me in detail the arrangements that had been made in the event of Harold Wilson dying. The news will be conveyed to a meeting of Ministers at Number 10, which will include the heads of all Departments, ie Ministers of Cabinet rank, as well as Cabinet Ministers themselves. Though there is no Deputy Prime Minister, George Brown is Deputy Leader of the Parliamentary Labour Party and will therefore have Harold's Party responsibilities.

Bowden as Leader of the House would be responsible for informing the House. As soon as Ministers know, letters or telegrams will be sent to every Commons Member of the Parliamentary Labour Party and a meeting will be summoned within twenty-four hours if the House is sitting or within forty-eight hours during a recess. No Lords will be present. At this meeting, nominations will be received and ballot papers will be duplicated on the spot. Four tellers will be appointed and the Party will proceed immediately to a vote.

It will be the usual exhaustive ballot procedure and if the first vote does not give an overall majority to one of the candidates there will be an adjournment for fifteen or twenty minutes in the same room to give candidates the opportunity to withdraw. There will then be another ballot and so on, until a new Leader of the Parliamentary Labour Party is appointed. The press will not be admitted until that is decided. The announcement will be made in a statement by Frank Barlow, as Secretary to the Parliamentary Labour Party, and will be conveyed to Sir Michael Adeane at Buckingham Palace. The Queen has been told that she is not to summon anybody to form a Government until she has heard who the new Leader is. Adeane understands this and the man elected Leader will be summoned. These arrangements have been agreed with the Liaison Committee of the Parliamentary Labour Party under Manny Shinwell's chairmanship and approved by Harold.

Friday 28 May
To the House of Commons this morning for a meeting of the Fabians.

After that to the *Daily Mirror* building to have lunch with Cecil King and Hugh Cudlipp. I had apparently gravely upset Cecil King by not having attended one of his functions earlier and the message reached Caroline through Lew Grade that he was hopping mad with me and had said, 'I snap my fingers and Harold Wilson comes to lunch but I can't get this man Wedgwood Benn. Who the hell does he think he is.'

Cecil King is a big and rather grim man and Hugh Cudlipp, the aging boy genius, is not all that attractive. I decided to talk frankly about the Office and how awful the civil servants were, how necessary it was to reorganise the whole thing, how the telephone service couldn't be put right for a long time and how the postal services need to be reshaped and to be forthcoming generally. I think I'm much too careful in talking to the press and probably most of my colleagues are much more free and easy and it pays off.

After lunch they got down seriously to the business of the fourth channel in which they are vitally interested since they are majority shareholders in ATV which is the one company that wants to take over the fourth channel. I told them that I would be sorry to see it allocated until I was absolutely satisfied that there wasn't some possibility of regional television performing a community function, buying programmes from programme contractors and broadcasting some University of the Air stuff. They didn't say much but were obviously disappointed and angry.

This highlights in my mind one of the great difficulties of being a socialist in the sort of society in which we live. The real drive for improvement comes from those concerned to make private profit. If, therefore, you deny these people the right of extending private enterprise into new fields, you have to have some sort of alternative. You have to have some body which wants to develop public enterprise but our present Civil Service is not interested in growth. It is geared to care and maintenance. The nationalised industries are not yet moving rapidly enough.

The thing to do is to find people who are keen on growth and give them the authority to grow on something other than a commercial basis. This seems to me to be the central problem of socialist practice today and I feel sure the answer lies in devolved authority. I don't believe that it is the drive for personal gain that makes private enterprise so energetic. I think it is the fact that when you are running your own show you have the authority to do what you want to do. And I'm sure the lesson for us is clear. We have somehow to create a multiplicity of public authorities and allow them to get on with the job. This is the case for splitting the Post Office up into its component parts as separate nationalised industries and for the progressive development of mixed enterprise where the state can work in partnership with those who are keen to break fresh ground.

Afterwards I had a talk with Brigadier Holmes and Toby O'Brien about my speech at the Postal Controllers' dinner tonight. Holmes was keen to get the 'feasible service' discussed, based on one delivery a day, and so was I. O'Brien was terrified that it would unleash a huge press campaign against us for having raised the postal charges and started to degrade the service at the same time. He thought the press, business organisations, the unions, the public and the Opposition would unite to attack us. I could well understand this and I felt the caution that goes with accountability. But I thought it ought to be done, so I cleared a press release setting out the possibilities quite clearly.

The dinner was a real postal occasion. The whole general directorate were there together with postal controllers from all over the country. The first speaker, Mr de Grouchy, made a characteristic Post Office speech in which he poured scorn on the automatic telephones as if they were new-fangled devices. He said the Post Office had always been run by broadminded ignoramuses at the top.

Replying, I drew attention to two occasions when the Post Office had been wrong in opposing innovation. One was the introduction of mail coaches in 1784 and the other was the statement in 1879 by Sir William Preece, the Engineer-in-Chief to the Post Office, when he said he saw no future for the telephone. I said we had a lot to learn from those who opposed change. Then I described the 'feasible service' and said we were considering it.

After me came Mr Jackson who was eighty-two – one of the last surviving surveyors.* He was a wonderful old man, upright, with a stern sense of duty, a good sense of humour and ready to argue all over again the case against mail coaches in 1784. He couldn't have done it better. I think I nearly overstepped the mark but I'm glad I said what I said. It was an enjoyable evening and it did bring to a head the conflict between innovation and conservatism which has been rumbling along inside the department since I've been there.

Monday 31 May
The Radio Services Department came to lunch with me today and I heard about the development of ship-to-shore radio for the purposes of conveying data from ships at sea to a computer ashore. This is being used by the Shell Company whose tankers – wherever they are in the world – can have information about their performance sent back to the UK, where it is processed on a computer. This service has only been going for a short while and the development of the technique is very exciting. It is possible that all payrolls of seamen can be dealt with in the same way, thus lifting the burden on the ships' officers.

This evening Peter Shore, Tommy Balogh and I had dinner together in St Stephen's Restaurant to discuss the general political situation and to prepare some useful advice for Harold. It was just like old times and was the first occasion on which we have actually discussed major strategy since the campaign last September.

---

* Controllers replaced postal surveyors, of whom probably the best known is Anthony Trollope, who were responsible for mail coaches and rural postal services.

The key questions are when should we have the Election and what should our strategy be? If the economic situation appears to be deteriorating it may prevent us from having an Election in which case we have two choices before us this winter: one is to have a siege Parliament, the other is to buy a year's time in the House by a temporary alliance. We agreed to meet later and discuss it again. Harold is keen that I should be included in these discussions. He only ever wants to hear from me when he thinks things aren't going well! But it is nice not to be entirely isolated in my departmental work.

Tuesday 1 June

I went to my room hoping to doze a bit during the all-night sitting. Unfortunately, I dozed too thoroughly and slept right through a division at 3.15 am without even noticing it. It shook my confidence in my ability to hear the division bell when I'm asleep. The whips were decent about it and quite understood.

At 5.30 I went into the tea room to talk to a group of Laabour MPs, John Horner, Idwal Jones, Arthur Probert and Tom Swain. George Brown came up, sat down and said to them, 'Can't you make the Postmaster General go away, I don't like him at all.' I thought it was friendly banter and then he turned on me and said, 'You have wrecked my incomes policy – you know that, don't you? As soon as the Commies started shouting at you, you gave way.' He said that I had ignored Ray Gunter's advice to adjourn the negotiations over the weekend and that he – Ray Gunter – was sore about it. He also said that I had telephoned Jim Callaghan on the Isle of Wight. Most of these statements were totally untrue but it was impossible to refute them because of all our colleagues who were there. They politely kept the conversation going although of course they could hear everything that was said.

I said, 'All right, George, let's go and have a talk about it in your room,' but he was tight as usual and turned away and joined in the general conversation. Afterwards, Tom Swain, Arthur Probert and John Horner said how disgusted they were by the episode. Arthur Probert said, 'It's a good thing that one of you was sober otherwise there would have been real trouble.' John Horner just squeezed my arm. The fact is that I am so used to George Brown that I was less shocked by it than they were. But as soon as the House rose and I got home at 6.30, I sat down and wrote a long letter to George. I decided to send it to him today. This is just to get the record straight. In fact I may even send a copy to Harold Wilson.

What is interesting is that it was the first time George Brown had spoken to me about the postmen's pay agreement since April, before

Go on then—I dare you!

After I missed the Division bell in June 1965

I began negotiations. I have been aware of this undercurrent of criticism and now know where much of it came from. Some of the phrases he used came straight out of the press and probably they were the same phrases he had put in the press. Happily, by going as monstrously far as he did, I am able to take it up and be on fairly strong ground.

Then we had the Post Office Board where there was a long discussion about the future of the postal services. For reasons of manpower it is necessary to reduce the demands the postal services make over the years to come and this drives us towards the idea of the 'feasible service' of fewer deliveries. In addition, we have got to consider how to save £5 million in the next twelve months to prevent a further increase in tariffs next year. This is going to require a tough line with the unions who are naturally opposed to what they would represent as a reduction of service. It also means that we've got to be strong on recruitment of women and part-timers. We agreed that negotiations with the union should begin next week and these must produce results soon.[17]

We also heard progress reports on the movement towards the new Advisory Council and on the telephone service where the quality of service is deteriorating.

Wednesday 2 June

To a Cabinet committee this morning discussing future legislation.

Lunch with the board of English Electric. The Director of Research was a bright and jolly man called Dr Eastwood and we had a long talk about the difficulty of selling new research projects to the product companies. In fact salesmanship is needed long before you get near the customer. The other directors of English Electric varied in quality. One, Mr Sutherland, was a red-faced, retired Indian Army colonel type who thought Britain was best and if you shouted at the foreigners they would soon know what was what. Then there was Sir Gordon Radley, ex-DG of the GPO, an engineer with a kindly temperament but firmly convinced that international communications could never improve on submarine cables and that satellites were rather a gimmick. Also Viscount Caldecote who is a Tory peer said that we should have launched our own communications satellites to compete with the Americans. In short, they were a typical British business board and not very impressive.

Charles Eames and Phyllis came to dinner with Caroline and me at St Stephen's. He said that he thought the United States – with its mixture of rootless émigrés – had been best qualified to take advantage of the opportunities created by the scientific revolution when the restraints imposed by poverty were removed. For there were no existing restraints imposed by tradition operating against innovation. It was an interesting idea.

Afterwards we walked back to the Commons and I took them into the Crypt. Before I went down there I checked that there was no division and relied upon the man who unlocked the Crypt gate to tell me if a division occurred. We were only there for four or five minutes and then walked through St Stephen's Hall. A few minutes later I saw a policeman and he told me that there had been a division a few minutes earlier. Peter Shore said at the same moment, 'It's a dead heat. 281 to 281.'

At that moment I realised what had happened and dashed into the Members' Lobby where the Chief Whip and some of his colleagues were standing. I said, 'I was in the Crypt and missed the vote.' At almost the same moment I heard that Norman Pentland had actually been sitting in the chamber discussing a constituency case and had been locked out and Stanley English had been down in the book stacks where there is no division bell. It was the most appalling moment. Everyone was extremely kind except for George Wigg who turned on me savagely. He cannot resist kicking anybody when they're down. The day was saved by the vote of the MP in the chair but it was on the Corporation Tax clause and could hardly have been more serious.

Charles and Phyllis were deeply shocked and appalled that the Government should rest upon such chance. When Caroline got home after midnight, the press were banging on the door – no doubt to check whether I really had been with my wife. I had said this clearly to the lobby journalists but probably they thought they might be on to something else and the fact that Caroline had been with me did not appear in the papers.

Thursday 3 June

Two things of interest today. First, Krishna Menon is to be invited to attend the Nehru Memorial Exhibition.[18]

Secondly, Ron Smith made a violent attack on me, speaking in Eire. He was referring to my speech to the postal controllers last week in which I had said there was a possibility of considering the idea of one delivery a day. He said that I was out to 'smash' the postal service and one or two other things just as bad. This is the explosion I expected but it has come rather late and the press, so far, has not taken it up. I think it was right to air it in the way that I did, since it creates a situation to which he now has to react.

There was still a lot of banter going on about my having missed the division yesterday and the awful thing is that I can't trust my normal mechanism and am afraid that I'll be standing next to a bell and forget what it means. I wrote to the Chief Whip to tell him what had happened and also to the Speaker, to Charlie Pannell, and the Serjeant-at-Arms to suggest changes in the system. With this tight parliamentary situation there has got to be improvement.

Home about midnight, extremely tired and looking forward to a break over Whitsun.

Friday 4 – Sunday 6 June

Stayed at home this morning and began clearing up the backlog of work before the holiday. This evening with the family to Stansgate. Mother was already there and so were Dave and June, Piers and Frances.

Sunday's *Observer* had a cartoon of me asleep with Melissa and Joshua standing by my bed with a bell and one saying to the other, 'Go on – I dare you.'

Tuesday 8 June

There was nothing doing at the Office and I decided to work at home instead. Among the papers I worked on was a minute about the appointment of a new vice-chairman for the BBC. I had decided some time ago to appoint Asa Briggs who is extremely well-qualified. Lord Normanbrook wanted Lord James or a man called Christopherson, the vice-chancellor of Durham University. The Director General sent me a minute pointing this out and a minute drafted for me to the Prime Minister in which I weakly recommended Asa Briggs but included long chunks showing how strongly Lord Normanbrook felt about the other nominees. I simply was not prepared to sign it. Normanbrook is not responsible for appointing the governors and it is my DG's job to support my nomination, not Normanbrook's. I checked with Professor Blackett. Christopherson is, as I thought, an Establishment figure and he – Blackett – thought Briggs was much better. But this is the sort of petty obstruction that goes on all the time.

This afternoon with Hilary to see the Nehru Memorial exhibition at the Royal Festival Hall which Charles Eames is preparing. It was a superb piece of design and, as with everything that Charles does, it was based upon the most detailed understanding. It was a most sensitive piece of work and we walked round it for about an hour and a half, discussing every detail. There was however one omission – the work of the Labour Party and 1945–51 Labour Government in finalising independence. Attlee deserved more of a mention than he got and so I came home and looked up some documents which I hope Charles will be able to use and integrate in some way into the exhibition. I lent him a copy of *Our Island Story*, *Our Empire Story in Pictures*, 'Let Us Face the Future – the 1945 Labour Election Manifesto' and my copy of the 1947 India Independence Bill. I also gave him a number of quotations about India including the hideous one on Gandhi by Churchill in 1931.*

Wednesday 9 June
Tommy Balogh came to lunch with me. He is very pessimistic about things. We agreed that it was necessary to keep the three of us – himself, Peter and myself – together to do an appreciation of the position for Harold.

We then discussed the Giro. I have been disappointed at the reaction of the Treasury and of the Ministry of Pensions towards this. The Treasury think the rate of financial return is inadequate and do not want to upset the banks. The Ministry of Pensions are not as interested as they ought to be in the use of Giro for paying social benefits. However, even in its modified form, the Giro is worth doing and I hope to get Cabinet approval next month and publish a White Paper. There is even the possibility that we might be able to do it without legislation.

* '. . . a seditious fakir of a type well known in the East, striding half-naked up the steps of the Vice-regal palace . . . to parley on equal terms with the representative of the King-Emperor.'

Afterwards Ryland came to see me and we talked about a number of things. These included my speech at the POEU next Monday, the provision of a low-cost communications system for the old and housebound, a new policy for telephone kiosks and a new look at the telegraph service. On the latter I am determined to try to get away from the loss of nearly £3 million incurred each year. It was a useful discussion and I felt I'd made some progress.

Home and worked till after midnight. Herbert Rogers rang up about the Labour Party meeting tomorrow night in Bristol. He was seething with hatred for the Government and said that Bristol had been denied a school, that he thought Wilson would soon be sending British troops to Vietnam, that Denis Healey was quite capable of introducing conscription, etc, etc.

Thursday 10 June

The Post Office Board met this morning and we discussed the financial review which shows that the postal prospects have worsened with the likelihood of a million pound loss this year, though the telecommunications figures are better than was expected.

We had a long discussion on the future of the inland postal service and revised the paper that had been submitted. The car radiophone is to be started on 1 July though the Ministry of Transport are still talking about a ban on using it while cars are moving.

After the Board meeting I met the National Guild of Telephonists led by Mr Barnfield who was demanding a £1 increase at once at all the points on the scale. Last year he signed a three-year agreement with us and it is impossible for us to make any concession. I think he knew this but was under heavy pressure from his members. It may be we shall be faced with guerrilla action in this field.

Then to Bristol where there was a special meeting of the GMC to which about fifty people came. I spoke for forty-five minutes and explained the policy of the Government and what had been achieved. Then we had a free-for-all in which some extravagant things were said. Some members blamed us for increases in bus fares, and one said that we were just bolstering up capitalism. Herbert Rogers launched into a violent attack against British policy in Vietnam. And all in all it was a rough passage. But a couple of young schoolteachers who were there, Price and Cox, did see the reality of the problems and made a lot of sense in what they said. There is an appalling gulf opening up between the Government and its active supporters, many of who seem to take a magic view of politics and suppose that you've only got to change the personnel in the Cabinet and everything will come right.

Saturday 12 June

I am reading the Bishop of Woolwich's latest book, *The New Reformation*. It is a most excellently argued book, saying that the Church as an institution is out of date and that it's got to re-create itself in real life, allowing its theology and its organisation to spring up much more from the real needs of the people. I think what he says has equal applicability to political parties. He's one of the most creative people I know.

Caroline went to Robin Day's wedding celebration party at the Garrick Club this evening. He has just come back from Australia where he married Katherine Ainsley and this was to give his friends a chance to meet her.

Sunday 13 June

This morning Kenneth Rose's column in the *Sunday Telegraph* included a little paragraph describing how Mountbatten had introduced Charles Eames to Harold Wilson as the man who nearly brought the Government down. Thus Harold learned that it was Charles Eames who was in the Crypt with me just before Whitsun.

The Nehru exhibition was opened on Thursday when I was in Bristol and Caroline had told me it was crowded with Establishment figures and was treated by the British as an opportunity for a flood of self-congratulation about our greatness in giving freedom to India. Clem and Harold were the great heroes with Mountbatten as the Establishment figure who yielded and the memory of this man Nehru was more or less submerged by what we had done. When Caroline mentioned it to an Indian he just giggled. She had an amusing encounter with the Cuban Ambassador who kept pulling her on one side and saying how Cuba wanted to be friendly with the United States and what difficulties she had with her other allies. Caroline thought that he must imagine that she would transmit this information straight on to the Foreign Secretary. She had met him once before but didn't really know him at all.

At the moment we are all feeling rather grim about the appalling concentration upon British achievement. There is an orgy of commemoration including Magna Carta, the Simon de Montfort Parliament, Waterloo, the First World War, the Second World War, Dunkirk, and so on. All of these are turned into royal occasions and thus strengthen the basically reactionary influence the monarchy has over our national life.

I read yesterday morning that the Beatles had been given MBEs. No doubt Harold did this to be popular and I expect it *was* popular – though it may have been unpopular with some people too. The *Daily Mirror*'s headline was 'Now They've Got Into The Topmost Chart

Of All'. But the plain truth is that the Beatles have done more for the royal family by accepting MBEs than the royal family have done for the Beatles by giving them. Nobody goes to see the Beatles because they've got MBEs but the royal family love the idea that the honours list is popular because it all helps to buttress them and indirectly their influence is used to strengthen all the forces of conservatism in society. I think Harold Wilson makes the most appalling mistake if he thinks that in this way he can buy popularity, for he is ultimately bolstering a force that is an enemy of his political stand.

The other thing this week that's in my mind is the developing situation in Vietnam, where the Americans are now deciding to invade in full strength and we are left in the embarrassing position of appearing to support them. I believe this is an untenable position and sooner or later we shall have to come out and say what we really think. The argument that we are keeping quiet in order to retain influence is of course fallacious. The real reason is quite different. On Friday night there was the first 'teach-in' at the LSE in London on Vietnam. It was based on the 'teach-ins' that have appeared in the United States and which are an aspect of the non-violent movement. I think they probably will have an influence and I'm told that whenever Harold Wilson's name was mentioned at LSE people booed. It may well be that when the time comes the Labour Government will have been held to fail not because it was too radical but because it was not radical enough.

Worked at home the rest of Sunday afternoon preparing a press release for tomorrow and then spent an hour or two with the family.

Monday 14 June
To Scarborough this morning for the POEU conference. I had decided that the right thing to do was to admit frankly the deficiencies of the telephone service and link it to a ten-point programme designed to put it right. The trouble with the Public Relations Department in the Post Office is that it is always boasting about successes and this can be an irritant to people who suffer poor telephone service – as I do myself. The more I think about politics today the more important it seems to me to tell the truth about the situation and not allow the public to live in a cosy dream which encourages them to believe that everything Britain does is best, that deficiencies and failures are just due to foreigners or the promises of politicians. The press is appalling, not because its comment is critical – that is necessary – but because it simply does not publish the facts and the truth.

The speech went down quite well at the conference and it married in with what Charles Smith had said in warning of near chaos in the telephone service in the future.

Afterwards I went round the Scarborough sorting office and telephone exchange and then had a meal with the POEU at the Crown Hotel.

Charles Smith is worried about the impending wage negotiations and feels that the Government is going to be driven towards some form of pay pause policy on the public sector because it is the only sector which it controls. I can see this coming and it is going to pose terrible industrial problems and turn many people away from us. But I frankly don't see the alternative unless we carry planning a great deal further and begin to control the economy in a true sense. Exhortation is too late. The public have got to be confronted with reality. Either we are stagnant or we have inflation unless we are prepared to go ahead with real planning.

Afterwards by car to York where I went over the sorting office from midnight till just before 1. It was exactly as it had been built thirty years ago with no mechanisation of any kind. Caught the 1 o'clock sleeper home.

Tuesday 15 June

Arrived home this morning on the sleeper and went to the Office. The Director General had gone to Ascot today and will be there tomorrow. It is just as Bevins said it was.

I worked through a few papers, talked to Joe Slater, went to the House of Commons and waited to hear Harold Wilson answering questions on Vietnam. It had been fully expected that he would be indicating some change of view but in fact he simply promised a statement and left it at that.

Wednesday 16 June

To the Post Office this morning and Mr Wolverson came in to discuss wage negotiations. I was concerned about the situation surrounding the postmen's negotiations, the repercussions of which are still with me. I asked him to see whether it was possible to conduct the joint survey of pay research reports with the union in such a way that the union didn't get to know or guess what would be the sum of money that we were asking the Treasury to authorise us to offer. For if they know that they can judge to what extent we've been successful and drive a wedge between us and the Treasury. I also discussed with him the conditions under which trade union leaders were sometimes told the extent of our authority in order to keep them sweet. This makes a mockery of genuine negotiations and renders it impossible to settle below the maximum. It was a useful discussion, particularly as there is no doubt that in the future we are going to be in real difficulties with the Government pay policy beginning to bite on the public sector.

Afterwards to the House of Commons where a Mr Sheppard came to see me. He had written to me eighteen years ago at Oxford asking if he could address the Oxford Union and I had written a non-committal letter back to say he couldn't but that if he would ever like to see me I should be glad to do so. He turned up last night at home saying he did want to see me and Caroline put him off. I rang him thinking it might be something important and he came this afternoon. He said that he had worked for twenty years on the greatest idea ever which he'd written down on a piece of paper. He handed me this in an envelope and when I opened it, it said, 'Everything everywhere moves. It always has done and it always will. EVERYTHING EVERYWHERE MOVES.' He wanted me to take this to the Russians and the Americans so they could share the truth equally. He was a real nut case but it was quite comic.

Tommy Balogh and Peter and I had a long talk this evening about Party strategy. I wrote a memorandum for them which is ultimately to go to Harold.

It was an all-night sitting and I simply dared not go to sleep. But I did discover that Harold, Jim Callaghan, Frank Cousins, and a whole host of other MPs had missed divisions recently. The only difference was that they didn't do it when the Party tied with the Tories. But I feel a bit better about it now.

The younger Labour MPs are most dissatisfied with the fact that the Finance Bill is occupying all the time of the House and with the appalling conditions under which they live and work. I think they're a good crowd and worth encouraging and I must see if I can do anything to help them. At about 5 o'clock this morning Raymond Fletcher [MP for Ilkeston] collapsed in the tea room and it was a horrible sight to see three people holding him down and hear him groaning. Whether it was an epileptic fit, as was rumoured, or not, I don't know. But this is the price we pay for such folly.

Thursday 17 June

The House sat till noon today. It was our sixteenth wedding anniversary and I telephoned Caroline.

When the House rose I went to the Post Office and then to lunch with Reuters. They struck me as a bright crowd who have built up a most formidable worldwide service. Our quarrel with them is almost insoluble. They get a preferential press rate of 1d a word. It was cut from twopence farthing a word to 1d a word during the war and ought now to be raised to at least 7d a word. They are sensitive about this but the issue will one day have to be faced. It is certainly not for the Post Office to subsidise Reuters' Commonwealth communications. If it is to be subsidised then the Commonwealth Relations Office should undertake it.

Having said that, I did feel this was a go-ahead organisation and I learned a lot. One of the interesting things was to hear that the London Stock Exchange was the only major stock exchange uncomputerised. This is because the jobbers don't want to be displaced but it greatly reduces the trading that can be done by foreign buyers and sellers on our exchange, since no up-to-the-second facilities can exist for quoting prices.

Caroline and I went out to dinner to celebrate our anniversary.

Friday 18 June

Up early this morning and by car to Basildon where I opened the new Standard Telephones & Cables factory there. This is American owned, a part of ITT and the top management was American. The European manager was a man called Admiral Stone who had been in Italy with Father in the war. When General Mason-Macfarlane was sacked by Churchill, Admiral Stone took over.

He told me one interesting piece of family history I didn't know. When Mike was killed in 1944, Father just came home without anyone's permission. General Brian Robertson, who was Earl Alexander's personnel staff officer, rang Admiral Stone to ask him where Father had gone. The Admiral said, 'I gave him compassionate leave.' Robertson replied, 'We don't have compassionate leave in the British Army in wartime.' The Admiral told Robertson that it was his fault and he must take full responsibility. I know that Father was so upset that he felt he had to come home in order to get on real active service.

Dashed back to London by car, collected Caroline and we went together to Cardiff. We stayed at the Park Hotel and went to the pre-Gala dinner organised by the South Wales Miners. They are Communist controlled – but a very nice crowd indeed. We had a delightful evening.

Saturday 19 June

Caroline and I were at the head of the procession with thirty-one bands from the city centre to Sophia Gardens where Michael Foot and I spoke. There was a little bit of Communist heckling but otherwise it went down well in lovely sunshine. Afterwards we had a bite of lunch and then wandered round the fairground and came home on the afternoon train – exhausted.

Sunday 20 June
Another lovely day. Joshua was in bed with bronchitis but the rest of the children played cricket in the garden and I worked in the office and dictated letters and my diary.

I almost forgot. On Friday, I had a letter in George Brown's own handwriting in answer to mine about the episode in the tea room, a report of which had appeared in *Private Eye*.

> Tony, Your letter has never been out of my mind. Although I do feel strongly about the matter I have absolutely no defence on the issue you properly charged me with.
>
> I'm only too well aware that a private apology for a public wrong isn't very satisfactory! But there's little else I can do. I'm very sorry, Yours, George.

So there it is. I was told I would get an apology from him for he always apologises. But it doesn't do much more than put the record straight on that issue.

Monday 21 June
The car broke down this morning so I got to the Office late. At 11 o'clock Mr Shina, the Minister for Parliamentary Affairs and Minister of Communications from India, came to see me. He was a jolly man of about sixty-five who had spent eight years in jail as a result of his work for the Congress Party. He knew Father and had come to see me as much because of Father as because I was his opposite number. I found him most delightful and we talked for about an hour.

The conversation began with his recollection of the struggle against Britain and then sharply changed tone as the subject swung to China, on which he was indistinguishable from John Foster Dulles speaking about Stalin at the height of the Cold War. It was an astonishing transformation. He found evil in the whole of their ideology, ascribed the most violent intentions to them, said the world must unite against them, compared Mao Tse Tung to Hitler, said the Chinese wanted to pick countries off one after the other, and generally speaking was unwilling to contemplate any policy but international isolation for China. He thus supported American policy in Vietnam and was extremely critical of what he called the left-wing influence in the Labour Party. I found it discouraging.

Afterwards I dictated another minute to the Prime Minister on Post Office reorganisation, seeking authority to make a speech on the subject which would open up the discussion and move us towards commitment. I am firmly convinced in my own mind that this is the right thing to do and believe that the opportunity lies within our grasp in the next twelve months. In this respect, I shall have the department working wholeheartedly for me and I may as well take advantage of their enthusiasm.

I had the Accountant General's department to a sandwich lunch today and then to the House of Commons where Ann Kerr [MP for Rochester and Chatham] and a colleague came to plead for lower TV licences for pensioners. This is frankly impracticable and I had to say so without sounding too heartless.

This afternoon George Brown came up to me in the tea room and said, 'Did you get my letter?' I replied, 'Yes, bless you, it was very nice of you to have written.' 'I hear you made a magnificent speech at the South Wales Miners' Gala,' he said, rather unconvincingly but when a man is trying to make it up you can't do more than be friendly.

I also saw Rawlinson this afternoon and told him that the Select Committee on Nationalised Industries would like to tackle the Post Office next session. He said that he had advised his people that this was all right. So the way is now clear for it. I think this may be the point of breakthrough.

Tuesday 22 June

The Post Office Board occupied us up till lunchtime. We had a discussion about the telephone service which falls well below acceptable standards. We also discussed the switch-over to all-figure dialling in place of letters and figures. This will pose certain PR problems but is necessary.

Sir Leon Bagrit, chairman of Elliot-Automation, Mr Anthony Milward, chairman of BEA,* and Mr Arthur Norman, chairman of De La Rue were our guests at the Board lunch. We had a short general discussion, at the end of which they were certain that the Post Office should be turned into a group of nationalised industries under a Ministry of Communications. This exactly confirmed my view and strengthened my opinion that we ought to get on with this job while the iron is hot. I am writing a long minute to Harold asking for consent to go ahead and prepare a detailed scheme. In order to do this, I shall certainly need permission to discuss the matter publicly and indicate which way my mind is going. I think this is probably the only really big thing I can tackle while at the Post Office and I don't want to miss it.

Afterwards to the House of Commons, where I met a big-talking Canadian gimmicky sales promoter who's full of a lot of crap about selling Britain abroad and whom Bessie Braddock foisted on to me. What it really amounted to was that he wanted British Government

---

* British European Airways, later absorbed into British Airways.

money to finance a scheme of his own. I wouldn't trust him as far as I could see him.

Later this evening Francis Noel-Baker [MP for Swindon], Terry Boston [MP for Faversham] and Donald Chapman [MP for Northfield] came to see me to urge me to allow the BBC to go ahead with local broadcast experiments. I said I was certainly prepared to consider this but we had not yet reached that stage in the review. But I must have something positive to announce soon, as I've made no progress whatsoever on the broadcasting front since I've been in office.

It looks as if my trip to Germany will have to be cancelled. The Hanging Bill comes up on Friday and Sydney Silverman [MP for Nelson and Colne] tells me that he is afraid we shall not carry it, as so many abolitionists are going away unpaired. I could never forgive myself for missing this vote if it were to lead to the defeat of the Bill. I shan't be sorry for three days off as I am so tired.

Wednesday 23 June

Caroline came in this evening and we went together to Harold's reception at Lancaster House for the Commonwealth Prime Ministers' Conference. There were crowds of MPs and among the many people we met there was Clem Attlee who was sitting on a chair being greeted by hosts of people who went by.

The great case for the Commonwealth today is what it does to this country. The effect of having all the African and Asian leaders in London negotiating with a Labour Prime Minister is to keep us in tune with world opinion. It is a real blessing and only an organisation like the Commonwealth can do it.

It is for this reason that I am so glad we have not got ourselves stuck inside Europe and cut off entirely from the great outside world. This is also why papers such as the *Daily Express* hate the Commonwealth so much, because they know what it is doing. It greatly strengthens Harold's hand against the Foreign Office and against the pressure from Washington. He has obviously decided to put on his Commonwealth hat and this has brought new developments in British policy towards Vietnam in recent weeks.

Thursday 24 June

I slept late this morning and Valerie came in for some work in the office. I had to go to the Post Office as Cooke had tabled a parliamentary question about the shortage of stamps. The Office quietly told me that they had incorrectly answered a previous question of his so I sought him out and explained this to him. He thinks that he's going to be able to prove that we failed to order sufficient stamps and that's why there's a shortage. In fact this is quite untrue. But how inefficient the Office has been in handling this whole question.

To the House briefly but the question didn't come up. Back to the Post Office where I worked quite late, clearing up various papers. They are trying to prevent me from getting the Gentleman stamps considered – these are the ones in blocks of six. So I decided to take over the whole question myself.

I also had Shepherd and Daniels in to discuss the joint Treasury-Post Office working party on the organisation of the Office. Sir Kenneth Anderson joined us and the whole thing was rather embarrassing. The DG was away and Anderson is known to be in favour of a separate telephone corporation which the DG is not. It really is like swimming through mud in that place.

Friday 25 June
To the House of Commons for the debate on the Bill to abolish hanging. The Tories filibustered and we didn't finish it but there were three divisions in which I voted.

Saturday 26 June
At home all day. This morning while cutting wood with my circular saw I let it slip and cut my thumb. This meant going to Hammersmith Hospital and having five stitches put in. A very silly thing to do.

Sunday 27 June
A violent attack on me by Crossbencher in today's *Sunday Express*. The first point of the criticism was on the postmen's pay settlement which it describes as having been a 20 per cent increase. It is obvious that I have got now to start counter-attacking on this front. I have held back for fear of annoying George Brown and in the hope that it would subside but it is obvious that it is going to go on and I cannot allow it to develop without dealing with it effectively.

Monday 28 June
After lunch I went to Fleet Building for rehearsals for the launching of the Early Bird satellite as a commercial telephone system. It was the most elaborate link-up with the possibility of all sorts of political and technical hitches. Harold Wilson arrived at about 4.15 with the Lord Mayor of London and a crowd of other people whom we had invited. I had to make an opening speech and then we picked up our telephones and President Johnson spoke, followed by Monsieur Jacinou from France, Chancellor Erhardt from Germany and Italian and Swiss speakers. Then Harold spoke.

Afterwards we went round the whole circuit again, linking telecommunications people. This time it was my turn to say something. While we were listening to the calls Harold and I exchanged scribbled notes like boys in class. He wrote 'This is the first time I've had three minutes to talk to LBJ without him interrupting 14 times.' Harold was in extremely good heart and looked rested and happy. The Commonwealth Conference has allowed him to put on a Commonwealth hat in place of the NATO hat which the Foreign Office is always trying to screw on to him. He has disengaged himself from his previous commitment on Vietnam with enormous skill. I am going to see him a couple of times this week and hope that I shall be able to win his support for my current projects.

I went to the Commons for a brief meeting with Tommy Balogh and Peter Shore. We discussed the new situation created by Harold's announcement that there won't be an autumn Election, the beginnings of a Tory campaign to get rid of Home, and the Liberal split over Jo Grimond's proposal that there might be a Lib-Lab arrangement. The economic situation remains worrying. Treasury pressure is of course along traditional lines: for a stop phase in the stop-go cycle. This would be completely disastrous and would end our five-year plan. It is the usual case of civil servants trying to sabotage Government policy and it must be resisted.

Then to Lime Grove to take part in the BBC 'Panorama' programme on the telephone service. They had made a fair film and I was interviewed by Michael Charlton. He really pushed the idea of making the telephone service into a private enterprise concern which I did my best to resist while keeping an open mind on the possibility that it might be reorganised on new lines, including various public corporations.

Tuesday 29 June
At 11 o'clock I went to Wren House to open a new international telephone exchange and then went round to see all the switchrooms. It was interesting but I find I have been put down for so many such engagements of this kind that I'm wondering if the department isn't trying to keep me so busy with them that I haven't got time to get on with my job. The fact is that many of the major projects such as the Giro, Post Office reorganisation and the data processing service are being held up as are the papers on broadcasting policy which I am anxious to get settled. The Director General and the general directorate as a whole are definitely acting as a bottleneck.

I have also discovered that my instructions on stamp policy have simply not been followed. I asked to see the artists' instructions to those who were designing the stamps of the new Post Office Tower.

I discovered that the instructions remained exactly as before and that no reference at all had been made to the fact that the Queen is prepared to receive non-traditional designs. The instructions all specified as usual, 'The Queen's head must be a dominant feature of the designs.' This is in strict contravention of what they know has been agreed and what I want. Unless you watch them like a hawk they simply don't do what they're told.

The same applied to the Battle of Britain stamps. I found that the stamps essayed by Harrison's at my request, incorporating six stamps in one block, had not even been prepared for submission to the Palace. I asked why and they said that I had agreed to a minute which had said this could not be done. I asked to see the minute and found that there was one tiny reference to the difficulty of producing 'multi-design' stamps in the time. This had been slipped in in the hope that I wouldn't notice it and would sign the minute and then it could be used to show that I had abandoned the idea. I found the letter to the Palace, re-wrote the minute completely and recommended the stamps by Gentleman printed in a block of six with the Queen's head only on the top right-hand one. As second choice I suggested a block of six in which the Queen's head appeared in all. I don't know what the outcome will be but now that we have agreed that rejected designs are also to be made available to the press there will be some public discussion of the stamps. It may be that this is all risky politically but I think that I am covered by the agreement reached with the Palace in March under which non-traditional designs were able to be submitted.

To the House of Commons after lunch where I heard Harold at questions. He is fabulously calm and cool and the Opposition simply can't get at him.

It was an all-night sitting, going on till about 5.45. I worked late on my parliamentary questions for tomorrow and then slept for four hours, punctuated by divisions.

Wednesday 30 June
To Number 10 at 10.30 to see Harold. He'd asked to see me about the appointments of the BBC and ITA governors. He wants Lord Annan as vice-chairman of the BBC and Asa Briggs on ITA. He thinks Professor Richard Hoggart at Birmingham might be unacceptable. But in fact, most of the hour and twenty minutes I spent with him consisted of a review of the general political situation. He feels that the decision not to have an Election this autumn has precipitated the Tory leadership crisis,[19] which is true. There is also a row going on between Jo Grimond, who would like a Lib-Lab pact and Emlyn Hooson, Liberal MP for Montgomery, who is trying to wrest the

leadership of the Liberal Party from the Bonham Carter dynasty.[20] All this is greatly in our favour.

We had a long talk about the launching of a Vietnam initiative and he gave me the background to it.

I then ran through some of the points that were on my list for discussion. I told him that the Giro was going well and hoped to bring it to Cabinet by the end of the month. Now that the banks have decided to close on a Saturday, this helps us and it is evident that the banks are just not prepared to provide the sort of service that we can and must provide. They will certainly protest about what we are planning to do but it may be that since they cannot or will not compete we shall get some joint clearing arrangement with them. If I can carry this through it would be a most notable achievement.

I also reported briefly on the national data processing service and raised the question of converting the Post Office into three national-ised industries. Somehow Harold is doubtful about this but I'm hoping that I shall make some progress.

On the future structure of the postal services he said he thought it was unwise to air ideas until a decision had been reached. This rather knocks out the scheme I had for trying to fly a kite about a one-delivery-a-day service. He had noticed that Ron Smith had attacked me on this and I felt that he was vaguely disapproving.

Afterwards back to the Post Office and then into the House for questions. I came top today and it was a rough session. The Tories concentrated on a number of points – mainly the shortage of stamps at the time that the new tariffs were introduced. Robert Cooke had a very savage question down and the Tory Front Bench reverted to the charge of 'incompetence'. Next they questioned me on the cost of the advertising campaign to explain the increases, which was £109,000. I had not been consulted on this and it seemed a lot of money to me. There was also another series of attacks on the BBC and Sir Hugh Greene. I decided that I would play it cool today and so I didn't hit back as hard as I might have done.

After questions I met Herbert Rogers and the group who had come up from Bristol on the Vietnam lobby. I gave them tea on the House of Commons terrace and we talked. The Commonwealth Prime Ministers' conference has made a big difference but I don't think it's permeated through to ordinary people on the Left yet that it has permitted Harold to disengage himself from such a close alignment with the American position. I tried to get this across.

In the central lobby I bumped into Matthew Coady of the *Daily Mirror* who said to me, 'You certainly are getting a shocking press.' I invited him to come and have a cup of tea in the Strangers' Cafeteria and we talked for an hour. He said that I had a reputation with the press lobby for being totally unapproachable and there was bitterness that they had supported me during my peerage case and now that I didn't think they could help me I wouldn't speak to them at all. This is not at all true but we have had strict instructions from Harold not to see the press and I have been rather rigid about it. Also it takes up a hell of a lot of time and leaks don't do you any good with your colleagues. However, I was grateful to Matthew for tipping me off and resolved to try to make some moves to improve relations.

Thursday 1 July

There was a serious fire at the Northern District Office this morning and a Nigerian postman was overcome by smoke and killed. I looked in there on my way to St Martin's-le-Grand.

After lunch I went to see Frank Soskice. Soskice is an impossibly reactionary man entirely in the hands of his civil servants. He said that if the Bill to abolish capital punishment did not go through next week 'I shall have to start hanging again'. It was an appalling thought that he should even be contemplating such a thing. And if it were to happen then undoubtedly Gerald Gardiner would resign from the Government and there would be a major revolt.

To the Office early this morning. I decided that I had better be careful about recommending the Battle of Britain stamps without the Queen's head. In view of the bad press I'm getting and the delicate political situation I could foresee that if these stamps were published – since the Queen is more or less constitutionally obliged to accept my advice – I would be violently attacked in the Tory press, and this would be presented as the final straw: 'Benn knocks Queen off stamps.' So I told my office to ring Sir Michael Adeane. They did this, having discovered that he was at Holyrood House. When they rang he was actually with the Queen presenting my letters and when he came out he said she was prepared for most of the recommendations but was not too happy about the Battle of Britain stamps showing five out of the six in the block without her head. That is to say she had rejected the headless stamps.

I was anxious to do this by consent and so my office indicated to Adeane that I would be perfectly happy if she chose the ones with the head on each stamp. This will therefore be the stamp that is issued in September, but the press will be shown the stamps that were rejected. It will focus publicity on the machinery of selection and I shall explain that I make recommendations to the Palace including the Stamp Advisory Committee's recommendations but of course the final choice remains with the Queen. Once this has happened I think it will pave the way for further moves next year with the pictorial stamps.

This out of the way, I went to the meeting of the seventeen organisations forming the Post Office Consumers' Consultative Council to replace the old Post Office Advisory Council. I welcomed them and said I thought the time had come when we should follow the pattern adopted by nationalised industries of having an independent consumer representative organisation working with us and I hoped that they would launch such a council.

Then I had a bravery award and afterwards the Director General came in and we had about an hour and a half's talk. He told me about his visit to Germany and we discussed the appointments to the BBC and the ITA and the future organisation of the Post Office. He is keen to keep telephones and posts together but he has let me see an important report written by Ryland and Shepherd some years ago, recommending that the telephone service be a separate nationalised industry. This I'm sure is the right line.

This evening Peter Shore looked in and he told me about his talks at Number 10 with Harold about Vietnam and how he had routed one of the Foreign Office people – Oliver Wright* – who works there.

Sunday 4 July
Pottered about in the garden this morning. It takes me about a day to recover from the pressure of the week's work. This afternoon I went back to Hammersmith Hospital to have the stitches removed from my thumb and then the whole family played cricket behind Wormwood Scrubs prison.

Monday 5 July
At 8 o'clock this morning Vernon Sproxton of the BBC came along to record a sentence by me about Reinhold Niebuhr, the American theologian, who is an old family friend.[21] He is doing a progamme on Niebuhr in October and is collecting a few comments from people who know him.

Then to the Post Office where I inaugurated the London radio car phone system. This was done with a call through to Richard Dimbleby, followed by a call from one of the finalists in the GPO telephonist competition back to me.

Afterwards to the Commons where Ian Aitken of the *Guardian* came to interview me. Charles Morris had fixed him on the basis of improving my relations with the press. I talked about the various problems that were confronting us but was extremely careful not to

* Private secretary to the Prime Minister 1964–6, knighted in 1974. Later held many Ambassadorial posts.

indicate firmly what way things were going. I spent the rest of the evening at the House and we rose relatively early, about 1 o'clock.

Tuesday 6 July

This morning Ian Aitken's article in the *Guardian* came under the heading 'Posts, Phones and Bank may be separated'. He then had a long piece in which he had gone far beyond anything that I had hinted to him. I'm afraid Harold won't be pleased and there may be rather a row about this. It just shows that it is not safe to talk to journalists. I've got somehow to improve my relations with the press and at the same time not leak anything to them.

I rang up Trevor Lloyd Hughes to have a talk to him about the bad press that we were getting and he said that he thought it stemmed from the original lobby meeting I had given last October or November when I had said that the posts were in an appalling financial state and then of course the statement had been delayed and delayed while the charges were battled through the Cabinet. It may well be that he is right.

The DG came to see me today. He told me that Wolverson would be retiring in September and he wanted Ryland to take his place. I told him of my idea for a study group on the postal services in the year 2000. This is something that Miss Goose stimulated me into doing. She thought that there was a real danger that we would simply mechanise our existing processes and that if we really were to get the major economies from mechanisation we would have to try to work on a much larger scale than we have hitherto thought right. The implications of this for the management and the organisation of the Post Office were tremendous.

I also had a brief talk with Sir Kenneth Anderson about Giro and he told me that he thought that we could move quickly now. Today Harry Hynd, Labour MP for Accrington, won the ballot for the Private Member's motion on 21 July and picked the Giro as a subject. This means that some decision will have to be taken within the next week. It looks as if it can be done without legislation and that means that the Cabinet ought to be pleased at the prospect.

This afternoon Caroline and I went to the GPO Interflora reception at the Waldorf. I am dreading tomorrow night when it goes on television. I desperately wish I'd never agreed to do it. It is the worst sort of Dale Carnegie commercial goo plus poor-quality Post Office PR, all souped up and presented by mediocre 1930s BBC producers.

Dr Jamal Shaer came to see me this afternoon. I knew him when he was here as president of the Arab Students' Union about ten years ago and then he went back to Jordan where he is a practising gynaecologist. He has been very active in the Ba'ath Party and has served a couple of periods in gaol as a result. He is in England on a visit to see friends and also in the hope of making contact with the Labour Party. He feels that the Labour Party's support for Israel has been a major barrier to understanding with the Arab socialists and wondered if there was any chance of overcoming it. I am very much out of touch now but decided to write to Fenner Brockway and John Stonehouse and also to the Labour Party to find out if they could see him. I also said I would send him a couple of issues of *New Outlook*.

Wednesday 7 July

This morning I decided to take the pay of cable ship officers to the Prices and Incomes Committee even though it had been approved by Ministers. After the postmen's pay trouble with George Brown I thought it wiser to be absolutely sure that he was prepared to support what I found necessary to do. In fact this was an over-abundance of caution but the percentage increases in this case are substantial and I could visualise him reading about them in the paper without having known anything beforehand.

I had a bravery award at half past two and then I hurried over to the House. The place is absolutely buzzing with the defeat of the Government last night. I was paired with Rawlinson but until I phoned him this morning and discovered that he had not voted I was not sure if I was one of the missing members. The Tories had prepared an ambush and they definitely caught us out.

Then Joe Slater came in to discuss the Board minutes for tomorrow with me and finally Joe, Wratten and I collected Caroline and we went to the GPO Interflora TV final. It was even worse than I expected, with a half-naked Hawaiian girl dressed in plastic flowers who insisted on putting a lei around my neck, although I had specifically asked that this should not happen. The thing was intensely embarrassing and I deeply regretted having agreed to do it. Caroline and I refused the dinner afterwards at the Beachcomber with all the gang of high-livers from the BBC, Interflora and the Post Office. Hilary's comment when I got home was the most revealing. He said, 'Dad, you didn't look at all authoritative, you were too eager, you were awful.' Thank goodness for one's children!

Thursday 8 July

To the Post Office this morning for the Board meeting where we went through a lot of work. When it came to the report prepared by Henrion on design in the Post Office, the Board launched into a bitter attack on it one by one. I let them all say their piece and then I told them that all progressive modern managements had design co-ordination of this kind and if they were not satisfied I was prepared to take it to the Council for Industrial Design and let them say whether they thought the scheme had merit. This does mean further delay but I am not prepared to have this thing frustrated by the Department. They were all buzzing with the rumours that had appeared in the *Guardian* about the division of the Post Office and were using it as a stick to beat me with. I refused to be disturbed by it.

To the Commons where I had a meeting with Mr Smart about the savings stamps. I had rejected the squirrel and the old sailing ship in favour of some new designs by Gentleman, and now Sir Miles Thomas, the new chairman of the Savings Committee, has refused to accept one of the Gentleman stamps. This really is too much but I shall have to try to ease it as best I can.

Caroline came in and we went together to a party in the Lords. It was rather tense being out of earshot of division bells but they promised they would tell me if anything happened. Afterwards Caroline and I sat on the terrace and talked to the Mayhews and the Dalyells until late and then home.

The Churchill stamps came out today and there will be an enormous demand for them.

Friday 9 July

I cancelled my visit to Scotland today because of the Prices and Incomes Committee meeting where I was taking the cable ship officers' problem. I went along and got a special accolade from George Brown for having brought this increase to the committee even though it only involved about seventy men and the total cost was £16,000 a year. But the percentage increase is simply enormous and if published the situation could become difficult. However, I got exactly what I wanted, in fact a little bit more than I had previously got, and I was pleased.

Hilary came to the Commons today. I got him under the Gallery and he heard a big row over the escape of the Great Train robbers and also many points of order about a possible statement on Vietnam.

Saturday 10 – Sunday 11 July

Had two days off which I appreciated but I did draft a long memorandum on Post Office reform which I intend to circulate round the Office and make the basis for a submission to the Government. I don't know how much support I'll get for it but I can see little point in doing what every other Postmaster General seems to have done – fume with frustration while in office and then write a strong pamphlet or book or article when he leaves office saying what ought to be done.

If this ought to be done then the time to try to get it done is when you are still in office.

In the *Sunday Times* Anthony Howard had a long article saying that there was a danger of a showdown between Lord Normanbrook and myself. I don't know where he got it from. I refused to see him earlier this week and I can't work out what the showdown is supposed to be about. Harold won't like it much since he is very anti-press – except insofar as he is able to use it himself. I suspect that this is a result of Lord Normanbrook's own lobbying which is a formidable threat to my position. Harold for some reason retains a respect for Normanbrook and I think underestimates the extent to which Normanbrook manipulates the machine to get what he wants. This may explain why the ministerial committee on broadcasting was rather unaccountably postponed recently. Caroline has a theory that Harold is impressed by pressure and that I ought to represent the reforms that I want to carry through as being in response to the pressure from the outside. That is to say that I ought to tell him that the Labour MPs are dissatisfied with the way the Post Office is being run (and that they are keen to do whatever we want to do at the BBC). Harold is more likely to listen to this sort of argument than he is to my own proposals for improving things. Caroline's argument is that I should always try to isolate my critics and never allow myself to become isolated. She is a shrewd political person – far more so than I.

Monday 12 July

This morning I dictated my major minute on Post Office reform and discussed it with Joe Slater who seemed pleased with it. The intention of this is to restore the impetus to the reform movement after the publication of the Treasury-Post Office working party report which is neutral and negative.

I also dictated another minute on the future of the postal services, trying to look ahead thirty-five years to see what effect mechanisation will have upon their basic structure. This I regard as an important operation.

I heard the Prime Minister did not sound too enthusiastic about hurrying the Giro decision in time for the debate next week, and I've got to get general support for it in time. It appears that this will now have to be done by means of circulating minutes to the Ministers principally responsible.

Today the External Telecommunications executive led by Colonel McMillan came to my Monday lunch. I thought they were a poor lot. Three of them had not got television sets which, for the heads of a big modern industry, was almost incredible. They were in favour of a change from Civil Service status though were not affected much by their links with the posts, and were more concerned to be outside the Government service than to be divided up. They were also heavily committed to cables as against satellites, mainly because they were brought up in the cable age and satellites were new and American. We discussed the switch to international subscriber dialling to the United States and a decision about this has to be taken in the next month or two. It would mean that people could phone direct to any subscriber in the USA or Canada at about half the cost, using existing equipment. I said that I believed this would more than double the traffic and thus we wouldn't lose any money. It is a decision comparable to Rowland Hill's decision to adopt a 1d postage and I'm sure it would pay off after a number of years.

After lunch I went to the House of Commons and Lord Normanbrook came to see me at his request about the article by Tony Howard that appeared in the *Sunday Times*. He said he was worried about it and thought the best thing to do was to have a talk. I assured him that I hadn't seen Howard or any of the BBC governors since I became the Minister. He was obviously much worried by the possibility that I might think that he was acting politically.

It was a perfect example of an Establishment figure – Tory in every instinct – genuinely deceiving himself into believing that he was non-political. But of course he isn't. His attitude came out revealingly when he was talking about concessions for television licences for pensioners as 'that sob stuff'. As soon as he said it he realised who he was talking to and he withdrew it but it gave an insight into the workings of his mind. I detest that man but I've got to work with him and Harold obviously doesn't want a row between me and him. The article has caused a great deal of comment in the House of Commons and lots of people have come up to speak to me about it. I have simply said that I refused to see Howard.

Today was the last day of the Finance Bill and we had to stay till 2 am.

Tuesday 13 July
To the Post Office about 10.30.

Mr Wratten and I had a talk about my minute on Post Office reform and he said that he thought it would be better to advocate a system under which there were two boards rather than three; and so I modified it to bring the banking services in with posts. I'm going to have it sent to the Deputy Directors General, the Engineer-in-Chief, the Comptroller and Accountant General, and the three operational directors, to collect their individual comments. I shall also seek the views of others who might be interested in it and then present the paper to the Home Affairs Committee or in a minute to the Prime Minister, as soon as the report of the Treasury-Post Office working party has been made available to him.

It all sounds revolutionary but it is not so different from what successive Postmasters General have said on leaving office. But it will take some years to carry through.

On to the House of Commons, home for a while and back to the Commons at 7 o'clock for the report and third reading of the Bill to abolish capital punishment. At the moment of dictating this – and it's nearly midnight – it looks as if we're getting to the end of the Bill and the majorities have been most encouraging.

I also did a bit of lobbying tonight about the Giro and I think that I shall be able to get this carried through. The expenditure involved in the next two years is absolutely trifling – a matter of £60,000 a year – and it will be three years before we start spending money in order to launch the scheme. After which it should be self-financing and bring in a better than 8 per cent return as it develops. It would be a major reform and I think would be a most welcome one.

I'm more worried about my Post Office reorganisation plans and frankly the leak in the *Guardian* last week is not helpful. It flies a kite and to that extent it may be useful, but it could also alienate Harold. At the moment he is not specifically interested and I shall have to work on him through Tommy Balogh and Peter Shore. Both of them see the case for it in terms of developing dynamic public enterprise capable of moving out into new fields.

Wednesday 14 July
James Fitton of the Stamp Advisory Committee came to see me this morning. He was dissatisfied with the two profile photographs of the Queen sent by the Palace, intended to be the basis for the new definitive stamps. He argued that many graphic designers had now moved into photography and what was required was to give them the opportunity to take their own photographs to use for all sorts of design purposes. I thought the opportunity might be a good one for writing a letter to the Palace which stressed this. I therefore dictated in his presence a long letter to Sir Michael Adeane which emphasised the importance of getting a good royal head and sought permission for sittings to take place. This is an extremely interesting letter to have on the record and Jean Goose burst into fits of giggles when she heard me dictate it.

After that the Director General came to see me to discuss my paper on Post Office reform. He said that he thought it read like an attack upon the Civil Service and I hastened to assure him that it was an attack upon the system and not upon those who ran it. Together we went through the paper in great detail and I made a large number of amendments to meet this point. None of them was of any particular substance but I think they probably did help to improve the presentation of the argument. We also discussed in some detail the actual way in which this reform might be done. The select committee on nationalised industries will be able to engage parliamentary interest in the coming year and I think the result will be helpful in neutralising parliamentary opposition to a change of status.

The staff attitude is much more difficult to foresee and it may well be that in the first instance the Post Office would have to go on as one body and gradually disentangle itself later on. I certainly wouldn't want it to fail because of the difficulties posed by the staff side that centred round the division of mails from telecommunications when they ought to be united on the transfer from Civil Service to a nationalised industry.

We went further and discussed the administrative reorganisation of the Office to provide for two Directors General, one to cover telecommunications and one mails and banking. This is something that I have wanted to do for some time and it is now perfectly clear to me that by proposing a far more extreme solution I have made the Director General conscious of the need for an administrative change even within the present set-up. As Mr Wolverson is going in September and there will be new appointments to be made, it should be perfectly possible to establish this arrangement rapidly. Given a White Paper and the select committee and new internal arrangements in the Office, the way ahead should be much clearer.

I gathered afterwards that the DG was happier having had a talk to me, although through the grapevine I heard that my paper was buzzing round the Office and creating a great deal of uncertainty.

Just before coming to the House I had Grady in to talk about the Giro. He says the Treasury are going to look at it benevolently and I think there is a good chance that I will be able to announce this in the debate next Wednesday. Everything depends on the Home Affairs Committee agreeing to this on Tuesday. On the present showing this seems likely.

This afternoon Caroline and I went to the Speaker's Party and had a talk to Sydney Silverman and congratulated him on getting his Bill through the Commons. By the end of the month I think hanging will have been abolished and it is a great achievement for him.

Thursday 15 July
This morning I went to an advertising agency with O'Brien to see the run-through of the television commercials that had been prepared

to recruit postmen. They weren't bad. This is the first time that advertising has been used on television for recruitment.

Afterwards I went up the Post Office Tower with Joe Slater and the DG. The view is superb but the organisation of the staircases and lifts is appalling. There are only two lifts, each holding fourteen, and these have to be used continually to take 400 people to the top and bring them down again.

This afternoon I heard about the strike by the Guild of Telephonists next week and made plans. This gave me a reasonable excuse for not attending the garden party at Buckingham Palace which delighted me. I wrote and apologised.

The telephone strike poses special difficulties. The men concerned have decided that they won't deal with any but emergency calls from 10 till midnight all next week. This will mean that the public will have their calls censored by the operators and is bound to cause trouble. There is no possibility of making a concession on the wage demand and I think I will have to show that we cannot be budged from our position. There is even a suggestion we might dismiss the men concerned but I cannot think that would be right.

Monday 19 July

At 11.30 am I had to go to the Cabinet Office for a key meeting on Giro. It was a tremendous battle mainly because *The Times* and *Financial Times* last Friday had predicted that the Government was going to introduce the Giro. This was untrue since no decision had been reached at that time. I rang Trevor Lloyd Hughes at Number 10 on Friday to find out what had happened and he told me that it had come from Herbert Bowden's weekly briefing of the lobby. But of course nobody at the meeting this morning at Cabinet Office knew that, and I was bitterly attacked by George Wigg and one or two others. The only point of substance was whether or not the banks would accept it and the Treasury were helpful. But I did win support in principle and things might have gone worse.

Lunch at the Post Office today was with the Statistics and Business Research Branch and they told me they would make available the surveys that had been taken in the past on the public attitude to the postal services. They were a bright new group of people; they've only been a department for some weeks and therefore are not fully settled.

I saw Grady this afternoon to discuss the Giro in the light of what had actually happened. The position is that I now have to clear it with Number 10 and with the Chancellor. Later I heard the Chancellor did support the line taken by the Treasury over Giro and so I sent a minute to Harold asking him whether it was all right.

Tuesday 20 July

To the Cabinet Office again this morning for the Home Affairs Committee to discuss the handling of tomorrow's Giro debate. Unfortunately the *Daily Mail* ran a screaming headline today leaking the story and again I'm sure people thought it was me. In fact it came from Keith McDowell the industrial correspondent and I think he had got it from the Federation of Sub-Postmasters. But it couldn't have come at a worse time because the Treasury were to discuss it with the clearing banks today.

I decided that the best thing to do was to send the draft of my speech to the Treasury to be cleared, particularly those passages concerning relations with the banks.

Caroline came in this afternoon and we went to the party at Number 10. Robert Maxwell was there and he told me that he was holding a press conference at noon tomorrow – *before* the debate on Giro – to publicise the book that his company Pergamon Press had published on Giro written by Paul Thomson, who had campaigned for it for years. I told him to cancel the press conference as no decision had been reached and it would be most unwise to hold it then. He really is rather a thrusting man who regards the House of Commons as a place where he can push himself.

Just about midnight I rang Ryland again and he told me that the notice I had put out about stopping telephonists' pay had caused bewildered resentment and that the strike had begun to spread to other parts of the country, notably Leeds and Bradford. But in London it had been slightly reduced. Although the UPW had said they would be perfectly happy to have their operators drafted in, some local UPW operators had been reluctant to do this. Ron Smith is of course anxious to crush the strike altogether in order to break the Guild of Telephonists. But I can't go along with that.

Stayed at the House till 3 am.

Wednesday 21 July

To the Post Office early and meeting about the strike. We agreed that we would have to take tougher action later but all that has happened so far is that supervisors have been told to invite volunteers to man the switchboards in the event of suspension being necessary. This gives me some room for manoeuvre. I must show that we can't be pushed around but am very reluctant to suspend anybody.

At 12.45 heard from Number 10 that the Giro was all right. It is a most interesting study of how a decision was made. Although this had been advocated by the Party in the past, nothing whatsoever had been put into the manifesto and it wasn't until two days ago that it first came to a committee of Ministers. Although Harold

Wilson knew about it – because I'd kept him informed – and the Treasury had studied the paper earlier this year, the thing was carried through in two days without ever having to go to Cabinet and undoubtedly it got through so easily because of the fact that Harry Hynd had won the ballot to introduce his Private Member's motion today. Looking back to the beginning of this Government I had put the Giro down as a suitable subject for a Private Member to raise although the department had not been keen on my doing so, so that I can honestly say that I have brought this major operation off with the minimum of trouble. I don't think most people realise the significance of it yet.

From 3.30 to 7 we had the debate on Giro and I wound it up. To my astonishment none of the anxieties of the banks were expressed by Tories and it was almost universally welcomed. I was delighted.

I stayed until about 2 am working on a speech for tomorrow's debate on the Post Office services and kept in touch with the progress of the telephonists' strike. It is spreading.

Thursday 22 July
The *Daily Mail* today described the Giro as 'Benn's Bank'. This was taken from a suggestion Jeremy Thorpe made and it was rather pleasing.

To the Office where we had a further talk about the strike of telephonists. I decided to prepare for suspensions to begin tomorrow, so we sent a message out to regional offices via the Defence telex network in order that all would be ready if necessary.

The DG came in for a long talk about reorganisation. The official Treasury-GPO working party members have completed their report and have sent it to the Chancellor who has written to Harold to say that on a quick reading of it, he doesn't think that it would be profitable to pursue reorganisation. The PM has evidently said that it is to go to the committee of permanent secretaries next week and the DG will be representing me there. I don't know exactly what will happen but it's pretty obvious that I shall have to put extra steam behind this to get it done. I am keen therefore that my major paper should be ready soon.

This afternoon, while going to the House of Commons I read the evening papers and saw that Home is about to resign. Yesterday I saw him and he was very cheerful and insisted that I went through a door before him. 'Your need is greater than mine,' he had said. This puzzled me at the time. If I had read the signs I would have known what it was that he was really saying.

The debate on the Post Office services went on from 8 to 10 and Marples opened it. All he did was to repeat his article in the *Sunday*

Telegraph, suggesting that the telephone service should be hived off. But it was useful to have it officially put from the Opposition. Marples hadn't really thought it out in any way. But what was clear from the debate was that Parliament was prepared to lose control of the Post Office and let it go its own way under permanent heads.

I spoke for the last twenty minutes and it went quite well until the very end when I foolishly made a joke about there having been three Shadow Postmasters General since the General Election and I wondered whether the Tory Party wanted Home for it. The Tories growled with rage and shouted 'cheap'. In truth I think it was rather cheap and it completely spoiled the end of my speech.

I had to stay at the House all night because of the rebellion by Back Bench Labour members against the increase for judges' salaries. Nobody would have minded a bit if they had just made their speeches but what was monstrous was that they hinted they were going to vote and thus kept many of us right through the night.

But I did have a chance to talk to Bernard Floud about the telephonists' strike. He has been personnel officer for Granada for many years and he told me that it was common for management to want to take violent action against unofficial strikers. In practice he said this only made things worse and it was a lot easier to start a strike than it was to finish one. This really decided me that the best thing to do was to let it ride a bit and I could satisfy myself that I was being firm in that there is no question of abandoning our position on the wage claim.

Friday 23 July
I heard today that the Guild of Telephonists' unofficial strike leaders had met and decided to call the strike off.

After lunch Sir Willis Jackson came to see me on behalf of the Television Advisory Committee to discuss colour TV. They want me to go ahead and make a statement that we will introduce colour television in 1967. But they are not yet agreed about what system it should be and frankly the whole technical side of television is so intensely complex that it is impossible to make progress at all. I agreed I would send him a questionnaire and ask for the views of his committee on these questions.

At 3 o'clock David Gentleman and his wife came to see me – at my request – about the launching of the Battle of Britain stamp next Tuesday. This is the block of six stamps with the Queen's head on the top right-hand stamp but not on the others. The Queen turned this recommendation down and now the department is panic-stricken because the press may start shouting.

We agreed that Gentleman's stamps without the Queen's head

would be shown with all his artwork at the press conference so that the press can see how stamps come to be designed. What is obvious from the artwork is that you start by designing the stamp and then add the Queen's head afterwards. I don't know how it will go on Tuesday but I am sure that this discussion has got to take place at some time or another and it couldn't be better than now when the one without the head has been rejected and when six Queen's heads, all side by side, will look so manifestly unsatisfactory from a design point of view. It will at any rate provide an opportunity for the press to discuss the whole issue and will pave the way for the exhibition in the New Year of Gentleman's album, showing how new stamp designs could be developed – a big philatelic event.

Saturday 24 July
This afternoon I went to the Bonnington Hotel for a conference organised by the National Executive, bringing together Ministers, MPs, economists, advisers and people from the nationalised industries, to discuss public enterprise. The first paper was on financial targets. I stood up for them and we had some sort of a disagreement about this. I didn't hold my own on the economic level but I think the main point I was making – namely that nationalised industries cannot be allowed to be starved of capital or underpriced – did go home.

Sunday 25 July
This morning to the Bonnington again for two more sessions. Last night we had discussed financial targets and purchasing policy and this morning we considered the way in which public enterprise could be made to develop. We had a first-rate discussion in which the most notable part was taken by Peter Shore who also wound up the whole conference. It was Peter who really devised the entirely new approach by the Labour Party to nationalisation. He was the man who thought of the idea of putting public money in at the points of growth in the economy instead of just acting as a dustbin for private enterprise that had failed. Now at last we have a chance to do this and of course that is the real significance of my Giro and the urgent necessity for the reorganisation of the Post Office as three nationalised industries. But few people understand this and it'll be a job to get the ideas carried through.

Monday 26 July
Back to the Office and at 11 o'clock Sir Martin Charteris, the assistant private secretary to the Queen, came to see me about the letter I had written to the Palace following James Fitton's visit a fortnight ago.

Fitton wanted some designer-photographers to be allowed to photograph the Queen to help prepare the designs for the next series of definitive stamps.

I looked Charteris up in *Who's Who* and found that he was educated at Eton and Sandhurst and had been a Regular Army officer and he gave his relaxation as wild-fowling. He was a tall, bony, bald man in his late forties. The Office was in a panic at his arrival and the staff were hovering around like a lot of birds.

Evidently the Queen was nervous at the thought of having a lot of photographers coming. I told him as much as I could about Fitton's idea and he suggested that Lord Snowdon should take the pictures. This suits me fine. The Queen doesn't like sitting for photographs and was doubtful about what I had in mind. It was agreed that Charteris would check with her that Snowdon could take the first series of pictures and I will arrange that some of the designers talk to him before he goes in so that he takes the sort of pictures in which they will be interested. The Queen is so busy that she can't have the photographs taken till October.

We also discussed the question of whether she should wear the crown or not. Brigadier Holmes said that the Garter King at Arms said she should either be wearing a coronet or have a crown over her head. I said that a stamp was not a heraldic emblem but a piece of modern design and I was sure the Duke of Edinburgh would take the same view. Charteris rather hesitantly agreed.

I also said that I hated using the word effigy as this suggested that I was asking for a death mask. All in all it was an amusing conversation because he had come suspecting foul play and I outcharmed him. It must certainly have relieved his anxieties for I'm sure the Palace is a lot more frightened of me than they have reason to be. The Office was also afraid that I would be rude to Charteris and were surprised to find that it was all butter. Anyway he went away perfectly happy and after I shook hands with him he turned and walked straight into the door which was rather comic.

The informal lunch today brought the Post Office Solicitor's Department to me and I cross-examined them about the powers that I had to move into new fields of enterprise. Originally they had told me that I would need specific statutory powers to do almost anything but I got them to admit that the Crown has the same powers as any individual and that since the PMG represents the Crown, he enjoys the same powers. It was just a matter of policy whether or not the Government insisted on legislation.

As we have got Giro without legislation, I think I am fairly safe and I won't have any more trouble on that score. I even said I thought that if we caught fish from our cable ships and sold them in post offices there could be no objection. They couldn't think of an objection themselves. I then made it a serious point and said that this Government did believe that public enterprise ought to enjoy the right to diversify and move into new fields that were enjoyed by private enterprise and they really couldn't see any difficulty about it. But they did say that if we became a public corporation or a series of nationalised industries, we might lose the powers of the Crown unless we vested them specifically in the statutes setting up the new authorities. This is a point to watch but it may be that if I remain Minister of Communications enjoying the powers of the Crown I could specially provide that by regulation I could confer these powers on the statutory boards. Alternatively one might give total power to the boards, subject to a directive from a Minister restricting them in any particular way that was thought necessary at the time. It was a most useful lunch.

At 4 o'clock I went to Fleet Building again for the press conference on all-figure dialling.[22] O'Brien was in a complete tizzy and the general attitude of the department was of baring their behinds for kicks from the press about this switch. I tried to take the offensive and to explain that this was inevitable, that it would bring advantages in terms of increased capacity, technical improvements by sectorisation, and open the way for direct international subscriber dialling. I also said that this was really a test of the public attitude to the telephone. If they continued to regard it as 'a contraption' obviously they would always be looking for ways in which it might go wrong. In fact the telephone was a precision instrument and I appealed to the press to present this change in the right way so that people would look at the phone in that light. The DG and Wolstencroft had turned up and sat at the back and I think they were surprised to discover how well I had understood it – and a little taken aback to find that I took the offensive against the press.

Back home about midnight and worked till 1 am in the office. Tomorrow the Battle of Britain stamps are revealed and this will create interest and controversy. I've done all I can to keep myself out of it and let it be argued out on design grounds.

Tuesday 27 July
Early to the Office this morning and I spent an hour looking at the layout for the press conference today to launch the Battle of Britain stamp. It was the first time that the Post Office had ever displayed stamps without the Queen's head. Some children's designs for the Churchill stamp were at the beginning, then followed the artwork by David Gentleman showing Battle of Britain stamps without the Queen's head with the words 'Great Britain', and some that had

actually been essayed with the words 'United Kingdom Postage'. This block of six with the Queen in the top right-hand stamp and the others without the Queen at all, and the words 'United Kingdom Postage', were of course the ones that I had sent to the Queen as my first choice but which she had turned down. Underneath all these stamps, which included most of Gentleman's work, were the words 'unaccepted' and typed under that were little notes to the effect that the artwork had been incorporated in the approved designs. It really was an outstanding display and right at the end were the stamps that had been accepted, which I had put in a special case called 'Accepted Designs'.

The real value of this exhibition this morning was to get the press – both national and philatelic – accustomed to the idea that very good stamps could be designed without the Queen's head.

At 11.15 am Andrew and Hazel Restall came to see me. Restall is a young designer and he has been appointed as Fellow in Minuscule Design. He was rather a hesitant young man in his early thirties and didn't quite know what the job involved. So I told him the whole story of how we had extended the criteria, got permission to submit non-traditional designs, wanted public discussion, and so on. I gave him wide terms of reference.

I heard from Brigadier Holmes (who is a bit of a yes-man) that the exhibition had created enormous interest and that a large number of photographs of the different stamps had been taken by the press. He said that Gentleman had told the newspapers that the Queen had seen the stamps without her own head on them so this may be a source of some controversy.

The press this morning came out with varied comments on the all-figure dialling conference. The best report of all was in the *Mail* and *Telegraph*. The *Sun* ran a stupid leading article saying that international dialling from Miami to London was not as important as cutting the waiting list. *The Times* has a fantastic editorial in which they put it all down to a socialist plot to prevent people from being identified by their telephone exchanges and trying to blur the difference 'between those who live in Chelsea and those who live in Bermondsey'. The *Guardian* talked about 'the crazy fad of internationalising everything'. For a newspaper that is in favour of the Common Market and the metric system this was pretty surprising too. But all in all it was not such a bad press and we got it across, and that's what really matters.

The DG came to see me just before lunch. We had a long talk about the Chancellor's statement in the Commons this afternoon involving a slowing down of public expenditure which will certainly affect the Post Office.

We then moved on to the promotions that were coming along. I told him that I was prepared to approve Ryland as Deputy Director General but only on the understanding that the work of the Deputy Directors General was divided into two and that Ryland would be in sole charge of telephones and Wolstencroft (who has less managerial ability) in charge of posts. It will be made clear what their terms of reference are and for the first time the telephone service and the postal services will each have a commander-in-chief. The DG reluctantly accepted this.

I also told him I wanted to keep Miss Goose and have her promoted as a principal in my private office. This is unusual but a Minister simply must have the people he trusts around him and it's no good chopping and changing to suit the convenience of the Office. The DG said he would agree to this 'on the understanding that if you go in the autumn I shall be free to take her away again'. I don't think he meant if the Labour Government was defeated but was obviously trying to persuade himself that I might be promoted. I told him there was no likelihood of that and I was happy in the Post Office and wanted to stay to finish the job I had started. The poor old DG took it as well as he could.

At lunchtime we heard that on the first ballot for the Tory leadership Heath had come out top and later in the afternoon that Maudling had yielded and would nominate Heath for the leader tomorrow with Enoch Powell seconding. So that is out of the way. Maudling would be much more frightening from our point of view and I think we shall be able to project Heath as a ruthless, ambitious machine politician without even the aristocratic backing of Home who could always count upon the deferential vote.

To the House this afternoon to hear Jim Callaghan's statement on the crisis measures necessary to save the pound. The place was packed and Labour Members heard the news with dismay. But Jim did as well as he could.

Wednesday 28 July

Contrary to my worst fears there was little about the Battle of Britain stamps in the papers. The *Sun* however had got a heading, 'Queen rejects stamps that left her out'. Then followed an article describing an interview with Mrs Gentleman which made the point with crystal clarity, left me entirely out of it, put it on the level of design, and also established the facts accurately and beyond dispute. From my point of view this couldn't have been better. The *Financial Times* also had an article on British stamp design policy which was extremely good.

To the NEC this morning. It began with a great row about the

crisis measures announced yesterday by Jim Callaghan. This argument rolled on for some time and was then deferred. We got through
the rest of the agenda quickly. The only point of interest was a
criticism by Joe Gormley and one or two others about the Bonnington
Conference. I waded in and said it had been the most useful weekend
I'd spent since the Election and I hoped we would have more conferences along these lines.

At about 10.50, Jim Callaghan and Harold Wilson having arrived,
there was a discussion on the economic situation in which Jim
explained what he had done. I had to leave before it had finished to
go to the Home Affairs Committee where the compulsory purchase
powers for the Post Office were considered.

At 2.15 the DG and Roger Morrison of McKinsey's came along
for half an hour's talk. Morrison had the preliminary report on the
structure, and he concentrated on the very points to which I had
drawn his attention. In fact he said practically nothing that I hadn't
said but we are paying him many thousands of pounds a month to
say it with greater authority.

The DG told me that this morning the committee of permanent
secretaries had met to consider the status of the Post Office and there
had been near unanimity that the transfer should be made to one or
more nationalised industries. However, they did not feel that it would
merit having a Minister and that it should be reorganised with
aviation, shipping and railways and roads to come under a big
Minister of Communications. Banking, they thought, should stay
with the Treasury. I don't care about the detail at this stage; it is
well above my level. But it looks as if I am almost home and dry.

Afterwards to the Commons for a family tea party. When they had
gone I settled down to work. Two good pieces of news: my plan for
having art in crown offices is to be started in twenty post offices in
the North East area on 1 October in co-operation with the North
Eastern Arts Association. Secondly, the *Philatelic Bulletin* is to be
reshaped and will be printed and published in its new form in
September.

Later this evening Tommy Balogh and Peter Shore and Miss
Hooper (Tommy's new assistant) came in for a general talk on the
situation. Tommy was worried about Jim's statement. He thought
that Harold should really dissociate himself somewhat from Jim and
reaffirm his dedication to full employment. Now that Heath is Tory
Leader, the Liberal position is really critically difficult and they have
even less incentive to get rid of us.

Peter said that George Wigg had told him, 'I could destroy Heath
given three hours.' Peter asked him what he meant and George
replied that he could destroy anyone within three hours including

Peter. It was a significant remark and I am slightly confirmed in my view that Harold would find it hard to get rid of George.

Friday 30 July
To the House of Commons this morning and Jon Akass from the *Sun* came to do a profile on me. He was a real Fleet Street journalist, wearing a brown corduroy suit and with a sad expression and huge bags under his eyes. We talked for nearly an hour and it certainly was an improvement on Susan Crosland.

Saturday 31 July
The article by Jon Akass in the *Sun* was extremely friendly and there was also good coverage in the press of the new Western District office showing the entirely automated nature of the postal services of the future. The image of the Post Office is beginning to change.

Monday 2 August
To the House of Commons where Herbert Bowden made the long-awaited and much-leaked statement about immigration restrictions. I suppose this was inevitable but it was distasteful.

Following that came the motion of censure moved by Heath. Here was the first 'study group' Conservative to become Leader and he made the sort of speech that might have been made at a Fabian Summer School, in which he went in detail through the economic record since the Election. It was so dull and statistical and so full of quotes that he lost the House and bored us all. Jim Callaghan by contrast was much tougher. I didn't hear Maudling wind up but Harold was subjected to continual barracking and did not have the ear of the House until the last four minutes when he revealed that Maudling had ordered plans for import quota restrictions just before he left the Treasury in October. This was a bombshell and the debate ended in uproar. But it was also just a little bit too clever to leave it to the end. Quite how you do tackle a House that doesn't want to listen to you I do not know so I am not disposed to criticise.

The row about the swastika on the Battle of Britain stamps is boiling up.[23] Jewish members have put down questions and John Hynd [Labour MP for Attercliffe] has written to the Prime Minister and Herbert Bowden has written to me. I think the answer is clear and I am seeing that it is furnished to everyone who asks. Here is a shattered swastika on the split tail plane of a shot-down bomber in the English Channel with four British fighters above.

There was a PLP meeting this evening at which Harold made a cheerful speech and was warmly praised by most of those who followed, except for Reggie Paget who said we had made currency

the master of industry. He could not support us and would have to
go back to Northampton and consider his position – perhaps never
to return. It was very sad and it does make you realise how vulnerable
a small majority is.

Afterwards Frank Allaun moved a resolution calling for more rapid
reduction in arms expenditure and Manny Shinwell announced that
the PLP-Government liaison committee was prepared to accept the
resolution so it went through without further debate. This evidently
surprised some people but I'm sure it was the wisest move. After all
we are engaged in a review of defence expenditure with that object
in mind.

Tuesday 3 August
This morning I opened the Western District Office just behind
Oxford Street. This is a £4.5 million semi-mechanised office, the
biggest and most mechanised that the Post Office has ever built and
equipped. Quintin Hogg and Lena Jeger came as the two local MPs.

Charles Morris told me that he had had a word with Ron Smith
who was angry about the reallocation of duties between the two
Deputy Directors General, one for posts and one for telecommunications. He felt he ought to have been consulted and saw this as the
first move to divide the Post Office into its constituent parts. I am
sorry about this but after my recent experiences with Ron Smith I
was not sure whether I could altogether trust him. At the same time
I had better see a little bit more of Ron as I would not like him to
be discouraged. I am clear in my own mind that this division has
got to be made formal and complete but until I know what my
colleagues' attitude is likely to be I have to be extremely careful
about it.

I went into the Commons for an interview with Mark Arnold-
Forster of the *Guardian* about my work at the Post Office over the
last nine months.

This evening I worked until about 1.30, completing the draft of
my major paper on Post Office reorganisation, which involved
reading the eighteen comments on the draft sent by headquarters
directors and compiling an appendix consisting of all the comments
made on Post Office reform over the last hundred years. I must admit
the arguments for three corporations are difficult to sustain against
those who say it would create a major upset to no good purpose. But
one effect of proposing such an extreme course is that it compels
people to accept the need for reorganisation; and if I could reorganise
the Post Office and get it removed from the Government service and
turned into a nationalised industry I would have achieved a lot.

Wednesday 4 August

Spent the lunch hour going over my parliamentary questions for this afternoon. One of them was about the swastika on the stamps and I had prepared an answer which I thought would settle it once and for all. One side effect of this controversy is that it has raised again the question of whether it is fair to the Queen to ask her to be on a stamp which has been chosen for its artistic merit. This may be helpful for my other cause later.

Afterwards I went to the smoking room and had an hour and a half's talk with George Brown who was friendly. I told him that I thought there should be an inner Cabinet of about four or five, made up of people who were responsible for the allocation of resources – Chancellor, First Secretary, Minister of Labour, etc. He said he was much attracted by this idea and hoped it would work out. I also began to interest him in my idea of Post Office reform. George, when he's being charming, is absolutely charming and I'm glad to have ended the session with such a friendly exchange.

After that I met Tam Dalyell who told me that he and Eric Heffer [MP for Walton] had just been to see Harold Wilson to propose that the nationalisation of the docks should take place in the new session following the publication of the Devlin Report on the ports and taking precedence over steel. I gather that Harold was interested in the idea and certainly with £150 million of public money about to be poured into the docks and the present labour dissatisfaction, I believe you could win public support for such a proposal. I said I would consider writing to Harold about this because there is a strong Bristol interest and also there is a departmental interest in that the Post Office suffers from dock delays.

Thursday 5 August

To the Office this morning and the Board met from 10.30 until 1.15. We went through a full agenda and three points of importance arose. The talks with the banks are going reasonably well on Giro and the White Paper will come out on 17 August.

Mr Wolstencroft produced a long memorandum arguing against a take-over by the Post Office of the relay wire systems, in response to a request I had made to him for this to be considered. I was not at all satisfied by the answer and to my astonishment the Engineer-in-Chief jumped in and said that he was sure the Post Office could lay a wire network much more efficiently and cheaply than the private companies. He thought that in the long run there was a strong case for having an electronic network throughout the country which would carry telephone, television, radio and other services that people might need in their homes, including perhaps pay-television.

We agreed therefore that he would set up a working party to examine this and I have until the end of the year to make up my mind whether to renew the licences from 1967. If I decide not to renew I have the power under the agreement to take over the relay companies lock, stock and barrel at valuation. It certainly is a tempting thing to do and although I don't visualise us actually doing it, we have a strong bargaining position if we choose to use it in dealing with the companies. We could force them to rationalise their operations and perhaps join in a joint enterprise with us.

In accordance with my general principle of expansion I had asked for consideration to be given to the idea of extending the activities of the PO factories so that they moved out of repairing into manufacture for sale. In response a working party was set up and the report was presented at the Board. It revealed that Post Office factories were extremely inefficient and expensive. It is estimated that an outside contractor could repair the 600,000 telephones a year that go to the factories much more cheaply.

Another unsatisfactory aspect of the factories it revealed was the fact that in Cwmcarn in Wales, which we have just re-equipped at the cost of about £8 million, the sick absences amount to about thirty days per worker per year. Indeed the Engineer-in-Chief went so far as to say that it would be more economic for us to close down the factory and put the work to outside contractors. I had no intention of doing this but I did say that we ought to get a price from a private firm quoted on the basis of a quarter of a million telephone repairs a year for a ten-year period, and then compare them with our known costs.

Then the DG came to see me and we had an interesting talk about the reorganisation paper which is now completed. The DG said that he was worried by the tendency towards commercialising everything, including the Post Office, which he thought would weaken its social service functions. But of course it isn't commercialising in the ordinary sense of private enterprise. It is trying to introduce some sane and sensible economic criteria into public enterprise in place of the awful old muddle and confusion that went on before. The fact is socialism cannot work if public industries do not make reasonable profits. Indeed in the end I think we shall plough profits from nationalised industries back to the Exchequer to help reduce the crushing burden of direct taxation.

Waded through tons of paper today in an attempt to clear up before I go on holiday tomorrow evening.

Friday 6 August

To the Office this morning and at 11 o'clock Charles Smith and Mr Jarvis came along to discuss the claim for higher pay for the factories grades. It was a complicated negotiation as it involved piece rates as well as basic time rate and had a bonus and a premium rate and a consolidated time rate and various other elements which I have not had to deal with before. In fact I had nothing that I could offer them but we discussed it fully. I hinted that it had come to light recently that the Post Office factories were much more expensive than outside contractors would be for the repair of telephone apparatus.

After lunch C. R. Smith, the Director of Computers, came to discuss the National Data Processing Service with me. I had received a memorandum from the General Directorate which came out in favour of the idea of the scheme but said that it doubted whether the Post Office had the power under the Post Office Act to run it. It also said that the £30,000 that it would cost to do a market survey ought to be carried by the Ministry of Technology. This would be an absurd argument to allow to develop.

I probed Smith about it. He was one of those who had sent in the most conservative answers to my memorandum about reorganising the Post Office. He told me that the negative attitude adopted by the General Directorate was their answer to what I had said about the Post Office being too big to run efficiently as one unit. If this was really so it certainly was an incredible way of indicating it to me, for the whole purpose of my reorganisation is to make it possible for the Post Office to expand without getting too big for management purposes. But still it was a revealing comment and I understand the way the department works much better as a result of it.

Smith also refused to give me his general comments on the Data Processing Scheme on the grounds that he was only the Director of Computers. He said that this was how the Army worked and he thought it was the best way of running things. It was a slightly tense interview but I learned a great deal about the Post Office and am glad it took place. Miss Goose was obviously very concerned with what had happened and said she knew I found it difficult to work within the Civil Service framework. She can say that again!

Parliament rose for the summer recess after the most gruelling session that I have ever experienced. But we have proved that we can govern and I think there is a reasonable chance that the Liberals will abstain in crucial censure debates, giving us another year at our job. Quite frankly I've got so much on my hands in the Post Office that I really would like one more year to finish it all off. My work will be done by the summer of 1966 and I should be happy then to move on to something else.

END OF TERM

'Wilson minimus—if I could have your attention for a moment...'

End of Term – August 1965.

Tuesday 17 – Tuesday 31 August
The family spent this period in Bandol. We left by train and boat and hired a car in Marseilles. We stayed in a pleasant family hotel and we enjoyed the sunshine and the complete escape from politics. I was able to get an English paper of one sort or another every day but otherwise it was a complete and very welcome break from the Post Office.

NOTES
Chapter Three

1. The Radcliffe Committee was set up following the Budget of 1957 to examine the monetary and credit system, with particular reference to the maintenance of high levels of savings and investment. It was chaired by Lord Radcliffe who also headed enquiries into security in 1961–2.
2. Conservative MP Peter Griffiths had beaten Patrick Gordon Walker in Smethwick in October 1964, in a campaign tainted by explicitly racist remarks. Gordon Walker, Harold's choice of Foreign Secretary, was thus deprived of a parliamentary seat. Harold immediately launched into an attack upon Griffiths when the House met after the Election, calling him a 'parliamentary leper'. It was the first explicit indication of official Prime Ministerial disapproval of racism in parliamentary politics. A seat had to be found for Patrick Gordon Walker and in January 1965, Leyton in East London became vacant on the creation of a life peerage for its Labour MP,

Reginald Sorensen. In a sensational result, Gordon Walker failed to win that seat too.

3. The Datel service had been introduced to provide rapid data transmission facilities under the auspices of the Post Office. Some Datel material represented computers speaking to computers but a great deal of the data transmission then and now concerns the movement of tapes and print-out physically by post.

4. Although everybody pays a licence fee for BBC television (and formerly for radio as well), that money is actually a tax paid to the Treasury which then finances the BBC. In periods when revenue from the licence fee exceeds the cost of running the BBC, the Treasury pockets the difference but where the licence fee falls below what is necessary, the government pays out a grant-in-aid. Thus the BBC is actually financed 100 per cent by government grant though the money is raised separately from normal taxation. The external service of the BBC has, however, always been financed by a grant-in-aid from the Foreign Office on the grounds that this service is the voice of the British Government abroad, and also because there are no possibilities of raising a licence fee from overseas listeners.

5. Arnold Wesker, the playwright, had expressed a desire that the Trade Union and Labour movements should take a greater interest in the arts. Through a union sympathetic to this idea, a resolution, number 42, was carried at the TUC. Encouraged by this, Arnold Wesker took over the Round House, an old railway engine shed in Camden Town, as a centre for the arts. It was known as Centre 42. In the end, it foundered under financial difficulties but the idea was absolutely right and it was my intention to use the Post Office through stamps and Crown buildings to promote the arts in the community as a whole. This was not very popular with my officials, particularly local Head Postmasters, who were afraid, I think, that they would be required to show nudes painted by local artists.

6. ELDO, the European Launcher Development Organisation, represented an attempt by Common Market countries to compete with the United States in the launcher business and put their own satellites into orbit. The French were keenest because they would be able to launch a French speaking satellite communicating directly with the Francophone countries in Africa and French Canada. The ELDO operation lacked a basic launcher but when the Blue Streak missile was cancelled in 1961, and Britain adopted the Polaris submarine from the Americans, the British Government offered the Blue Streak to ELDO, later withdrawing from the project. The British ELDO launcher was eventually dropped in favour of the French rocket which later put the French satellite into orbit. British skulduggery in dealing with its Continental allies on ELDO led to a great deal of disenchantment with Britain's commitment to high technology, to Europe and indeed to financial integrity.

7. In 1940 when my younger brother David was twelve, there were rumours that the school might be evacuated to Canada. My brother wrote to my mother that he did not wish to leave the country and said, in a childish way, 'I would rather be bombed to fragments than leave Britain now.' My mother, struck by his language and courage, wrote to *The Times* and the

letter was reported to Churchill who, in June 1940 in the middle of the Blitz, sat down and with his own hand wrote a letter to my brother congratulating him on his courage and said it had been an inspiration to us all. He sent my brother a copy of his book *My Early Life* and my brother replied, delivering the letter himself to 10 Downing Street. I should add that my brother's original draft to Churchill had to be censored by the family because it contained the phrase, 'Thank you for your book which I shall always remember as a relic of my early life.' This was not thought appropriate for a twelve year old in writing to the PM at the height of the Battle of Britain.

8. The Pilkington Committee, chaired by Sir Harry Pilkington, met from 1960 to 1962 and its report was very critical of independent television services. It recommended that the Independent Television Authority should buy all programmes from contractors and sell advertising time centrally, with surplus revenue accruing to the Treasury.

9. A. V. Alexander, former MP for Hillsborough, Sheffield, and later Alexander of Hillsborough, was First Lord of the Admiralty in the 1929–31 Labour Government, was reappointed First Lord of the Admiralty by Attlee in the 1945 Government and in the reorganisation of the Defence Ministries in 1946 was made First Minister of Defence with overall responsibility for the three service ministers. He was a Labour and Co-operative member and was also a member of the Water Rats, an organisation of people in entertainment.

10. After this dinner at the Crossmans' home in Westminster, Dick, Tam Dalyell and I described the evening in our respective diaries. I record extracts from the others as a light-hearted example of comparative diary entries.

Dick Crossman

We had the Wedgwood Benns to supper. Tony was as frustrated as ever in the Post Office. He told me what he thought should be done about the BBC. He feels the licence can't be increased from £4 to £6 at the moment without upsetting people. Instead we ought to try to raise the money by giving the BBC the right to raise some of its revenue by advertising on television. He is also anxious that the BBC should run radio with advertising as a main source of income.

I had to tell him frankly that I thought these ideas would be unacceptable to the Cabinet, who had simple views about the BBC as a public service radio and wouldn't see his proposals as progressive. And I didn't see our colleagues wanting to introduce legislation to ban Radio Caroline – the pirate radio station – unless and until the BBC produces as good pop music itself. It was a pretty good evening. I knew Wedgy Benn was enjoying it because he is one of the few politicians who likes taking punishment. (Richard Crossman – *Diaries of a Cabinet Minister* 1964–6)

Tam Dalyell

Arrived in the evening at Vincent Square to find Dick and Tony Benn going hard at it on the Government's plan for broadcasting. To save money, and the embarrassment of a Labour Government having to put

up the licence, Dick wants to do away with BBC2 – which shocks me since I go along with the 'Reith View' of the BBC. (I had the unworthy suspicion that Dick's real vendetta was less against BBC2 than a capricious desire to make things awkward for Hugh Greene.) Tony was at least Dick's equal and naturally knew more about the subject. In spite of the fact that Dick thought he was a bit potty in wanting to throw open BBC television to trade unionists to put their case, I think Tony is on a good line. Why should not the unions have their say? I was impressed by Tony's grasp of the Post Office's potential role in relation to the electronics industry. Twice I tried to get him interested in Borneo and the Far East and told him that I was a bit angry that neither Tony Greenwood nor Barbara Castle who had sat on countless Movement for Colonial Freedom platforms would lift a finger. They were obviously embarrassed in having a row with Denis Healey. . . . Dick said I should apologise to Tony for trying to drag him into my Borneo plotting but I shall do nothing of the kind. In fact, I think it's pretty ironic that here's sober me, trying to get the army out of Borneo and all those leftwingers in the Cabinet, meekly going along with the Chiefs of Staff: I thought Tony was a good bet but you can't expect the Postmaster General to run the Ministry of Defence! Dick thought afterwards that Tony's self-righteousness and virtue must irritate his civil servants no end, and he said, 'He would drive the Dame frantic [Dame Evelyn Sharp, Crossman's Permanent Secretary] and she would do him. Of course he's a tremendous presenter of a case, but he hasn't fully grown up yet. Gaitskell had no time for him . . . but he has tremendous energy, which makes up for his third class honours degree.'
(Tam Dalyell – unpublished diaries)

11. Healey's remark was a reference to the stand taken by Reginald Paget, on the right of the PLP, and Konni Zilliacus, on the left, against the Government's nuclear defence policy based on Polaris submarines, which was set out in a White Paper in March 1965.

12. By long established convention any changes made in the electoral system are undertaken by what is called a 'Speaker's Conference', in which the Parties send senior representatives and the Speaker in theory presides. The Boundary Commission which operates at a practical level is also chaired by the Speaker and in this way such matters are supposedly independent of narrow Party political interest.

13. Cable & Wireless, in which the Government had a majority shareholding, had historically been responsible for Colonial telecommunications throughout the British Empire. After the Empire became transformed into the Commonwealth, Cable & Wireless tried to continue but found it difficult to maintain its monopoly or position in newly independent countries. My interest was that it opened up the possibility of a mixed enterprise in which a Government holding would be dominant but some private capital might be brought in in order to finance expansion. Cable & Wireless was in a similar position to BP, a majority shareholding of which had been acquired by Churchill as First Lord of the Admiralty in the summer of 1914.

14. My grandfather, John Benn, was first elected to Parliament as a Liberal

for St George's in the East, in the East End of London in the General Election of 1892 with the support of Gladstone on a programme that included Home Rule for Ireland. Subsequently in 1906, my father was himself elected for the same constituency and remained MP for St George's in the East, Tower Hamlets division, until redistribution in 1918 led to his adoption and election in Leith near Edinburgh.

15. The money transmission functions of social security payments (the 'social wage') should have been handled through the Giro. It was significant that although the Government was setting up a publicly owned bank, which it could be reasonably expected to use itself, officials argued that we could not discontinue the arrangements with the commercial banks. Had the Giro been supported by the Government, this would have assured its future from the start and made it one of the most powerful banks in the country. Subsequently of course, the Giro did become the mechanism for payment of social security benefits.

16. The Labour Government had agreed, despite its very narrow majority, to proceed with the nationalisation of the steel industry. However, two Labour Back Benchers, Desmond Donnelly, MP for Pembroke, and Woodrow Wyatt, MP for Bosworth, refused to support it. Faced with a difficult parliamentary situation and without himself being at all enthusiastic about the re-nationalisation of the steel industry, George Brown, Minister for Economic Affairs, made a concession in the debate which secured the support of Wyatt and Donnelly. In 1971 Donnelly joined the Tory Party.

17. With the peaks and troughs which the postal service experienced – 6 million letters were mailed in London alone after 6 pm every night – it was argued by the Post Office managers that women and part-time workers would have to be employed. The union resisted this move in order to preserve any available overtime for their low-paid full-time male postal workers.

18. I knew Krishna Menon during his period as High Commissioner in Britain and as Indian Minister of Defence (1957–62), attending with him the seminar on Portuguese Colonies in Delhi in November 1960. He was a barrister and had actually been a Labour councillor for St Pancras, 1934–47. He was one of Pandit Nehru's closest associates.

19. After the electoral defeat of 1964, it was clear that Sir Alec Douglas-Home was thought unsuitable by many Tories to continue to lead the Party but with a second Election impending change was considered risky. In this period, one of the most vigorous and active figures on the Opposition Front Bench was Edward Heath who had special responsibilities for the Finance Bill and fought against the Labour Government with great vigour and panache. In fact, Sir Alec did resign in the summer of 1965 and a leadership contest developed between Heath, Reginald Maudling and Enoch Powell – Heath winning with an overall majority.

20. Violet Asquith, elder daughter of Prime Minister Herbert Asquith, married Sir Maurice 'Bonjy' Bonham Carter, Asquith's private secretary, in 1915. Their daughter Laura married Jo Grimond in 1938. Thus Lady Violet, herself one-time President of the Liberal Party Organisation, was the daughter and the mother-in-law of Liberal leaders. Other Bonham

Carters active in the Liberal Party included Violet's son Mark who was MP for Torrington, 1958–9. Broadly speaking the Asquith-Bonham Carter family were part of a political dynasty at the centre of British politics for sixty years until Grimond's resignation in 1967, when he was succeeded by Jeremy Thorpe.

21. Dr Reinhold Niebuhr was a famous American theologian, the writer of *Moral Man and Immoral Society* and other influential books. In the late twenties he was the pastor of a parish near Henry Ford's works and this experience made him a socialist, although he resigned from the American Socialist Party at the outbreak of the Second World War because he was not a pacifist.

22. Until this time, telephone numbers in big cities began with three letters which were the name of the exchange, e g VICtoria, followed by four numbers. With the increase in demand for the telephone it was considered better to move to an all-figure number dialling system which would facilitate adjustments to telephone exchanges. Moreover, as most countries around the world had already abandoned the three-letter four-figure system and did not have letters on their dials, they could not phone Britain direct. When I introduced this I was accused of socialist dogmatism, designed to blur the class differences between MAYfair and BERmondsey, which supposedly manifested my bitter hostility to the ruling class.

23. The stamps which David Gentleman designed to celebrate the twenty-fifth anniversary of the Battle of Britain included pictures of Messerschmitt and Dornier bombers from the Luftwaffe sinking into the Channel with RAF Spitfires and Hurricanes above them. But the Board of Deputies of British Jews objected to the appearance of a swastika in any shape or form on the stamps and I was sharply criticised for having approved the stamps. In the event, those stamps were honoured and praised all over the world and I believe it was a storm in a teacup.

4
From Office to Power
September 1965–June 1966

Wednesday 1 September
Arrived home about six o'clock in the evening and found things in
perfect order. Valerie had been looking after all the correspondence.
Everything seems to die in August.

I rang Wratten this evening and he told me there had been nothing
happening in the Post Office in the last fortnight. There were two
'silly-season' stories, one, an allegation that the telephone operators
had been listening in to the Queen's telephone calls when she was
at Badminton.

Thursday 2 September
Mr Speaker Hylton-Foster* died today, precipitating something of a
political crisis because, with Labour's tiny majority, we could hardly
afford to elect a Labour MP as new Speaker.

At the Office I went through the backlog of papers and saw the
Director General for half an hour. The department is fighting hard
not to have to do too much cutting back in line with the current
economic policy of the Government and I obviously have to keep the
pressure on there. They seem to think that the important thing is to
establish their right to be regarded as a nationalised industry. This
is constitutionally correct but it doesn't absolve us from the necessity
of co-operating with the measures which the Chancellor proposed.

Saturday 4 September
Hilary and I set off by train this morning to the constituency where
Harold was speaking tonight. We stopped at Bath and saw the
Roman baths and the museum of costume and then went on by car

* Conservative MP for York, 1950–9, Westminster, 1959–65. Speaker 1959–65.

to Kingswood where I opened a fête for the Made For Ever youth club.

Then on to Unity House where about forty people had gathered to see me in what Herbert Rogers had described as a deputation. In fact it was a gathering of Communists and others from all over Bristol who launched a most bitter attack on Government policy covering Vietnam, economic policy and almost everything else they could think of. Only eight of them were members of the Party and, with the exception of Herbert Rogers and Joyce Perham, none of them lived in Bristol South East.

I listened to them for about forty-five minutes and then began answering the points raised. At this they started shouting and abusing me and the whole thing was a complete shambles.

After that I went to the hotel and then on to Harold's meeting. Hilary was allowed to sit in Caroline's seat on the platform and as the platform was introduced one by one to the meeting there was a round of applause for Hilary which absolutely thrilled him. Harold spoke for about an hour and a quarter. It was heavy stuff but the reception was astonishing and it indicated that the heart of the Party was solid and did not intend to let the Government down.

Hilary and I went back in the Prime Minister's motorcade to the hotel and Marcia said that Hilary could stay for dinner with Harold. At 10.45 we started dinner which went on till about midnight. Aside from Harold and Mary, Alf Richman, who is on Harold's staff, Marcia and two Bristol trade unionists, Hilary and I were the only others there. It was a delightful evening and we had a long talk about the Speakership. Marcia suggested we make Desmond Donnelly Speaker and we had an amusing talk about the possibilities. Harold is optimistic that a Tory Back Bencher might be induced to do it. Before we finally parted Harold gave Hilary an autographed photograph and Hilary went to bed in seventh heaven.

Sunday 5 September
To the Post Office this morning and Lillicrap came to see me. I am extremely keen to get some progress on broadcasting decisions and asked him whether he could get the ministerial committee held soon. The key person here is the Lord President, Herbert Bowden, and he has been slow in moving. I know Harold is keen to make some progress, since he wants to refer to the University of the Air at the ITA dinner on 16 September.

After him Grady came in and reported on the good progress he has made with the Giro. He is confident of the co-operation of the banks, of really big business accumulating. I asked him what he thought about the major reorganisation plans that I have put forward.

He was agreeable to the idea of a popular banking corporation and thought that the Trustee Savings Banks might be brought in.

I went over to Number 10 to see Harold, but the war between India and Pakistan had made it necessary for him to hold a lobby so I went instead to the Home Policy Committee where the Conference agenda was being discussed. It was a complete shambles, since no one had thought out what we wanted the Conference to do this year and we were simply concerned with agreeing our attitude to the resolutions that have been tabled by constituency parties. I had a brief talk with Peter Shore on the telephone to see if we could begin to get the heads of agreement on the themes we would need to put in our next manifesto.

Back to Number 10 at 5 o'clock and had a talk to Harold about a number of things. He is only lukewarm about the Post Office reorganisation scheme but a top-level ministerial committee, which he will chair himself, will meet soon to discuss it. This is as far as I could hope to get at this stage. I am not sure whether I can carry the committee but I think that even if all else fails I shall get a proper enquiry into Post Office organisation and this will be an achievement by itself.

We also discussed the need for developing political themes for the next twelve months and Harold wants Tommy Balogh and Peter and myself to meet and discuss them.

Harold raised the press story that Harold Evans,* Macmillan's old PRO, might be appointed by Lord Hill as new Director General of the ITA. George Wigg is hot under the collar about this and I went to see him afterwards, and he abused me in his usual manner. I don't know why I put up with it except that a row with George is not worthwhile. He has been consistently wrong on all the issues which I have discussed with him recently and it is only because of his formidable character as an enemy that I accept the way in which he treats me.

Tuesday 7 September

Wratten came to see me this morning and showed me the Post Office Tower stamps that had been approved in my absence. For the first time ever these stamps have printed on them the name of the printer, Harrison, and of the designer. The press conference today released them, and since there was no criticism I propose to make this the standard thing in the future. It elevates the status of the designer and recognises the technical competence of the printer, both of whom have been regarded as backroom boys in an enterprise that has been

* Journalist and editor of the *Sunday Times* and subsequently the *Times*, 1967–82.

conducted anonymously and appears to the public as being purely concerned with pumping out more pictures of the Queen's head.

Caroline suggests the words 'United Kingdom Postage' ought to be printed on the guttering of the stamps, i.e. between the perforations and the design itself as well, whether or not the Queen's head is on them. It is an interesting idea.

To Bristol for the night. I watched the first TV film of the developing war between India and Pakistan which is so grave. All my instinct is pro-India but I think they may have made a grave mistake. To alienate the Muslim world will cost them dear. China now has an opportunity to intervene and drive America to India's support, thus branding India as a tool of American imperialism, and opening up a new front against Western capitalism which will tip the scales in favour of China and against Russia in the battle for intellectual leadership of the Communist bloc. In addition, the strains of the war and the humiliations of the likely military defeat for India could lead her to a military dictatorship and, in time, to a Communist revolution that would see the end of the Indian democratic experiment.

Wednesday 8 September
Caught an early train to London, went straight to the Post Office and from 10.30 till 3 the Post Office Board met for its longest agenda yet.

We discussed the acute manpower shortage affecting postmen, counter clerks and telephonists, which is accompanied by a deterioration in the service. Next, the restrictive practices insisted on by the UPW, which are affecting counters and which I must now take up with the union directly. We shall have to introduce less frequent balancing by staff of monies paid in and withdrawn at post offices, and one or two other changes. We also discussed the paper by the Engineer-in-Chief, pointing to the possibility of direct broadcasting from satellites straight to the television aerials of the general public, which has enormous political significance.

After lunch I went to the Cabinet Office again where Peter, Tommy and I discussed the themes for the next twelve months at the specific request of Harold, who is beginning to prepare the way for the next Election campaign. It was not very fruitful as Tommy was full of colourful and obscene abuse of Ministers who he thinks are obstructing imaginative policies.

This evening we had a meeting at home of parents who want a parent-teachers association started at Holland Park School. We made good progress.

Thursday 9 September

To the Western District Office this morning to preside at a meeting of eighty manufacturers of Post Office equipment to persuade them to buttress our new postal consultancy service by forming a manufacturers' association.

Wratten told me that the Director General intends to retire if reform is agreed. Though sad for him, I think it is probably right. Wratten, of course, is – like most younger members of the Office – wholly committed to the success of this venture. He said that in the past it had been thought too far-fetched to be considered seriously and that the senior officials were somewhat dazed at the thought that it might happen. He himself suspected that it was inevitable and had concluded that it would arise from mounting criticism of the Post Office, leading to an enquiry. The only difference is that I have anticipated this by coming to my own conclusions before public opinion had crystallised, instead of waiting till I was out of office and writing a Fabian pamphlet saying what should be done.

Looking back on nearly a year in office, I think probably the only contribution that I have been able to make to the Post Office is to create an atmosphere in which people with ideas have felt that this was the time to bring them forward, knowing that they would be sympathetically considered. Brigadier Holmes, who is leaving headquarters to become director of the London Postal Region, said to me today, 'Before I go, may I say as an individual, rather than as an official, that it has been an inspiration to work with you this year.' It was a decent thing for him to have said and if there is any truth in it I feel I have done my job.

Sunday 12 September

To Chequers all day for the Cabinet meeting which heads of department were invited to attend. It was my first visit to Chequers and it is a beautiful house. But the whole place is like a hotel and if any reminder were necessary of the fleeting nature of high political office, this gives it. Indeed even the bedrooms were like hotel bedrooms, with little brass squares outside into which names on cards could be dropped and with basins screwed against the wall like some one-star hotel in Blackpool. One could have a wonderful time at Chequers, handing over the whole house to somebody who knew the Elizabethan period and telling him to remove the excrescences of 1930s modernisation and restore the place to a decorative style appropriate to its age. He might at the same time add central heating, for I'm told that the house is as cold as can be and those little brassy electric fires in every room are also a real eyesore.

Monday 13 September
The Battle of Britain stamps came out today and they are a terrific collector's item with demand the highest ever. All the swastika silliness is over now.

Dinner with Dick Crossman at the Athenaeum and he couldn't have been nicer. We discussed the tensions between Marcia, George Wigg and Tommy Balogh, who are the three favourites at the court of King Harold. Dick is now in charge of a liaison committee and our object was to plan a strategic appreciation, our campaign themes and (with the utmost secrecy) the outline of the manifesto.

I raised two points. One was the urgent necessity for finding some way of injecting new policy ideas from Ministers into the manifesto, even before the Cabinet machine had ground them through. Secondly, the risk that if Harold's parliamentary majority was eroded by by-election defeats the Queen might deny him a dissolution until she had tried to see whether Heath alone or Heath and Grimond could form an alternative Government without an Election. Even if Heath couldn't he would be bound to say he could and we would be put in the most absurd position, fighting an Election on our Government record, but as an Opposition. Dick took this seriously enough to suggest we raised it with Harold to see whether he could do anything to prevent it.

Tuesday 14 September
Straight to Number 10 this morning for the meeting which the PM chaired to consider my paper on Post Office reorganisation. Also present were George Brown, Jim Callaghan, Herbert Bowden and Douglas Houghton.

I introduced it mainly in terms of efficiency, pay and productivity, and tariffs. Jim spoke and pooh-poohed it. He said the Treasury was marginally in favour but he thought the difficulties – especially on the staff side – were too great to risk. George thought I had overstated the ease with which a nationalised industry could negotiate productivity deals and feared that this might mean some further weakening of Government prices and incomes control. Douglas Houghton welcomed it firmly, said that all change was exciting and that the Post Office unions were a great embarrassment to the Civil Service staff side. Bowden was very conservative – as he always is on everything – and said there was no question of legislation. Harold summed up skilfully, saying the idea was attractive in principle, that an official committee should study how it should be done, should report to a ministerial committee under Douglas Houghton, which would report to the Cabinet as early as possible. Meanwhile nothing whatsoever was to be said about it.

This was as far as I could hope to get first time round and once it is really underway it would be hard to stop. One by-product of it means that we should set up an Economic Development Committee for the Post Office under the NEDC.[1] The only black part of the morning was that Douglas Houghton launched into another violent outburst against the postmen's pay settlement. I didn't reply since the argument helped me marginally and it would have diverted attention from the main issue.

Afterwards I had a talk to Harold about the risk that Heath might be asked to form a Government.

Thursday 16 September

Worked at home this morning and after lunch to Number 10 to be photographed with Harold and Dick Marsh outside the Cabinet Room. This is for the *Observer* colour supplement, to be published on the first anniversary of the Election.

In conversation Dick Marsh said he thought George Woodcock* was a megalomaniac who regarded himself as above politics and thought that he should be regarded as assistant Prime Minister to be consulted about everything.

Then to the Post Office where I looked in at our Flower display, dashed to Fleet Building where Mary Wilson was opening the Civil Service Flower Show, and back home to get ready for tonight's Guildhall dinner to celebrate the tenth anniversary of ITA. I had been dreading this for months. I fought hard against commercial television in 1954 and accept the Pilkington Committee view that the ITA ought to get all the advertising revenue and buy the programmes from the programme contractors. The thought of an orgy of self-congratulation by the millionaires and the Establishment, at which one would be expected to imply 'how wrong I was, etc', filled me with gloom. I worked immensely hard on my speech and tried to get some sort of balance between congratulation and the airing of legitimate anxieties.

I decided that I would not wear a white tie and tails. Not only are they ridiculous, but for a Labour Government to appear – especially on television – in this garb seems to me to separate us even more from our voters and confirm the latent suspicion that we are just the same as the Tories. In addition there are some people who haven't got tails and they are always so grateful to see that someone at the top table isn't wearing them either. I asked Harold if he minded and he said no, though one would be accused of inverted snobbery. Anyway I didn't wear them and was the only one and was conscious

* General Secretary of the TUC, 1960–9.

of a wave of disapproval. Whether it's worth the effort every time this happens, I don't know.

The dinner was just as I feared, with a bishop in purple silk, a High Commissioner, Lord Mayors, and George Woodcock (immaculate in tails), telly millionaires and a sprinkling of performers.

Harold made a folksy speech and ended with some more muddled promises about the University of the Air. Charlie Hill was a caricature of himself, gruff, breathy, vulgar and reeking with plain commonsense that concealed controversial opinions and the full dollop of self-congratulation. I like him very much and he certainly is easier to talk to than Normanbrook, who seemed to be a poor old fuddy-duddy and doesn't know what's going on.

All in all, rather a depressing evening.

Friday 17 September
The press this morning gave the National Plan[2] a big build-up and I think the Tories are making a big mistake by mocking it and dismissing it as a Party gimmick. Coming so soon after the rescue of the pound and the better prospects for the trade deficit, it looks ahead positively and I think will command a great deal of interest and support. Today's NOP poll gives us a lead again and it may be that Harold is right when he says that Heath is not such an asset for them as we had thought.

Monday 19 September
Mr Downes came to see me this morning on his appointment as Director of Postal Services. We talked about the need to have a productivity negotiation with the UPW. We discussed the survey of public opinion to see what proportion of the mail is urgent and prepare the way for our reshaping of the services.

We need to alert the postal staff casually to the likelihood of a feasible one-delivery-a-day service and the necessity for a split from the telecommunications services and the new status idea so that they are not so shocked as they might otherwise be. It looks now as if the next year will be crucial for the reorganisation of the postal services as a whole and I am looking forward to the task with enormous interest.

The papers today had a tremendous leak about Dick Crossman taking over from George Wigg as Government co-ordinator on Party publicity. Dick said it had killed the appointment stone-dead.

Dinner with Dick, Peter and Tommy at the Athenaeum. Since the Gallup Poll puts us 6.5 per cent ahead this morning we are bound to re-examine the assumptions on which we had planned our Election advice to Harold. All the evidence suggests that this autumn would be a great deal safer than hanging on till March or trying to survive another year or eighteen months, which may be parliamentarily impossible. Harold has been much influenced by advice that we ought to go on but this new factor is bound to encourage him to re-examine the situation.

We are at the mercy of our rebel fringe. If Harold were to say that Britain should have a strong Government to deal with the problems that now confront the country and to give it authority against the unions or the employers or anyone else who seeks to obstruct it, it might be a powerful point. Moreover, he would be going to the polls before he was actually defeated in Parliament, which would be psychologically better. In the spring unemployment will be higher and the municipal elections are bound to be disastrous since we are fighting seats that we won in the unexpectedly favourable atmosphere of 1963. In any case, it is unlikely that we can survive the winter as the Liberals are bound to want to destroy us. Against this are the facts that the majority of the electorate do not want an Election, there might be some Labour apathy, and we may destroy our one great asset: that we are going on against all sorts of odds.

Before we broke up we agreed that it would be unwise to be too firm in our recommendations to Harold but the new situation opens fresh options to him which ought to be considered dispassionately and whatever else he does he ought to be striking a more confident note, saying, 'We don't want an Election but if anybody makes any trouble for us at all, we shall appeal to the country and win it.'

I went to have a look at the Post Office archives and was appalled by the Dickensian atmosphere in the sub-basement where these poor people try to gather some sort of historical records. All the vehicles, equipment, stamps, uniforms and papers will need to be co-ordinated into an effective Post Office museum and historical library.

This evening Caroline had the Comprehensive Schools Committee. It is composed of a formidable group of educationalists and this week they launch their campaign to support and monitor the Government introduction of comprehensive education. It is creating great interest. This is being launched later this week and will create great interest.

Wednesday 22 September
At 12.30 Charles Smith came to lunch and Ron Smith joined us at 1.15. With just the three of us there, it was less inhibiting than the weekly informal committee.

I had been so strictly ordered to keep quiet about my nationalised industries plan that I confined myself to presenting to Ron the difficulties that the PMG experiences, ie he has no effective control, no access to old papers, no independent voice, and no continuity of appointment. Also it is impossible to enter into mixed enterprise arrangements since Civil Service and private enterprise don't mix.

I asked Ron Smith whether he would see a little Neddy as being the proper place to air the PMG's problems. Charles of course agreed with me but Ron is so obsessed by the defeatism that has gripped the postal services and the fear that they will be left with the unskilled end of the business that he just muttered about the resistance of his staff.

Friday 24 September
Arrived at Blackpool last night and found myself in a room at the Imperial Hotel which is quite a period piece. The National Executive met all morning to go through its ordinary agenda and give consideration to the work of conference.

The first big row came over the foreign policy debate and centred round whether Michael Stewart should be invited to speak from the platform. In the end it was agreed that Ray Gunter would move the draft statement formally and Michael would be invited to open the debate from the platform. We then went through the draft statement and I got some important amendments accepted. First, the admission of China to the United Nations should be included in the statement. Unaccountably this had just been forgotten. Second, we should give more emphasis to our loyalty to the UN than our loyalty to our alliances or the Commonwealth. Third, we should not only be interested in the divisions that were growing up in Western Europe but in the whole of Europe, and so the word 'Western' was removed from the draft.

The next discussion of interest was on Party constitutional amendments where Mikardo had done his homework and proposed that we accepted a number of them. Of course nobody was ready to make a change and it strengthened the case for a constitutional commission to look at the constitution of the Party after the conference. I intend to pursue this at the Executive meeting once conference is over.

The third discussion centred round the Party's submission to the Speaker's Conference, recommending the reduction of the voting age to eighteen, which unaccountably had been completely forgotten. Sara Barker, who had prepared the document, gave the most unsatisfactory answer and we agreed that words dealing with this should be inserted into the submission before the end of the month. There are obvious political advantages in this, quite apart from the moral case and the fact that people are maturing and marrying younger.

This evening I had dinner with Geoffrey Goodman of the *Sun*, Peter Jenkins of the *Guardian* and another journalist. We discussed the state of the Conference and what we expected would happen.

Bed about 12 and read a book on Charles Bradlaugh.

Saturday 25 September

Caroline rang this morning. Everybody turned up at the press conference yesterday to launch her Comprehensive Schools Committee except for the *News of the World* and the *Observer*. A significant combination.

A pouch had come from London and I worked on it in my bedroom all morning. One of the difficult Office decisions that I have to take is to accept Bootle for the Giro in place of Huyton in Harold Wilson's own constituency. He has been pressing me on this but there is an overwhelming case for Bootle and I shall have to tell him.

This evening I had dinner and talked for three or four hours with journalists John Beavan, Victor Knight and Anthony Shrimsley of the *Daily Mirror*. Most of the discussion was on the relations between the press and politicians and Victor Knight told me that in the past he had actually been shown some Cabinet documents by Tory Ministers. I daresay I am naive about this but I was astonished. He also said – the others agreed – that most Ministers made it clear when they disagreed with their Cabinet colleagues on points of policy. One valid point they made was that the secrecy which surrounded National Executive and Cabinet proceedings was in many cases absurd. Journalists had a job to do and wanted to file a story and even innocuous and non-secret information was withheld from them just because of a political dislike of the press. Looking back on yesterday's National Executive, most of what happened could easily have been revealed and it may be worth raising at tomorrow's Executive the proposal that we should tell the press almost everything that happens.

I suggested that we ought to have a seminar with Crossman and Macleod, the press lobby, Ministers and ex-Ministers to discuss the workings of press relations between politicians and the lobby to see if we couldn't hit on a better system. Quite frankly, I am uncertain as to what to do, sometimes feeling that I am much too indiscreet and sometimes feeling that I am absurdly highminded.

Sunday 26 September

Peter Shore arrived in Blackpool this morning and I had breakfast with him. Afterwards, Marcia brought us the first text of Harold's speech which we discussed. Then we went in to see Harold. I suggested that he should try to draw a distinction between the Tory Party as the champion of those who own industry and the Labour Party as the natural ally of the managers and the people who run it. I also suggested that he should address the Liberals over the head of the Liberal MPs.

After lunch we had a long meeting of the Executive – the last before Conference begins. There was a tremendous clash between

Jack Jones, Dan McGarvey* and Ian Mikardo against George Brown about the proposed legislation to make it obligatory for wage claims to be notified in advance.

The other most interesting argument was about whether we should accept a resolution from the floor which rejected the idea that the integration of public schools could be achieved by taking state places in fee-paying schools. Dick Crossman said that if we accepted the resolution, it would kill the Public Schools Commission stone-dead. Alice Bacon said she would rather do nothing at all than do this. George Brown said that Dulwich College had 90 per cent free places and surely we couldn't object to that.

In the end, with only George Brown, Dick Crossman and Eirene White, from the Women's Section, against it, the Executive decided to accept this resolution which effectively puts paid to what Crosland is planning. I was delighted. We also agreed to accept a composite resolution in favour of comprehensive education which included a reference to the active discouragement of streaming.

Monday 27 September
The Conference began this morning with a debate on pensions. Nobody wanted to speak. It was obvious that the choice of pensions to start the day had been a great mistake and Peggy Herbison had to come in early and the Conference adjourned about 12.20.

I had lunch with Jennie Lee, Lena Jeger, Beattie Plummer,† the Greenwoods and the Castles and it was like the old days of the Keep Calm Group at Margate.

Afterwards I went and met Caroline at the station and on to the Conference where we heard Dick Crossman. Then to the Fabian tea where I took the chair for Michael Stewart who was talking about the UN. Michael gave a perfect civics talk on the UN that would have been suitable for sixth forms. He's a nice, sincere guy who is basically right-wing but is humane and civilised. The audience seemed to enjoy it.

Afterwards we moved off to the UPW party in honour of the POEU who have returned to affiliation to the Labour Party after thirty-seven years. Then we dragged our way back to the overseas reception, where we met Naranja, the Kenya High Commissioner, and Olaf Palme who is just about to become the Swedish Minister of Transport and Communications.

From there we came back to the hotel where there was an amusing confrontation between Caroline and Tony Crosland who had read

* President of the Amalgamated Society of Boilermakers, Shipwrights, Blacksmiths and Structural Workers, 1965–70. Knighted just before his death in 1977.
† Baroness Plummer, widow of Leslie Plummer, MP; close friends of Harold Wilson.

The *Punch* cartoon of 1938 when my father, William Wedgwood Benn MP, defended Duncan Sandys during the famous Official Secrets Act debate.

the newspaper reports about the new Comprehensive Schools Committee but obviously knew nothing about it. His first inclination was to be scornful and when Peter Shore showed him the list of sponsors, he was somewhat taken aback.

Tomorrow the Executive election results will be announced first thing. Tony Greenwood and Barbara Castle are terrified but I'm sure that nothing will go wrong.

Tuesday 28 September
Caroline and I had breakfast in our room this morning and went on the National Executive bus to Conference. We had the TUC fraternal greetings and then the results of the elections. There were few

changes. Barbara Castle came top on the constituency section, I remained at second and Tony Greenwood had dropped to third.

After that we had the debate on the parliamentary report which Harold Wilson opened with a speech that lasted nearly an hour. It was not a bad speech but he presented bouquets to all his colleagues rather like a headmaster and the reference to me was slightly scornful: 'Of course, the Tories play cops and robbers with the help of Tony Benn who obligingly provides the division bell.'

Harold's final passage defended why he had done so little to change the mood of Britain in respect of honours, formality, etc. It was a poor passage in which he boasted that he had not made any baronetcies or hereditary peers! I found it rather revealing and I think there is a little tension between him and me on this as he thinks that I am a woolly liberal. At the same time he has accepted the Establishment view too much. He said that successive Tory Chief Whips had corrupted their parliamentary parties by the use of honours. As a postscript to this Robin Day asked him tonight straight whether he was charging Ted Heath – a former Tory Chief Whip – with corruption. Harold said he was, and I am sure this is going to be the big news tomorrow.

This afternoon Caroline had a talk with Roy Jenkins who would like to become Home Secretary. I had to go to the Conference as it was the private session where I was put down to deal with the Young Socialists. Bessie Braddock moved the change of rules which would restrict the freedom of the Young Socialists, with a speech that Reg Underhill had written for her. Afterwards a succession of delegates came and denounced this, finishing up with Sydney Silverman who made a classic liberal appeal for freedom of thought and resolution and said that the Labour Party was treating young people as second-class Party members.

It was in this atmosphere that I had to get up and speak and it was an extremely difficult speech to make. I paid a genuine tribute to Sydney Silverman but tried to pose the problem of how you could create a youth movement that was vigorous and critical and forward looking, without creating an entirely new movement which would split the young from the mainstream of British democratic socialism, depriving us of their vitality and them of our strength. In the end the NEC won by 6,900,000 votes to about 800,000. What I hated more than anything else was being congratulated by Ray Gunter, Len Williams, Sara Barker and all the right-wing members of the Executive.

Finally back to the hotel at 12.45, feeling pretty tuckered out.

Wednesday 29 September
This morning we had the foreign affairs debate at the conference. Michael Stewart spoke for nearly an hour at the invitation of the

Executive. It was an uninspired speech but not a bad one, and I think that the Conference listened to him intently and with respect. He made the United Nations his main theme and the record of achievement there is not a bad one.

Afterwards there was a series of speeches from the floor, many of them critical on Vietnam, as would be expected. The best was Harold Davies who gave us a touch of his old self about his mission to Hanoi.[3] It was wildly cheered and was a very interesting speech because it represented a clear breach of collective Government responsibility. I'm sure the Foreign Office will be absolutely furious about it but Harold Davies remained true to his own background and beliefs, and I cannot see why, if you become a Minister, you should have to pretend that you've abandoned all that you've ever stood for in pursuit of some vague constitutional doctrine. But I'm sure the knives will be out for him in certain quarters.

Harold Wilson came to wind up. All I can say about his speech was that it failed to rise to the occasion. He made jokes about the Tories, he was funny, but also in a way cheap. He quoted himself several times and although there was nothing in particular that you could put your finger on, and he did give an effective answer to much of the criticism that has been directed against the Government, it just failed to be more than a Party answer. It didn't give a vision or an analysis. The main resolution criticising the Government on Vietnam was defeated by 4 million to 2 million after a card vote which Ray Gunter tried to resist.

We had lunch at the hotel with Gerald Gardiner and Elwyn Jones and the usual gang. Gerald was extremely funny. 'I was once told, years ago, that Cabinet Ministers were allowed to see their own MI5 files,' he said. 'So I asked my department to get hold of mine, thinking that this would give me a good opportunity to judge the efficacy of MI5. After all I would be able to judge what they said about me in comparison with what I knew about myself. However, the civil servants hummed and hawed a lot and so I kept saying to them every week or so, "Where is my file?" In the end I said I wanted it by tomorrow and they said I would have to see the Home Secretary. Frank Soskice was embarrassed and said that he couldn't agree and that he wasn't allowed to see the files either. When they wanted to show him anything, they photographed a page and gave it to him but he never saw the complete file. He was so upset about it that I just let it drop.' Gerald went on to say that he had heard that someone who had insisted on seeing his complete file had been told that it had been destroyed the day before.

It was a most amusing story because not only did it reveal the essential naivety of Gerald Gardiner but it was a direct confirmation of what one suspects: that there is no political control whatsoever over the security services. They regard a Minister – even the Home Secretary – as a transitory person, and they would feel under no obligation to reveal information to him. Indeed I do not know how the Home Secretary could physically get hold of an MI5 file short of sending a platoon of policemen along to take it out of the filing cabinet without the consent of those who were responsible for guarding it. It also said an awful lot about Frank Soskice as I can't believe that a Home Secretary could be fobbed off with just a page from an MI5 file if he insisted on seeing the whole thing. I had assumed that my difficulties in the Post Office were because I was not the person responsible for security. But I can see I would have a fight if ever I were sent to the Home Office. That is a job that does need cleaning up and where a tough Minister is required to take control.

Gerald was friendly but incredibly distant and Caroline thinks that he really has distilled himself by his long study of the law to such a point that he has succeeded in abstracting all political feelings about the Law from his mind, leaving only a legal computer in charge.

Elwyn Jones told a story about meeting a Pakistani High Court judge who had advocated at the Commonwealth Judicial Conference that criminals should have operations imposed on them as a punishment for their crimes, as in Saudi Arabia. Elwyn said that when he did a television interview with this judge, he shook him by the hand and said, 'I think I'd better do this while I've still got my hands left.' Elwyn also described Cyril Osborne's comment in his Commons speech against the Wolfenden Report on homosexuality in which he said, 'I warn those Members who are going to vote for this reform that none of their seats will be safe at the next Election if they persist.' When someone jumped up and asked, 'What about lesbians?' Cyril Osborne replied, 'I can only do one at a time.'

This afternoon I sat in my room dictating letters and then went back to the conference to hear the debate on immigration. We got there as Reg Freeson, MP for Willesden East, was making a most rational case against the White Paper[4] and was followed by Bob Mellish who was quite hysterical in his real working-class way, speaking for the Bermondsey dockers against immigrants. The interesting thing was that it was probably the only real debate on immigration that has been made public for some time. It wasn't the cultured exchange between middle class Right and Left, it was a real reflection of the Party and all its feelings. Alice Bacon was extremely good in putting over the White Paper for the first time in its proper way.

In the evening, Caroline and I went to the POEU party. Harold repeated a joke about my stamps. This was more than Caroline could bear: that Harold has dropped into the habit of just making slighting references to me instead of referring to the serious work that we're doing. So when Harold came up afterwards and said to Caroline, 'I hope you didn't mind about the stamps,' Caroline said, 'Yes, I do, and I wish you wouldn't go on doing it.' I turned away quailing and Harold realised this was a serious point and quickly turned it. But I will be interested to see whether he does it again. I'm sure he doesn't like being criticised and he could see that she wasn't teasing.

This evening from 8.30 until 12.30 we sat in the hotel and talked with Judy Bernstein from the Research Department and John Lyttle, also of Transport House. John was absolutely opposed to the immigration white paper and said that Harold's language in dealing with it when he referred to the 'social explosion' would be a self-fulfilling prophesy. John was passionately anti-Marcia, whom he regarded as a pernicious influence and anti-Dick Crossman and pro-George Wigg and George Brown. Meanwhile he told me that I ought to get to know Jack Jones of whom he thought highly.

I was waylaid by Abdul Minty of the Anti-Apartheid Committee, who told me that they had received two letters at the Anti-Apartheid office and that they had contained enclosures appropriate to the other which proved that they were being opened. I told him to write to me about it and as one of the letters was from David Ennals, I told David Ennals that he ought to look up the White Paper on the interception of communications and the Sandys privilege case[5] of 1938 and see Frank Soskice about it. Apparently this opening of letters to Anti-Apartheid has only begun recently which suggests that the Home Office have taken a new line.

I also had a talk to Dick Clements' mother, Sonia Clements, who told me that at the *Tribune* meeting this evening Michael Foot and Sydney Silverman had both come as near as they could to saying that they had reached breaking point and could not support the Government under certain circumstances – Sydney on immigration and Michael on the possibility that steel nationalisation may be excluded from the current legislative programme. If this is so, then I don't think this Government is going to last through the winter and it may be that Harold would do better to reverse his view and have a General Election now.

Thursday 30 September
Up at 5.30 with Caroline. At 6 o'clock we left to visit the Blackpool Post Office with the Head Postmaster, Lister Goodall. He took us round and we talked to a number of postmen preparing their delivery. Then at about 6.30, I went into the canteen where we all had a mug of tea with eighty of them. The military atmosphere was confirmed

by the postman, higher grade, who said, 'Shall I call the men to order now, sir?' But they were all in a jovial mood.

Caroline went off to London and I went on to the Conference, where we had the huge debate on incomes, prices and productivity. George Brown began it with a powerful speech and the debate was thrown open with the outcome still in some doubt, as the AEU had switched to join the TGWU in opposing the proposed compulsory early warning system. Jim made a good speech in winding up. The union resolution was defeated by over a million votes.

I came back to the hotel about 5 and went to see Harold to tell him the Giro office could not be in Huyton in his own constituency. He and Marcia went out of their way to be pleasant to me and I've no doubt whatsoever in my own mind that this was because Caroline had ticked him off last night at the POEU party.

Coming out, Bob Maxwell came up and said that he was determined to take up the question of modernising the Party machine. Frankly I don't want to get mixed up with Maxwell because it's really just a part of his campaign to get on the National Executive and he was honest enough to say it. On the other hand he has got the resources and though I would never take a penny from him, if he does get some facts and figures out it certainly would be helpful.

Finally a short talk with Dick Crossman who said that he thought Frank Cousins had made his own position impossible by standing absolutely outside the prices and incomes policy and making it as clear as he conceivably could that he dissociated himself from Cabinet policy. He thought the only decent thing Frank could do would be to resign and that he seriously thought he might.

Friday 1 October
Back from Conference. Caroline and I went out in the evening to the party given by Shen Ping at the Chinese Embassy to celebrate the anniversary of the liberation of China by the Communist regime. It was a splendid party and clearly the Chinese are moving more and more into the diplomatic world. I talked to the candidate from Luton who told me that he had been in China and was much impressed by the genuine participation of people in the life of the community. He thought the rule that top management had to spend one day a week doing manual labour was a good one and I wish I could introduce it in the Post Office. But somehow I don't see myself as a cleaner or a postman without the thing becoming just a huge press gimmick. Certain techniques are applicable to a revolutionary society which are not applicable to an established society. But the idea is a good one and even if I didn't learn anything about the job it would certainly help to maintain a closer contact between top and bottom.

He described in detail the self-criticism that went on, where every-body was brought together and invited to criticise management. Here again the Post Office is so geared to the Establishment that I just can't see people getting up and saying what they really think. I must think of some practicable alternative.

Sunday 3 October
Worked most of the day dictating, and writing to members of the Executive to see if I can win some support for a new look at organi-sation, finance and publicity. I know Bob Maxwell is intending to do serious research and he is a potential ally. The big struggle with Maxwell is whether you allow him to use you or whether you use him. My firm intention is to keep some sort of control myself. But when you're wrestling with a millionaire you do start with something of a disadvantage.

Tuesday 5 October
To the Office early this morning and the DG came to see me for our first talk for three weeks as he has been on holiday. I had listed about six points I wanted to discuss with him but he spent the first half hour telling me about his holiday and we got through only one of the points before I had to leave at 11 to present British Empire Medals to the Post Office recipients in the honours list. It was a rather revolting task, made all the more so by the fact that they were such good people and they were so overjoyed to be decorated.

Then I had lunch with Charlie Pannell at the Ministry of Works. Afterwards we went to see a film about the construction of the Post Office Tower and Charlie went to sleep and started snoring loudly – as he did during the Cabinet meeting at Chequers!

A lot of stamp designs that had been submitted for the Robert Burns stamp were brought to the office. They include some superb designs and many without the Queen's head. Sir Kenneth Clark, the chairman of the Stamp Advisory Committee, has resigned. He says that this is because he has served for thirty years on the stamp committee and feels it is time for a change. But I think it is not unconnected with the present policy. I must be careful that this does not get out to the press and be presented as a dispute over our current stamps.

Friday 8 October
Caroline and I went off by car about 10.15 and got to the Post Office Tower well before eleven for the official opening. Among the guests who came were Clem Attlee, who is our oldest and most senior ex-Postmaster General, Charles Hill, Lord Normanbrook, Sir Billy

Butlin – who will be running the restaurant – and of course the top brass from the Post Office. Despite the grave Rhodesian crisis which is reaching its climax today with Harold Wilson's last meeting with Ian Smith, Harold arrived with Mary Wilson, Sergeant Kelly (their detective), Marcia Williams and Brenda Dew, Peter Shore and Derek Mitchell.

Just after 11.30 we went into the apparatus room where Mr Harnden, the Director of the London Telecommunications Region, introduced the ceremony and then I spoke, followed by Harold who finished by making the inaugural telephone call to the Lord Mayor of Birmingham. Then to the base of the Tower where Harold Wilson unveiled the plaque commemorating the opening ceremony. We went up the tower but it was so misty we could hardly see anything at all. Marcia took some pictures of Harold and Mary with Caroline and me. Afterwards we went to the VIP lounge where there was a merry party and Caroline and I broke away to go back to the apparatus room where all the staff and press were celebrating.

Today the press was full of Caroline's survey of thirty people who had sent their children from private schools to state schools. This survey had been done with enormous care and had of course included a number of opposing comments from different people. The Comprehensive Schools Committee has come at exactly the right moment and literally dozens of people, including headmasters and some chief education officers, have written for further information.

This evening Caroline spoke at a teach-in for sixth formers. The subject was the education of women and she enjoyed it very much.

Monday 11 October
Went to Bristol. Spoke at the University Labour Club lunchtime meeting and it was absolutely packed out. The Left Club, who have broken away and formed a joint group with Communists, Trotskyites, anarchists and dissatisfied Labour people, turned up in force to heckle me. But a number stayed for questions for two hours.

At 7 o'clock to Kingswood primary school where I had to give away the prizes. Mr Dobbs, the headmaster, was a remarkable man and the children made the school report by reading their own compositions about different aspects of school activities. They were confident and articulate and it was the best school prize-giving I've ever attended.

Tuesday 12 October
Up at 6.30. Back to London, looked in at home and then to the Office where O'Brien and Mr Downes were waiting to discuss my draft Aberdeen speech. They were horrified at the fact that I had

admitted the existence of postal delays and wanted me to erase all those references. But I absolutely refuse to do this. The Office just wants me to be an uncritical PRO for their activities and I won't.

Andrew Restall, the Fellow in Minuscule Design, came to see me. Restall has got access to printing facilities and is thinking of printing an album of stamps. He is looking at the whole problem from scratch, thinking about the possibility of decimal stamps and is anxious to be practical. I was a bit discouraged when he said that most designers wanted the Queen's head on the stamps, and just objected to the Dorothy Wilding definitive portrait. Still, this we can tackle in due course. I think it's worthwhile having the Fellowship.

Colin Cross came to see me at 3 o'clock to discuss his nasty article in the *Sunday Express* on the state of the Post Office. The fact is that you can't win as PMG. I don't say this in the spirit of bitter resentment that Bevins expressed. But the Post Office is not an efficient organisation, it is something that the press like to attack, and the Tories have a deliberate political reason for trying to spotlight the failures of public enterprise. I am tempted to draw in my horns and concentrate on the absolutely minimum number of major issues. One of the most unattractive features of the job is that I have to go to the House of Commons week after week and defend incompetence and failure by a huge department. I am tempted to start saying that I won't answer that question as it is a matter of day-to-day management. But I think the House would tear me to pieces if I did.

This evening Harold did a ministerial broadcast on Rhodesia and did it very well. Last week the press has been full of Ian Smith and on the whole he has had a sympathetic hearing here. No doubt Harold felt this had to be neutralised and he bent over backwards to suggest that he had the full support of the Tories in what he was doing. There will be a big row at the Tory Conference this week and no doubt Heath will be forced into a position of semi-opposition. It is going to be the biggest Commonwealth crisis for many years and it is possible that the Commonwealth will not survive a break unless Britain takes action – even military action to prevent the UDI.*

Thursday 14 October
To the Aberdeen Head Office this morning about 9 after spending yesterday visiting Edinburgh. We gathered in the Head Postmaster's office with the Lord Provost, Hector Hughes [MP for Aberdeen

---

* Unilateral Declaration of Independence, the term used to describe the secession of Rhodesia from the Commonwealth and separation from the British Government.

North] and Forbes Hendry [MP for West Aberdeenshire] and we went on to the new public office.

I had decided to make a major speech on Post Office policy and I gave some preliminary findings of McKinsey and said that we must try to get managers to take a more direct interest in cost reduction and the optimum utilisation of labour. I also hinted that there would have to be a new look at promotion policy and finished up by welcoming the select committee investigation of the Post Office this coming year. Most of this went over the heads of the Aberdeen audience where there are few postal difficulties and there are certainly no recruitment difficulties. But I had been looking for an occasion to say it for some time.

In fact the real news today didn't come from my trip in Scotland at all but from a letter written by Mitchell at Number 10 to Wratten about stamp design. It was an astonishing letter for any civil servant to have written for it contains within it a clear statement that the Queen might under some circumstances 'reject the advice of her Ministers'. This of course does not come directly from the Palace but Adeane had conveyed this impression to Mitchell and Mitchell had conveyed it to the Prime Minister, who has decided to frighten me off by conveying it to me.

There are many angles of this letter which require a great deal of thought. The first is that it looks as if my new stamp policy has been torpedoed. Whether or not the Queen cares personally about it, Adeane and all the flunkies at Buckingham Palace certainly do. Their whole position depends upon maintaining this type of claptrap.

Realising that they were dealing with somebody who didn't intend to be bullied and couldn't be flattered, Adeane decided to get at me sideways by going to Harold Wilson and threatening political controversy which he knew would be sufficient to effect an order by Harold to me to stop. This is exactly how the Palace works. It doesn't want to appear unpopular, yet at the same time it does not want certain things to happen and it uses the threat of controversy to stop any changes from going too far. Whether or not Adeane will go so far as to say to Heath or Salisbury* or Home 'You'd better watch that Postmaster General, he's trying to take the Queen's head off the stamps', I don't know. They certainly aren't gentlemen when it comes to political in-fighting. But, at the present, Adeane obviously thinks this is the best way to operate.

For my part, particularly after all the unfavourable press comment that I have had, I am not sure how far I would want to go with the new stamp policy. It is only peripheral and I would be prepared to

---

* Marquess of Salisbury, leader of the House of Lords 1942–5 and 1951–7.

give it up if I could get out of the Palace an official order to stop it. For a piece of paper written in that way would be of priceless constitutional interest. What I am not going to do is to allow myself to be stopped without getting that particular order.

This evening I began to turn my mind to the best way of dealing with this letter. I do not intend to raise it with Harold Wilson. It is too unimportant to worry him with and I don't want him to give me orders to do anything. I want them directly from the Palace.

Saturday 16 October

The line that I have decided to take on the Mitchell letter is this: that I am puzzled by what has happened and cannot understand it. I can draw attention to the fact that at the audience the Queen had assured me she had no feelings on the matter and that in Adeane's letter in March he had said, 'The Queen has an open mind on the matter'. I can then go on to describe what has happened since and can give Mitchell a categorical assurance that no stamps have been specially commissioned without the Queen's head, that the Queen's right of veto is not at issue, and that nothing further will happen until I have approached the Palace further.

I also decided that I would write directly to the Queen herself. Since Adeane had chosen the roundabout way through himself, Mitchell, Harold Wilson and Wratten, I decided to go straight back to the Monarch and drafted another letter expressing my astonishment that there should have been any confusion, asking for clarification and saying that if it is the Queen's wish, I will cancel the whole thing and make an early public statement in the House of Commons about it.

I know this is the last thing in the world she will want and she will be in a cleft stick. The Palace wants her to be popular, doesn't want controversy and, above all, doesn't want to be thought to be a barrier to change. That is because the Palace is, in itself, such a barrier to change that if it can conceal it by appearing to sponsor modernisation that suits it down to the ground. I drafted this letter with immense care so that it looks absolutely obsequious but contains a threat of cancelling the stamp policy.

Sunday 17 October

A usual family day at home. I went to see Mother this morning. After lunch, we all went to the park and sat in the hot October sunshine. It was far better than days in June or July. The boys played football and Melissa played with a balloon. It was a lovely day.

Monday 18 October
To the Office this morning and gave Mrs Funnell my two letters about stamp policy to type, one to Mitchell, the Prime Minister's Private Secretary, and the other to the Queen direct. When Wratten saw these he was somewhat concerned. He said the draft was too tough. He had little objection to my writing to Mitchell in any terms that I liked – so long as I made it clear that it was my draft that he was signing! But he did think that to write to the Queen direct (and to hint that Adeane might have been lying) and to draw crudely to her attention the fact that it was suggested that she had changed her mind, was a bit much. On reflection, I think he was right and so I decided to put the letter to the Palace in cold storage and mention in the letter to Mitchell that I had in mind writing to the Palace for further clarification. This probably is the right thing to do.

I called Downes in this morning and put to him as a serious and immediate possibility the idea of converting the fully paid and printed paper rates into fast and slow service, ie first- and second-class mail. There is a case for doing it immediately before the next tariff increase so we would have an opportunity of seeing its effect. If we had it operating for a year, the tariff increase could be used to correct any failures or weaknesses that might emerge. Downes was much struck by this and said he would think about it.

Tuesday 19 October
To dinner with Tommy Balogh where we were joined by Dick Crossman, Peter Shore, Marcia Williams and Gerald Kaufman. Dick had just come from a meeting of his strategic planning committee and we discussed tactics and the beginnings of the manifesto for the next Election. We agreed that Heath was not as formidable as we had feared at the time he was chosen leader. He is too like Hugh Gaitskell – a basic splitter who insists on getting his own way at the cost of Party unity – and is humourless and cannot roll with the punches as Harold can.

Dick brought me home and said that Harold had told him that 'Tony is being very difficult about the stamps'. I received today a note that Harold wanted to see me about this and so this is obviously going to be the moment of truth.

Wednesday 20 October
We had a Board meeting all morning. Afterwards I went to see David and Rosalind Gentleman about stamps. They have produced superb examples of what could be done. I told them of the difficulty over the Queen's head but this is soluble in the context of a small white or black silhouette which can be placed in the top right-hand corner

of the designs submitted. In fact we agreed that the real line to take now was that it was the Dorothy Wilding portrait we objected to since that made design impossible, and if we could have this simple little silhouette, the problem might be solved. I intend to take some of the examples when I go to see Harold on Monday.

Saturday 23 October
Surgery at Unity House, Bristol, this morning. It went on for two and three quarter hours. There was a woman who'd had a miscarriage while on holiday in Austria and had had to pay the hospital bills; a philatelist whose first-day cover had been ruined; a Post Office engineer who said he had been passed over for promotion; an architect with a planning problem; an upholsterer whose factory had been burned down and who had now got into trouble for putting up a portable building one-twentieth of which was outside the building line and wanted help because he had an important export order. There was a manufacturer of ladders who was worried about rising British Railways charges; a woman who had fallen in the street and wanted to claim damages from the Corporation; a real working class Tory who had come to argue about compulsory purchase procedures; and there was a telephone call from someone who wanted to know whether educational welfare officers had any part to play in the new Home Office family service courts. In fact it was a perfectly representative surgery.

Afterwards back to London.

Caroline was at the opera, the boys were at a music camp and Melissa was staying in Harlow so I had a completely clear evening to start my stamp project. The Office had given me the stamp designs submitted in the course of the current year. I worked for four hours photographing all these designs with my Polaroid. The fact is that the Office normally guards them like gold or diamonds and I have the greatest difficulty in getting them. They are historic designs because we are passing through a period of great change.

Sunday 24 October
I began turning my mind seriously to the problem of how we could represent our national identity by means of a small symbol on each stamp. One idea was the small black or white silhouette of the Queen which could be fitted into any design that was submitted. Another would be the 'E II R' symbol with crown or the crown itself. Another might be a small union jack or a royal coat of arms.

David Gentleman came to the house with all his designs. He had added a complete set of definitives along the lines of the suggestion I had made of a white silhouette on backgrounds of different colours.

They really looked effective and would prepare the public for the idea of the silhouette as the royal symbol on commemorative and pictorial stamps. He agreed to go away and work on other types of symbols – the basic design plus the head, the crown, the cipher, the coat of arms, etc.

I still have somehow to get round the two difficulties imposed by Harold Wilson's instruction via Mitchell that I must not commission stamps without the Queen's head and must not show stamps without the Queen's head to the press without the Queen's permission. I think I am getting near the point when I shall have to seek another audience.

Monday 25 October
To the Office this morning with all David Gentleman's designs and Mr Downes, the DPS, came to see them. He was immensely excited by the fertility of Gentleman's ideas. Two ideas occurred to me and rather recommended themselves to Downes. The first was that Gentleman should attempt a series of stamps dealing with horses! These might be sporting prints or famous racehorses and could easily be produced at short notice. The other was that we might ask Lord Snowdon to become chairman of the Stamp Advisory Committee in place of Sir Kenneth Clark. This would be an appointment justified on merit and would also guarantee that there was a continuing link with the Palace. I rang Gentleman and he is going to do the sporting prints and thought that Snowdon would be a good chairman.

I then dictated a long and informal letter to Harold Wilson which I intend to send through Marcia, reassuring him about the Queen's head and suggesting the Snowdon appointment. Provided there is no risk of political trouble, I think he will back me. In fact it looks as if the row will clear the air and I hope I can have another audience with the Queen to reassure her. If Snowdon becomes chairman he can open the next stamp exhibition and it will be impossible to criticise it if he does so. All in all, I think we are seeing our way through a potentially difficult problem.

This afternoon we had the PMG's Informal Committee. We discussed the possibility of the fast and slow postal service and they all reacted in characteristic Post Office way, saying that it was impossible and would cause terrible operational difficulties.

Tuesday 26 October
To the PLP meeting this morning, where there was a brief discussion on the Speakership of Horace King.* With typical Labour tactless-

* First Labour Speaker in the House, MP for Southampton, 1950–7. Created Lord Mowbray-King, 1971.

ness Ted Short said that the choice of Horace King had been forced on the Party by the Tory insistence on him and the views of 5 per cent of Labour members, who thought he should be Speaker regardless of the parliamentary consequences to us. This bald statement was greeted with some horror.

After that there was a short debate on parliamentary procedural changes and the Back Bench revolt against Bowden's conservatism began to be felt. Bowden and Len Williams are the two most conservative forces in the Party.

This afternoon Horace King was elected Speaker. The ritual now seems so dated and irrelevant.

This evening I went to dinner with Dick and Marcia. Tommy, Peter and Gerald were there too. Coming home Marcia told me that Mitchell had told Harold that I was going to resign over the stamps issue and that Harold was genuinely puzzled and worried. Marcia also said that Mitchell had tried to knife her and that Harold intended to get rid of him.

Wednesay 27 October
To the Executive this morning where we were told that there would be a joint meeting with the Cabinet on 6 February. It was also agreed that at all future meetings we should spend half our time on politics and I raised the desirability of making time to discuss organisational matters as well. This was the first move in the Penny-Farthing* campaign supported by Dick Clements, Paul Johnson [editor of the *New Statesman*] and others.

Then to the Speaker's memorial service in the Abbey where one felt that the high priests of the tribe were laying away one of the Establishment figures. Not very personal or moving, but the music and setting were lovely.

Thursday 28 October
On the train back from Bristol I met a Sister Millicent Olga, an Anglican nun, who wants to become a counter clerk again and told me she had once written to ask whether it would be possible. I am rather keen on the idea if it can be done without too much difficulty.

Friday 29 October
David Gentleman came to the Office this morning. Downes, O'Brien, Gentleman and I had a talk about the essaying of his stamp designs. He had found some sporting prints of horses designed to win royal

---

* A term coined by Harold Wilson in the fifties, and invoked in 1965 to characterise the archaic state of the Labour Party machine.

support. He also had photographed some little symbols, including the royal crest in various forms, as well as some new profiles of the Queen.

I dashed to the Commons at 11 as the House was sitting and Sir John Ricks and Mr Shepherd came over. We had to discuss whether legislation could be provided, in the Bill that the Minister of Transport is sponsoring, to remove restrictions on nationalised industries. I wanted the Post Office to be given exactly the same freedom as any other private industry but they said that although I had complete inherent power representing the Crown, my financial powers were limited by the Post Office Act. I said that I should be given a statutory duty and I decided to dictate a memorandum laying down my reasons for wishing the change and I will take it to my colleagues in EDC.

Then Tommy Atkins, the print director of the International Publishing Corporation, came along to tell me about the new photon computer typesetting machine which IPC have bought from America and which they claim will make it possible to print whole pages of the telephone directory at the rate of about 2 million letters a minute. I promised I would get our Office to make contact with them.

Saturday 30 October
Up early and Caroline and I went to Bath by train. In the next compartment on one side was Mark Bonham Carter, former MP for Torrington, going to a Liberal function in Bristol and in the other compartment was Ted Heath going to a Tory function in Bristol.

At Bath we were taken to meet the Mayor, Mrs Evans, in the Guildhall. Then we went to Claverton Church where there was a short ceremony in connection with the re-dedication of the tomb of Ralph Allen, the postal pioneer. Caroline and I went to see the Roman baths and at the lunch in the Pump Room I spoke about Ralph Allen. I said that he was what in modern parlance would be called 'a whizz-kid' and that no doubt his idea for crossposts was thought of as 'a gimmick'. After the lunch we just had time to look in at the Assembly Rooms to see the wonderful museum of costume.

The Mayor lent us her car to go to Hanham where Tony Crosland opened a sale of work. Afterwards we went to the wedding reception given by Paul Stephenson and his bride in Portland Street.

In the train back, Ted Heath was again in the next compartment and champagne and strawberries had been provided for him. There were four policemen and the station master at Bristol station which was a little odd considering he was only Leader of the Opposition. But that's the way the Tories run things.

Stephen and Hilary are back from their music camp and we had a family evening watching television.

Sunday 31 October

The main news at the moment is the conclusion of Harold Wilson's mission to Rhodesia. I am terrified that he will reach some sort of a settlement with Ian Smith. But I ought to have more confidence in him. The idea of a Royal Commission with a Rhodesian judge as chairman is a little worrying. But the longer the UDI is postponed the better.

Monday 1 November

To the Cabinet Office where we had a meeting of the Broadcasting Committee. We postponed a decision about BBC finance and went on to local broadcasting where it was agreed that I could go ahead with my project for local radio. It was also agreed that we should have a national broadcasting advisory council which would have special responsibilities in respect of new local stations. These were two notable successes and so I didn't press pirates or any of my other issues. I came away feeling very cheerful.

Back to the Post Office and then to the House of Commons. I heard Harold make his statement on Rhodesia which was really a triumph. Despite the uneasy feelings some of us have, there is little prospect of a settlement and he can claim to have done everything a man could do. Heath just ate out of his hand, he really is the most inadequate Opposition Leader.

The House sat till 2.30 in the morning and it is extremely exhausting. The atmosphere is intensely oppressive and one has this awful feeling one will miss a division. I tried to work.

Tuesday 2 November

Attended the Regional Directors' Conference this morning. This was the first one that I had attended for a year and the DG asked me to speak. I told them what we had achieved and then began discussing problems of the Post Office's status, the division in management responsibility, and the future of the postal services.

They were all extremely critical of the idea of a split at the regional level between Posts and Telecommunications. These are the people who would lose status by having a divided responsibility. I argued as hard as I could but was more concerned to hear their opinions. After about an hour and a half of discussion, I drew up a chart on a board, showing the way that the command structure would work, with departmental policy in the centre going up to the present

Director General and two arms each side representing Posts and Telecommunications.

At this point Mr Harnden, the director of the London Telecommunications Region, said, 'I'm grateful to the Minister for drawing that diagram because it proves conclusively how little he understands of the way the machine really works.' I thanked him, saying, 'It was most kind of you to speak so plainly. One of the difficulties for somebody like myself who comes from politics into the Civil Service is the excess of courtesy he experiences. It is rare that one gets a blow straight between the eyes of the kind that Mr Harnden has directed at me and I greatly appreciated it.' Mr Harnden was extremely embarrassed and in that general atmosphere of laughter, I left. It is obvious I won't make any progress with them but nothing they said convinced me that this decision would be a wrong one.

At 5 o'clock I went to see Harold in his room at the House of Commons, with my stamps. I thought he was a little uneasy to begin with and this was no doubt because Mitchell had told him I was being difficult. I opened all my stamps and showed them to him and he was absolutely captivated by them. The ones he liked best were of the old railway trains. I should have guessed this since he wrote his thesis at Oxford on the early days of the railways. In fact he was absolutely certain that I had had these specially designed to win his support. He over-rates my political sense. He also laughed very hard about the sporting prints which he agreed were the best way of presenting new ideas to the Palace.

With regard to the Queen's head, he said that he had spoken to the Queen personally about it and that she didn't want her head removed from the stamps. 'She is a nice woman,' he said to me, 'and you absolutely charmed her into saying yes when she didn't really mean it.' He went on, 'I don't think you ought to go back and argue it out with her again because I'm sure you would win and she really wouldn't be happy.' He thus disposed of my claim that the network was operating to prevent this from happening. For my own part, I suspect that Harold more or less invited her to say no in order to keep in with the Palace. But, coming from him, there was no argument and I told him that it would create no problems as I could put a head on every stamp and showed him the cameos. He relaxed and realised that this would present no political difficulties for him.

Marcia came in at this stage and so did Brenda and they looked at the designs and were delighted with them, especially with the costumes. But when Marcia heard about the Queen's view she burst out and said that it was a scandal that in modern England the Queen should have any say about anything at all, and why did she choose the stamps, what had it to do with her and couldn't Ministers reach their own decisions. I told her that I agreed with her entirely but if there was likely to be political trouble it wasn't worth it, and I would accept this. I do like Marcia, she's got all the right instincts and she does Harold a great deal of good.

Anyway, Harold said he would be seeing the Queen tonight at his audience and would tell her that we'd made great progress and probably the right thing to do would be to go along for another audience soon. I told him I wanted an exhibition but he was doubtful about the wisdom of having the press see stamps without the head again in case this put pressure on the Palace. Obviously this is what the Palace had said to him and it may well be that I shall just have to accept that we will get these beautiful new stamps out with the head in silhouette and the rest will have to go by the board. It's much more important to keep in with Harold and it would be silly to run any risk of a row politically. You may be sure the Palace would leak it all to the Tories if they thought it would help. The Palace regard me as a complete revolutionary – dating back to my peerage days – and feel that I must be restrained.

At 8 o'clock I went back to Downing Street for dinner with Dick, Gerald, Peter, Tommy and Marcia. Mary waited for us in the living room in the flat where they live and she was sad at having to live away from home. She really doesn't want to be the Prime Minister's wife and would love to be the wife of an Oxford don. This is not an affectation, it's perfectly genuine. She is a nice and unaffected woman. *Private Eye* are bringing out 'Mary Wilson's Diary' as a book and we discussed whether any action could be taken to stop it. Harold said that nobody had read *Private Eye* for over a year now as it was so scurrilous! It's one thing to run a comic column called 'Mary Wilson's Diary' and it's another thing to publish a book which many innocent people will think has been written by Mary Wilson. I think some legal action is called for and would succeed.

Harold came in straight from his audience with the Queen and told me that he had been there for an hour and a quarter. 'We spent ten minutes on Rhodesia, and an hour and five minutes on stamps,' he said. I'm sure this reflects the proportion of the Queen's mind which is devoted to Rhodesia as compared with stamps. He told me that she was perfectly happy to accept a silhouette, and to accept the rulers of Britain, including Cromwell and Edward VIII, but that her head had to appear on everything and the press was not to see any stamps without her head. He told me that the thing that had really annoyed the Palace was my recommendation that in the Battle of Britain stamps she should accept a block of six with her head in the top right-hand corner but not on the other five. I pointed out that these were the very stamps that I had shown her when I knelt at her feet on the floor at Buckingham Palace and that she had been delighted with them. 'Ah,' said Harold, 'but the Queen was quite unable to resist your youth, enthusiasm and charm. You were clearly a working man's Lord Melbourne.'

Anyway there it rests. The plain truth is that the Palace has won on the main point and I have been defeated by Palace pressure exercised through the network on me, using the Prime Minister as an intervening force. Harold, who is so busy using the Queen on Rhodesia and wants it to be known that he enjoys the closest possible relations with her, is prepared to sacrifice this for a quiet life, and freedom from political criticism. Within its limited power the monarchy and all it stands for is one of the great centres of reaction and conservatism in this country.

We had dinner without Mary and discussed the Queen's speech next week. Peter made the point that the Bill to extend the powers of nationalised industries ought to be made much bigger, to feature more in the programme. I agreed strongly and told Harold that this Bill had been played down to a minimum. I told him that my department had given me no information about this and that I found it was almost too late to include the Post Office in it.

I also said I would like the Post Office to buy the Exchange Telegraph Company which is going to close down its parliamentary reporting service in the House. Harold was intensely interested in this and so was everybody else present. He picked up the telephone and dictated a minute to one of his secretaries in the basement. It is now obvious that I shall get official backing for a much wider Bill and I put it to Harold that we ought to have a Ministry of Public Enterprise which would encourage a bigger role for an enlarged public sector. He was much taken with this idea.

For the first time for months I was able to make contact with Harold on a host of issues that went far beyond the Post Office. One of the most frustrating things about the Post Office is that I have been limited in my range of subjects to those contained within my department.

I heard a little bit more about Derek Mitchell's attempt to get Marcia Williams out of Number 10. There is a big tussle going on. Marcia is infinitely the most able, loyal, radical and balanced member of Harold's personal team and I hope he resists efforts to dislodge her.

Wednesday 3 November
To Number 10 in the evening to hear Ted Heath doing a TV broadcast. He was odiously ingratiating and the programme had begun with the applause after his speech at the Tory Conference, and had shown pictures of him sitting and smirking. Edward du Cann, the

Tory chairman – cardboard man, as he is known – then introduced Heath who ogled the viewers. He only made two firm points, one anti-trade union and the other attacking us for failing to help the owner-occupier. But he ended by saying, 'The difference between the socialists and ourselves is that they believe in the State and we believe in the family.' Whether this was intended to draw attention away from his own bachelor status or was meant seriously, it didn't go down well.

I heard more about the petty troubles at Number 10. Evidently Marcia had made some slightly disparaging remark about one of the garden girls – that typing pool of debs who service Prime Ministers – and the girl had written to Mitchell saying she would resign. There is a frightful row developing. The whole thing is pathetic and reflects the sort of petty jealousies that must exist in any court. But Harold, I think, will stand firm by Marcia and so he should.

Thursday, 4 November

To Number 10 again for the Cabinet meeting where I had to make an oral report on the Exchange Telegraph position. I began to say a word or two about it when I was interrupted by those who wondered whether it was worth saving at all. This was not for me to decide. Also the Board of Trade are the sponsoring department for newspapers and industry generally and so it was agreed that Douglas Jay would make the necessary contacts with the firm. I'm glad to be relieved of the job but it's nice to know that I have got powers if it is necessary for me to do anything about it.

After lunch I went to the House. Speaker King is getting through questions at a spanking pace and it does mean that Members have a chance of getting their questions answered.

This evening I took all the stamps that I had photostated and photographed in black and white and colour and stuck them into an album. Now that the headless stamps are going to be banned, I'm keen to have a complete set of design work and copies of stamps during this period that reveal what the designers would have done if they had the power to do so.

The Westminster by-election* result today showed the Tory majority cut to 6,000 from 17,000 in 1959 and 10,000 when Hylton-Foster stood as Speaker last year. Not a bad result. The Liberal lost his deposit with only 1,500 votes.

---

* Held as a result of Speaker Hylton-Foster's death in September 1965. His successor was John Smith.

Friday 5 November

Caroline and I had lunch with David Bruce, the American Ambassador. Afterwards up to Holland Park School where we had an appointment with Alan Clarke, the headmaster, about the formation of a parent-teacher association. He was agreeable to the idea and, like Len Williams, had to convince us that he had thought of it first.

Caroline and I went to the Russian Embassy. We met Rogov whom Caroline is absolutely convinced is the leading security man in the Embassy. He always looks so embarrassed and behaves quite differently from the way he did when he was here before. He also manages to let out that he knows a great deal about us. Last time it was a businessman from Cincinnati who had been to the Soviet Union to sell laundry equipment and who had been asked to work for the CIA while he was there. This time he had been in Socchi in Russia and had noticed the fact that we had been to the Botanical Gardens where I had transplanted a lemon on to an orange tree or something. He just knows too much.

Paul Johnson was at the Embassy. He noticed a microphone sticking out of a wall light and called into it, 'This is Paul Johnson of the *New Statesman*. I have noticed your microphone and I am breaking it off.' Mr Vassev said that he very much hoped that I might take a delegation to the Soviet Union to discuss post and telephone matters. I am suspicious, but I would like to see them and it would be an interesting trip.

We came home to celebrate Guy Fawkes day with lots of fireworks in the garden.

Monday 8 November

Morrison and Stewart of McKinsey's came to see me this morning to discuss the progress they have made. Before we got on to managerial reorganisation, they pointed to a significant saving that they thought possible. If 538 of the smaller Crown offices were sold off and sub-postmasters were asked to take on the work they reckoned there would be an annual saving of nearly £2 million and a great capital gain from the sale of the property. Sub-postmasters would pay their staff less, would have a lower standard of accommodation and would be subsidised to some extent by their shopkeeper activities. In effect, this advice and recommendation was based on the idea that public enterprise had to get out of this area because it simply couldn't compete efficiently and involved a downgrading of the quality of service.

The unions would fight this like tigers and so would I. If we accept this, then of course you could probably do better by selling the whole

Post Office to private enterprise and making a large capital gain in the process. It provided another vivid example of the handicapped conditions under which public enterprise has to work today.

Then we went on to discuss major reorganisation. I think there is no doubt that they have discussed this with the DG and they regard their loyalty as consultants to the Director General and not to me. I am in the position of chairman of the company – as they see it – somebody to be kept informed but not central to the exercise. This is the intensely frustrating thing about office, that a Minister really is not in charge, and the department would much prefer to work without me altogether.

Peter Bessell, Liberal MP for Bodmin, came to see me at 5 o'clock to ask about the possibility of licensing walkie-talkie radios for fishermen and lifeguards. At the moment many Japanese sets come into the country which people use illegally and we have to prosecute. He wanted a waveband for unlimited use of this kind. The department is obscurantist about this and for some reason simply doesn't want to grant it. I am determined that we shall have a completely clear band for use by private individuals and then manufacturers can make the sets that will fit this range.

Tuesday 9 November
Parliament was opened this morning but I didn't attend the ceremony, going instead to the meeting in Room 14 where the Parliamentary Labour Party and the National Executive traditionally meet on the day of the Queen's speech. Manny Shinwell had just begun when Michael Foot got up and asked if there would be an opportunity for a debate on the omission of steel from the Queen's speech. There followed a procedural wrangle in which Manny Shinwell appeared to resist the idea of a further Party meeting tomorrow. However, in the end he did concede that it would be possible.

Harold then spoke and outlined the programme, and said how big a programme it was. He thanked us all and said that naturally some people would be disappointed about steel but we had to take the priorities. There were one or two questions but the meeting was quiet, with a certain sense of suppressed dissatisfaction under the surface.

After that I had lunch with Peter Shore and then went into the House to listen to the debate. Ted Heath attacked me again in much the same terms as he has done in many of his public speeches. I always get singled out along with Frank Cousins, and he also made much play of Dick Crossman.

At 8 o'clock we had the first of our informal dinners in our house with Dick Crossman, Tommy Balogh, Marcia Williams, Gerald

Kaufman and Peter Shore, Caroline and Valerie. It was a typical evening. Dick was in a peculiarly negative mood. Everything we suggested he knocked down and he left at 11 o'clock without anything particular being decided. He was extremely rude to Tommy and Tommy was fairly sharp in reply. But after Dick had gone we did work out the main areas of policy for the next Election manifesto and I was deputed to write a short paper. Of course the whole Election may be overshadowed by the Rhodesian situation. A Unilateral Declaration of Independence could produce serious political problems for us and although Dick didn't want to discuss it, we shall have to give some thought to it soon.

Thursday 11 November
This morning UDI was declared in Rhodesia. We have been waiting for it for a long time but now it has come there is a sense of relief. Harold is in a difficult position and the dominating factor in his mind is the risk of a Tory attack upon him and severe electoral consequences at home. To tackle this problem with a majority of one is unbearably difficult. I would like us to take stern action and not rule out the use of force. But this is completely out of the question with the Cabinet as now constituted. I went to the Commons to hear Harold make his statement on Rhodesia.

The Erith by-election result came out and although the Labour candidate, Jim Wellbeloved, did well, the Liberal vote slumped and the Tories picked up more votes than we did, making a net swing of 2 per cent against us. It shows how unreliable the polls are and threatens our position in the Kingston-upon-Hull by-election caused by the death of Henry Solomons.* The real danger to us is a Liberal collapse in favour of Heath. I think in a General Election we should probably win but there is not a sufficient margin of certainty to make it worth Harold's while going to the country.

Monday 15 November
The Times this morning had a centre-page news story about the possible break-up of the Post Office into three public corporations. It must have come from Ron Smith because it referred back to my Aberdeen and POEU speeches in which I'd hinted that we were prepared to re-examine relationships between the Government and the Post Office.

Today the first issue of the *Comprehensive Schools Committee Bulletin* came out attacking Crosland for the non-comprehensive schemes that

* Solomons gained Kingston-upon-Hull (North) for Labour in 1964 with a majority of 1,181.

he had approved and it was reported in the press. Happily Caroline's name was kept out of it but the attack emerged forcibly.

Ruth and Seretse Khama came to have dinner with us tonight. Seretse has been in hospital over the weekend with diabetes and looked pretty poorly. Ruth was just as much fun as ever. Seretse is much happier now that he is Prime Minister and next year he'll become President of Bechuanaland when it becomes an independent republic. He has established warm relations with Jomo Kenyatta, Kenneth Kaunda and Julius Nyerere and no longer feels like a reactionary chief surrounded by revolutionaries. All in all I found him in better form than for many years past.

The whole day today in the Commons was occupied with Rhodesia as we passed through both Houses the Enabling Act that will permit the Government to take sanctions. The Tory Back Benchers showed their true colours in both Houses. In the Lords, Lord Salisbury emerged as a querulous old man, completely isolated from the Establishment which for so long he had led and symbolised. But the Enabling Bill went through. I went to hear it getting the Royal Assent in the House of Lords at 2 am and I found the whole ritual ludicrous with Gerald Gardiner in a three-cornered hat and all the ridiculous ceremonial. While waiting for the debate to end, Tony Crosland and I had a talk in the Tea Room. He was angry about the attack on him in the *Comprehensive Schools Committee Bulletin* and said that all the facts were wrong. We also discussed the public schools, where he is hoping to press on with the scheme for integrating them and feels that he is the only radical in the Government. It is all bunk but obviously the arrows of criticism had gone home and that's not a bad thing.

Tuesday 16 November
This evening I had dinner with Dick Crossman and the usual gang. Marcia was depressed. Today a scurrilous letter has been sent from Huyton to many MPs, including myself and Joe Slater, with an undecipherable signature, saying, 'Who is Marcia? It is time that Harold Wilson cleared his name', etc, etc. It is a perfectly vicious letter and may easily leak to the press. I'm sure that the right thing to do is to ignore it. John Rankin, MP for Govan, came and had said he would like to put down a parliamentary question about it but I dissuaded him from doing it.

Wednesday 17 November
This morning by car to Farnborough where I opened Fleet Building, Lord Thomson's new headquarters which will handle the advertising contract for the telephone directories. He got the contract last July

and has set up an enormous organisation to handle it. When I saw
it I realised exactly why he cared so much about it. With the help
of 300 salesmen and a computer data processing system, he will have
the best intelligence service in the country and will be able to print
out from the computer the most superb and continually corrected
information about every profession, occupation, trade and business.

In my speech I twitted Thomson about being a peer and we had
lunch together. He's a charming old boy and we discussed the House
of Lords. He admitted frankly that as a poor boy in Canada he had
determined to make good, and he was interested in money not
because he needed it but because it was a symbol of success. 'In a
society like ours, the only way you can tell success is by profit,' he
said. I told him why I was opposed to the hereditary system and
gave as my reason the fact that it prevented people like him from
getting to the top. He admitted, 'I may be a bit confused about
this.' We also discussed his motivation and the motivation in public
enterprise. I rather like him and I am enormously impressed by his
drive and energy. We discussed – entirely without prejudice – the
idea of setting up a joint subsidiary company, half-owned by the Post
Office and half by Thomson's, to exploit all the possibilities created
by the telephone directory contract.

Home at 11 o'clock and found Stephen working on his project on
the Irish potato famine of 1846–8. He is starting to work hard at
school.

Thursday 18 November
To the Post Office this morning for a meeting of the Board. A paper
was presented which recommended the appointment of Henrion to
be in charge of all design. Sir Kenneth Anderson exploded. He
attacked the idea of having an outside commercial man to dispense
this massive patronage and I really had to get tough. In the end, it
was agreed that he would come in and act as a consultant.

Then there was a paper responding to my plan for a fast and slow
service which posed all sorts of difficulties and said it would be
impossible to experiment. It was agreed to leave this over to a seminar
but I'm sure that I'm on to a good thing and don't mean to give
way.

I worked over lunch and at 2.30 Dr Konrad came to see me. He
is a psychologist who had done a report for the Post Office on alpha-
numerical codes covering telephones and postal coding. The Office
want to do a postal coding system which will consist of two parts:
the first for despatch or outward sorting, consisting of postal districts
in London and a simple extract code for other cities, the second part
for inward sorting or despatch and they suggested that one digit

followed by two letters would be best [eg W1A 4WW]. In my opinion this is confusing.

Downes and Wolstencroft had been at lunch with him and no doubt stoked him up on their side. In the end he was prepared to accept that it might be the subject of further research. Mr Downes said that if there was a change now it would set them back for six months and the coding in Croydon would have to be stopped, an argument that they had never used before, having previously told me that the coding could be organised in any way that suited Dr Konrad. I decided to drop my opposition to it.

At 4.30, Dr Camm, formerly of ICI, came along and agreed to become chairman of the Post Office Users' Council.

Friday 19 November
To the Office this morning where Lord Hill, Sir Sidney Caine and Sir Robert Fraser of ITA came on a deputation to discuss their request that the ITA have all restrictions on hours lifted from them. This is one of the old grumbles. The reason for it is simply that due to advertising the ITA makes money with every extra hour it broadcasts whereas the BBC loses money. Mr Lawrence from the Radio Services Department was there and so was Mr Wratten. My brief included a particular reference to the desire of the Department of Education and Science to reserve hours which they might wish to use for the University of the Air.

I listened carefully and probed various possibilities. The most attractive was that we should grant the ITA unlimited broadcasting hours if in return they would give us, say, four hours a day for educational broadcasting, plus the money to finance it. They would get this money by charging programme companies extra rental in return for the extra hours.

Calculating roughly on a piece of paper, I worked out that we should need about £4 million a year and this would mean raising the rentals by about half as much again as they now are. This was a crude bargain that I was suggesting and Hill and Fraser thought about it carefully. The real objection to it would come from the Treasury who would argue that I was hypothecating revenue – appropriating money by a special tax for use for a special purpose without it going through the normal Treasury consolidated fund. I would like to go to the Ministerial Committee on Broadcasting and say that I had got them four hours educational broadcasting a day and the money to finance the education programmes without any extra charge on the Treasury or without the Treasury losing any money at all.

Lawrence was furious that I had aired this idea and fulminated outside to Wratten. I called Lawrence in later and discussed it with him. He is an obstinate and difficult man. In some ways my civil servants are impertinent. Since I don't mind argument and am not prepared to be dislodged by it I suppose I can't grumble. But I cannot think that many Ministers would accept the sort of attitude that I get from them.

During the lunch hour I went to see the new designs for the pillar boxes that have been brought out by designer David Mellor and which are very good.

Monday 22 November
The first snow of winter. The Engineer-in-Chief and some of his senior engineers came to one of my informal lunches, the first time I've had the engineering department and they were a little bit stodgy.

At 4.15 the Ministerial Committee on Broadcasting met and again faced the problem of BBC finance. We went through the report paragraph by paragraph and when we came to alternative ways of financing the BBC there were only three: an increased licence at the end of 1966, a tax subvention from the Treasury, or some advertising. The Treasury absolutely refused to consider a tax subvention and an increase in the licence is impossible. I therefore put forward the idea that the BBC Light Programme should be allowed to advertise under suitably authorised conditions. Judith Hart raised some doubts about this as she dislikes advertising. So do I, but I'm absolutely convinced that the only way of saving public service broadcasting is by giving it some form of revenue which will grow with it. It will also kill the pirates stone-dead.

The Committee agreed that this should be included in the White Paper in the form of 'an assurance to the BBC that any proposal they might make to advertise on the Light Programme would be acceptable to the Government under strictly controlled conditions'. I regarded this as a tremendous success and if it goes through Cabinet, as I think it will, it will be the beginning of the reshaping of British broadcasting under public service conditions with some mixed revenue, with a real chance of establishing the fourth channel on entirely new lines. All that remains to be decided now is colour, the fourth channel and how to handle the University of the Air.

Afterwards I wandered round the House and talked to a few people. Charles Morris told me that he thought that many of the leaks about new status were reaching the UPW from the DG and the staff at the Post Office. Charles told me an amusing rumour which is apparently going round that I am to replace Frank Soskice as Home Secretary. There is obviously not a jot or tittle of truth in it but it will make Roy Jenkins angry.

Tuesday 23 November

The Director General came in for a talk this morning that lasted for over two hours. Joe Slater obligingly came with me and between us we beat him down on a number of issues.

First, I insisted that when I go to Japan in January, I must take a postal man as well as a telecommunications man.

Secondly, I told him that we were absolutely firm on a broadcasting advisory council and on local sound broadcasting by non-profit making trusts. I also told him that the BBC advertising on the Light Programme would be a feature of the White Paper. He warned me that the Board of Governors might resign en bloc and we discussed what consultation there ought to be with the BBC. This whole broadcasting argument with the department is a classic example of Civil Service fighting a rearguard action against determined ministerial policy making.

The third point we discussed was the reorganisation of the department. I told the DG that I really did insist upon a Director General of Telecommunications and a Director General of Posts. I said that I wanted him to prepare a scheme as quickly as he could. The DG went out at about 12.15, after having had a double whisky and appearing to accept what had been decided. Now I must keep the pressure up.

At 2.30 I saw Sir Kenneth Anderson. He has put in a powerful paper on the future organisation of the Post Office saying that the Giro, Savings Bank and investment accounts ought to be organised together under a banking corporation with dynamic and aggressive business practice. This is a contradiction of the Treasury paper which said that the Savings ought to be left under the Treasury to be administered as a Government department. I was encouraged by Anderson's enthusiasm and told him that I agreed entirely with what he had said.

From there to the House of Commons to hear the Rhodesia statement by Harold and to see the Tories splitting up and splintering before our eyes. Heath is a pathetic figure, kicked this way and that, and is incapable of giving firm leadership. Home and Selwyn Lloyd are really running the Tory Party now and are much firmer on Rhodesia than Heath. Our massive lead of 18.5 per cent in the Gallup Poll reflects a failure by Heath and the fact that Harold is emerging as a father figure for the whole nation. But I don't see any prospect whatsoever of Harold beating Smith unless he's prepared to use stronger measures.

I went to dinner with Dick, Thomas, Peter, Marcia and Gerald. We had an interesting discussion about the fact that when a Minister attending a committee dissented from the brief given him by his permanent officials the minutes of the meeting always contained what the departmental brief said rather than what the Minister said. The case in point was yesterday when George Darling* at the Ministerial Committee on Broadcasting said that the Board of Trade was opposed to our scheme under which dealers would help us deal with licence evasion. But he said he disagreed with his Board's line. I must look in the minutes to see whether it contains what the Board wanted it to contain or what George Darling himself said.

Later in the evening Marcia came in and she was skeptical about Harold's so-called fantastic success on Rhodesia. She thinks that Harold has completely taken off and got out of touch with the real problems at home and she clearly feels cut off from him. Marcia is the best thing about the court at Number 10.

Home about 12.15 and found Caroline still had a few people here from the Comprehensive Schools Committee.

Wednesday 24 November
To the National Executive this morning. There was a poor attendance and we got through our business quickly. Ian Mikardo raised the question of the Party's attitude towards a lowering of the voting age to eighteen. Mik said he favoured a decision to lower it partly on grounds of principle and partly because of its political impact. I strongly supported him. It then turned out that everybody at the Executive was in favour. I asked that this should be minuted and Dick Crossman suggested that Len Williams should announce it in the press conference after the Executive was over. Thus an important political and constitutional decision was reached, virtually without discussion, accidentally and without notice and without the presence of the Prime Minister, the Deputy Prime Minister, the Chancellor of the Exchequer and a number of other senior Ministers. This is how many important political decisions are actually reached.

This evening I worked in my room at the House and watched the television programme about Reinhold Niebuhr. It was quite good but I wish there had been a lot less old newsreel and dull still pictures and more of him talking.

It is now after midnight and the debate on the Rhodesian Orders in Council are still going on.

During the course of the next fortnight discussions took place with the Television Advisory Committee and the manufacturers of broadcasting equipment concerning the technical aspects and costs of introducing colour television. I worked on the

_____

* Minister of State at the Board of Trade and Labour and Co-operative Member for Hillsborough, 1950–74.

phasing in of the new first- and second-class postal system in place of the ordinary and 'printed paper' regulations, the most radical change in postal services since Rowland Hill's day. In Parliament the Post Office Savings Bank Bill giving 5 per cent interest on special investment accounts was piloted through with little opposition.

Thursday 2 December

George Wigg telephoned to say that telephone communications between London and Zambia were appalling and would I do something about it. I went to the Office and asked for a full report on the communications with Zambia, told the department that I wanted the independence stamps issued by the Rhodesian Government declared invalid, and discussed with Mr Downes the preparation of franks to give the BBC wavelength on all letters to Rhodesia.

Early this afternoon a man from the *Daily Mail* came to interview me about micro-bugs. The *Mail* had carried a story about a micro-bug radio microphone, which is the size of a matchbox and can transmit to an ordinary VHF transistor at the range of about 200 yards. Lillicrap told me that these will soon come down to about £20 or £30 each and would pose a terrible problem for the Post Office which could never detect them. I dictated a short minute saying that no further licences were to be given to people using these radio mikes, that I should have a list of those who had licences, that anyone discovered using them should be reported personally to me and I called for a select committee and legislation. This really is the arrival of 1984 and must be taken seriously. Before the interview Lillicrap admitted that he had licensed the use of radio mikes by detective agencies and so I'm glad I laid down the rule that I did.

Then Ryland came with information about communications with Zambia and it is clear that the best thing we could do would be to send some engineers out, which I reported to George Wigg.

I learned today that Bevins was never shown a copy of the Ryland Report. He thus left the office without ever knowing that two of his most senior officials had recommended that the telephone service be made a nationalised industry. If this is true – and Wratten told me it was – it is the most astonishing revelation about the way in which the Office treats its Ministers.

Monday 6 December

To the Post Office this morning where Downes and Sir John Ricks came to discuss my request that on the back of envelopes to Rhodesia we should put a little stamp showing the time, wavelength and duration of BBC medium wave broadcasts from the new transmitter in Bechuanaland. Ricks was obstructive and said we had no power, nothing could be done about it, it would take four weeks and we could be taken to court, and he relied upon a judgement by Quintin Hogg's father in 1923, which said that the PMG could not put advertising material on envelopes. My contempt for lawyers grows every day. They are simply not concerned with what is required and how it can be done but on searching the entrails of the tribe to see every conceivable reason why things shouldn't be done.

Thursday 9 December

I had my first informal talk to the Post Office staff at Fleet Building. 1,500 people had balloted for tickets and only about 300 were able to be accommodated. The whole thing was a little bit stiff and formal. It was different from having a political candidate speaking at a public meeting, as I was the boss. But I think the experiment was a success and I intend to repeat it.

This evening we had our weekly political dinner party at home: Dick Crossman, Gerald Kaufman, Marcia Williams, Tommy Balogh and Peter Shore. The main discussion was about the date of the General Election. Dick was strongly in favour of postponing the Hull by-election and going in March. I am against that and think we should probably carry on, unless the prospect is absolutely disastrous (and I'm not sure it is that). We do better the longer we are in power. I don't think the public want an Election. Dick was wildly political and said that what we needed was a really fraudulent Budget, but fears a really tough one from a Crippsian Callaghan. Tommy thinks that it will be necessary to take another £100 million out of the economy in the coming year to keep the pressure down but if that is all that is at stake, I can't see the reason why we shouldn't ride the storm. Then of course the local elections won't be too good and there is the risk of losing another Member and actually finding our parliamentary majority gone.

I came under heavy fire from Marcia for having decided to prosecute the pirates. The sooner I can get out my policy statement on sound broadcasting, the better. I am strongly in favour of having a pop channel, but letting the profits accrue to us and help to keep the BBC licence fee down. I think this will be acceptable now.

Saturday 11 December

This evening Stephen had a party with his friends. They just bumped about and giggled like a lot of colts. The record player blared out and I could see my ceiling rising and falling by about two inches with the dancing above. Meanwhile I dictated letters and brought my diary up to date.

"WE SHALL NOT STAND IDLY BY!"

Confronting the pirate radio enemy in 1965.

Sunday 12 December

This morning I went to see Joe Cort who is passing through London with his four children on the way to take up his chair of medicine in Canada. His wife Ruth, who has disseminated sclerosis, went back to America four months ago and is apparently slightly improved as the result of treatment there. Joe himself was hounded out of America by the McCarthyites as a Communist and is driven back to America by his wife's illness, having won his case at the Supreme Court to restore his American citizenship.

I had wondered whether, in fact, MI5 would report on my visit to his house. But dismissing these thoughts from my mind, I went to see him and caught up with his news. He is a real wandering Jew. His father, Boris Korotky, was an officer in the Czarist army. His uncle was shot by Stalin as a Trotskyite in the 1937 purge and his other three uncles were killed in the Red Army in the Second World War. It is a fantastic story and I feel sure it is not over yet.

After lunch at home I heard Radio 390 which was broadcasting a recorded appeal by the managing director for people to write to me in a protest against my decision to prosecute the pirates. The telephone rang shortly afterwards and it was Harold Wilson who had been listening to the same programme and he was extremely worried.

I told him that we were making progress on the broadcasting White Paper with its proposals for advertising on the Light Programme and the establishment of municipally owned local radio stations which might even help to make a profit to reduce rates. He was clearly relieved. He indicated that I shouldn't prosecute at this stage.

Monday 13 December
To the EDC this morning where the new investment grants were discussed. From there I went to the greetings cards manufacturers' exhibition and made a short speech. They are hopping mad about the standardisation of envelopes and extremely worried – so they say – about my proposal for a Post Office Christmas card. I decided to brazen it out and said that we had been in the greetings business for over a century. To confirm this, I produced a number of our greetings telegrams at which they booed cheerfully. Afterwards, talking to them and looking at their hideous cards, I came to dislike them even more. One of them made a particular point of attacking charity Christmas cards because of the inroads that they might make into their business. This, despite the fact that they print and sell a thousand million Christmas cards a year. Pressure groups with a narrow financial interest are hideous.

Back to the Office where about 700 postcards and letters had come in as the result of Radio 390's appeal. There were certain continuing themes. First of all, the listeners hated the BBC because of its facetious announcers and the middle class tone of the programmes. They wanted music and not chatter. Secondly, quite a number of them would be perfectly happy if only the BBC Light Programme would provide them with this type of broadcast. Thirdly, it was obvious none of them knew the reason for the announcement I had to make. I decided therefore to write a standard letter and have it sent back to everyone who had written to me. It would certainly do the BBC a great deal of good to read these letters and postcards and I think I may send them to Frank Gillard, the head of sound broadcasting. It was also clear that the political pressures that would build up against a prosecution of the pirates would be difficult. *The Times* had a bitchy *Sunday Express*-type article saying that I was 'damaging my image' by this action.

Tuesday 14 December
To the Christmas press conference at the Western District Office. I had had it moved there to try to change the superior image created by Mount Pleasant.

Dinner at Number 10. Harold couldn't join us as he was with the Nigerian Prime Minister but Mary Wilson and Brenda Dew and

Marcia were there, as well as Dick, Tommy, Peter and Gerald. We had a splendid discussion about the political situation. Marcia thinks it was a great mistake for Harold to have gone to Rhodesia. Dick is still in favour of a March Election but the leak in the *Sunday Express* that he was an advocate of an early Election has more or less killed it in Harold's mind. I am in favour of going on. Gerald was critical of my pirates' prosecution. I showed him the draft letter and he made one or two suggestions.

Wednesday 15 December
To the Executive this morning. We got through the business in half an hour and there was some discussion about pit closures which George Brown dealt with.

This afternoon I came first for parliamentary questions and there were ninety-five questions down – an all-time record for the Post Office. I had a rough run but did much better than on previous occasions.

The pirate letters are continuing to flood in and there must now be 2,000 or more. I decided to make it clear that there would be a gap between the warning and the prosecution of the pirates and I think the prosecutions cannot begin until after the White Paper on broadcasting. But it was necessary to make a statement about prosecutions in order to take the heat off the Foreign Office which is under heavy pressure from European countries.

Thursday 16 December
All morning at the Post Office attending a seminar on reorganising the postal services on the basis of a fast and slow service. Mr McDougall, the new Head of the Postal Planning Branch, presented it very well. At the end I tried to force them to a decision.

I had a long talk to Jennie Lee at the House. She is having exactly the same difficulties with her civil servants that I'm having with mine. She has a plan for a Government-managed corporation to run the fourth channel, which will provide outlets for her University of the Air and give scope for entertainment programmes from 8 pm onwards which should supply the revenue to finance her University. I think we are working on the same lines. We both agreed that the officials were delaying everything and thought that we should go and have a chat to Harold.

Friday 17 December
This afternoon we had the Post Office Board for three hours. The first item of interest was a paper from the DG suggesting that because of the difficulties in which the Post Office found itself it would be

unwise to proceed with publication of our 'Aims and Purposes of the Post Office'. I take a perfectly contrary view. The greater the difficulties in which we find ourselves, the more necessary to get clear what our aims and purposes are. I therefore said I would raise this with the staff representatives in January and intend to go ahead with it and publish the information in the annual White Paper on Post Office prospects.

The second paper was on hidden subsidies which revealed the most astonishing information about the extent to which we do subsidise other departments. It includes £46,000 for postal and telephone services for the royal family, £1.4 million as a result of our decision not to force Post Office civil servants to claim sickness benefit due to them and £8 million which is the effective subsidy that we are paying to the airways in higher charges than are strictly justified to carry our airmail. I insisted that all this information should be published in the same prospects White Paper.

Monday 20 December
Today the top-level ministerial committee on Rhodesia rejected the Order in Council allowing me to put 'Devices and words that the PMG thinks proper' on to letters to Rhodesia to publicise the BBC transmitter wavelengths.

Tuesday 21 December
James Fitton and Paul Reilly of the Stamp Advisory Committee came to see me. They have been extremely irritated by my commissioning the Gentleman album and also by the fact that I have not always accepted their recommendations on stamps. Sir John Wilson, Keeper of the Queen's Philatelic Collection, had told them that the Queen would never accept stamps without her head on them. I described frankly what had happened at my audience in March and Paul Reilly said with some feeling, 'There have certainly been second thoughts since then.' The plain fact is that I shan't get the Queen's head off the stamps and it's probably rather foolish of me to go on knocking my head against a brick wall.

Afterwards the General Directorate came to lunch in my room and we had a jolly time discussing almost everything but the Post Office.

Wednesday 22 December
To see Mother early this morning, then to the Commons where I waited all day for the debate on television standards. Hilary and Joshua came and sat under the Gallery to listen. Only about ten Members were present but it was an opportunity to explain why it is that a Postmaster General can't intervene in programme content.

I heard that Richard Dimbleby was dying and Granada asked me to record a tribute to him.

Back home about 7.30. The Cabinet reshuffle was announced this evening. Barbara Castle is to be Minister of Transport in place of Tom Fraser and Roy Jenkins Home Secretary. I am quite happy to be at the Post Office for a few more months to carry out the changes that I have started. Yesterday I sent a long letter to Harold reporting on the Post Office in 1966 and giving him an idea of what was coming. It didn't call for any decisions but I thought there was no harm in making a private report to him.

Thursday 23 December
Shopping this morning. Mother had her hip operation and is all right.

Afterwards I went to the Post Office typing pool to say Happy Christmas. Then to the Post Office Tower where we had a private office party for about eighty people, including the children. We had a lovely view from the top of the Tower and then tea. Joshua disappeared after tea and I walked up four flights and along various corridors, asking if anyone had seen him. Finally a man said, 'I did see a little boy with long hair and long trousers who said that the lift needed oiling.' It was Joshua. There he was coming down in the lift, having been up to the top of the Tower.

Friday 24 December
Jim Callaghan rang me up this morning to tell me that he had seen a note in the paper about a businessman called Leonard Machin who had been unable to get an urgent export to Australia because he had been told by the GPO that all calls to Australia had been booked up for greetings for three days. I finally tracked him down in Jersey, asked him for the number he wanted, fixed with my office for him to get his call and by 11 o'clock he had it. I rang Jim Callaghan to thank him. Then I rang back Machin and he was absolutely delighted. He promised that he would tell the press how wonderful we had been. It's about time we did have good publicity.

This afternoon the Christmas ritual began. We went to our neighbour, Mrs Chambers, and then on to Dave and June's and back via the hospital where Mother is, and to see the candles in Campden Hill Square. Then this evening Caroline and I decorated the tree. It is our thirteenth Christmas in Holland Park Avenue and we are very fond of it.

Saturday 25 December

Big family party at home. This evening we had our phone call from Cincinnati. After everyone else was in bed, Hilary and I went out with two bottles of whisky and visited the Trafalgar Square Post Office and the King Edward Building Post Office, both of which are open twenty-four hours a day. I think it was appreciated.

Monday 27 December

This afternoon the press rang to find out details of the incident in which Machin got his telephone call to Australia. We shall get a little credit for it.

Tuesday 28 December

Up early this morning and drove to Stansgate. The place was icy cold and within a few minutes of getting there the main electricity fuse went. So we had no light, heat or power. I rang the Electricity Board and they were there within three hours. After that we huddled round electric fires we'd brought from London and managed to get the central heating going, which gradually took the chill off the house. The place was in a terrible muck and we more or less camped but it was pleasant to get away from London and Stansgate is about the only place where I can relax and forget about the Post Office and politics and almost everything else.

Wednesday 29 December

This morning I came up to London to have lunch with the Japanese Ambassador. Wesil, Jones and Wratten came too – the four of us who are going to Japan on Sunday. The Ambassador was accompanied by some members of his staff. It was a rather inconclusive lunch since the diplomatic people knew nothing about posts and telephones and I knew nothing about Japan.

Afterwards I went back to Stansgate.

Thursday 30 December

Back to London this morning and this afternoon I went into the Office with Stephen and Hilary and seven friends. Mr Pitman the controller of the foreign section at King Edward Building took them round the sorting office, down to see the railway and then to see the Roman wall. Afterwards I gave them tea.

The Director General has sent me another minute strongly recommending that we don't reorganise the management until the status is settled. This is becoming an extremely obstinate clash of wills between him and me. But it can wait till I get back from Japan. Also he had produced a minute from the Prime Minister recommending Beattie Plummer for membership of the ITA but he simply mentioned my recommendation and then at length listed Lord Hill's objections to having a Party politician and a peer. How Hill has the affrontery to do it I don't know. But since I know that Harold wants Beattie Plummer I didn't bother to change the minute.

There was another minute from Sir John Ricks saying that it was impossible for me to dispense with licences to sell stamps since this was specifically provided for in the 1891 statute. In recent years dispensations have been given for hotels and hospitals and frankly the whole thing is a lot of nonsense. How I hate lawyers! They regard their function always as being to obstruct.

Friday 31 December
As I dictate this I can hear the television upstairs and Big Ben has just struck midnight. 1965 is over.

It has been a good and busy year but I think the lesson I must learn now is to concentrate more on the essentials of my job. It is tempting in the Post Office to spend a great deal of time on stamps, design and details and to allow these to crowd out the important managerial, financial and administrative matters. Having battled with the department for twelve months I am becoming much more modest about what is possible and should be lucky if I leave the department having made one or two really major changes. These must be a change of status, and a change of management structure and perhaps the beginning of a reshaping of the postal services to meet sharply rising costs. All the rest must take second place.

Secondly, I must try to take more trouble with the press. I have a great contempt for it but it is a powerful influence in society and no one who is interested in the politics of a parliamentary democracy can afford to ignore it. Touting round and giving lunches and being friendly with the hope of getting a good press is something that is hard to combine with self-respect but as a realist, I recognise that this does have to be done and I shall try in 1966 to see that what I am working on is more clearly understood.

Next I think I must put my vendetta with the Palace into cold storage. Whatever my views may be, it is clear that Harold's intentions are that we should be more royal than the Tory Party and he finds the Queen a very useful tool. This may give him a certain short-term advantage and he is exploiting it as hard as he can. I doubt whether he is so foolish as to be taken in by smiles from the Queen and the flunkeys at Buckingham Palace and for that I am grateful. But I am sure that in the long run his attitude simply strengthens the reactionary elements in our society and cannot help those who want to make change.

It is obvious that I shall have to abandon my hopes of getting the Queen's head off the stamps. *Private Eye* had a superb cartoon this week about pornographic stamps which sold like hot cakes but which led to disaster because in one issue – by a printing error – the monarch's head had been omitted. I'm not sure that *Private Eye* isn't right.

Sunday 2 January 1966

To the airport with Wratten. The Japanese diplomats had come to see me off. Mr Jones and Mr Wesil were also there and we boarded the VC10 at about 11 o'clock. I worked on my brief most of the way across the Atlantic.

The captain invited me into his cabin for the last part of the journey and I sat right behind him as he came into New York. The cloud was very low and I saw the co-pilot scrabbling through written instructions as to how to approach the city and heard the crackle of the radio giving instructions. The landing was exactly like a wartime landing in an old plane. It absolutely shook my confidence in the improvements that have been made in flying in the last twenty years. Indeed as we landed, the co-pilot said, 'I think we turn left near the hotel and try to find our way to the terminal building from there.'

We were met by BOAC and Government officials who swept us through customs and kindly arranged for us to catch an earlier flight for San Francisco. It is incredible to think one can get from London to San Francisco in one day. Increasingly when I come back to America I feel what a very old civilisation it is. There are so many newer countries in the world that America, as the oldest republic in the world, has become established and almost conservative.

Monday 3 January

Up early, breakfast at 6.30 and read the *San Francisco Chronicle*. This was full of highly critical articles about Vietnam, most intelligently written. It is a great deal better than most English provincial morning newspapers. The rest of the party went out sightseeing this morning and I went to buy some books about Japan.

The plane took off at 7 pm for Honolulu. It was a six-hour trip. We were taken to the Royal Hawaiian Hotel which was built in the thirties and is in the grand style. I went for a brief walk along the Waikiki beach. The moon was up and there were all the hotels stretching out along the bay towards Diamond Head.

Tuesday 4 January
Up at 6 o'clock this morning and had breakfast on the beach.

The British Consul collected us in his car and took us round the island. It is beautiful with some high hills covered in green foliage right to the peaks. The American influence is absolutely dominant with no signs whatsoever of any previous local civilisation, although flat-faced Polynesians are to be seen everywhere. The main source of revenue is the tourist trade, followed by Pearl Harbour (which is particularly busy with the Vietnam war) and lastly the growing and selling of pineapples.

We took off at 1 pm in the same BOAC Boeing 707 for Japan. It was at this stage in our journey that all sense of time disappeared. As we took off we put our watches back five hours to 7 am and six hours later, as I was sitting talking to the captain on the flight deck, the day changed from Tuesday 4 January to Wednesday 5 January. I must therefore stop this day's diary in the middle of the day and start again.

Wednesday 5 January
The day started in the middle. We continued our flight on to Japan, arriving there at about 4.30, local time. At the airport there was a tremendous crowd to meet us: the Ambassador, Sir Francis Rundall, had come with members of his staff; Mr Kohri, the Japanese Minister of Posts and Telecommunications; Mr Tanaka, the Vice-Minister; Mr Kaya from the Ministry of Foreign Affairs; and representatives from Japan's International Telephone Corporation and the Broadcasting Corporation. There were about five men with movie cameras and flashlights and they walked backwards in front of us so that one of them fell right over, which led to a great deal of giggling. Everybody bowed low as we went and the tough little Japanese police thrust people back in a most determined way.

We exchanged courtesies and then the Ambassador bundled me up into his Rolls Royce with the union jack flying and, preceded by a white police car with a red light flashing and horn wailing, the procession of vehicles started the eleven-mile journey into Tokyo along the new super-highway. We could see Mount Fuji on the skyline eighty miles away. It was dark as we came into Tokyo and to our hotel, the Imperial.

The Ambassador stayed for a moment and told me that my visit had greatly flattered the Japanese. They really were pleased that the world recognised their achievements and would bend over backwards to help me in every way they could. We also briefly discussed the Vietnam war. The Ambassador said that the Japanese were particularly anxious to avoid a confrontation between the United States and

China, mainly because it would interrupt their trading activities. He was rather cynical about them and said that their interest in trade was such that they tried to contract out of all conflicts and that this simply was not possible for a country that was now the fifth largest industrial power in the world. He said that he had had to put considerable pressure on them to get them to stop trading with Rhodesia. He also said that they were getting a bad name with the Afro-Asians because of the high level of their trade with South Africa.

After he had gone Mr Ellingworth, the head of Chancery and Mr Hohler, the Ambassador's private secretary, stayed for a while to discuss my programme with Wratten, Wesil and Jones. Although they were exceptionally respectful and called me 'sir' every two minutes, they were at the same time rather bored and shocked, I thought, to have anything to do with the Post Office, which from their point of view must be the most unimportant Government department ever. They behaved rather like Eton schoolmasters at a meeting with some minor grammar school group. Indeed the whole atmosphere reminded me of a visit to Eton. There was the bluff pipe-smoking jovial Ambassador, looking rather seedy but fundamentally decent, and round him these effete-looking men. It is the final end of the public school man now that the Empire has gone – to finish up in British Embassies around the world, representing all that is least dynamic about British society, although no doubt they have first-rate intellects and a fundamental decency.

After they had gone, the four of us went out for a walk along Z Avenue and Ginza Street and we saw the flashing neon signs of Tokyo. This is the last day of the New Year holiday and many of the girls were wearing kimonos; they looked charming.

Thursday 6 January
Nine o'clock in the Embassy car to the compound just opposite the Imperial palace where the Ambassador and most of his staff live and work. Four or five members of the Ambassador's staff were there and the four of us. The Ambassador's study was panelled and dark. The other FO men became increasingly like schoolmasters. There was the tall thin ascetic-looking one – Ellingworth – who was probably the senior classics master. There was the big ruddy man – Figgess – who looked like the maths and rugby expert. Then there were the two prefects – Hohler and another private secretary who had long hair and kept crossing and uncrossing his legs and calling everybody 'sir'. The conversation was unbelievably stilted and the collective lack of dynamism unbearable. Many meaningful glances were exchanged between them and we felt in outer darkness. They're still puzzled by our arrival and do not quite know what to make of the whole business.

With the Ambassador in his Rolls Royce, again with a white police car flashing and screaming ahead of us, we went to visit the Minister of Posts and Telecommunications, Mr Kohri. When we got to his department, there was a fresh group of newsmen and flash photographers and people walking and bowing backwards as we went into the lift and entered the Minister's room.

Mr Kohri greeted us and we sat down in a little circle. He began by drawing attention to an ashtray in porcelain on the table and I thought it was a gift. Actually it was just a way of passing the time. He drew attention to it as a special piece of Japanese pottery but added with typical modesty, 'Do look at this rather worthless piece of china.'

Then a whole series of senior officials were brought up in line, shook hands and bowed to me and then shook hands with the others. These were all under-secretaries and were treated like schoolboys getting a prize. They then withdrew and sat in the background while Mr Kohri addressed me in English in a prepared speech in which he described his pleasure at our visit.

I replied briefly to say how much we appreciated his reception and how anxious we were to learn from Japanese experience. Then he gave me the most beautiful stamp album and I gave him our rather indifferent one. He received it with great delight and said that he had been watching with interest the rapid development of British stamps which no longer consisted solely of pictures of the Queen's head but were getting bigger and included new and more varied items of design. It was the first time I had had a compliment about our new stamp programme and I valued it a great deal.

Mr Kohri joined me for a lunch party and after lunch we sat in a room in which there was a tape recorder, and we had a discussion about various postal problems which was intended for reproduction in the magazine *The Post*, circulated among communication and postal workers. The Minister made a particular point of mentioning the hardworking postal staff and his desire to do justice to them. I realised then that he was hoping to use my visit to improve his relations with the unions, with whom he has had many difficulties. I therefore took advantage of this comment by him to say how close the relations were with the unions in Britain, how I attended the conferences of both the major unions, had regular meetings with the staff leaders and were bringing them into long-term planning.

At 6.15 we left the Ministry, exhausted and an hour and a quarter behind schedule. We had a quarter of an hour to freshen up in the hotel and then went off to a Japanese restaurant in a particular quarter of the town where the Minister was waiting to greet us again and to entertain us to a traditional Japanese dinner, complete with geisha.

The geisha girls were bowing as we went in. We took off our shoes, put on slippers and climbed up the stairs and into a room where we sat with the women standing and bringing us drinks and bowing and scraping. A few minutes later we went into the dining room which was absolutely plain except for a very low table and on each side were cushions with the backs of chairs behind them and separate arm rests which was on the floor, entirely matted with tami mats. The geisha girls, aged from twenty to about sixty, then gathered round and knelt between our seats. There were thirty of them (each being paid up to £20 for one evening of work) and they were dressed in kimonos with huge stiff hairstyles that I understood later were in fact wigs. Their faces were completely whitened with chalk, their lips were bright red and they would have been picked up in ten seconds if they had put their faces out of a door in London. They leaned across, put the food on our lacquered wooden plates, gave us saki – rice wine – to drink in tiny egg cups, and tried to make conversation. It was the ultimate in feminine humiliation and I was most embarrassed by the whole thing.

I had been allocated one called Maryanne who was about my age. She told me that she had been a geisha since she was eighteen, that she was a Catholic, that she lived with her mother and her chronically ill sister and that she worked through the geisha house which acted as an agent for her in the particular district where the restaurant was. Halfway through the meal some girls played three-string balalaikas and there was some formal stiff fan-dancing by two of the other girls and then later some singing. I'm glad to have seen it once but I would never want to do it again.

Back to the hotel at 10.30, where the four of us had a serious conference going over the work of the day.

Friday 7 January
At 10 o'clock we went to the National Telephone Corporation (NTT) where we were greeted by the president, Dr Yonezawa. I presented him with the Trimphone and we sat down to talk. He made many points, among which several were particularly relevant. The division of telephones from posts has helped the growth of the telephone service because it has permitted greater flexibility of organisation: it took three years to disentangle. There is no accountability to the Diet for day-to-day management, only limited control by the Minister covering loan policy, but the Diet has to approve tariffs by full legislation. After that the president has absolute power. The Corporation, which is entirely publicly-owned, seeks harmony between

public service and commercial enterprise and all profits are ploughed back into the business.

At 12.30 we had lunch with Sir Francis and Lady Rundall in the British Embassy. Also there were Mr Colin Harris, the senior counsellor and his French-born wife. The Ambassador told me that he and his wife had seventeen servants to look after the two of them. Mrs Harris said that it was wonderful that the British Embassy had one more staff than the American Ambassador and it was important to make the Japanese realise how important Britain was. Sir Francis went to great pains to explain that the Foreign Office drew its people from all sections of the community – 'We had one boy here from a grammar school – although of course he went through Oxbridge because Oxbridge gets the best people.' Quite what hope there is of altering the image of Britain abroad while our diplomatic representatives continue to be of this kind, I do not know.

After lunch we went to the KDD, which is the separate International Telephone Corporation. This is private enterprise, and is extremely profitable. They said that they were separate from NTT because the amount of capital was limited under Government auspices, the Government link might be embarrassing in dealing with countries abroad and that whereas the domestic telephone system was a monopoly, overseas was mainly a business matter and should be handled by businessmen. They told us that they thought it might be better if NTT were also a private company.

From there we went at about 4 o'clock to NHK, the Broadcasting Corporation. We sat in a long room, on opposite sides of the table as is customary in Japan. The Corporation is similar to the BBC in structure and has a Commission appointed by the Government which is the supreme organisation. The finance comes from a listeners' and viewers' fee which is actually voluntary but which the NHK collects from almost everybody in the country by means of collectors who go round every two months. It is making good progress in educational broadcasting and has established a College of the Air.

They treat audience criticism seriously and there are a thousand public meetings all over the country held each year in which executives of NHK meet the audiences and discuss the problems. This basic democratic structure is an interesting one and I shall certainly take it back to the BBC – though I can't see them adopting it.

From NHK we went back to the hotel briefly and then to the airport where Japan Airlines provided us with a free trip to Osaka. It was dark all the way and we flew over the snow-covered slopes of Mount Fuji, illuminated in the moonlight. It was a fantastic sight.

At Osaka we were greeted by Mr John Lloyd, the British consul-general, with all the regional directors of the posts, radio, telecommunications and other organisations lined up at the airport. I gave a brief interview to the local pressman who, because of his deadline, had written and typed out the interview in advance and asked me just to look at it to see if it was all right. I made a few corrections but I think it had actually been printed before we arrived.

To the Osaka Royal Hotel and worked a little, going to bed at about 1.45.

Saturday 8 January
Up early and finished my notes for today's speech to the Economic Federation in Osaka. There were about eighteen ancient businessmen who were the heads of the major companies and the oldest man was over eighty-five. I spoke for about twenty minutes. Then came the questions and almost all of them were about nationalisation. These men, who are engaged in a continual drive for profits and are battling with the trade unions which are now demanding a decent wage, regarded the Labour Government as if it were the Japan Socialist Party. It was like meeting middle Western Republican businessmen in the United States. I don't know if I did any good but I talked frankly and explained our new attitude towards public enterprise and participation.

Afterwards to lunch, Japanese-style, with the governor of Osaka, Mr Sato, the deputy mayor and others. Mr Sato was formerly a Buddhist priest, is a philosopher, and was once Minister of Defence. He was a charming man.

From there we drove straight to Kyoto which took us about an hour and a half. The British consul-general came with us. The fact is that these British officials cling to you like limpets and you never meet any Japanese. It's like the royal family – wherever you go you only meet other members of the royal family. It's good of the officials to accompany us but we miss half the value of it. Lloyd seemed an arrogant man who behaves as if he were Lord Mountbatten: personally very pleasant, courteous, but extremely superior in the way he behaves to the Japanese. This comes, I think, from having been here before the war.

In Kyoto we saw one of the beautiful wooden Buddhist temples and then went on to the Kyoto central post office.

Then to the Miyako Hotel where we had half an hour for a cup of tea and a rest before going out to dinner as guests of the six regional directors in a perfectly beautiful restaurant with a formal garden approached up a hill. Kyoto has 3,000 geisha girls as against 200 in Tokyo. The food was as usual – better to look at than to eat. But the atmosphere with the postal people was one of great camaraderie and good feeling. The *maikos* (young trainee geishas of about sixteen or seventeen) were far more amusing than the geishas we had met before and after they had done their fan dancing the regional director of posts – an extremely cheerful and amusing man who looked exactly like a Buddha – went on the stage, knelt down next to the woman playing the balalaika and began singing vigorously himself. This led the chief of the postal inspection bureau to disappear for a moment and come back dressed as a samurai with a sword and do a samurai sword dance. I cannot quite imagine the officials of the Post Office participating enthusiastically in an entertainment of this kind. This led to demand for a song from the English visitors so we sang 'Lloyd George knew my father – father knew Lloyd George', followed by 'Bless 'em all'. The geisha girls knew 'You are my sunshine' and began singing. The whole thing was very jolly.

Sunday 9 January
At 9.30 we set off from the Miyako Hotel on a day of sightseeing. We began by visiting the Katsura Imperial Villa which was built about 300 years ago for the eldest son of the Emperor, with the most beautiful Japanese garden to be found in the country. It was extraordinarily peaceful and although every aspect of it was artificial the effect was to create a sense of carelessness that belied the incredible precision of every part of it.

After that we went to the Kokedera Temple, founded in 1731 with a garden that contains nearly a hundred different types of moss. The abbot, the Reverend Kaikó Fugita, took us round. I think that all religious ceremonies have more or less dried up and he lives on the considerable profits of the tourist trade.

We then went to the Heian Shrine where I got my fortune told and Mr Ishakawa translated it to say that the moon would show the road ahead for me!

Finally to the Kinkakuju Pavillion, built in 1397 as a villa for one of the Shoguns and later converted into a Zen temple. This is the famous golden pavillion which was in fact reconstructed in 1950 after it had been burned down by a Japanese Buddhist monk who was jealous of its beauty.

Then to the station, to return to Tokyo on the superb new Tokaido Express train. This does the 350 mile journey to Tokyo in less than three hours. We tested the radio telephone on board.

Monday 10 January
At 9.30 we went to the board room of the NTT building for about two hours of further discussion.

Then to the Fukuday Restaurant for lunch given by the president of NTT. At the end we were given the most beautiful lacquered vases and plates and Dr Yonezawa's book on the microwave circuit on which the Japanese are far ahead of us. The meal looked beautiful and tasted horrible, as is usually the case.

We spent the afternoon at the Tokyo telegraph office and the television relay centre and at 7 o'clock we went to the Korinkaku Restaurant for a dinner given by the presidents of NTT, NHK and KDD. Afterwards there were some wonderful Japanese dances including the chrysanthemum dance, the cherry-blossom dance and some samurai and geisha dancing. We have two more days of work and then the plane home. It certainly has been immensely worthwhile.

Tuesday 11 January

At 2.30 we drove to the Nippon Electric Company works where we saw a film on postal mechanisation. The segregator was a complete copy of our Thristle-Elliott machine and the letter sorter and stamp canceller had been bought directly from the Germans. It was rather irritating to see the Japanese selling what is basically our equipment and was the only example of actual copying that we came across.

After that we drove in the car to the Nippon Tamagawa factory and during the journey I had a chance of talking to the president of Nippon at great length.

He told us that he had decided to join with the American Hughes Aircraft Company which is the principal agent for Comsat and has prepared the Early Bird satellite. Although Nippon Electric are enormous, they felt that they needed the umbrella of the Hughes Aircraft and have set up a subsidiary company studying multiple access. Later, in the factory, we saw the Star System which is being worked on by Dr Rosen of Hughes Aircraft and Dr Morito, the chief development engineer of Nippon Electric. This provides almost unlimited multiple access on Early Bird with very little modification to the satellite which becomes in effect a switchboard in the sky. The control apparatus has to be on one of the ground stations but if this system is adopted by Comsat it will give the Japanese an enormous advantage over British manufacturers, who are still fooling about wondering what possibilities exist.

Moreover, if multiple access comes in there will be far more ground stations than would otherwise be necessary because almost every country could justify having one and might even find some use for satellite transmission across areas of their own countries. So not only will there probably be more than a hundred tracking stations all over the world, but the Japanese and Americans are likely to get the contracts for all of them. This will give them a lead into the telecommunications industries of the countries concerned and Britain would more or less be out in the cold. That is what I tried to get across to British manufacturers a year ago but they absolutely refuse to form a consortium and are busy competing with each other for a market that simply doesn't exist for them.

The link between telecommunications and computers was very important in Nippon Electric. In general I got the feeling that their factory was more efficiently run than any British factory that I have attended. The export sales manager who drove back with us in the car said that fifteen years ago they were busy coming to England to study what Standard Telephones & Cables were doing but now were so far ahead that frankly they had nothing to learn either from England or America. I have a feeling that they are right. It is impossible to overlook the fact that the competition from Japan in the future is going to be formidable. British manufacturers would be well advised to alert themselves to this.

In two respects I was angry. One was to hear the president say that the pulse code modulation (invented by a British engineer twenty years ago) was the best system in the world and to know that Nippon Electric were producing it already for NTT whereas in Britain we were still footling with the field trial. The other annoying thing was that Dr Rosen of Hughes Aircraft admitted to the president that he had got the idea of communications satellites from Arthur Clarke, the British science fiction writer, in 1945 and here again Britain had been trailing behind. Our great weakness is the gap between invention and development and we simply have to close it.

Today's news of the death of Prime Minister Shastri of India just after concluding the Kashmir agreement with Ayub Khan is tragic.

Wednesday 12 January
Up early and at 8 o'clock three British newspaper correspondents came to see me from *The Times*, the *Financial Times* and the *Telegraph/Economist*. A fourth man from Reuters didn't turn up. They were obviously still skeptical about our trip so we told them of our studies in posts, telephones, broadcasting and organisation and tried to indicate that it had been immensely worthwhile from our point of view.

We spent the day at NHK TV and radio training school.

At 6.45 we all went to dinner at the British Embassy. There were a number of interesting people there and when they left at 9.30 the Ambassador suggested that we sit down and have a little talk about our trip with his staff. It was clear from the discussion that the Embassy had been extremely impressed by the amount of energy we had put into our visit and that much of this had fed back to them from the Japanese side. I think we really did create an impression of dynamism and the Ambassador was pleased because it has expanded his contacts into wider fields. He said he would be interested to get a copy of the report that we will write. I must admit I rather warmed to the Ambassador this evening. He was very jovial and I think was pleased with us which naturally made me feel rather more amicably disposed towards him. I thanked him for his help and said how much we'd appreciated the services offered by the Embassy.

It is now almost Thursday morning and the day after tomorrow I shall be home. This has been the most crowded fortnight I ever remember and enormously worthwhile. For me the most interesting and important part of the visit has been the study of a divided administration. NTT, the telecoms side, is obviously successful and posts is extremely inefficient, partly because it is a Government department and is just incapable of acting rapidly enough to cope with the problems that face it. This has completely solidified my thinking on the organisation of the Post Office and I intend to press ahead with this as hard as I possibly can.

Thursday 13 January
At 10.30 we set off in a procession to the airport, headed by the white police car. There was a tremendous committee of people to see us off but not including the Minister who was busy with the budget.

Friday 14 January
At 4.15 we caught a BOAC flight 921 from Hong Kong and climbed high above the city, cut along the China coast and crossed Vietnam near the border between the South and North. I went into the cabin to talk to the flight crew and they said that they could often see firing and ships from the American fleet and even aircraft engagements. But we were at 35,000 feet above it all and we could see nothing below.

We arrived at Delhi at 10 o'clock. John Freeman[6] was waiting with his Rolls and we got through the formalities without the slightest difficulty. He was just the same John Freeman, looking incredibly immaculate and just like a Foreign Office man. He described Shastri's funeral and said that Mountbatten had come with a retinue of nine people and George Brown had come with one.

He confirmed that Indo-British relations were severely strained and that Wilson's statement in September criticising the Indians for crossing the line in the war with Pakistan had been extremely unpopular. According to John, Kosygin said bluntly that he expected the Indians and Pakistanis to stop their fighting and concentrate on keeping the Chinese out on their northern border. This is the real explanation of the Soviet interest in ending the Kashmir dispute.

John took the view that China represented a long-term serious threat and he also said that the Russian interest was to disengage the British from India. I said that surely the Russians were working with us in the sense that they were trying to improve Indo-Pakistan relations and were trying to play some part in ending the Vietnam war. John agreed in part but was speaking of Russia in the old Cold War language and of China in language that was even more unpleasant. He thought that the West simply had to contain China and that if the Americans got out of Vietnam then the Chinese would certainly take over.

We had a talk about Harold who had evidently done brilliantly at the Lagos conference on Rhodesia. John thought that Harold was a new Lloyd George and immensely clever and was debasing the monarchy by using it. When Heath had been in Delhi recently he had admitted frankly to John that he was finding it difficult to deal with Wilson. John hoped that Harold would visit India and felt sure that he would do well if he did.

Back to the hotel and bed at 1 o'clock.

Saturday 15 January

We left at about 9.30 and drove past the bullock carts and poor, poor countryside to Delhi airport, which is nothing more than a shack and was absolutely full of incredibly emaciated Indians seeing off a group of immigrants who were coming to Britain for work. We couldn't use the VIP room because the Vice-President of the UAR was leaving by the same plane. The contrast between the standard of living in India and in Japan is most marked. Somehow as other countries get richer year by year, the poverty of India seems more shocking. It is hard to see how they are going to lift themselves out of it.

At 10 o'clock we caught the Air India Boeing 707 headed for London.

About an hour before we got to Beirut, I wrote a little note to the UAR Vice-President saying that I heard he was travelling on the same plane and I had many Egyptian friends including Fawzi, who was once Foreign Minister. I handed the letter to the guard and was invited back to meet the Vice-President.

He is a handsome, rather dapper man of about fifty and had been one of the original colonels in charge of the cavalry at the time of General Neguib's take-over of Egypt in 1953. I told him that Father and Mother had visited President Nasser and he knew about Father's negotiations in 1946.* I told him how much we admired the progress

---

* My father, as Secretary of State, headed the Labour Government delegation visiting Cairo in 1946 to revise the Anglo-Egyptian Treaty of 1936.

in Egypt and he said that it was essential to catch up with the technology of the West. I said that it was grand for a country with an ancient history to be able to enjoy technological progress, since the earlier civilisation could be made to blossom again and that we in Europe were just barbarians. He was friendly and after about fifteen minutes' talk I shook him by the hand and went back to my seat.

We landed in Beirut and had about an hour there. One of the nicest things was to see a platoon of Canadian troops wearing the blue berets of the UN. One or two of them were also wearing kilts and a big fat corporal played the bagpipes which the Arabs gathered round to listen to, since they play the pipes as well. The UN forces are the only forces I believe in and I could have stood and watched them for ages.

Back home by 8.45 pm where the family was waiting to greet me. By Delhi time it was 3 am and I was pretty punch-drunk with exhaustion. So after giving away my presents, I went to bed just before midnight or 6 am Delhi time.

From the Post Office point of view the trip was enormously worthwhile. We have made many friends among the Japanese and I think that Post Offices as a world community, making possible contact on a person-to-person basis are potentially more important even than the Foreign Offices of the world, which are concerned with the old-fashioned idea of contact between Government and Government.

Tuesday 18 January
At 10.30 the whole general directorate came to hear me give a general report on my visit to Japan. I went over the points of interest on the postal, telecommunications and broadcasting side and paid special attention to the evidence we have seen of high research expenditure by all the bodies we met.

The reaction of the general directorate was interesting. The DG was interested in a bluff sort of way. Ryland and Wolstencroft were extremely absorbed. The Engineer-in-Chief, Barron, was determined to discount everything I said on the basis that we were doing it too, or we knew about it or if they were doing it it wouldn't work or that if we tried it there would be difficulties. I must say this made me sick and I think it was evident to him and to the others that I felt strongly about this attitude.

It confirmed me in two things. First Barron is not the best man for being in charge of the Engineering Department and secondly that the Engineering Department, under any boss, is bound to be inadequate unless it is firmly under the control of the man responsible for the telephone service. You cannot have a separate engineering empire operating in the way in which it does now. I resolved to bring to a head my decision about these two matters when I see the DG in a day or two.

Wednesday 19 January
Post Office Board this morning. It is obvious that the POEU wage claim, which may reach 15 per cent, cannot possibly be justified and we would even have some difficulty in justifying the 3.5 per cent norm. Since we have all received instructions from George Brown and Ray Gunter that support for the incomes policy is more important than conciliation, it looks as if this may well be one of those issues on which there has to be a show-down. I just hope it doesn't come before an Election. Harold will, I think, be the first to crack if this type of confrontation is accepted as a piece of deliberate policy.

The number of failures on STD attributable to the Post Office had risen to 9.9 per cent and over the whole of this last year the situation had been worse than in 1964. The Engineer-in-Chief said this was because the manufacturers couldn't supply us with equipment rapidly enough. I seized on the point of manufacturers' delays and asked how long it would be before things got better. I have some sympathy with the manufacturers because if the programme had been prepared on an adequate scale they would have been able to expand their capacity progressively, instead of finding themselves confronted with this enormous demand at short notice.

Afterwards I caught the train to Hull and went in the freezing weather to speak for the candidate Kevin McNamara. They thought there would be a majority of between 2,500 and 3,000. The second meeting was more packed than the first, with quite a bit of heckling about Vietnam which I managed to silence reasonably effectively.

Back by train to Leeds where I arrived at 11 pm and it was bitterly cold as I went across the windswept station to the unheated sleeping car.

Thursday 20 January
Arrived home about 7.45 am and had a hot bath.

Worked at home this morning, then with Caroline to the House of Lords where we had lunch with Mervyn Stockwood. He looked much better than when I last saw him and although he was rude to Caroline – by ignoring her as he does all women – it was nice to gossip. He told me that Bishop Pike of California was here for six months trying to get over being an alcoholic.

At 5 o'clock the DG came to see me. He described briefly the emergency action that we shall have to take if a threatened railway strike takes place and he apologised for his outburst at the Board meeting yesterday when I had suggested that we might buy some foreign equipment in modernising our plant to meet the soaring demand.

Friday 21 January
This afternoon I went to Bristol for the joint ward meeting of St George East and West. There was a whole series of criticisms of Labour Government policy ranging from Vietnam through to the prices and incomes policy, the failure to provide a new comprehensive school for East Bristol and a number of other things, including increases in the cost of living. I dealt with them as best I could but frankly it was not a representative meeting of Labour voters or even of Labour members. It was the old faithfuls who have turned up for years and helped me win all my elections and are ageing militants characteristic of safe Labour constituencies. I'm sure it's worth having meetings of this kind but one has to see them in perspective.

Monday 24 January
I had a series of meetings this morning about local broadcasting. Firstly, the NUJ are opposed to the idea of local broadcasting but think that if it were done it ought to be done by the BBC so that there would be no loss of advertising revenue to commercial radio stations.

After them came the newspaper proprietors who are also opposed to local broadcasting but think that if it is inevitable, it ought to be done by local commercial radio stations of which the newspapers should become principal shareholders. It is interesting – but not surprising – that everybody looks at national problems from the point of view of their strict personal financial interests.

Olaf Palme, the Minister of Communications in Sweden, telephoned me from Stockholm to ask about pirate radio stations. They are just about to take a much tougher line and had heard rumours that we were going to legalise them. I was able to assure him that this was not true. He told me that he had a broadcasting White Paper coming out at about the same time as mine and that he was also reorganising the postal service. I really would like to go to Stockholm for a couple of days to have a talk to him.

Wednesday 26 January
To Oxford to attend the Nuffield seminar which was great fun, as it always is. My subject was 'On becoming a Minister' and I talked frankly about the experience and said that no book I had ever read on the British constitution had been any help or had given me any indication of what to expect.

Afterwards I had dinner in college and sat next to the Warden, D. N. Chester. He told me that there was a great row in the Civil Service about Barbara Castle's leak that she intends to get rid of her Permanent Secretary. He was frank and said that Ministers could not interfere with staffing 'as they are only temporary'. This exactly confirms what Peter Shore has said in his new book* about temporary versus permanent politicians.

Afterwards I stayed with Marilyn and David Butler.

Friday 28 January
The enormous majority of 5,000 in yesterday's by-election in Hull has created a completely new political situation. Heath is in serious trouble with his own Party and the criticism there is bound to grow. Harold is sitting pretty with a majority restored to its full strength and a retained option on the date of the Election. Peter Shore is in favour of dissolving immediately, Dick Crossman of going in March or May, but I'm not sure Harold will do it. Much of our support in the country now comes from the fact that we are carrying on and we haven't yet written such a firm record as to make it absolutely certain we would be returned. Moreover the Tories and Liberals will now be reluctant to defeat us in the Commons, even if that were possible.

To the Office this morning where I had Mr Gill of External Telecommunications to see me. He has just come back from the International Satellite Committee meeting in Washington. I questioned him keenly about the Japanese development on multiple-access that I had seen at Nippon Electric. He told me that he thought British manufacturers were working on the problem but I remain unconvinced. They are still too busy competing with each other and I just don't believe there is enough fundamental research going on.

Saturday 29 January
This afternoon Caroline, Hilary and I went to the Albert Hall for the political rally addressed by Harold Wilson, Dick Marsh and Bessie Braddock and with Walter Padley in the chair. The speeches were not of very good quality. Hilary met Clem Attlee which will be quite a historic thing for him to remember in his old age.

Tuesday 1 February
I had a talk to Downes about the Post Office Christmas card. He had put in an absolute negative in the best Postal Services department fashion. He came in grim-faced and I talked him out of it. We will have a card with a Christmas stamp and simple greetings, selling at

* *Entitled to Know*, 1966

6d. In addition, we will offer blank stamped cards at the same time to all charities who could then overprint their own message and sell them for a shilling – pocketing the profit or pricing it still higher. This will gravely undercut the greetings card manufacturers, without actually competing with their own lousy products. I know I must keep the pressure up if it is to be done in time.

Later to the Ministerial Committee on Broadcasting, where we discussed the official committee report on the University of the Air. By relying on ITA figures the report had virtually proved that the University of the Air couldn't be broadcast on a future fourth channel without an enormous cost to the Treasury. I was briefed to support this view, but having read my brief made no reference to it. We simply agreed what we wanted – three hours of prime time per day on the fourth channel. It was a great victory for the politicians over the civil servants. If ITA won't do it, we shall set up a new corporation to run the fourth channel over which programme contractors are bound to fight to get access to colour in the time available. The advertising revenue will accrue directly to the corporation which will then buy the programmes and leave time for the University of the Air. The Treasury tried to stop it and will no doubt put up a strong fight. But Harold is committed and God knows it requires courage to take on the big interest groups, who include the *Mirror-Sun* group, and deny them and the public more pure entertainment.

Dick was funny at the committee, denouncing the idea of financing by advertising on the grounds that universities had to have clean money from the Treasury. But of course the Treasury lives on the immoral earnings of drinking, smoking and television advertising and many of our most ancient universities have endowments that bring them the rents from slum property.

Then to dinner at Number 10 with the usual crowd: Harold and Mary, Marcia and Brenda, Dick, Peter, Tommy and Gerald. We didn't talk about the date of the Election but it is clear that Harold is keeping all options open and we discussed the way of drafting a manifesto under the guise of preparing a long-term policy document for presentation at Conference. He told me that he was now convinced about the need for my reorganisation of the Post Office into three parts so I felt cheerful about that.

One thing I learned tonight from Harold: the Foreign Office statement issued when Johnson resumed the bombing of North Vietnam on Monday expressing Her Majesty's Government's 'understanding and support' was not authorised by Harold. He was fuming about it and had sent two serious rockets to Michael Stewart. But did even Michael know? Apparently the Foreign Office put it to Number 10 but Harold's Private Secretary did not put it to Harold.

Wednesday 2 February
More of the family are in bed with flu. I hope my attack can be delayed for a few days.

Spent most of the morning going over my broadcasting White Paper with Lillicrap. During the lunch hour Ryland came to ask me to approve a press notice about the purchase of British Crossbar exchange equipment. The fact is that wrong decisions were taken about exchange equipment years ago when the Post Office tried to leap over Crossbar and go straight to electronics. It was a bright idea but didn't work and it meant maintaining and now even expanding the production of obsolete Strowger equipment which no one else in the world uses, until our electronic exchanges come into operation.

To the Commons for the first meeting of the EDC Ministerial Committee on the status of the Post Office, chaired by Frank Soskice. Everything possible went wrong. My August minutes setting out the case for the change had not been circulated. Whether this was sabotage or inefficiency or both I do not know. Secondly Frank Soskice began by saying that the change of status had been approved in principle and there should not be discussion on the merits. This thoroughly annoyed Diamond, Albu and the others who were there. When I tried to make the case it was purely oral and the whole meeting broke up into arguments about alternative schemes with some favouring one nationalised industry and others the grant of freedom to telecommunications, leaving posts as they are.

After about an hour and a quarter of this I offered to write a new paper and we agreed to meet again. The whole thing must now be salvaged by direct intervention from Harold.

Thursday 3 February
To the Commons to see George Brown. He now claims that he is planning to settle the railway strike and is being stopped by Ray Gunter and Barbara Castle. He behaved monstrously to his officials, sending a senior civil servant out for bottles of gin and whisky and five minutes later ringing his own department in Storey's Gate to find out where the poor chap had gone. He really showed off. George is completely erratic and irrational and an impossible old boozer – rarely being sober after lunch.

Afterwards I went to the Emergencies Committee under Roy Jenkins' chairmanship to discuss plans for dealing with the possible rail strike.

Home at 10 and I knew flu was on its way.

Friday 4 February
Awful night. Woke with a temperature of 102 and stayed at home.
Worked in the basement office part of the morning and afternoon
and telephoned the department about issues that cropped up. It looks
as if I shall miss Chequers on Sunday.

Sunday 6 February
Feeling slightly better and Peter Shore came to collect me to take me
down to Chequers. If he hadn't done this I certainly shouldn't have
got there.

The place was crowded with the whole Cabinet and National
Executive – about sixty in all. Harold started by saying that all
options must be kept open. We were not there to discuss the date of
the Election.

Then George Brown gave a general introduction to the document
that had actually been prepared by Peter but for which Terry Pitt
was most elaborately praised. Tom Driberg queried whether there
would be a statement on overseas policy. Then Jack Jones asked
whether it would be possible to cut defence costs and asked whether
one could divorce defence and foreign policy from economic policy.

After that we came to part one of the document, which was on the
state of the economy. Jim Callaghan said that the debt problem was
not insoluble but he did not expect that the growth rate could be up
to 4 per cent before 1968/9. He asked us not to be impatient and
said we would have to have priorities within the public sector. He
warned us that public expenditure was going up 9 per cent this year
and we had to keep our promises in the Election within limits. He
predicted that tax rates might have to go up and said that personal
taxation was already too high. He rather pooh-poohed the idea of
abolishing the rates because of the burden on the Exchequer.

After him Jack Jones stressed the need for productivity as against
the restriction of incomes. He asked the Cabinet to abandon the early
warning legislation and said that what was required was more worker
participation in management and that management must be prepared
to buy improvements in productivity. He warned us against losing
our Labour image. Bill Simpson suggested that we make a special
place for public enterprise in the document and Jim Callaghan said
that of course steel was beyond dispute.

Then Mikardo spoke about the need for more discriminatory
investment policy. He warned that the Cabinet would not get the
early warning system through the House of Commons since a number
of Labour Members simply would not vote for it. He also wanted the
Industrial Reconstruction Corporation to extend public ownership.

We broke for lunch and I sat opposite Tony Crosland who admitted that he now had some doubts about the binary system for higher education[7] and rather regretted the philosophic speech he had made in defence of the binary system when he had only been at the Ministry a short time.

After lunch Dick made a most effective speech about the need for a policy covering the whole physical environment and the need to share social furniture between different groups. He thought it was ludicrous to have a large playing field for a school and then find the local authority wanted more open space for general recreation, etc.

Barbara then made a speech about transport in which she said that we must democratise car ownership and extend it more widely, spend more on the roads and get the physical integration of freight traffic on rail and road. She wanted to get away from the concept of paying our way in transport.

We then moved on to the social services, where Douglas Houghton talked about the need to re-examine family allowances and to rationalise social payments with fiscal policy. He warned us that social security – especially pensions – was mainly concerned with women, since 5.5 million out of the 7.5 million pensioners were women. Crosland said a word about school building and how difficult it was to provide new schools to replace old ones with his present budget. He broadened it out to say that we needed to have a poverty programme covering housing, social services and education under a separate agency – rather taking a leaf out of President Johnson's book. He went on to say that he was sure that there was more money that could be raised by taxation and that we were not at all at the limits of it as compared with other European countries.

Next came Kenneth Robinson, who again complained of the great difficulty in meeting needs under his present budget, which would have to be expanded two and a half times in order to provide for all the hospital beds required at the end of the century and to replace the pre-war hospitals.

We had tea and afterwards Jennie Lee spoke about the University of the Air and Peggy Herbison reported on pensions progress.

We turned to consider the next section which was on revitalising democracy and I spoke about the need for modernising Parliament in controlling the powers of the House of Lords. Fred Lee gave a short report on fuel and power and said that the coal industry had actually got wider powers and a better future than sometimes appeared from Alf Robens and others. But, said Joe Gormley, the miners were depressed about the future. Finally George wound up and he stressed a number of points which were all sensible. The meeting ended at about 6 o'clock.

Marcia came round and whispered that Harold wanted 'the group' to stay behind – Dick, Peter, Gerald and myself. Tommy Balogh, of course, was not at Chequers. We had a meal with Harold and discussed the Election strategy. It is pretty apparent that the Election will come soon and we were told to come to Chequers again next Sunday by which time Peter Shore has to prepare a draft manifesto.

Home about midnight, feeling extremely tired and full of flu.

Tuesday 8 February

At 11.20 I had to go to Cabinet about the University of the Air. Jennie had produced a paper asking for the fourth channel and a new public corporation to run it with access by programme contractors for most of the day which would yield an advertising revenue and make available two or three hours a day for the University of the Air programmes. There was general support for this but in view of the heavy financial commitment involved it was decided to have another look at it and to publish a White Paper containing details of the university courses that would be provided without specifying exactly on which channel they would be broadcast. This must have been a terrible set-back for Jennie but, in the circumstances, I think it was more or less inevitable.

Thursday 10 February

Lunch with the Press Association. This is one of their regular directors' meetings and after the lunch was over some of the proprietors of local newspapers put questions. I was told this was just to be a general talk about matters of common concern. In fact the only thing they were interested in was my policy on local broadcasting. They are afraid that local commercial stations are going to be authorised. I hedged but it is obvious from what they said that there will be great resistance to the proposals made in the White Paper. This is too bad. I shall have to alert the Cabinet but hope that they will agree we should stand firm.

At 5.30 we had the second meeting of the EDC Ministerial Committee on the status of the Post Office. Frank Soskice began by saying that the Prime Minister had expressed great interest in this for possible inclusion in the manifesto. This had an electric effect on the meeting. We went round the table and Jack Diamond said that he thought there was a case for making the whole Post Office a nationalised industry but not for a split. Austen Albu said he thought there was a case for splitting telecommunications but for leaving posts as a Governmental department. Dick Marsh had come round entirely to my side. Stephen Swingler* was still doubtful but on the whole sympathetic and Ernest Thornton† was only concerned with the staff.

I replied powerfully citing all the absurdities of Civil Service status and on the basis of that it was agreed that it would be in order for us to come out in favour of a change of status, provided we were prepared to leave open the question of the number of boards. That is what I want to do anyway. We agreed to reserve the question of banking for a Cabinet decision.

I agreed to write a memorandum to go to EDC with a report from Frank Soskice. With luck it can go through EDC quickly and on to Cabinet where I hope Harold will bless it and allow me to make a statement. Once this statement is made in the House of Commons it can appear in the manifesto and I shall have opened up this enormous change in the organisation of the Post Office, which is fifty years overdue.

After that meeting I had a meal with Peter Shore and then Ioan Evans came to see me. He has taken on the job of being my PPS and I think he will be very good. I briefed him on all the work we were doing under the strictest pledge of secrecy.

Friday 11 February
To the Office early this morning, where we had a half-an-hour meeting on the headquarters organisation that we should set up to deal with the rail strike which starts on Monday. I agreed the text of a statement cancelling the parcels service and modifying other services.

At 10.30 we had a Board meeting confined entirely to the question of external telecommunications. We agreed to go for the high altitude synchronous satellites on the Early Bird model in preference to the medium altitude orbiting satellites. We also agreed to oppose the extension of a telecommunications cable from Malaya to Ceylon and to work for a satellite link instead.

To the House at 4 o'clock to vote in favour of Humphry Berkeley's Bill legalising homosexual practices between consenting adults in private which was carried by a big majority.

We heard on the news that Harold had summoned the NUR to Number 10 and right through the evening I listened to all the bulletins. At 12.40 an announcement was made. The Executive had

---

* Labour MP for Newcastle-under-Lyme and Parliamentary Secretary in the Ministry of Transport.
† Labour MP for Farnworth and Parliamentary Secretary in the Ministry of Labour.

agreed to call off the strike. It was a great achievement for Harold and done without making any concessions of note.

Sunday 13 February
Peter Shore turned up at 8.30 this morning and drove me to Chequers. He had a draft manifesto which was first-rate. Dick, Tommy and Gerald were there and so were Marcia and Brenda. We went through it section by section making suggestions, broke for lunch and finished it by about 4.10. It is obvious now that the Election will come next month, although Harold is still not saying it definitely.

The manifesto should be a very good one. Harold was rather tired but we had an amusing time. I thanked him for bringing my Post Office reorganisation forward.

We talked at lunch about George Brown and Jim Callaghan and how both of them would like to be Leader of the House of Commons and got as near as we could to discussing various other changes. When the question came up of who would succeed Harold if he were knocked down by a bus, I asked Harold outright and he said that the first thing he would want to know would be who had paid the man who drove the bus.

Home in time for tea with the family.

Monday 14 February
A major development on the broadcasting front. This morning I was handed a letter from Lord Fulton, Vice-Chairman of the BBC, to the Prime Minister, expressing grave anxiety at the prospect of advertising on the BBC and saying it would precipitate a crisis of confidence between the BBC Board of Governors and the Government. A letter from Hugh Greene repeated the warning about advertising. I was also shown a letter from Lord Fulton to the Director General asking for a £6.10s licence fee, starting on 1 August.

In view of the Cabinet meeting tomorrow to consider my broadcasting White Paper, I thought it necessary to act fast. So I went to see Herbert Bowden and told him of this. He strongly supports the idea of some advertising on the BBC Light Programme and was in favour of standing firm. Next I went to see Harold who has confused the whole thing in his mind with his current dislike of the bias in BBC programmes. It is in fact important to keep these two issues completely apart, in case the BBC Board of Governors got into their heads the idea that the Government was in any way restricting their licence revenue out of political irritation with them. But it looked to me as if Harold would stand firm.

Tuesday 15 February

To Cabinet this morning at 11 o'clock where my broadcasting White Paper was the main item. I presented it and of course the whole thing got bogged down on the BBC financial proposals. Those in favour of advertising on the BBC included Harold, Dick Crossman, Barbara Castle, Bert Bowden and one or two others. Those wholly opposed were Douglas Houghton, Frank Cousins and Tony Crosland.

I argued as powerfully as I could and it was agreed that Harold would see Lord Fulton and Hugh Greene tomorrow with Bowden and me present. In a way I didn't expect to make much more progress on the first occasion on which this idea was discussed. It is always a shock for people to think about something as new as this when they don't see it as part of a concerted plan under which the ITA would have to accept some non-commercial programmes. I feel sure that, given a bit of time, I shall get it through.

There are rumours all the time about Christopher Mayhew's resignation, based on the supposed decision by the Cabinet to buy F-111 planes instead of maintaining British aircraft carriers. I don't think from Harold's point of view it would do much harm if it looked as if he was being firm against the right wing of his own Party in insisting on defence cuts.

Wednesday 16 February

To Number 10 where Harold saw Fulton and Greene. The Lord President, Herbert Bowden, was there. Despite Harold's threat to talk tough he was in fact very gentle and said he well understood the BBC's view but the problem of the steadily increasing licence fee was one that he had to take into account and it was true that advertising was one of the options, though no decisions had been reached. He thus protected me from what is currently the BBC view that I am trying to get advertising inserted into the BBC single-handed. My standing with the BBC will continue to be low until this White Paper is published and the whole thing can be seen in its proper context.

After lunch, as I went back to the Post Office, I realised that there must be some other way of solving this problem. I promptly dictated a minute to Harold setting out a new line of argument under which there would be no general licence increase until January 1968 and meanwhile the BBC would get a £3 extra licence for colour transmission, would be paid for broadcasting University of the Air programmes, would get stronger anti-licence evasion measures taken, would be able to get money for building new studios and local radio stations, and for supplying them with sustaining programmes. In addition, the Government would grant it permission to have some advertising under strictly controlled conditions on the Light

Programme if the Board of Governors asked for it. This would then transfer the argument for public consideration and would leave the BBC Governors faced with a choice of cutting back or doing this.

I think this is a satisfactory solution provided it is accompanied by my second proposal, namely that the ITA would be denied the fourth channel and would be allowed longer hours of broadcasting on the present channel on the understanding that they carried University of the Air programmes for nothing and also had to provide some public service broadcasting of an experimental kind without advertisements. Bowden is in favour of it. The only person who is likely to have any doubts is Jennie Lee who will be bitterly disappointed that the University of the Air cannot have the fourth network.

At 5 o'clock I had Hardy Ratcliffe, the Secretary of the Musicians' Union, and Brian O'Malley to see me. Without telling them any of our plans, I did discuss the prospect of getting needle time extended. They told me that the Musicians' Union was principally interested in finding outlets for live music and that restricted needle time was only a means of preventing the BBC or any other broadcasting station from confining itself entirely to records.

From there I went to the Communications Group of Labour MPs which had been specially summoned to discuss broadcasting policy. Frank Allaun was in the chair and it was most interesting. Arthur Blenkinsop, a member of the BBC Advisory Council, opened by saying there should be an early White Paper to provide for the BBC to run local radio stations, which should not advertise or in any way seek to replace the pirates who should be crushed.

Charles Morris and Charles Mapp who thought the BBC should take advertising so that the public sector would not be starved of resources.

Hugh Jenkins said that the ITV levy [advertising surplus] should be paid by the Treasury straight to finance the fourth channel, which should also be allowed to do some prestige advertising. He thought the BBC sound programme monopoly should be broken by local radio that was not under BBC control, financed by some local advertising and networked. He thought a £6.10s licence fee would have no political impact on the prospects of the Party in an Election.

Bernard Floud said the public was only interested in the pirates and in keeping the licence fee down. He thought there would be a big row if the pirates were squashed.

Chris Rowlands and Terry Boston were both strongly opposed to publishing a White Paper. They thought the alternatives were some capitulation to commercial advertising which they hated but thought would be popular, and some increase in the licence fee which they wanted but thought would be unpopular. Harry Randall and Norman

Buchan were also against publishing a White Paper for such the same reasons.

Chris Rowlands thought that an increased licence fee would have an impact on the public and he was afraid that I might be tempted by the desire for electoral popularity to come down in the wrong direction. I hit back hard at this and said that broadcasting had been my interest for some years in Parliament. I would never publish a White Paper in which I didn't believe and when I did publish one I would argue for it strongly both inside the Party and nationally. I thought it was a great mistake to suppose that it was a black and white issue in which you went for the commercial solution or swingeing and regular increases in the licence fee. Chris Rowlands more or less had to apologise after that.

It was interesting that there was a majority in favour of some advertising solution if it could be done properly but it was agreed that we shouldn't publish a White Paper at all. This is impossible and I could not accept it.

Friday 18 February
Lunch with William Rees-Mogg of the *Sunday Times* at Brown's Hotel. He had asked to see me some time ago and we had a general talk about politics with a little bit about the Post Office thrown in.

In the evening the whole family with the Gibsons went to see *At the Drop of Another Hat* with Michael [Flanders] and Donald [Swann] at the Globe Theatre. It was a delightful evening and they sang a special song about a pillar box. Afterwards we all went backstage and chatted for a bit. The children loved it.

Sunday 20 February
Collected Peter Shore this evening to go to Number 10 at Harold's request to go over the manifesto. It is obvious that the Election is imminent, although Harold pledged us to deep secrecy and didn't actually say so outright.

He began talking about his colleagues. Harold is terrified that if Jim Callaghan became Leader of the House of Commons he would conspire against Harold and weaken his position and we tried to reassure him that he was all right and had nothing to fear. It is extraordinary how a man in his position should have anxieties on that score.

He then talked about all the people he had offered jobs to and what had happened. Alf Robens wanted to be Ambassador in Washington but Patrick Gordon Walker wouldn't promote him. Harold said that if only he had agreed to do so we would have had less trouble with the Coal Board! He then went on to say that he had

offered Michael Foot the Home Office but that Michael had refused
on the grounds that he was not prepared to accept collective Cabinet
responsibility for Vietnam. He would be making some major changes
after the Election but he made it as clear as he could that I would
not feature in this. He was incredibly indiscreet and it was interesting
that every reference he made to his colleagues referred to their weaknesses. Caroline thinks, and I am sure she's right, that the way in
which he manipulates people is by concentrating on their weakness.
I must say I found the evening extremely unattractive. My opinion
of Harold was lower tonight than it has ever been before. He really
is a manipulator who thinks that he can get out of everything by
fixing somebody or something. Although his reputation is now riding
high, I'm sure he will come a cropper one day when one of his fixes
just doesn't come off.

Monday 21 February
To EDC this morning where I had the whole agenda. The first item
was the Post Office prospects White Paper. They leapt on it and tore
it to bits and left me to rewrite it.

They then moved on to the status of the Post Office and again I
made practically no progress. Everybody had a different view and no
one there had read the papers or had thought about it carefully. It
was all over by about 11 and I am back where I started. However,
this always happens when ideas are considered for the first time. I
went back to the office and rewrote the whole White Paper, adding
a reference to new status, and dictating it to Mrs Funnell on to a
typewriter.

Jim Fitton came to see me this afternoon to look at the stamps for
the April pictorials. We planned out the stamp exhibition on
18 March, showing some of the new heads that have come in for
consideration for the new definitive stamps. Fitton is rather a fusser
but during this extremely delicate period when I am changing British
stamps, I think I'd better keep fairly close to him.

I worked at the Office till about 7 o'clock, came home and had a
lovely talk to Caroline. She thinks that I'm not half tough enough
and that what I must do is to become rather more independent of
Harold. I'm sure she's right but it's difficult to do when you are a
member of the Kitchen Cabinet.

Tuesday 22 February
To the Office this morning and Andrew Restall came to show me his
work. He had done a great deal of fundamental work on the shape
and layout of stamps, the proportions between side and top and
the need for some type of basic house style, including typography,

denomination and descriptive matter. He is interested in new types of printing, including lithography, and has devised some interesting ways of getting the head to look embossed though in fact flat.

To the House this afternoon, where Denis Healey made a statement on the defence White Paper and Christopher Mayhew made his resignation speech. It went on for forty-five minutes and was far too long. He has exposed himself, like everyone who resigns, to a great deal of criticism on the grounds that if what he now says he has always believed, he should have resigned a long time ago. Alternatively if he was prepared to stay if he could get one aircraft carrier, then all the rest of his argument was invalidated.

I have come to the conclusion that there must be at least three conditions met for a resignation to be right and effective. First, it must be simple and clear and important enough for everybody to understand. Second, it must be a resignation over an issue that is getting more important and where the stand taken will be more meaningful in a year or more's time than it is at the time the resignation takes place. Thirdly, it must be a resignation that is more than a gesture of defiance or disappointment and you must carry a large definable body of opinion, particularly within your own Party, with you, and not just contribute to a general splintering of loyalties. You could also argue that a resignation is no good unless it is followed up by a vigorous campaign in support of the views that you hold. Just to go to the Back Benches gets you nowhere. It is also arguable that nobody should resign until he is satisfied that the Party of which he is a member has become the greater of two evils.

Mayhew's speech was important because it focused public attention on the fact that this country has become entirely dependent on the United States and cannot act in a military sense apart from the United States. For the right wing of the Labour Party to say this is significant, since it has been denied so often in the past. It may also help to awaken public interest in the truth about our military and economic position in the world. I think most people realise now that a continuation of permanent British bases East of Suez is bunk, or at any rate a declining policy. Harold is afraid of admitting this partly because he still believes in it and partly because he is afraid that to cut our world commitments would be a preamble to our admission into the Common Market which he does not favour. Indeed on Sunday night he made it clear that his Cabinet appointments next time would bear strongly on the balance of opinion within the Party about the Common Market. He is afraid of being isolated in a minority and forced to go into the Common Market by a Cabinet which consists principally of Common Marketeers.

Thursday 24 February

To the Cabinet where it was decided, after a short debate, to go over to decimal currency in 1971.

News from Ghana today that President Nkrumah has been deposed by a military coup. Everyone here is cheering because Nkrumah was such a hated figure. Much publicity is being given to the release of the political detainees. But of course they will soon be replaced in prison by Nkrumah's supporters. However wild and uncontrollable the cult of personality has become in Ghana I feel sure that history will treat Nkrumah much more kindly than now appears from the British press. It is hard to escape the conclusion that a newly independent country requires a tough leadership and a focus of loyalty, and although he has no doubt been corrupt and wasteful and has isolated himself from the people, I suspect that in terms of fundamental development Ghana has not done too badly.

Friday 25 February

I wrote a letter to the Queen's Private Secretary telling him that the Gentleman album was completed, that Andrew Restall had done a great deal of work and that I wanted to put all this on show in the Stampex exhibition. It so happens that the stamps will be shown in the middle of the Election campaign which is politically dangerous but I think I will make it clear that these are just sample stamps and there is no question of them being issued in their present form.

After lunch Lord Fulton and Hugh Greene came to see me for a follow-up discussion about BBC finances. To my amazement, they said that after ten days' work, they had realised that they could get away without an increase in the licence fee for two or three years. This despite what the official committee had said about it being impossible for the present licence fee to be held without drastic cuts in the services. I asked Greene how it was to be done and he said there would be cuts in central administration. This is the one thing we had always thought should be done but which the civil servants and others had said was impossible. They also said they could do it without cutting the services. It means that we are now able to give a pledge that there will be no licence fee increase for two years. I then went on to think of ways in which further revenue might be made available for them. I tried to explore more fully the possibility of finding revenue from advertising that didn't involve the BBC itself advertising. Greene was intensely suspicious and said that they really didn't need the money. What a complete volte-face!

On colour they were prepared to consider a supplementary licence fee and they were also prepared to buy some ITA colour programmes for BBC2, which would make colour all the more attractive.

We then discussed the possibility of a music network and I said that the BBC had exposed itself to pirate competition by policy refusal to meet what most people wanted – background music on at least one of the three radio channels provided by the BBC. Fulton was interested in this and Greene gave all the old standard arguments against it. Greene knew quite well what was in my mind but I didn't say anything at all about our intentions and was able to confirm that no decisions had been reached.

After they had gone I received the papers for Monday's meeting which showed that George Brown has come out in favour of new status for the Post Office.

I called the DG and insisted that there must be internal organisation changes in the Post Office to be announced within the next two weeks. The minimum requirements were the renaming of the DG to become Permanent Secretary, the appointment of two Directors-General, one for Posts and one for Telecommunications, the decapitation of the Engineering Department which would then come under the DG Telecomms, and the disappearance of the Engineer-in-Chief to become Chief Scientific Adviser. He didn't like it much but I told him that it was essential and an approach will be made to the Treasury next week after status has been cleared.

Monday 28 February
To the EDC this morning where my PO prospects White Paper was approved but where my plan to change the Post Office into public corporations was shelved for the Election which is expected to be announced today. I entered a dissenting view but was so completely over-ruled that there was nothing I could do about it. The important thing is that in principle it has been agreed and will come up after the Election.

This afternoon Caroline and I went to a party given by the Dean of Westminster, to celebrate the publication of the Westminster Abbey stamp. It was a real feudal occasion in the Jerusalem Chamber with all the clergy in their red cassocks and robes.

This evening Harold Wilson announced that the General Election would take place on 31 March.

Tuesday 1 March
To the Cabinet this morning. The BBC had sent in a further letter saying that they had proposals to make that might enable the licence fee to be held stable for two years. This provided the Cabinet with an excuse for killing my proposals in the broadcasting White Paper, and I was told to negotiate further with the BBC on this. Thus the second of my projects has been lost as a result of the Election. I think

Harold was afraid that any suggestion of advertising would create a great deal of controversy. But it is rather discouraging.

This afternoon Jim Callaghan opened the debate on the economic situation and introduced a mini-budget. This included a special subsidy for mortgage owners, to be financed by a tax on betting. It was wildly popular.

To dinner at Number 10 with Harold, Dick, Gerald, Marcia, Brenda and Peter and Terry [Pitt]. We went over the manifesto, line by line, and after the vote I returned to Number 10 and stayed there till midnight.

Home at 12.15 and then out to Michael Flanders' birthday party.

Wednesday 2 March
I heard today that the Tories have put down broadcasting as a subject for tomorrow's debate and of course I have nothing whatsoever to announce. So the Cabinet which thought they could push broadcasting under the carpet until after the Election have really been caught. I shall have to cope with the situation as best I can. The only thing I can do is to make some progress on colour. At 5.15 I went to see Harold about this and he suggested a general line for my speech. He said that I ought to come out – in general terms – in favour of colour television. But this simply isn't good enough and is to be referred to Cabinet tomorrow.

One amusing incident today. I saw Marcia just before I went in to see Harold and told her that I had dreamed about her on the previous night. She told me that she had dreamed that Harold was dead and had not believed it until she had been shown the body. She said she hadn't dared to tell Harold this story. But then Harold had told her this morning that last night he dreamed that Hugh Gaitskell had been sitting in at a committee – all white. What an extraordinary combination of dreams.

Joined Caroline at the Youngers' for a dinner party. The Pallisers were there. Michael Palliser is going to replace Oliver Wright as Private Secretary at Number 10. His wife is Spaak's* daughter and they are passionate Common Marketeers.

Thursday 3 March
Early to the Post Office. The broadcasting debate began at 3.30 and I wound it up. There was a great deal of criticism for our failure to reach decisions but during my speech I was able to announce colour and to indicate our lines of thinking on other problems.

The PO prospects White Paper came out this afternoon and of

* Paul-Henri Spaak, Belgian Socialist Foreign Minister.

course the press comment was 'higher postal charges soon'. This was an inevitable consequence of publishing the figures but I was absolutely determined not to do what Bevins had done and conceal them.

Friday 4 March
Went to Bristol for the meeting of local Party officers. Bert Peglar was in the chair with Fred Newman, the Reverend Peter Allen, Dr Robert Glendinning, Herbert Rogers, Joyce Perham and myself. Bert said there was a strong feeling in favour of Herbert Rogers remaining as the agent for the forthcoming Election.

I said we should have a campaign committee which authorised the expenditure and it was agreed that Bert Peglar should be the chairman of this committee, and that Fred Newman and Herbert and I should be on it. The next item was the planning of the campaign itself.

I shall have to devote the next three weeks to campaigning in Bristol. I have by no means neglected the constituency or the problems of my constituents but I have not attended the local Party as often as I should.

Sunday 6 March
Worked in the Office all day, going through the big thick booklet on the achievements of the Government since October 1964. It is a formidable record. This has been prepared by the Government machine and I transferred the main points on to cards for use during the campaign.

This evening at 9.15 I went back to Number 10 for a final look at our manifesto and also for a strategic discussion about the Tory manifesto which was published today. This includes a great war on the trade unions, the remodelling of the Welfare State, strict control of immigration and pledges for greater increases in expenditure, coupled with the determination to cut taxation. We discussed the best way of handling this.

Monday 7 March
To Transport House this morning for the meeting of the Executive at 10.30 to go through the manifesto. We got through it quickly, with the minimum of discussion about the prices and incomes policy which had been carefully worded to avoid trouble. There was some discussion about the nationalisation of the docks but the general view was that we should include a pledge on this. The only actual disagreement was over the phraseology of the sentence dealing with our entry into Europe. I voted with Mikardo and Tony Greenwood

and Barbara Castle and one or two others against the firm commitment that 'Britain should be ready to enter Europe'.

The reference to 'a major reorganisation of the Post Office' had
remained in the final draft. I came to the conclusion that without
being able to elaborate, this phrase would be meaningless. I therefore
passed a note on what this would involve to George Brown: 'Dear
George, Much as I would like a reference to be made to reorganisation
of the Post Office in the manifesto, I think it might raise difficulties
and lead to questions that we couldn't answer. Regretfully I have
therefore concluded that it should not be there.' George looked
puzzled but had the phrase deleted. For the rest of the day I worried
about whether this was the right thing to have done. The manifesto
was published this evening and got a good press.

Sunday 13 March

I talked to someone yesterday who said that he would probably abstain
in the Election. Not to put too fine a point on it, he finds Harold
Wilson phoney and entirely without principle. I record this only
because it is a fact in the political situation that one has to take into
account. After having started extremely well in the Party and
attracted people from left and right to his leadership, he has, since
he's been Prime Minister, appeared to be too cunning and crafty and
smart, and to be somewhat lacking in principle. It may well be that
these are the qualities needed to be a Prime Minister – and to win
elections. I am not expressing my own opinion about this, but I think
it's interesting to put on record that the more successful Harold
Wilson becomes the less attractive he is to the sort of people who
campaigned most actively for him as Leader of the Party when Hugh
Gaitskell died. One also has a feeling about him that since his success
in the eyes of the public, encouraged by the press, is greater than is
perhaps justified by his real achievements, so, when the moment
comes for mistakes and failures, these too may be made to seem far
greater than they are. This is rather the same thing as happened to
Harold Macmillan.

This evening Peter and Liz Shore looked in after his meeting in
Stepney. We discussed the effect of a large Labour majority. The
polls suggest that this is likely and I think it would be an excellent
thing to have a vocal left wing in the House of Commons, as it would
mean that Harold could be subject to pressure from the Left as well
as from the Centre.

Friday 18 March

Harold and his entourage arrived in Bristol where there was a big
meeting in the Central Hall.

Afterwards Harold asked me to go to TWW with him where he was interviewed by ITN and by the local television channel. Coming back in the car, he told me about the row he was having with the BBC. He feels that they are arrogant and are strongly biased against him and the Labour Party. The thing that irritated him was their refusal to interview him one day except on the subject that he had picked for his morning press conference.

Monday 21 March
Drove to Bristol. Long talk to John Guinery about the Election. He said the lobby did not like Harold Wilson because they felt that he was manipulating them and, although they had to report what a Prime Minister said, they resented being managed. Walter Terry's invention of the phrases 'instant politics' and 'non-events' – like the winter emergency committee, and so on – had apparently struck home.

Friday 25 March
To the Party headquarters this morning and then to Taunton for five meetings in the Tiverton constituency. Then on to Collumpton doing 'Any Questions' with Quintin Hogg. It was the first 'Any Questions' I had done for a long time and I thoroughly enjoyed it. Quintin was in a mellow mood and I think has begun to realise that with a Labour Government for the next five years, he may never hold high office again.

Saturday 26 March
Spoke at an open air meeting in Exeter for Gwyneth Dunwoody and then on to Okehampton to speak for Frank Paton fighting North Devon, to Launceston to speak for Reg Wills [Cornwall North] and to Bugle Penwithick to speak for Reg Scott [Truro]. In the evening I addressed a meeting at Constantine and another at Falmouth for John Dunwoody. Paul Carmody drove me throughout the day and dropped me at the station to catch the sleeper back to London. The Falmouth meeting was tremendously exciting and one feels the Election has begun to catch fire.

Sunday 27 March
Flew to Manchester and was driven to Blackburn where I spoke for Barbara Castle at a crowded meeting in the Windsor Hall. I caught the sleeper home. At Preston station I saw Frank and Elizabeth Longford. He is a bit depressed because he thinks that in the reshuffle he will be reshuffled out. I strongly doubt whether Harold will make

many changes in his Government, despite all his protestations to me and others earlier.

Thursday 31 March
Polling Day. To headquarters at about 9 and from 9.30 am to 6 visiting all the polling stations and committee rooms. We had lunch at the 'Hole-in-the-Wall' and then went out again with our loudspeaker, doing final knocking up. After the polls closed we cleared up the headquarters, went back to the hotel and began watching the BBC Election programme. It was evident that a big Labour victory was coming, although the size of the majority was predicted in the first place as 150 and began falling.

At 11.30 we went to the St George Grammar School for the count and wandered round. They count terribly slowly in Bristol.

Friday 1 April
From the time we got to the count till our result at 1.35, we wandered round with a radio and an earpiece hearing the victories pouring in. At 1.35 am the result was announced and my majority had increased by 1,600 to almost 11,500. But it was only a small swing to me because of all the new housing. Then we had the traditional ritual with the car pulled up to the Walter Baker Hall where a television set had been installed. I met and talked to my supporters and then went off to do an interview for Welsh television. Bed at 4 o'clock.

Up at 8 and drove to London. The results continued on the radio in the car and it was clear that we had won the General Election with a majority in the mid-nineties. All was well at home when we got back. Wilson, my driver, came over with a letter signed by Derek Mitchell at Number 10 saying that, in accordance with precedent, all Ministers were to regard their offices as being placed at the disposal of the Prime Minister so that he could reconstruct his Government. However, I was asked to supervise the current work of the department. I don't know that I shall go into the Office until I know where I stand. My authority has now completely expired and although I am in law still Postmaster General and have been asked to carry on in practice as Postmaster General, the civil servants won't take any notice of me and I don't see any particular point in trying to test my strength against theirs.

One of the most interesting things about the new Parliament is the inrush of new Members, most of them young, many of them professional, and all of them keen and eager. They will be very different from the old Left and from the solid trade union members. The Labour Party is in the process of transforming itself into a genuine national party.

Sunday 3 April
Forty-first birthday and the children came in with gifts in the morning. Mother came over for tea and we had a family party. No news yet of the reconstruction of the Government.

Monday 4 April
Just after lunch a phone call came, asking me to go and see Harold. I went across and had five minutes with him. After a brief exchange of congratulations he said, 'I'm going to offer you a Ministry but I rather hope you won't take it. It is the Ministry of Works which is technically a little senior to the Post Office.' I asked whether it was in the Cabinet and he indicated that it was not. I asked whether he was reducing the size of his Cabinet and he said no. 'The Minister of Works is thought of as being marginally senior to the Postmaster General but its housing functions will be taken away and it would be left with Royal Parks and Government Procurement and the Palace of Westminster.' I thought quickly and decided that if I wasn't going to be in the Cabinet there was no point in moving. Anyway I didn't want to be under Dick Crossman as overlord of Works and Planning, and I wanted to finish my Post Office work. So I said, 'If you're not offering me a place in the Cabinet I think I'd rather stay where I am.' Harold looked uncomfortable and said, 'I have decided not to make many Cabinet changes and to try to get away from the idea of major reshuffles. Instead I will move people every year – one or two of them, like the Football League. The Ministry of Technology is the real glamour job and I can't think that Frank Cousins will stay long. He's not fit anyway. I'm not promising it to you but of course it would be easier to move you if you hadn't already been moved recently. Also you have a big job of industrial reorganisation with the Post Office and Arnold Goodman has told George Wigg that you are the only person who can really settle the television problem. The Cabinet is an ageing one and there will be room for you later on.'

I suppose I should have looked a lot angrier than I felt but I'm not sure that bullying gets you anywhere. Anyway I didn't conceal my disappointment when I said that I would rather stay where I was for the moment and finish what I had started. I told him that I was extremely interested in Technology and he said, 'You would have to learn the difference between a cyclotron and a megaton.' I told him that although I had had a liberal education, the scientific side of the Post Office had interested me greatly and the present arrangement under which the electronics industry had been transferred to the Ministry of Technology for purposes of sponsorship was not a satisfactory one. When I had been in Japan I had seen how

Above: Members of the 'Left' on the Labour Party's National Executive Committee during the 1960s: Crossman, Castle and Tom Driberg at Conference

An economist in the corridors of power: Thomas Balogh, who advised the Labour Government 1964-8

The funeral of Sir Winston Churchill, 30 January, 1965. The Establishment pays its respects: heads of state and members of the British royal family outside St Paul's Cathedral

August 1965: Edward Heath, new Leader of the Conservative Party the first Tory Leader ever elected by Conservative MPs

With Jennie Lee, Under Secretary at Education, with whom I worked closely in 1965-6 on the 'University of the Air', later the Open University

With the Queen, leaving the GPO Tower in May 1966. We had tea together at the top of the tower in Billy Butlin's revolving restaurant

Above: Meeting the Union: At the Clapham headquarters of the Union of Post Office Workers. On my right are Ron Smith, General Secretary of the UPW and Caroline; Joe Slater, Assistant PMG, is to the left of me (smoking cigarette); Charles Morris, my PPS, is behind him

Left: With Reginald Phillips of Brighton whose collection of early Victorian stamps was bequeathed to the GPO and led to the establishment of the Philatelic Museum

May 1967 — with President Johnson at the 'Water for Peace' Conference in Washington, surrounded by security men. Next to LBJ is Stuart Udall, US Secretary for the Interior

Concorde roll-out in Toulouse, December 1967, when I announced that the British model would also have an 'e' — for England, excellence and *entente concordiale*. The remark did not go down well in Scotland — until I pointed out the 'e' was also for Ecosse

Union protestors at the Atomic Energy Authority plant at Risley, where a pay increase had been held up by the Government's restraints on prices and incomes

much active support a Government could give to industry. I pressed at this so that my keen interest became embedded in his mind.

Afterwards I went to Horse Guards where my driver was waiting and I told him that I was going back to the Post Office. When we arrived, I told Wratten that I had been given a choice but had decided to stay in the Post Office and he was genuinely pleased. Then I had the DG in and I told him that I'd been offered another job but had decided to stay on. He was shaken to the core. He was certain that I would be promoted and they had evidently spent a lot of time in the Department preparing position papers for my successor. The DG informed me that he would be retiring at the end of July and that Sir Kenneth Anderson was going on 5 June. So there are two top vacancies to be filled and I shall take advantage of their departure to make other changes. I had Mrs Funnell in and dictated a memorandum to myself covering the areas on which I expected to make substantial progress in the next few months.

Afterwards, home and picked up Caroline and we went to the party at Transport House to celebrate the victory. It was a pleasant evening though Harold didn't turn up. The next few months are going to be extremely difficult and are going to call for all my skill as a negotiator but I shall have a chance of modernising the Post Office along the lines that I know to be necessary.

Tuesday 5 April
Into the Office early this morning and I had a talk to Wolstencroft about the postal services. As I expected, all the things I had asked him to do on the reshaping of the tariff structure had been entirely neglected because they were not expecting me to return. Wolstencroft was discomfited to find that I had come back.

I had a talk to Ryland and we went over some of the problems on the telephone side. Afterwards I asked Sir Kenneth Anderson to come and see me but he telephoned Wratten and exploded. He said that he had never been appreciated and that I had not realised that he was really my best friend and that I had abused his confidence in revealing the deficit concealed by the Conservatives and that he was sick at the way the DG had treated him, though he did admit the DG had played a wonderful delaying game, and so on. He has decided to retire on 5 June and it's obvious that he's completely out of action from now till then. I'm sorry if I'm in any way responsible for this but it is a remarkable reflection on the state of the Office. I mustn't assume that all the General Directorate agree with each other because I think there's probably just as much trouble between themselves as there has ever been between them and me.

This evening I went to a concert at Holland Park School.

Wednesday 6 April

Charles Smith came to lunch with me and I took him over to the 'Master Gunner'. I told him everything that was on my mind, including the demotion of the Engineer-in-Chief and new status for the Post Office. I told him that I might not carry my colleagues with me but this was what I was hoping to do. He was sympathetic and I am certainly going to deal with the trade union leaders on a different basis in the future. My discretion has become absurdly limiting.

Ioan Evans, my new PPS, came over. He suggested that I give two tea parties to meet the new MPs, which is a good idea. We also agreed that we should have to see that parliamentary questions included questions favourable to us and we discussed the possibility of rather better relations with the press.

At 5 o'clock I went for an hour's talk to Frank Gillard about broadcasting problems. I adopted the new policy of being forthcoming, on the understanding that it was entirely confidential. Frank told me about his plans to have Radio 247 run by the BBC to beat the pirates. It sounds as if he can offer a service from 5 am to 2 am with entertainment music on the medium wave band for the teenage audience, by opting out of the Light Programme, which would remain on VHF. His only problem is money. But it's mad to raise the licence fee to provide something that could be provided for nothing by advertising. All this points to a separate pop network which is used as a revenue raiser, where the Post Office rent the programmes, studios and transmitters from the BBC and pay them an enormous sum, thus ensuring that they are not corrupted by the advertising.

Friday 8 April

Drove to Stansgate with the whole family today. Mother followed with Dave and June and their babies. We had nine days there and for the first time since the war really tackled the problem of accumulated junk. The incinerator was burning almost throughout the whole week and we cleared out the cupboards full of books and suitcases and assembled and sorted the material. Mother's annexe is a great success, although there are a few tidying jobs to be done. The weather was good over the first weekend but it settled down to snow and rain and was icy cold for most of the rest of the week during which we worked indoors as much as we could. The place is lovely and I'm looking forward to getting down there for the summer. It was a wrench to come home.

Tuesday 19 April

To the Office and at 10 o'clock Mr Wolstencroft, Mr Downes and Mr MacDougall, Deputy Chief Inspector of Postal Services, came to discuss postal buses and postal tariffs. A scheme for combined postal and passenger minibuses in two parts of Wales should be available in a month and I hope to introduce it later this year.

To the Dorchester today to give lunch to the Mexican Minister of Communications, Dr Segura. He is an academic professor as well as being a Minister, modest and intelligent. He is here to study the possibility of buying British equipment. However, at lunch he seemed reluctant to discuss the reason for his visit and afterwards Ryland and I agreed that it had been unsatisfactory in that we had not pushed British exports enough. It did reveal a weakness in our organisation. I asked Wratten to prepare a minute to the Director General, asking for an overseas liaison officer to be appointed to ensure that every visitor who comes to this country is given the opportunity of seeing all possible sources of British supply and of working closely with the Board of Trade and Technology on these matters.

This afternoon Ryland and Lillicrap came and we had a long discussion about eavesdropping and the new menace of microbugs. I want a select committee to sit on this but apparently the Home Office are worried that if a select committee is set up, it will lead to awkward questions about the devices used by the security services. This seems to me to be just making a monkey out of the House of Commons and trying to preserve secrecy over an important area of public interest for one particular reason. I couldn't get Ryland or Lillicrap or Wratten, for that matter, to see the importance of a serious approach to this problem. For my part, I want regulations making it an offence to eavesdrop using radio microphones or to intercept telephone conversations and listen to and record them. But I can see that I shall have some difficulty about this. No doubt every other department will brief its Ministers against me and I daresay I shouldn't carry this through a ministerial committee.

Wednesday 20 April
To ITN this morning where I saw the film of bugging devices marketed in America and was then interviewed by Andrew Gardner. I wasn't able to go very far as the Home Office and Board of Trade have to be won over before I can promise anything. But I did say that it was a great menace and we were considering various ways of dealing with it.

After that to the Commons for the traditional service for Members of the Government, taken by Mervyn Stockwood and Donald Soper. It was a pleasant ceremony though Mervyn was as egocentric as ever and his sermon was largely about his own political and spiritual experience.

This evening was the Eve of Parliament reception at Number 10, when Harold read the Queen's speech. Afterwards I had a meal with Peter Shore and we agreed to begin cautiously to get a small dining group of younger Ministers to keep in touch with each other on the political level. We've got to be sure that Harold knows about it, both to safeguard ourselves against the charge of plotting and to make him realise that there are forces at work that he cannot ignore.

Thursday 21 April
I hurried to the Commons for the opening of Parliament. It was the first time ever that television cameras had been admitted to the Commons chamber. I found Members in a high state of anger about the lighting. Anyway it was an historic occasion and I'm glad I attended. Unfortunately it has set back the move for televising the House of Commons and we shall have to find some way round the difficulties.

After the Queen's speech we went to the Party meeting where a number of points were raised by Members. John Mendelson, the MP for Penistone launched into a bitter attack on Government policy on Vietnam and questions were raised about the prices and incomes policy. After lunch I heard a bit of Harold's speech and then settled down to prepare my own speech for tonight's adjournment debate. Mikardo is attacking Harold, Herbert Bowden and Ted Short for interfering in BBC and ITA political programmes and the job of replying was off-loaded on to me. I had to see Harold briefly.

Mik was violent and I answered by putting on record – I think for the first time – the nature of the different relationships that exist between the broadcasting authorities and the politicians. But I was careful not to deny any of the charges that he made and I also put in my own opinion that the widest spectrum of views ought to be represented on television.

Friday 22 April
This afternoon to the Commons for the Ministerial Committee on Joint Research and Development to discuss our attitude towards joint space projects in Europe. I presented the usual departmental view that there is no justification for British participation in space, based on the fact that we co-operate with the International Satellite Committee and therefore can see no advantage in space work of our own or with Europe. But having said this, and when the meeting was more or less at an end, I said I wanted to express a view that I held strongly: namely that the handling of space matters by the Government was completely chaotic, that we never met to discuss together the implications of the space decisions we were now taking, and that it was time we looked at it again. To my delight and

astonishment Eddie Shackleton and almost every other Minister there (except from the Treasury) supported me and it was agreed that Sir Solly Zuckerman would prepare a paper on how space was handled now.

Fred Mulley, who was in the chair, was a bit overwhelmed. It is clear that one Minister should be put in charge of space policy and I think the Minister of Technology is the obvious person.

Monday 25 April
Waited this afternoon for the first question of the session on pirate radio but it was never reached. The Americans are sending a powerful ship over to compete with the existing pirates and the whole thing is becoming immensely disreputable. People just don't believe the Government when it says it's going to act. It is a mixture of legislative difficulties due to the bottleneck in parliamentary time, and a certain weakness of will and indecisiveness at the top about what we should do. I am clear about my own line and as soon as the White Paper comes to Cabinet, I shall be in a position to put it forcefully.

Tuesday 26 April
This afternoon I gave my first tea party for the new MPs. About fifty turned up and they were touchingly grateful. The fact is that the Party has done nothing to greet them and I was the first MP who had taken the remotest interest in them. They gathered round and asked me a lot of questions from 'How do you get a pair?' to 'How do you put down a parliamentary question?' I'm glad I did this as it has given me a chance to meet them and they look a bright lot.

Afterwards I went to see the Chief Whip to find out whether he would mind if I gave them an evening to try to deal with their queries. But he took this as a rebuke at his own failure and said he would rather I didn't.

Thursday 28 April
At a press conference yesterday about the choice of stamps for the world football cup, the designer, David Caplan, gave away to the press the fact that the Foreign Office had banned the first choice because it contained the North Korean flag. This, of course, is the big story in the papers today.

Post Office Board all morning and we made real progress. We agreed on the general outline of the new tariff structure which will bring a two-tiered fast and slow service in 1967 at fourpence and threepence halfpenny. If I can carry this through with my colleagues it will be a major reconstruction of the postal services and should safeguard postal finances for some years ahead.

Arnold Goodman came to lunch with me and I went over the broadcasting White Paper with him. He was in full agreement with the main outlines of it but thought that I ought to be more positive in saying that there was no case for a fourth TV channel at this moment. He also thought that the University of the Air ought definitely to be limited to BBC2 as this would maintain its integrity and would also permit experiment on a relatively small scale to begin with. I trust his judgement and hope that he will be influential in talking to Harold.

To the Commons this afternoon for the second tea party for new Members and then to hear U. Thant, Secretary-General of the United Nations, speak in Westminster Hall.

Friday 29 April

I had a phone call from a man in Devon. He said that he had been unable to buy any 3d stamps the previous night, so instead bought 6d stamps and cut them in half with scissors and would I authorise them to go through the post. I was helpful but said that I had no authority to authorise this and that he should have put the 6d stamps on and then written to me for a refund. Later I discovered that in fact he was a stamp dealer and had not had thirty important bills to send out – as he told me – but actually sent out 600 of these half-stamps which he now claims are worth £15 a piece. I think he ought to be prosecuted.

Sunday 1 May

To Bristol, where I spoke at the May Day meeting. Frank Longford had come down in place of George Brown. Only about 350 people turned up.

Afterwards I went to the Agricultural Workers' sixty-year celebration rally in Weston-super-Mare and spoke there. Then I was driven to Gloucester, and, with an hour to wait for the train to London, I went and inspected the sorting office and then caught the sleeper, very tired. It was the warmest May Day for twenty-six years.

Monday 2 May

This morning I had the PMG's Informal Staff Committee and we went over a number of points of interest. There was no pressure on new status – thank goodness. I did raise two points of general interest. One was to seek their views on the practicability of introducing industrial democracy in the Post Office. What it would mean, how could we do it, and so on. They promised to think about it further. The other point I raised was the need for a rationalisation of the structure of trade unions and staff associations in the Post Office.

There are twenty-three of them, which is far too many. They had doubts about this, so I promised that I would draft out what I had in mind and send it round to them as individuals for comment.

This afternoon Charles Smith came back with his negotiating committee about the POEU wage claim. We have offered 5 per cent for the general engineering grades to recognise their contributions to productivity but only 3.5 per cent for the factory grades. He claimed this was a breach of the agreement which we had reached last October that would have lined the two up. I was a little worried in case we had broken our pledge so we met and talked about it afterwards with Ryland and I wrote him a letter reaffirming the offer that I made. Quite frankly I cannot go further than this.

Tuesday 3 May
To the Stamp Advisory Committee this morning. This was the first time I had ever met all the members. Fitton was in the chair and Professor Guyatt, Mr Milner Gray and Sir John Wilson, the Queen's philatelist, were there. The stamps we were looking at were, first, the stamps on British technology, which were disappointing and secondly, the Hastings stamps which were very good, carrying a small cameo of the Queen's profile in gold.

Sir John Wilson just muttered all the time about the size of the Queen's head and said with a thick Scottish accent, 'People seem to forget that it's the symbol of the country, that it must be significant, that it must be big, that it must be important and we can't accept anything less than that.' I kept my mouth shut but I was impressed by the amount of effort they had put into it and am glad I have attended one meeting.

To the Commons this afternoon for the Budget.

This evening Caroline and I went to dinner with Lew Grade and his wife. Hugh Cudlipp and his new wife were also there and Robin and Mrs Gill of ATV and Tom Moore, the president of ABC in America, and his wife.

I had a long talk with Hugh Cudlipp in which he launched into a vicious attack on Harold as somebody who had entirely failed to give any leadership to Britain and was always sitting on the fence. He pointed particularly to Harold's failure to back up George Brown's prices and incomes policy over the last year. I defended Harold as best I could but the place where I ran into difficulty was on Hugh Cudlipp's passion for Europe. I said I took a completely pragmatic view of this. We also had a discussion about the trade unions in which Hugh Cudlipp got himself into the usual muddle of being anti-union and at the same time proposing a solution which could only mean much stronger trade unions.

Wednesday 4 May

This evening Caroline and I went to the *Time-Life* party for Henry Luce III who had just been appointed head of the London Bureau. We got caught by Vassev and Rogov who had evidently been invited because *Time-Life* wanted to reopen their Moscow Bureau. Caroline just teased Rogov, who she is absolutely convinced is a Soviet agent and who, she believes, thinks that she is a CIA agent.

I decided to ask him bluntly about the Brooke case.* He said that Brooke was a man of no importance who had taken this commission to make contact with unimportant Soviet subversives and there was no suggestion the British Government was involved. The whole thing was sad and unnecessary. I said it was causing great concern in this country and if Brooke and the groups that he was associated with were so unimportant, why on earth did they bother. He said that he had discussed it frankly with the Prime Minister and was awkward and embarrassed about the whole thing.

Thursday 5 May

This morning to Willesden to visit the factory of the Hall Telephone Company which is a subsidiary of Elliot-Automation. I was shown round their works, which didn't look to me efficient or modern, where they are making pay-on-answer kiosks.

Afterwards we went to lunch with Bagrit and some of the other executives. We had a completely inconsequential talk at lunch and just as we were leaving they launched into a great attack on Post Office purchasing policy. They say that we gave them a development contract on the pay-on-answer box and then put the whole thing out to open tender afterwards, which meant they didn't get the manufacturing contract. I'm not sure competitive tendering is a good thing if it prevents manufacturers getting a long run. But it may well be that the Hall Telephone Company is not efficient on the productive side, however imaginative its designers may be. Bagrit is a bit of a disappointment in some ways. He's thoughtful and stimulating and a big talker but I'm not sure whether he's an efficient businessman.

Afterwards back to the Office, where I heard that the Gentleman album had been cleared by the Palace with a letter from Sir Martin Charteris saying the Queen was not at all satisfied that the small cameo was sufficiently significant. She also had doubts about the use of the royal crest on stamps – even those in the 'rulers of Great Britain' series. But I now have my go-ahead to show the stamps to the press and hold the seminar, all within Harold Wilson's ruling. I

---

* British college lecturer in Russian, imprisoned by the Soviet authorities for espionage in 1965.

have long believed that once this album came out, British stamps could never be the same again. I am completely covered since they are experimental and I am not committed to using any of them.

My main job this evening concerned the Clay-Cooper fight. The BBC and ITA have written to ask me to intervene and declare it a national event so that they would be entitled to broadcast it live. Viewsport, who are part-promoters, want me to force the BBC to make it available to the European broadcasting organisations. I decided to issue a statement declining to intervene on behalf of the BBC or Viewsport but saying that I should be glad to meet all of them together if they thought it would help.

Friday 6 May

Flew to Edinburgh this morning for the opening of the new post office there. I had lunch with the senior officials and the Duke of Edinburgh arrived at about 4.15. I had to make a short speech and he made a good off-the-cuff knockabout speech on the subject of the Post Office and we then moved on to the reception. He was pleasantly relaxed and informal and did the job competently. But somebody who does nothing but attend official functions is only capable of a degree of small talk.

Sunday 8 May

Up early and about fourteen people came to the house for discussions about the big fight: Harry Levine, the promoter; Jarvis Astaire, from Viewsport; Lord Brabourne from pay-TV; Curran and Dimmock from the BBC; Bragnell and Rogers from ITA; Wratten and Lawrence and Armitage from the Post Office.

I introduced the issues briefly and went round the table to let each of them say what he thought. Then I repeated all their arguments in summary as best I could. It was obviously impossible for the fight to be shown live on BBC or ITA as it would kill Viewsport, and I said that the only possibility of compromise was for the BBC to agree to take it the following afternoon and allow a live radio commentary. By this time they seemed agreeable to it. Meanwhile Valerie had been typing out the statement I proposed to make at the end and brought it up at just the right time. We went through this and they all agreed.

Finally we had a joint press conference at which I explained what we had done and let each of them make their own points. The television news people poured into the house.

Monday 9 May
Joshua's eighth birthday.

To Swansea for the sub-postmasters' conference. The official coming with me, Pentecost, missed the train due to his own incompetence and I was on my own. The sub-postmasters are discontented with their lot, feeling that they are not paid enough. I did my best to point up their importance and then spoke a little about the problems facing them and us. But the plain fact is that the sub-postmaster idea was based on the small retail shop in very different times and they are feeling the pinch from us as well. It may well be that we shall have to reorganise the nature of our contract with sub-postmasters and try to get post offices put as departments of bigger shops that are entirely self-financing.

Tuesday 10 May
To the Ministry of Defence to lunch with Eddie Shackleton. We met to discuss British space policy and I promised that I would write a note to Harold saying that I thought it ought to be organised rather differently inside the Government.

Norman Hunt* came to see me this afternoon. He is on the Civil Service Commission and had thought of suggesting to the Commission that they should engage McKinsey's to do a job evaluation. In strictest confidentiality I lent him a copy of the McKinsey report on the Post Office and he took it away, promising to bring it back by hand.

This evening I had dinner with Frank Gillard and Hugh Greene in Frank's flat. We discussed the whole range of ideas that are in my White Paper. Hugh Greene was absolutely dead set against the BBC accepting advertising, and against the pop music network which is my alternative to it. The plain truth is the BBC does not regard itself as a public enterprise in broadcasting which should be growing and developing. That's why it doesn't try hard for exports or think of going into pay-television or consider my advertising proposal. It just wants to be the BBC and to rest on a shrinking island of purity and integrity and is even happy that the rest of the broadcasting outlets should go to crude commercial organisations. Now that I have this idea clear in my mind, it is obvious that I must create a new type of organism for sound and the fourth channel and the BBC will just have to be left on its own to cope as best it can.

---

* Member of the Fulton Committee on the Civil Service, 1966–8. Became Lord Crowther-Hunt in 1973.

Wednesday 11 May

To the Ministerial Committee on Parliamentary Procedure to discuss the new Select Committee idea. I was shocked but not surprised to hear people saying that the committees ought to be a sop to parliamentary opinion and would be all right so long as they were innocuous. That of course is a real Government view and it's amazing how some Ministers are already forgetting that they were ever in the Opposition, let alone Back Benchers.

Ron Smith came to lunch with me at the Post Office and I discussed frankly with him my hopes for a change of status, although I told him that I wasn't at all sure whether it could be carried through. He said that he thought he could get his Executive to agree to one nationalised industry so long as there was no division into three corporations. I am coming round to the same view now partly because it would be simpler to do, partly because with distinct management authority for posts and telephones I don't think a division is all that worthwhile, and partly because I know the Treasury will fight like a tiger to stop me getting a banking corporation and in those circumstances there is really nothing that I can do to defeat it. So if we all go out together with a new management structure, the GPO will be greatly improved.

Friday 13 May

I decided today to go ahead with the children's competition for the Christmas stamp, even though the local education authorities are opposed to it. It will give us an idea of the sort of quality you might expect from children.

I have also given my instructions for the Post Office Christmas card. I went through some old colour prints and there is an excellent one of the Post Office Headquarters in 1829 with St Paul's in the background. To go with it, I have designed a modification of the Post Office Tower stamp, showing the London skyline with the Post Office Tower and the two will be perfectly respectable. It's a risky thing to have done but the Office has a way of pushing you up against a deadline and you are usually forced to accept that nothing can be done.

To the Post Office Tower for a lunch for former Postmasters General and senior Post Office officials. Of the PMGs five came – Billy Listowel, Ness Edwards, Ernest Marples, Reg Bevins and myself. The most senior former civil servant was Sir Donald Banks who was the first Director General of the Post Office in 1934. He told me that at that time the Postmaster General would come into the Office about twice a week when Parliament was sitting for a glass of port at noon. All the minutes for him to sign would then be laid around a long table in his office and he would walk round and sign them one after the other, have another glass of port and then disappear. In fact, he spent as much time on Post Office work as a Chancellor of the Duchy of Lancaster does on Duchy work. At that period senior civil servants worked from 10 am to 4.30 pm, five days a week, and had eight weeks' paid holiday a year. Life was leisurely. At least it was in Britain. But it was during those years that the rest of the world caught up with and overtook us.

Billy Listowel told me at lunch that he had tried to get the Monarch's head off the stamps in 1945 but had been told that it was impossible and had dropped the idea under heavy pressure.

This evening to Ralph and Ann Gibson's together to read *The Importance of Being Earnest*, en famille.

Sunday 15 May
It was a lovely day today and we all sat in the garden most of the morning. Michael and Betsy Zander came in for a drink.

Tuesday 17 May
Caroline went to the BBC today for the recording of the second instalment of 'Charolotte's Web' in the Jackanory series.

This afternoon the Queen came to visit the Post Office Tower. I had to greet her at the entrance and we went up into the VIP lounge where I introduced her to all the senior civil servants. Then she was taken through the apparatus rooms and up in the lift. I gave Wratten my movie camera to take some pictures on the observation platform as we walked round. Afterwards we went up and had tea with Billy Butlin, revolving in his restaurant. She was obviously not interested in the technical aspects but I think enjoyed seeing London from such a height. I suggested that there ought to be a state banquet in which all the guests went by the top table every twenty minutes.

As we came down she discussed the issue of bird stamps. She did not much like the six stamps put together and said she would prefer to have only four. I promised that this is what we would do. It was a minor concession but made me seem reasonable.

Wednesday 18 May
Helsby came to see me early to discuss the Post Office management reorganisation. The DG, who was there, supported him in opposing my proposals. But I did guess from seeing Helsby that the change of status is now widely assumed to be taking place at some point. Once this is agreed I shall have much less difficulty in carrying through the other changes.

First for parliamentary questions again. Had a rough time on the delay in the broadcasting White Paper but held my own. When one Tory said how much he disliked the new stamps I replied, 'The Honourable Gentleman is one of the small group of mis-atelists,' a word I had made up to describe a stamp-hater.

Thursday 19 May
To the Office and then to the Post Office Tower for the public opening with Billy Butlin. I said that there was a new definition of a Cockney: 'someone born within sight of the new Post Office Tower.' We went up and looked round with a party of people.

To the Guild Hall for the fiftieth anniversary of the National Savings Movement attended by the Queen and the Duke of Edinburgh. It was full of pageantry and flummery and a complete waste of time.

At the House of Commons my old friend Dan Leon was waiting to see me to find out if I could help him to get an English publisher for his book on the kibbutz, for which I had written a preface some time ago. I told him I'd do my best.

There was a fiasco tonight because the Speaker was late and the closure couldn't be moved.

Friday 20 May
Lunch at the American Embassy, then on to see the exhibition at the US Trade Centre on protective signalling devices. This is the exhibition which Mr Jamil, the American manufacturer of microbugs, wished to use to demonstrate various bugging devices. It was interesting and had some bearing on our own security problems.

Back to the Post Office where I presented some bravery awards and then on to see Frank Longford at the House of Lords to discuss the televising of the Lords. My view on this is completely cynical – that if the Lords are televised (which they want to be for reasons of publicity) this will force the Commons to be televised as well.

This evening Caroline and I went to the state banquet at Hampton Court for the Austrian President. I sat opposite Sir Michael Adeane and next to Mrs du Cann and Caroline was opposite Lady Adeane and next to Edward du Cann.

I spent most of the evening talking to Adeane and it was very amusing. I began by asking him about the effect the Conservatives' decision to elect their own Leaders had on the Queen's prerogative in choosing a Prime Minister. He said that of course the Palace had had this problem three times in the last ten years and had hoped that the new Conservative system of choosing a Leader would take the load off their shoulders. I pointed out that the Election system was at its best in Opposition but could create serious difficulties in

Government if the Party mafia decided to elect a man to be Prime Minister who was not acceptable to the majority of the Cabinet. This point had not occurred to him. I asked him about his own expertise in this field and said, 'What would happen if you were knocked down by a bus?' He replied that he thought the Queen could just about manage it now.

I asked him about the official view of Anastasia, the daughter of the Tsar, and he said that he thought there was nothing in this. There was an old tradition of pretenders to the throne in Russia and that in any case there was no money to be picked up. I then asked him whether there would be any family embarrassment created if it was suggested that the Queen went on a state visit to the Soviet Union. He said that he thought the memory of the massacres at Ekaterinburg would certainly have prevented George V or VI from going and he thought it still might be difficult. I then asked why it was that there had been no embarrassment with the German relatives who had fought against us in two world wars. Adeane replied, 'Oh but the German royalty are all very decent chaps.'

Next we moved to Edward VIII and I said I thought it would be inexpressibly tragic when he died and his funeral took place. There would be a national sense of guilt that we were prepared to honour a man in his death but not during his life. Adeane hastened to point out that, certainly within the last few years, the Duke of Windsor's decision to live abroad was his own and he was happy in his house in Paris. He also said that experience in Belgium, where King Leopold continued to live, showed how embarrassing and difficult it could be to have a former King on the premises. I said I thought that there would be some feeling about the Duchess of Windsor when her husband was taken away from her in death and put back in his position in the long line of King Emperors. He completely misunderstood my point and he said that there was a place prepared for the Duchess of Windsor as well in the vaults.

Then he raised the question of stamps and I asked him how he had liked the album. He said that the rule about having a monarch's head on the stamps had, he thought, always referred to the ruling monarch and he had some doubts about the use of previous rulers. I said that it would be easy to put the Queen's head on every single monarch's stamp although it might not look good. I asked him whether there would be any difficulty about having Cromwell or Edward VIII among the rulers and sounded so reasonable and earnest that I feel sure I disarmed him. I told him that the Secretary of State for the Colonies had once sent a circular out to colonial territories, pointing out that the royal crest or cipher, which he had suggested to me might be tried, would be appropriate in cases where the Queen's head was not used. He was so keen to seem up-to-date and 'with it' that he said he couldn't understand why people didn't like the new stamps. So I sloshed him between the eyes by telling him what Archbishop Lord Fisher of Lambeth had written to me[9] and he didn't know what to make of it. This was a story that told heavily against what I was trying to do but indicated the grave and serious way in which I undertook my duties.

Afterwards we walked in the sunken gardens briefly and then came home.

Saturday 21 May

We went to lunch with the Croslands today. This was in the nature of a peace-offering. Ever since I asked Susan Crosland not to publish the profile that she had written about me in the *Sun* and ever since Caroline became active in the Comprehensive Schools Committee, things have been a bit frosty. But they were quite agreeable and we enjoyed our talk. Susan's younger daughter is going to Holland Park in the autumn and they are keen that she should get to know some friends there.

The Cooper-Clay fight took place this evening and Clay won, having opened the cut in Cooper's eye so that the fight had to be stopped in the sixth round.

Sunday 22 May

Today's *Sunday Telegraph* said that a group of MPs thought that I was being cowardly about the pirates and were pressing Harold Wilson to get rid of me as a weak Minister and find someone strong enough to deal with them. This was more than I could stand as I have tried to get a pirate Bill into the legislative programme in three separate sessions and the Cabinet had got cold feet, with Harold Wilson having the coldest of all. He enjoys the pirates and has always been trying to find some way of taxing them. This of course would be guaranteed to consolidate their strength and the Treasury would then never let us kill them.

So I rang him at Chequers and blew up. I said I was absolutely sick of the delay in getting the broadcasting policy out, that the ministerial committee had not met since the Election and that the pirate issue was reflecting on the integrity of the Government. The whole thing was becoming disreputable. I have never spoken to Harold like that before and I think it shook him. But being nice and quiet and easy doesn't help you much. Caroline has been saying this for a long time and I think she's right.

Monday 23 May

I had a word with Edmund Dell about the future of the telecommunications industry and he told me in greater detail than I had ever heard before of the report that Jones (an ex-Post Office engineer now at the Ministry of Technology) had written and sent over to the Post Office last year. I asked for a copy of this report. It contained, as I suspected, all the criticisms that I had formed in my own mind about the industry and the way the Post Office pursued its procurement policy. It is little short of scandalous that I should not have been told of this report. In fact a year has gone by with practically no action on this front. This is one of the difficulties of having a Minister who is not authorised to deal sternly with his own department.

At one o'clock Wratten and I set off for Sweden, collecting my passport (which had expired) from home on the way, We caught an SAS Caravelle, leaving London at about 3 o'clock.

We were met at the airport by Olaf Palme, the Minister of Communications, a former secretary to Tage Erlander and tipped as a future leader of his Party and Prime Minister. I had met him on a number of occasions at Labour Conferences with Peter Shore.

Mackenzie, a diplomat from the British Embassy, also met us and he and Wratten drove to the Grand Hotel in the Ambassador's Rolls. Wratten told me afterwards that Mackenzie had said to him that Olaf Palme was just like Harold Wilson in that nobody trusted him. He also said that he might well be the next leader of his Party but would never be Prime Minister – thus confirming his conservative sympathies. I have never known a Foreign Office man who was any good and Mackenzie joins a long list of Tory failures.

I drove back with Olaf Palme and he outlined the organisation of his Ministry. He has a permanent secretary – which is a political appointment – a Director General of posts and telecommunications combined, and others responsible for legal affairs etc. There are only about seventy people in his department. I got back to the hotel just before 6 and dictated this in the lovely room overlooking the harbour. The sun is shining over the water and Stockholm looks as beautiful as ever.

This evening I went to dinner with Olaf, his officials and the General Secretary of the postal workers' union. We discussed Vietnam and Palme said the Swedish Government had taken a strong view against American bombing and had won wide public support. The Opposition did not agree with this view but dare not express their criticism because the public was so strongly behind the Government's attitude. We talked about the problem of microbugs and walkie-talkies and after dinner Olaf walked back to the hotel with us.

Tuesday 24 May
At 9 am I walked over to the Ministry of Communications for the morning's discussions. We gathered in a conference room with Olaf. The ministerial machinery was interesting. There is a meeting with the King in Council once a week where all decisions are formally ratified. The Cabinet meets once to three times a week and no minutes whatsoever are kept. In addition, there is a Cabinet lunch every day at which most decisions are taken on an entirely informal basis. These are conveyed to the departments by the Ministers concerned.

All files of the departments are open to the public unless declared secret on grounds of national security, criminal record or medical record. The public can see anything they like once the current negotiations relating to it are completed. The Ombudsman, elected by Parliament, has direct access to the files of the department and publishes an annual report. Any members of the public can go to the Ombudsman.

We adjourned to the Ronda Restaurant where we had lunch with a number of officials, including two from the British Embassy.

The main discussion at lunch was about the new republican movement which has grown up among the young members of the Social Democratic Party, supported by young Liberals and with some measure of support from young Conservatives. This is not personally directed against the King, who is popular, but is an expression of the general democratic spirit. They feel it is wrong to have a King in a democratic country.

Olaf Palme had been in charge of the constitutional development before he became Minister of Communications last October and he told me that when he had announced his plans he had included a reference to the possibility of reviewing the functions of the head of state. But others at the lunch thought it unlikely that the Swedish Labour Party would actually make an issue of the monarchy, which was popular.

In the afternoon we met the legal adviser to the Ministry who had flown back from Helsinki specially to give me a briefing on pirate radio. There was legislation passed in Sweden in 1962 along the lines of the legislation we now propose but it was not really effective. Earlier this year it was decided to introduce stronger legislation which would give the Government power to seize mainland property attaching to those engaged in pirate broadcasting to the equivalent value of the ship at sea and its advertising revenue. This law was passed about four weeks ago and at this stage it was realised by the pirates that the game was up.

However, Olaf himself was threatened with a bomb attack and at his 1 May meeting in Malmo about 25,000 people turned up to see the bombing. In fact, this was organised by teenagers and all that happened was that some eggs were thrown at him. This swung public opinion in favour of the Government. Olaf admitted that the pirate radios were popular among teenagers but thought that once they had been withdrawn there would be little memory of what they had been like after a few months. What is interesting is that he found it necessary to have tougher legislation than we presently envisage in order to be effective. With the music network which is now in the process of being settled, the political effect of dealing with the pirates is not as bad as was feared and they are satisfied they have found an answer to the problem.

We adjourned at about 4 o'clock and I went with Olaf to the Riksdag, which is the Parliament. We walked round and I looked in to see both chambers debating. Then he took me to the Prime Minister's office and Erlander came out for a moment and we had a short chat. He said that he had been hoping that Harold Wilson would pay a private visit for talks with him on European matters during the first weekend in August, and that Harold had replied positively. Erlander said that this visit would help him with his own municipal elections in September. He is a charming man of about sixty-four or sixty-five and will soon be retiring as Prime Minister. The next parliamentary elections are in 1968 and among the likely successors as Leader of the Party is Olaf Palme who at thirty-nine is very much the young dynamic Minister and an intimate friend of Erlander himself.

At 5.30 we drove to the airport for the flight from Stockholm to Copenhagen which took about two and a half hours in a prop jet. Then another one and a half hours to Amsterdam where we caught the BEA jet to London, a journey of only forty minutes. As I dictate this, the engines are being cut back and the descent into London begins.

Wednesday 25 May

To the NEC this morning where we got through the business in twenty minutes and George Brown introduced a discussion on the Common Market. It was highly geared to a Party audience and there were no trumpet calls for European integration. He dismissed 'theology' and said the Government was only engaged in a probe. He admitted that the present French Government was opposed but thought that after de Gaulle died the position would change. Certainly we should do nothing to encourage de Gaulle's disruptive tactics against NATO. The whole thing was so anodyne that there was virtually no discussion. Instead, we went on to the seamen's strike and Jack Jones spoke critically to Harold who answered back largely in the language of self-justification.

Lord Brabourne came to lunch to press for an extension of pay-TV on the basis of six months' experience. He probed to see if pay-TV could get the fourth channel. The case for pay-TV is a strong one, but the case for a private business monopoly is extremely weak. Brabourne is an aristocratic and well-connected front man for a powerful pressure group and he's always seeing Ministers, including George Brown, Herbert Bowden and others.

I watched Caroline doing her Jackanory story. It was great.

Tommy and Peter and I had dinner together and Dick joined us later. I really let my hair down about my present frustrations and made it pretty clear that I thought Harold ought to give more support than he does. I agreed strongly when Dick said that it was only through being disloyal and leaking and making rows that you could get anything done. This rather shocked Peter who still thinks that basically Harold is on the right side. I am coming increasingly to suspect that Harold doesn't want trouble and the person who makes the most trouble will get his own way. I think I went a bit far indicating this but it won't do any harm if it gets back to Harold. Indeed last Sunday's telephone call to Harold has already activated Herbert Bowden, and the broadcasting White Paper will be authorised next month. It is all beginning to prove Caroline right.

Thursday 26 May
Arnold Goodman came to discuss broadcasting. He said he thought the ITV should have all the hours they want (with which I agree) and saw a possibility of a public corporation running pay-TV on the fourth channel. It might later take the University of the Air, which he thinks should start on BBC2. He promised to canvass Harold in support of the outlines of my White Paper.

To the Commons for the debate on the Emergency Regulations (Rhodesia) and had a long and pleasant talk to Dennis Howell* about pay-TV. He said he thought the sporting world liked the idea of pay-TV and big screens but hated Jarvis Astaire who was setting himself up as a monopoly promoter. The Clay fight had made a large profit for Astaire and he and Levine had only managed to sign Cassius Clay on by promising to pay a direct subsidy to the Black Muslims in Britain. The fight game sounds a lot dirtier than politics.

* Under-Secretary for Education and Science with responsibility for sport.

Friday 27 May
A slight difficulty is coming up about the seminar on stamp design. Fitton is so angry that the Gentleman album was not done through the Stamp Advisory Committee that he has persuaded the Committee to boycott the seminar. Also the *Sunday Times* magazine is going ahead with its item on stamps and if it shows anything that has not already gone to the Palace there could be an explosion there because designs would come out before they were finalised.

I rang Godfrey Smith, editor of the *Sunday Times* colour magazine, and got his agreement that I should see the layout before it goes to the printers and shall write to the Palace and tell them what is coming up so that there is no difficulty. I am also sending the whole album to Harold with a letter, bringing him up to date. It's going to be a tricky operation but once it is over I shall have breached the ramparts.

Saturday 28 May
Caroline was going to Paris today and I took the children to Stansgate by car. I took a little bit of work to do but only managed to read the draft papers for my colleagues on broadcasting prepared by my department. They nearly drove me crazy. They listed every conceivable objection to the proposals that I had made and then ended up by saying 'nevertheless I ask my colleagues to agree' etc, etc. I realise that I shall have to write these papers myself.

Thursday 2 June
The world football stamps came out yesterday, showing a minute black silhouette of the Queen's head. They represent the second major breakthrough in my policy and will pave the way nicely for the Gentleman album.

At 9 o'clock this morning to Thomson House to see the layout for the *Sunday Times* colour supplement feature on British postage stamps. Fortunately they have included a number of different items and have not concentrated unduly on the Gentleman album. They are showing our old definitives, some colonial stamps, the Stanley Gibbons pictorial stamps and the Rulers of Great Britain with a few others from the Gentleman album. I suggested removing the birds without the Queen's head and including Rosalind Dease's costume stamps in pairs. Godfrey Smith was there to meet me. It was kind of him to give me this opportunity and most of my anxieties about this are now allayed.

At 11.30 to see Douglas Houghton about the next stage in the battle to get the Post Office status changed. We had a brief discussion about my plan for establishing a Fellowship to study the way in which the Post Office might provide a link between the social services and those in the community who need their help. My department have been much opposed to this project. They warned me that the social services departments were deeply suspicious of the project. However, Houghton was keen and more or less cleared the way for me to go ahead. It just shows you shouldn't believe what the network tells you other Ministers are thinking. We had a pleasant talk about a whole host of general political issues. I like Douglas Houghton and although he's considered right wing, he is in many respects a reformer and he was rather skeptical about the reforming zeal of some of his colleagues.

After I left him I went and had lunch with Geoffrey Goodman, the industrial editor of the *Sun*. In accordance with my new policy of being frank, I talked openly about all the issues that were current, including Vietnam, the lack of impetus shown by the new Government, the difficulties over prices and incomes, broadcasting, and so on. I draw the line at any critical comment about any named colleagues but do not see why I should become a mere spokesman for the Government on every private as well as public occasion.

On to the Emergencies Committee called to counter the seamen's strike. Returned home. The strike is not making any great difference to ordinary life, although it is doing grave damage to the economy. The Ministry of Labour are, as usual, absolutely obsessed with the necessity of being non-provocative and I am not even allowed to suspend the parcels service to Northern Ireland for that reason. I cannot see the logic of this but the policy is not for me to make.

Friday 3 June
I had a note from the DG in response to my proposal that Ron Smith and Charles Smith might come along to a special meeting with the Post Office Board to discuss the meaning of industrial democracy and see if we could carry it a stage further. He suggested this meeting should be entirely informal and I agree with this. Industrial democracy is in the air at the moment, and I think the Post Office is an absolutely perfect model on which to start.

Monday 6 June
Today an invitation came in from Marcia Williams for me to go to Chequers on Tuesday for the night, to have dinner with Harold and then continue our talks the following morning. Harold realises, at last, that he is in real trouble and that is why he has summoned his old 'friends'. I think the time has come for a bit of frankness and I spent part of the evening drawing up a list of discontents, so that the least I can do is to tell him frankly what people are thinking. There

is an apparent loss of impetus by the Government. On key issues such as Vietnam, East of Suez and prices and incomes there is disagreement in the Party. There is uncertainty or inaction on other issues, notably Rhodesia and Britain's relations with the European Community, Britain's world role, parliamentary reform and Party organisation. There has been serious mishandling of the Parliamentary Labour Party since the Election, and, finally, our sense of purpose needs rearticulating.

Caroline had her Comprehensive Schools Committee meeting this evening and I worked late.

Tuesday 7 June

Left home at 8 o'clock to go to see Mother with a bunch of flowers from the garden for her sixty-ninth birthday.

I looked in at the Commonwealth Relations Office for twenty minutes to talk to Judith Hart who, like me, was invited to go down to Chequers this evening. First I went to John Grigg's for dinner and left about nine o'clock. I got to Chequers at 10.45 and found Harold, Marcia, Gerald, Peter and Tommy Balogh all comfortably settled in the white drawing room. Judith joined us at about 11.30.

We talked until well after 3 o'clock, ranging over the whole field of politics. Harold was badly shaken by the appalling press that he got over the weekend, suggesting that he had lost his grip on the Party. He had called us in because he felt the time had come to listen to his friends. I found a curious ambivalence in my attitude to him. If one wanted to talk as a friend it meant identifying every problem from his viewpoint and trying to help him to overcome the criticism to which he was subjected. But I am not sure that I am not one of the critics.

He began with his now famous theme that the British public was bored with politics and wanted him to be the doctor who looked after the difficulties so that it could go on playing tennis. I challenged that fundamentally and said I thought it was an elitist view of politics and was incompatible with a radical Government. Maybe the public didn't understand economics and was sick of the abuse of Party politics, but it was interested in real politics and it was our duty to pick those issues which related to matters we thought important and actually make them controversial. I cited the educational issue as an example and said that I thought the status of women in society might be another.

Harold didn't much like this but his idea that the public will go on comfortably enjoying rising living standards while the Labour Party worries about the affairs of the nation is getting dangerously close to Harold Macmillan's 'You've never had it so good' and that the Tories are the Party born to rule.

On Vietnam, Harold indicated that he hoped at some stage another initiative might be possible but he was obviously not prepared to say anything whatsoever that might divide him from the Americans. About the only move he will make is to tone down the praise for American action which Michael Stewart is continually giving.

On East of Suez he was bitter at what he called the cynical coalition between the extreme Right represented by Christopher Mayhew and the pacifists and fellow-travelling Left. He was obviously worried by the Party meeting which is to take place next Wednesday and wants our advice on what sort of speech he should make. We all went as far as we could in pointing out that he must identify with the Left and articulate their anxieties.

He was optimistic that the situation in Rhodesia might be settled within two months. Since Judith was there and knew all about it, I didn't think there was much I could offer there.

On prices and incomes it appeared that he thought there was some solution which would enable Frank Cousins to stay on. Since he had more or less offered me Frank Cousin's job in October, I felt this was a hint to me that I wouldn't get my move.

I stressed the need for better handling of the Parliamentary Labour Party and said that I thought the Leader of the House ought to perform the role Herbert Morrison performed, by spilling his authority over into Transport House with a new General Secretary in charge. Harold said he was in favour of a Commission to look at the Labour Party, which he thought George Brown might chair and of which I might be a member. But I will believe that when I see it. We all pressed him to get rid of Len Williams by ennobling and promoting him so that he wouldn't actually be in situ while the enquiry was going on. He had doubts about this.

We also discussed the seamen's strike which is causing him some anxiety, although he kept referring to it as a 'toothache'. In fact it is much more serious than that and with the cost of the sanctions against Rhodesia and the real difficulty in maintaining the prices and incomes policy, and the disappearance of the import surcharge in the autumn, the short-term economic position is very tricky indeed. Tommy Balogh kept referring to this.

I finally went to bed at 3.35 with the first light of dawn beginning to illuminate the distant Buckinghamshire horizon. My bedroom was the one that Harold Macmillan used throughout his period of office.

Wednesday 8 June

Up just before 8 and had a bath. Breakfast was brought into my room by the WRAF orderly. Then I went for a short walk round the house and took some movies. At 9.30 the same group gathered in deckchairs on the patio overlooking the garden at the front of the house. Coffee was brought and we talked till 12.

We ranged round the same subjects and it was generally agreed that this group should start meeting again so as to keep in touch with Harold and advise him. I think he still has the idea that he's going to be able to talk himself out of his difficulties. But I am not sure it will be as easy as that. One of the factors about being an isolated person is that your triumphs are personal and no one shares them, but your defeats are personal and there are not all that many people prepared to share them either.

Having said that, I must admit he was very agreeable and it was pleasant to feel that one had access to him over a wide range of subjects. I told him that Jim Callaghan had more or less stopped my Post Office reorganisation and that I needed his support on my broadcasting White Paper. He was pretty noncommittal and this was clearly not the time to make a scene. But I do mean to make a scene on both these things if I'm not given backing.

We had lunch and I told him about my plan to appoint a Fellow to study the relations between the social services and the public using the agency of the Post Office on both the postal and telephone sides. After lunch I managed to get a short movie picture of him on the steps and then at 1 o'clock my driver, Wilson, drove me back to London. I was dog-tired, had a thumping headache and was terribly behind with my work.

I had a short time at home and then went to the Ministerial Committee on Broadcasting, where I had a tremendous battle on local sound broadcasting and on the new music network. In the end, I more or less scraped through on both. I was authorised to talk to the BBC and the Institute for Practitioners in Advertising on the possibility of the music network. I was also more or less authorised to hint that we were looking carefully at the possibility of an alternative to the pirate stations. But I made no progress on the promise to get legislation to deal with the pirates. I did make one suggestion that the Bill might be integrated with the Bill to deal with licence evasion which already has a place in the current session.

This committee, however, is not the full Cabinet and it will be a matter of running the gauntlet in Cabinet again. Whether I shall be able to do any effective canvassing or not, I don't know. We cannot postpone our broadcasting White Paper much longer but if some of the more negative members of the Cabinet got their way, there would in fact be no broadcasting policy of any sort to announce.

Thursday 9 June

All morning dictating my revised paper on the future organisation of the Post Office. I finally concluded that one public corporation with separate executive Boards of Management would be the right solution. Douglas Houghton is keen and I believe that if anyone can carry it through, he can.

Afterwards to the Emergencies Committee. The seamen's strike may be entering a new phase but fortunately I do not have acute departmental difficulties yet.

Saturday 11 June

Caroline and I arrived in Manchester early for the Lancashire Miners' Gala and were driven to Wigan for breakfast. There we met up with the various miners' leaders and marched for about an hour through the streets to the fairground where the Gala was being held. These occasions have become folk festivals and I spoke for ten or fifteen minutes to a small group of about 150 who happened to be gathered around the platform. Meanwhile the rest of the festival was going on over a huge field, with few people listening to what was said on the platform. Caroline crowned the Gala queen and we finally got away in the Mayor's car after it became obvious to us that Joe Gormley had lost all interest in getting us back to Manchester and would have been a most unsafe driver had he tried to do so.

Sunday 12 June

Worked all afternoon on my reports on the Japanese and Swedish visits and in the evening Caroline and I went to the American Embassy for a show. Barbra Streisand sang at the end. She is a very striking woman and has tremendous power and personality. The theatre was crammed with celebrities and Ministers and we had a chance to talk to one or two people.

Monday 13 June

To the Office this morning. Sir John Ricks, the solicitor, and Mr Lillicrap came to discuss the problem of pirates. I want a prosecution as soon as I can but Ricks is incredible in finding reasons why it can't be done.

I invited Matthew Coady of the *New Statesman* to lunch and we had a talk about the Party's present difficulties. The fact is the Government and Harold have had an appalling press over the last few weeks. Somehow all the magic seems to have rubbed off and he is under serious attack. He has not really entrenched himself with the Right and has alienated himself from the Left. Lew Grade came to see me and put in his demand for a limited colour service, a second channel, and the usual list of ATV demands. I had seen him at Harold's request.

After that David Butler and Tony King looked in for a moment, having just come out of their talks with Harold Wilson about the Election campaign. They told me that Harold had said to them that he had not taken any interest in the date of the Hull by-election last January as an indicator for the General Election. This I know to be untrue and so do they.

Stayed in the House all evening and came back by tube at 12.15.

Tuesday 14 June
This morning I spoke at the telecommunications session of the Commonwealth Press Union. Gavin Astor of the *Times* was in the chair. I talked about the technical developments in communications, particularly the role of satellites. I also raised the question of the Commonwealth press rate and pointed out that a penny a word was not satisfactory. The speech went down well to a mixed group of proprietors and journalists. I saw Sir Harry Brittain, a founder of the Commonwealth Press Union, who said that he remembered as a boy, in 1878, being taken to see a piece of apparatus which someone told him was a telephone. At that time there were only eight of them connected in London.

Dick Clements of *Tribune* came to have lunch with me, the first time I've really seen him since the Election. He was talking about the need to keep the argument going inside the Labour movement. He was absolutely certain that the Labour Government would be re-elected in the next Election and possibly in the Election after, and that this gave us scope to maintain a real opposition and dialogue within the Party. He had retained his faith in Harold Wilson but this of course dates from the old days of Left-wing collaboration. The fact is that some of the new Left don't realise that Harold ever was associated with the Left and this is, in part, his difficulty. We discussed Party organisation which he thought ought to be much more regionalised with less power in the centre and with more democratic regions.

Afterwards I worked on the presentation to the Chancellor of my case for having two Directors General. Jim looked rather tired. I put to him, with great force, the absolute necessity of having one man in charge of the telephone service and another in charge of posts. I pointed out that this was the view of McKinsey's, this was my view, this was the view of my predecessors – those of them who have written memoirs – and I think I made some impact. Helsby had obviously reported against it and had told the Chancellor that German was against it too.

I didn't use my trump card – namely that I would take it to Harold Wilson if he didn't agree. Then I raised with him the question of changing the status of the Post Office to a nationalised industry. He said his main anxiety was that there shouldn't be a new centre of authority in the financial world not under his control. I reassured him that he could have all the control he wanted over the investment, financial and monetary policy of the Post Office Savings Bank, so long as it had managerial independence to run itself in an efficient way. I had a feeling that Jim was weakening and that I would get this through.

Afterwards I dashed over to Transport House for the first meeting of the Science and Industry Sub-Committee where the subject was the development of industrial democracy in Britain. I had asked to be allowed to go on the committee because I was keen to make some progress in the Post Office. Jack Jones was in the chair. We laid our plans for the weekend conference in the autumn.

Then Caroline and I went to the new *Times* building for a reception given for the Commonwealth press. I had an interesting talk with Lord Devlin about the possible application of the press council principle to broadcasting and also about the legal difficulties I was experiencing with the pirates. He said he had met me at Uncle Ernest's house thirty-five years ago.

I was dropped off at Dick Crossman's house for the reconvened meetings on Party strategy. Tommy Balogh, Peter Shore and Gerald Kaufman were there, with Judith Hart joining us for the first time. She is very able and I like her immensely. Dick was utterly sunk in gloom and said he didn't care what happened to Rhodesia, he thought the incomes policy was nonsense and that unemployment was coming anyway and that it would be much better to have unemployment than to try to hold incomes down. It was Dick the teacher emerging, but it is wearing.

We were frank with Dick and I told him that he was a complete obstructionist on every reform other than his own. He glories in being a departmental Minister and is saving up all that he has to say about politics for his book which he says he is going to start writing in three years time. He keeps the most elaborate diary.

Tommy is entirely obsessed with the day-to-day economic problems but is very useful on it. He's also rather exaggerated in his comments, reiterating today that Gerald Gardiner should have been publicly hanged for having advocated an increase in judges' salaries.

We ranged over a number of subjects but dwelt heavily upon

Harold's own personal position. Evidently he did badly today at question time when he tried to score off Mayhew and was heard in silence. Even when he turned to attack the Tories our own people didn't support him. It would be foolish to say that Harold is finished but the magic has definitely gone and however clever he is now, he is not going to be able to restore himself to the position he occupied six months ago. Indeed I think it would be wrong to try, for a reputation based upon political skill is bound to be a bubble reputation. If he wants to carry people with him, they must see him as an instrument of a cause greater than he is, or as someone with a vision of the future.

Tommy and the others reiterated the fact that Harold didn't use his power. Indeed Judith said that she thought he had an inferiority complex based on the fact that for years he had had to manipulate on the National Executive and in the Shadow Cabinet because he knew that he was always in a minority. I think it may well be the case that Harold has got a profound inferiority complex and that means that those who want to help him have got to persuade him to be tough and strong.

Dick crudely said he thought we needed a cabal that would make difficulties which had to be listened to. I think he may well be right but I'm not sure that if there were such a cabal I would want to be in it with Dick, who is so entirely unpredictable.

At the end of the evening, Judith and Peter and I agreed to start meeting regularly. Dick is profoundly defeatist and thinks that the Labour Government is really finished and is getting to be more concerned about his book, explaining why it happened rather than how it can be corrected. Pen Balogh is the wisest of all and sees it clearly, more so even than Tommy.

Wednesday 15 June
Today was one of the best days that I've had since I've been at the Post Office. Everything seemed to go right.

It began with the Stamp Advisory Committee at the Design Centre at 10 o'clock. It was only the second time I had attended and I went there knowing that the whole committee had decided to go on strike against the Gentleman album and our proposed stamp seminar. They were angry that the album had been commissioned without their consent, they were angry that they had not seen it, they were angry at the idea of the seminar, and they were determined to teach me a lesson. From my point of view the meeting couldn't have gone better. Their own approved designs for British technology were a complete shambles. I had kept entirely aloof from this exercise. When the designs that were produced were handed round they were obviously very bad. Jim Fitton is a disastrous chairman and when Mr Beaumont from the Post Office read out the comments of the technological authorities who had been consulted about the stamps, they contained a list of fatal defects of technological detail on each of them. In the end it was only just possible to scrape together a few that would make a first choice.

Then came the Battle of Hastings. The Committee had previously chosen for essaying a double Gentleman design and some others which were no good. At my suggestion Gentleman had extended this double stamp into six, all printed in a block showing a whole section of the Bayeux Tapestry, divided by perforations. These were produced and everybody liked them. Thus Gentleman had scored a notable triumph before we had really started. The Committee was unanimous in recommending the entire Gentleman series. In doing so, they had also approved a small head.

Next came Gentleman's album, which I laid out on the table. I explained that the seminar had arisen out of my audience with the Queen and that these were experimental designs and that a discussion would be useful. Then the criticism began. The designer Abram Games said that they were like a lot of cigarette cards. I should add that it was Gentleman's Churchill stamp that had displaced his own design. Others were equally critical. At about this time Lady Sempill discovered that I was the Postmaster General and became acutely embarrassed because she had been fulminating quietly against me for an hour and thought I was just a young clerk from the Post Office. She never recovered from that discovery because the rest of the meeting she devoted to wondering what I might have heard that she might have said. She left early.

I went on to say how important I thought the seminar was and I had hoped that Jim Fitton would take the chair but I understood that he was going to be away and couldn't do it and I was awfully sorry. He then admitted that he was going to be in England but didn't want to be committed to the designs. He said he didn't like them. So I said, 'Well, if you don't like them, you'd better say so at the seminar. The great advantage of having the stamps that are experimental is that no one is committed to them, and if you like to say that you think the head is too small and the crest is unacceptable and the solution is no good and they are like cigarette cards – say it at the seminar.'

This statement had an electric effect, for all of a sudden these people realised that it was to be a seminar and that they could say what they liked. Then one of them thought and said, 'But the press will be there and they will hear what we say about the experimental stamps. You can't have the press there.' 'Oh,' I said. 'That's easy to deal with. I shall simply say at the beginning that the press may report and write about the discussion and about the stamps but I shall ask them to respect the individual views of those who take part and not quote individual opinions.'

By then the ranks of the Stamp Advisory Committee had broken, and they all wanted to be in on the act. When I promised them a second seminar in the autumn to show their own work on the new definitive series and Andrew Restall's work and the work of his students, they were completely captured. The only rearguard action was a further expression of regret that the press should be allowed to hear the discussion. One of them said, 'Wouldn't it be better if we decided what to do about the stamps before we told the public?' I said that the whole purpose of my policy was to encourage public discussion and not to regard stamp design as something that had to be kept secret. That more or less clinched it.

Just before I left, the Post Office Christmas card which I have designed was circulated. I thought it wise to get out before the comments were made. It is entirely my own project. Five million of these Christmas cards will be printed, sold in post offices, and we shall make a profit and pioneer our entry into the greetings business.

Yesterday, I received a letter from Sir Michael Adeane, the Queen's private secretary. The text is extraordinary, so I will dictate it into my diary.

Windsor Castle, 13th June 1966

Dear Postmaster General

Thank you for your letter of 10th June which I have shown to the Queen.

Her Majesty is interested to read about the seminar which is to be held this month and about the *Sunday Times* colour supplement, which is being published in July, and she hopes that the wide public interest in British stamp design which you have aroused in this country and which is now being re-echoed in the United States of America, will continue to have fruitful results. You can rest assured that this is far from being a subject which Her Majesty regards in any way as 'routine'; she looks forward to the design which you should submit because she realises, better than most people perhaps, that the postage stamp, which we invented, remains one of the best ways of reminding the world of what we are and what we are doing.

I, too, enjoyed our meeting at Hampton Court and am grateful to whatever deity arranges the seating round dining room tables. I hope it may be repeated before too long. Yours sincerely, Michael Adeane.

That letter ends the first chapter in the reconstruction of British stamps. All Palace opposition is now over and once the stamps are shown to the public and widely seen and discussed in the press, things will never be the same again. I care much less about the Queen's head issue now than I did. The little black head that we put on is perfectly satisfactory. Indeed the little gold head may be even better. It may be I shall get away with the royal crest on the Rulers of Great Britain series next February as a special case. But even if I have to put a little gold head on each of those we shall have got back into the absolute lead in world stamp design. It is immensely satisfying.

From the Design Centre to the House of Commons, for the end of the much publicised PLP meeting on our East of Suez policy. I got there in time to hear Norman Atkinson who made a good speech for the Left and Jack Ashley who said that he agreed with the motion but didn't want to vote, and Phil Noel-Baker who said that he didn't believe in East of Suez and the UN peacekeeping force was the only one in which he was interested. Harold spoke for an hour in answer. It was a speech that was far too long and he gabbled over it. It may read well but there was much too much self-justification and self-quotation to make it really good. He didn't hammer the major points and he didn't really answer some of the questions that had been put. But he scored an overwhelming vote of over 200 to 54. I think it was a mistake to vote because a vote tends to close an argument, whereas a dialogue where the weight of argument is able to stand on its merits is much more effective.

I had lunch with Barbara Castle. She raised with me again her idea that Ministers ought to stand down from the National Executive at Conference this year. She says that we are no good on the Executive and we ought to make way for Back Benchers. I think in the back of her mind is the fear that she might be defeated and that she is losing her role as the leader of the Left. I doubt if she would be defeated. But I told her frankly that I would rather be defeated than give up my place. I said that in the Executive I had scope that I didn't have as a non-Cabinet Minister and that I was using the Executive to help me with some practical Post Office problems. Barbara was embarrassed with this and told me that she had spoken to Jim Callaghan who said that he wasn't going to stand down because he wanted to be chairman of the Party. This reminded me that I shall be chairman of the Party one year before Jim Callaghan because his service was broken when I knocked him off the Executive on my way back on it. I added that I had left the Executive once under the most inauspicious circumstances and I didn't intend to leave it again when I had just got back. I said I had no intention of asking Harold Wilson's opinion as I had no intention of accepting it unless it confirmed me in my decision to stand again. Dick Crossman could leave the Executive if he liked, having been chairman and being a departmental Minister who had abandoned interest in politics. Tony Greenwood was wobbling all over the place – that was evident. Anyway I spoke frankly to her and I would be surprised now if she decided to give up.

I told her that I thought her whole line on the democracy of everyone owning their own vehicle was wrong and she ought to talk about everyone's right to use vehicles and move towards the renting of them, rather than the ownership of them. She said that she would like to discuss this later.

At 6.30 the Communications Group met and Hugh Jenkins opened it by giving his views on the need for a national music programme to replace the pirates and on local broadcasting. As a result of a secret briefing I had given him some weeks ago, his plan was exactly the same as the one in my White Paper and to my delight the overwhelming majority of the Communications Group agreed with it. Even Christopher Rowlands, who is an entire BBC man, said he thought that if there was to be a national pop service, it ought to be run and organised by the BBC and receive advertising. I was overjoyed. I was called to say a word or two and I stressed all the difficulties and said that none of them might easily be overcome but I would like to hear the views of the group on a series of questions which I then posed. A division was called in the middle of this and we are going to resume it next week. Hugh Jenkins will then write to Harold conveying the view that I am simultaneously presenting in my White Paper. It will greatly strengthen my case.

As I came out of the division lobby, Jim Callaghan said he wanted to see me but he had Macleod with him at the time so I went and had a meal with Hugh Jenkins and then Jim and I had an hour's talk on the terrace.

This was the final success of the day. Jim told me that although Sir Laurence Helsby was opposed to my managerial reorganisation of the Post Office with two Directors General and so was Sir Ronald German, he had decided to come out on my side. He said that he had told them that a young and keen Minister ought to be allowed to organise the department in the way he thought right and that even if I was wrong no possible disaster could follow. I had expected a 'no' from Jim and was preparing to take it to Harold personally. He said that he would have difficulty with Helsby, to which I replied, 'Oh I can't believe that the Chancellor of the Exchequer can't get his own way on anything he wants.' 'You would be surprised,' he said. 'I have the most terrific tussles with my department. But Helsby refused me a knighthood for someone the other day and so he will have to pay the price by assenting to your reorganisation. He owes me a knighthood and this will do in exchange.'

I then went on to raise the question of the nationalised industry status and I said that this was essential for efficiency. Jim said that he could see that I was looking at it from the point of view of running an efficient industry but he was looking at it from the point of view of Government control of the economy and he could not tolerate any freedom of action in the banking field that might weaken his financial control over monetary and credit policy by the Savings Bank. Of course I absolutely agree about that and told him so, but said that I felt sure his needs could be met. He said that he hadn't made up his mind but I got the feeling that things were going my way. He is the only obstacle to an early announcement and I told him that the unions were coming round to my way.

He then asked me about the Executive and told me that Barbara had been on to him. I told him exactly what I had told Barbara and we agreed that we should both continue to stand. Neither he nor I were prepared to ask Harold Wilson's advice since this was a political matter within our own discretion. He strongly urged me to go on, saying that he was fifty-four and had only ten more years in politics, whereas I had longer and ought to stick it.

The truth is that after all the disloyal and horrible things I had been saying to Tommy Balogh and others about Jim Callaghan, I warmed to him this evening. He told me that sterling was a nightmare to him and that he never thought he could manage the first six months. 'But you can't die twice,' he said, 'and although we still have terrible problems, I am less worried than I was.'

It was the first time I'd had a friendly political talk to Jim since he came to speak at the Bristol May Day meeting in 1964. It does make politics easier if you have a chance for informal exchanges. He sympathised with my difficulty in arriving at Cabinet meetings and trying to find a seat and being called to speak before I even had time to put down my papers.

During my meal with Hugh Jenkins, Arthur Palmer, MP for Bristol North East, came up. He is on the nationalised industries committee and asked me – out of the blue – whether I didn't think there was a case for nationalising the Post Office. Jim was there so I had to be careful. I said that Clem Attlee had been very much in favour of this in 1931, which was an entirely unexceptionable remark based on historic fact. I said there was a case on either side. But after Jim Callaghan had left, I settled on Arthur Palmer and gave him the whole story. I said how keen I was to go before the Select Committee myself. Jim had said – just before he left – that he thought I should be allowed to go too. I shall take this one up with Harold who has not answered my minute requesting permission to do this. Arthur is obviously an ally on this and I am gradually feeding my friends with the right ideas.

So that is the end of the story of Wednesday 15 June. Success with stamps, the Party Communications Group coming out in favour of my White Paper – without knowing it, an agreement by Jim to my management reorganisation, and a move towards nationalised industry status. No Minister could ask for more from one day.

Thursday 16 June
Peter Shore told me how the work in the Ministry of Technology was proceeding. He is an extremely thoughtful person and for the first time I began to see the role of the Ministry in its proper light. Today it took over most of the Ministry of Aviation and is now one of the biggest departments in Government. Remembering what Harold Wilson told me about Frank Cousins at the Ministry of Technology, I thought I had better keep myself alert.

I had a word with Charles Morris, who told me that he was now directly concerned with the leak procedure which Harold Wilson is presiding over. Apparently Harold is very worried about the volume of leaks, and the relations between every Minister and the press are being scrutinised most carefully. I am being much less discreet in my consultations with people with whom I have to deal but still careful with the press. There has certainly been no complaint about me in this respect for over a year.

Then I went and sat in the whips' office and had a long talk to John Silkin [Labour MP for Deptford] and Gerald Kaufman about the honours list, which we all hate, and about the possibility of reforming the House of Lords on the basis of Privy Councillors without ennoblement. I also talked to Arthur Palmer, Bernard Floud, and Brian O'Malley about the progress of the Select Committee on Nationalised Industries and put them all on the track of a nationalised industry status for the Post Office. To my delight Dr Camm, chairman of the Post Office Users Council, had earlier this afternoon volunteered the information that this seemed the right solution for the Post Office to him. Everything is going my way but I shall just have to be patient and not hurry it too much.

At the end of the day I caught Jim Callaghan's eye as he was leaving the chamber, and he called me into his room. 'I must tell you that I have run into some trouble about your management reorganisation,' he said. 'Helsby has declined to accept my decision and has appealed to the Prime Minister. I am therefore minuting the Prime Minister in support of your proposal and Helsby is appealing directly to him against it. I will see that you get a copy of my minute to the PM and you can then take direct action yourself.' It is astonishing to me that the Chancellor of the Exchequer should be having trouble with his own civil servants, but obviously my Post Office problems are not unique. I can't think that Harold will possibly override Jim and me united on this issue, but I shall have to keep my powder dry.

Home about 2 am, only to realise that it was the beginning of our seventeenth wedding anniversary.

Friday 17 June
I took James Margach of the *Sunday Times* to lunch at St Stephen's. He said that there were no more leaks under this Government than under any previous Government. He also told me that the lobby was angry that Harold Wilson paid so much less attention to them now that he had been elected with a comfortable majority than he used to in the old days. I rather sympathise with Harold. The fact is that seeing the press takes an awful lot of time and for any busy Minister it is hard to find that time. Margach thought that Harold's attitude to the press stemmed from his background as a civil servant and this also explained his obsession with leaks.

At 3.15 the new ministerial committee on the status of the Post Office met under Douglas Houghton. I presented my new paper in which I had come out in favour of a single corporation with three management boards. To my delight, Jack Diamond and Austen Albu gave me strong support and it looked as if we were going to get through without another meeting. However, we were notified that the Ministry of Technology were now in favour of a telecommunications corporation and Edmund Dell was unable to attend to put the point. Also the Ministry of Public Works and Buildings were worried about the risk that they might lose Post Office work. Finally, Austen Albu said that for prices and incomes' reasons it might be difficult if we acquired nationalised industry status too soon and began paying our new chairman £15,000 a year. I pointed out that it would take some time for the legislation to go through and I didn't think this was an immediate problem. On this happy note we adjourned.

I tried to talk to Marcia Williams today to tell her that Jim Callaghan had agreed to support my management changes in the Post Office but that Helsby had announced his intention of appealing to the Prime Minister. Tommy said it was important to get in with the Prime Minister early.

Monday 20 June
To lunch at Camelford House, which is the headquarters of London Telecommunications Region, and spent half an hour with the staff representatives. They were all intensely dissatisfied with their pay

and conditions. I tried to explain that in a situation where you had full employment and labour was short, you couldn't solve recruitment problems by just increasing incomes. But the pressure was obvious.

At 6.30 I went to a meeting for new MPs. I found some of them very cynical. They had all sorts of tricks they wanted to use without any regard to their obligations to their constituents. It was a case of the politicians being more cynical than the PR men, which is unusual.

Back to my office, where I worked on papers till about 11.45. I managed to have a short word with Harold, who said that Helsby had seen him today and had not even mentioned the Chancellor's support for my management proposals. Harold had agreed that these should be postponed until the future status of the Post Office was clearer. When I told him what had happened, he promised to put a stopper on Helsby. I wish I could have got in earlier.

One point of note today: in speaking about the seamen's strike, Harold referred to the Communist influence. This has caused a great deal of dissatisfaction among the Labour Left, and Peter Shore rang to tell me that he thought it was completely bonkers. I think I share that view. Indeed, I am beginning to wonder whether Harold Wilson is not becoming like Lloyd George. We shall have to see.

Tuesday 21 June
I saw the DG and told him that I wanted to get all my Post Office decisions initiated at the time of the annual report on 20 July, including the status announcement, the appointment of the Directors General, the split in the regions, the rationalisation of telecommunications tariffs, the new call box policy, the new structure of postal services, and so on.

To the Commons and this evening to Number 10 for a buffet supper that Harold had laid on. Among those who came were Peter Shore, Ron Brown [MP for Shoreditch and Finsbury], George Wallace [MP for Norwich North], Gerald Kaufman, Marcia, Percy Clark, and Dick's PPS, Geoffrey Rhodes and members of the PLP permanent staff. Harold began by giving his usual analysis. The public 'are not interested in politics and want to play tennis and clean their cars and leave things to the Government. By contrast the Party wants to do things and change things, and the main thing is to keep it on the move like a caravan so that it does not have time to stop and fight'.

The discussion roamed on for some time, so I plucked up my courage and said that if there was a conflict between what the public wanted and what the Party wanted, I was on the side of the Party. Anyway, I didn't agree that the public wasn't interested in politics. They may be sick of Party bickering but they are interested in a whole host of issues that are essentially political and it was the Party's job to show the connection between issues that concerned the public and the political ideology and decisions that we expressed. It was for us to propagandise and campaign, just as it was the job of the Labour pioneers to convince the people fifty years ago that unemployment had something to do with politics.

What worries me is that Harold may be going to preside over a period of decline just as serious as occurred under Macmillan and accept the same basic philosophy of 'never had it so good' affluence that Macmillan accepted. Consensus is no substitute for putting key issues and institutions deliberately into the crucible of controversy. If we don't change things fundamentally, we shall have failed in our job even if we survive as a Government – which is not by any means certain.

Wednesday 22 June

To the Executive this morning. As usual the business went through rapidly but we didn't have a general discussion because the PLP meeting on prices and incomes had been arranged for 11. This was an excellent meeting. George Brown made a first-rate speech and the debate was good. Even the critics were constructive and it was packed to the doors. It is impossible to underestimate the significance of an empty chamber in the Commons for most debates, which is crowded for Party meetings. That is where power now resides and I am coming round to the view that the press should be allowed to attend them.

The Commons sat all night on the Finance Bill and I had to wait for the adjournment on pirate radios. It was a timely debate. Today a boarding party seized Radio City on Shivering Sands fort and the managing director was shot and killed. Gangsterism has moved into the pirates and the Government's failure to act is now an absolute disgrace.

The debate began at 5 am. Hugh Jenkins made a good speech in which he put forward positive proposals that were almost identical to my White Paper. In replying I reaffirmed our intention of acting and discussed publicly the problems associated with providing an alternative.

Thursday 23 June

To Fleet Building this morning for the long-awaited stamp seminar. I took the chair myself and it was well attended. Milner Gray said that he was against the Queen's head and it was clear that most of the artists were. Fitton intervened regularly and rather violently and it was obvious that, as chairman of the Stamp Advisory Committee, he felt on the defensive. I am sure that the seminar justified itself up to the hilt in that the discussion from now on will be intelligent and informed.

I lunched with the stamp designers and afterwards they singled out a dozen entries from the 4,500 submitted by children. Some were excellent.

Then back to the exhibition where I took the press conference. When challenged directly, 'Will you be taking the Queen's head off our stamps?' I replied, 'I cannot visualise the time . . .' This was deliberately ambiguous and will not prevent us from submitting the Rulers of Great Britain series to the Palace for next February. I felt I was marginally betraying my cause, but things have to change slowly.

By now I was so sleepy I could hardly think straight. I worked till 10 and came home.

Friday 24 June
To the Post Office briefly and then to the Tower where I entertained Kai Lindberg, the Danish Minister of Communications, for lunch. He was tall, immensely fat and incredibly dull – without doubt the most boring man I have ever met in my life. He moved slowly, said practically nothing and only gazed occasionally at the fabulous view you get from the Tower. It was the nearest thing to having lunch with a model from Madame Tussaud's.

Briefly home and then to Bristol for the New Bristol Group. John Ollis had come specially and so had Stephen Macfarlane, Gordon Priest and Angus Buchanan. What was meant to be a funeral really became a conception and we agreed to have a public meeting in the autumn to launch a further edition of our paper, *Output 3*, and hope to gather enough interest for others to take it over. We had a splendid discussion that went on late. Bed, tuckered, having had twenty two and a half hours' sleep all week.

Sunday 26 June
Up early and cleared up and dictated for Valerie. This afternoon Caroline took Hilary to the anti-Government Trafalgar Square demonstration on Rhodesia. The children wrote a pop song, music by Stephen and words by Melissa, called 'Marie'.

Monday 27 June
Stayed at home working this morning. Wilson arrived at 12.30, with the new grey Humber Super Snipe equipped with the radio-tele-phone. It is comfortable and the radiophone is a tremendous success and help.

Lunch with *Newsweek* and the *Washington Post* at New Zealand

House. They asked me all sorts of questions about the Common Market, East of Suez, and the malaise in Britain. I was much franker than I would ever have dared to be with British journalists, relying on them to regard it all as background and not to quote me. They told me it was non-attributable. I just hope I don't get into trouble.

My appointment with Harold Wilson this afternoon was cancelled because there was a row in the House over Denis Healey's weekend reference to de Gaulle as being 'untrustworthy' and Jim Callaghan's admission that he had deleted three words from Hansard last week because he thought they might contain a slur against farmers. The House was at its most petty municipal level and I found the whole thing rather revolting.

Ioan Evans came to see me to report on the growing feeling that the Government's inaction against the pirates was becoming a scandal. I felt this strongly all along and had rather given up hope of making progress. However, stirred by Ioan, I rang Harold at Number 10 and told him that something must be done. He said that I should put in a joint paper with the Home Secretary to Cabinet. I said I didn't want to go to the Home Secretary as it could only delay things and that I proposed to put in a paper on my own the following morning. I then sat down straight away and wrote the Cabinet paper, giving the new factors and asking for permission to introduce the Bill at once and have it enacted as soon as possible. It was an all-night sitting tonight and although I had a couple of hours' doze between about 2 and 4, I was talking to people and sitting in the Chamber and sitting on the terrace most of the time.

Tuesday 28 June
The House rose at about 8 and I came home for an hour: just time for a bath and breakfast.

Back to the Commons, where I sat almost all through the debate on the seamen's strike. Harold Wilson began by naming the Communists who had intervened. It made me sick and reminded me of McCarthyism. The Left attacked him almost unanimously with powerful speeches by Michael Foot, Eric Heffer and Ian Mikardo. In a sense Harold said nothing that was new, since every trade union leader knew it and we were all afraid that by going in for these tactics, he would simply make the anti-Communist smear a weapon that every Tory could use against us in the future. All that can be said for his approach is that since the Communists are politically trying to use industrial discontent to break the prices and incomes policy, it is desirable that people should understand this. I am over-sensitive because of the McCarthy period. I am not much convinced by this argument and still feel it was an undesirable thing to have done.

Home about 10.30 and straight to bed.

Wednesday 29 June

To the Office briefly and then to the Commons where Harold Wilson dissociated the Government from the American bombing of Haiphong and Hanoi. Heath criticised him for it and the Left was less than generous. Very few people realised the immense significance of this act of dissociation. From now on, things will never be the same, and we are perhaps witnessing the beginnings of the new policy.

Thursday 30 June

At 10.30 Lord Normanbrook came to see me. The first issue for discussion was our plan for a new music corporation that would provide twenty-four hours of pop and be financed by advertising. He came out with his own Radio 247 scheme, which would cost £200,000 and would simply mean providing a musical option for those parts of the day when 'The Dales' or 'The Archers' were on the Light Programme. We discussed the whole problem fully and although we didn't agree, I think he did understand that the plan I put forward was an attempt to preserve the purity of the BBC, while at the same time dealing with the pirate stations. We then moved on to the idea of a National Broadcasting Commission and the only anxiety he had about that was whether the effect of it would be to weaken the control and power of the BBC Board of Governors. I was able to reassure him that we didn't intend to interfere with programme matters, and on that note I left.

I dashed to Number 10 for the Economic Committee and waited an hour in the ante-chamber before my item was called. It went through in about three minutes and means that tomorrow I can make the announcement about the impending legislation to deal with the pirates.

Afterwards I was asked to wait in Marcia's room as the PM had something he wanted to say to me. While I waited I read my horoscope in the *Evening News*. 'Follow your instincts. This is a lucky day for you.' At that moment Harold came in and I went and had a chat with him in the Cabinet room. 'Frank Cousins is resigning when the Prices and Incomes Bill is published this weekend,' he said, 'and I want you to take his place.' I did not react except to say how sorry I should be to leave the Post Office at this critical moment and on the eve of the announcement of historic changes. 'Well', said Harold, 'that is always liable to happen. You have done an excellent job in modernising an old industry and few people know what has gone on. Now you must start learning and for six months you will have to keep your head down and read, and no gimmicks.' (That from Harold!)

So that is it. Unless Frank Cousins changes his mind the announcement will be made on Sunday and I am in the Cabinet with a chance to create a new department that can really change the face of Britain and its prospects for survival.

NOTES
Chapter Four

1. The National Economic Development Council, known as Neddy, was set up by Harold Macmillan in 1962, and comprised Ministers, representatives of industry and trade unions meeting on a monthly basis to discuss broad economic and industrial problems. In 1964 the NEDC had special responsibilities for the discussion and development of the National Plan (see Note 2) and it was agreed to establish a series of Economic Development Committees – little Neddies – for certain industries. The original concept of NEDC was tripartite in character and subsequently representatives of the City and of consumers were appointed to the national body. Tripartitism characterised the thinking of a succession of governments from the time of Harold Macmillan to the end of the Callaghan period in 1979. Subsequently, although NEDC continued, its tripartite influence diminished.
2. In 1964 George Brown, carrying with him into the Department of Economic Affairs certain planning functions from the Treasury, launched a National Plan which provided for a steady period of economic growth to give confidence to those engaged in investing in industry, and it was supported by the CBI and TUC. The National Plan was based on certain forecasts, the veracity of which were later questioned, and after the economic pressures of the summer of 1966 the Plan was abandoned.
3. Harold Davies was MP for Leek, 1945–70 and confidante of Harold Wilson, being his PPS, 1966–70. He was Parliamentary Secretary in the Ministry of Pensions, and Ministry of Social Security, 1964–7. In July 1965 he undertook an unsuccessful visit to Hanoi on behalf of Harold Wilson. He was created Baron Davies of Leek in 1970.
4. This White Paper on Immigration was the basis on which the 1968 Commonwealth Immigrant Act, which imposed immigration restrictions on UK citizens from the colonies, was founded. It was interpreted both here and in the countries affected as a racialist measure.
5. In 1938, Duncan Sandys, then MP for Norwood, tabled a question about the air defences of London which indicated that he had received information from official sources. The officer responsible for supplying this information was charged under the Official Secrets Act and Duncan Sandys appealed to the Speaker on grounds of privilege. The case was referred to a Select Committee on the Official Secrets Act which in 1940 declared that information disclosed to a Member for the purpose of the proceeding in Parlia-

ment was itself privileged, a very important ruling which has often been cited since. In a parliamentary debate on the case in 1938, my father strongly supported Duncan Sandys and described his treatment as an infringement of the Bill of Rights.

6. John Freeman was Labour MP for Watford, 1945–55, and subsequently became editor of the *New Statesman*, 1961–5. He was British High Commissioner to India 1965–8 and British Ambassador in the United States, 1968–71. He became most well-known for his brilliant series of 'Face to Face' television interviews on BBC.

7. As Secretary of State for Education, Tony Crosland had made an important speech in which he favoured a division between universities and the polytechnics, which had the effect of creating two classes of higher education institution, with different status and funding methods. It was a denial of the comprehensive principle in higher education which we had worked so hard to bring about in secondary education and the policy determined the direction of higher education in the 1960s.

8. One of the reforms pioneered by Dick Crossman as Leader of the House was the introduction of parliamentary select committees relating to specific departments – Treasury, Defence, and so on, in addition to occasional select committees already in existence. This innovation was very much resisted by Whitehall and some Ministers, but has become an integral part of the relationship between the House of Commons and the Government of the day.

9. After Lord Fisher of Lambeth, Archbishop of Canterbury, 1945–1961, had retired and became a curate in the West Country, he read about my proposal to remove the Queen's head from postage stamps and wrote me an angry letter. He said that as the Archbishop who had participated in the sacrament of coronation and had had the honour and privilege of placing the crown on the Queen's head, he thought it inconceivable that anyone should think of removing it from our stamps. I replied courteously and my last exchange with Lord Fisher was during the Common Market referendum when he wrote me a warm letter of support, saying how opposed he was to Britain joining the Common Market.

5
'White Heat'
July 1966–December 1967

Friday 1 July
Up early this morning to the Post Office for the last time as PMG.
I took my movie camera and got some photographs of Mr Parrot
and Mr Rice in their red uniforms and top hats.

I spent the whole morning listening to McKinsey's presentation of
their findings on the postal services. Roger Morrison and Alan
Stewart spoke for about two hours and produced an enormous
number of tables and charts, proving conclusively that the techniques
of management used were totally inadequate.

I had a sandwich in the Office and then to the Commons where
my parliamentary answer announcing legislation against the pirates
came out. Peter Shore looked in at 11 o'clock and we talked for an
hour and a half.

Sunday 3 July
I rang Number 10 this morning and had a word with the PM's
Private Secretary, to make sure the announcement was really going
to take place today. He told me that it had actually been advanced
and that Harold would be talking to the lobby at 4.30. At lunchtime
I told Stephen and Hilary and in the afternoon Melissa and Joshua.
At 5.30 the news flash came over the radio and within a few minutes
the front garden was jam-packed with photographers and reporters
and BBC and ITV crews.

I sat and wrote twenty-eight thank-you letters by hand to all the
people in the private office and some others in the Post Office.

Monday 4 July
At 7.30 my driver, Mr Wilson, took me to the Post Office, where I
arrived just before 8 and I handed in my keys and bag and collected
my ashtray and mug and camp bed. Wratten was punch-drunk and
said that he felt everything would stop now. Mr Atkins, my mes-

senger, clutched my hand in both of his. It was all very sad and I felt the wrench of leaving.

At 8.30 I arrived at Millbank Tower and went straight up to my room. I was the first person to arrive and I had half an hour to get settled before the meeting at 9 am to discuss parliamentary questions. Peter Shore and Edmund Dell were there too. We went over questions for a time and then Frank Cousins came in to say goodbye. He was relieved in a way to have gone and yet obviously under considerable strain. I like Frank but I think that his heart is in the trade union movement. He really thinks the union movement is more important than the Labour Party or the Government, and that is where he wants to go back to and do his job. He reminded me that in 1960 he had said that my resignation would ruin my political career as Gaitskell would crucify me. 'I was wrong,' he said, 'and I'm glad that you've got this opportunity.'

It's funny to be on the site where I was born* and to look out over the same scene from a greater height. I can see the Post Office Tower in the distance and St Paul's. After lunch to the Commons, where Sir Otto Clarke, my Permanent Secretary, came to see me. He is one of the most brilliant Treasury men, rather erratic but exceptionally able. We discussed the amalgamation with Mintech of most of the Ministry of Aviation and the shipbuilding functions from the Board of Trade.

Caroline and I went to dinner with Kenneth Harris of the *Observer* this evening, and the editor, David Astor, was there. He has just come back from Washington where Secretary of State Dean Rusk had tried hard to persuade Astor that Britain ought to send troops to Vietnam. However, the view of Secretary of Defence, Robert McNamara, had been quite different and he had said, 'We need Britain internationally and domestically because Wilson's support for the Johnson administration is absolutely necessary,' implying that the sending of British troops would undermine support for the US in Britain.

We talked about prices and incomes, and the Labour Government and de Gaulle's view of the world. Astor is a sentimental old liberal who thinks that we ought to give up the bomb altogether and try to persuade de Gaulle to do the same, and that the prices and incomes policy wouldn't succeed – generally speaking not incisive or effective. But he is a fundamentally decent guy.

Home to bed about 2 o'clock and found a red box waiting for me.

---

* Millbank Tower was built on the site of 40 Grosvenor Road, later 40 Millbank, where I was born in 1925.

Tuesday 5 July

I got to the office at 9 o'clock and found everybody sitting there and looking as if they had been there for hours. I think the shock of arriving after me yesterday had been too much for them. I sat in my room most of the morning going over today's parliamentary questions. Number 10 rang up to say that I should not be taking questions before I was sworn in as Minister. I told my secretary to ring Number 10 and say that I had not the slightest intention of being absent from the House at questions and letting the Parliamentary Secretaries do the job.

As it happened we had a quiet time. Some of the Tory MPs who had put down questions simply to get at Frank Cousins didn't bother to turn up and the others were very quiet. In fact there was a general note of welcome which made a pleasant change from the Post Office. Afterwards I had a word with David Price – my Tory opposite number – and agreed with him that we should have to see what prospects there were for a parliamentary committee on technology. For my part I should welcome this very much and it is just a question of persuading Harold.

Then went off to Buckingham Palace to swear in. Before we went in, I had a chance for a short talk with Frank Cousins, who had come to the Palace to shake hands on his resignation. I asked him whether he would be staying on in the House of Commons and he told me that the Nuneaton Party wanted him to do so and lead the Left in a general attack on the Government including on Vietnam.

I saw Michael Adeane at the Palace and he congratulated me on my appointment and said that he had written about the possibility of issuing Rulers of Great Britain as a stamp series next February. He said he thought that a gold Queen's head might be acceptable but the royal crest might not. Thus I mark the end of my attempt to get the Queen's head off our stamps. Adeane made it clear that it would have to appear on every one. I'm sure Ted Short won't take any interest in stamps but I'm awfully glad that I wrote to Adeane about this particular series the day before I left. It will pave the way for other series of famous playwrights and authors and painters and scientists.

We went into the Council and stood in a row while John Silkin swore his oath as Privy Councillor and I affirmed as Minister of Technology. Going down on one knee and holding up your hand and then having to pick up the Queen's hand to kiss it is absurd but it didn't offend me as deeply this time as it did the last. Herbert Bowden then read out a list of business and the Queen said 'Approved' at the end of each one, trying to suggest that she had thought about each and this was her considered view. If she had laughed and joked and we had felt that we were going through a little ceremony which we all knew was ridiculous, it would have been so much more fun. Instead of this, the empty shell of a procedure was conducted as if it was the most important political business. Afterwards, she made a few remarks to us and as I shook hands with her she said, 'I'm sure you'll miss your stamps.' I replied, 'Yes indeed I shall. But I shall never forget your kindness and encouragement in helping me to tackle them.' She gave me a rather puzzled smile and I bowed and went out backwards.

At 8.30 Peter and Liz Shore and Caroline and I arrived at the Post Office Tower Restaurant and Tommy and Pen Balogh came a little later. We had a splendid but wildly extravagant celebration dinner. The weather was gloomy until sunset and then it cleared and we had a wonderful view of London. Tommy was in cracking form and told us all about his childhood in Hungary. He was the son of a Hungarian director of statistics in the Ministry of Transport and is a hereditary politico-economist. He was at this extraordinary high school where Nicky Kaldor* and a whole host of other Hungarian émigrés were taught.

Wednesday 6 July
At 10.30 I went up to the Neddy meeting which was a high-level affair. The first business was the consideration of the little Neddy report on the mechanical engineering industry where there are 4000 firms of whom 75 per cent employ less than fifty people. The report was rather gloomy in its forecasts. I said that I thought the most important job might be to communicate rapidly to all the management by the use of television and suggest that we should take away two hours a week from the BBC and use it for Neddy's own purposes. George Brown got rather anxious and thought I was very offbeat but I think it was a useful point and I'm glad I made it.

I had to leave at noon to go to the Party meeting on Vietnam where Harold made a good speech, saying that no country in the world had done as much to bring about a settlement as Britain and that it was difficult in the circumstances when Hanoi absolutely refused to talk to anybody. He said that Attlee had had more influence in 1950 with Truman because we had troops in Korea but that he, Harold, was not prepared to commit any British troops to Vietnam. He also said that one of the difficulties of his job was that he couldn't say exactly what he was doing when he was engaged in confidential negotiations. It was convincing but I couldn't see why we needed to

* Cambridge economist, adviser during the Labour Government 1964–70 and 1974–9. Created a peer in 1974.

come out so formidably in support of the United States in public. There was a vote and the Left got 45 out of more than 250.

At 4.30, I had a deputation from the senior civil servants' union, the First Division Association, protesting about the appointment of Sir Charles Cunningham from the Home Office to be Deputy Chairman of the Atomic Energy Authority. I could only really listen and promise to consider the points they made about promotion opportunities for AEA administrators. This ended at 5 and I worked for two and a half hours on my papers. There is a mass of stuff to absorb and I have obviously got to re-cast my day in order to leave four hours clear for reading every night. At the moment it is overwhelming.

Home at 11 and settled down to three hours' hard work in preparation for tomorrow. I'm going to have to spend months and months meeting people and picking things up and learning all I can if I'm going to be any good at the job.

Thursday 7 July

At 11.30 I attended my first Cabinet meeting.[1] I found myself sitting on the Prime Minister's extreme left in the corner with Douglas Jay on one side of me and the Chief Whip, John Silkin, on the other side. I had been to the Cabinet before but I was always called in to discuss something specific – and to be sitting in that room and feeling that I was now in the Cabinet was extremely exciting.

Then to the Commons where I sat next to Ted Short. I asked him how things were going and he said it was difficult to take over the Post Office at that particular moment. The status proposals will go forward as before but the management structure would have to wait. This means that my plan to get rid of the Engineer-in-Chief and give telephones independence has been frustrated. Obviously the Office organised itself the very day I left and managed to stop it all. I'm not a bit surprised. This is the price you pay for ministerial changes. Power returns almost immediately to the civil servants and they see to it that projects they don't want advanced don't get advanced. Afterwards I dashed to Montague Burton's and got a couple of cheap suits off the peg.

Solly Zuckerman came to see me. He told me about the new arrangements that are being made for handling space matters and about the British lead in desalination by the Atomic Energy Authority.

Caroline came to the office and we went to a party at Lancaster House for the French premier, Monsieur Pompidou. I had a long talk to Lord Nelson, who is the chairman of English Electric. He told me that one of the factors in high costs for British exporters was the liberal safety margin built into all British equipment, which found no parallel in foreign products. Whatever the justification for this might be at home, it did raise costs by about 10 per cent abroad and he thought we ought to have a general look at the problem.

Then to the Commons where I heard the end of the debate on Vietnam. Douglas-Home wound up and gave a good analysis of the problem of Anglo-American relations. Harold spoke for our side and I was so tired I dozed off during part of it. But it still lacked that quality of greatness which one expects in a Prime Minister and there was a certain cheap Party political note, especially at the end when he quoted Enoch Powell, which somehow destroyed the validity of his argument and left me feeling rather sour. It is a curious weakness in a man who is expected to rise above Party considerations and speak for the nation.

Friday 8 July
At 11 o'clock I was called in to the Cabinet room for the meeting between the French party, led by Pompidou, and the British side led by the PM.

I now have ministerial responsibilities that involve nuclear and other relations with France. I didn't have to say anything but it was interesting to see Pompidou, the French banker, looking shrewdly across at Harold, and Harold trying to be friendly by talking about technical co-operation. At the end Harold said that the Foreign Secretary wished to say something about the French nuclear tests. So Michael Stewart said how much the British Government regretted the fact that the French were testing nuclear weapons despite the Test-Ban Treaty. Pompidou said that his Foreign Minister, Couve de Murville, would reply and de Murville said, 'I am grateful to the British Foreign Secretary for pointing out that now the British have completed their nuclear tests they think it is unnecessary for the French to complete theirs,' dismissing it with a touch of scorn. It was most amusing. Harold then said, 'Let's go to lunch,' and that was the end of the matter.

On the way out Eddie Shackleton called me on one side and warned me about Solly Zuckerman. 'Remember that he is a man without any sense of loyalty whatsoever,' he said. 'He wants to be loved and I'm sure there is a place for him, but if you encourage him do it discreetly.' This sort of high level gossip is, I suppose, part and parcel of high politics. If I were C. P. Snow I would note it in my diary for my novel about Whitehall. As it is I find it rather unattractive.

At 12.15 I went to see George Brown at the DEA in response to his invitation to have a talk about the way in which I saw my work at Mintech. Before we began, I told him of the impression I had formed of the Anglo-French talks. He was depressed about them, He had just met a journalist, Michael King (Cecil King's son), who had returned from Paris where he had received a pre-trip briefing from the French delegation. They had spoken with scarcely veiled contempt about Harold Wilson and when asked about George Brown's attitude in support of British membership of the Common Market, had said, 'George Brown does not speak for Britain.'

George felt that after the dissociation from the Vietnam bombing the time had come when we had to reassess our entire foreign policy and look again at the close relations with America. As it was, we were getting separated from the United States without really establishing any close relations with Europe. George hoped for ministerial meetings with the French to try to find our way into the Common Market.

At 1 o'clock I went to the Post Office where my old private office had laid on sandwiches and beer so that I could meet them all again. They presented me with a beautiful little reading lamp which will be just what I need for my bedside for reading official papers late into the night.

Don Wratten took me aside and told me what had happened in the week since I left. Helsby was coming to see Ted Short in the afternoon and it was clear than the changes in the management structure would be killed. On stamps Short was strictly conservative. The office had put a draft letter in front of him addressed to the Queen, assuring her that her head would always stay on the stamps. Wratten said that the DG was almost delirious with excitement at my departure and that Ted Short has asked him to delay his retirement for three months which he was likely to do. This was so depressing that I really couldn't bear it and I was glad to hurry away after having said goodbye to all my friends there.

At 4 o'clock George Brown phoned to tell me to forget everything that he had said earlier today, as the Pompidou meeting had gone a great deal better at the later stage.

At 5 John Adams, the Controller of the department seconded from the Atomic Energy Authority, came and explained his plan for establishing a United Kingdom Industrial Technology Authority which would link all the research institutes with the Atomic Energy Authority, plan the technological goals and provide a proper structure for assessing projects that came up for consideration.

Thus ended my first week at the Ministry of Technology. It has been an absolutely hectic one and at this stage I still don't feel I know enough to be authoritative. I shall have to establish my position by learning the background and the task of asserting firm control over the whole department will necessarily be a long one.

Otto Clarke is an extremely able man and I foresee many clashes with him. It really is difficult coming into an industrial field of which I have no knowledge at all and trying to make sense of it in time to be able to bring some serious impact on the direction of policy. Thank God Peter Shore is there. I intend to see that he and Edmund Dell are brought into all major decisions and not allow myself to be isolated with my civil servants.

Monday 11 July

This afternoon I had a briefing on the AEA and Sir William Penney came in to meet me. He is a very easy-going man in his late fifties. We talked about two projects of immediate interest to him. The first is the need for the AEA to co-operate with the CEGB in the design of atomic power stations and get away from the ridiculous idea of competitive tendering by separate nuclear power consortia; and the second was about the use of Capenhurst* to generate cheap electricity for the smelting of aluminium.

At 6.30 we had the first of the informal weekly meetings which I intend to institute in the office. I took the chair. Peter and Edmund were there and so was Otto Clarke, my private secretary William Knighton, Patrick Blackett and John Adams. I told them that we should meet once a week at a fixed time, to review the work in which we were involved in Cabinet committees, official committees and EDCs. I would require documents to be circulated so that we could keep abreast of the work in which we were all engaged.

I said our objectives would be to keep an eye on the structure of the department as we took over aviation and shipbuilding and we would need to develop a departmental policy on Europe and in the following areas: take-over bids (especially from abroad) and mergers; the utilisation of Mintech resources; the provision of technological services; the policies for each industry; the development of a techno-economic team for assessing projects; procurement policy; the development of the engineering aspects of the National Plan; the role of public enterprise, and information policy.

At 8.30 I went over and had a meal with Peter Shore and Tom Williams [Labour MP for Hammersmith South] at the Commons. Tom is now engaged in defending one of the gangsters charged with murdering someone at an affray in Mr Smith's Club, Catford, and he talked for about an hour on gangsterism in Britain. He said that this particular South London gang was strongly entrenched and almost all the restaurants, dance halls, strip clubs and so on in

---

* Atomic Energy Association nuclear establishment responsible for the enrichment of uranium.

Central London were paying protection money to the gang. A lot of this money was getting into pirate radios. He said that witnesses to the murder in which his client was involved absolutely refused to give any evidence in court and that one member of the jury had been threatened at midnight. In all he gave the impression that London was in the grip of a gang war quite as serious as that which held Chicago in the 1920s and 30s. His own remedy was virtual abolition of short sentences and the concentration upon serious criminals by means of indeterminate sentences.

Later Peter came to my room at the Commons and we had a talk about the deteriorating economic situation.

Tuesday 12 July
Straight to Cabinet at 10 am, where we discussed the economy. The situation is really pretty serious. The press are beginning to criticise Harold for not taking action.

I went back to the office where Clem Leslie, the new PR consultant, came for a talk. He was chief Information Officer at the Treasury for many years and before that was with Herbert Morrison. He is an Australian, an almost elderly man now, modest but tough and effective. He said he didn't think that his role was necessary now that I was there. I told him that, far from not being necessary, it was even more so as my relations with the press were not good.

He told me that, firstly, we must make the Ministry's job better known and this would involve thinking it out ourselves and explaining it on every occasion. Secondly, if we want to make an impact on industry, we shall have to approach it with some modesty. I do not come from an industrial background and they will be suspicious of an amateur telling them what to do. Similarly, it will be necessary to approach the trade unions modestly. Thirdly, real effort must be made to raise the status of engineers. We would have to explain what an engineer does and show that a dreamer without an engineer behind him is no good at all.

On the general question of public relations, he said that we would have to concentrate on areas where we expected to get short-term results. He said we must have something to say on electronics, on which there had been very little said so far, and that we must get on with the redeployment of publicly-owned research and development. In this connection, he thought a visit to the United States would be a good idea.

Finally he asked me what my relations were with George Brown. I told him frankly that George didn't particularly like me but I had a great deal of admiration for him. Leslie said that the DEA had been spreading some pretty poisonous stuff about Mintech in the past and he thought it was essential that they should take a higher view of our importance. I found it a useful talk. I like Clem Leslie and invited him to join our informal weekly meetings.

Wednesday 13 July

The first Advisory Council on Technology met under my chairmanship this morning. Bruce Williams presented a paper on the relationship between research and development and economic growth. His main argument was that R & D was no guarantee of economic growth and that it might be better to buy know-how from abroad rather than spend a great deal of our resources on maintaining our own R & D disconnected from industry. People have attended these meetings for nearly two years and I think they are getting rather impatient. At the next meeting we must present them with a list of our own resources and also show that we have established a techno-economic group capable of assessing the value of the projects on which we are engaged.

Seretse Khama came to my office. Seretse is in London for economic discussions on the eve of independence for Bechuanaland of 29 September. He told me about the residual difficulties with the Queen's commissioner and the way in which the Colonial Office in London had tried to get him to dismiss his economic adviser on the grounds that he was too left-wing. He said that he thought it unlikely that the British Government could topple Smith. For his part he was being subjected to strong pressure from South Africa which wanted to absorb the protectorates into a new semi-independent Bantustan status. He said the Rhodesian Africans were a great nuisance in exile and that if they wanted to do anything, they had better go home and start a revolution. Seretse is a dear friend but he is not exactly a revolutionary himself. But I find his comments on life interesting.

After he had gone I had a talk with a Mr Nixon of the American computer giant IBM, who came to enquire about our policy in the light of the disclosures that we were giving a 25 per cent preference to British computers in public procurement. Edmund Dell let this out in talking to the *Sunday Times* which published it last Sunday week and has caused a certain amount of embarrassment because it could be presented as unfair and anti-American.

At 8.30 I went to Dick Crossman's house for dinner with Judith Hart, Peter and Tommy. We had a discussion about the economic situation which is deteriorating rapidly. By being able to talk relatively frankly amongst ourselves we were able to isolate points of agreement.

Thursday 14 July

Went straight to Cabinet this morning at 10 am.[2] Afterwards to lunch at Lady Pamela Berry's.* Dick Crossman and Ann were there and so was Mervyn Stockwood, Sidney Bernstein, Mrs Bruce (the American Ambassador's wife) and others. As soon as lunch was over Lady Pamela tried to put Dick and me on the spot about the economic crisis. Having just come from Cabinet we were both determined to keep our mouths shut, but Dick developed an interesting line of argument showing that almost all our social policies ran counter to the idea of rapid growth. He pointed out that pushing industry into development districts, maintaining the green belt, standard tariffs for the electricity and gas, and a whole host of other things which we accepted uncritically as being part of a civilised community actually held back growth. If you wanted a massive growth you ought to accept Enoch Powell's laissez-faire doctrine. It was stimulating – Dick always is – and it diverted us from more dangerous topics. Mervyn was rather wet.

This was the first time we had been to lunch with Lady Pamela and we ate with gold knives and forks and the food was superb. She has been trying to get me along for some while.

Back to the office and I called in Otto Clarke to discuss the Geddes Report which had recommended that the shipbuilding industry be grouped in larger units by mergers, but remain under private ownership. I insisted on Peter being there. This did not create a favourable impression but I'm glad I did it as Peter strengthened my hand. I told Otto that I had looked at the outline of the report and had come to the conclusion that if the Government was going to put such a large sum of money in to shipbuilding we ought to put it in equity and not just loans and grants which would prop up a potentially profitable industry without bringing any return to the taxpayer. Clarke said this would throw the whole thing into a state of complete chaos and that it would lose confidence in the shipbuilding industry. Clarke promised to do a paper for me.

Afterwards Peter was absolutely delighted and said that this was the end of consensus politics. I think he rather overdid it but I'm glad that I did explain forcibly to Clarke that this was the policy on which we were elected and the sooner the department understood this the better.

---

* Daughter of the Earl of Birkenhead and wife of Michael Berry, later Lord Hartwell, editor of the *Daily Telegraph*. Well known as a 'society hostess', it was my one and only lunch there!

Saturday 16 July

Travelled up to Durham last night for the Miners' Gala. Breakfast in our room early and at 8.30 we heard the first bands approaching. We went downstairs and watched from the balcony. The sky was overcast but fortunately it did not rain and there was the fabulous spectacle of all the lodges carrying their huge and beautifully decorated banners passing with their bands one after the other. The children from the villages danced ahead of each party and behind the banners came the old miners with their wives and families. This year there were only forty-nine lodges represented compared with 150 at the peak fifteen years ago. Thirty pits had closed in the area within the last year or so and it is obvious that the gala is slowly turning from a significant political event into a folk festival. But it is nonetheless moving for that.

On the balcony were Michael Stewart and his wife and George Brown. George beckoned me on one side and said he wanted to talk to me urgently. He was in a state of tension. In brief, he feared that the Treasury would come forward with major deflationary measures at home and that he intended to resign from the Government tonight. He told me that he had only told Harold Wilson, Roy Jenkins and me. 'You may just as well make your speech under the same misery that I am going to make mine,' he said. I replied that if he did this it would mean the end of the Government – so I profoundly believe. The Cabinet simply would not have a majority in the House of Commons if George Brown had decided to opt out on these grounds. George's own remedy for the economic situation would be infinitely preferable. Just after we had talked he had a phone call from Harold Wilson on the eve of his departure for Moscow and after that he seemed a little bit more relaxed. He told me that his resignation would become effective on Wednesday when the economic statement was made. All this worried me very much until I had a chance to reflect on it. Then it occurred to me that George was overwrought and that it was unlikely either that the Cabinet would accept such Draconian measures or that he himself would in the end decide to go. Political unity at this moment is more important than anything else.

In this atmosphere it was rather difficult to make a convincing speech at the gala but I concentrated on the long-term need for injecting modern technology into British industry and he talked about short-term needs for everybody to pull together and get us round our current difficulty.

Sunday 17 July

I rang Peter Shore to discuss the crisis and Peter Shore rang Tommy Balogh and it was agreed they would both come here at 7.30. In fact Peter arrived early and we had an opportunity for a quiet talk.

In Peter's view the deflationary effect of the Selective Employment Tax will be so great when it comes that for strictly economic reasons one only needs to take a relatively small sum out of the economy in addition. He is afraid that we shall oversteer as a result of panic measures. We discussed exactly how this ought to be taken out of the economy in order to be effective and preserve social justice, and safeguard essential items of social expenditure as well as the development programme for the nationalised industries and business confidence for future investment. We thought it necessary that if there was to be any sort of limitation on incomes, special measures would have to be taken to deal with higher ones in order to maintain social equity. Tommy arrived later, looking shaken. Apparently he went to see George Brown last night and George roundly abused him in a way that Tommy found hard to take. With his bad heart condition I began to wonder whether he could stand the strain.

I went to bed about 11 and settled down with my reading light to read into the night.

At this moment, my thoughts are roughly this. I shall fight against the sort of Treasury cuts which would be socially inequitable and damaging to the growth of the economy. This is really a political crisis and when we have to choose what to cut it will be a test of our own political faith. The economists can't help us at this stage, beyond giving us a general indication of the lines on which we should go.

From the point of view of public presentation we must seem to be speaking the truth and it is reasonable that we should ask everybody to make a contribution to solve the problems, provided that the weakest are protected and the essential basis of future growth is not affected. Nothing could be worse than to pretend that we could get out of this difficulty without real effort and sacrifice for ordinary people at work.

However, having said that, the unity of the Cabinet at this moment is essential. We have a large majority in the House of Commons that could be eroded if a majority of the Cabinet decided to opt for a right-wing set of choices rather than a left-wing set. No one is going to vote against Harold Wilson because he is too radical, whereas the Cabinet might lose some of its members if it went in the other direction and a split could melt the majority in the Commons. I am therefore strongly opposed to resignations on this issue. But if there are resignations and the Government in its present form fails, and there is any question whatsoever of a National Government, then we should go out at once. We should then be confronted with an Election under curious circumstances with a much better chance of saving the unity of the Party than we had in 1931. These are all rather random and disjointed thoughts.

Monday 18 July

I took Barbara Castle for an early lunch in the canteen. I told her that in my view the real danger was that we should go too far and that with Selective Employment Tax the package might be too deflationary. She absolutely agreed with me and so we decided to talk to George and Tony Crosland. We also agreed that it was important not to form a clique in the Cabinet which might lead to trouble. I didn't tell her about George Brown's impending resignation.

Afterwards I went back to the office and had Otto Clarke to see me to ask his views about the economic situation. He is so arrogant. When I asked him what he thought should be in the measures, he gave me the complete Selwyn Lloyd package, including prescription charges, reduced subsidy for school meals, cuts in educational expenditure and lower housing subsidies. I didn't argue with him but felt gloomy that I should be dependent on that sort of advice.

At 6 pm Peter and Clarke came in for a further talk about the package. Clarke had been to a meeting of Permanent Secretaries called to prepare some papers for the Cabinet tomorrow.

To the Commons this evening and had a meal with Peter who urged me strongly that in my contribution to Cabinet I should keep off the proposal that the pound should be floated. Peter and I don't see eye to eye on various things. He is an East of Suez man on the grounds of Indo-British relations and I am not. He is also a parity man and I am not. He retains a high regard and affection for Harold Wilson which is, in my case, fast evaporating. I do not think that Harold has a long-term vision of the sort of society we want to create and the short-term tactical dodging at which he is adept may have been perfect for the 1964–6 Parliament but has no place in the developing strategy for the next four years.

I decided to float around and talk to a few Ministers. I saw Fred Lee whose main concern was that there should be appreciable defence cuts. I went to see George Brown and found him in a state of high excitement. Barbara Castle was with him. He repeated definitely that he was going. He said he had warned Harold a year ago that he was not prepared to put up with another episode of this kind and that Roy and Tony agreed with him. Barbara said she thought there would be a majority in the Cabinet in favour of his view but George said that it was impossible that this could carry the day as Harold was so heavily committed publicly to maintaining the value of the pound. Barbara said she thought Harold would accept the majority view and George said, 'No, this involves his leadership. Do you want me as Leader, Barbara?' Barbara replied firmly, 'No.' 'Then Harold will win,' said George.

He stressed that he was not looking for the leadership but that the issue in question was so important that he didn't think there could be a change without involving a change of Leader. I asked George whether all this linked in with our possible entry into the EEC. George said that in his view it made Europe a little bit easier, though it couldn't come for some time. This thoroughly worried Barbara who is anti-EEC and I tried to establish that the European issue was not really relevant to the question of devaluation. George agreed, and on that basis Barbara was able to support his view, feeling that it left the final option on EEC membership open. George stressed that the economic package would be more or less the same, whether we took the course that he recommended or not. I left George reiterating his firm determination to resign.

Next I went to see Dick Crossman who said that *he* was ready to resign since he felt that he had done his job and had no ambitions beyond the present Parliament. I tried to urge him not to but I don't think that he was seriously intending it. I pointed out that the leaks had suggested that Harold's threat to Cabinet members would be 'accept the axe or quit'. Dick had not heard this. Finally, at 1 am I was talking to Dick Marsh in the tea room and he said that he was for savage cuts, slashing everything in order to give us a chance of starting again from scratch.

Tuesday 19 July

Meeting at 10.30 to discuss the Rolls-BAC merger. Afterwards Bruce Williams stayed on to discuss the economic package. He too was afraid that it was going to be too much and said that our role as a banker and our expenditure east of Suez was more than we could really manage. He thought the future of the Labour Party was at stake.

Eddie Shackleton came to lunch and I asked him whether he thought that our commitments East of Suez were necessary. He was of the opinion that they could be cut but that the plain truth was that in most of the parts of the world where our troops were present, the people there wanted to keep them. This was an interesting comment from a Defence Minister.

At 2.30 the package of cuts arrived and I studied it briefly.

From 5 till 8.30 the Cabinet met. The big question was devaluation versus deflation. I spoke for devaluation. The Cabinet were very narrowly divided on it and I made a speech in which I argued that we really couldn't cut again. Harold was upset about it because he clearly intended to deflate. It was pointed out by Jim, quite rightly, that if you did devalue, you would also have to deflate, so you couldn't escape the package but there would be a chink of light. Otherwise, he said, it was like going along the same dark tunnel for ever. There was a break for a few minutes in the middle of Cabinet and Harold said he was glad the meeting had gone against devaluation as he himself would have to consider his position if it had gone in favour. The question now is whether George Brown will resign.

Wednesday 20 July
To the Cabinet again for another four-hour sitting, ending at 1 o'clock.

Sandwich lunch at the House of Commons and then went to hear Harold make his statement at 3.30. George Brown was not sitting on the Front Bench and this became the subject of immediate comment. I had a word with Austen Albu and Bill Rodgers.* Bill had just come back from seeing him and his eyes were red with tears. They all said what a tragedy it would be if he went and Austen said George had a death wish and somehow wanted to get out of politics altogether. A round robin of Members was quickly drawn up and conveyed to him.

At 6 o'clock the Mintech Board met and we ran over current work. I asked for a paper on the attitude we should adopt towards Europe and one on the need for assessing our technological goals. The discussion was mysterious because John Adams, the Controller, seemed quite unable to articulate what he thought should be done. The Permanent Secretary was also very mysterious and it was only afterwards that I learned that John Adams had put in a paper on this very subject and Otto was sitting on it and didn't want the matter discussed. I will have to be tough with Otto if I am going to assert my authority over the department.

This evening I had a talk to Peter and got home to bed after midnight. Caroline told me there had just been a news flash to the effect that George Brown had withdrawn his resignation and was carrying on.

---

* Labour MP for Stockton-on-Tees, Under-Secretary of State at the Department of Economic Affairs and one of the founders in 1981 of the Social Democratic Party.

Thursday 21 July
Caroline and I went to the GLC party at County Hall. I had a long
talk to Bernard Floud who is a member of the Select Committee on
Nationalised Industries. I told him the whole story about the Post
Office. He said that the MPs on the committee treated the whole
business superficially and most of them didn't bother to turn up at
all. He said that the clerk of the committee kept in touch with the
Post Office who suggested the lines of enquiry that the MPs might
like to pursue. Thus a new network was established under which the
Post Office officials alerted the Commons officials, who geared the
elected Members to ask only those questions that were convenient to
the officials. I realise that I am getting precious close to saying that
parliamentary democracy, which is our proudest boast, is not working
in the country, but on reflection I find it hard to escape this
conclusion. The answer, of course, is a really dynamic political party
that is elected knowing the difficulties that will face it and determined
to get control of the Whitehall machine and really use it to carry
through fundamental changes. I just don't believe that this impetus
exists within the Labour Party or within the Labour Cabinet, and it
may well be that I am in a minority and that it does not exist
anywhere, that we are going to go on floating, governed by civil
servants with Ministers from the two parties coming in and out by
a curious quirk known as the electoral cycle.

Friday 22 July
Lunch with Nigel Calder, the editor of the *New Scientist*, at Kettners.
He is the son of Ritchie Calder, for whom I have the highest respect,
and himself a physicist. He told me about the Massachusetts Institute
of Technology attitude towards engineering which he had discovered
when he was over there. MIT had evolved a new philosophy for
engineering, based on the idea that computers enabled the routine
work of the engineer to be done automatically and thus released the
engineer so that he didn't concentrate solely on a particular project,
but was invited in as a consultant to consider the whole problem
itself. This I found very creative thinking. It means that all the
disciplines are harnessed to particular purposes and are not allowed
to run to seed in their specialisation. It is a principle that I intend
to apply as far as I can to the work of the department.

I got on with him very well. I put to him my big problem which
is how we stop ourselves from becoming a party of cancellers, who
get the economists in to rule out all the projects advocated by the
enthusiastic scientists and technologists. He produced Bruce
Williams' thesis that it is better to back a number of projects with a
low possibility of success but a higher rate of return than the same

number of projects with a high probability of success but low rate of return. The real difficulty here is how a society where all the major frontiers of knowledge are being pioneered by agencies financed by the Government can acquire a genuine risk capital approach, and not look too critically at every single project.

Back to the Commons where I voted for the Abortion Bill, which was carried by 223 votes to 29 – a notable victory.

Then to the DEA where I sat in while George Brown interviewed the CBI about the wage and prices freeze. George put on one of his pyrotechnic displays against Sir Maurice Laing,* John Davies,† Sir Stephen Brown and others. He shouted at them, bullied them, wheedled them, giggled at them, but in a way – although it was a sensational performance – I felt they were hardened to it and am not sure that it was as impressive as George thought it was. He has not really got the stability to be Prime Minister, though he is in many ways an attractive and fullblooded figure.

This evening Caroline and I went to Tommy Balogh's party. Tommy is depressed by the events of the week. I had a long talk to Nicky Kaldor. He said that as far as he was concerned Harold had been brilliant during the last Parliament but that this time he was just concerned with maintaining himself in power and had no strategy whatsoever. We moved on to talk about Otto Clarke who they said was an absolutely brilliant and ruthless figure. They said if I wanted to get the most out of him, I would have to draw him on a number of alternative solutions and then pick up the one that I wanted pursued, and pretend that it was his idea. I really don't see why I should do that but I was glad to get an inside view of him. They said that in the end one just couldn't help liking him because he was so eccentric.

George Wigg and Marcia were there and I think I must be in their bad books for having come out so strongly against Harold on devaluation this week. They are loyalists above everything else.

Saturday 23 July
Worked at home all day. I feel so tired at the end of the week that I just don't get on with my work. But I did plough through my letters and dictated my diary.

Wednesday 27 July
To the National Executive this morning and we started with a discussion of the recent economic measures. Harold explained what

* President, then Vice-President, Confederation of British Industry 1965–70.
† Director General, Confederation of British Industry 1965–9, later Conservative Cabinet Minister.

had happened and why and then we had Jim Callaghan and George. There was a host of criticisms from the trade union members. Jack Jones was absolutely opposed to what had been done and made it clear that the TGWU was not prepared to support the Government. Frank Chapple* of the ETU said that it would be extremely difficult for elected trade union leaders to help the Government since the inevitable effect of them doing so would be to let the leadership pass into the hands of unofficial groups. I have never felt a more fundamentally hostile atmosphere from the trade union side. Hardly any of the constituency people spoke at all and the battle was fought entirely between the three leading members of the Cabinet and the trade union leaders. One immediate issue that came up was the recommendation that we should pay a substantial increase to our staff. In the circumstances it was agreed that we would have to apply the standstill to them as well.

Back to the office where I was drawn by the artist for the *Eastern Daily Press* and then hurried on to the Machine Tool Trades Association lunch with the leaders of the major machine tool manufacturing companies. I found myself sitting opposite Sir Arnold Hall of Hawker Siddeley. He is an extremely able and cultivated man and I like him very much. A number of leaders of the engineering industry were there as well. It was my job to make a speech afterwards and I described the work of Mintech and the importance of the machine tool industry and then went on to develop my thesis, which I am going to make a major theme throughout the coming months. It is simply this: what has gone wrong with Britain in the industrial field is not due to two years of Labour Government, thirteen wasted Tory years, six years of socialist misrule, the War, the depression, the First World War. The origins of our difficulties go back much further. Germany overtook this country in the 1880s and indeed we began losing our lead in about the fifties or sixties of the last century.

The reason was that at that time we opted to become an imperial country instead of continuing as an industrial one. I recalled in my speech that in my childhood I had been taught a great deal about the engineers of the late eighteenth and early nineteenth century but that after that the school books concentrated on viceroys and generals, civil servants and diplomats, and this country had simply opted out of industrialism. Thus all the schools had geared themselves to producing the sort of people the empire needed. When I said this there was a spontaneous burst of applause and one or two people came up afterwards and said I ought to publish the speech. In fact

* Assistant General Secretary (GS in September 1966) of the ETU, later known as the EETPU. Created a life peer in 1985.

it was a pre-introduction model of a major speech which I intend to make on every possible occasion from now on.* The truth is that Britain must now give up being an imperial country and become an industrial country again and only in this way can we reshape our society, and encourage people to regard work in industry as the most worthwhile job they can possibly do. It is significant that this September the Colonial Office is wound up and the Ministry of Technology gets into its stride. If I'm asked to speak at Conference, this is certainly what I shall say.

To the Commons this evening to hear the end of the economic debate. George Brown was absolutely overwrought, and although his speech had touches of brilliance it was also full of the most awful gaffes. Having seen him in action so often, I wasn't at all surprised but a number of Back Bench colleagues who had never seen him like that were completely shaken by it. Tam Dalyell told me that for the first time since the Election the confidence of the whole Party was now shaken in the leadership. Harold is under continuous fire and George is obviously exhausted. Jim is in a sense discredited by the failure of his Budget to control the situation and the Party is dismayed. We shall have a tough time at the TUC and at the Labour Conference.

Thursday 28 July

The Cabinet lasted from 9.45 until 1.15 today, discussing the wages and prices standstill. I had a nice little note from Jim Callaghan saying, 'You have joined at the worst time I ever remember. It can be more enjoyable than this.'

This afternoon I had the AEA trade union side coming to see me about the future of Aldermaston.† Fortunately I was able to say that Mintech is not responsible for any military work at all and that of course the AEA have to organise themselves in the best way possible. I told them that we were looking at Government resources as a whole and were trying to redeploy them in a sensible way.

Friday 29 July–Sunday 31 July

The whole family drove off to Stansgate, arriving at 10.30 on Friday. All day doing nothing on Saturday. It takes an awful time to unwind after a week's work and I have nightmares in which I am required to see General de Gaulle about the future of Concorde, or arrive late in the office unshaven, not having read my Cabinet papers.

An old Post Office pillar box was delivered today at Stansgate –

* See Appendix IV.
† Atomic Weapons Research Establishment in Berkshire, at which nuclear weapons were, and are, produced.

it weighs about half a ton. I had ordered it as Postmaster General
and it was to cost five or six quid. But as I had left by the time it
was delivered they decided to give it to me as a gift. With a sledge
hammer we broke off the bottom and gradually moved it over and
erected it. I am very proud of it.

Pleasant sunny day on Sunday and we sat on the lawn. I didn't
even open my red box. We drove home, getting back about 6.15.
Parliament rises at the end of next week and I shall be glad of a
break.

Monday 1 August

I went to the Science Exhibition organised by the Dean of
Westminster. Lord Adrian opened the proceedings and I walked
round with him. It was well organised – much better than the Science
Museum in Kensington, I thought. One of the most interesting things
was to discover that geology had been completely paralysed in this
country until about 1800 because the Church had laid down that the
creation was in 4004 BC and nobody had been sufficiently interested
in geology to challenge it. It was only then that the dating of fossils
began and with it the dating of the earth. Thus do unchallenged
beliefs and disciplined minds check the development of human
knowledge.

Tuesday 2 August

This evening I had a meal with Tommy Balogh at the Reform Club.
He is gloomy and we both agreed that Harold had effectively cut
himself off from all his friends. We also agreed that the real danger
to him was not George Brown or even Jim Callaghan but Roy Jenkins,
who has cultivated the press to such a point that they would come
out as strongly for him as they did for Heath, were he ever to have
a chance. He obviously hopes to be made Chancellor of the Exchequer
when Jim Callaghan moves, as everyone expects he will, from the
Treasury in the autumn reshuffle.

Unfortunately the line that Dick, Barbara and I took in support
of devaluation in 'recent discussions' has meant that we have been
marked down by George Wigg as unreliable. For this reason Tommy
thinks it would be impossible for us to resume the pleasant evenings
at the Crossmans at 9 Vincent Square. The fact is that Harold has
cut himself off from us and has no real friends on the other side in
the controversy. I am so out of sympathy with the continuation of
our banking and world roles that I don't know that there is any
advice I can give within the orbit of existing policy. Probably Tommy
is right in saying that we all need a holiday and can come back afresh
to our problems afterwards.

Pen came to collect him later on – she is so wise and wistful. I think she realises what has actually happened and that Tommy's uncritical support for Harold has somehow come to an end. But if not Harold, who is to be Leader?

Wednesday 3 August
This morning I went to the second Neddy meeting. George Brown was tied up with the Prices and Incomes Committee, so Douglas Jay took the chair. He was infinitely less effective than George and the whole meeting went to bits. Fred Catherwood began with a long survey of the economic situation in which he considered the problems created by our role as a world banker, our heavy overseas Government expenditure, and the continuing outflow of private capital. He then went on to the position created by the July measures and said that industrial efficiency was the key. After this came speeches from John Davies of the CBI, who said that he was anxious about the future of world trade; and Aubrey Jones* who said that it was clear that the public were opting for leisure and that it was also clear that we didn't know how to run the economy well.

There was a sharp clash when George Woodcock said that the TUC would not be prepared even to discuss what the right level of employment should be. It wasn't made any better by Alf Robens who came in later and said that, in his opinion, without 2 to 3 per cent unemployed you couldn't get any labour discipline. Alf also said that the villains of the piece were in the room and particularly referred to the postmen whose increase I had authorised last year. I took no notice of it. Later in the discussion I did join in and tried to argue that at the Productivity Conference in September we ought to concentrate on the problems of management which seemed to me to be the most important ones in connection with productivity.

I had lunch with Sir Denning Pearson, the deputy chairman of Rolls Royce and discussed with him the general problem of our research operations. He said that the worst people in the world to decide their own programme were research scientists and that we ought to latch businessmen on to each of our research stations. This is in line with my current thinking.

Thursday 4 August
I had Matthew Coady to tea and explained my idea of the role of Mintech as the spearhead of an industrial Britain in opposition to the old concept of imperial Britain. He saw it as an attack on East

* Chairman of the National Board for Prices and Incomes, 1965–70, and former Conservative MP and Minister.

of Suez and said that if I put it in this way, it would be absolute dynamite. This, I think, is the great weakness of the lobby: they are thinking in terms of personalities and not in terms of themes. Coady is violently anti-Harold and has got a piece coming out tomorrow on 'Labour's Crown Prince', suggesting that Roy Jenkins is the obvious person to take over from George Brown and ultimately the leadership itself. This confirms my view that Roy is working hard with Bill Rodgers, Bernard Donoughue* and the old Campaign for Democratic Socialism–Europe Group to take over the leadership of the Party at some stage. I didn't say any of this to Matthew Coady but I'm interested that he should, quite independently, have been beginning to see Roy's star rising on the horizon.

I also had a long talk to Neil Carmichael [Labour MP for Wood-side], who told me that there was a great lack of confidence in the leadership at the moment and that it extended to Left, Right and Centre. There is also an embarrassing position developing over twenty-seven Labour MPs who abstained last night on the Prices and Incomes Bill, and if disciplinary action is taken it will lead to even greater difficulty for people like himself who would have liked to have voted against it but didn't out of loyalty. He also told me that he thought Roy was making a bid but that those who were pro-Harold needed a bit of reassurance and direct contact with Harold. Some fences needed to be mended, he said.

Friday 5 August

This afternoon I had two hours' talk with Otto Clarke. He produced his plan for the organisation of the Ministry and I asked particularly where Bruce Williams would fit into it. He said that Bruce Williams was part-time, and that you couldn't rely on anyone who was part-time and he was looking for someone new to head his economics department. I told him frankly that I had to have somebody who was politically sympathetic on whom I could rely to give me advice and it was absolutely essential that all the papers on which I had to reach a decision should come to me with Bruce Williams's advice on them. This I think rather shook him. He wants to record the Mintech Board meetings as just weekly philosophical discussions which is not at all what they are intended to be.

Clarke is a slick operator and conveyed to me what the Chancellor had said about the aircraft industry as if he, Clarke, were the Prime Minister and he was giving me my orders. I can see that I am going to have a proper row with Clarke soon and at the same time establish

* Lecturer at London School of Economics and senior policy adviser to Harold Wilson 1974–9. Later created a peer.

a reasonable working relationship with him. Just at the moment Mintech is becoming a little too much for me. All the decisions are so complicated and technical and I'm not really qualified to judge them. No doubt it'll get better later but it's all very worrying.

Saturday 6 August

We all went down to Stansgate for the weekend. Slept late this morning and Peter and Liz arrived with their two younger boys to spend the night. They are our closest political friends. Peter and I had a long talk. He told me that he'd been to Number 10 and had had tea with Harold and Marcia and Tommy and that afterwards he had a proper talk to Marcia. Apparently the events of the last few weeks have absolutely shaken Harold to the core. He is convinced that a deliberate plot was conceived to get rid of him. He sees it operating like this: Roy Jenkins and his gang decided to get rid of George Brown and to make Jim Callaghan No. 2, with a view to getting Roy in as No. 1. Evidently my opinions expressed at the time of the crisis had thoroughly upset Harold and he was bitterly hurt that nobody had wanted to speak to him and get his advice before the Cabinet meeting announcing the cuts.

Number 10 lives in an atmosphere of intrigue, encouraged by George Wigg who is a completely crazy adviser, Marcia who gets a bit hysterical and Gerald Kaufman who just sits wisely and nods. What Harold needs is a frank talk from his friends, but at the moment he won't allow his friends to meet. He's afraid that if Dick, Barbara, Tommy, Peter, Judith and I meet, we may turn out to be against him. I find the upper strata of politics less and less attractive. It's not exactly that I'm naïve, but I really am only interested in politics in order to get my job done. Peter is of course a wise bird, having been a political civil servant for a long time. He suggested that I should go and see Harold soon, in order to mend my relations with Number 10.

Sunday 7 August

We had another pleasant day and Peter and I went over one or two joint projects affecting Mintech. This afternoon we drove back to London. I rang Tommy and he suggested I should ring Marcia, and he said, 'Harold was wounded at what you did but is also very loving.' It was a typical Thomas remark. I rang Marcia and said perhaps I could come and see Harold at his convenience. She said he'd been waiting for me to come and see him ever since the crisis broke. I said I didn't want to bother him and wasn't at all sure what had gone on. Marcia said, 'At your level he expects you to bother him whenever you want to.' He would also like me to ring him before Cabinet when anything important is coming up to find out the line that he wants to take. On balance, I'm glad that I struck out on my own, since I had been Harold's adviser for too long and it is a good thing that he should see me in my own right.

Tuesday 9 August
This morning I had Sir Frank Kearton of Courtaulds, Ronald Grierson of Warburgs and Ben Cant* – members of the new Industrial Reorganisation Corporation[3] – to come along to talk for about an hour and a half about the work of the Corporation in anticipation of Thursday's debate. Kearton is very nice and I have great confidence in Cant as well. Grierson is a rather flabby city type. We went over the ground carefully and I got all the information I wanted. I had the impression that the opposition to IRC would probably diminish. The bitter criticism of it before the Election stemmed much more from political reasons than from any other.

I went to the Commons and answered questions. Then I had Mr Banks and Mr McDonald of the Institution of Civil Engineers to come and talk to me about the relationship between their institution and Mintech. They said that there should be more women in engineering, especially those who have qualified and have then married, that Mintech should have closer links with universities which ought to appoint practising engineers to chairs, and that Mintech ought to consider the possibility of setting up young engineers' clubs in various cities, and consider the appointment of an engineering adviser to me in Mintech. I found them tough but shrewd and kindly – the embodiment of the nineteenth-century engineer.

After them came Mr Gill, the chairman of the Society of British Aerospace Constructors, and Sir Richard Smeeton, the new Director General, who wanted to talk in general about the aircraft industry. They were dull, I thought, and clearly look to the Government to point the way forward for the industry by approving a number of major projects. But the key to all this is whether we can sell our aircraft abroad and no amount of Government support can possibly be justified if we can't get the money back.

This evening we had the report stage of the Prices and Incomes Bill and it went on right through the night. I managed to get a couple of hours' sleep. Some Labour members abstained and I had a talk to the Chief Whip about it. He is keen not to withdraw the whip and suggested that those who abstained should simply be refused permission to come to Party meetings.

I also had a talk to Tony Crosland at breakfast and he said that he was getting awfully sick of Cabinet Ministers telling the press

* Industrial adviser to the Ministry of Technology, 1964–70.

what jobs they would like in the Government. The main culprits are Roy Jenkins who uses John Harris and Roy Hattersley, Labour MP for Sparkbrook, as his agents in dealing with the press; Jim Callaghan, whose ambitions for the Foreign Office are now so well known as to be almost boring, and possibly Dick Crossman, who would like to take over from George Brown.

Wednesday 10 August
All night sitting. I went home for a bath and straight back for Cabinet.

Hilary came to the Commons this evening and I introduced him to seven Cabinet Ministers. Tonight was the night of the big reshuffle which came as a great surprise to everybody. Dick Crossman became Leader of the House of Commons in place of Herbert Bowden, who went to the Commonwealth Office in place of Arthur Bottomley, who went to Overseas Aid in place of Tony Greenwood, who went to Housing in place of Dick Crossman. Michael Stewart and George Brown changed places. Nobody can make out the reason for the change. Various explanations have been offered. One is that George Brown made it a condition of staying on in the Government at the time of the recent threatened resignation that he should get the Foreign Office and that Harold acceded to it.

There is a great deal of dismay about the future of the DEA although it may be that Michael Stewart, with his quiet Fabian manner, will keep the thing going on a rather better basis than George could have done. There is some anxiety about George at the Foreign Office but he has always wanted the job and Harold presumably didn't feel able to stand out against him. I think Dick Crossman's appointment is the best news of all as we probably shall get some parliamentary reform and he will now be acting as the liaison between the Government, the Parliamentary Party and the National Executive. He is thus the Herbert Morrison of the new Government. The Party did not receive this news well.

Monday 15 August
Shopping and clearing up in the morning and this afternoon took Hilary, Melissa and Joshua to Stansgate, arriving at 3 o'clock. It is nice to be here with almost two clear weeks ahead.

Thursday 25 August
The whole family – without Stephen – went to the Bradwell Nuclear Power Station this morning. They had laid on a superb tour for us and we saw the station which cost £58 million to build and is of a Magnox type, now obsolescent. We walked right into the reactor and

saw the gantry that moved the nuclear fuel. We were frisked by Geiger counters, saw the heat exchanger and the turbines and then had lunch with the senior officials of the CEGB who had come to see us. It was altogether an enjoyable day.

The thing that interested me was the difference in attitude between Joshua, who is aged eight, and myself. I had to drive out of my mind all my primitive knowledge of how power stations worked – whereby you burned the coal, heated the water and the steam turned the turbines – and try to think of the implications of atomic energy. Joshua took it entirely for granted. It seemed natural to him that if you had a nuclear power station, you would be able to generate electricity and because he wasn't consciously thinking about the processes, he got an awful lot more out of it than I did.

Wednesday 31 August
For the first time since the holiday began I went up to my little attic room in Stansgate and started working on my red boxes which have been accumulating. I haven't read the papers or listened to the news for just over two weeks and it was a wrench to come back to it all. It may be better next time I have a holiday to maintain just an hour or two's interest in my work each day, so that I don't get into the position where it is an absolute agony to break away from the escapism of a holiday and go back to real work.

Monday 5 September
To the office this morning to start work in earnest. One of the first issues that has come up has been the application by the Vauxhall Motor Company to increase its prices to be announced at the Motor Show. I sat on this.

Lunch with Peter Shore and Jeremy Bray at the Tate Gallery and then went to see Dick Crossman. Together we watched on television Harold's courageous speech at the TUC and we went back to Dick's room to talk about parliamentary reform. This is one of the things he is keen to carry through and I'm sure that his appointment makes a lot of sense. We are certainly going to get a Science and Technology Committee of the House of Commons, which will look at my department and Tony Crosland's. I think we shall also get a rearrangement of business so that the House meets in the daytime instead of at night, and the televising of Parliament.

Tuesday 6 September
By helicopter this morning to the Farnborough Air Show. I have never been to Farnborough before and I went round and looked at the planes which made the aircraft industry a little bit more real to

me in terms of actual products. After lunch I watched the display and was put next to the Duke of Edinburgh for a few minutes. I had a brief talk to him and was impressed by what he knew about the aircraft industry. He certainly knew more than I did.

The news of the assassination of President Verwoerd of South Africa came to us as we were watching the air display and it creates a new situation in Southern Africa which may well have an impact on the Rhodesian situation.

Wednesday 7 September
A long talk to Sir William Penney this morning on the future of the AEA. With Edmund Dell's help we have begun to relate this to the future of our nuclear power station exports. Given goodwill from the Ministry of Power, the CEGB and the Treasury, it will, I think, give the whole industry a fresh focus and provide part of the answer to the very difficult problem as to what to do with the AEA.

Afterwards by hydrofoil from Westminster pier to Dagenham where I drove the millionth Cortina on to the dock and made a short speech. Stanley Gillen, the Managing Director of Ford (UK), took me round the works and I saw the new wholly automated engine plant. It was the first time I had been inside a motor car factory and I was immensely struck by the vastness of the production line. The automated engine plant took rough castings straight from the foundry and passed them through machine tools that turned them and drilled them and bored them and polished them so that they came out the other end ready for the basic assembly of the engine. At this point, they were bolted on to a conveyor and went by as all the other components were added. There were very few men involved in the whole process. Finally they were hot-tested. Gillen was brought over from America last year to try to tidy up the British Ford Company and he was obviously a very tough American business executive.

I looked in to see Tommy Balogh on my return and he is now rather cheerful. He thinks that the freeze may give us an opportunity to develop a real plan for our wages and incomes and prices, which will allow us to come out of this squeeze with a socialist economy and in this way we may have stumbled into socialism.

Thursday 8 September
To Bristol this morning for the opening of the Severn Bridge by the Queen. Here was a major engineering achievement, a beautiful bridge, marvellous architecture, and they'd got the Lord Lieutenant of Gloucestershire and the Lord Lieutenant of Monmouthshire and military bands and the royal family, while the actual people who'd constructed it were pushed into the background.

There were many distinguished people looking on as the ribbon was cut. I was there in my capacity as an MP, sitting among the MPs and merely observing it, but as Minister responsible for the engineering profession, I found it extremely interesting.

I hurried back and there was a meeting at Number 10 to discuss the Productivity Conference. Afterwards, in the evening Caroline and I went to Harold's reception at Lancaster House for the Commonwealth Prime Ministers. We talked to a number of people there and Tony Hart – Judith's husband – suggested that we ought to make a move to get an Academy of National Technology established, with a status comparable to that of the Royal Society.

Friday 9 September
I caught the 1.45 train from Paddington and opened the Engineering Industry Training Board premises in Bristol. This was the first time I have spoken in Bristol as Minister and I made my speech about education. Then I was driven to Gloucester where I spoke at the first Regional Policy Conference organised by Transport House. I was told by the regional organiser that Number 10 had ordered that all Ministers' speeches and the question and answer sessions should be tape recorded and sent to Number 10, 'so that the sort of questions that would be likely to come up at Conference could be analysed'. Although I couldn't object, I did resent what appeared to me to be a form of political security checking. Presumably Gerald Kaufman and George Wigg and others will be listening to it to find out whether or not Ministers are putting the right line across. I delivered a perfectly good, tough speech and on the whole, despite some criticism, the general atmosphere was good.

Monday 12 September
First thing this morning Mr Bargash, the Minister of Development of Morocco, came to see me and it was quite clear from what he said that the Moroccans would like to get out of the French sphere of influence and establish closer relations with us. In practice, we have no money we can give them by way of aid but I have the feeling that if we sent a group of experts out to look at some of their projects, it might open up long-term export possibilities for us. This might be quite a useful way of using our QSEs [Qualified Scientists and Engineers]. His main concern was with the Rif re-afforestation schemes and the Sebou river dams.

At 4 o'clock I went to the Home Policy Committee at Transport House and afterwards I walked back to the Treasury with Jim Callaghan. It was the first time I have talked to him since the July measures and he asked me if I had had any knowledge of the alleged conspiracy to unseat Harold during July. He told me that Harold told him that this had been organised while he, Harold, was in Moscow, that Roy Jenkins and Tony Crosland were behind it and that I had fallen for it along with the Left who were very naive. Indeed, hearing the same story told to one of the supposed ringleaders in such a way as to acquit him and implicate others indicated the paranoid thinking in Number 10.

In fact I had talked to Barbara Castle and George Brown and others at the time but there had been no notion whatsoever of a conspiracy and I do not believe that one existed. My own view is that Jim Callaghan genuinely wanted to leave the Treasury and that his press leak on this subject had led to a great deal of supposition about his ambitions. But since he was not on the side of radical measures in July he could hardly hope to gain by having those radical measures imposed on the Cabinet by a minority. Roy Jenkins is certainly ambitious and may well have his eye on Number 10 in the long run and I would be much more suspicious about Roy than about almost anybody else. But even so, I do not think a conspiracy took place and I think that Harold must be badly advised by George Wigg and Marcia. It shows what an extraordinarily insecure atmosphere exists at the top in politics.

Jim then went on to say things about Harold which I was very careful not to comment on. He said he thought that Harold was extremely devious and that he had had to say to him, 'Don't forget, Harold, that the shortest distance between two points is often a straight line.' I somewhat doubt whether Jim really did say this but he thought that lack of confidence within the Cabinet was now a very serious factor. I confined myself to saying that if on major issues a Cabinet Minister couldn't come to his own conclusions and advocate them without it being regarded as an act of disloyalty, things would be very difficult.

Jim is very disappointed to have been anchored in the Treasury after the reshuffle and I feel sure that the leaks which were put out in August to the effect that this was being done as a punishment can't exactly have helped his morale. He also indicated that he was very unhappy about the existence of DEA, that it had delayed decisions so interminably that he didn't think in the long run it could work.

This evening Caroline and I went to the Soviet Embassy and we met the new Soviet Ambassador, Mr Smirnovsky, and his wife. They are both aviation engineers, having worked with the Ilyushin Group during the war. I liked him and thought he was a very straightforward person. We also met a number of leaders of the Soviet aircraft industry who had come over to study the Farnborough Air Show.

They expressed interest in common research and development on some problems and also in the development of our small aircraft. I doubt if there is a big market for major UK aircraft in the Soviet Union. They asked us to dinner and I had the feeling that they think I am a member of the Government worth keeping in touch with. I said nothing political at all, except how very able George Brown was. They, of course, have grave doubts about him, following the visit of Khrushchev here in 1956 when there was a slanging match between the two of them.

Tuesday 13 September

At noon Mr Webb, the Head of NASA, came to see me with Dr Draper, formerly of the Massachusetts Institute of Technology, who was responsible for the guidance system of missiles including the Polaris missile. Webb said the American space effort had reached such a scale that the pay-load they were going to put up could take over a number of scientific research projects which exceeded the capacity of American universities to provide. He wanted co-operation with us. I was extremely non-committal on the subject of expenditure but expressed a general interest in sharing the dissemination of information so that the technical fallout could be spread more evenly among the Western countries. Webb's main object of course is to build up a Western space capability in Europe to rival that of the Soviet Union and particularly to see that the French don't break away on their own and monopolise all the space technology in Europe. His first idea had been to suggest links directly with the Germans, following Chancellor Erhardt's visit to President Johnson last December when the joint space probe was proposed. He had then thought that it would be worthwhile looking in to see us and I tried to say enough to keep the options open without committing us to any expenditure which we couldn't afford.

I had my first meeting with NACMMI, the National Advisory Committee for the Motor Manufacturing Industry. All the bigwigs of the industry, including Lord Rootes of Rootes Motors, Sir Patrick Hennessy, chairman of Ford's, Sir George Harriman of British Motors, and Sir Donald Stokes of Leyland, were there, plus representatives of the Confederation of Shipbuilding and Engineering Unions, the Ministry of Transport and the Board of Trade, the Iron and Steel Board and my own department. It was a very difficult meeting indeed, as they were extremely anxious about the position in the light of the credit squeeze and particularly the effect of the imposition of a deposit of 40 per cent on hire purchase payments.

They told me that without a firm expanding home market it was impossible to develop exports and that they disliked the idea of using the motor car industry to act as a regulator for the economy. I said I was naturally interested in what they said and would convey any message that they gave me but that the policy was set and it was impossible to have an expanding economy unless we got more exports. From the nation's point of view therefore, a much bigger export drive was essential if we were to sustain the level of home demand that would make it possible for them to have a large home market. On this contradictory note one got stuck.

Wednesday 14 September
I had a talk with an Under-Secretary in the department, Richard Bullock, about the possibility of Government stock-piling as a means of maintaining the output of the machine tool industry during this current squeeze. The departmental view is strongly opposed to this but it is a matter on which Harold has expressed an interest so I was very keen that the idea should be fully explored and not treated too negatively. I also concluded that the time had come when we would have to look at a more radical solution for the machine tool industry in order to meet the problem of rising imports in times of boom and too low capacity in general.

In the afternoon, I went to Dick's weekly meeting where I drew attention to the anxiety about the car situation and Dick was extremely rude and angry. He is now in one of his socialist-maso-chistic moods and this I think is going to create a certain amount of trouble for some of his colleagues.

Thursday 15 September
This morning I had Maddock in to discuss the ways and means by which we could stimulate a real drive on information retrieval so as to make more new technological information available for industry. Maddock is a first-rate chap and I have great confidence in him. I realise that my big problem is that I am so ignorant of industry. It is extremely difficult to do this job without a real working knowledge of industry and its main figures, and I've never acquired this over the years and must work at it very very hard indeed from now on. I think it does mean meeting more industrialists and talking to them on an informal basis.

Friday 16 September
Cabinet and then to the office, where I had a talk to Otto Clarke about the carve-up of the Ministry of Aviation and the possible use we might make of Lord Mountbatten on information retrieval. I am rather sceptical of Mountbatten's value but he is a big name and it might be quite useful to link him with Mintech.

Sunday 18 September

Lunch with Tony Crosland. Tony was in a very curious mood. He stressed how he was trying to cut down on the work he was doing and how important a complete holiday was. He said that he was devolving more and more work to his department, that the comprehensive battle was won and he was leaving it to Assistant Secretaries to approve the various reorganisation schemes that came up.

After lunch we sat and talked and I told him I did not like the idea of having to make every discussion in Cabinet a vote of confidence. I raised the question of the conspiracy and asked him if he had any knowledge of it and he denied it entirely. He said, quite frankly, 'I never was an admirer of Harold Wilson but I think he's probably as good a peacetime Prime Minister as this country ever gets, even though over the last four months we appear to have been entirely without a strategy and I think he's been very bad. But in time he will learn to be less gimmicky.'

He thought that Jim Callaghan might conceivably visualise himself as Leader some time and he thought Roy Jenkins was ambitious too, but that none of these things was in sight over the next five years. I don't know whether Tony Crosland is discreet or not but there is always a certain risk in talking even to Cabinet colleagues. I don't particularly want this to get back to George Wigg.

Monday 19 September

At the office this morning Mr Seidman of the US Bureau of the Budget came to discuss the Post Office reorganisation. He is going to the Post Office as well but wanted to get a briefing from me and I gave him the background. He said that Roosevelt had considered a similar reform but it had never been contemplated seriously because of congressional opposition. I told him the whole story and that my view was now unofficial since I didn't actually know what was happening. But it does show that when you start reforming, people begin coming from abroad to find out why.

Tam Dalyell came to tell me about the difficulties in his constituency due to the BMC redundancies at Bathgate. We discussed the possibility of a training scheme which would enable some workers to be kept on to raise the level of skill so that the development areas would be less vulnerable in the future.

This evening I went to a reception and heard a characteristic story about a British instrument firm which supplied equipment to America but had not changed its design or scientific features for years. It had never sent a man over to meet its customers and was likely to lose the contract.

Wednesday 21 September

Got up very early and went to London airport for my visit to Scotland but it was very foggy, with no prospect of the fog clearing, so I called off the flight. While I was there I met Lord Reith, the first Director General of the BBC, who is now seventy-seven but full of energy. He was recently elected rector of Glasgow University – by the popular vote of the students – and is now throwing himself into reform of university structure. He expressed tremendous interest in the Post Office changes and hinted more than once that he would like to be the first chairman of the Post Office Corporation. He made a remark that was absolutely characteristic, 'I think I can give a promise, on behalf of the Almighty, that I shall be active for five years.'

Went to Dick Crossman's meeting and afterwards he told me that he was going to suggest that he, Barbara, Peter and I had dinner together every week and that he and Barbara and I should actually discuss Cabinet business before it comes up. In view of Harold's incredible sensitivity to groups and his paranoid fear of conspiracies, I said immediately that I wouldn't be prepared to contemplate such a thing unless it was approved by Harold. He said that it would be impossible for Harold to approve it but he would of course make what he was going to do clear to Harold. But, quite frankly, I'm not prepared to take this risk, although I would like to see Dick and Barbara and others to discuss things more often than I do.

Thursday 22 September

Lord Mountbatten came to see me. He was anxious that the Ministry of Technology should take on the National Electronics Council. This was something he thought of when he gave up the Defence Department – he being a trained electrical engineer. He had set up this Council and then found it was too much for him and tried to get Frank Cousins to take it on. Frank wouldn't and so he has come to get me to do it.

There is absolutely no enthusiasm in the office for this because Mountbatten has always worked on the principle that he would only have absolutely top people on his committee. That is to say the chairmen and managing directors of all the major electronic firms and Permanent Secretaries and Ministers. Sir Richard Clarke was very obsequious and smiling and smirking and afterwards I said to him that I thought it had all been very high level waffle. But of course Mountbatten's name with its royal connections was so compelling that nobody dared to think of standing in his way. No doubt this is how he got such an organisation off the ground.

We began a discussion on productivity which was interrupted by the visit of Dr Kotzina, the Austrian Minister of Works and Technology. The Foreign Office brief obligingly said that he was a lawyer who had 'fought on the Eastern Front' during the war. This meant that he was in the German Army against Russia. He was nearly sixty and relatively new at his job and didn't seem to have a great deal to offer.

Friday 23 September 1966
To Number 10 for a discussion under Harold's chairmanship of the Productivity Conference and afterwards he asked me to stay. He said that his reshuffle in August had been the smartest piece of work he'd ever done 'as there are now six crown princes instead of just one'. This, I think, was his real motive and it confirms retrospectively what one has feared about his analysis of the July crisis. He also said that the only reason he had reshuffled on that day was because George Brown had told his press adviser and it had to be announced before it leaked. I asked if Mintech would have a new Minister of State in the next reshuffle and he said that it was very difficult, as he was up to the legal limit of Ministers of State and Ministers and he had to fit in Patrick Gordon Walker and he didn't intend to let Fred Lee go, and so on and so on. So it looks as if things are going to be delayed for a while.

I said how pleased I was that Dick Crossman had taken on the job of Lord President, since it would mean that parliamentary reform would move forward and that he would occupy the sort of position that Herbert Morrison occupied. I fancy Harold was a little worried at the suggestion that Dick would brief the press on matters on which he himself preferred to give guidance. We then had a long talk about the work of my department. It was the first time that I'd talked to him since he made me Minister of Technology and it was useful to demonstrate that I was hard at it and knew my stuff.

Afterwards I went back to the office and then in the afternoon went to the Ministry of Technology Water Pollution Laboratory at Stevenage, my first visit to one of our research stations. I met the senior staff and then there was a general meeting of all staff. I spoke for five minutes about the Ministry of Technology and what it did and tried to emphasise that our job was to help British industry to be competitive – giving a commercial tilt to the whole affair, which I think was probably a new emphasis.

The questions that came out were interesting. One was about the possible use of procurement by the laboratory to stimulate the use of British equipment. Another was from a man who would like to see the laboratory give much more positive help to local authorities and to industries in order to see that their basic work was applied. They were keen on a stronger link with industry and would like to carry on their research to the point of production. Some of them would actually like to be consultants to industry, in addition to their work in the laboratory, and others thought that if they could get something more as individuals out of the patents that were taken out by the laboratory, this would encourage them as well.

All in all, the visit was well worthwhile from my point of view because it involved an exploration of the centre ground between Government research and industry, which is the key to our success as a department. I shall have to do some more work on this problem.

The diary entries from now until the end of 1967 are rather different in character from those in both my earlier and later diaries. Due to the severe pressure of Ministry of Technology work, at the end of September 1966 I ceased to keep a full record of events over the following fifteen months, and made only brief daily notes which I dictated in diary form some years later, with the advantage of hindsight. It is important that readers should understand the nature of this part of my diary which is quite different from that relating to the period up to September 1966 when it was dictated daily to a secretary to type, and after 1 January 1968 when the daily dictation was resumed – this time on tape. Some of the major political events during these African months do not feature because the entries made about them at the time were too short or cryptic to be significant and I did not wish to rely on my memory to fill in gaps.

October 1966 opened with the Labour Party Conference in Brighton and Harold called me in to his room, as usual, to help him prepare his speech. This was the first time that he received a hostile reception as Leader and it was largely due to the cuts, introduced in July, in public expenditure which had created a great deal of unpopularity for the Government and had led to 1000 BMC car workers demonstrating outside the hotel as he walked towards the Conference centre. Wilson took a loudspeaker and talked to them and took a few of them into the hotel, later telling me how courageous he had been.

It was also at this Conference that we had a special Cabinet in Harold's room where Part 4 of the Prices and Incomes Act which, for the first time, gave the Government statutory powers to restrain wages, was activated. This was the first statutory pay policy of that Government and it embittered the trade union movement, especially shop floor workers and activists, and played a part in separating the Government from its own supporters in the trade unions.

As for the rest of the Conference, there was not much to report except that while I was there, Sir Otto Clarke, my Permanent Secretary, came down to discuss the future of the nuclear industry and Peter Shore and I told him that we were not prepared to continue with the absurdity of having competing tenders when the reactor orders were so few and far between, and that in practice the industry could only survive if there was a single reactor group under public ownership.

One other event perhaps worth commenting on was that Radio Caroline, the pirate radio station, hired a very beautiful woman to come to the ITN party and to head for Sergeant Kelly, the PM's bodyguard. This publicity stunt created something of a stir.

Monday 10 October

I opened the Design Conference and took the chair. Then on to the Economic Development Committee, where there was a division on whether we should go ahead with the plan to nationalise the aircraft industry. The plan was that the Government should buy BAC and merge it with Hawker Siddeley and have a minority holding in the new, united company.[4] Later I flew to Wick in the HS125 with Bill Penney and James Marjoribanks, our Ambassador to the Common Market, and others who wanted to see Dounreay – all part of the 'technological approach to Europe'.

Wednesday 12 October

Judith Hart came to see me about Rhodesia. She was absolutely convinced that there would be a sell-out and she wanted my advice about resignation. I told her not to resign but to say, just before she thought the sell-out would occur, that there would be no breach of our solemn pledge – and then get sacked.

To the Design Conference dinner, and sat next to Lord Snowdon who was extremely friendly.

Wednesday 19 October

The chairman of the USSR State Committee for Science and Technology, Vladimir Kirillin, and his party had arrived from Moscow and came to the Ministry of Technology for talks, designed to encourage the building up of technological agreements with the Russians. Caroline and I had given a dinner at home for Kirillin and his party and had received gifts from them, and some query arose as to whether the presents were bugged. So we had to send them for electronic sweeping by the security services.

Made my first speech in Parliament as Minister of Technology in the debate on the Industrial Reorganisation Corporation Bill. The great argument was whether the Government should intervene in industry or not, the Tories taking a very strict view on disengagement. The Industrial Reorganisation Corporation actually began with a memorandum which Ben Cant and Pat Blackett wrote and submitted to the Advisory Council on Technology of Mintech in 1964 and was then taken up enthusiastically by George Brown at the DEA and by Harold.

Saturday 22 October
Driven to Chequers for the meeting on Europe at 10.45 am which lasted until 7 pm There were nineteen Ministers there, and numerous officials who left in the afternoon.

There was a great row in the morning when Sir William Armstrong, Joint Permanent Secretary at the Treasury, said that he didn't see any prospect at all of Britain being able to be in the Common Market unless and until we had devalued. George Brown got quite hysterical at this thought, because he knew that the Cabinet would be opposed to devaluation, George himself being in favour, and that this would affect our chances of entry. William Armstrong was really in the doghouse for saying this. We agreed that Harold Wilson and George Brown would visit the six countries of the Common Market to do a 'probe'. Harold was not prepared to let George go alone because he didn't trust George and he thought that George didn't trust him. I came to the conclusion that Britain would be in the Common Market by 1970.

Monday 24 October
I had a talk to Otto Clarke about Europe and he believed that we would never get investment until we were part of Europe. Once businessmen knew that we were going in to the Common Market, then investment would absolutely soar.

He also said to me that the British Civil Service was so much better than any of the civil services of the Common Market countries because we had run an empire from Whitehall, and so when we went into Europe our Civil Service would run rings around the Europeans. I had doubts about that.

Kirillin came for a long talk and we discussed how to bring together our two economies and get scientific and technical collaboration. I took him to see Harold Wilson.

In the evening we went to the Soviet Embassy and as George Blake,* the spy, had just been 'sprung' from Wormwood Scrubs there were a lot of rumours around that he might actually have been in the Embassy at the time of the party.

Tuesday 25 October
Dr Glenn Seaborg, chairman of the US Atomic Energy Commission, came to see me. He is a tall, quiet, craggy American academic and was a distinguished wartime physicist. Our relations with the US Atomic Energy Commission are very close. Not only do we have

---

* Foreign Office official imprisoned in 1961 for forty-two years for spying for the Soviet Union.

defence relations – as a result of which all British atomic security is vetted and overseen and double checked and approved by the Americans – but also we owe a tremendous amount to them in the sphere of technology.

Thursday 27 October

Caroline and I had dinner with the Gulbenkians at the Ritz. Christopher Soames* and his wife and Sir Alec Douglas-Home and his wife were there. I sat next to Soames's wife Mary, the daughter of Churchill. She told me how bitterly angry and disappointed the family were that Lord Moran had been so unfair as to publish a book† about her father's health. An enjoyable evening – Gulbenkian is an amusing man.

Wednesday 2 November

Met Arthur Norman, Chairman of De La Rue, the big manufacturing company, who told me that he was planning a big expansion for 1970 because he knew that it would be an Election year and no Government would dare go into an Election without a boom.

I had a talk with Jim Callaghan. Jim said, 'What is Harold up to on Europe?' He simply didn't know.

Monday 14 November

To the Foreign Policy Association lunch at the Dorchester and afterwards met the Confederation of Shipbuilding and Engineering Unions. I was beginning to think about a big programme of consultation with trade unions. It was absurd to me that a big industrial department should have very close links with industrial management but in effect no real consultation with the unions. I had been the first Postmaster General to go to the UPW headquarters and speak at union conferences and try to get to know them really well, and I decided to do the same at the Ministry of Technology.

Wednesday 16 November

Harold produced his plan for a European Technological Community. He had been much struck by an article in the *Economist* about this in September when we had our Chequers meeting on Europe. The whole discussion of what a European Technological Community meant was

---

* Former Conservative MP, subsequently Ambassador to France and Vice-President of the EEC Commission.
† *Winston Churchill, The Struggle for Survival*, 1966 by Charles Moran (Churchill's private doctor).

extremely vague from beginning to end but it was Harold's way of keeping the pressure going on Europe.

When later Peter Shore came out with a serious proposal, saying that a real European Technological Community would mean that we only procured from European sources, this was turned down contemptuously by Whitehall who often wanted to buy American, knowing that the Europeans wanted to buy American too.

Friday 18 November

To the Science Museum for Engineers' Day. The Queen was there and Ayub Khan, the President of Pakistan, and I took her round. What was interesting to me was that because we had the Queen – which was the department's idea – it meant that the event was covered by the court correspondent, who knew nothing about engineers. The result was that there was no serious reporting of the event at all except what the Queen wore and who came in which carriage or car. It was a perfect example of how a royal visit will kill anything serious.

Wednesday 23 November

Had lunch at the National Research Development Corporation with Harold Wilson. He was tremendously proud of having set it up when he was President of the Board of Trade in 1948. Sir William Black, Chairman of Leyland, was there and I heard that he earned £70,000 a year from Leyland.

The Comprehensive Schools Committee, working hard to change the policy of the Labour Government on education, regularly use my office at home down in the basement. Then they leave and I come home with Cabinet papers and work there all evening, and at weekends. Some papers put out by the Department of Education and Science clearly reflect the influence of the Comprehensive Schools Committee and it is an interesting lesson in the operation of pressure politics.

Sunday 4 December

Harold came back from HMS *Tiger* with a document half agreed with Smith. Wilson had been negotiating with Smith on board *Tiger* in the Mediterranean to try to end the Rhodesian crisis. We had a Cabinet specially summoned and everyone was there except Barbara Castle. I had great anxieties as to whether it was right to agree with what Harold had brought back, but I did.

Monday 5 December

Rhodesia rejected the terms agreed with Harold at the talks on HMS *Tiger*.

Tuesday 6 December

Lunch with Solly Zuckerman at London Zoo. We talked about nuclear weapons and he told me that he was keen that Denis Healey and the Defence staff should not be able to get away with further expenditure on nuclear weapons by hardening the Polaris submarine warheads.[5] He said that he and Lord Rothschild were really at one on this.

We also talked about the European Technological Community. Solly Zuckerman is passionately pro-French and he has got many contacts in Paris. Throughout my dealings with him, I always found that he was very keen on the European link and on sharing our nuclear power with the French. He has some influence, though, like all advisers, he feels very frustrated.

Friday 9 December

Went to Newcastle for early morning talks with Danny McGarvey of the Boilermakers at his headquarters. At 9.30. I met the Northern Economic Planning Committee. Then Dr Monty Finniston and I went round his International Research and Development Company. The company is a research organisation doing contract research and he was very keen it should have Government support. All over the United Kingdom there are people who want public research establishments set up not only to provide employment but also to give status. I was beginning to doubt however whether it was sensible to go on spending a great deal of money on research which didn't appear to be very wisely used, and the department was very much against it.

From there I went to the Swan Hunter shipyard and had lunch with Sir John Hunter, the chairman. He is regarded as one of the best of the shipbuilders, an absolutely typical tough nineteenth-century figure. It was his manager, Tom McIver, a sort of non-commissioned officer type, who really understood the business. You had the combination of the rich, slightly aristocratic and at the same time nouveau riche shipbuilding magnate, and the man who has come up from the ranks and really does all the work.

Then to Durham Technical College, followed by Durham University, to talk to the Young Socialists – a fairly stormy meeting – and finally to the Sunderland Fabian dinner in the evening.

Caught the sleeper home. I really was exhausted after such a day.

Thursday 15 December

I called Stokes and Harriman in together to discuss the Chrysler/Rootes crisis. I put to them three simple questions. Do you want to see Chrysler take over Rootes? Do you think it is worth

attempting a British solution – a regrouping that would include
Rootes and British Motors and Leyland, in which there might be
some Government participation? Would you be prepared to bring
about a merger between your two companies to try to absorb Rootes
if the Government were prepared to help?

*Rootes was a well established British motor car manufacturer under the control
of Sir William Rootes. Owing to inadequate investment and poor design, the
company had got into difficulties which were accelerated by the stop-go policies
followed by successive Governments, including the Labour Government with its
July 1966 measures. During the previous Tory Government, the American
Chrysler company had bought up a part of the Rootes equity on the clear
understanding that Chrysler would respect the independence of Rootes and there
would be no change in the balance of share ownership without the consent of
the Government.*

*In the autumn of 1966, Rootes was clearly in serious trouble and Chrysler
offered to buy the remainder of the shares making it, in effect, into the British
component of the international Chrysler Corporation. General Motors already
existed in Britain and so did the Ford Motor Company, and it became clear
that if Chrysler were to gain complete control of Rootes, there would be three
American giants operating in Britain, putting the survival of the British motor
industry at risk. I was engaged in negotiations with the object of bringing about
a merger between the British Motor Corporation (BMC) and Leyland which,
backed by Government investment, would be in a position to buy Rootes and
establish a British motor giant on a scale likely to be able to compete with the
Americans. However, owing to the conflicts between BMC and Leyland, which
were worsened by tension between Sir George Harriman, the chairman of BMC
and Sir Donald Stokes, the chairman of Leyland, this project came to nothing.*

*In the event, I was obliged to agree that Chrysler would acquire a majority
holding in Rootes. But, by way of guarantee that British interests would not be
neglected, Chrysler accepted that there would be an investment by IRC which
would provide a British Government presence on the Board. These negotiations
were very difficult and delicate throughout. I was disappointed at the outcome
and the House of Commons did not welcome the announcement when it was
made. Subsequently, of course, Leyland acquired BMC and British Leyland
was established but too late to have any influence on the Rootes company.*

Then to the National Physical Laboratory, which is an absolute
monastery of academic scientific research. The NPL was set up originally in about 1900, at a time when Britain was dropping behind
Germany in the research race, to do practical research for British
industry. During the First World War, the Department of Scientific
and Industrial Research was established to carry the same work
forward and the Ministry of Technology is part of the same history.
But over the years the NPL had become very pure. I visited the ship

research division where they were doing research on the shape of hulls and other problems, but none of it had any appliction to the shipbuilding industry.

Monday 19 December

Had the CBI group in, talking about their visit to the USSR designed to strengthen relations with the Russians under the technological agreements.

The CBI were not very keen to have much to do with Government and, under the general heading of 'Captains of Industry', had hit upon a formula for visits between top industrialists and Russian industrial Ministers, which was quite a good idea. I was keen that relations with the Soviet Union should be developed on *that* basis. A department can do very little when it comes to pushing British business and we have to leave it to the industrialists.

Thursday 22 December

At Cabinet I saved the Harrier vertical take-off jet, one of the most brilliant British aeronautical innovations, which Denis Healey always tries to cancel on every possible occasion.

The Rootes-Chrysler deal was approved by the Cabinet with general commendation. I tried to promote the idea of a special concession on electrical cars by taking off the tax and purchase tax so as to encourage their development.

In the evening I did a long and – given my limited knowledge of French – painful broadcast for the BBC French Service.

Sunday 31 December

1966 began with the last three months of Wilson's first Government and I made considerable progress on my Post Office projects. The stamp programme was accepted and has been a great success. The Giro was also approved and work began on the investment accounts. Relations with the unions were restored. With the Post Office job pretty well completed, I left just as the final reorganisation work began to be undertaken.

Then we had the March Election and the great Labour triumph. But shortly after the Election things began going wrong for the Government. We had the seamen's strike where Harold said he would not be blown off course, and thoroughly demoralised many Labour people by his attacks on the radical leadership of the Seamen's Union. Then we had the 20 July measures, which were really the death knell for the National Plan because it was then that we decided to opt for a balance of payments surplus rather than for economic growth, and this involved paying an enormously heavy price without getting any great political advantage from it. We also went for the prices and incomes statutory policy which did us a great deal of damage in the Movement.

We got embroiled in the Rhodesia problem and although the *Tiger* talks were an attempt to solve it, they didn't succeed and that did us a great deal of damage politically.

British entry into the EEC was seriously discussed by the Government and I began to get my teeth into the problems of the Ministry of Technology which are immensely complicated, particularly as I am not a scientist or an engineer. And having no knowledge of the City I found the financial side all very difficult too. But industrial problems are very exciting. I realised that the main contribution that I could make was to bring my political skills to work in the department and to remember that my great expertise was supposed to be persuasion and the organisation of consent to achieve what I wanted. At the end of 1966, I still found the job pretty rough, requiring me to work extremely hard – much harder than I anticipated.

Tuesday 10 – Wednesday 11 January 1967
Off early to Dusseldorf by plane and I was given a huge police escort to Bonn for talks with Gerhard Stoltenburg, the German Minister of Science and Industry. The Germans are tremendously keen on co-operation in space, but we are not. Bill Penney and I went to the Julich Nuclear Research Station, of which the Germans are very proud and where, we suspect but have no proof, they may be doing some secret military work.

Tuesday 17 January
To the office early, preparing for the Rootes-Chrysler statement I was to make later in the day. It was very sternly criticised on the Labour side, the Tories not actually attacking it and I was left appearing to be putting forward a Tory scheme.

Saturday 21 January
In the afternoon to Birmingham for the British Jewellers' banquet at the Grand Hotel. George Woodcock was there. He is a very cynical man – maybe if you get to the top in the trade union movement you have to be cynical, but not as much as he is. He once made a speech saying that life was full of shoddy compromises, and I think, early on, he had a conception of how the trade unions should develop and be run which never came to reality, partly because history wasn't ready for it, and partly because he didn't have enough drive. It has made him very bitter. He is also a terrible old bore.

Wednesday 25 January
Ronnie Grierson announced he was resigning. He is a very emotional man. With Grierson, it was like passing the parcel – you just hoped that he wouldn't be with you the day that he resigned. In the evening he phoned and withdrew his resignation.

Thursday 26 January
Had a row over Cabinet Ministers' memoirs. It had been reported in the papers that Dick Crossman and Barbara Castle had signed contracts to write their memoirs and a Minister raised this at Cabinet on the grounds that it made some people very uneasy to know that their colleagues were keeping a record of everything.

Dick did admit that he had a contract to write and publish his diary. He had got a woman from Nuffield to edit it for him but out of respect to the Party he had arranged that they were not to be published until after the General Election. But there was still anxiety because if there had been a very narrow Labour or Tory majority followed by another Election, and in the interval between the two Elections, Dick Crossman's memoirs – with confidences about his colleagues – were published, it could have done enormous damage to the Party.

Barbara then admitted that she had also signed a contract to write her memoirs.

Harold declared that he intended to write three books. 'One,' he said, 'I will write immediately we leave office and that will be an absolutely factual record of the Administration. Later, when I retire, I shall publish a much fuller account in which I will give far greater detail – this is when I have retired from public life. Thirdly,' he said, 'I shall write a book about what really happened with instructions that it should not be published until after my death.'

I said that there were some of us who felt resentful that *we* hadn't been approached to publish our memoirs, and I said that I, too, was a diarist.

Tuesday 31 January
To Cabinet where we discussed Malta and great anxiety was expressed that Dom Mintoff, leader of the Malta Labour Party, might become Prime Minister. Although we were sympathetic to Mintoff politically, because after all he was a member of the Socialist International, the official view was that if he became Prime Minister, it would weaken Malta as a NATO and a British base; and therefore we were told that the Cabinet would try to help the Government of Borg Olivier [Malta Nationalist Party] to see that Mintoff didn't win.

Friday 3 February
Cabinet meeting, at which we discussed the Defence White Paper.
Denis Healey made out that he was making great cuts whereas he
wasn't at all. He was just holding expenditure at the level that it had
been when we came to office and in fact only cutting down on
enormous planned expansions in the defence budget which we had
inherited and couldn't have realised anyway. Denis is much over-
rated as Secretary for Defence.

Saturday 4 February
Spent two hours trying to set the combination on my new safe which
every Minister has to have at home. We couldn't open it, but Joshua
finally managed it – not bad for an eight year old.

Monday 6 February
Premier Kosygin's visit to Britain, and his plane was diverted from
Gatwick at the last minute so the whole Cabinet was diverted too. I
drove at 110 miles an hour at one point to get there. Then to Claridges
with Soldatov, the Ambassador, and Kosygin.
   I might add here that the security services bugged Kosygin during
his visit. I know this because I got a mysterious memorandum from
the security services, reporting something they had picked up on tape
that Kosygin had said about Pompidou. I didn't find it very useful,
as it happened, except that it indicated how very close Kosygin and
Pompidou were, due to de Gaulle's Eastern policy.

Tuesday 7 February
Met Brian Faulkner, the Northern Ireland Minister of Commerce,
and we discussed the development of Northern Ireland. I realised
how much more scope Northern Ireland Ministers had, unlike for
example the Scottish Secretary or the Welsh Secretary in this country,
because not only does Northern Ireland get more than Scotland and
Wales as a result of the Imperial Settlement following the 1920
Government of Ireland Act, but also because Faulkner was able to
concentrate all his money where he needed it and didn't have to
spend it in accordance with rigid rules laid down from London.

Wednesday 8 February
I went to Elliot-Automation with Kosygin and on the way in the car
he kept looking out of the windows – I think it was the first time he
had been to Britain – and asking me, 'What is the cost of that house?'
This is as we were going up through Hendon to Boreham Wood.
'How long would a man have to work as a worker to be able to afford
one of these houses?'

In the evening we went to the Kosygin reception at Lancaster House, followed by dinner at the Soviet Embassy. George Brown got tight and kept shouting, 'I want to go home. Are they all Bolsheviks?' and similar remarks.

I received an invitation to go to Moscow for the May Day Parade and for talks. Sir Geoffrey Harrison, our Ambassador in Moscow, was absolutely opposed to a British Minister attending the May Day Parade because, he said, it would cause great political embarrassment.

Thursday 16 February

Saw Harold about aviation security. As I had taken over the Ministry of Aviation, I acquired the security branch and I had to go and see George Wigg again about it. It is really intolerable. I do dislike George Wigg – he is an evil man.

Wednesday 22 February

Talked to Roy Jenkins about George Wigg and security. I said to Roy, 'You have been Minister of Aviation and had these responsibilities; what is George Wigg's position? Is he authorised by Harold Wilson to do what he likes and does he really control the security services?' Roy said, 'Don't worry about Wigg, it is not like that at all. The security services don't trust him.'

Friday 24 February

Shimon Peres of the Israeli Labour Party came to see me. It was the first time I had met him. He is known as a hawk in Israeli circles. He talked, as one would expect, very intelligently about Israel's economic position and he said, 'Our great hope is to get integrated into the advanced industrial framework of the West, by producing specialist components, by selling our know-how,' and so on.

Wednesday 1 March

In the afternoon I had another talk with George Wigg, who is absolutely obsessive about security. I later asked Otto Clarke whether George Wigg really controlled the security services and he said, 'No, the security people can't stand him and they don't tell him anything important,' confirming what Roy had told me.

Thursday 2 March

To Cabinet, where we discussed Party discipline arising out of abstentions on the defence debate. At the PLP meeting later, Harold made his 'dog licence' speech – that each MP is allowed to bite once like a dog but if they abstained or voted against the Government again they would be in trouble. This was a remark that he had thrown off at Cabinet in the morning and I must say that I didn't like it very much, and I liked it even less when he said it at the Party meeting. It caused tremendous offence because it was very insulting to imply that we were all dogs and he was our trainer. It also gave me a great insight into his attitude towards the Labour Party, namely that we were there to support him and that he licensed the Party, whereas of course we license him because we elect him.

Friday 3 March
Had a meeting on the position at Shorts. The Treasury were pressing us to issue an order saying that Shorts could never produce a complete aircraft again, and indeed to get rid of the little Skyvan which is the utility vehicle that Shorts made. I was anxious to keep open the possibility that Shorts might be allowed to produce aircraft, mainly because of the Northern Ireland employment problems.

Talked to Christopher Cockerell, the inventor of Hovercraft. He is an extremely difficult man and he has been a stranger in the department over the years because he felt people weren't taking enough interest in him. He was right in a way. But he is not the best man to advise the British Hovercraft Corporation which has been set up. We haven't made a penny out of Hovercraft and probably won't for years to come.

Tuesday 21 March
The *Torrey Canyon* oil tanker disaster occurred off the coast at Land's End. There had never been a monster accident like this and it began to make people wonder more publicly about technology and mergers and economic growth. Harold tackled it with great military enthusiasm, sending a Minister down to take charge and flying by helicopter from the Scillies to have a look at it.

Thursday 23 March
There was a big splash in the papers on the Bristol Siddeley contract scandal. We had discovered that Bristol Siddeley had been over-charging for the repair contract of Viper engines right up to and during the 1964 Election, and we suspected that the Tories had concealed it.

Sunday 26 March
The Bristol Siddeley row was in all the papers. John Stonehouse had made a statement indicating that the manufacturers had co-operated with the Government. So I got Mr Haines, Mintech's Director of Contracts, to come to see me and we spent an hour and a half

together. He was a very quiet solid man who used to be a tax official, and he was extremely upset by what had happened because he felt that it would reflect on his own officials. I tried to get to the bottom of it and at the same time reassure him as best I could that we were not getting at him.

Monday 3 April
My forty-second birthday.

I went to Bristol to see Concorde, then to Bristol Siddeley Engines and had a long interview with TWW news on Bristol Siddeley, which is now the centre of a great storm. John Stonehouse is being panned by the press as a result of his statement.

Caroline went to lunch with Hubert Humphrey's wife. In the evening we went to Number 10 for the dinner for Senator Hubert Humphrey, the Vice-President. Humphrey was an old tub-thumping radical who had been the hero of Americans for Democratic Action since he had worked in Minnesota, where he was Governor. His name had been given to me twenty years ago, when I went on my debating tour of the US, and he was an idol of the British Left in a curious sort of way. But I must say, talking and listening to him, particularly on the Vietnam war, he was unspeakable and terribly disappointing. Afterwards we went back to Dick Crossman's house with the Shores and the Baloghs.

Tuesday 11 April
I had a security briefing on Russia, warning me about all the things that might happen if we went. They cited the case of a man from the Anglo-Soviet Friendship Society, the official body sponsored by the Foreign Office, who went to Moscow and was drugged, and placed in a compromising homosexual situation and photographed. The security services always warn you about this sort of thing.

Went to Cabinet, where we were discussing the specialist select committees. There is still a great deal of opposition about them from some politicians, notably Dick Marsh, who has a contempt for Parliament and is really a tycoon who, when he gets into office, feels that the Commons has no knowledge of anything. It has divided us in quite an interesting way.

Thursday 13 April
The GLC elections, and Labour were absolutely routed. We were losing support as a Government, and this was rubbing off on Labour councillors who were very resentful against the Government. But there was a school of thought, of which Gerald Kaufman was one of the leading exponents, that the Labour Party doing badly had the

great effect of sweeping out the most ghastly reactionary old Labour councils and bringing in new leadership – a very cynical view.

Talked to Douglas Jay about the USSR and to Peter Shore about Ulster. Peter is very pro-Protestant. He's a Liverpool lad and I think that deep down inside him is a hostility towards Liverpool Catholics, which must in part explain his attitude.

Monday 17 April

I went to the airport and flew on BEA to Moscow with Tommy Balogh, Ieuan Maddock, Harry Slater* and William Knighton. Caroline was invited but Harold had personally vetoed it.

We were met by Kirillin and the Ambassador, Sir Geoffrey Harrison, and Gvishiani† and I was put up at the National Hotel. We had a short walk round the Kremlin – it was very cold – and we had dinner at the Embassy with Sir Geoffrey and Dr Alexander, who is the Science Attaché and generally thought by the Russians to be an intelligence man.

Then we had a meeting in the Embassy's secret conference room, which is in the basement and is suspended from the ceiling so that it does not rest on any foundations. From a corner of the room came the recording of a cocktail party playing continuously and Ieuan Maddock worried them very much by saying that he could bug the room easily by stripping off the noise of the cocktail party and picking up the vibrations of the suspended room through the earth. But once you are in a room like that you can't honestly think of anything secret to say! We discussed our strategy until 1 o'clock in the morning by which time I was extremely tired.

Tuesday 18 April

I went to the State Committee and had first talks with Kirillin. We discussed what sort of a framework of co-operation we needed. The Russians have a most elaborate system with the French, known as the 'Grande Commission', represented at the very top by Pompidou and Kosygin. Below that, a 'Petite Commission' of Russian and French Ministers meets more regularly at official level and below that there is some further complex structure. I suggested something much more informal and I was asked to draw it on the blackboard. Then we had lunch in the British Embassy. I cabled for instructions as to whether we could go ahead with the agreement in this form which was what I wanted but which I knew the Foreign Office didn't

* Assistant Secretary responsible for technological agreements.
† Vice-Chairman of the USSR State Committee for Science and Technology, and son-in-law of Kosygin.

want: they didn't want anything done in detail. They are absolutely opposed to these links with the Russians and I had to battle and battle to get them established. I just wouldn't be discouraged.

Then we went to the Institute of the Tele-Mechanics where we were greeted by Academician Trapeznikov, a very distinguished man who was studying control theory and trying to relate cybernetics to biology and neurology. As we walked around his Institute there was a girl sitting with wires on her arms, picking up electrical impulses. She was opening and closing her hands and on the oscilloscope you could see the electrical impulses being recorded while people were trying to find out how the brain sent a message to the hand.

In the evening we went to dinner with Kirillin and his wife and daughter, Ola, at their flat, along with the Ambassador, and Gvishiani, Academician Artsemivitsch and Academician Keldersh. Madame Santalova was the interpreter.

I had been told by the Ambassador that Russian Ministers never invite British Ministers to their flats or homes and he was absolutely amazed when this invitation came in but it was, of course, because I had asked Kirillin to my home in London. It was lovely. We sat and talked in a tiny little flat where he and his wife and child lived. Kirillin is one of the Vice-Premiers of the Soviet Union and an eminent scientist. We sat in his little library while the meal was being laid and we ate together, then he showed us home movies of his trip to England and having snowballs thrown at him by the children.

It was a marvellous evening and afterwards he told us stories of Azarbaijan Radio, a great joke in Russia. Azarbaijan Radio apparently invites listeners to write in with questions like, 'Why do the Americans produce better automobiles than the Russians?' Azarbaijan Radio replies, 'Why do the Americans persecute the negroes?' indicating that there is no good answer.

Artsemivitsch, who is a leading nuclear scientist, was interesting. 'Science, we say in the Soviet Union, is defined as "Satisfying your curiosity at the expense of the State",' which is an amusing definition.

We talked about fusion. I had great anxieties as to whether we should go ahead with the huge Culham fusion programme* which wasn't producing results. Artsemivitsch said, 'Well ten years ago we said it would take us twenty years to make fusion work and we still say it will take twenty years to make fusion work, so we haven't altered our view in any way!'

---

* Culham was the AEA laboratory working on fusion technology for the generation of electricity.

Wednesday 19 April

Had talks all morning with Gvishiani, who was studying management and had applied for a PhD in management science. He looks a bit like Nasser. He related one wonderful story that in America he had been invited to dinner by a friend at a famous restaurant called the Four Seasons and when they got there he was told that they had no table. His American host went to the head waiter and whispered something about his guest and immediately they were flashed to the best table in the restaurant. Gvishiani asked his host what he had said and he replied, 'I went to the head waiter and said, "Look, I have got a very distinguished Egyptian colonel to take to dinner".'

I went to the Kremlin for lunch with Kosygin and Gvishiani and I sat next to Elyutin, the Minister for Education. His wife is a teacher. I asked Elyutin about the special schools in Russia and he said, 'Well, these are supposed to be schools for specially gifted children, but as a matter of fact they are schools for the children of specially gifted parents,' which was a marvellous way of indicating that educational privilege had crept back into Russia.

In the evening we caught the plane to Kiev, leaving Tommy Balogh to visit Gosplan. We stayed at the Dnipro Hotel in Kiev which is beautiful and I walked round the city in the evening.

Thursday 20 April

I went to the Institute of Cybernetics and met Academician Glushkov, one of the most brilliant cyberneticists in the Soviet Union and a member of the American Computer Society. We had a Ukranian lunch with them and at the Institute I was shown a computer they had built. I wasn't, of course, in a position to judge how good their technology was, but Ieuan Maddock, who was with me, said it was many years behind Western standards. They showed me one computer which had been specially programmed to put together every day of the week with every day of every year back to 1700. They said to me, 'Minister, tell us when you were born and we'll tell you what day of the week it was.' So I told them I was born on 3 April 1925. The computer creaked and groaned and produced the reply that it was a Friday. I said that was quite right, because I knew the day. So they asked, 'How do you know that it is correct?' and I replied very flippantly, 'Well, I don't remember 3 April, but I remember how excited I was on Thursday 2nd.' This was translated into Russian and then back into English and into Russian again and they thought it was rather a flippant joke for a senior Minister to make.

Sightseeing in Kiev and shopping with Mme Santalova. Then we caught the sleeper back to Moscow. On the train, sitting in the compartment next door was Academician Kornichuk, who is the President of the World Peace Council. I went in and introduced myself to him and Academician Glushkov, who happened to be in the train, came into the compartment and translated. We all sat and talked and I asked Kornichuk about the work of the Peace Council and how he was getting on in bringing the Israelis and the Arabs together. He replied, 'Ah they are impossible, impossible. We tried very hard but the Arabs walked out when the Israelis appeared.'

He was very drunk. He was on his way to Moscow to be given the Lenin Prize for a play that had made him famous, which he had written during the war. He was a sort of Kingsley Martin of Russia – an old intellectual on the Left with an international reputation. He started attacking computers in exactly the way that John Betjeman might attack them. Glushkov translated, 'My comrade says that if computers are in general use they will destroy man's genius and his spirit and his imagination.' Glushkov, who was a young chap, laughed and was very amused by it. It was great fun.

There was a lot of champagne and singing in the corridors and Kornichuk and Glushkov and I ended up joining in, with some British songs included to make me feel at home. I was of course stone cold sober and getting rather tired by this time.

Friday 21 April
The train arrived in Moscow at 9 o'clock and I had a very discouraging telegram, which I might have predicted, from the Foreign Office, signed by George Brown.

Tommy Balogh was waiting at the hotel to see me and said that we must have a discussion together before the final talks with the Russians. I said, 'Well, look, I am all tired and dirty,' so he came into my suite and sat on the bidet in the bathroom while I was quietly having a bath and he told me what he hoped to achieve and how we must plan it. It was only later that I realised we had disregarded all the warnings in the security briefings. The Russians would have photographs of me in a bath and the Government's economic adviser sitting on the bidet! We had a laugh about that.

Final talks and drew up the protocol with Kirillin. Then we drove to the airport and got back to London in three and a half hours.

Saturday 22 April
I went to see Harold about the Russian visit and he was very pleased with what had happened. I told him the story about my bath but he didn't think that was very funny.

Monday 24 April

I was de-briefed on the USSR. Otto said to me, 'You must remember, Minister, that our trade with Russia is only 1 per cent of what it is with Denmark, and it is not an important market.' And that was the attitude of the Board of Trade people throughout – they never cared about this operation. Nor did the Foreign Office.

Thursday 27 April

The Nutting book came up at Cabinet. Anthony Nutting had written a book on Suez, the crisis which had led to his resignation from the Eden Government, and this raised the whole question of the Official Secrets Act and whether it applied to Ministers. It was in line with the earlier discussion about ministerial memoirs but in the end we agreed we couldn't do anything about it.

Caroline and I went to the Salvation Army lunch at the Dorchester and met General Coutts, an awfully gentle man of the Salvation Army, and Jack Warner,* whom I have known for years. Also there were Sir William and Lady Armstrong, Sir William Armstrong's father and mother having both been in the Salvation Army. The lunch was to launch their appeal, under the heading 'For God's Sake Care', to fight poverty in Britain today, and I had written a short piece in a book which they were using to boost the appeal.

Sunday 30 April

I went to Chequers where we had Cabinet all day on the Common Market and we voted by 13 to 8 for an unconditional application. I made a speech which created a favourable impression with the pro-Europeans, who thought me anti-European. I said we had to cut Queen Victoria's umbilical cord.

Those of us who favoured the application were not too worried about the conditions because we were a defeated Cabinet. Going back to the war, we had tried as a Labour Government to solve the country's economic problems and we had left in a balance of payments crisis in 1951. The Tories had tried and had left in a balance of payments crisis in 1964. We had tried and had had to put the brakes on in 1966, and we were now looking for solutions to our problems from outside and somehow we were persuaded that the Common Market was the way of making progress.

Tuesday 2 May

I went to Number 10 for one of the political evenings with Harold and the gang, as a member of Harold's kitchen cabinet.

* The actor, best known as 'Dixon of Dock Green'.

Wednesday 3 May

Ibuka of Sony and some Japanese businessmen came to see me. I was very much impressed with Ibuka. Sony had started after the war as a tiny little company set up by Japanese ex-servicemen, who received a grant and concentrated absolutely rigidly on manufacturing tape recorders and electronics. A few years ago, engineers at Sony had realised, before Polaroid discovered it, that it was possible to manufacture a camera that would produce a picture immediately. They had gone to the Sony board for permission to develop this and the Sony board had discussed it very carefully and had come to the conclusion that it would not diversify. Sony was in the electronics business, they had no camera outlets and their experience in that field was unknown.

This made a great impression on me, first of all because of the single-mindedness of the Sony management, and secondly because, unlike British scientists who would have griped that they had invented it but the Americans had developed it, Sony just pushed it on one side. That is the secret of the Japanese industrial success.

Thursday 4 May

A meeting was held to discuss whether we should close down the fusion work at Culham. A report had recommended by a very narrow majority that the fusion work was not succeeding and should be discontinued.

I had this difficult decision to take: some of the best brains in Britain were working at Culham and yet it was a near certainty that we weren't going to produce any practical results, although, predictably, the scientists there had moved away from fusion research to plasma physics which was purer and much more interesting and merited Government money. I was torn between closing it altogether or accepting the minority report recommendation that we should cut it back 50 per cent.

Friday 5 May

I got up early and flew by HS125 jet to Pershore to visit the Royal Research Establishment at Malvern.

Malvern is the great defence electronics establishment, where much of the radar computer work is done. It is also doing some computer work on traffic problems, another example of the way in which the scientific community realises that cuts in finance are coming, and tries to develop something else which will get funded.

When I got back to London, Lord Hinton* looked in at the office

---

* Chairman, Central Electricity Generating Board, 1957–64.

for a talk on the Atomic Energy Authority. He is a very distinguished engineer and a nice old boy. When he gave the inaugural lecture as the President of the Institute of Mechanical Engineers, he described his life story. He had come from a middle class family but some disaster when he was a child had prevented him going to university, and he was sent to be an apprentice at the Great Western Railway workshops in Swindon. After five years his mother came into some money and could afford to send him to Cambridge, where he qualified as a graduate engineer. But when he went back to try to get a job with the railways they said, 'You will appreciate, Mr Hinton, now that you have got a degree we can't make use of you.'

Tuesday 9 May
Joshua's ninth birthday and the usual family excitements.

I went to the Cabinet and saw Tommy Balogh, who told me that he had to decide whether to stay as an economic adviser or go back to Oxford because Oxford would not keep his place for more than three years. He decided to go back.

Wednesday 10 May
In the evening went to the State Banquet at the Royal Naval College, Greenwich, for King Faisal of Saudi Arabia.

Had to hurry back to vote in the Common Market debate in the House of Commons and there was a massive vote in favour of application. Almost all the Tories and the majority of Labour MPs were in favour.

Thursday 11 May
I appeared before the Science and Technology Sub-Committee on reactor policy. I was the first Minister ever to appear before a select committee to explain his policy and I was very pleased about it.

I wanted to do it very much but I had had a great struggle with the department who were terrified of the select committees, particularly Otto Clarke who was absolutely opposed to them. I could see in the select committee arrangement great benefits for an active Minister, because he could retain contact with Parliament, and indeed win parliamentary support for a policy that he wanted to pursue. But for the civil servant it meant that he had to be questioned and even asked to give his opinion on what he thought about the Minister's policy. The idea that a government department was working for Parliament as a whole, instead of for the Minister with whom civil servants were enmeshed in a web of secrecy, was not at all to their liking.

There was an Economic Committee to discuss Skyvan, which I

was trying desperately to keep alive. The Shipbuilding Bill had its report stage and third reading.

Monday 15 May
Went to have a look at Shell-Mex House. The department wanted very much to move out of Millbank Tower to Shell-Mex House in the Strand and I said I wouldn't go. I said, 'I was born here and I like it here.' They said, 'Oh, you'll find it's marvellous in Shell-Mex House.' That was because the senior officials found it a nuisance coming to visit the Minister at Millbank, but I simply wasn't going to budge. I agreed to look at it, but it was awful.

Friday 19 May
In Canada with Ieuan Maddock, William Knighton and an Under-Secretary, Gordon Bowen, for the Water for Peace Conference and had dinner with Sir Henry Lintott, the High Commissioner, and Lady Lintott, at his splendid residence.

At 12.45 I had lunch at the Canadian House of Commons and visited the National Aircraft Establishment, which was struggling to cope with its own brain drain. We think of the brain drain in Britain as being the loss of British engineers to the New World, but many of them go to Canada and are then sucked away to the United States.

In the evening I went to the Canadian House of Commons again and then met the High Commissioner and the British Old Vic Company who were performing *Measure for Measure* and for whom there was a reception. In Canada, I met the actress Jane Asher, whom I was told is a friend of one of the Beatles.

Saturday 20 May
Up at 6 and to Montreal to see EXPO '67. The British exhibition was excellent, combining our history with modern technology. They had the Olympus engine from the Concorde and some rather amusing, self-deprecatory and nostalgic exhibits, trying to create the feeling of Britain.

The French exhibition was all very glittery and boastful. The German was impressive. The Russian had lots of machine tools but, unlike the Russian exhibition we had seen in New York in 1959, there were Russians actually at work here.

We went on the Hovercraft up the St Lawrence, the first time I had been in one. We went right over an island in the middle of the river – it was an astonishing experience.

Then I flew on to Toronto, to Chicago and on to Cincinnati to meet up with Caroline.

Sunday 22 May

To Washington and I met the Water for Peace UK delegation and said we were here to describe our own achievements and to sell our products.

Then I went to talk to Sir Patrick Dean at the Embassy, a man I very much dislike – a typical British Ambassador, arrogant and smooth, pursuing his own policy and regarding Ministers as mere visitors.

I asked to see Robert McNamara at the Department of Defence and was taken to the Pentagon. It is impossible to convey adequately the tremendous respect with which McNamara is regarded in Washington. Here was the great American defence establishment, overwhelmingly the most powerful in the world, and McNamara, one of Kennedy's men, had come in and established civilian control and crammed through programme budgeting. It was like going into an emperor's court – the centre of military power in the world.

I said that we in Britain knew of his military achievements but we didn't know as much as we would like to know of his control of the Pentagon, and I asked him whether he was interested in the Concorde or supersonic aircraft for military purposes. He said he wasn't.

I had lunch at the Embassy and then in the afternoon Caroline and I visited the British stand at the Water Exhibition and went to a number of receptions.

Tuesday 23 May

Caroline went to Capitol Hill to see the Senate and the White House.

It was the official opening of the Water for Peace Conference at the Sheraton Hotel and Stuart Udall, the Secretary for the Interior, and President Lyndon Johnson attended. Lyndon Johnson made a speech, saying he was setting up a Water for Peace Office in the State Department which convinced me that this was just an arm of American foreign policy and wasn't what I was interested in. I wanted a direct contact, not through Foreign Offices, which are very narrow tubes through which to conduct international relations, but direct from our Ministry of Housing and Local Government to their Interior Department, between Mintech and their Department of Commerce, Science and Technology, and so on. I felt that the whole thing was an unattractive Lyndon Johnson publicity stunt.

We dashed out after the opening and went back to the British stand, where President Johnson came round to meet us. He looked absolutely drained of energy, totally exhausted. The only other man I have ever seen who looked quite as white and tired was Kosygin. The leaders of the US and the USSR really do carry a load far beyond the capacity of a single person. What was interesting was the way the American President moved, with no protocol but absolutely maximum security.

He was surrounded by about five or six security men with their backs to him, moving as he moved, and they had walkie-talkies into which they were talking all the time, describing where he was, looking round, saying check this and check that. It was like a Roman emperor with the Praetorian Guard, only the Praetorian Guard was defending him with an electronic network of security, rather than with actual weapons, though I have no doubt the men were armed.

Friday 26 May
Flew to New York and met Sarnoff of the Radio Corporation of America, RCA. This was a meeting that I had wanted for some time, to pursue my idea of planning an international computer merger, beginning with the ICT joining with English Electric which had technical computer links with RCA and using that as a way of building up a tripartite computer consortium, bringing in the Germans and French, if possible. The British would dominate the European end of it, but the European end would dominate the Americans because the British, French and German group would be stronger than the RCA computer group.

Sarnoff, the son of General Sarnoff who founded RCA, was absolutely terrified about these talks because of anti-Trust legislation. He had lawyers with him and they prevented him saying anything at all.

Then I went back to Washington to give a lecture in the Rotunda at the British Embassy, before returning finally to New York.

Back to London overnight absolutely exhausted, having flown Boston–New York; New York–Washington; Washington–New York–London.

Wednesday 31 May
Melissa came to have a meal at the House and was kissed by George Brown – she was thrilled. She met Barbara Castle, Douglas Jay, Elwyn Jones and Jeremy Thorpe and she was as happy as could be.

Thursday 1 June
Cabinet from 10 am till 12. George Brown was in charge because Harold was in Washington, where he was being received with all the trumpets appropriate for a weak foreign head of state who has to be buttered up so that he can carry the can for American foreign policy.

Had dinner with Dick Crossman, Barbara Castle, Peter Shore and John Silkin. Barbara was absolutely furious, and lost her temper with

Dick Crossman about Harold Wilson, whom she is always attacking but absolutely faithfully follows.

Friday 2 June
Denning Pearson, deputy-chairman of Rolls Royce, came about the Concorde contracts. I had been trying hard to get Rolls Royce and the British Aircraft Corporation to take some risks in connection with the Concorde. I was absolutely fed up with the fact that on the research and development side we were picking up all the bills, and whatever the escalation of costs, the Government had to pay. I had worked out a scheme which I put to him, whereby the production contracts would lose money if escalation occurred.

Denning Pearson wouldn't look at that because he knew quite well that the Government was over a barrel on Concorde. We couldn't stop Concorde, because of the treaty with the French and for political reasons, so he didn't care what we tried to make him do.

I flew to Paris for the air show, visited the stands at Le Bourget, gave a reception for the press, and met the air correspondents for the first time. The aircraft business is very difficult to understand.

Saturday 3 June
Went to the air show again. Met Pompidou briefly and Pierre Messmer, the Minister of Defence, who was in charge of Concorde. Group Captain Townsend, Princess Margaret's old boyfriend, was there.

It was a beautiful display. The French do these things in a fantastic way – far better than we do. The Farnborough Air Show is just a pre-First World War country cricket match compared to the Paris International Air Show. Of course the French planes and French technology dominated. The F–111 came over, folding its wings. The paratroopers dropped, the French Hovercraft was available for us to see, the Concorde was presented as a French plane – it was a marvellous example of the glory of France being exploited.

I came home and had my first ever automatic landing in British aircraft. I saw the pilot with his hands just by the stick but in fact it landed itself.

Wednesday 7 June
Michael Michaels, head of the Atomic Energy Division, came to see me and he explained in great detail the French anger at British atomic policy. Michael Michaels is an old civil servant, has a lot of experience and knows the atomic business very well. He pointed out to me that the French were deeply insulted that during the war they were kept out absolutely from any joint nuclear work by the Amer-

icans and the British, even though some very experienced French scientists had been part of the wartime atomic team. Then after the war we had drawn all our know-how from the Americans: the French had been left out again. This was the explanation of part of de Gaulle's hatred of the Anglo-Saxons.

De Gaulle had later proposed a NATO triumvirate in the hope that the French could be brought into this nuclear business but the Americans would have none of it and neither would we. France therefore greatly resents the British lead in this technology, drawn largely, though not entirely, from the Americans and they are resentful at our refusal, on the grounds that they might use it for their nuclear weapons programme, to supply them with nuclear fuel.

In the opinion of Michael Michaels, Harold's European gambit – the European Technological Community and the approach to Europe – cannot be resolved unless there is some sort of an understanding about nuclear sharing which would be for us, the British, a tremendous experience because we would have to break our special relationship with the United States and establish instead a relationship with the French. This would really mean changing sides in the NATO battle – joining the French against the Americans. Michael Michaels explained it to me brilliantly.

I suspect that Heath must have learned this secret when he was trying to negotiate the Common Market in 1962 and later that was why Heath was talking about an Anglo-French nuclear force, because he knew that, when it came to the talks with Pompidou, this would have to be the nature of the deal.

Dined with Dick and Peter, John Silkin, Barbara and Tommy. Working until 3 or 4 every morning.

Thursday 8 June
Cabinet. I spoke for an arms' ban on Israel[6] until there was a ceasefire in the Arab-Israel war.

Then in Cabinet we came to discuss public expenditure and Harold declared his view that we wanted more money for people and less money for the social services. That was his theory of the 'jingle of cash in your pocket' and he was beginning to respond to the criticism about high taxation under the Labour Government. This, plus the dog licence speech and the 'Dr Wilson theory', were really an indication really of the abandonment by the Cabinet of the idea that we were the Party of equality, the Party of socialism.

Tuesday 13 June
Stanley Gillen came to see me to tell me about Ford of Europe. He said that Ford had decided to try to build up a European Ford instead of basing the company on individual countries, like Ford of Britain or Ford of Germany. He said that it wouldn't mean very much change: we should have the headquarters in London and, he said, 'I thought I'd tell you as a courtesy.'

I was amazed. I said, 'Surely this is a very big decision? This indicates that you are going to build up a huge multi-national company in Europe which will still be guided from Detroit, but it will mean that there will be even less coincidence of interest between the British Government and Ford of Britain and you will surely federalise much more. You will be producing components in Britain and similarly in Germany, for the whole of European Ford.'

He was a bit surprised, I think, that I had looked ahead as far as this and really anticipated the corporate planning that they knew they would be doing. It was the first time that I had dealt with Ford on the question and it was another valuable lesson that I learned about the multi-national companies.

Tuesday 20 June
Had lunch at Number 10 with Gough Whitlam, the new Leader of the Australian Labour Party, a big tall man feeling his way. He didn't create a profound impression: he was enormously respectful to Harold. But the special relationship between England and Australia has begun to go and the Australians look more to the Americans for their links.

Tuesday 27 June
Meeting with Signor Moro,* the Italian Prime Minster, and Signor Fanfani, the Foreign Minister in London for talks. Fanfani was the politician who invented the great phrase 'technological gap', which mesmerised everybody, like C. P. Snow's 'two cultures' (scientists can't talk to non-scientists) and McNamara's 'management gap'. These fashionable phrases spread among leading figures all over the world, and everyone talked about them.

Peter Jay† came to lunch and was sceptical of the work of the Ministry of Technology because, being a brilliant Treasury man, he was interested in macro-policy and not micro-interference or intervention. It was the only time he did come and see me and I felt that he didn't understand or appreciate what we were doing.

* Later murdered by the Red Brigade in Italy in May 1978.
† A Principal in the Treasury, becoming economics editor of *The Times* in 1967.

Had a talk on nuclear industry and I tried to get Dick Marsh, Minister of Power, to agree to the single consortium but he, backing up the CEGB, wouldn't support it. Had cocktails with the air correspondents and then dinner at Number 10 with the Italians, and Caroline had a long talk to Signor Fanfani.

Wednesday 28 June
I went to the Society of British Aircraft Constructors' dinner; it was the first time that I had addressed the aircraft industry since we had taken over the Ministry of Aviation. I was determined to indicate that there was a difference between the Ministry of Technology attitude to aviation and the old Ministries of Aviation in the past. I said in my speech that in the old days Ministers of Aviation could get money as easily as pinching pennies off an old man's drum, but now it was going to be different and we had to justify every penny. Those present were absolutely livid at this speech. They thought it was offensive, and it led to a major row, but it was the turning point. It was a warning that there would be no more Concordes and that we would expect them to take some risks.

Thursday 29 June
I went to the GMC in Bristol: a small meeting which was very bitter, very anti-Government. I spoke and did my best to argue the Government's case but the rank and file of the Labour Party were pretty fed up with the Government.
  I was nominated to the National Executive.

Friday 30 June
Lord Nelson came to the office with Lord Caldecote, Managing Director of BAC, to put the case for leaving guided weapons out of the BAC-Hawker Siddeley merger. They were happy to let us have the old airframe side: guided weapons are of course profitable because they are electronics.

Tuesday 4 July
Announced plans for the sonic bang tests. When Concorde was started in 1962 we had already had supersonic fighters – the Lightnings for example. There should have been tests over the United Kingdom so that people got an idea of what a supersonic bang was like, but they were not laid on at the time because they were supposedly unpopular. Roy Jenkins then took office as Minister of Aviation and later claimed that he wanted to stop Concorde. I don't frankly believe he did, because I saw the early Cabinet papers in 1964, when it was pointed out that the cancellation charges would come to

£25 million, and there was the risk of the French taking us to the International Court. I think it was just an absurd excuse for continuing. But Roy Jenkins never had a sonic bang test. Neither did Fred Mulley. No one did until I said that we must have one, because people are entitled to know what the noise is like. So I laid sonic bang tests on over London and other places.

I met the Board of Shorts and they were pressing for the extension of the Skyvan programme. I had to explain that we would support the Skyvan as long as we could but we really did have to sell some. We had only sold two or three and Shorts were still hoping that they would be able to develop a new aircraft, which the Treasury wouldn't support.

Wednesday 5 July
Bill Penney came in to talk about the centrifuge separation method for producing enriched uranium. This centrifuge as a way of producing uranium was based on a development by Dr Zipper, a German scientist, during the war. In order to produce enriched uranium, centrifuges have to turn at enormously high speeds, posing a mechanical problem rather than a nuclear one, and once you have solved that, you can enrich uranium without the tremendously expensive and bulky gas diffusion process.

Penney said that the centrifuge project has enormous military implications because the risk of the spread of nuclear weapons is much greater than before. It means that countries like South Africa, which have natural uranium, might be able to develop enrichment plants on a small scale almost completely undetected, near their natural uranium field. I could see that the effect on the Non-Proliferation Treaty and on other areas would be great. Penney told me that all that had held up the centrifuge system from operating was that there had been no parts able to rotate at the required speed without breaking down. So the development of this use of centrifuge was really a mechanical engineering refinement. Our fear was that if anyone knew that the British AEA was using the centrifuge to enrich uranium, then all the work that had been stopped or never started on centrifuges elsewhere would begin with renewed vigour. We ourselves, after announcing that we were going ahead with a bigger atomic programme for peaceful purposes, had stated that we would be expanding Capenhurst for the purpose of enriching uranium by gas diffusion, and everybody was waiting for the second stage of the Capenhurst development to begin. In physical terms, civil engineers and so on were all ready to move in and build it. But it was now unnecessary to expand Capenhurst and we were afraid that the secret would leak out simply because of the fact that Capenhurst wasn't going ahead. Anyone who knew the score would be able to read into that the fact that the AEA had the centrifuge. It would mean that Britain could meet its own enriched uranium needs without being so dependent on the Americans and that the big French plant at Pierre Lagge would be the most expensive piece of junk ever.

The Dutch had boasted that *they* had found a better way of enriching uranium and that they were using the centrifuge, but the Dutch had no nuclear know-how and nobody believed them. The Germans were thought to be involved. When I visited the Julich reactor with Stoltenburg earlier in 1967, this was where the Germans were working on it.

It was so important that I went to see Harold at 11.45 that night to tell him the news, and explain to him the implications of it all this, which he took on board. Then I went home and I worked till 3.30 am.

Friday 7 July
I drove to Birmingham for a university dinner and found myself sitting next to Sir Anthony Eden – Lord Avon – the university Vice-Chancellor. I had never talked to him before and I recalled old memories and tried to pick his brain. I can't remember anything he said, which is probably because nothing he said was ever memorable. Rather a pathetic figure.

Tuesday 18 July
I had dinner with Brigadier A. R. W. Low* and Arnold Weinstock. Arnold Weinstock is an extremely bright guy. He sees the whole of business in terms of money and he reduces every problem to cash flow. He's clever at devolving: he never overloads himself, he just sits and thinks and looks at books, and then gives instructions and expects them to be followed. He doesn't bother himself deeply with detail and his politics are absolutely primitive: he thought the Fabian Society was a Communist organisation and that the LSE was teaching wild revolutionary doctrines, and so on. He's very naive in a way, but being very important, everybody is respectful to him. The only person who isn't is Caroline, as a result of which he likes her very much.

Wednesday 19 July
Cabinet meeting on public expenditure, during which there was a sonic boom. It was very funny. I told the Lightning jet crew to fly

* Lord Aldington, former Conservative Minister, MP for Blackpool North, 1945–62.

over London at 12 noon as we were sitting in Cabinet. It was a tremendously hot day and all the windows were open. I was afraid that there would be a frightful din so I passed a note to Harold saying that there would be a sonic bang at midday and should I tell the Cabinet? He said, no. So I sat there dreading it. At 12 o'clock, which we heard on Big Ben, there was a great sound like a clap of thunder. It did cause a shock, and was different from subsonic noise but it wasn't as bad as one had expected. But Miss Nunn, who was in the Cabinet secretariat, hadn't known what was happening and went very pale.

Thursday 20 July
Cabinet on public expenditure. This was the great exercise where we cut items in our public expenditure and saved £350 million. The whole question of whether there was a risk of devaluation obsessed us throughout this period of Labour Government.

Saturday 22 July
To Chequers for a meeting of Harold's kitchen cabinet with Dick Crossman, John Silkin, Marcia, Judith Hart, Barbara Castle, Tommy Balogh and Gerald Kaufman. For the first time we did discuss, amongst ourselves, the possibility of devaluation. At a meeting like this, with Gerald Kaufman who was just a press officer present, matters that were not even discussed at Cabinet were considered. But I think every Prime Minister probably has to operate like that.

I got home at 2 am in a thunderstorm.

Monday 24 July
Petrilli of the Italian Industrial Reorganisation Institute came to see me. IRI was started by Mussolini when he came to power in the 1920s and found that Italian industry had collapsed and had to be saved by public enterprise. Petrilli was a bright, dynamic managerial type, on a visit to build up his reputation, because he was engaged on a major project in the Mezzogiorno – the Alfa Romeo plant he was trying to get agreed in the south – and he wanted to be seen as a major international figure with full press coverage. This is a characteristic of Ministers visiting another country. Everybody falls into the spirit of the game: that is to say, you recognise that you won't make much progress in the talks, but you understand the Minister's need to build himself up at home and therefore all press facilities are laid on.

Had an adjournment debate on the European Community at 2.15 in the morning and I recorded it on my tape recorder, probably the first debate in Parliament ever to be recorded – strictly illegally.

Tuesday 1 August

Offered Sir Hugh Tett, who had just retired as chairman of Esso, the chairmanship of the Atomic Energy Authority. He was very courteous and friendly and I thought it would be a good thing to have an industrialist rather than a scientist in the job. But he refused it and told me that Esso, knowing that he had been paying high rates of taxation as the chairman of a British company, had decided to reward him on his retirement – he was still quite young – by giving him a world-wide consultancy for which he would be paid an enormous sum. The money that we were prepared to offer him for the chairmanship of the AEA simply wasn't attractive.

I went to see Harold with Bill Penney about centrifuges. What occupied a lot of my time and attention at this point was the whole question of security. I was in the curious position of reading in the *New Scientist* a full description of the centrifuge, all of which was quite accurate, and at the same time getting a paper saying the same thing but under the heaviest security classification: 'TOP SECRET: ATOMIC: UK EYES ONLY.' Each sheet was numbered, brought in for me to read and then taken out again – and the only thing that was secret was that we knew it could be done.

Friday 4 August

Because of unemployment in the North East, we were anxious that Swan Hunter should tender for two container ships which were on order, and I had had authority to offer a subsidy for this purpose to Sir John Hunter who hadn't bid for it on the grounds that it wouldn't be profitable.

I called in the directors of Swan Hunter and as quick as a flash they realised that we had to give them the money for employment reasons, so they simply stuck out for more. I think originally we offered them half a million. They stayed for three hours and we tried to arrange it so that we could supervise the accounts. But in the end they went away with a million quid. Absolute bribery.

Sunday 27 August

The *Observer* had a typical Concorde cancellation story. They have been running it for years.

Harold phoned to say that he had offered Eric Heffer [MP for Walton] a job in the Ministry of Technology as Parliamentary Secretary, but Eric Heffer had turned it down on the basis that he didn't have confidence in the Government's economic policy and unless Jim Callaghan was dismissed from the Treasury, he wouldn't take it. I admired him for that.

Monday 28 August

In the reshuffle, Peter Shore was appointed Secretary of State for Economic Affairs, although Harold Wilson took overall personal charge of the department. Tony Crosland left to become President of the Board of Trade, a post from which Douglas Jay was sacked because of his anti-Common Market attitude. Peter Shore felt that he was in a slightly weak position with Harold over and above him.

Tuesday 29 August

I went to Chequers for a discussion about economic planning with Peter Shore, Tommy Balogh, Marcia Williams and Gerald Kaufman and a big dog which they call Paymaster, which I must say is an appropriate way of referring to George Wigg.

Harold was thrilled to be in control of Economic Affairs as a counterweight to the Treasury. There was some serious talk about devaluation and clearly this was Harold's way of entering directly into the economic situation.

Wednesday 6 September

I worked till 5 am on the airframe merger problems and Concorde and to the office for all-day meetings, with no real solution in sight. The truth was that I was not interested in buying BAC and then having it as a minority holding in Hawker Siddeley. BAC wanted much more for their shares than we were prepared to pay and even that price was wildly extravagant. Hawker Siddeley were not prepared to accept the BAC share on the basis of our valuation.

We were still in disagreement about the guided weapons: you get the worst of all possible worlds by having an airframe merger of this kind.

Thursday 7 September

I had sandwiches and went to meet Chamant, the French Minister of Transport, and Stonehouse for talks about Concorde. This was the first real round of discussions and Chamant appeared to know very little about Concorde: officials had to give him information all the time, and I had a feeling that he hadn't been candid with the French Cabinet, and that de Gaulle just insisted that the plane be kept going with no questions asked.

Tuesday 12 September

I went to Chequers for a conference on Dick's Lords' Reform scheme for the total abolition of the hereditary principle. On the question of whether we should have two tiers or one, there was a great floundering among the constitutionalists. I personally wasn't keen on the plan. I am instinctively opposed to attempts to reform, rather than abolish, the Lords and when I heard that there was some possibility that peers who had renounced would have the right to get back their peerage and return to the House of Lords, I thought it was intolerable.

Saturday 23 September

I went to see Alun Chalfont in his Chelsea flat to tell him about the centrifuge project ('Acarus'). Harold asked me not to tell George Brown, presumably because this was so secret and George Brown was considered a security risk. Chalfont was extremely interested. He was only a Minister of State at the Foreign Office and he was being told something that the Foreign Secretary couldn't be told. I thought it was a bit strange. At any rate he is a great defence expert and no doubt Harold felt that he was reliable. Chalfont said that George Brown was on the way out anyway, and that de Gaulle might veto our Common Market application on 23 October. He is very well informed.[7]

The Labour Conference took place from 2–6 October 1967 at Scarborough, and the issues discussed included the Common Market, education and transport, the economy and Vietnam, on which the platform was defeated by the Conference because of discontent with the Government support for the United States. As usual I was drawn in to help Harold Wilson with his parliamentary report, in which he returned to the central theme of technology.

Wednesday 11 October

I heard a rumour that Donald Stokes was going to make a bid for British Motors.

There was a TUC meeting with Peter Shore about the brain drain of scientists to America, a report having been published the day before.

Appointed Sir John Hill to be Chairman of the Atomic Energy Authority.

Sunday 15 October

Went to Chequers in the evening for British Motors–Leyland talks with Harold. Harriman and Stokes were there and Harold said we wanted to bring them together. He said that what we were looking for was that subtle combination of a buccaneer and a statesman. Donald Stokes was a bit of a buccaneer and Harriman was a statesman, and he went on and on trying to persuade them. It was intolerable that a Prime Minister should have to try to persuade two industrialists to agree to something that was in the national interest, but it was a personality clash that prevented any co-operation.

Tuesday 17 October
Bill Penney said an amusing thing at dinner: 'You know, parliamentary democracy in Britain is in a very bad way. I look around and think, if there was a coup d'état who could possibly organise it? I say to myself, well the army isn't efficient enough, the police aren't nationally organised – it must be the Ministry of Technology who are going to take over.'

Monday 23 October
Met Bykovsky, the Soviet cosmonaut, who was rather a shy young man. These are the princes of the modern age – a phrase Caroline coined – the great young heroes who are ordinary, nice, modest people.

Tuesday 7 November
Went to the memorial service in Westminster Abbey for Clem Attlee who died on 8 October. The whole Establishment was on show. Middle-class Labour leaders are recaptured by the Establishment when they die and there is no reference to their political work. Attlee is 'forgiven' for being a socialist and the past is forgotten.

Had lunch with Kingsley Martin and Dorothy Woodman in their flat in Victoria Street.

Wednesday 8 November
Devaluation was discussed at the Steering Committee on Economic Policy. I said we had no choice. The veto on discussion was removed and the consensus of opinion was for it.

Thursday 16 November
Cabinet decided to devalue.

Spent all morning on a package of cuts while I had this terrible guilty secret, which I had to keep quiet until it was announced.

Friday 17 November
Went to the Risley AEA site in Manchester with John Hill, new chairman of the AEA, for meetings with the staff. They were angry because there had been some hold-up in a pay claim, due to our prices and incomes policy and they marched about with slogans saying, 'We want some of the American loan': it was rumoured we were going to have a loan to tide us over. It was a rough meeting and what was interesting was that my civil servants had never seen

a Minister being shouted at, though I was used to it. They were shocked.

Saturday 18 November

Devaluation from $2.80 to $2.40 announced. A great moment of defeat for the Government but I felt cheerful about it as a matter of fact, because this was, after all, what we had tried to prevent for three years and this delay was itself a great defeat for Harold. The following day he did his absurd broadcast on television saying, 'The pound in your pocket won't be devalued.'

Tuesday 28 November

Had lunch with Hugh Cudlipp, who was critical of Harold and who thought he should resign – he had no time for Harold at all. He said that the cuts were quite inadequate, £500 million wasn't enough, and so on.

Tuesday 5 December

John Hill came in to see me, particularly to discuss the question of the 'hardening' of the Polaris missiles and penetration aids and the multi-head missiles. It was a big and highly secret issue. One of the arguments propounded in favour of hardening was that Aldermaston had a highly skilled staff engaged in refurbishing nuclear warheads for the Polaris, but this work had tailed off because all the Polaris missiles had been completed, and unless we went on with hardening, there wouldn't be enough work to keep this highly skilled group going and the existing nuclear weapons programme would, in effect, break down.

I put this to him and asked him if this argument was true. Well, he hummed and hawed a bit, but my judgement was that it wasn't and that was a useful piece of information.

Then to the Nuclear Policy Committee, where the same issue came up. Denis Healey, of course, was strongly in favour of hardening; the Foreign Secretary and the Treasury were against on financial grounds; and I was against on policy grounds. Solly Zuckerman was also very much opposed.

Monday 11 December

To Paris in the HS125. Collected Sir Patrick Reilly, the Ambassador, in Paris and went to Toulouse for the roll-out of the 002 Concorde. It was icy cold.

Chamant met me and I made a little speech. I didn't speak in French, but I did say that as a tribute to this occasion we would now in future have a British Concorde which would be spelt with an 'e'.

The white-heat of Anglo–French technology: Wilson and de Gaulle,
December 1967.

There was great cheering. I said, 'That is "e" for excellence; "E" for
England and "e" for "*entente concordiale*".' This went down very well.

In fact, there was a hell of a row about this. The press said it was
a capitulation to de Gaulle, whom had I consulted, and so on. When
I sat and thought about it I realised that this wasn't taken as a joke.
I had an angry letter from a man who said, 'I live in Scotland, and
you talk about "E" for England but part of it is made in Scotland.'
I wrote back and said that it was also 'E' for 'Ecosse' – and I might
have added 'e' for extravagance and 'e' for escalation as well! I then
discovered that the British Concorde had always been spelt with an
'e', but after the French vetoed British entry into the Common Market
in the early sixties, the Government gave an order that the Concorde
was to drop the 'e'. So I had only reinstated the original spelling.

But it was a great day and, except for the icy cold, it was well
worthwhile. It was nice to see Concorde out of the hangar. After
worrying so much about Concorde, you wondered if you would ever
see it.

Friday 15 December
Went to Cabinet where there was a major row over South African
arms, with a bare majority against it. Harold was saved by a few
votes, including mine, George Brown being strongly in favour of
resuming arms sales.

Saturday 16 December

Harold phoned and said, 'Don't brief the press on the South African arms question.' I thought how responsible, but actually Harold had already arranged a briefing to build up further support for himself.

Sunday 17 December

The Mayhews came for their annual Christmas visit. Chris Mayhew thought that Roy Jenkins should replace Harold – that, of course, is the view of the Right.

Monday 18 December

Total victory. No arms for South Africa. Harold made a statement in the Commons making it clear we would not supply them. It would be a disaster if we had decided to vote arms for South Africa. We would have split the Party up the middle.

Friday 22 December

John Silkin phoned and we decided to keep in touch to defeat the Junta. This was our reference to Roy, George and Michael Stewart and others who were trying to get rid of Harold. Undoubtedly there was an attempt to get rid of him.

Saturday 23 December

Crosland in for a drink before lunch. He denied there was any plot, though if there was, he was undoubtedly involved in it, probably with Jim Callaghan.

Monday 25 December

Christmas Day. Melissa woke up at four and climbed into Joshua's bed. She was so excited.

 Came downstairs and opened stockings and gifts.

Wednesday 27 December

Packed the car and drove the whole family to Stansgate to find a plague of mice when we arrived, but it was nice to be away from all that workload.

Sunday 31 December

1967 was a most demanding year. The Ministry of Technology acquired the Ministry of Aviation and took on board all the great aviation problems; Concorde was an almost daily problem because of the escalation of costs, pressure for cancellation, difficulties with the French, and so on.

 It was the year of devaluation, when we finally realised we couldn't hold the exchange rate and later wondered why we had ever tried to do so.

For me it was a year of great physical exertion. Considering the hours I went to bed, no wonder I was tired. I wasn't spending my time wisely and sensibly, that is quite clear, and if ever I am Minister again, I shall try to organise my programme to have more free time, more free weekends, more opportunity to think and talk, and less absolutely frantic work. Otherwise the job isn't done properly. It is only now, looking back on it, that I can begin to see what my objectives were.

During the course of the year I did develop links with the trade unions, which was one of my major objectives; did begin to carry through the shipbuilding policy; did introduce a completely new policy for the aircraft industry, which made me unpopular with the aircraft manufacturers but needed to be done; and I also learned a lot more about multi-national companies like Ford and how they operate.

I introduced the Industrial Expansion Bill, which was a great struggle, pushed ICT leasing through, pioneered the Shipbuilding Industry Bill. I handled the difficult Bristol Siddeley scandal and saved Skyvan for Shorts. I contributed – wrongly, I think, looking back – in the debate on whether we should enter the Common Market. It was a year full of travel – to Russia to consolidate technological agreements, to France for Concorde, and to Washington. And I was beginning to be aware of the grave dissatisfaction of the Party with the leadership.

NOTES
Chapter Five

1. For the first eighteen months that I was Minister of Technology my diary, which I had previously dictated to my personal secretary, omits detailed description of Cabinet meetings. This was a policy I adopted in line with the traditional secrecy then associated with Cabinet proceedings, a secrecy that has since been undermined by many published memoirs and records.

2. This Cabinet, and the following one on 19 July 1966, accepted proposals from the Chancellor of the Exchequer intended to halt speculation against sterling. The programme was designed to remove an estimated £500 million from the economy and imposed a six month freeze on prices and incomes.

3. The Industrial Reorganisation Corporation was established by the Labour Government in December 1966 to promote industrial efficiency by mergers and public investment, with the power to take equity.

4. One of the proposals awaiting me at the Ministry of Technology related

to the future of the British Aircraft Corporation and Hawker Siddeley. It had been suggested that the Government should buy BAC and then use its holding to become a minority shareholder in a joint company with Hawker Siddeley. This proposal had very little merit in my mind so I tried to get it agreed that we would acquire both companies and set up a Corporation of a kind that was later achieved in the 1974–9 Government. However, my proposal was not accepted and in the event the merger was dropped.

5. In late 1966, a proposal came forward that the Polaris warhead should be hardened and penetration aids added to allow the missiles to get through the supposed Soviet defensive screen. Lord Rothschild was appointed to chair a committee to examine this and when it reported later, he, Solly Zuckerman and I came out against the hardening. That was the last I heard of the matter until the 1974 Labour Government when Harold Wilson made casual reference to a 'refurbishing' programme, which must have been an early version of the Chevaline project and which was approved by Jim Callaghan without consulting the Cabinet.

6. Tension between Israel and the UAR and Jordan developed into war in early June 1967. An interesting side-light on this discussion was provided in the summer of 1973, when I was talking to Crossman about the Official Secrets Act and remarked that, as Cabinet Ministers, we did not know any secrets. He replied, 'Oh, yes we did – we knew what attitude the Cabinet was taking on issues like the supply of arms to the Israelis in 1967, information that was of great value to them. I told the Israelis, "We cannot rely on the British Government ever to support Israel." Harold was very angry when I did that.'

7. Alun Gwynne-Jones was the defence correspondent of *The Times*, 1961–4 and was generally thought to be a liberal. He was made a peer as Lord Chalfont and appointed by Harold Wilson in 1964 to the Foreign Office as Minister of State, for which his knowledge on defence and disarmament was thought to qualify him.

Principal Persons

(I) Political and Official

Each person is named according to his or her status as the diaries open. A full list of Government Members at the beginning of the 1964 and 1966 Labour administrations, some of whom do not appear here since they do not feature prominently in this volume, is given in Appendix V. The terminology used here and throughout the main text conforms to usage at the time.

ALBU, Austen. Minister of State at the Department of Economic Affairs, 1965–7. Labour MP for Edmonton, 1948–74.

ALLEN, John Scholefield. Political and economic research assistant to the Labour Party before the 1964 Election. Subsequently attached to the Cabinet Office, 1964–70.

ALTRINCHAM, Lord *See* GRIGG, John

ANDERSON, Sir Kenneth. Deputy Director General and Comptroller General at the GPO from 1952 until his retirement in 1966.

ARNOLD-FORSTER, Mark (1920–81). Senior journalist and political commentator on the *Guardian*, the *Observer* and ITN, 1946–81. Distinguished service with the Royal Navy while engaged on secret missions during the Second World War. Married to Val Arnold-Forster, journalist. Family friends.

ATTLEE, Earl (1883–1967). Clement Attlee, Leader of the Labour Party, 1935–55 and Prime Minister, 1945–51. MP for Limehouse, subsequently West Walthamstow, 1922–55. Created an Earl, 1955. Married to Violet Attlee who died in 1964.

BACON, Alice. Minister of State in the Home Office, 1964–7 and Education and Science, 1967–70. Labour MP for Leeds, 1945–70. Chairman of the Labour Party, 1950/1. Created Baroness Bacon of Leeds and Normanton in 1970.

BALOGH, Thomas (Tommy) (1905–85). Oxford economist of

Hungarian birth, close adviser to Harold Wilson in the 1950s and early 1960s, and Economic Adviser to the Cabinet, 1964–8. Created a life peer in 1968. Minister of State at the Department of Energy, 1974–5, and Deputy Chairman, British National Oil Company, 1976–8. Married to Penny Balogh.

BARKER, Dame Sara (1903–73). National Agent for the Labour Party, 1962–9.

BARRON, D. A. (1907–80). Deputy Engineer-in-Chief at the GPO, 1960–5. Engineer-in-Chief, 1965–7.

BERKELEY, Humphry. Conservative of liberal views, MP for Lancaster, 1959–66. Left the Conservative Party in 1970; in 1974 unsuccessfully fought North Fylde for Labour. Joined the SDP in 1981.

BING, Geoffrey (1909–77). A barrister, successively Constitutional Adviser, Attorney-General and Presidential Adviser in Ghana, 1955–66. From 1945–55 he was Labour MP for Hornchurch. Assisted Tony Benn in the early days of the peerage battle.

BLACKETT, Patrick (1897–1972). Chief Scientific Adviser at the Ministry of Technology. Pre-eminent nuclear scientist. President of the Royal Society, 1965–70. Created a life peer in 1969.

BONHAM CARTER, Violet (1887–1969). Leading Liberal, President of the Liberal Party, 1945–7. Active in the League of Nations and United Nations. Daughter of Liberal Prime Minister, Herbert Asquith, mother-in-law of Liberal Leader, Jo Grimond. Created a life peer in 1964, as Lady Asquith.

BOWDEN, Herbert. Opposition Chief Whip, 1955–64, and Lord President of the Council and Leader of the House of Commons, 1964–6. Labour MP for Leicester, 1945–67. Retired in 1967, when he was created a life peer, Lord Aylestone, to become Chairman of the Independent Broadcasting Authority. Joined the SDP in 1981.

BRADDOCK, Bessie (1899–1970). Labour MP for Liverpool Exchange, 1945–70. Long-standing member of the National Executive.

BRAY, Jeremy. Joint Parliamentary Secretary at the Ministry of Technology, 1967–9, dismissed by Harold Wilson in 1969 for writing a book, *Decision in Government*. Labour MP for Middlesbrough West, 1962–70, for Motherwell and Wishaw, subsequently Motherwell South, since October 1974.

BROCKWAY, Fenner. Life-long campaigner for peace and founder of the Movement for Colonial Freedom in the 1950s. Labour MP for East Leyton, 1929–31, and for Eton and Slough, 1950–64. Leading member of the Independent Labour Party between 1922 and 1946. Created a life peer in 1964.

BROWN, George (1914–85). Deputy Leader of the Labour Party, 1960–70, and in that capacity member of the National Executive and Chairman of the Home Policy Committee. Held office in the 1945–51 Government, finally as Minister of Works. First Secretary of State at the Department of Economic Affairs, 1964–6, and Foreign Secretary, 1966–8. Ardently pro-Common Market: tried to negotiate Britain's entry in 1967. Labour MP for Belper, 1945–70. Created a life peer, Lord George-Brown, in 1970. Resigned from the Labour Party in 1976 and later joined the SDP.

BUTLER, David. Political scientist and broadcaster, whose special subject is the study of elections; the first person to coin the term 'psephology'. Has published a study of every British General Election since 1951. Life-long friend. Married to Marilyn Butler.

BUTLER, 'Rab' (1902–82). Foreign Secretary, 1963–4. Held office in Conservative/National Governments from 1932; Chancellor of the Exchequer, 1951–5, Leader of the House of Commons, 1955–61. Home Secretary, 1957–62. Conservative MP for Saffron Walden, 1929–65. Created a life peer in 1965.

CADBURY, Kenneth. Director of Clerical Mechanisation and Buildings at the GPO, 1964–5, Director of Inland Telecommunications, 1965–7. Became Deputy Managing Director of Communications for the Post Office, 1978–9.

CALLAGHAN, James. Chancellor of the Exchequer, 1964–7, Home Secretary, 1967–70, Foreign Secretary, 1974–6, Prime Minister, 1976–9 and Leader of the Labour Party until 1980. Held junior posts in the 1945–51 Labour Government. Chairman of the Labour Party, 1973/4 and Labour MP for South, South-East and again South Cardiff, 1945–87. Father of the House, 1983–7. Made a Knight of the Garter, 1987.

CASTLE, Barbara. Minister of Overseas Development, 1964–5, Minister of Transport, 1965–68, First Secretary of State at the Department of Employment and Productivity, 1968–70. Chairman of the Labour Party, 1958/9. Secretary of State for Social Services, 1974–6, dismissed by James Callaghan when he formed his Government in 1976. Labour MP for Blackburn, 1945–79. Leader of the British Labour Group in the European Parliament, 1979–85.

CATHERWOOD, Fred. Industrialist and Chief Industrial Adviser at the Department of Economic Affairs, 1964–6. Member of the Advisory Council on Technology and Director General of National Economic Development Council (Neddy), 1966–71.

CHURCHILL, Sir Winston (1874–1965). Prime Minister and Minister of Defence, 1940–5, Prime Minister, 1951–5. Parliamentary career began in 1900 as Conservative MP for Oldham, and ended in 1964 as Conservative MP for Woodford, Churchill sitting as a Liberal MP, 1904–22. Out of Parliament for only two years, 1922–4. His personal support for the peerage renunciation campaign, both as Prime Minister and later, played a significant part in its success.

CLARK, Percy (1917–85). Director of Publicity of the Labour Party 1965–79.

CLARK, Valerie. Personal Secretary to Tony Benn, 1963–7.

CLARKE, Sir Richard (Otto) (1910–75). Permanent Secretary at the Ministry of Technology, his last Civil Service appointment. Formerly a senior Treasury official.

COUSINS, Frank (1904–86). General Secretary of the Transport and General Workers' Union, brought into the Labour Cabinet as Minister of Technology in 1964. Resigned in 1966 over the wage freeze and returned to the Union until his retirement in 1969. Labour MP for Nuneaton, 1965–6.

CROSLAND, Anthony (1918–77). Minister of State for Economic Affairs, 1964–5, Secretary of State for Education and Science, 1965–7, President of the Board of Trade, 1967–9 and Secretary of State for Local Government, 1969–70. In the 1974–9 Labour Government he was Secretary of State for the Environment till 1976 and then Foreign Secretary, in which post he died suddenly in February 1977. Labour MP for South Gloucester, 1950–5 and Grimsby, 1959–77. Married journalist Susan Barnes in 1964. A personal friend since the war years.

CROSSMAN, Richard (1907–74). Minister of Housing and Local Government, 1964–6, Lord President of the Council and Leader of the House of Commons, 1966–8, Secretary of State for Health and Social Security, 1968–70. Chairman of the Labour Party, 1960/1. He later published three volumes of diaries describing his years as a Cabinet Minister. Labour MP for Coventry, 1945–74. An Oxford academic, he wrote *Government and the Governed*, 1939. Became editor of the *New Statesman*, 1970. Married to Anne Crossman.

CUDLIPP, Hugh. Succeeded Cecil King as Chairman of Daily Mirror Newspapers, 1963–8. Deputy Chairman, then Chairman of International Publishing Corporation, 1964–73. Created a life peer in 1974.

DALYELL, Tam. PPS to Richard Crossman 1964–70. Labour MP for West Lothian, 1962–83, and Linlithgow since 1983.

DELL, Edmund. Joint Parliamentary Secretary at the Ministry of Technology, 1966–7, Joint Under-Secretary of State at the Department of Economic Affairs, 1967–8, Minister of State at the Board of Trade, 1968–9, and at Employment and Productivity, 1969–70.

Secretary of State for Trade in the 1974–9 Government, resigning in 1978 to take up an appointment as Deputy Chairman of Guinness Mahon; later joined the SDP.

DIAMOND, Jack. Chief Secretary to the Treasury, 1964–70. Labour MP for Blackley, 1945–51, Gloucester, 1957–70. Chaired the Royal Commission on the Distribution of Income and Wealth, 1974–9. Created a life peer in 1970 and became Leader of the SDP in the House of Lords.

ENNALS, David. Secretary of the Labour Party's International Department, 1958–64. PPS to Barbara Castle, 1964–6. Under-Secretary of State at Defence, 1966, and at the Home Office, 1967. Minister of State at the Department of Health and Social Security, 1968–70. In the 1974–9 Government he was Minister of State at the Foreign and Commonwealth Office and Secretary of State for the Social Services, 1976–9. Labour MP for Dover, 1964–70 and Norwich North, 1974–83. Created a life peer in 1983.

EVANS, Ioan (1927–84). PPS to Tony Benn as Postmaster General. A Government whip, 1968–70. Labour MP for Yardley, 1964–70, Aberdare, 1974–83 and Cynon Valley, 1983–4.

FLOUD, Bernard (1915–67). Labour MP for Acton, 1964–7.

FOOT, Dingle (1905–78). Solicitor-General, 1964–7. Labour MP for Ipswich, 1957–70, previously Liberal MP for Dundee, 1931–45. Brother of Michael and Hugh Foot.

FOOT, Hugh. Minister of State for Foreign Affairs in the Lords, 1964–70. Ambassador to the United Nations, 1961–2. Created a life peer, Baron Caradon, in 1964.

FOOT, Michael. Back Bencher during the 1964–70 Labour Government. Held posts in 1974–9 Government as Secretary of State for Employment, 1974–6, Lord President of the Council and Leader of the House of Commons, 1976–9. Deputy-Leader of the Labour Party, 1979–80, and Leader, 1980–3. Member of the National Executive, 1971–83. Labour MP for Devonport, 1945–55, Ebbw Vale, 1960–83, and Blaenau Gwent since 1983. Author and journalist; close friend and biographer of Aneurin Bevan.

GAITSKELL, Hugh (1906–63). Leader of the Labour Party, 1955–63. Held office, 1945–51, as Minister of Fuel and Power, Minister of State for Economic Affairs and Chancellor of the Exchequer. Labour MP for South Leeds, 1945–63. Succeeded Arthur Greenwood as Treasurer of the Labour Party in 1954 and in that capacity and as Leader sat on the National Executive until his death.

GARDINER, Gerald. Lord Chancellor, 1964–70. Created a life peer in 1963. He was Chairman of the National Campaign for the Abolition of Capital Punishment and from 1973–8 Chancellor of the Open University.

GENTLEMAN, David. Designer of stamps for the GPO in the 1960s. Member of the Design Council, 1974–80.

GERMAN, Sir Ronald (1906–83). Director General at the GPO from 1960 until his retirement in 1966. Formerly Postmaster General for British East Africa, 1950–8.

GOODMAN, Arnold. Prominent lawyer, adviser to Harold Wilson, 1964–70, undertaking a number of missions on his behalf. Particular interest in Open University and the Arts. Created a life peer in 1965.

GOOSE, Jean. Assistant private secretary to Tony Benn as Postmaster General, 1964–6.

GORDON WALKER, Patrick (1907–80). Foreign Secretary, October 1964–January 1965. He was defeated in the 1964 Election as Labour MP for Smethwick, a seat he had held since 1945, and was therefore a Cabinet member without a constituency. Fought and lost Leyton, 1965 but elected Labour MP for Leyton, 1966–74. Returned to Cabinet as Secretary of State for Education and Science, 1967–70. Created a life peer in 1974.

GORMLEY, Joe. President of the North West area of the National Union of Mineworkers, 1961–71, and subsequently of the NUM, 1971–82. Member of the National Executive, 1963–73. Created a life peer in 1982.

GREENE, Hugh (1910–87). Director General of the BBC, 1960–69. *Daily Telegraph* correspondent in Germany in the 1930s, appointed Head of BBC German Service in 1940.

GREENWOOD, Anthony (1911–82). Colonial Secretary, 1964–5, Minister for Overseas Development, 1965–6, and Minister of Housing and Local Government, 1966–70. Chairman of the Labour Party, 1963/4. Labour MP for Heywood and Radcliffe, subsequently Rossendale, 1946–70. Son of Arthur Greenwood, a Labour leader of the thirties and forties. Created a life peer in 1970.

GRIERSON, Ronald. Director of Warburgs, Deputy Chairman of the Industrial Reorganisation Corporation, appointed by the Labour Government, 1966–7.

GRIGG, John. Journalist and author who inherited the title Baron Altrincham in 1955 and disclaimed it on 31 July, 1963.

GRIMOND, Jo. Leader of the Liberal Party, 1956–67. Liberal MP for Orkney and Shetland, 1950–83. Created life peer in 1983. Son-in-law of Lady Violet Bonham Carter.

GUNTER, Ray (1909–77). Minister of Labour, 1964–8, and Minister of Power for two months in 1968 before resigning from the Government. Member of the National Executive, 1955–66. Labour MP for Essex South East, 1945–50, Doncaster, 1950–1, Southwark, 1959–72. Resigned from the Labour Party, 1972.

HAILSHAM, Lord. As Quintin Hogg sat as Conservative MP for St Marylebone, 1963–70, after disclaiming his peerages in 1963 during the contest for the Conservative Party leadership. Previously sat as MP for Oxford City, 1938 to 1950, when he succeeded his father as 2nd Viscount Hailsham. Held ministerial posts in the House of Lords during the 1951–64 Conservative Governments, including Secretary of State for Education in 1964. Returned to the Lords with a life peerage in 1970. Lord Chancellor, 1970–4 and 1979–87.

HARRIMAN, Sir George (1908–73). Chairman of the British Motor Corporation from 1961 and of British Motor Holdings, 1967–8. President of British Leyland Motor Corporation, 1968–73.

HARRIS, John. Labour Party's Director of Publicity, 1962–4. Special Assistant to Michael Stewart, 1964–5, and to Roy Jenkins, 1965–70. Created a life peer in 1974, and was Minister of State at the Home Office, 1974–9. Joined the SDP in 1981.

HART, Judith. Joint Under-Secretary of State for Scotland, 1964–6, Minister of State for Commonwealth Affairs, 1966–7, Minister of Social Security, 1967–8, Paymaster General, 1968–9, Minister for Overseas Development, 1969–70. In the 1974–9 Government she was Minister for Overseas Development, 1974–5 and 1977–9. Member of the National Executive, 1969–83. Labour MP for Lanark, 1959–83, Clydesdale, 1983–7. Married to Tony Hart, scientist and leading anti-nuclear campaigner.

HEALEY, Denis. Secretary of State for Defence, 1964–70. Chancellor of the Exchequer, 1974–9. Deputy Leader of the Labour Party, 1980–3, member of the National Executive, 1970–5, and later again as Deputy Leader. Labour MP for South East Leeds, 1952–5, and East Leeds since 1955.

HENRION, F. H. K. Consultant Designer to Tony Benn as Postmaster General, 1965–6. Member of the Council of Industrial Design, 1963–6.

HERBISON, Peggy. Minister of Pensions and National Insurance, subsequently Social Security, 1964–7. Chairman of the Labour Party, 1956/7. Labour MP for North Lanarkshire, 1945–70.

HEATH, Edward. Succeeded Alec Douglas-Home as Leader of the Conservative Party in 1965 and continued until his defeat by Margaret Thatcher in 1975. Prime Minister, 1970–4. Back Bencher since 1975. Minister of Labour, 1959–60, Lord Privy Seal, 1960–3, and Secretary of State for Industry and Trade and President of the Board of Trade, 1963–4. Conservative MP for Bexley, subsequently Old Bexley and Sidcup, since 1950.

HELSBY, Sir Laurence (1908–78). Joint Permanent Secretary to the Treasury (with Sir William Armstrong) and Head of the Civil Service, 1963–8. Created a life peer in 1968.

HILL, Dr Charles. Chairman of the Independent Television Authority, 1963–7, moving to the BBC as Chairman of Governors, 1967–72. Physician, the original 'Radio doctor', and Liberal and Conservative MP for Luton, 1950–63. Created a life peer in 1963.

HOLMES, Brigadier Kenneth. Director of Postal Services at the GPO, 1960–5. Director of London Postal Region, 1965–70. Author of a history of the Post Office.

HOME, Earl of. Foreign Secretary, 1960–3, in the House of Lords. Before inheriting his peerage in 1951, the Earldom of Home, he was Conservative/Unionist MP for Lanark, 1931–51, using his courtesy title of Viscount Dunglass. He succeeded Macmillan and renounced his title in 1963. Prime Minister from October 1963 until October 1964, and MP for Kinross and West Perthshire, 1963–74. In 1974 he was created a life peer and re-entered the Lords as Home of the Hirsel.

HOUGHTON, Douglas. Chancellor of the Duchy of Lancaster, 1964–6, Minister without Portfolio, 1966–7. Chairman of the House of Commons Public Accounts Committee, 1963–4. Labour MP for Sowerby, 1949–74. Created a life peer in 1974.

JAY, Douglas. President of the Board of Trade, 1964–7. 'Resigned' in the reshuffle of August 1967 and returned to the Back Benches. Leading anti-Common Marketeer in the Labour Government. Labour MP for North Battersea, 1946–83.

JEGER, Lena. Labour MP for St Pancras and Holborn South, 1953–9 and 1964–74 and for Camden, Holborn and St Pancras South, 1974–9. Member of the National Executive, 1968–80. Created a life peer in 1979.

JENKINS, Roy. Minister of Aviation, 1964–5, Home Secretary, 1965–7, Chancellor of the Exchequer, 1967–70, Home Secretary, 1974–6. In 1976 he became President of the European Commission. Deputy Leader of the Labour Party, 1970–2, in which capacity he sat on the National Executive. Labour MP for Central Southwark, 1948–50, for Stechford, 1950–76, Leader of the SDP, 1981–3, and SDP MP for Hillhead, 1982–7.

JONES, Elwyn. Attorney-General, 1964–70. Labour MP for Plaistow, 1945–50, for West Ham South, 1950–74 and for Newham South, February to May 1974, when he was created a life peer, Lord Elwyn-Jones, and appointed Lord Chancellor, a post he held until 1979.

JONES, Jack. Assistant General Secretary of the Transport and General Workers' Union, 1963–9, succeeded Frank Cousins as

General Secretary in 1969. Member of the Labour Party National Executive, 1964–7, when he went on to the Trades Union Congress General Council. Vice-President of Age Concern since 1978.

KEARTON, Sir Frank. A distinguished public servant. Chairman of Courtaulds, 1964–75, and served on the Atomic Energy Authority, and the Central Electricity Generating Board, 1955–81. First Chairman of the Industrial Reorganisation Corporation, 1966–8. Member of the Advisory Council on Technology. In 1975 he became the first Chairman of the British National Oil Corporation.

KENNET, Lord (Wayland Young). Parliamentary Secretary at the Ministry of Housing and Local Government, 1966–70. Joined the SDP in 1981.

KING, Cecil (1901–87). Chairman, International Publishing Corporation, 1963–8. A director of the Bank of England, 1965–8. Chairman of Daily Mirror Newspapers Limited, 1951–63.

KNIGHTON, William. Principal Private Secretary to Tony Benn at the Ministry of Technology, 1966–8. Subsequently became a Deputy Secretary.

LEE, Jennie. Parliamentary Secretary at the Ministry of Public Building and Works, 1964–5. Under-Secretary, then Minister at the Department of Education and Science, 1965–70 during which time she was responsible for establishing the Open University. Chairman of the Labour Party, 1967/8. Created a life peer in 1970. MP for North Lanark, 1929–31, and Cannock, 1945–70. Widow of Aneurin Bevan, Deputy Leader of the Labour Party.

LILLICRAP, H. G. Director of Radio Services at the GPO, 1964–7 and Senior Director of Planning and Customer Services, 1967–72. Chairman of Cable and Wireless, 1972–6.

LONGFORD, Earl of (Frank Pakenham). Lord Privy Seal and Leader of the House of Lords, 1964–8. Colonial Secretary, 1965–6. Created a peer, Lord Pakenham, in 1945 in order to hold office in the 1945–51 Labour Government but subsequently succeeded to his brother's title, Earl of Longford, in 1961.

MACLEOD, Iain (1913–70). Leader of the House of Commons, 1961–3, and Chairman of the Conservative Party during that period. Served in the 1951–64 Conservative Governments as Minister of Health, Minister of Labour and Colonial Secretary. Chancellor of the Exchequer, June–July 1970. Conservative MP for Enfield, 1950–70.

McMILLAN, Colonel Donald. Director of External Telecommunications Executive at the GPO, 1954–67, became Chairman of Cable and Wireless on his retirement in 1967.

MACMILLAN, Harold (1894–1986). Prime Minister from 1957 until his retirement in October 1963, previously Minister of

Defence, 1954–5, Foreign Secretary, 1955, and Chancellor of the Exchequer, 1955–7. Created Earl of Stockton, 1984. Conservative MP for Stockton-on-Tees, 1924–9, 1931–45, and for Bromley, 1945–64.

MADDOCK, Ieuan. Atomic scientist who worked at the Atomic Weapons Research Establishment, Aldermaston, and directed the research programme for the Nuclear Test-Ban Treaty, 1957–66. Controller at the Ministry of Technology, 1965–71, and subsequently Chief Scientist at the Department of Trade and Industry.

MARSH, Richard. Parliamentary Secretary at the Ministry of Labour, 1964–5. Joint Parliamentary Secretary at the Ministry of Technology, 1965–6, and Minister of Power, 1966–8. Minister of Transport, 1968–9, when he was dismissed by Harold Wilson. Labour MP for Greenwich, 1959–71. He resigned his seat and became Chairman of British Railways Board, 1971–6. Created a life peer in 1981, and left the Labour Party.

MASON, Roy. Minister of State at the Board of Trade, 1964–7, Minister of Defence, 1967–8, and of Power, 1968–9, and President of the Board of Trade, 1969–70. In the 1974–9 Labour Government he was Secretary of State for Defence, 1974–6 and Secretary of State for Northern Ireland, 1976–9. Labour MP for Barnsley, 1953–87.

MAUDE, Angus. Conservative MP for Stratford-on-Avon, 1963–83, and for Ealing South, 1950–58. Paymaster General, 1979–81. Director of the Conservative Political Centre, 1951–5, and appointed Deputy Chairman of the Conservative Party in 1975. Created a life peer in 1983.

MAXWELL, Robert. Owner of Pergamon Press and Labour MP for Buckingham, 1964–70. Chairman of the Mirror Group of Newspapers since 1984.

MAYHEW, Christopher. Appointed Minister of Defence for the Royal Navy in 1964, resigned in 1966 in protest against naval cuts. Labour MP for South Norfolk, 1945–50, and for Woolwich East, 1951–July 1974, when he resigned from the Labour Party to join the Liberal Party. Sat as a Liberal MP for Woolwich East for three months. Created a life peer in 1981.

MELLISH, Robert. Joint Parliamentary Secretary at the Ministry of Housing, 1964–7. Minister of Public Building and Works, 1967–9. Government Chief Whip, 1969–70. Opposition Chief Whip, 1970–4. Labour MP for Bermondsey from 1946 to 1982, when he resigned from the Labour Party and sat as an Independent until the by-election in March, 1983, which was won by the Liberals. Created a life peer in 1985.

MIKARDO, Ian. Labour MP for Poplar, 1964–74 and for Bethnal Green and Bow, 1974–87. MP for Reading and South Reading, 1945–59. A distinguished leader of the Labour Left, he was Chairman of the Labour Party, 1970/1. A close associate of Aneurin Bevan and sometime chairman of the Tribune Group of Labour MPs.

MITCHELL, Derek. Private Secretary to Alec Douglas-Home and to Harold Wilson, 1964–6. Subsequently a senior official at the Treasury.

MORRIS, Charles. PPS to Tony Benn, Postmaster General, 1964–6, and to Harold Wilson, 1970–4. Minister of State in the Civil Service Department in the 1974–9 Labour Government. MP for Openshaw, 1963–83.

MORRISON, Lord (1888–1965). Deputy Prime Minister, 1945–51, and Deputy Leader of the Labour Party, 1945–55. Foreign Secretary, 1951. Labour MP for South Hackney, East Lewisham and South Lewisham intermittently between 1923–59. Chairman of the Labour Party, 1928/9. Leader of the London County Council, 1934–40. Served in the wartime coalition Cabinet. Created a life peer in 1959.

MOUNTBATTEN, Admiral of the Fleet, Earl (1900–79). Chairman, National Electronics Research Council. First Sea Lord, 1955–9. Chief of Defence Staff, 1959–65. Supreme Allied Commander, South-East Asia, 1943–6, appointed last Viceroy of India, 1947. Created Earl Mountbatten of Burma, 1947.

MUMFORD, Sir Albert. Engineer-in-Chief at the GPO from 1960 until his retirement in 1965. President of the Institution of Electrical Engineers, 1963–4.

NELSON of Stafford, Lord. An industrialist, Chairman of the English Electric Company, 1962–8, and member of the Advisory Council on Technology.

NORMANBROOK, Lord (1902–67). Chairman of the Governors of the BBC, 1964–7, previously Joint Secretary of the Treasury. Secretary of the Cabinet, 1947–62, Head of the Home Civil Service, 1956–62. Created a life peer in 1963.

O'BRIEN, Toby. Chief Public Relations Officer with the GPO, 1953–68, subsequently a public relations consultant.

PADLEY, Walter (1916–84). Minister of State for Foreign Affairs, 1964–7. President of the Union of Shop, Distributive and Allied Workers, 1948–64. Chairman of the Labour Party, 1965/6. Labour MP for Ogmore, 1950–79.

PAGET, Reginald. Labour MP for Northampton, 1945–74. Created a life peer in 1974.

PANNELL, Charles (1902–80). Minister of Public Building and

Works, 1964–6. Labour MP for Leeds West, 1949–74. Created a life peer in 1974.

PENNEY, Sir William. Chairman of the Atomic Energy Authority, 1964–7. A wartime pioneer of nuclear weapons. Director of the Atomic Weapons Research Establishment, Aldermaston, and Rector of Imperial College, London, 1967–73. Created a life peer in 1967.

PITT, Terry (1937–86). Head of the Labour Party's Research Department, 1965–74. Special Adviser to the Lord President of the Council, 1974.

POWELL, Enoch. Minister of Health, 1960–3. Resigned as Financial Secretary to the Treasury in 1958 in protest at the Budget. Conservative MP for Wolverhampton South West, 1950–74. Resigned in 1974 over Conservative policy. Ulster Unionist MP for Down South, 1974–87.

REYNOLDS, Gerry (1927–69). Under-Secretary of State for Defence, 1964–5, and Minister of State for Defence, 1965–9. Former head of Local Government Department of the Labour Party. Labour MP for Islington North, 1958–69.

ROBINSON, Kenneth. Minister of Health, 1964–8. Minister for Planning and Land, 1968–9. Labour MP for St Pancras North, 1949–70. Later Chairman of London Transport Executive. Chairman of the Arts Council, 1977–82.

ROGERS, Herbert. Election agent for Tony Benn, 1951–79. Secretary of the East Bristol Independent Labour Party from 1912. Agent for Sir Stafford Cripps, MP for Bristol East and after wartime work in the Government became Secretary of the Bristol South East Labour Party.

ROSS, William. Secretary of State for Scotland, 1964–70, and 1974–6. Labour MP for Kilmarnock, 1946–79. Created a life peer in 1979.

ROTHSCHILD, Lord. Scientist and Chairman of Shell Research Ltd, 1963–70. Member of the Central Advisory Committee for Science and Technology, 1969. Subsequently Director General of the Central Policy Review Staff ('Think Tank'), 1970–4.

RYLAND, William. Director of Inland Telecommunications at the GPO, 1961–5. Deputy Director General, 1965–7, Managing Director, Telecommunications, 1967–9. In the reorganised Post Office Corporation Ryland became Chairman, 1971–7.

SHACKLETON, Lord. Minister of Defence for the RAF, 1964–7. Leader of the House of Lords, 1968–70. Created a peer in 1958. Former Labour MP for Preston, 1946–50, and Preston South, 1950–5.

SHEPHERD, E. W. Director of Finance and Accounts at the GPO, 1960–7, Senior Director of Finance, 1967–73.

SHINWELL, Emmanuel (Manny) (1884–1986). Chairman of the Parliamentary Labour Party, 1964–7. Minister of Fuel and Power and Minister of Defence in the 1945–51 Labour Government. Labour MP for Linlithgow, 1922–4 and 1928–31, for Seaham, 1935–50, and for Easington, 1950–70. Chairman of the Labour Party 1947/8. Created a life peer in 1970.

SHORE, Peter. Head of the Research Department of the Labour Party, 1959–64. PPS to Harold Wilson, 1965–6. Joint Parliamentary Secretary at the Ministry of Technology, 1966–7, Secretary of State for Economic Affairs, 1967–9. Minister without Portfolio, 1969–70. Became Secretary of State for Trade in 1974. Secretary of State for the Environment, 1976–9. Labour MP for Stepney, subsequently Stepney and Poplar, and then Bethnal Green and Stepney since 1964. Married to Dr Liz Shore who after leaving general practice rose to become a senior medical officer at the Department of Health and Social Security.

SHORT, Edward. Government Chief Whip, 1964–6. Postmaster General, 1966–8. Secretary of State for Education and Science, 1968–70. Deputy Leader of the Labour Party, 1972–6. In the 1974–9 Labour Government he was Lord President of the Council and Leader of the House of Commons. Labour MP for Newcastle-on-Tyne Central, 1951–76. Created a life peer, Lord Glenamara, in 1976.

SILKIN, John (1923–87). Government Whip, 1964–6 and Chief Whip, 1966–9. Minister of Public Building and Works, 1969–70. In the 1974–9 Labour Government he was Minister for Planning and Local Government, subsequently Minister for Agriculture, Fisheries and Food. Labour MP for Deptford 1963–87.

SLATER, Joe (1904–77). Assistant Postmaster General, 1974–9. Previously PPS to Hugh Gaitskell and Harold Wilson. Labour MP for Sedgefield, 1950–70. Created a life peer in 1970.

SMART, Henry. Director of Savings at the GPO from 1958 until his retirement in 1968.

SMITH, Charles Delacourt (1917–72). General Secretary of the Post Office Engineering Union, 1953–72. Formerly Labour MP for Colchester, 1945–50. Created a life peer in 1967, and was Minister of State at the Ministry of Technology, 1969–70.

SMITH, Ron. General Secretary of the Union of Post Office Workers, 1957–66, and member of the General Council of the Trades Union Congress. Later a member of the board of the British Steel Corporation.

SNOW, C. P. (1905–80). Scientist and author. Created a life peer in 1964 and served as Joint Parliamentary Secretary at the Ministry of Technology, 1964–6. Between 1940–60 was a Civil Service Commissioner with responsibility for scientific recruitment.

SNOWDON, Earl of. Architect, designer and photographer. Consultant to the Council of Industrial Design since 1962. Married to Princess Margaret, 1960–78.

SOSKICE, Frank (1902–79). Home Secretary, 1964–5. Lord Privy Seal, 1965–6. Served in the 1945–50 Labour Government as Solicitor-General. Labour MP for Birkenhead East, 1945–50, for Neepsend, 1950–5, and for Newport, 1956–66. Created a life peer, Lord Stow Hill, in 1966.

SOUTHERTON, T. H. Controller of the Factories Department at the GPO, 1964–7. Director of Telecommunications Management Services, 1967–73, and Senior Director of Data Processing, 1975–8.

STEWART, Michael. Secretary of State for Education and Science, 1964–5, Secretary of State for Foreign Affairs, 1965–6, Secretary of State for Economic Affairs, 1966–7, Foreign and Commonwealth Secretary, 1968–70. Held junior office in the 1945–51 Government. Labour MP for Fulham East, subsequently Fulham and then Hammersmith and Fulham, 1945–79. Created a life peer in 1979.

STOKES, Sir Donald. Managing Director and Deputy Chairman, subsequently Chairman, of Leyland Motor Corporation from 1963, and after the takeover of British Motors Corporation became Chairman and Managing Director of British Leyland in 1973, President in 1975. Created a life peer in 1969.

STONEHOUSE, John. Parliamentary Secretary, Ministry of Aviation, 1964–6. Under-Secretary of State for the Colonies, 1966–7. Minister of Aviation, 1967. Minister of State at the Ministry of Technology, 1967–8. Postmaster General in 1968 and Minister of Posts and Telecommunications, 1969. Labour Co-operative MP for Wednesbury, 1957–74, and Walsall North, 1974, until his resignation in 1976.

THORPE, Jeremy. Leader of the Liberal Party, 1967–76. Liberal MP for North Devon, 1959–79.

TILLING, Henry. Private Secretary to Tony Benn as Postmaster General, 1964–5. Deputy Director of Finance at the GPO, 1965, and subsequently became Secretary of the Post Office, 1973–5, and Chairman of the Scottish Postal Board, 1977–84.

TREND, Sir Burke (1914–87). Secretary of the Cabinet, 1963–73. Created a life peer in 1974.

UNDERHILL, Reginald. Labour Party Assistant National Agent, 1960–72. National Agent, 1972–9. Labour Party official since 1933. Created a life peer in 1979.

UNGOED-THOMAS, Sir Lynn (1904–72). Labour MP for North

East Leicester, 1950–62, previously Llandaff and Barry, 1945–50. Solicitor-General in 1951, and a Chancery Judge, 1962–72.

WESIL, D. Deputy Director, then Director of the North East Postal Region of the GPO, 1966–70. Senior Director of Posts, 1971–5.

WIGG, George (1900–83). Paymaster General, 1964–7, with responsibility for advising Harold Wilson on security. Labour MP for Dudley, 1945–67. Created a life peer in 1967 and became Chairman of the Horserace Betting Levy Board.

WILLIAMS, Bruce. Economist and academic. Economic adviser to the Minister of Technology, 1964–7. A member of the Advisory Council on Technology until his appointment in 1967 as Vice-Chancellor of the University of Sydney.

WILLIAMS, Len (1903–73). General Secretary of the Labour Party, 1962–8. Formerly Assistant National Agent, National Agent and Deputy General Secretary, 1946–62. Governor General of Mauritius, 1968–73.

WILLIAMS, Marcia. Personal and Political Secretary to Harold Wilson since 1956. Created a life peer, Lady Falkender, in 1976.

WILLIAMS, Shirley. PPS to Minister of Health, 1964–6. Parliamentary Secretary at the Ministry of Labour, 1966–7. Minister of State, Education and Science, 1967–9 and the Home Office, 1969–70. In the 1974–9 Labour Government she was successively Secretary of State for Prices and Consumer Protection, for Education and Science, and Paymaster General. Member of the National Executive, 1970–81. Labour MP for Hitchin 1964–74, for Hertford and Stevenage, 1974–9, Founder of SDP in 1981, President in 1982 and SDP MP for Crosby, 1981–3.

WILSON, Harold. Leader of the Labour Party, 1963–76. Prime Minister, 1964–70, and 1974–6. Resigned in 1976 and did not hold office again. President of the Board of Trade, 1947–51, when he resigned with Aneurin Bevan. Chairman of the Labour Party, 1961/2. Labour MP for Ormskirk, 1945–50, and Huyton, 1950–83. Created life peer, Lord Wilson of Rievaulx. Married to Mary Wilson, poet and writer.

WOLSTENCROFT, A. Deputy Director General at the GPO, 1964–7, Managing Director of Posts and Giro, 1967–8. Became Secretary of the Post Office, 1970–3.

WOLVERSON, W. (1905–74). Deputy Director General of the GPO from 1960 until his retirement in 1965.

WRATTEN, Donald. Private Secretary to Tony Benn as Postmaster General, 1965–6, Head of Telecommunications Marketing Division, 1966–7. After the reorganisation of the Post Office he became Director of Telecom Personnel, 1975–81.

YOUNG, Wayland. See KENNET, Lord.

ZANDER, Michael. Lecturer in Law at the London School of Economics and legal correspondent on the *Guardian* in 1963. Professor of Law at LSE since 1977. Gave great assistance to Tony Benn during the peerage campaign, 1960–1. Left the Labour Party to join the SDP.

ZUCKERMAN, Sir Solly. Zoologist. Long-time Government adviser. Chief Scientific Adviser to Harold Wilson, 1964–70, and to the Secretary of State for Defence, 1960–6. Chairman of the Central Advisory Committee for Science and Technology, 1965–70. Created a life peer in 1971.

(II) Personal

BENN, Caroline. Born in Ohio and graduated from Vassar College with postgraduate degrees from the Universities of Cincinnati and London. Founder member of the main comprehensive education campaign group in Britain, and editor of *Comprehensive Education*. Author of many educational publications including *Half Way There* with Professor Brian Simon (1970) and *Challenging the MSC* with John Fairley (1986). President of the Socialist Educational Association. Adult education lecturer since 1965, currently teaching an Open University preparation course. Former member of the Education Section of the UNESCO Commission and of the Inner London Education Authority, and governor of several schools and colleges. Married Tony Benn in 1949. Four children: Stephen, born 1951, Hilary, born 1953, Melissa, born 1957, Joshua, born 1958.

BENN, David Wedgwood. Younger brother, a barrister, worked for the Socialist International and later for the External Service of the BBC. Head of the BBC Yugoslav Section, 1974–84. A writer specialising in Soviet affairs.

BENN, June. Former lecturer; novelist writing under the name of June Barraclough. Married David Benn in 1959. Two children, Piers, born 1962, and Frances, born 1964.

FLANDERS, Michael (1922–75). Actor and writer. Contemporary of Tony Benn at school. Family friend with Donald Swann, who together formed the duo well-known for its musical stage entertainment.

GIBSON, Ralph. University contemporary, a barrister who was later made a judge. He and his wife, Ann, are close friends of the family.

KHAMA, Sir Seretse (1921–1980). Founder and President of the Bechuanaland Democratic Party from 1962, becoming Prime Minister of Bechuanaland (Botswana) in 1965, and President of the Republic of Botswana in 1966. A barrister educated at Oxford,

Seretse had become chief of the Bamangwato tribe in 1925, aged four. He was removed from the British protectorate by the Labour Government in 1950 over objections to his marriage to Ruth Williams, a white British woman, in 1948. Became close friends with the Benns who lent support in the 1950s. Seretse Khama was god-father to Melissa Benn and Tony Benn god-father to Anthony Khama.

LAMBERT, Phyllis. A Canadian architect, a college contemporary of Caroline Benn, and long-time friend of the family.

STANSGATE, Lady. Margaret Holmes, born in Scotland in 1897, the daughter of Liberal MP, D. T. Holmes. Married William Wedgwood Benn in 1920. They had three children (the eldest son, Michael, was killed while serving as an RAF pilot during the war). A long-standing member of the Movement for the Ordination of Women, the first President of the Congregational Federation, served on the Council of Christians and Jews, and of the Friends of the Hebrew University. Fellow of the Hebrew University. Joint author of *Beckoning Horizon*, 1934.

STANSGATE, Lord (1877–1960). William Wedgwood Benn. Son of John Williams Benn, who was Liberal MP for Tower Hamlets and later for Devonport, and Chairman, 1904/5, of the London County Council of which he was a founder member. William Wedgwood Benn was himself elected Liberal MP for St George's, Tower Hamlets, in 1906. Became a whip in the Liberal Government in 1910. Served in the First World War and was decorated with the DSO and DFC, returning in 1918 to be elected MP for Leith. Joined the Labour Party in 1926, resigned his seat the same day, and was subsequently elected Labour MP for North Aberdeen (1928–31) in a by-election. Secretary of State for India in the 1929–31 Labour Cabinet. Re-elected as Labour MP for Gorton in 1937. He rejoined the RAF in 1940 at the age of sixty-three, was made a peer, Viscount Stansgate, in 1941, and was Secretary of State for Air, 1945–6, in the post-war Labour Government. World President of the Inter-Parliamentary Union, 1947–57.

SWANN, Donald. School contemporary and family friend who wrote the music for and performed in many shows, including *At the Drop of a Hat*, which he and Michael Flanders staged in London and took on a world tour. Composer of church music.

WINCH, Olive (Buddy). Miss Winch was with the family as a children's nurse from 1928 until 1940, when she left to undertake war work. A life-long friend.

Chronology

1963
18 Jan	Hugh Gaitskell dies
25 Jan	Anglo-Polish Conference, Warsaw
14 Feb	Harold Wilson elected Leader of the Labour Party
28 Mar	Parliamentary Report on Peerage Law reform approved
4 April	Anglo-German Conference at Königswinter
2 May	Bristol colour bar and bus boycott
5 June	John Profumo resigns
31 July	Peerage renounced
20 Aug	By-election. Re-elected for Bristol South East
1 Oct	Re-elected to National Executive Committee
10 Oct	Harold Macmillan resigns
18 Oct	Lord Home becomes Prime Minister and to renounce peerage
22 Nov	President Kennedy assassinated

1964
9 Jan	Discussions with Wilson over 'New Britain' speeches
27 Mar	First meeting with Chinese chargé d'affaire in London
14 June	Demonstrations over Rivonia trial of Nelson Mandela and others
11 Sept	'New Britain' manifesto discussed
15 Oct	General Election. Re-elected for Bristol South East
19 Oct	Appointed Postmaster General
4 Nov	Lyndon Johnson elected President of USA
17 Dec	Elected Chairman of the Fabian Society

1965
24 Jan	Winston Churchill dies
10 Mar	Audience with Queen on postal stamp design

2 April	National Philatelic Museum plans
15 April	Postmen's pay negotiations
28 June	Early Bird satellite trans-Atlantic telephone
21 July	National Giro announced
27 July	Edward Heath elected Leader of the Conservative Party
24 Sept	Comprehensive Schools Committee launched
11 Nov	Ian Smith makes Unilateral Declaration of Independence in Rhodesia

1966
5–13 Jan	Official Visit to Japan
31 Mar	General Election – Labour landslide. Re-elected for Bristol South East
17 May	Queen visits Post Office Tower
23 May	Talks with Olaf Palme in Stockholm
17 June	Approval of Post Office as public corporation
30 June	Pirate radio legislation approved by Cabinet
3 July	Appointed Minister of Technology in the Cabinet
10 July	Cabinet reshuffle
19 July	Economic cuts agreed at Cabinet
25 Aug	Visit to Bradwell Atomic Power station
22 Oct	Cabinet meets at Chequers to discuss Britain and the Common Market

1967
6 Feb	Soviet Premier Kosygin arrives in London
15 Feb	Ministry of Aviation merged with Ministry of Technology
2 Mar	Second Reading of the Shipbuilding Industry Bill
3 April	Vice-President Hubert Humphrey at Number 10
17–21 April	Official visit to the USSR
21 May	Official visit to Washington
3 June	Paris Air Show
28 Aug	Reshuffle. Peter Shore appointed Secretary of State for Economic Affairs
12 Sept	Lords reform discussed at Chequers
21 Sept	Centrifuge discussed at Number 10
8 Oct	Death of Clement Attlee
18 Nov	Pound devalued
11 Dec	Concorde rollout at Toulouse

APPENDIX I
The Lords: Make this the Beginning of the End

Article for Tribune, *7 June 1963, celebrating the peerage victory and outlining its significance.*

Last Thursday the Prime Minister presented a Bill in the Commons to permit a man to renounce a peerage, become a commoner, and like any other commoner offer himself as a candidate for the House of Commons.

This Bill, looked at one way, makes a very minor change in the hereditary system, and has been described as 'common sense', and 'an example of the British genius for adaptation'. But is it? And if it is such a small change why has it taken over ten years to get it carried through? This campaign has led to three parliamentary committees, five separate petitions, the presentation of five previous Bills, and has occupied both Houses for seven full-length debates. It has also been fought out in a by-election and occupied two Judges for two weeks in overturning the result.

All this didn't happen by accident. The leadership of the Tory Party put up a bitter resistance to this change until the last possible moment. And they did it because they knew that anything that weakened hereditary privileges in any way would weaken them. They used every argument – including the 'defence' of the Monarchy – and preferred to seat a defeated candidate than give way.

Now at last they have been forced to act. The turning point was the Bristol by-election. The Tory vote was cut to half and the Cabinet saw the red light. Like the Duke of Cambridge, they had to admit 'there is a time for everything, and the time for change is when it can be no longer resisted'.

The Government's motives now are simple to understand. They hope that if this anomaly is corrected before Labour comes to power the Labour Government will leave the Lords alone.

Whether their strategy succeeds depends entirely upon us. If we are content to leave things as they are no one will be more delighted than the Tory Central Office. The House of Lords will be told to play it quiet during the first four years of the Labour Government and then to use their delaying powers to sabotage Harold Wilson's programme in his last critical year before the next election when it will be too late to over-ride their obstruction.

This present victory must, therefore, be the starting point for a fresh effort to purge the Lords of all their hereditary element and to give the Commons power to over-rule any Second Chamber without delay. This can and must be done within the first year of the Labour Government while some of the major social and economic legislation is being prepared.

The effect of this change will be far more than constitutional. It will symbolise a change of mood and tempo and indicate our determination not to allow entrenched privilege to hold this country back any more.

It should also re-awaken interest in the necessity for radical changes in some of our other institutions where privilege is a major factor in preserving backwardness. Full-scale parliamentary reform, civil service reform, local government reform, legal reform and educational reform are absolutely essential as a pre-condition for the advance of Britain.

For me the most encouraging part of this long battle has been the proof that democracy can be used to mobilise ordinary people to get things done. The machinery of parliamentary democracy only works when you use it and discover how much power you have. That's what the Bristol Campaign was all about.

APPENDIX II
The 'New Britain' Campaign

Memoranda written for Harold Wilson in June 1964, proposing themes and tactics for the General Election.

1. The Choice for Britain

Introduction

With Parliament in its last dying weeks and a very long recess ahead and no party conferences in the autumn to revive political interest, it will be for the Labour Party to raise the political temperature by its own actions and at a time of its own choosing.

One key element in this campaign must be the themes set by the Leader's speeches. A connected series, like the major speech series that began in January, is probably the best way of doing this.

It is necessary now to go over to the attack – but in a new way. A formula is required that is both forward looking and aggressive. The Conservative version of this is of course their attack upon public ownership and socialism – painting a gloomy and frightening picture of Britain under a Labour Government.

Is it not time that we developed our own particular answer to this by a series of speeches pinpointing the principal issues of the Election, stressing the choice that has to be made, and drawing a picture of a Tory Britain in 1970, based on a projection of their record over the last thirteen years? Beside this we could then bring out our own objectives and the means we intend to use to achieve them. This contrast should enable us to demonstrate why the Tories can't do better and why we believe we can.

The Economic Choice

Would it be possible to project forward for five years the average increase in production, exports, investment and research based on the increase over the last thirteen years, and compare what we find with a similar projection for other major industrial countries? In this way we would reveal an estimate of our continued decline in relative economic strength and draw some very frightening conclusions. Having said this, the case for purposive economic planning would almost make itself.

This technique for analysis could also be effective if broken down on a regional basis, showing the relative decline of certain regions. In personal terms you could actually estimate that another quarter of a million Scots, for example, would want to move south. Who would they be? Where would they come from, and what effect would the loss of their skills have on Scottish recovery? If they came south, where would they live, etc., etc.

Similarly, the estimated increase in unemployment due to techno-logical redundancy could be used to hammer home the need for planning and public ownership as an instrument for creating new jobs to absorb those likely to be affected. This would involve using the scientific revolution to alert people to its dangers, as well as its advantages.

The Ownership of Industry

The natural answer to the nationalisation charge is that under the Tories there would be a progressive growth of monopoly by takeover bids and amalgamations, eliminating competition and small busi-nesses, and opening the way to wider foreign control. If any sensible projections of past trends were possible, a rough picture of the owner-ship of industry in 1970 should be interesting.

Transport

The transport crisis lends itself especially well to the technique of projection since statistics are readily available and the trends emerging from them are so clear and startling. The decline of the railways, the rise in road vehicles, the multiplier effect on road conges-tion, the erosion of public transport generally, and the insufficiency of the road building programme, all point to a major seize-up.

If you felt inclined, a reference to road safety would be well worth making. There is a rising tide of anxiety about this and the Govern-ment really is lagging in a number of important directions: for example, in vehicle inspection control, medical standards for drivers, and an ever-weakening police enforcement. Everyone knows the number of people who have been killed and injured in the past but to project these figures forward and say that between now and 1970, 35,000 people will be killed, nearly half a million gravely injured, and a million and a quarter less seriously hurt, poses the problem in a very dramatic way.

Education
This subject too lends itself to forward projection. The rise in school population, the shortage of teachers and the growing pressure on university places can all be contrasted with what has been achieved since 1951. Tory promises can be more effectively discounted by saying that we prefer to judge them by what they have done rather than by what they say they will do. One very vivid statistic that could be used to underline the need for comprehensive schools would be to estimate the number of children who will fail the 11-plus examination between now and 1970. Similarly, the number of qualified students who are likely to fail to gain admission to universities is worth estimating.

Social security
Here the projection should be based on extrapolating from the trends of wages and benefits, the widening gap between those at work and those who are sick, unemployed or retired.

In the same way, by allowing for the increase in the number of retired people as a proportion of the whole population in 1970, a very effective picture can be drawn of the new poverty in our society and hence a powerful case can be made for our comprehensive graduated social security system and the income guarantee.

Prices
Taken alone, a projection of the likely increase in prices and fall in the value of money between now and 1970 might prove the most useful argument of all. Broken down into land prices, food prices, or in even more detail, a specific warning could be given of the effect of Tory policy on different groups in the community.

Housing
Taking the expected increase in the population and the predicted shift of population to the most congested areas, it should be possible to estimate the number of families requiring homes to be contrasted with the Council house building programme if continued at the rate of the last thirteen years. From this, the size of the waiting lists could be calculated.

For would-be owner-occupiers it should be possible to project the rising cost of land, building materials and labour and thus estimate the mortgage payments they would have to meet for an average house.

The Choice of Parties

If, in each and every one of these speeches, the problems looming ahead can be revealed in a way that is easily intelligible, the Government's obvious incapacity to meet them can also be demonstrated. The arguments outlined above can be simplified into a series of propositions like this. A TORY BRITAIN IN 1970 MEANS... Britain falls behind... Redundancy rises... More overcrowded classes... A longer wait for a house, etc., etc.

One can then say again and again that Britain cannot afford another five years of Sir Alec Douglas-Home and Mr Selwyn Lloyd and Mr Henry Brooke, and so on.

Conclusion

If reliable estimates can be made covering theme and other items of policy, they will not be susceptible to effective Tory counter attack, since they will all be based upon their record up to date. If they try to deny them we can ask why we should expect that they will do any better in the future than they have done in the past.

At the same time, our themes will not be purely negative since each and every one of them will pinpoint an issue of supreme importance for ordinary people and underline the need for a new Government with new ideas and energy to carry them into practice.

2. The Impact of The American Elections

This year will be the first time for many years that the American and British General Elections have coincided. We ought therefore to give special consideration to the way in which the American elections might impinge upon our own campaign. Speeches made by President Johnson or Senator Goldwater are bound to touch on such international issues as South East Asia, and Cuba, and indeed the reliability and policy of their allies.

We must also consider the impact that the possibility of a Goldwater victory might have upon the Government attack on us on Polaris. If they could argue that we were putting the safety of this country in the hands of a man like Senator Goldwater it might be of some advantage to them. Our obvious counter is that Senator Goldwater would never permit us to acquire these missiles from the USA unless we were prepared to bring our policy into line with his policy on some issues where they now differ.

Whatever we can actually do about this it might be worthwhile taking soundings from the headquarters of President Johnson and Senator Goldwater on these issues. If we could get an American to write to each of them asking certain questions it would give us an idea of what line they are likely to be taking in their public speeches and would alert us to any danger of which we should be aware in advance. For this reason I have listed below some questions which I think we ought to put, anonymously, to the two camps.

1. Are you in favour of putting pressure on the British Government to cease trade with Cuba and China and, if so, what form could this pressure take, and how far would you be prepared to go with it?

2. Are you in favour of sharing American nuclear know-how with Britain, while it pursues its present policy? This is at present done through the Nassau agreement under which they will receive American nuclear submarines and missiles and plans of warheads. Would you be prepared to continue this arrangement or not?

3. Are you in favour of going on with the proposed multilateral nuclear force even if it is opposed by the British and French Governments? Would you go so far as to enter into an arrangement with the German Government on a bilateral basis for establishing this force to provide the United States and Germany with a joint nuclear force – always on the understanding that the ultimate veto power rested with the United States?

Later on we might send further questions and assess the answers, but these are the most important ones and it would be very helpful to us to have this information in our hands as an intelligence survey. We have got to be very careful that we are not caught out on this. It might be that some of the answers given would be very helpful to the cause that we are trying to establish.

3. The BBC

Introduction
It appears that the BBC is interested to hear our views on broadcasting policy over the next few months. There are some important points worth stressing in our contacts with them. These are:

1. We obviously attach great importance to the need for keeping political interest high during August and early September when Parliament is in recess and before the campaign proper has started. We should do our best to provide them with news items and to encourage them to give full coverage. I think our own line should be that the Labour Party is attacking the issues confronting the

nation, rather than the Prime Minister and the Government direct. During this period we might even encourage the BBC to have a series of programmes called 'Looking at 1970', in which the problems of the next five years are taken up one by one and examined and the parties are given an opportunity of saying what they want to do about them. This would be serious stuff but would help to establish us as a party concerned with the future.

2. We ought now to tell the BBC that we should be very interested in the televising of the Opening of Parliament this year. This has been done once before and there is no reason why it should not be done again. There are obvious advantages in this if we win the Election since it will get wide publicity and will help to establish us in the public mind. We could also make use of the occasion to invite a number of distinguished people to come and attend the Opening of Parliament and there might even be a Government reception for them in Westminster Hall afterwards. This would differentiate our view of Parliament from the entirely feudal view which at the moment holds sway.

3. We should ask them to consider making provision for more ministerial broadcasts after the Election. If a new Government is elected, there will be changes of policy on many fronts and it is absolutely essential that our Ministers should have the right of access to the public to explain these. Ministerial broadcasts are not supposed to be controversial and not all our broadcasts would be. But we should not object if they decide that it is necessary to offer a full right of reply to the Opposition if they wish to take advantage of it.

4. Consideration might be given to the televising of Parliament after the Election, on the initiative of the BBC. With so much of the press hostile to us it would be especially necessary for us to have access to the public direct and this might be the time to start an experiment along these lines. It could begin with the tape recording of parliamentary debates using the existing microphone system and when this had been tried out and played back to MPs privately we could consider whether to go ahead experimentally and allow Question Time to be broadcast in sound only. If this succeeded we could move ahead to the televising of Question Time and certain other highlights of parliamentary debates.

APPENDIX III
A Year at the Post Office

The Postmaster General's Minutes to Post Office staff, November 1964–October 1965.

Date	No.	Title	Action by Department
9.11.64	1,77	Machinery of Government	No action called for unless something goes wrong.
	2.	Chair of Communications	With Engineer-in-Chief.
	3.	Executive Aircraft	PMG agrees too costly.
	4,72	Joint Satellite Station Consortium	We are arranging meeting and not leaving it to Technology.
	5.	Post Office Billing	PMG accepted no prospect of comprehensive billing.
	6.	Radio Phones in Trains	PMG accepted no early development possible.
	7.	PO Direct Mail Address Service	No answer needed.
	8.	Two-Speed Tape Recorders	PMG has had one demonstration: another to follow.
11.11	9.	Constituency Correspondence	No operational objection to extending MPs' 'free' postage.

Date	No.	Title	Action by Department
	10.	PO Christmas Cards	PMG decided not to proceed.
	11.	Staff Name Plates	Raised on, and at present with, PMG's Informal Committee.
	12,56,71	Art in Crown Offices	Under way.
	13.	Postal Buses	Following first report, a pilot scheme is being worked on.
	14.	Standardisation Generally	Outstanding.
	15.	Unit Trust	Chancellor not in favour.
	16.	Design of Pillar Boxes	PMG satisfied with reply: to see David Mellor's pillar box.
	17.	Forward Planning	PMG not finally accepted report that such a post could not be integrated with present organisation.
13.11	18.	Election Procedure	Answer not on file.
	19.	Staff Exchange	PMG asked for further report suggesting extensions.
	20.	Savings Stamps Design	Competition in abeyance: Savings Stamps to be put to Advisory Committee.
24.11	21.	Radio Telephone Answering Service	PMG approved outline plan: preparations for market research being made.
	22.	Packing of Parcels	Department report co-operation with Packaging Research Organisation.
30.11	23.	Scientific Developments	Answered.
	24.	Hours of Counter Work	General enquiry being made.

Date	No.	Title	Action by Department
	25.	Advertisements in Telephone Directories	No separate answer, but Board to seek tenders for new contracts.
	26.	Telephone Answering Service	PMG agreed to market survey.
	27.	Parcels Charges	PMG satisfied.
	28.	Magazine Delivery	No answer needed.
	29.	Directory Enquiries	PMG accepted that no charge be made: to be informed of result of study of problem of making directories more effectively usable.
	30.	Stamp Machines	PMG satisfied: to be kept informed.
	31.	London Airport	PMG satisfied.
	32.	Design Policy	Mr Henrion appointed.
	33.	Minuscule Design	Fellow appointed.
	34.	Telephone Advertising	PMG approved experimental scheme.
	35.	Wages Structure	PMG accepted that change in wage structure would not be likely to help, but asked for suggestions as to where over-scale rates would help recruitment.
7.12	36.	Colour on Pay-TV	Colour and Pay-TV will not go together on wire: PMG has asked about radio pay-TV.
	37.	Uniforms	PMG to be told when conclusions are reached on the cloths being developed and tried.
	38.	Chemical Cancellation of Letters	PMG accepted this must wait.
	39.	Coded Telegrams	PMG to be told of developments in scheme for more direct transmission.

Date	No.	Title	Action by Department
	40.	Alarm Systems	Department reported on systems in use.
10.12	41.	Direct Catering	PMG has had reports.
	42.	Collection of Mail	Recommendation against morning collections concentration.
	43.	Land Buying	PMG has asked Ministry of Land and Natural Resources to include a compulsory purchase power in their legislation.
	44.	Rural Post Boxes	Posting Boxes may be put on buses where appropriate.
	45.	Telecommunications for the Lonely	On the Board: conclusions not yet reached.
12.12	46.	Wireless Licence Evasion	More frequent licence combing.
	47.	Christmas Stamps	Left over until next year.
	48.	National Data Processing Service	Department support this, and are consulting Technology.
	49.	Value Engineering	Trials by Engineer-in-Chief approved.
1.1.65	50.	International Commission	PMG has agreed to suspend action for the present.
	51.	Cybernetics	Outstanding.
	52.	Structure	Treasury/PO group examining.
19.1	53,80	Telephone Interpreter Service	Board of Trade asked if they would support this: no further report received: letter sent to Board of Trade.
22.1	54.	Co-operation on Parcels	Department and British Railways preparing for discussions.

Date	No.	Title	Action by Department
	55.	Exhibition in Tokyo	Board decided against participating.
28.1	56.	See 12	
11.2	57.	Copyright Act	Decided that legislation would not solve problems connected with broadcasting records.
	58.	Standardised Envelopes	Department are getting on with action.
12.2.	59.	Redevelopment of Defence Resources	Statement of staff needs sent to Sub-Committee.
	60.	High Value Packets	Still live: DDG(P) asked to prepare scheme.
	61.	Pillar Boxes and Postal Carts	PMG satisfied.
19.2	62.	Franking Machines	PMG satisfied: information requested on talks with Joint Committee.
	63.	PMG's Powers to Join Outside Enterprises	
23.2	64.	Educational Broadcasting	PMG has written to colleagues giving available information.
24.2	65.	PO Advisory Council	Not a Board item.
25.2	66.	Industrial Research for the Post Office	Outstanding.
	67.	Debate on the Resolution	Completed.
	68.	Contracts in Development Districts	Subsidiaries of Ring Companies cannot be excluded from 'reservation' orders.
1.3	69.	Bulk Supply Agreements	Discussions.
9.3	70.	McKinsey Consultancy	No answer necessary.
26.3	71.	See 12	
	72.	See 4	

Date	No.	Title	Action by Department
	73.	Estimation of Telephone Demand	Now a Board item.
	74.	Relay Services	Outstanding.
	75.	Machine Tools	Answer sent to Ministry of Technology for information.
	76.	Factories Functions	Factories undertake manufacturing within capacity.
	77.	See 1	
	78.	Skilled Manpower	Information supplied.
	79.	Organisation	DG has asked for discussions.
7.4	80.	See 53	
	81.	Co-operation with Technology	Part answer.
	82.	Giro	Discussions continuing.
12.5	83.	PMG's Power to Join in Outside Enterprises	Reply to 63: PMG asked for draft paper to HAC: no answer.
27.5	84.	Local Broadcasting Paper	Done.
	85.	Post Office Buildings	Answered.
	86.	Travellers Cheques in Crown Post Offices	No answer.
7.7	87.	Telephone Directory Entries	MPs – answered.
9.7	88.	Call Boxes and Kiosks	Answered: credit cards for non-subscribers.
	89.	Post Office Reorganisation	Discussions proceeding.
13.7	90.	Long-Term Future of Postal Services	Paper provided for Board.
4.8	91.	Office Minutes	Action taken.
6.8	92.	Licence to Sell Stamps	No answer.
	93.	Restrictive Practices	

Date	No.	Title	Action by Department
24.9	94.	Post Office History	
	95.	A Year's Work Done	No answer required.
	96.	A Year's Work Ahead	No answer required.
6.10	97.	Compensation	
	98.	Redirecting Mail	
	99.	Exports of Postal Equipment	
11.10	100.	Communications Code	Discussion requested: no answer.
	101.	Internal Communications	
	102.	Postal Overtime	
21.10	103.	Post Office Planning and Local Authorities	Action being taken by APS with PD/SB.
	104.	Minor Building Works	
	105.	Hidden Subsidies	
	106.	Promotion Policy	
21.10	107.	Post Office Counters	
	108.	Customers' Education	
	109.	Telephone Service – Fringe Services	

APPENDIX IV
The British Revolution, 1966

Extract from a speech to the Institution of Mechanical Engineers at the Dorchester Hotel, 17 November 1966.

The fundamental economic problems of this country are not new. They go back a hundred years or more. The plain truth is that this country failed to follow through the lead that it acquired in the first Industrial Revolution.

Joseph Whitworth drew attention in his report on the New York Industrial Exhibition of 1853, to the eagerness with which the Americans applied machinery to every department of their industry. But his warning was not heeded. Neither was the warning of Doctor Playfair. In his famous letter to Lord Taunton in 1867 he reported on his experiences in the Paris Exhibition. This is what he said: 'I am sorry to say that with very few exceptions, a singular accordance of opinion prevailed that our country has shown little inventiveness and made little progress in the peaceful arts of industry since 1862.'

Similarly, one of the trade union members of the Mosley Industrial Commission that visited America in the autumn of 1902 reported 'an all round readiness to accept new ideas, and a general hankering for machinery and appliances'. These warnings have been repeated regularly since then. But even today industry is not yet accorded the respect in society necessary for industrial success.

For a hundred years from 1850 we were busy building an empire. From 1850 to 1917 we established seventeen new orders of chivalry to honour ourselves but unfortunately forgot to found any schools of business management or advance engineering training as rapidly as we should have done. Our universities – or some of them – are still too disconnected from the business of preparing people to earn the nation's living.

Technological change has already completely outdated the nineteenth century pattern of education. It requires us to educate all our children and also to make provision for retraining ourselves during our working life at least once and maybe twice or three times. If I say that we must raise the school-leaving age to sixty-five, you will get some measure of what technological change requires of us in terms of educational response.

Technology through the agency of the motor car, and the roads and bridges over which it travels, is one of the major forces undermining the whole basis of local government and forcing us to think about better structures to replace it. The trade unions too are being changed as old crafts and skills are being replaced by new machines and techniques which call for a new response, new organisation and new ideas. The Civil Service is finding that the demand made upon it by technology will require a radical rethinking of its recruitment, training and role. Government and Parliament must also adjust themselves in a hundred ways to meet the new situation which technology has created.

These changes are, by any definition, revolutionary. And the driving forces behind them are engineers. To talk of technology as if it existed in a vacuum is meaningless. Technology is the sum total of what engineers do. It seems to me therefore quite plain that the whole body of engineers are revolutionaries. Your work, while being entirely constructive in its primary effect, is almost entirely destructive in its secondary effect.

I hope this analysis will not come as too great a shock to you. I am, of course, a member of a political party that has long been committed to the need for social change. But compared to the changes that the engineering profession has achieved in the last ten years, our achievements are modest indeed. As an old political agitator I must yield to you the credit for launching the British Revolution of 1966. It has all been achieved without bloodshed, indeed without being noticed in some cases.

It rather confirms the curious definition of an engineer that I found in my *Oxford English Dictionary* last night: 'One who contrives, designs or invents. An inventor: a plotter.' Once this conviction got hold of me I turned back to my history books to see whether this analysis did not perhaps help us to understand earlier periods. The idea that kings and queens in the Middle Ages, or presidents and prime ministers in more recent years, really shape the destiny of many may now require a critical reappraisal.

Though engineers were few and far between, and many hundreds of years often marked the stages of engineering progress up until 1800, it is arguable that human history could best be understood by reference to the level of technology obtaining at different times.

APPENDIX V
Her Majesty's Government
Complete List of Ministers and Offices

The Cabinet, October 1964

Prime Minister and First Lord of the Treasury	Mr Harold Wilson
First Secretary of State and Minister for Economic Affairs	Mr George Brown
Secretary of State for Foreign Affairs	Mr P. Gordon Walker
Lord President of the Council and Leader of the House of Commons	Mr Herbert Bowden
Lord Chancellor	Lord Gardiner
Chancellor of the Exchequer	Mr James Callaghan
Secretary of State for Defence	Mr Denis Healey
Home Secretary	Sir Frank Soskice
Secretary of State for Commonwealth Relations	Mr Arthur Bottomley
Secretary of State for Scotland	Mr William Ross
Secretary of State for Wales	Mr James Griffiths
Secretary of State for Colonial Affairs	Mr Anthony Greenwood
President of the Board of Trade	Mr Douglas Jay
Lord Privy Seal and Leader of the House of Lords	The Earl of Longford
Secretary of State for Education and Science	Mr Michael Stewart
Minister of Housing and Local Government	Mr Richard Crossman
Chancellor of the Duchy of Lancaster	Mr Douglas Houghton
Minister of Labour	Mr Ray Gunter
Minister of Technology	Mr Frank Cousins
Minister of Agriculture, Fisheries and Food	Mr Frederick Peart
Minister of Power	Mr Frederick Lee
Minister of Transport	Mr Thomas Fraser
Minister of Overseas Development	Mrs Barbara Castle

Ministers not in the Cabinet, October 1964

Minister of Aviation	Mr Roy Jenkins
Minister of Pensions and National Insurance	Miss Margaret Herbison
Minister of Health	Mr Kenneth Robinson
Minister of Public Building and Works	Mr Charles Pannell
Paymaster General	Mr George Wigg
Postmaster General	Mr A. Wedgwood Benn
Minister of Land and Natural Resources	Mr Frederick Willey
Minister of State for Foreign Affairs (UK Representative at United Nations)	Sir Hugh Foot
Minister of State for Foreign Affairs (Disarmament)	Mr A. Gwynne-Jones
Deputy Secretary of State for Defence and Minister of Defence for the Army	Mr Frederick Mulley
Minister without Portfolio	Mr Eric Fletcher
Economic Secretary to the Treasury	Mr Anthony Crosland
Minister of State, Department of Education and Science	Lord Bowden
Minister of Defence for the Royal Air Force	Lord Shackleton
Minister of State, Foreign Office	Mr George Thomson
Minister of State, Foreign Office	Mr Walter Padley
Minister of State, Commonwealth Relations Office	Mr Cledwyn Hughes
Minister of Defence for the Royal Navy	Mr Christopher Mayhew
Minister of State, Home Office	Miss Alice Bacon
Attorney-General	Mr F. Elwyn Jones
Solicitor-General	Mr Dingle Foot

The Cabinet, March 1966

Prime Minister and First Lord of the Treasury	Mr Harold Wilson
First Secretary of State and Secretary of State for Economic Affairs	Mr George Brown
Secretary of State for Foreign Affairs	Mr Michael Stewart
Lord President of the Council and Leader of the House of Commons	Mr Herbert Bowden
Lord Chancellor	Lord Gardiner
Chancellor of the Exchequer	Mr James Callaghan
Secretary of State for Defence	Mr Denis Healey
Home Secretary	Mr Roy Jenkins
Secretary of State for Commonwealth Relations	Mr Arthur Bottomley
Secretary of State for Scotland	Mr William Ross
Secretary of State for Wales	Mr Cledwyn Hughes
Secretary of State for Colonial Affairs	Mr Frederick Lee
President of the Board of Trade	Mr Douglas Jay
Lord Privy Seal and Leader of the House of Lords	Earl of Longford
Secretary of State for Education and Science	Mr Anthony Crosland
Minister of Housing and Local Government	Mr Richard Crossman
Minister of Labour	Mr Raymond Gunter
Minister of Technology	Mr Frank Cousins
Minister of Agriculture, Fisheries and Food	Mr Frederick Peart
Minister of Power	Mr Richard Marsh
Minister of Transport	Mrs Barbara Castle
Minister of Overseas Development	Mr Anthony Greenwood
Minister Without Portfolio	Mr Douglas Houghton

Ministers not in the Cabinet, March 1966

Chancellor of the Duchy of Lancaster	Mr George Thomson
Minister of Health	Mr Kenneth Robinson
Minister of Pensions and National Insurance	Miss Margaret Herbison
Minister of Public Building and Works	Mr Reginald Prentice
Minister of Aviation	Mr Frederick Mulley
Postmaster General	Mr A. Wedgwood Benn
Minister of Land and Natural Resources	Mr Frederick Willey
Minister without Portfolio	Lord Champion
Paymaster General	Mr George Wigg
Chief Secretary to the Treasury	Mr John Diamond
Minister of State, Economic Affairs	Mr Austen Albu
Minister of Defence for the Royal Navy	Mr J. P. W. Mallalieu
Minister of Defence for the Army	Mr Gerald Reynolds
Minister of Defence for the Royal Air Force	Lord Shackleton
Ministers of State, Foreign Office	Mr Walter Padley
	Mrs Eirene White
(UK Representative at United Nations)	Lord Caradon
(Disarmament)	Lord Chalfont
Minister of State, Home Office	Miss Alice Bacon
Minister of State, Commonwealth Relations Office	Mrs Judith Hart
Ministers of State, Board of Trade	Mr George Darling
	Mr Roy Mason
	Lord Brown
Minister of State, Scottish Office	Mr George Willis
Minister of State, Welsh Office	Mr George Thomas
Ministers of State, Education and Science	Mr Edward Redhead
	Mr Goronwy Roberts
Attorney-General	Sir Elwyn Jones
Solicitor-General	Sir Dingle Foot
Lord Advocate	Mr Gordon Stott
Solicitor-General for Scotland	Mr H. S. Wilson

APPENDIX VI
Labour Party National Executive Committee 1963–7

1963/4

Mr Anthony Greenwood, MP	Chairman
Mr R. J. Gunter, MP	Vice-Chairman
Mr H. R. Nicholas	Treasurer
Rt Hon Harold Wilson, MP	Leader of the Parliamentary Party
Rt Hon George Brown, MP	Deputy Leader of the Parliamentary Party
Mr L. Williams	General Secretary

Trade Unions' Section
Mr J. M. Boyd (Amalgamated Engineering Union)
Mr D. H. Davies (British Iron, Steel and Kindred Trades Association)
Mr J. Gormley (National Union of Mineworkers)
Mr A. V. Hilton (National Union of Agricultural Workers)
Mr D. McGarvey (United Society of Boilermakers, Shipbuilders and Structural Workers)
Mr F. W. Mulley, MP (Clerical and Administrative Workers' Union)
Mr W. E. Padley, MP (Union of Shop, Distributive and Allied Workers)
Mr W. Perrins (National Union of General and Municipal Workers)
Mr W. H. Rathbone (National Union of Foundry Workers)
Mr W. Simpson (Amalgamated Union of Foundry Workers)
Mr E. S. Taylor (Amalgamated Society of Woodworkers)

Socialist Co-operative and Professional Organisations' Section
Mr A. Skeffington, MP (Royal Arsenal Co-operative Society)

Constituency Organisations' Section
Mr A. W. Benn, MP
Mr L. J. Callaghan, MP
Mrs B. Castle, MP
Mr R. H. S. Crossman, MP
Mr T. Driberg, MP
Mr I. Mikardo

Women Members
Miss A. Bacon, MP
Mrs E. M. Braddock, MP
Miss M. Herbison, MP
Miss J. Lee, MP
Mrs E. White, MP

1964/5

Rt Hon R. J. Gunter, MP	Chairman
Mr W. E. Padley, MP	Vice-Chairman
Mr D. H. Davies	Acting Treasurer
Rt Hon Harold Wilson, MP	Leader of the Parliamentary Party
Rt Hon George Brown, MP	Deputy Leader of the Parliamentary Party
Mr L. Williams	General Secretary

Trade Unions' Section
Mr J. M. Boyd (Amalgamated Engineering Union)
Mr D. H. Donlon (National Union of Railwaymen)
Mr J. Gormley (National Union of Mineworkers)
Mr A. V. Hilton (National Union of Agricultural Workers)
Mr J. L. Jones (Transport and General Workers' Union)
Mr D. McGarvey (United Society of Boilermakers, Shipbuilders and Structural Workers)
Mr W. Perrins (National Union of General and Municipal Workers)
Mr W. Simpson (Amalgamated Union of Foundry Workers)
Mr E. S. Taylor (Amalgamated Society of Woodworkers)

Socialist Co-operative and Professional Organisations' Section
Mr A. Skeffington, MP (Royal Arsenal Co-operative Society)

Constituency Organisations' Section
Rt Hon A. W. Benn, MP
Rt Hon L. J. Callaghan, MP
Rt Hon B. Castle, MP
Mr R. H. S. Crossman, MP
Mr T. Driberg, MP
Rt Hon A. Greenwood, MP
Mr I. Mikardo, MP

Women Members
Miss A. Bacon, MP
Mrs E. M. Braddock, MP
Miss M. Herbison, MP
Miss J. Lee, MP
Mrs E. White, MP

1965/6

Mr W. E. Padley, MP	Chairman
Mr J. M. Boyd	Vice Chairman
Mr D. H. Davies	Acting Treasurer
Rt Hon Harold Wilson, MP	Leader of the Parliamentary Party
Rt Hon George Brown, MP	Deputy Leader of the Parliamentary Party
Mr L. Williams	General Secretary

Trade Unions' Section
Mr F. J. Chapple (Electrical Trades Union)
Mr A. Cunningham (National Union of General and Municipal Workers)
Mr F. Donlon (National Union of Railwaymen)
Mr J. Gormley (National Union of Mineworkers)
Rt Hon R. J. Gunter, MP (Transport Salaried Staffs' Association)
Lord Hilton (National Union of Agricultural Workers)
Mr J. L. Jones (Transport and General Workers' Union)
Mr F. W. Mulley, MP (Clerical and Administrative Workers' Union)
Mr W. Simpson (Amalgamated Union of Foundry Workers)
Mr E. S. Taylor (Amalgamated Society of Woodworkers)

Socialist Co-operative and Professional Organisations' Section
Mr A. Skeffington, MP (Royal Arsenal Co-operative Society)

Constituency Organisations' Section
Rt Hon A. W. Benn, MP
Rt Hon L. J. Callaghan, MP
Rt Hon B. Castle, MP
Rt Hon R. H. S. Crossman, MP
Mr T. Driberg, MP
Rt Hon A. Greenwood, MP
Mr I. Mikardo, MP

Women Members
Miss A. Bacon, MP
Mrs E. M. Braddock, MP
Rt Hon M. Herbison, MP
Miss J. Lee, MP
Mrs E. White, MP

1966/7

Mr J. M. Boyd	Chairman
Rt Hon Jennie Lee, MP	Vice Chairman
Mr D. H. Davies	Treasurer
Rt Hon Harold Wilson, MP	Leader of the Parliamentary Party
Rt Hon George Brown, MP	Deputy Leader of the Parliamentary Party
Mr L. Williams	General Secretary

Trade Unions' Section
Mr L. V. Andrews (Union of Post Office Workers)
Mr T. G. Bradley, MP (Transport Salaried Staffs' Association)
Mr J. Chalmers (Amalgamated Society of Boilermakers, Shipwrights, Blacksmiths and Structural Workers)
Mr F. J. Chapple (Electrical Trades Union)
Mr A. Cunningham (National Union of General and Municipal Workers)
Mr F. Donlon (National Union of Railwaymen)
Mr J. Gormley (National Union of Mineworkers)
Mr J. L. Jones (Transport and General Workers' Union)
Rt Hon F. W. Mulley, MP (Clerical and Administrative Workers' Union)
Mr W. E. Radley, MP (Union of Shop, Distributive and Allied Workers)
Mr W. Simpson (Amalgamated Union of Foundry Workers)

Socialist Co-operative and Professional Organisations' Section
Mr A. Skeffington, MP (Royal Arsenal Co-operative Society)

Constituency Organisations' Section
Rt Hon A. W. Benn, MP
Rt Hon L. J. Callaghan, MP
Rt Hon B. Castle, MP
Rt Hon R. H. S. Crossman, MP
Mr T. Driberg, MP
Rt Hon A. Greenwood, MP
Mr I. Mikardo, MP

Women Members
Rt Hon A. Bacon, MP
Mrs E. M. Braddock, MP
Rt Hon M. Herbison, MP
Mrs E. White, MP

APPENDIX VII
Abbreviations

ABC	American Broadcasting Company
AEA	Atomic Energy Authority
AGD	Accountant General's Department
APMG	Assistant Postmaster General
ATV	Associated Television Ltd
AUEW	Amalgamated Union of Engineering Workers
AWRE	Atomic Weapons Research Establishment
BAC	British Aircraft Corporation
BBC	British Broadcasting Corporation
BEA	British European Airways
BOAC	British Overseas Airways Corporation
BP	British Petroleum
CBI	Confederation of British Industry
CEGB	Central Electricity Generating Board
CLP	Constituency Labour Party
CND	Campaign for Nuclear Disarmament
DEA	Department of Economic Affairs
DEP	Department of Employment and Productivity
DG	Director General
DHSS	Department of Health and Social Security
EDC	Economic Development Committee (Little Neddy)
EEC	European Economic Community
EFTA	European Free Trade Association
ELDO	European Launcher Development Organisation
ETU	Electrical Trades Union
EETPU	Electrical, Electronic, Telecommunications and Plumbing Union
FBI	Federal Bureau of Investigation
FLN	Front Liberation Nationale (of Algeria)
GEC	General Electric Company
GLC	Greater London Council

GMC	General Management Committee
GPO	General Post Office
IBM	International Business Machines
ICI	Imperial Chemical Industries
ICT	International Computers and Tabulators
ILP	Independent Labour Party
IMF	International Monetary Fund
IPC	International Publishing Corporation
IRC	Industrial Reorganisation Corporation
IRI	Industrial Reorganisation Institute (of Italy)
ITA	Independent Television Authority
ITN	Independent Television News
ITT	International Telephone and Telegraph
ITV	Independent Television
LCC	London County Council
LSE	London School of Economics
MI5	Military Intelligence 5
MIT	Massachusetts Institute of Technology
MLF	Multi-Lateral Force
MOD	Ministry of Defence
NACMMI	National Advisory Committee for the Motor Manufacturing Industry
NASA	National Aeronautical Space Agency
NATO	North Atlantic Treaty Organisation
NCB	National Coal Board
NEC	National Executive Committee
NEDC	National Economic Development Council (Neddy)
NHS	National Health Service
NOP	National Opinion Poll
NPL	National Physical Laboratory
NRDC	National Research Development Corporation
NUM	National Union of Mineworkers
NUJ	National Union of Journalists
NUR	National Union of Railwaymen
NUS	National Union of Seamen
OAU	Organisation of African Unity
O&M	Organisation and Methods
OPEC	Organisation of Petroleum Exporting Countries
PIB	Prices and Incomes Board
PLP	Parliamentary Labour Party
PMG	Postmaster General
PO	Post Office
POEU	Post Office Engineering Union
POSB	Post Office Savings Bank

PPS	Parliamentary Private Secretary
PRO	Public Relations Officer
R&D	Research and Development
RCA	Radio Corporation (of America)
SDP	Social Democratic Party
SET	Selective Employment Tax
STC	Standard Telephones and Cables
TEMA	Telecommunication Engineering and Manufacturing Association
TGWU	Transport and General Workers' Union
TUC	Trades Union Congress
TW3	'That Was The Week That Was'
TWW	Television West and Wales
UAR	United Arab Republic
UDI	Unilateral Declaration of Independence
UN	United Nations
UNESCO	United Nations Educational, Scientific and Cultural Organisation
UNICEF	United Nations Children's Fund
UPW	Union of Post Office Workers
USDAW	Union of Shop Distributive and Allied Workers
WEA	Workers' Educational Association
ZANU	Zimbabwe African National Union
ZAPU	Zimbabwe African People's Union

Index

See Principal Persons, *p. 519, for biographical details*